1600–1750   Music

Earliest opera, *Euridice* (Peri and Caccini)
The Triumphs of Oriana, English madrigals (incl. Weelkes: *As Vesta was*)

Byrd: *Ave verum corpus (Gradualia)*
Monteverdi: *Orfeo*

Monteverdi: *Vespers*
Gesualdo: *Responsories for Holy Week*

Schütz: *Veni, Sancte Spiritus*

Byrd dies (80)

First public opera house opens, Venice

Monteverdi: *The Coronation of Poppaea*
Monteverdi dies (76); Frescobaldi dies (59); Cavalli: *Egisto*
Carissimi: *Jephte*

Lully becomes chief composer at French court

Schütz: Passion settings; Cavalli: *Ercole amante*
Buxtehude becomes organist at St Mary's, Lübeck; Cesti: *Il pomo d'oro*
Lully: *Le bourgeois gentilhomme*
Schütz dies (87)

First German opera house opens (Hamburg)
Purcell organist of Westminster Abbey

Lully: *Armide*

Purcell: *Dido and Aeneas*

Purcell dies (36)
Earliest pianoforte made
Beginning of greatest period of Stradivari's violin-making

Handel in Italy; Bach in Weimar

Handel in London — *Rinaldo*
Vivaldi: Concertos op. 3
Corelli dies (60); Couperin: First harpsichord book
Bach in Cöthen; Couperin: *L'art de toucher le clavecin*
Handel: *Acis and Galatea*
Bach: *Brandenburg Concertos*
Rameau settles in Paris, *Treatise on Harmony*
Bach in Leipzig — intensive cantata composition
Bach: *St John Passion*; Handel: *Giulio Cesare*
Vivaldi: *The Four Seasons*; A. Scarlatti dies (65)
Bach: *St Matthew Passion*
Pergolesi: *La serva padrona*; Rameau: *Hippolyte et Aricie*; Telemann: *Musique de Table*

Handel: *Messiah*

J. Stamitz appointed concertmaster at Mannheim

Bach: Mass in b
Bach dies (65)

Art and literature

Caravaggio: *Christ and the Apostles*
Shakespeare: *Hamlet*

Cervantes: *Don Quixote*

Rubens: *Self-portrait with Isabella*

Bernini: Colonnade of St Peter's, Rome

Rembrandt: *Nightwatch*

Velázquez: *Maids of Honor*
Milton: *Paradise Lost*

Molière: *Le bourgeois gentilhomme*; Levau and Mansard: Versailles

Racine: *Phèdre*

Wren: St Paul's Cathedral, London

Watteau: *Embarkation for Cythera*

Canaletto: *The Bucintoro*

Gainsborough: *Mr and Mrs Andrews*

History and philosophy

Galileo discovers the laws of dynamics

Harvey demonstrates the circulation of blood
30 Years' War begins (Germany)
Mayflower sails to Plymouth (Mass.)

Harvard University founded
Descartes: *Discourse on Method*

Louis XIV comes to French throne

Pascal: *Pensées*
Newton discovers the laws of gravity

Spinoza: *Ethics*

Leibnitz: *New Essays on Human Understanding*

Frederick the Great becomes king of Prussia;
  Maria Theresa becomes head of Holy Roman Empire

Timeline markers: 1600, 1625, 1650, 1675, 1700, 1725, 1750

The Cambridge Music Guide

The Cambridge Music Guide

edited by STANLEY SADIE
with ALISON LATHAM

The right of the
University of Cambridge
to print and sell
all manner of books
was granted by
Henry VIII in 1534.
The University has printed
and published continuously
since 1584.

CAMBRIDGE UNIVERSITY PRESS

Cambridge
London New York New Rochelle
Melbourne Sydney

Published by the Press Syndicate of the University of Cambridge
The Pitt Building, Trumpington Street, Cambridge CB2 IRP
10 Stamford Road, Oakleigh, Melbourne 3166, Australia

© 1985 John Calmann and King Ltd
This book was designed and produced by
John Calmann and King Ltd, London

First published 1985

Filmset by Keyspools Ltd, Golborne, Lancs
Printed in Great Britain by Butler & Tanner Ltd, Frome

British Library Cataloguing in Publication Data
The Cambridge music guide
  1. Music – History and criticism
  I. Sadie, Stanley   II. Latham, Alison
  780'.9   ML160

ISBN 0 521 25946 0

Abbreviations in music examples:
bn., bassoon; cl., clarinet; cont., basso continuo; db.,
double bass; fl., flute; hn., horn; m. (mm.),
measure(s); ob., oboe; orch., orchestra; pf., pianoforte; str., strings; tpt., trumpet; trbn., trombone; va.,
viola; vc., cello; vn., violin; ww., woodwind.

In the Listening Notes and lists of works, capital letters
denote major keys, lower-case ones minor keys.

Contents

Map 10

Preface 11

I The Elements of Music 13

Notation 14
Rhythm 17
Melody 19
Key, tonality 24
Harmony 26
Counterpoint, polyphony 29
Color, dynamics 31

II The Instruments of Music 32

Voice 33
Strings 34 Bowed 34 Plucked 36 Keyboard 39
Wind Instruments 41 Woodwind 42 Brass 49 Organ 52
Percussion 53
Electronic instruments 55
Orchestras, bands and ensembles 55

Listening Note II.A Britten: Young Person's Guide to the Orchestra 56

III The Structure of Music 59

Musical form 59 The main forms 62
Genres 69 Orchestral 69 Chamber 71 Keyboard 74 Sacred vocal 77
Secular vocal 80 Dramatic 82

IV The Middle Ages *Judith Nagley* 87

Music of the church 88
Secular song 90
Early polyphony 93 Léonin, Pérotin 93
The motet 95
Ars Nova 96 Vitry 96 Machaut 97
Secular polyphony 99 Landini 100 Ciconia 100

Instrumental music 101
England 101   Dunstable 101

Listening Note IV.A Guiot de Dijon: Chanterai por mon corage 92
Listening Note IV.B Pérotin: Viderunt omnes, excerpt 95
Listening Note IV.C Machaut: Messe de Nostre Dame, Kyrie 98
Listening Note IV.D Landini: Ecco la primavera 99
Listening Note IV.E Dunstable: O rosa bella 102

V   The Renaissance *Judith Nagley* 104

Introduction 104
The Franco-Flemish composers 109   Dufay 109   Binchois 113
Ockeghem 113   Josquin 114   Isaac 117   Janequin 118   Lassus 118
Italy 120   Palestrina 120   The Gabrielis 125   Marenzio 126   Gesualdo 127
Spain 128   Victoria 128
England 129   Byrd 129   The English madrigalists 133
Ensemble music 136
Keyboard music 137
Lute music 138   Dowland 138

Listening Note V.A Dufay: Ce moys de may 111
Listening Note V.B Josquin Desprez:Nymphes des bois 116
Listening Note V.C Lassus: Alma redemptoris mater 120
Listening Note V.D Palestrina: Missa brevis, Kyrie 122
Listening Note V.E G. Gabrieli: Canzon XIII (1597) 126
Listening Note V.F Marenzio: I must depart all hapless 128
Listening Note V.G Byrd: Ave verum corpus 132
Listening Note V.H Weelkes: As Vesta was 135
Listening Note V.I Bull: Coranto "Alarm" 138
Listening Note V.J Dowland: I must complain 139

VI   The Baroque Era 140

Monteverdi 145
Early and middle Baroque in Italy 153   Frescobaldi 153   Cavalli 154
Carissimi 155
Northern Europe: early–middle Baroque 155   Schütz 155
Buxtehude 160
England 161   Purcell 162
France 166   Lully 166   Couperin 158   Rameau 170
The Italian late Baroque 175   Alessandro Scarlatti 175   Corelli 177
Vivaldi 177   Domenico Scarlatti 181
Late Baroque Germany 182   Telemann 182   Bach 184   Handel 204

Listening Note VI.A Monteverdi: Orfeo, excerpt 147
Listening Note VI.B Purcell: Dido and Aeneas, excerpt 165
Listening Note VI.C Rameau: Hippolyte et Aricie, excerpt 172
Listening Note VI.D Vivaldi: Violin Concerto in A minor, op. 3 no. 6, 1st movement 180
Listening Note VI.E Bach: Brandenburg Concerto no. 4 190
Listening Note VI.F Bach: Prelude and Fugue in C minor, from the "48", Book I 192
Listening Note VI.G Handel: Acis and Galatea, excerpt 209
Listening Note VI.H Handel: Messiah, excerpt 216

VII The Classical Era 218

Gluck 223   Stamitz 225   C. P. E. Bach 227   J. C. Bach 228   Haydn 230
Mozart 242   Boccherini 260   Clementi 261   Beethoven 262

Listening Note VII.A Haydn: Symphony no. 104, 1st movement 236
Listening Note VII.B Haydn: String Quartet in C, op. 76 no. 3, 2nd/3rd movements 240
Listening Note VII.C Mozart: The Marriage of Figaro, excerpt 249
Listening Note VII.D Mozart: Piano Concerto in G, K 453, 1st movement 252
Listening Note VII.E Beethoven: Symphony no. 3, 1st movement 268

VIII The Romantic Era 281

Schubert 285
Early Romanticism in Germany 299   Weber 300   Mendelssohn 302
Schumann 307
Romanticism outside Germany and Austria 315   Chopin 315
Liszt 320   Berlioz 325
Italy 334   Rossini 334   Donizetti 336
The operatic masters: Verdi and Wagner 337   Verdi 337
Wagner 345
Brahms 356

Listening Note VIII.A Schubert: String Quintet in C, D 956, 1st movement 297
Listening Note VIII.B Schumann: Dichterliebe, excerpt 312
Listening Note VIII.C Chopin: Mazurka no. 45 318
Listening Note VIII.D Berlioz: Roman Carnival, overture 328
Listening Note VIII.E Wagner: Tristan und Isolde, prelude 354
Listening Note VIII.F Brahms: Symphony no. 1, 1st movement 361

IX The Turn of the Century *Paul Griffiths* 366

Russian nationalism 369   Tchaikovsky 369   Balakirev 375
Mussorgsky 376   Borodin 378   Rimsky-Korsakov 378   Rachmaninov 379

East European nationalism 381   Smetana 381   Dvořák 383   Janáček 386
Vienna 388   Wolf 388   Bruckner 388   Mahler 391   Strauss 399
Northern Europe 405   Sibelius 406   Elgar 408
France 411   Debussy 411   Ravel 417
Italy 419   Puccini 419

Listening Note IX.A Tchaikovsky: Symphony No. 4, 1st movement 372
Listening Note IX.B Mahler: Das Lied von der Erde, 5th movement 396
Listening Note IX.C Strauss: Till Eulenspiegel 400
Listening Note IX.D Debussy: Prélude à "L'Après-midi d'un Faune" 412

X   Modern Times   *Paul Griffiths*   422

The Second Viennese School 426   Schoenberg 426   Berg 433
Webern 434
The radical alternative 438   Stravinsky 438
The Central European crossroads 448   Bartók 448   Hindemith 454
Weill 456
Orff 457   Poulenc 457   Les Six, Satie 457   Falla 458
America: the "ultra-moderns" 458   Ives 458   Cowell 463   Varèse 464
The American mainstream 466   Copland 466   Carter 468
Bernstein 470   Menotti 471
Latin America 472   Villa-Lobos 472   Ginastera 472
Britain and the Soviet Union 472   Vaughan Williams 472   Holst,
Delius 473   Prokofiev 474   Shostakovich 477   Britten 480   Tippett 484
Since 1945 486   Messiaen 486   Boulez 489   Stockhausen 491   Henze 495
Berio 496   Cage 496   Lutoslawski, Penderecki 499   Xenakis 500
Ligeti 500   The Minimalists 500

Listening Note X.A Schoenberg: Pierrot lunaire, excerpt 431
Listening Note X.B Webern: Six Bagatelles no. 4 437
Listening Note X.C Stravinsky: Symphony in C, 1st movement 444
Listening Note X.D Bartók: Concerto for Orchestra, 1st movement 452
Listening Note X.E Ives: Three Places in New England, no. 2 460
Listening Note X.F Britten: Serenade, excerpt 483
Listening Note X.G Messiaen: Vingt regards sur l'Enfant-Jésus, no. 18 487
Listening Note X.H Stockhausen: Gesang der Jünglinge, excerpt 492

XI   The Traditions of Popular Music   *Wilfrid Mellers*   502

Blues and ragtime 508   Blues 509   Ragtime 510   Piano jazz 510   Blues
singing 511
Jazz 512   New Orleans 512
American musical 515

9

Swing era 517   Cabaret singers 519   Instrumentalists 519
White country music 520   Bluegrass 520
Rock 522   Music theater, rock musicals 525

Further Listening 529

Further Reading 531

Glossary 534

Acknowledgements 540

Index 541

Preface

The principal aim of this book is to enhance people's pleasure and understanding in listening to music. Although it is designed in the first place for those with little experience or musical knowledge, I hope that its mixture of musical description and background information may also prove attractive and helpful to the general music lover.

The approach here to the repertory of music is perhaps slightly different from those commonly found in introductory books. Description and elucidation remain the first considerations; but the reader will find that considerable emphasis is placed on history and context. I do not find myself especially sympathetic to a philosophy in which every work of art is regarded as an independent entity that can profitably be discussed simply for what it is: "what it is" – and thus the understanding of it – depends on when it was created, how men and women were thinking at the time, and the purpose for which it was created, as well as the techniques used in its creation. The mystical complexities of a Bach or the heroic strivings of a Beethoven assume a greater significance if we can begin to realize why these men were drawn to the mystical or the heroic.

The book begins with three chapters on the materials of music. The first treats "elements" (pitch, rhythm, harmony, key, etc), chiefly for the benefit of those not familiar or not fully familiar with them. It is not of course exhaustive but is designed to equip the reader sufficiently for what is to come, introducing concepts one at a time and assuming no prior knowledge. It includes an outline of the principles of notation that should be helpful to the student unfamiliar with printed or written music at least to an extent that he or she should be able to make something of the music-type examples appearing later in the book – though these will serve their purpose best if an instructor can, wherever the character of the example allows, make some kind of attempt at conveying their essence on a piano or with recordings. The second and third chapters discuss respectively musical instruments and the structures of music, again to a level that should enable the student to understand what ensues.

The main part of the book, Chapters IV to X, discusses the music of seven different eras, in chronological order from the Middle Ages to the present day. The principal author of the first two of these is Judith Nagley and of the last two Paul Griffiths, both of whose contributions I acknowledge with warm thanks. I myself, however, supplied the introductory sections to all seven of these chapters. In them I have made some attempt, not (of course) to give a comprehensive account of the social or the cultural history of the period concerned but to draw attention to features of contemporary social and cultural history (indeed political, intellectual and religious history too) that seem to relate in significant or suggestive ways to the music that is to be discussed, and also to outline the new stylistic weapons that composers forged to enable them to rise to the challenges of a changing world. The aim is to give the reader a sense of music as a part of the fabric of life, as something that changes as the world does, and so to heighten his or her understanding of it through this broader human context.

It is with these objectives in mind, too, that in the main text of the central chapters we have laid more stress than usual on biography. Without biographical discussion it is rarely possible to explain the purpose for which a piece of music was composed, on which its style and structure may acutely depend. Except in the earliest chapters, where the material scarcely exists, and the latest, where the familiarity of the modern world renders it progressively less necessary, a biographical account (sometimes brief, sometimes fuller) is included for important composers; and so that the scope of each composer's contribution

1 Map of Europe showing the principal centers of musical importance.

can clearly be seen, we also give in tabular form a summary list of works. A tabular biographical outline is also supplied for the most important composers. I believe that biography can be inherently interesting, that it can cast light on the society to which a composer belongs, and that, taken with the music itself, it may serve to stimulate the reader's interest and increase his or her involvement. I hope that the enthusiasm and the love of music that I and my co-authors feel, and have made no special effort to hide, may also infect the reader.

Many people come to music first of all through popular music of some sort. Our final chapter – written by Wilfrid Mellers, to whom I am much indebted – discusses the traditions of popular music in a way that in its different context may be seen as analogous to that pursued in the main historical chapters. I hope and believe that this chapter may provide a valuable way in for students more familiar with popular music than with other kinds.

The absence from this book of any substantial discussion of non-Western music ought not to be regarded as a symptom of ethnocentricity. The Western musical tradition (with its relatively recent Afro-American infusion, as treated in Chapter XI) is quite big enough, rich enough and complex enough to be the subject of an entire book. There are in the world other traditions of high complexity and richness, too, and to treat them cursorily or perfunctorily would be unwarrantedly patronizing. This book is in any case primarily for Westerners, who may be expected to be closer to their own traditions than to others'. Occasional remarks will be found at various points (especially in Chapter II) to remind the reader that the musical culture of the West is not the only one.

I would not like to claim that this book is a history of music as well as one about its understanding and enjoyment. It might, however, be described as a book "towards" a history of music. A history has to be comprehensive in a sense that this book does not aim to be: yet during the writing of it my co-authors and I have tried, by the careful selection of material within the composer discussions, and by the provision of a certain amount of "connecting tissue" outside them, not only to leave no serious gaps but also to give some indication of the lines of historical development and continuity.

Supplementary to the main text is a series of Listening Notes, printed at appropriate points in the chapters concerned. These – which follow no uniform scheme, since different music needs to be listened to in different ways – are designed to be read (with help and guidance from an instructor where that is suitable) while the music is actually being heard. Many of them are supported by more general discussion of the works in the main text. Suggestions for further listening, based on representative works referred to in the text, are offered on pp. 529–30.

It is never possible in the discussion of music (or any other specialized topic) to avoid the use of technical vocabulary. Much of this is explained as it is introduced; but all of it is covered in the Glossary (pp. 534–9), which through its cross-references to the main text has something of the nature of an index of musical topics. There is also a general index, chiefly of names.

Lastly, I should like to acknowledge the collaboration, at every stage in the preparation and editing of this book, of my close colleague and constant helper Alison Latham, who (among other tasks) prepared the tabular material and the Glossary; also the work as picture editor of Elisabeth Agate, whose imaginative contribution speaks for itself. We are grateful to Elisabeth Ingles for her patient work on seeing the book into print.

STANLEY SADIE

Chapter I

The Elements of Music

In every society, in every period of history, men and women have made music. They have sung it and danced to it; they have used it in solemn rituals and in light-hearted entertainments; they have listened to it in fields and forests, in temples, in bars, in concert halls and opera houses; they have made it not only with their voices but by adapting natural objects and banging them, scraping them and blowing through them; they have used it to generate collective emotion – to excite, to calm, to inspire action, to draw tears. Music is not a fringe activity or a luxury one: it is a central and necessary part of human existence.

Every human culture has found a musical style, and a means of expressing it, that arise from the needs, the history and the environment of that culture. In Black Africa, for example, where the native population has in general a stronger and

2 Dame Gladness leading a round dance: miniature from *Le Roman de la Rose*, c1420, by Guillaume de Lorris and Jean de Meun. Österreichische Nationalbibliothek, Vienna.

subtler command of rhythm than populations elsewhere, and where there has been a crucial need for quick communication over large distances, the musical culture is more closely concerned with drums and drumming than any other culture in the world. The "gong-chime culture" of Indonesia (the most important instruments are in effect sets of gongs) owes its existence to the fact that the region found its musical character during the late Bronze Age. The ancient courtly cultures of the East – such countries as China and Japan, India and Vietnam – developed musical traditions of high elaboration and refinement while the rural populations used music of much simpler kinds. In Western (European and American) music, the chief concern of this book, musical traditions arose chiefly from chant used in the early church, from the sophisticated art forms developed at the courts of kings and nobles, from the needs of the wider audiences that industrialization created, and from the technologies of the electronic age – while the rural population, and in more recent times the urban industrial one, has developed a more demotic or popular one of its own (see Chapter XI).

What, then, *is* music? It has been defined as "organized sound". A musical tone is the product of regular vibration in the air, and is perceived when an inner part of the listener's ear is made to vibrate in sympathy. A noise, by contrast, is the product of *irregular* vibration. Of the banging, scraping and blowing we mentioned above, the first may produce music or noise, according to the object banged and the ways in which it vibrates. Normally, scraping or striking a taut string, or causing a column of air to vibrate, will produce a musical tone. Any musical composition, or piece of music, will be made up of a very large number of musical tones, intended to be heard in a carefully ordered pattern.

The basic systems of ordering are three: *rhythm*, which governs the movement of music in time; *melody*, which means the linear arrangement of tones; and *harmony*, which deals with the simultaneous sounding of different tones. There are other important elements too, such as color and texture. We shall discuss these in turn, but need to start with an outline of the notation of music so that graphic expression of its shapes and patterns can be used to illustrate the discussion.

Notation

In non-literate societies, there is no need for musical notation, nor any possibility of it; all music is passed on by ear, one generation learning a repertory or store of tunes by listening to an older generation singing or playing it. The same applied for a time with ecclesiastical chant, in our literate, Western society; but eventually, so that repertories could be stored, reproduced or distributed, a system had to be devised to indicate how music should be performed. This was at first done with little signs ("neumes") that could be written above or below the words and which showed in a symbolic way a number of standard small groupings of notes. Many other notation methods, however, have been devised in different cultures, suited to the kinds of music each culture favored and usually based on the local form of script. Many notation systems tell the performer not what tone is to be sounded but where to put his fingers on the instrument he is playing to produce the one that is wanted. This kind of system ("tablature") is still widely used, especially for the guitar.

Pitch

There are two basic facts that any musical notation has to convey: first, the *pitch* of a tone; second, its *duration*. As regards pitch, we define tones as *high* or *low*. Musical notation, in the standard Western system, shows pitch by the positioning of the symbol (or note), representing each musical tone, on a five-line *staff* (or stave) of fixed pitch. The staff shown in ex. I.1 carries an indication, in the sign at the left (the *clef* sign, providing the key – *clef* is French for key), of the level at which the pitch is fixed. This is a traditional script sign for the letter G, and it means that the second line from the bottom represents the note called by that letter (which is created by a vibration of about 390 cycles per second – or, as generally given nowadays, 390 Hertz or Hz). This, the G clef, is also called the *treble clef*. The first note shown on the staff signifies the note G; the notes that follow move up in sequence to form a *scale*. They are placed alternately on the lines and in the spaces between the lines. Where the music needs to run off the top or the bottom of the staff, small extra lines (called leger or ledger lines) are added, as we see for the last three notes of ex. 1. Music that

ex. I.1

is lower pitched is written in the F clef or *bass clef*, where the symbol on the fourth line up signifies an F, the note nine below the treble-clef G. The C clef, fixing the note halfway between these, is used for instruments of intermediate pitch. Ex. I.2 shows the notes on and close to the treble and bass clefs. The notes are labeled alphabetically, in upward sequence, with the letters from A to G, which are then repeated.

ex. I.2

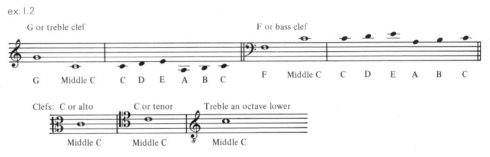

The study of pitch has occupied scientists and musical thinkers since ancient Greek times. The mathematician Pythagoras – famous for his discoveries in geometry – is believed to have been the first to discover the basic facts about pitch intervals. The simplest interval is the *octave*: this is the interval at which pitches seem to be duplicated. If you sing or play a simple scale, the eighth note seems in some clear but indefinable way to be "the same" as the first, only higher. When women and men sing together, the men automatically sing an octave lower than the women; women use the treble clef, men generally use the bass.

Pythagoras found that there exists a natural 2:1 ratio between tones an octave apart. A string two feet long, set in vibration, will produce a particular tone; halve the length to one foot (and keep the tension the same), and the resulting tone will be an octave higher – or double the tension (and keep the length the same), and the sound will also be an octave higher. This applies equally to a column of air; a tube two feet long will produce a tone an octave lower than a tube one foot long. We now understand this phenomenon in terms of vibration (which Pythagoras and his followers had no means of measuring): the longer string or the longer tube creates vibrations at half the speed of the shorter. The note to which most symphony orchestras tune their instruments is A, which is 440Hz (this is the second note in

Octaves

ex.I.1); the note an octave lower is 220Hz, two octaves lower is 110, an octave higher is 880. On a full-size modern piano, the lowest note is an A, 27.5Hz, and the highest A – seven octaves higher – is 3520Hz; the human ear can cope with musical sounds almost an octave below the lowest A before they degenerate into mere rumble, and more than two octaves above the highest.

Scales

The notes shown in ex. 1 are, on a piano keyboard, the white notes; these form what is called a *diatonic scale*. The seven intervals between its eight notes are made up of five full steps (of a whole tone or two semitones) and two half steps (of one semitone); the half steps fall at E–F and B–C. This kind of scale was used well into the Middle Ages. Then intermediate steps began to be used, and, as the diagram of the piano keyboard (ex. I.3) shows, the five larger steps of the diatonic scale were filled in, with black notes. The note midway between C and D is called C sharp (notated C♯) or D flat (D♭). This shows how the octave is divided into 12 equal steps (or semitones), forming what is called the *chromatic scale* (ex. I.4). The sharp and flat signs are called *accidentals*; they can be contradicted by the natural sign (♮).

ex. I.3

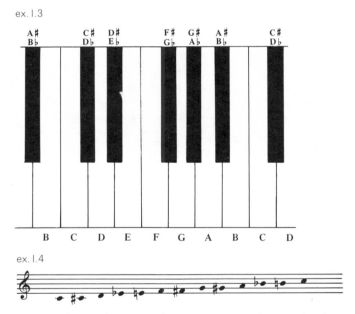

ex. I.4

Intervals

No relationship among the notes is as close as that between two an octave apart, but some of the *intervals* (as they are called) are closer in feeling than others. Pythagoras found, as well as the 2:1 octave relationship, a 3:2 relationship for notes a 5th apart, and 4:3 for a 4th (see ex. I.5). There are simple number ratios for all the basic intervals between notes of the scale. These intervals are defined by the number of notes they include, counting both the bottom one and the top one: the octave is eight notes, from one A to the next, the 5th five notes (A–E), the 2nd two (A–B). Some intervals – 2nds, 3rds, 6ths and 7ths – need to be identified as "major" or "minor" as they may include different numbers of semitones: C–E, for example, is a major 3rd, made up of four semitones, while D–F, of three, is a minor 3rd. Intervals of 4ths and 5ths are described as "perfect" when made up of five and seven semitones respectively; in the white-note diatonic scale there is one 4th (F–B) and one 5th (B–F) of six semitones and these are called, respectively, "augmented" and "diminished". Ex. 5a shows the intervals in semitones up from C; ex. 5b shows them with their inversions (that is, the intervals that complement them in the octave).

ex. I.5

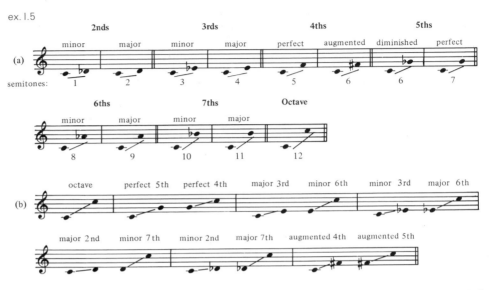

Most historic Western music uses the diatonic scale as its primary material, drawing mainly on the seven-note octave but adding notes from the additional five as they may be needed. Over the last hundred or so years, the use of the extra, chromatic notes has become increasingly frequent, most of all in and since the compositions of such men as Wagner and Debussy. In the present century, in fact, compositional systems have been devised, and widely used, that take as their starting-point the principle of using all 12 tones equally.

The traditional Western division of the octave into seven and 12, though it has some basis in natural, scientific fact, is not universal. Many folk cultures use a five-note division (called *pentatonic*); a familiar example of a pentatonic melody is *Auld lang syne*. Pentatonic scales are widely used, for example in China, parts of Africa and South-east Asia, and in much European folksong. Then more complex divisions of the octave are also found, for example in India, where there are 22-note scales – though in these, and the 31-note divisions that have been proposed, the notes become so close that the ear has difficulty in telling what notes are intended. Intervals smaller than a semitone have also been used in Western music, especially by eastern Europeans (who find "microtones" in some of their folk music) and such modern experimental composers as the American John Cage.

Rhythm

The most basic element in music is *rhythm*; some musical systems, in fact, use rhythm alone. While painting and architecture depend on space, music depends on time. Our perception of time in music is related, first, to the establishment of a regular pulse (for which there are models in nature and everyday life, like a person's heartbeat, breathing or walking, or the ticking of a clock), and second, to the use of accent and duration, by means of which groupings can be constructed.

Pulse, tempo

The most usual way for a composer to express the rhythmic structure of his music – that is, the timing of the notes – is for him to indicate the *pulse*: this is done with a conventional word, probably an Italian one (see the list below), to suggest the speed or tempo, though he may be more precise and state exactly how many beats are required per minute, using a metronome marking (a metronome is a clockwork pendulum, calibrated so that it can be set at different speeds). Then he will also indicate how the beats are to be grouped, whether in twos, threes or fours (these are by far the most common):

ONE two ONE two ONE two ONE two . . .
ONE two three ONE two three ONE two three . . .
ONE two THREE four ONE two THREE four ONE two THREE . . .
(The capital letters denote the accented beats; in groups of four, a secondary, lighter accent falls on the third beat.)

Meter

Counting in this manner shows the *meter* of a piece of music – that is, the beats and their groupings. The actual rhythms of the music are heard with the meter as an understood background; in some kinds of music, for example music for dancing,

---

Tempo markings

prestissimo	very fast indeed
presto	very fast
allegro	fast, cheerful
vivace	vivacious
allegretto	moderately fast
moderato	moderate
andantino	moderately slow
andante	slowish but moving along
larghetto	slowish, broadly
largo	broadly
adagio	slow
lento	slow
grave	gravely

Italian terms are chiefly used for tempo as it was Italian composers who dominated European music when tempo marks came into use. None of them is precise in meaning; several are more indications of mood than of speed.

There are also a number of terms used to modify a tempo mark; these are the most important:

assai	enough
molto	very
poco	a little
più	more
meno	less
ma non troppo	but not too much

The following indicate a gradual change in tempo:

rit. (= *ritenuto, ritardando*) } *rall.* (= *rallentando*) }	becoming slower
accel. (= *accelerando*)	becoming faster

ex. I.6

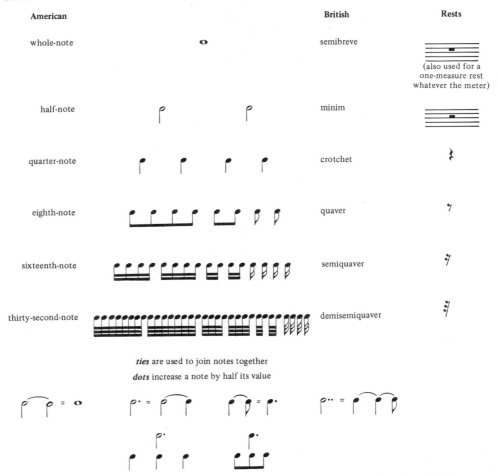

The American note names work on a mathematical basis of proportional lengths (as do the German); the British (like most other European) preserve something of the original Latin names.

Eighth-notes and shorter ones may be written with "beams" (as shown on the left of ex. 6), to improve legibility and to indicate metrical groupings; the grouping with beams may be shorter (as shown just right of center) as long as it conforms to the metrical divisions, or the notes may be shown separated (as on the right). Note the "flags": none on a quarter-note, one on an eighth, two on a sixteenth, and so on.

for large-scale communal singing, or above all in popular music, the meter or beat will tend to be strongly emphasized. Marches provide a good example of a meter in twos, or duple – obviously, as we all have two legs. Familiar instances of duple meter are *She'll be comin' round the mountain* and *Greensleeves*. Waltzes are always in triple meter; other examples are *The Star-Spangled Banner* and *The First Nowell*. In quadruple meter are *O come, all ye faithful*, *Swing low, sweet chariot* and *Way down upon the Swanee river*. (It is worth trying to hum through some of these, thinking about the meter and the accents; try other songs you know, too, to increase your awareness of meter.) Some music is without meter at all: early church chant is often performed without meter, taking its rhythm from the words (we do not know if that is how it was originally performed), and there are types of non-Western and advanced Western music that do without it.

If the pitch of a note is the "vertical" element when we look at musical notation, then the horizontal element is rhythm. We have seen how the height of a note on the staff shows its pitch; its placing in horizontal distance along the staff – reading from left to right, as one reads words in Western languages – shows when it is to be sounded and for how long.

The modern system of rhythmic notation is believed to have been devised in its essentials by a thirteenth-century writer, Franco of Cologne. He suggested a series of notes of different shapes to express different durations; the shapes have of course changed over seven centuries, but the principle and some of the details remain. His two main note values were the long (in Latin, *longa*) and the short (*brevis*), with the half-short (*semibrevis*) for quicker-moving passages; sometimes there were two shorts to each long (or half-shorts to each short), sometimes three. Over the centuries, note lengths have grown slower, so that nowadays the basic longest note is the old half-short, which is called a whole-note or, in British usage, a semibreve. In place of the variable 2:1 or 3:1 ratio between successive note values, we now use a fixed 2:1 system. But provision has to be made for the possibility of dividing notes into three, and for that purpose we have the additional convention of adding a dot after a note, which augments its value by half. Ex. I.6 shows the standard note values. Musical notation has to provide not only for notes but also for silences of exact length: so there exists a system of *rests*, equivalent in length to each of the note values.

Regular meter is conveyed in notation by means of a *time signature* or *meter signature*. This, consisting of one number above another, is placed at the beginning of each piece to tell the performer how the beats in the piece are grouped and what the duration of each of them is. The lower number indicates the unit: 4 (the most common) represents a quarter-note, 2 a half-note, 8 an eighth-note (16, even 32, is possible but very rare). The upper number shows how many of this unit are in each *measure* or *bar*; the measures are ruled off by vertical bar-lines. The first note of each measure has a natural metrical accent.

The commonest time signature is 4/4 (often notated by its equivalent C, a relic of early time-signature systems, sometimes taken to stand for "common time"): some typical groupings of note values in measures of 4/4 are shown in ex. I.7. Also much

ex. I.7

used among duple and quadruple signatures are 2/4 and 2/2 (or its equivalent ₵). Easily the most common triple time signature is 3/4. All these are what are known as "simple" time signatures, in that their unit beats are divisible by 2. Sometimes, however, the unit beats need to be divisible by 3, and have to be dotted notes; these are called "compound" time signatures, and of them the one most often used is 6/8. This means that there are six eighth-notes in each measure, divided into two groups of three; 6/8 is a duple meter (it is the meter of *Greensleeves*), but a compound duple one. 9/8 and 12/8 are the standard compound triple and compound quadruple meters. All the most common time signatures are charted in ex. I.8.

ex. 1.8

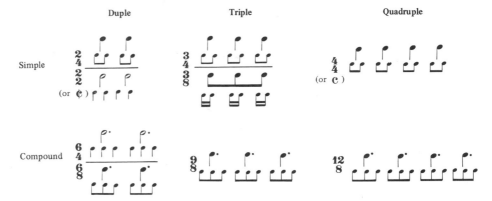

3 Rhythm in action: the
conductor Pierre Boulez in
rehearsal, 1971.

Melody

Melody has been defined as a "succession of notes in a musically expressive order". Certainly, to most people's minds, melody is the heart of music; no aspect of musical skill is as much prized as the ability to compose melodies that are shapely, expressive and memorable.

Anything that involves a perceptible sequence of tones may be regarded as a melody – from a nursery song to a line of ecclesiastical chant, from a folk dance to the angular music declaimed in a Stravinsky sacred work, from a Bach fugue subject to last week's hit song. Generally, however, we think of melody in terms of tunefulness, in the capacity of a line of music to impress itself quickly and clearly on the memory; in that sense, some of the examples just cited might fail to qualify. The present discussion is concerned primarily with this more limited conception of melody.

ex. I.9

(a) Oh, say can you see, by the dawn's ear-ly light, What so proud-ly we hail'd at the twi-light's last gleam-ing? Whose broad stripes and bright stars, thro' the per-il-ous fight, O'er the ram-parts we watch'd were so gal-lant-ly stream-ing? And the rock-et's red glare, the bombs burst-ing in air, Gave proof thro' the night that our flag was still there. Oh say does that star- span-gled ban-ner yet wave o'er the land of the free and the home of the brave?

(b) Should auld ac-quaint-ance be for-got And ne-ver brought to mind? Should auld ac-quaint-ance be for-got And days of auld lang syne? And days of auld lang syne, my dear, and days of auld lang syne, Should auld ac-quaint-ance be for-got And days of auld lang syne?

(c) L'hom - me, L'hom - me, L'homme ar - mé, L'homme ar-mé, L'homme ar-mé doibt on doubt - er, doibt on doubt-er. On a fait par-tout cri - er Que chas - cun se viegne ar - mer D'un hau - bre - gon de fer. repeat A - B

The armed man, the armed man: dare one hesitate? On all sides they are crying that each person should arm himself with a coat of mail.

(d) Sah ein Knab ein Rös-lein stehn, Rös-lein auf der Hei - den, war so jung und mor - gen-schön,

lief er schnell, es nah zu sehn sah's mit vie - len Freu - den. Rös-lein, Rös-lein, Rös-lein rot,

Rös - lein auf der Hei - den.

A boy saw a little rose standing on the heath; it was so young and morning-fresh that he ran quickly to see it, and saw it with great delight – little red rose on the heath. (In the succeeding verses he goes to pick it; it threatens him with its thorn; he picks it, and the thorn pierces deep into his hand; he long remembers the little red rose on the heath.)

Ex. I.9 shows four melodies: *The Star-Spangled Banner*, of which the tune was composed by J. S. Smith in the late eighteenth century; the traditional *Auld lang syne*; the fifteenth-century *L'homme armé*; and Schubert's *Heidenröslein*, written in 1815. Each of these melodies is built out of a series of short phrases, planned sometimes to answer one another, sometimes to repeat or echo. All are vocal melodies, so that there is a relationship between music and words; mostly, a phrase in the music corresponds with a line in the poem. *The Star-Spangled Banner* consists of two-measure and four-measure phrases, in a 2+2+4 pattern, so that each pair of short phrases is answered by a longer one; the first group of this kind is immediately repeated, then comes a *sequence* (a phrase repeated at higher or – as here – lower pitch) of two measures, followed by a phrase which echoes at its close one heard earlier. Finally, the concluding phrase takes the music to a clear climax with the ascent to the high note just before the end. The use of upward-leaping phrases and dotted rhythms is typical of music intended to be stirring (compare for example the French national anthem, the *Marseillaise*).

The phrase structure of *Auld lang syne* is much simpler: 4+4+4+4. Further, the last four measures match almost exactly the second four, while the third four follow the first quite closely. The rhythms are also very consistent, but they are largely determined by the meter of the verse. Here again there is a high note near the end to provide a sense of climax.

The other two melodies will not be so familiar. *L'homme armé* ("The armed man") was one of the earliest melodies to achieve wide popularity; composers in the fifteenth and sixteenth centuries built entire works around it. Its composer is unknown and it may have a folk origin. It is quite subtly constructed, with phrases less square than the other melodies: the pattern is 4+1, 4+2; 4+4+4; (repeat of the first part). The groups marked *x* and *y*, though not exactly matching, help make a clear unity of the melody – as too does the rhythmic near-correspondence of the four-measure phrases of the second part with the opening four measures. The overall pattern, *A–B–A*, is (as we shall see in Chapter III) a common one, in music of all kinds and periods.

In the Schubert song, *Heidenröslein* ("Little rose on the heath"), the opening four-measure phrase is answered by another – beginning the same way, then taking a new twist in the second measure by changing the C to C♯, and a further new twist by adding two further measures before reaching a point of rest. Then two further two-measure phrases, the first of them a clear echo of measures 3 and 4, carry the music away from the resting-point of D to G. Note the point of climax on the high note (with a pause sign over it, showing that the singer may linger there) close to the end; note too the smooth movement of the whole melodic line, which tends to go by stepping from one note to another rather than skipping. Writing of this kind, called *conjunct*, is normally used in gentle, lyrical contexts, while more *disjunct* melodies, with many skips, are used to make a more strong, energetic effect.

A number of general points about melodies can be made on the basis of the songs we have looked at (though it would be necessary to examine very many more to see anywhere near the full variety of melodic character even in Western music). First, we can note that melodies are made up of individual phrases, usually of two or four measures; often the composer aims to have some variety in phrase length and to balance shorter and longer phrases. Second, the music heard at the beginning recurs at some later point; it may be as an immediate repeat or as a recall after other, contrasting music. Third, there are likely to be resting points in the course of the melody, some momentary, some more strongly defined; these are called *cadences* (after a Latin word meaning "fall"), and there is virtually always a decisive one at the end. Fourth, there may be patterns, of line or of rhythms or both, that recur in the course of the melody and give it a clear sense of unity. Fifth, there is often some kind of climax point, with a rising phrase and a high note, close to the end.

We shall be returning to the subject of melody, and its character at different times in musical history, later in this book, but particularly in Chapter III, where we shall consider the role of melody – of every kind, from the extended to the fragmentary – in relation to larger musical structures.

> Cadence

Key, tonality

One matter of particular importance in the discussion of musical form – that is, the way elements are arranged in a musical work to make it coherent – is *tonality*. If you hear or play any of the four melodies we have just been considering, and break off shortly before the end, you will find that you instinctively and unmistakably know what the final tone should be. The music is drawn to a particular tone as if with a gravitational pull. If, as with the first two melodies, that tone is C, the music is said to be "in C". Had we written *The Star-Spangled Banner* beginning one note higher, on A rather than G, and kept all the same relationships between notes, it would have ended on D and been "in D"; we would have *transposed* it from C into D.

It is not, however, simply a matter of the last tone. The fact that the melody is in C affects the role each tone plays in it. C is the central tone, the *tonic*, but G is almost as important: note how the music comes to rest on G at the words "light" and "fight", and later (more decisively) at "there" – and it is a G that provides the climax (on "free") at the end. When music is in C, G is called the *dominant*, and is almost always treated as the obvious alternative tonic – for in all but very short pieces the composer will generally change the tonal center or *key* from time to time. Of course, all this applies equally at different pitches: for music in A, the dominant is E, and for music in E♭ it is B♭. Any melody, indeed any piece of music, may be transposed from one pitch to another without changing its internal note relationships; it will merely sound higher or lower.

> Tonic, dominant

We saw earlier (p. 15) that the diatonic scale consists of a sequence of notes equivalent to the white notes on the piano keyboard. This group of seven different pitches (the octave duplication does not count), which provided the basic material of music well into the Middle Ages, still can provide all that is necessary for music that does not change key at all (*Auld lang syne*, for example, has no notes with accidentals, and *The Star-Spangled Banner* adds only sharps to the note F when it leans towards the key of G). The white notes on the piano make up the scale of C major. Make all the F's into F sharps, and the notes make up G major; sharpen the C's as well, and it is D major. Or flatten the B's, and a scale of F major results. The process of adding sharps and flats may be continued up to six of each – six sharps is F♯ major, six flats G♭ major (which are different ways of saying the same thing,

ex. I.10

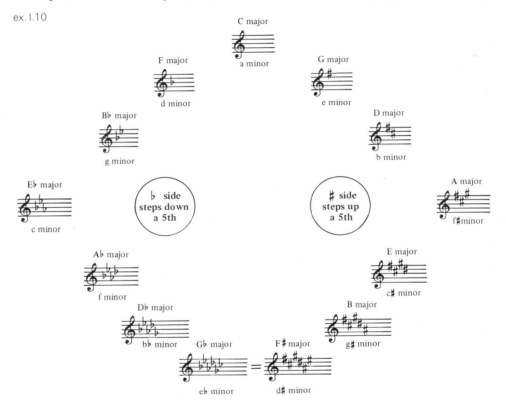

because on the piano F♯ and G♭ are the same note). There is, then, a "circle of keys", which is mapped out in ex. I.10. This shows the *key signature* for each key: when a composer wants to write in (say) D major, all the F's and C's will need to be sharpened, so instead of laboriously writing them in every time, they are shown in a key signature at the beginning, with the understanding that all the sharps or flats specified will be observed throughout.

Key signatures

Major, minor

So far we have dealt only with major keys – those in which, when the notes used are equivalent to the white ones on the piano, the music gravitates towards C. Some, however, work differently: when the same selection of notes is used, the music gravitates not towards C but towards A. These are the *minor* keys. The tonal center in a minor-key piece is a minor 3rd (three semitones) below that of its major equivalent; A minor is called the *relative minor* of C major, and C major the *relative major* of A minor. In reality, the scales are not identical, even though the key signatures are; in A minor, for example, the note G (and to a lesser extent the note F) often needs to be sharpened if the melodic line is to run smoothly. The minor key relative to each major is shown in ex. 10. Ex. 9c, *L'homme armé*, although it comes from a period before the major and minor keys were established, is akin to a minor-key piece: its first section (and its last) end on D, when in a major piece they would be expected to end on F (and the middle section on A rather than C). It is generally thought that music in minor keys is more sad, more serious, perhaps more threatening in character than that in major keys (though of course there is plenty of sad major-key and cheerful minor-key music).

It will be clear from the special relationship we have noted between a key and its dominant, and from the circle of keys shown in ex. 10, that some keys are more closely related than others. When C is the tonic, G, we saw, is the chief complementary key; but F is also close – one step in the flat direction (or anti-clockwise in ex. 10), while G is one step in the sharp direction (and C, of course, is the dominant of F: which is why we call F the *subdominant* of C). A piece of music in C major is likely to change key first of all to G, but it may well change, too, to F, to A minor, and to the relative minors of G and F (E minor and D minor). Composers use such key changes for contrast in feeling and to help establish the form of a piece – for the changes are perceptible to the listener and create natural divisions between its sections. In a longer piece, or one where the composer is aiming for dramatic effects, changes to more distant keys (ones further round the circle from the tonic of the piece) are usual. The process of changing key is called *modulation*.

Modulation

Tonality came to be recognized as an important element in musical composition around the year 1600. But well before then the pull of a tonic, or a home note, was an important factor in composition. The home note was not, however, always C or A when the diatonic scale A–B–C–D–E–F–G was used. Back in ancient Greek times, music theorists had devised a series of *modes*, in which the whole-step and half-step intervals between notes were differently placed; each had its own name and its own supposed expressive character. Medieval theorists took this up and they too devised a series of modes (to which they gave Greek names), six in all, with the whole steps and half steps differently related to the final note. The Dorian mode, for example, had D as the final note when the white notes were used. Medieval and Renaissance composers were also keenly aware of the different expressive character of each mode.

Modes

Harmony

So far, we have been discussing music as if it were a single line of sound. In fact, for about the last thousand years almost all composed art music in the Western world has involved two or more simultaneous sounds. The term used for the combination of sounds is *harmony*.

The earliest forms of harmony in Western music (and probably in any music) arose when traditional church chant was sung not by all the monks together but by only some of them while others sang something different – usually either a fixed tone or in tones moving parallel with the chant melody (see ex. I.11). This was regarded as adding a clothing to the melody, and an element of depth to the music. Harmony still has that function, as we hear when, for example, a hymn is sung with organ accompaniment, or a guitar plays in support of a voice, or a pianist adds a left-hand part below a right-hand melody. The organ, the guitar or the pianist's left hand will normally play combinations of several notes, or *chords*.

Chords

ex. I.11

(chant in white notes, added part in black notes)

te   hu - mi - les   fa - mu - li   mo - du - lis   ve - ne - ran - do   pi - is

Ideas have varied a great deal as to what combinations of notes make good harmony. Ex. 11 shows that in the tenth century the interval of a 4th was specially favored. Other types of early harmony move mainly in 5ths; movement in parallel 5ths is also used in some kinds of folk singing. By the Renaissance the *triad* had become the main unit of harmony. This is a three-note chord built up in 3rds, or by filling in the central gap in the interval of a 5th. The triad has remained the basic element in Western harmony until well into the present century; it is used not only with the notes in their basic order, 1–3–5, as shown in ex. I.12a, but also in *inversions* – that is, with the same notes but in a different vertical order, as shown in ex. 12b.

Triads

ex. I.12

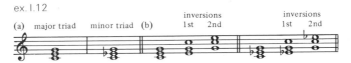

Anyone who has tried picking out a melody on the piano and adding chords to it knows that an acceptable harmony can be made for many melodies just by using two or three triads. Ex. I.13 shows the opening of *Auld lang syne* harmonized with three triads, those on the tonic, the dominant and the subdominant. *The Star-Spangled Banner* is a more developed melody, and though it too could be very simply harmonized it sounds much better with a wider range of harmonies, as ex. I.14, with its opening measures, shows; two of the chords there (marked ★) are inversions. The full stirring effect of the melody can be made only with its proper, rich harmony. The way a note is harmonized often changes its sense in a piece of

ex. I.13

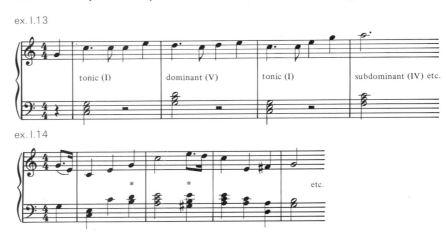

music; ex. I.15*a* shows the same note with several different harmonies beneath it (some are simple triads, others have additional notes), and if you listen to these you will realize that your expectation of what (if anything) is likely to follow differs from one to another.

ex. I.15

Consonance, dissonance

Ex. 15*b* shows two of these chords with the chords that naturally succeed them. The first chord of each of those pairs is a *dissonance*: it embodies a feeling of clashing or of tension, which needs to be resolved. The chord that resolves a dissonance is normally a *consonance* or a smoother-sounding chord. The tension generated by dissonances can provide a sense of movement and energy to a piece of music. Sometimes a composer resolves one dissonance on to another, and then a third, and so on, holding the listener in a state of tension until the moment of resolution. Bach and Handel used that method to give their music rhythmic impetus; Wagner went very much further, sustaining the tension by moving from one dissonance to another for entire acts in his operas (sometimes as much as two hours of music – it can be exhausting to listen to!).

Ideas have, of course, differed a great deal from time to time about which intervals are consonant and which are dissonant. In traditional Western triadic harmony, two tones a semitone (or minor 2nd) apart, or the inversion of that (a major 7th), form the strongest dissonance in our system; also quite dissonant – although found smooth enough, it seems, in the tenth century – is the 4th. These are shown, with their usual resolutions, in ex. I.16*a*. In the fifteenth century, even a full major triad was felt inappropriate for the final chord of a piece and an "open 5th" was preferred (ex. 16*b*); full triads were usual for concluding chords in the period 1600–1900, but in the twentieth century composers have tended to treat dissonance more freely – ex. 16*c* shows the final chords of three works by Stravinsky. But by this time, the early twentieth century, new ideas were replacing the principles of triadic harmony; some composers, like Bartók, were using 4ths rather than 3rds as a basis for constructing chords.

If harmony can help provide forward movement in music, it can also do the

ex. I.16

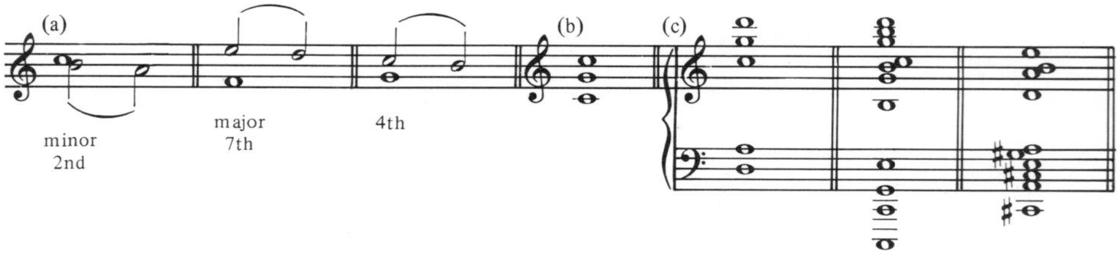

opposite and provide a musical equivalent of punctuation marks. We saw, in the melodies of ex. 9, that there are natural stopping places or cadences – strong ones at the end of each, rather weaker ones at various points on the way (generally coinciding with the ends of lines of verse). When they have a clear air of finality they are called "perfect cadences" or "full cadences", and generally lead from the

4 Rehearsal of an 18th-century sacred work in the presence of monks: ink drawing. 18th century, by Joseph Bergler the younger, Kupferstichkabinett, Berlin.

dominant to the tonic; the most important secondary kind, called "imperfect cadences" or "half cadences", lead to the dominant. There are examples of both kinds in ex. I.17, a partial harmonization of a line of *Auld lang syne*. Cadences of

ex. I.17

these kinds are the most basic material of harmony, for harmony is not simply single chords but progressions of chords, and it derives its character from the way successive chords relate to one another.

Counterpoint, polyphony

Much music, as we have seen, consists of melody with accompanying harmony. But much, too, consists of melodic lines that are heard against one another, and are woven together so that their individual notes harmonize. The word derives from the idea of note-against-note, or point-against-point – for which the medieval Latin is *punctus contra punctum*. Music that uses counterpoint is called *contrapuntal*. An important and more general term for music made up of several strands is *polyphony* (from the Greek word for music of "many sounds"); two terms related to it, and often opposed to it, are *monophony* (which applies to music of "one sound", or a single line of melody) and *homophony* (music of "like sounds", meaning all the voices moving in the same rhythm, like a melody with each note harmonized).

Techniques of counterpoint, of composing one line against another, were particularly important to the composer in the late Middle Ages and the Renaissance, when it was usual for church music to incorporate traditional chants. Ways were devised of composing melodies to be sung against these chants, or of weaving the chants into the musical texture of a piece (the term *texture* is a useful one for distinguishing between music that is mainly harmonic, or homophonic, and music that is mainly polyphonic or contrapuntal). The late Renaissance period, the sixteenth century, is generally acknowledged to have been a "golden age" of polyphony, when with composers like Josquin and Palestrina these techniques were brought to the highest point of refinement. Central to this kind of polyphony was the idea of *imitation* – that is, of one voice (or instrument) imitating the musical line sung (or played) by another. Ex. I.18*a* shows a brief passage in simple counterpoint, where the two lines each have some melodic character but "go" together (in no sense is the lower simply a harmonization of the upper); ex. 18*b* shows a brief

Imitation

ex. I.18

passage in imitative counterpoint, where two phrases (*x* and *y*) are heard first in one voice and then imitated in the other. The concept of imitative counterpoint is not of course unfamiliar to anyone who has tried to sing *Three Blind Mice* or *Frère Jacques*; these are rounds, and the music is in *canon*, a special kind of imitation that is continuous and very exact. In most imitative counterpoint the imitation continues for only a few notes and it is usually at a different pitch.

There was another golden age of counterpoint in the early eighteenth century,

5 The importance of music in royal ceremonial is shown by this engraving of trumpets and kettledrums in procession: from the *History of the Coronation of James II and Queen Mary* (1687) by Francis Sandford.

with J. S. Bach as its greatest figure. This is a more elaborate, faster-moving type of counterpoint than that of the sixteenth century, more instrumental than vocal. Composers have continued to use counterpoint to enrich and add variety to the texture of their music, and to give their music a sense of greater depth and intellectual weight – for music in which all the interest lies on the surface is apt to seem thinner than music where the interest, sometimes at least, irradiates the entire texture.

Color, dynamics

Composers can, as we have seen, create variety in their music by several different means: by its texture, its rhythmic character, its speed, its key structure. Two other weapons in the composer's arsenal are tone color and dynamic level. A tone sounds quite different when played on different instruments or sung by the human voice: in the next chapter we will look more closely at the instruments a composer has at his disposal. He can also – with most instruments, but not all – ask the player to produce sounds at various levels of volume. These he indicates, as with speeds, by a series of Italian terms (see table).

abbreviation	term	meaning
ff	*fortissimo*	very loud
f	*forte*	loud
mf	*mezzo forte*	moderately loud
mp	*mezzo piano*	moderately quiet
p	*piano*	quiet
pp	*pianissimo*	very quiet

Some composers wanting extreme effects have gone further, in each direction; in a few scores *fff* and *ffff* are to be found, as are *ppp* and *pppp* – Tchaikovsky even asked for *pppppp* at one point in a symphony. There are also terms for other effects that involve dynamic levels:

cresc.	*crescendo*	growing (louder)
dim.	*diminuendo*	diminishing, getting quieter
sf	*sforzando, sforzato*	
sfz		forced, accented
fz	*forzando, forzato*	

Chapter II

The Instruments of Music

At the beginning of Chapter I, we saw that musical sounds are produced by regular vibration in the air. Human beings have devised numerous ways of creating this vibration: first of all by singing, later by playing instruments.

The simplest, most primitive kinds of instrument are lumps of wood or stone, fashioned so that the player can strike them. Lumps of different sizes were found to produce sounds of different pitches, and hollow objects to produce a fuller sound than solid ones (because the air in the cavity takes up the vibration in resonance). A skin stretched across a hollowed-out object gives a still better sound; this in fact creates a drum. The simplest *wind instruments* came into being when someone thought of blowing across a leaf or a straw, through a hollow bone or horn, or into a reedpipe. Anthropologists have found animal bones with holes made in them which would enable a player to produce sounds of different pitch. The earliest *string instruments* probably grew out of the discovery that a taut string, when plucked, could produce a musical sound, and that the sound could be magnified by the attachment of a box of some sort to the object bearing the string.

Primitive peoples used the materials available to them to make instruments of various kinds. In countries where bamboo grows, for example, a series of cut lengths of bamboo can be made into an instrument to be struck, and will produce a range of pitches. With a thin piece of cane attached, or with a carefully shaped opening at one end, a length of bamboo can be made into a wind instrument. With slivers of wood pared loose (remaining attached each end) and with a couple of wedges inserted under them, it can become a "string" instrument, with the hollow tube serving as resonator.

Virtually all instruments belong to one of four categories. The simplest are the *idiophones* ("own-sounding"), where the body of the instrument is set in vibration by the player and is itself the sound-producing object. Examples are bells, cymbals, xylophones and rattles. When a skin or membrane – rather than the instrument's actual vibrating body – is struck, the instrument is a *membranophone*; this group includes little other than drums, though kazoos also belong to it and so does the comb-and-paper. Wind instruments are called *aerophones*; this category includes trumpets, flutes, clarinets and organs. String instruments, or *chordophones*, range from the piano and the harp to the violin and the guitar. To these four classes a fifth has lately been added, *electrophones*, instruments that produce their sound by electric or electronic means, like the electric organ or the synthesizer.

Plate 1 *Opposite* King David playing a positive organ, with hurdy-gurdy and cymbalum: miniature from the *Rutland Psalter*, English, *c*1270 (the type of lavishly illustrated manuscript mentioned on p. 87). British Library, London.

CCE NOMEN

domini ue nit de longin quo et claritas eius replet

orbem terrarum. INVITAT. Regem uenturum do

minum uenite adore mus.

Epła ad Ro
mai

Hora est iam nos de somno surgere. et aperti sunt oculi nostri surgere ad xpm quia lux uera

est fulgens in celis. V. Egdiet uirga.

SPICIENS

A LONGE ecce uide

o de i potentiam uenien

tem. et nebu lam totam terram

tegen tem ite ob uiam

e i & dicite Nuncia

nobis si tu es ipse

Qui regnaturus es

Voice

The human voice may not exactly be an instrument, but it is certainly the oldest means of music-making, and it remains the most natural and the most expressive. Unlike the other sources of sound to be discussed in this chapter, the voice is actually a part of the body of the performer; he or she is thus more dependent on natural gifts (if a singer's voice fails, he cannot buy a new one). The "vocal cords", which we cause to vibrate when we sing, are folds of skin in the throat. We make their vibrations resonate in the cavities of the chest or head, and can automatically adjust the shape and size of those cavities by muscular control according to the note we want to sing and the syllable we sing to it.

Female

We saw in Chapter I that the pitch of a woman's voice is normally in the treble clef and a man's in the bass. But there is a good deal of variation. A high-pitched woman's voice is called *soprano*, a low one *contralto* or simply *alto*, and an intermediate one *mezzo-soprano* (meaning half-soprano and sometimes called just *mezzo*). The normal pitch ranges of these voices are shown in ex. II.1, but voices

ex. II.1

vary greatly and many singers can range wider without loss of quality. The soprano voice is probably the most prized of all. The vast majority of the great women's roles in opera are for sopranos; a significant exception is Carmen, Bizet's sultry gipsy, which is a mezzo part. Sopranos may be gentle and lyrical, or bright and bell-like with a capacity for rapid, high singing (called *coloratura*), or grand and brilliant (like the heroines of Wagner's operas). In a large modern choir the sopranos are usually the largest group, not only because it is the commonest voice among women but because the soprano voice is generally the lightest and more are needed if the sopranos are to hold their own against the other groups.

Male

The highest normal male voice is the *tenor*, the lowest the *bass*; between them lies the *baritone*. The pitch ranges are shown in ex. II.2. For the last two hundred years the tenor has been regarded as the main voice for heroic singing and for expressing

ex. II.2

ardent love. Opera composers tend to have tenor heroes and bass villains, though the richness and masculinity of the bass voice have often led to its use for kings or warriors or sympathetic fathers; there is also a tradition of comic bass parts. The strong, warm sound of the baritone voice has been much called upon for dramatic and heroic roles.

All these different voice types are used in large choirs; most of the repertory of choral music is composed for "SATB" (soprano, alto, tenor and bass). Often, boys (known as trebles) are used in preference to sopranos, especially in European church music, much of which was composed at a time when it was considered improper for

Plate 2 *Left* Page showing neumatic notation (see pp. 14, 90) from a Benedictine antiphoner, German, 12th–14th century. Badisches Landesbibliothek, Karlsruhe.

women to sing in church. Boys tend to produce a strong and firm, sometimes even raucous sound, less soft and sweet than that of girls or women. In earlier times, too, the alto part was regularly sung by men, as it still is in many church choirs; good male altos produced a light, sharply defined sound that is well suited to contrapuntal music. Some men singing these parts use what is called "falsetto" (meaning an unnatural, "put on" high voice), but with others this type of singing is a natural extension of the top of the tenor voice; it is generally called *countertenor*.

Castrato

There is another type of high voice of great historical importance which needs to be mentioned here. In the sixteenth century the custom developed, in southern Europe, of castrating boys who had musical gifts and particularly fine voices, to prevent their voices from breaking. Italian church choirs began to use these *castrato* voices, and in the seventeenth and eighteenth centuries *castrato* singers dominated serious opera. The combination of a boy's vocal quality and a man's lungs evidently produced a sound of extraordinary beauty, power and flexibility. *Castrato* singers took the roles of heroes, warriors and lovers for two centuries (for example Handel's Julius Caesar and Gluck's Orpheus). Most of them had roughly the same range as a mezzo-soprano; the roles they took are nowadays best sung by a woman. The practice of castration began to be regarded as abhorrent in the eighteenth century and was abandoned during the nineteenth.

Strings

The term "string instrument" (or "stringed") is often taken to mean only those instruments that are played with a bow – that is, the violin type. It also applies to many plucked instruments, like the guitar or the harp, as well as keyboard instruments like the piano (where the strings are struck) and the harpsichord.

Bowed instruments

Chief among the bowed instruments are the violin and the other instruments like it – the viola, which is a large violin of slightly lower pitch, and the cello (its full name is violoncello), a much larger instrument pitched an octave below the viola. To these we may add the double bass, which is larger still but structurally rather different from the others.

Violin

The violin is basically a resonating box with a neck attached, across which, with a system of pegs and bridges, four strings are attached. The strings are made of gut, often with silver wire wound round them, or of steel; they are held taut and stretched across a piece of wood (the fingerboard) in such a way that the player can press them down with the fingers of his left hand and so, in effect, shorten their vibrating length. With his right hand he draws his bow across the strings, bringing its horsehair (made sticky with rosin) into contact with one of them and causing it to vibrate. The vibration passes through the bridge and, through the soundpost, into the hollow body of the instrument (the soundbox), which amplifies it and transmits the vibration to the air and to the listener as a musical note.

Violins have existed since the sixteenth century. The great age of violin-making was in the seventeenth century and the early eighteenth, the time of such men as Stradivari and Amati, who built instruments of incomparable sweetness, richness and power of tone. It was at this time too that the violin became the basic instrument in the orchestra and in chamber music, a position in which it is still unchallenged because of the beauty and the expressiveness of its sound and its unrivaled agility. Its capacity to draw a silvery line of tone and to play with great brilliance and rapidity make it specially prized as a solo instrument. Many composers (Bach, Beethoven, Mendelssohn, Brahms) have written concertos for it.

The four strings of the violin are tuned to the tones shown in ex. II.3a. Since the

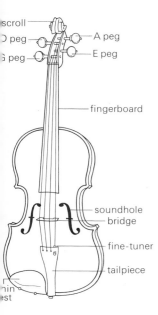

6 Diagram of a modern violin showing principal features.

ex. II.3

(a) Violin   (b) Viola   (c) Cello   (d) Double-bass

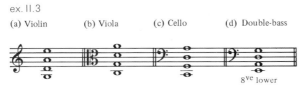

player can modify the length of the string only by shortening it, by pressing it against the fingerboard, all he can do is raise the pitch from these four "open notes", so the first note shown (G) is the lowest of which the instrument is capable. The highest is more than three octaves higher, produced by pressing the E string at the end of the fingerboard. The violin offers an almost infinite range of possibilities for varying the sound: among the most important are *vibrato* (when the player's left hand has a controlled wobble, greatly enriching the tone), double stopping (playing on two strings at once) and plucking or *pizzicato*.

Viola

The viola is tuned a 5th lower than the violin (ex. 3b); the instrument is itself some six inches longer. Its tone is rather darker and less sweet, less brilliant than the violin's. The viola is only quite rarely used as a solo instrument, its main role being to play a middle, accompanying voice in the string texture. In England it was once called the "tenor", and in France it is still called the "alto" – which makes clear the kind of part it is usually asked to play.

Cello

By the rules of acoustics the viola, since its pitch is a 5th below the violin's, ought to be half as big again as the violin. But then it would be impossible, when the player tucked it under his chin to play it, to reach the other end or to support its weight. So the viola has to be made smaller than its acoustical ideal. The cello, however, is built rather closer to its proper acoustical size, since it is played not under the chin but held between the player's knees. Its tuning is shown in ex. 3c. Otherwise its technique is exactly like that of the violin or viola, except in left-hand fingering – because of the longer strings, the points at which the player has to press them down, or "stop" them, are much further apart. The cello is an instrument of outstanding eloquence and warmth, with a rich middle register and an intensely expressive top register; many composers have written for it music of a specially personal quality, like Dvořák and Elgar in their concertos.

Double bass

In the modern orchestra, a deeper foundation is needed than the cellos can provide; this is supplied by the double bass. The most usual tuning is shown in ex. 3d; note that the strings are set not a 5th apart, as with the upper instruments, but a 4th, for the distances that the player's hands have to travel between notes would otherwise be too great. The instrument's tone is inevitably somewhat gruff when it is heard alone, but coupled with the cello an octave higher it sounds firm and clear.

Viols

The way that the shoulders of the double bass slope gently up to the neck mark it out as less closely related to the violin family than to the viol family. The viols developed about the same time as the violins, or a little earlier, and were much used for chamber music in the sixteenth and seventeenth centuries; their gentle, slightly reedy tone makes them ideal for the contrapuntal music that was popular at that time. Viols are made in several sizes, of which the main three are the treble, the tenor and the bass; they have six (occasionally seven) strings, tuned as shown in ex. II.4.

ex. II.4

Bass viol

The viol could not produce the brilliance or the attack of the violin and, in the late seventeenth century, it began to fall out of favor. All of them, even the smallest, are played with the instrument held vertically, between the knees like a cello. Unlike violins, viols have frets (strips of gut, wood or metal) on the fingerboard against which the strings are stopped.

Plucked instruments

Most of the plucked string instruments work on exactly the same principle as the bowed ones – they have a resonating body, and a neck along which the strings are stretched with a system of pegs and bridges; the player stops the strings against a fingerboard (with frets) attached to the neck to shorten the strings' sounding length and so produce the full range of notes.

Guitar

The best known of these is of course the guitar. The modern guitar has six strings (earlier ones had four or five), tuned as shown in ex. II.5a. Its body has a flat back

ex. II.5

(a) Guitar   (b) Lute   or

with incurved sidewalls; the strings are nowadays of nylon, with the lower ones wound in metal. The instrument is specially associated with Spanish and Latin American music, but its appeal has always been wide and it is used in folk music in many countries. The guitar can be plucked or strummed, either with the fingers or, if a sharper sound is wanted, with a device (a plectrum) made of some hard material.

Lute

Historically, the most important of the plucked instruments is the lute. An instrument of great antiquity, it is probably of Arabic origin. In the sixteenth century it was the most popular domestic instrument, like the piano later or the guitar today, and was used for solo music and for accompanying songs or ensembles. The classical lute generally has a flat soundboard and a bowl-shaped or pear-shaped body; there are several different sizes with necks of various lengths and shapes but typically lutes have six strings tuned as shown in ex. 5b. Larger-sized lute-type instruments, like the archlute, chitarrone and theorbo, usually with long necks and many strings (often a dozen or more), were much used in the seventeenth

7 *Right* The most important instruments in the lute family.

cittern

lute

mandolin

electric guitar

sitar

shamisen

chitarrone

guitar

banjo

8 *Above* Pedal harp by Salvi, 1974.

century, particularly in ensembles and for accompanying.

There are numerous other instruments of the lute type, some historical, some modern. Among the best known are the mandolin, a small instrument originating in Italy with a pear-shaped body and four or five double wire strings, whose thrumming adds a special color to Italian (and particularly Neapolitan) folk music; the banjo, a favorite instrument among black American minstrel groups and also much used in parlor music, with a round body and usually five wire strings; and the ukelele, a Hawaiian instrument like a small, four-string guitar. The most important non-Western instrument of this kind is the *sitar*, the best-known of all Indian instruments. It has a long neck, a bowl-shaped body made from a gourd resonator, five playing strings, two "drone" strings (lower-pitched ones that sound constantly) and a dozen or more strings that vibrate in sympathy with the plucked ones, adding a kind of halo to the sound. The Japanese *shamisen*, a three-string instrument with a square soundbox, is used in both folk and art music.

Harp

Of an altogether different type is the harp, which unlike the guitar, the lute and the other plucked instruments has a place in the modern orchestra. The harp is another

9 *Girl with a lute:* painting by Bartolommeo Veneto, early 16th century. Isabella Stewart Gardner Museum, Boston.

ancient instrument, known in biblical times and in many widely separated cultures, notably in Africa and South America. The orchestral harp is a highly developed instrument with about 45 strings, tuned to a diatonic scale. At its base is a set of seven pedals with which the player can tauten the strings and raise their pitch by one or two semitones; one pedal controls all the C strings, one the D strings, and so on. The harp has always had an important place in folk music, especially in Ireland and Wales; it entered the world of art music in the late eighteenth century, first as an alternative to the piano for elegant young ladies, later to add color and atmosphere to orchestral music with its delicacy and its gentle washes of sound.

Zither

Another group of plucked instruments are the zithers, which generally consist of a wooden box across the top of which a series of strings are stretched. Zithers take many forms and are used in folk music in many parts of the world. The biblical psaltery was of this kind; so is the Japanese *koto*, an ancient instrument (it dates back to the eighth century) for which there exists a large and sophisticated repertory.

Other versions are known in countries as far apart as China and Iran, Turkey and Switzerland. Zithers seem to be specially favored in mountain regions. Some such instruments, struck with hammers rather than plucked, are called dulcimers. A version played in eastern Europe, particularly Hungary, has been used in Western art music, chiefly by Hungarian composers; this instrument, the cimbalom, is often heard in café bands in central and eastern Europe.

Keyboard instruments

Piano, harpsichord

Another, rather better-known example of a struck string instrument is the piano. Here the striking is done at one remove, through a complex mechanism operated by a keyboard. The piano was invented just before 1700 by an Italian, Bartolomeo Cristofori, who wanted to build an instrument that – unlike the harpsichord, the most important keyboard instrument of the day – could be played soft or loud, or *piano* and *forte*: hence its full name, pianoforte (or fortepiano).

Both the piano and the harpsichord consist of a set of tuned strings held taut in a wooden case, with a sounding-board underneath; both possess keyboards in which the keys for the diatonic notes are at the front (they are usually of white ivory) and the keys for the other five notes, the sharps and flats (usually of black ebony), are set a little further back from the player. The harpsichord, however, is a plucked instrument. When the key is depressed by the player, a piece of wood (the jack) is thrown up and a piece of quill (in modern instruments plastic) that is attached to it plucks the string. The player has no control over the speed at which the jack is projected, so cannot affect the force with which the string is plucked. Each tone on the harpsichord, accordingly, sounds at the same volume, regardless of how hard the key is struck; though on larger instruments there may be two keyboards and two or more sets of strings and jacks, so that the player can change from one to the

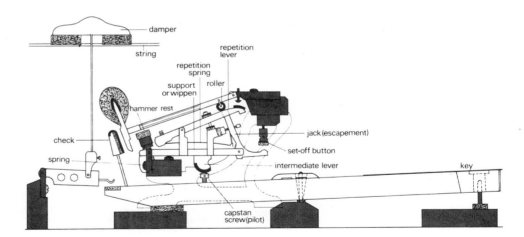

10 Action of a modern grand piano: on pressing the key the movement is transmitted via the pilot to the intermediate lever; the jack then acts on the roller of the hammer which rises towards the string. The moment the backward projection of the jack contacts the set-off button the jack moves back permitting the hammer to escape and to continue in free flight to strike the string and then begin its descent; it is then caught and retained by the check and repetition lever as long as the key remains depressed. If the key is partly released the hammer is freed from the check, and the roller is acted on directly by the repetition lever; it is thus possible to strike the string again by depressing the key a second time (the jack will re-engage with the roller only when the key has been fully released so that a full hammer stroke may be made).

other to obtain a different quality and weight of sound. The action of the piano, by contrast, allows the pianist to control, by the force he applies, the speed at which the hammer strikes the strings and, accordingly, the volume of each tone.

The harpsichord went out of fashion in the late eighteenth century, a time when composers increasingly felt that variation in volume was important for the kind of expressiveness they wanted in their music. It was revived in the present century, when performers began to realize that, if we wanted to hear music in the sense intended by its composers, it was necessary to use the kinds of instrument they had in mind when writing it, and that any "improvement" the piano had to offer in terms of variety of volume was not relevant to music never intended to possess such variety.

The piano became the principal domestic instrument during the nineteenth century; virtually every cultured home in Europe and the USA had one. It also became the instrument that many composers of the time played and used for much of their most original and most personal music (Beethoven and Chopin, for example). It has a huge repertory, most of it solo music, some of it chamber music with strings, some of it accompanying (mostly the human voice); the piano has no real place within the orchestra, but there are many piano concertos, in which the piano plays with the orchestra and is sometimes pitted against it.

The instrument has changed considerably. In the late eighteenth century, its tone was crisper and lighter, less warm and less "singing". Its sustaining power and its volume have greatly increased. These changes were made necessary not only by the changes in musical style but also by the rise of public concerts in large halls, where the music has to be loud enough to carry to a substantial audience. To support the extra string tension needed to permit this extra volume of tone, wooden frames gave way to iron ones in the early years of the nineteenth century. The traditional "wing" shape, derived from the harpsichord and convenient for accommodating strings long in the bass and short in the treble, has remained in use for concert grands and large domestic pianos. The upright piano, in which the frame and strings are mounted vertically, has long been the normal piano for use in the home, occupying much less space and producing an ample volume for an ordinary living-room. In

11 *Man playing the harpsichord:* painting by Gonzales Coques (1614–84). Private collection.

12 Beethoven's last piano,
by Conrad Graf, a gift from
the maker.
Beethovenhaus, Bonn.

the piano's early days, the "square piano" – in fact in the form of a rectangular box
on legs – was favored for home use.

The harpsichord too has domestic equivalents, the virginal or the spinet; these
worked on the same principle, with plucked strings, but were smaller and had only
a single keyboard. Another domestic keyboard instrument is the clavichord, whose
delicate, intimate tone is produced by the impact of a tongue of brass (operated
directly from the keyboard) on the string.

Wind instruments

The basic principle of any wind instrument is that an air column in a tube is made to
vibrate to produce a musical tone. There are three main ways in which this can be
done: first, by blowing across a sharp edge on the tube; second, by attaching to it a
reed that will vibrate; and third, by the player's using his lips in the role of a reed.
The choice of method affects the kind of sound that the instrument will produce.
Other factors influence the sound – the nature of the reed, the materials of which the
instrument is made, and the bore of the tube (whether it is uniform or widens

towards the far end: that is, whether it is a cone or a cylinder). Wind instruments are usually divided between so-called woodwind and brass. This usage helps clarify the role of each in the orchestra, though it is inexact – some "woodwind" instruments are made of metal, and the category "brass" includes some of wood.

Woodwind

The simplest of all wind instruments are the flute type, in which the player directs his breath at an edge, creating eddies of air that set the column in vibration. (The principle is the one that enables someone blowing across the top of a glass bottle to produce a faint sound; pour water into the bottle, reducing the effective size of the tube, and the tone will rise in pitch.) Every culture uses flutes of some sort – there is the highly developed Arab *nay* and the Indonesian *suling*, while other less obvious varieties include the ocarina as well as the nose-blown flutes of Polynesia. Flutes divide into two main types, the end-blown (like the recorder) and the side-blown (like the true flute).

Recorder

The recorder has a long history in Western music, probably dating back to the fourteenth century. It is built in various sizes, to play at different pitch levels: the four main ones are the soprano (or descant), the alto (or treble), the tenor and the bass (the lowest tone possible on each is shown in ex. II.6). Recorders have traditionally been made of wood, or occasionally of ivory, until recent times when

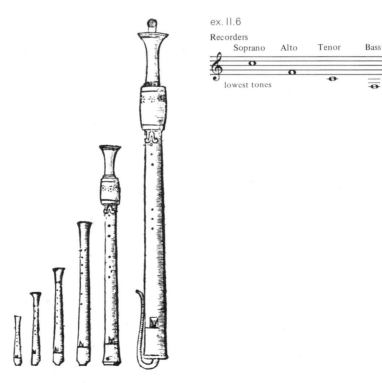

ex. II.6

Recorders
Soprano   Alto   Tenor   Bass

lowest tones

13 Part of a consort of recorders: woodcut from *Syntagma musicum* (1619) by Michael Praetorius.

their massive use in schools has led to the manufacture of smaller types in plastic. The instrument has a beak-shaped mouthpiece at the top, with a whistle-like aperture a little below it to provide the edge that sets up the vibration. Its main body, which is cylindrical, has holes which are covered or uncovered by seven fingers and one thumb to produce different tones. With all the holes covered, the tube sounds at its full length and gives its lowest tone, but by blowing in a more tightly focused way the player forces the tube to vibrate in two halves and produce a tone an octave higher.

The recorder has no place in the normal modern orchestra, but is an important member of the Baroque orchestra. Its chief repertory comes from the Renaissance and the Baroque periods; around 1700, particularly, many composers wrote sonatas for it. Bach and Handel included parts for it in many of their works. Its cool, clear, piping sound was less well suited to the music of the era that followed and it fell out of use during the second half of the eighteenth century. Like the harpsichord, it was revived in the twentieth so that music could be played on the instruments for which it was intended – and also, in the case of the recorder, to answer the need of music educators for an instrument that could be readily and rewardingly played by children.

14 Modern flutes: alto (*top*), concert, and piccolo, by Rudall Carte & Co.

Flute

The history of the flute goes back to ancient Rome or even beyond. By the Renaissance it was a simple cylindrical tube with six finger-holes. It came into greater prominence during the late seventeenth century when a group of French makers devised improvements, adding an extra finger-hole controlled by a key (if it were in the acoustically correct position the hole would be out of reach) and making the bore partly conical. Unlike the recorder, the flute was difficult to play in tune, especially the chromatic tones. Various attempts were made to improve it by adding more keys, but the first fully successful one came only in the 1840s with the work of Theobald Boehm, who devised an ingenious system (soon adapted for other instruments) using rings as well as keys.

Early flutes were normally made of wood, or occasionally ivory; wooden flutes are still used, but metal ones – of silver or alloy, occasionally gold or platinum – are much more common. The tone of the instrument, when gently played, is cool and limpid; its lowest register can achieve a soft, delicate, almost sensuous expressiveness. But its extreme top can add sharpness and brilliance to an ensemble. Composers have often used the flute coupled with violins, to which it can give an extra, airy delicacy, or with another woodwind instrument. Flutes are made in various sizes, the most common being the piccolo (essentially a half-size flute, and very shrill) and the alto flute, a 4th lower than the normal instrument. The compasses of these are shown in ex. II.7 (it should however be mentioned that for any wind instrument there is no absolute upper limit; much depends on the player, the instrument and the circumstances).

The flute has a large repertory of solo sonatas from the beginning of the eighteenth century. When the recorder fell into disuse, the flute remained, being

15 Playing a one-key flute: engraving from *Principes de la flûte traversière* (1707) by Jacques Hotteterre.

ex. II.7

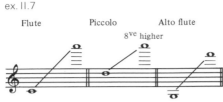

particularly well suited to the character of mid- and late eighteenth-century music and popular among amateurs. Two flutes became the standard in the orchestra by 1800. The nineteenth-century solo repertory is of small interest, but in the present century its flexibility and its delicate, unassuming sound have won it much favor, especially among French composers.

Oboes, bassoons

16 *Below* Modern oboe and english horn, by Howarth of London.

17 *Right* Oboist: detail from "Dance of the Nymphs" in the series *History of Psyche*, Gobelins tapestry, 1690. Musée du Louvre, Paris.

All the other orchestral woodwind instruments of today are reed-operated. There are two types of reed: the single reed, a blade of cane which is tied to the mouthpiece and made to vibrate against it when the player blows, and the double reed, consisting of a pair of blades which vibrate against each other when the player blows. The oboe is the principal double-reed instrument of soprano pitch.

The word "oboe" comes from the French *hautbois*, meaning literally "high wood", or a loud instrument made of wood. It was applied to an instrument called the shawm used in the Middle Ages and the Renaissance, particularly for dancing and processions. Double-reed instruments of this type are used in many cultures, for example the North African *zurna* and the Indian *shahnai*.

Like the flute, the oboe underwent much improvement from French makers in

the late seventeenth century, with the addition of keys to improve its tuning. Until then it had been used more in bands than in orchestral music, but it now found a firm place in the orchestra where, by the middle of the eighteenth century, it was the first woodwind instrument firmly to establish itself. Two oboes have been a basic part of the orchestra ever since. In the nineteenth century Boehm's improvements were drawn upon for the oboe and further key-work was added.

It is perhaps surprising that an instrument capable of such sweetness of tone and intensity of expression as the oboe should not have inspired a larger solo repertory in the nineteenth century. The eighteenth century however supplied some, and so has the twentieth. Oboes of various sizes have been built. The most important are the english horn (or *cor anglais*), curiously named since it is neither English nor a horn – it is a tenor oboe, pitched a 5th lower than the ordinary instrument and having a richer, more throaty tone – and the oboe d'amore (or "love oboe", presumably so called for its warm sound), pitched a minor 3rd below the standard instrument. The oboe d'amore was much used in Bach's time; the english horn is called for in many scores of the nineteenth and twentieth centuries. The compasses of the three instruments are shown in ex. II.8.

ex. II.8

Various attempts have been made to build a satisfactory bass oboe; but the existence of the bassoon, a double-reed instrument and the true bass of the woodwind group, makes it unnecessary. It has a warmer, smoother, less reedy sound than the oboe and its immediate relatives. Its ancestry lies less with the shawms or their bass equivalents, the pommers, than with the more gentle-toned dulcian, first known in the sixteenth century. As with the other woodwinds, the bassoon was given a more rational form by the French makers of the late seventeenth century, and further improved in the eighteenth by the addition of more keys. The size of a bass instrument poses special problems: the long tube (nine feet) of the bassoon needs to be doubled back on itself and the finger-holes have to be bored obliquely through the wood if the player is to be able to reach them. Boehm's reforms did not work well for the bassoon, but there were other changes which improved its tuning and its flexibility.

The bassoon came into the orchestra during the eighteenth century as the bass to the oboes; the standard classical orchestra has two bassoons. The solo repertory is not large but several composers of the Baroque and early Classical periods wrote sonatas or concertos for the instrument. It has always had something of a reputation as "clown of the orchestra" because of its capacity for comic effects, but bassoonists are apt to resent this since it can also be eloquent or somber. Pitched an octave lower than the bassoon is the double bassoon, whose 18-foot tube is twice doubled back on itself; this instrument provides a deep and resonant bass to the woodwind section of the orchestra. The compasses are shown in ex. 8.

18 Modern German bassoon by Wilhelm Heckel.

Clarinet

The clarinet has a shorter history than the other orchestral woodwinds. Its predecessor is an instrument called the *chalumeau*, which, in the early eighteenth century, seems to have served as a model to the Nuremberg maker who apparently built the earliest clarinets. It has a single reed, fastened to the mouthpiece, against which it vibrates. The tube, normally of African blackwood, is cylindrical. Because of the acoustical properties of a cylindrical tube with a single reed, the player, when he blows more acutely, does not make the sound rise an octave (as with the other instruments we have been considering) but an octave and a 5th. Since players have only sufficient fingers to uncover enough holes for an octave, the clarinetist has to use special keys to fill the gap between the basic tones produced by the full tube length and the next series an octave and a 5th higher. This acoustical feature has other implications, making the clarinet's timbre rather different from one register to another – rich and oily in the lowest, a little pale in the middle, warm, clear and singing in the medium-high, quite shrill at the top.

19 *Young man holding a clarinet*: painting, 1813, by Johannes Reekers. Frans Halsmuseum, Haarlem.

20 Modern clarinets: sopranino , soprano in B♭ (Schmidt-Kolbe system, by Fritz Wurlitzer), soprano in A, basset horn in F, bass in B♭, by Leblanc.

The strength of its upper registers quickly secured the clarinet a place in the military bands of the eighteenth century. It still plays a central part in bands. The instrument was slower to find its way into the orchestra and was not regularly used until close on 1800. There is a little eighteenth-century chamber music and wind ensemble music with the clarinet, as well as a few concertos (Mozart contributed notably to its repertory). But nineteenth-century composers found its romantic tone appealing and made much use of it for poetic effects in their orchestral and operatic music. In the twentieth century it held an important place in jazz bands in

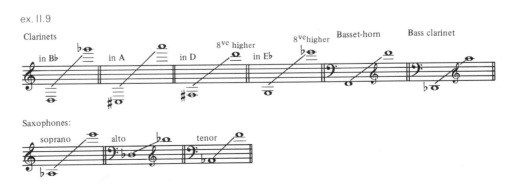

ex. II.9

21 Woman playing a crumhorn: detail from the painting *The presentation of Christ at the Temple*, 1510, by Vittore Carpaccio. Galleria dell'Accademia, Venice.

the hands of men like Artie Shaw and Benny Goodman.

Clarinets are made in a variety of sizes. All are transposing instruments; this means that the tone that is heard differs from the one the player sees in his music and plays. This curious system enables a player to change from one size of instrument to another without altering his fingering technique. The standard clarinet is said to be "in B♭", which means that when the player plays C the tone that sounds is B♭. There is also a clarinet in A, more convenient for music in certain keys. Smaller, shriller instruments in D and E♭ are used for special effects and in bands. A larger tenor clarinet usually pitched in F and called the basset horn was used by Mozart and others. The most important of the various sizes is the bass clarinet, pitched an octave below the standard one. The compasses of all these are shown in ex. II.9.

Saxophone

Another single-reed instrument is the saxophone, invented by Adolphe Sax in the mid-nineteenth century. The saxophone is made of metal, with a conical tube. Sax built seven different sizes of instrument (and two versions of each); the alto, tenor and soprano have been the most popular. The saxophones never quite found a regular place in the orchestra, though a few French composers have successfully used their suave tones. They are however used in military bands, and above all in jazz, where their smoothness and flexibility find a natural home.

Other reed instruments

With a number of reed instruments, the player has no direct contact with the reed. One is the Renaissance crumhorn, a wooden instrument with finger-holes and a broadly curved end. The reed is fixed inside a "windcap" into which the player blows. The tone is not exactly refined but the instrument, which is made in several sizes, serves well for dance music and for accompanying convivial songs.

Familiar instruments that use this "free reed" principle include the harmonica (or mouth organ), the accordion and the bagpipe. The harmonica consists of a number of small reeds (usually 40 or 48) mounted in channels so that the player can blow (in some models also suck) air through them. With the accordion the air is passed by the squeezing of a bellows, the reeds are made of metal and tones are selected on a keyboard and a range of buttons (each offering a pre-selected combination).

With the bagpipe, one or more pipes with reeds are inserted into a bag, which the player inflates through a blowpipe and presses under his arm to drive the air through the reeds and make them vibrate. One of the pipes with a reed has finger-holes, enabling melodies to be played. The bagpipe is a folk and military instrument, not used in art music; it is generally associated with Scotland and Ireland, and with laments and martial music, though in fact bagpipes are known in many countries and probably originated in the Middle East or the Mediterranean.

Brass

The so-called brass instruments – they may be of other metals, or even wood or horn – work on a principle similar to that of reed instruments: but here it is the player's lips that act as the reed. The player presses them to a cup-shaped (or funnel-shaped) mouthpiece against which they vibrate, setting the air in the tube in vibration. Anyone who has tried blowing in this way into a simple piece of tubing, like a hosepipe, knows that a musical (or fairly musical) sound can be made but that only a limited number of tones can be sounded. That is because the length of the air column cannot be varied. But it can be made to vibrate in sections – halves, thirds, quarters and so on. These tones form what is called the *harmonic series*; ex. II.10 shows the tones that can be obtained from a tube about eight feet in length (at least

ex. II.10

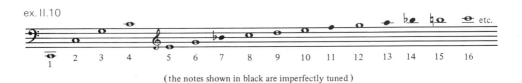

(the notes shown in black are imperfectly tuned)

in theory: physical reasons sometimes limit the number). The lowest tones are produced with the lips very relaxed, the highest with them very tight.

Instruments of this type were used in ancient civilizations, commonly for ceremonial or ritual purposes, because the sound produced is generally loud and noble. Animal horns were often used, for example the original Roman *buccina* and the Jewish *shofar*; the alphorn, used in mountainous countries for long-distance signaling, is of wood. An early metal example is the Scandinavian *lur*, a long, conical instrument in the shape of a bent S; several pairs of them have been found by archeologists.

The impossibility of playing even a simple scale on a brass instrument (except at the very top of its compass, which is insecure and strenuous for the player) kept such instruments out of ordinary music-making for several centuries. The only one that found a place was the cornett – not to be confused with the modern cornet – which was wooden and had a series of finger-holes that enabled the player to alter the sounding length. He therefore needed to use only the two or three lowest harmonics. It was prominent in the sixteenth and seventeenth centuries, and much used for ceremonial church music, including the playing of hymns from church towers in harmony with trombones. But the difficulty of playing it well and the strain it imposed on the player led to its falling out of use as soon as there were other instruments to replace it early in the eighteenth century.

Cornett

Horn

The first true brass instrument to establish itself in the orchestra was the horn (usually called French horn, but in fact many are German in origin). In the early eighteenth century it was mainly used for special effects, in outdoor music or pieces referring in some way to the hunt. By the middle of the century there were normally two horns in an orchestra. The style of music then being written could accommodate the instrument's limited range of tones, and a pair of horns added warmth and fulness to the orchestral sound. At the end of the century it was occasionally used as a solo instrument (notably in Mozart's three horn concertos). In the nineteenth century the horn's romantic qualities, especially its ability to sing a noble melody, brought it into special favor among orchestral composers; it was also useful for supplying unobtrusive inner harmony. Four horns were often used, sometimes six or even eight.

By that time the horn could play more than just the tones of the harmonic series. Structurally, it had originally been simply a coiled, slightly conical brass tube, with a flared opening (or bell). But in the eighteenth century, so that it could play its limited number of tones in the prevailing key, the player would use a "crook" – an extra coil of tubing – to supplement its basic length. For a symphony in F major, for example, the hornist would fit his "F crook", and the instrument would be able to produce a series of tones suitable for music in F major. (By pushing his hand firmly into the bell, he could also obtain some neighboring tones, but their quality was poor.) Early in the nineteenth century a system of valves was devised which made crooks unnecessary: the valves enabled the player to switch extra lengths of tubing

22 *Below* Hand-horn player, lithograph, *c*1835, by C. Tellier.

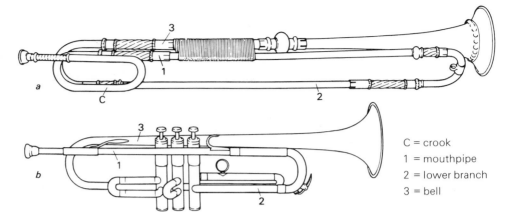

24 *Right* Diagram
comparing a Baroque and
a modern trumpet.

C = crook
1 = mouthpipe
2 = lower branch
3 = bell

into action by pressing one, two or three of a series of pistons and so alter instantaneously the series of tones available to him. This meant that the horn could now manage a full range of tones. Since that time, changes in the instrument have been slight, mainly affecting the design of the valves and the bore of the tube, which has been widened to give a smoother tone and greater facility of execution. The horn is in fact the least "brassy" of the brass instruments and blends readily with the woodwinds and even the strings.

Trumpet

The highest-pitched of the brass instruments (their compasses are shown in ex. II.11) is the trumpet. A simple cylindrical tube, either straight or twice doubled back on itself, it began to be used in orchestral music during the Baroque period, when the fanfare-like phrases it could play – for like the horn it could manage only the tones of the harmonic series – fitted well with the cut of the melodies. During the late eighteenth century a pair of trumpets came to be used regularly in the larger orchestras, especially in music of a formal or ceremonial kind, or where there were military associations. As on the horn, crooks were used to adapt it to the key of the music.

ex. II.11

Valves were applied to the trumpet, too, early in the nineteenth century, freeing it from the crook system and enabling it to play a full range of tones. Since then composers have taken advantage of its brilliant and forthright sound and its ability to penetrate, or ride over, the full orchestral ensemble. Two or three are used in the full symphony orchestra. Also sometimes found is a larger, bass trumpet, and the cornet, a gentler-toned instrument looking like a short, stubby trumpet, less noble in sound but much easier to play (French composers have used it in the orchestra, but it is more commonly used in bands). The trumpet itself, of course, is much used in jazz; indeed its most famous exponent ever is certainly Louis Armstrong. In jazz, and occasionally in orchestral music, the trumpet's tone is modified by the insertion of a mute – a kind of large plug – in its bell. Mutes of various shapes and materials affect its tone, enabling the instrument to do anything from moaning to snarling.

23 *Left* Triple horn in
F/Bb/F alto, with five
rotary valves, by Paxman
(first manufactured in
1965).

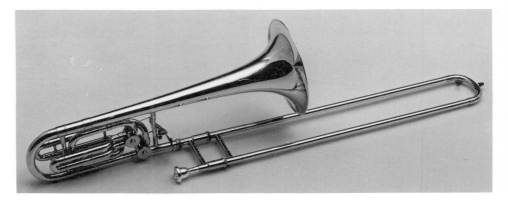

25 Modern American bass trombone in Bb/F/Eb, with two thumb valves (Vincent Bach model), by Selmer.

Trombone

The "heavy brass" instruments are the trombones and the tuba. A trombone (or sackbut, to use its early name) has no need for valves as it has a movable slide; by altering the length of the tube and (as with the horn or trumpet) varying his lip pressure, the trombonist can play any tone in his compass. Trombones used to be made in three sizes, but the alto fell out of use and nowadays a single instrument fitted with a valve so that it can encompass the music of both the tenor and the bass is widely used. In the Baroque and Classical periods trombones were much used in church music, and their noble, solemn tones are now often called upon when an effect of grandeur or ritual is wanted – and they are heard too in noisy, brilliant climaxes. Three trombones are usually found in the orchestra today.

Tuba

At the bass of the brass ensemble comes the tuba, a large instrument of the horn type with a wide bore and three or four valves. Tubas are made in numerous sizes; the most usual orchestral one has about 16 feet of tubing (not including the lengths controlled by valves). There are still longer military ones, but also several shorter types, including the euphonium (a tenor tuba). They are made in a variety of shapes, some of them (like the sousaphone – named after the composer – and the helicon) winding round the player so that he can support it the more easily when marching. Its tone is deep, sonorous and well rounded, lacking the bite and edge of the trombones.

Organ

The organ is a wind instrument, although the player fortunately does not have to blow it. The air is supplied by pumps and bellows. An organ may have hundreds, even thousands, of pipes: one (sometimes more) for every tone in every stop. "Stop" is the term used for the group of pipes that produce a particular quality of sound. The player has at his command a series of buttons that he can pull out to engage each of them (hence the expression "pulling out all the stops"). The pipes may be of wood, tin or other metals; they may be flue pipes (on the edge principle) or reed ones; they may be narrow or wide, open or closed, round or rectangular in section. Each type produces a different characteristic or sound. Every country, and in some of them every locality, has its own traditions of organ building and its own preferences over tone quality.

A large instrument may have three keyboards, or even more, operated by the hands, and a further one (a pedal board, laid out the same way but larger) for the feet. Traditionally, the action of an organ – the series of links between the keyboard and the air supply to each pipe – was purely mechanical; but nowadays electrical

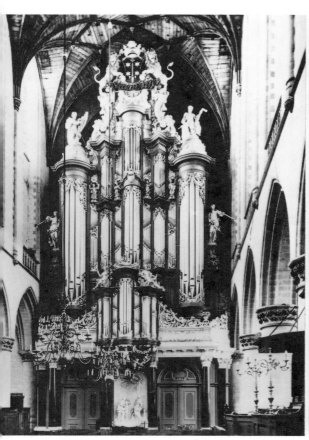

systems are widely used. And electronic organs, without pipes at all, have reached a point of development where almost any sound can be accurately and cheaply reproduced – a threat to the traditional pipe organ despite the latter's beauty, variety and grandeur of tone.

The organ's repertory dates back to the Middle Ages; it reached a peak in the early eighteenth century, with the incomparable music of Bach, and includes several masterpieces from the nineteenth and twentieth centuries. A few composers have written organ concertos, notably Handel, but the organ has never had a regular place within the orchestra; its natural home is of course the church and its natural repertory sacred music.

Organs, old and new:
26 Organ by Christian Müller, 1735–8, Groote Kerk, Haarlem (*left*).

27 Organ by the Holtkamp Organ Co. (inaugurated 1967), University of New Mexico, Albuquerque (*right*).

Percussion

Percussion instruments are those that are sounded by being struck, or in a few cases shaken. Most are made of wood or metal. Some, called untuned percussion, produce on impact a noise rather than a definite musical tone; others, the tuned percussion, sound a recognizable pitch. Percussion instruments tend to be used more for rhythmic purposes than melodic, and some of them can also provide a good deal of drama.

28 Modern percussion
instruments.

tam tam

bass drum

timpani

cymbals

side drum

xylophone

glockenspiel

tubular bells

Drums

The most important percussion instrument in Western music is the drum, in particular the kettledrums, or timpani. Pairs of kettledrums have been used in orchestral music since the early eighteenth century, often in association with trumpets to add a touch of pomp and brilliance to the music. The kettledrum is a large bowl-shaped vessel, usually of copper, with a skin held taut across the top. It sounds a tone of definite pitch, determined by the tension of the skin, which is adjustable either with hand-screws or with a foot-operated mechanism. They are generally used in pairs; often one is tuned to the tonic of the music to be played, the other to the dominant. The quality of the sound is affected by whether a padded stick or a hard one is used.

Untuned percussion

Other types of drum include the bass drum, much used in bands, which provides a deep, unpitched thump, and the side drum, a small instrument with strings that rattle against the head when it is struck, producing a sizzling sound. These types are basic to the rhythm sections of jazz and dance bands; so is the cymbal, a resonant brass plate that can be played either with a drumstick or – as is common at dramatic climaxes in orchestral music – clashed one against another. Another instrument often heard at climactic moments is the large gong or tam-tam: struck with a soft, heavy beater, it can produce a solemn, awesome noise that menacingly grows in volume for a few moments after the impact. Gongs play a large role in the music of Indonesia, where the gong-based orchestra is known as the *gamelan*; the type of gong used there, unlike the tam-tam, sounds a definite pitch.

Tuned percussion

Tuned percussion instruments include the bells, or chimes, a series of metal tubes suspended in a frame; they are often called upon to imitate church bells. Smaller bells are represented on the glockenspiel, a series of metal bars struck with small hammers. A similar instrument operated from a keyboard is called the celesta because of its sweet, "celestial" sound. Wooden instruments of this type produce a harder, drier tone. Chief among them is the xylophone, a series of wooden (or synthetic resin) bars laid out like a piano keyboard with metal resonators underneath. It is struck with small mallets, either hard (to give a crisp, clipped sound) or softer (for a mellower one). A larger version, lower in pitch, is the marimba – the name comes from Africa, where (as in parts of Latin America) such instrument types are common. A metal instrument of this kind, with disc resonators made to revolve by a motor and so producing an effect of vibration, is known as the vibraphone or vibraharp (or simply "vibes"); it is much used in jazz.

Electronic instruments

Almost any sound can be analyzed by electronic means and then re-created. Were it not for the central importance of the human element in music-making, and the traditions of musical expression with which a player gives meaning and vitality to the music he makes, we might expect all the instruments we have been discussing to be replaced before long by electronic ones. That is not likely to happen: but the people who have experimented during the present century with electric methods of creating sound have already added enormously to the range of sound and the means of organizing it.

The most important of the early electronic instruments is the *ondes martenot*, operated from a keyboard and a small control panel; it produces a smooth sound like a de-personalized human voice. More recent are the electric piano, which can sustain tones in a way that the real piano cannot, and the electric guitar – well known from rock music – where the string vibration is resonated by the electric apparatus; also the electronic organ (mentioned above). But also under the heading of electronic instruments may be mentioned the tape recorder, with which an ingenious and imaginative musician may devise new ways of making and shaping musical sounds, and ultimately the synthesizer, which has an almost unlimited capacity for the generation of sounds or the modification of existing ones. We stand on the brink of a new world of sound creation – a prospect that must be exciting to the composer, although the creation of sounds as never heard before is not the same thing as composing fresh, original and worthwhile music.

Orchestras, bands and ensembles

The orchestra

The orchestra as we know it dates back to the late seventeenth and early eighteenth centuries, when regular groups of musicians began to be employed to play in opera houses and at courts. As early as 1626 a royal band of 24 string players had been assembled by King Louis XIII of France. Later, wind players were added to the strings; often they were brought in from a local military band. Orchestras varied greatly in size, depending on the wealth of their patron or employing organization, the kind of music to be played and the size of the building in which the performances took place. Generally, however, an orchestra of the mid-eighteenth century might be expected to have a dozen violins, eight other string players, a flute, two each of oboes, bassoons and horns, an accompanying (or "continuo")

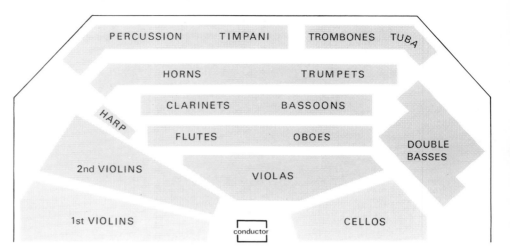

PERCUSSION   TIMPANI   TROMBONES   TUBA

HORNS   TRUMPETS

CLARINETS   BASSOONS

HARP   FLUTES   OBOES

DOUBLE BASSES

2nd VIOLINS   VIOLAS

1st VIOLINS   conductor   CELLOS

29 Typical layout of a modern orchestra.

harpsichord, and for important occasions a pair of trumpets and kettledrums.

By the beginning of the next century, when larger halls were in use and music of a grander kind was being composed, an orchestra in an opera house or concert hall could well have 24 violins, ten violas, six each of cellos and double basses, and two each of flutes, oboes, clarinets, bassoons, horns, trumpets and kettledrums, with a few extra instruments – a piccolo, an extra horn or two, two or three trombones – as required. A modern symphony orchestra at full size might typically have 32 violins (divided into 16 firsts and 16 seconds), 14 violas, 12 cellos and 10 double basses, with a piccolo and three flutes, three oboes and an english horn, three clarinets and a bass clarinet, three bassoons and a double bassoon, six horns, three trumpets, three trombones and a tuba, two harps and four to six percussion players.

A typical arrangement of a modern orchestra on a concert platform is shown in fig. 29. It used to be normal to place the two violin groups on opposite sides of the conductor, so that answering phrases in the music came from different directions; but players prefer the arrangement shown as it is easier for them to play accurately together.

Bands

Wind bands go back to the Middle Ages, with the employment of town musicians or "waits"; there also existed, in the Renaissance period, military bands of shawms, trumpets and drums. In the seventeenth century there were ceremonial bands of cornetts and sackbuts (trombones), and also oboe bands with oboe-type instru-

---

Listening Note II.A

Britten: *Young Person's Guide to the Orchestra* op. 34 (1946)

Benjamin Britten (1913–76) composed his *Young Person's Guide to the Orchestra* as music for a film about the instruments of the orchestra. It is in the form of a theme and variations, the theme being a dance by Henry Purcell written in 1695 for use in a play called *Abdelazer*.

The theme (ex. i) is presented in six brief sections, the first and last of them identical and both scored for full orchestra; of the sections in between, the first is for woodwind instruments alone, the second for brass, the third for strings (including the harp) and the last for percussion. Now the variations begin:

A   The two *flutes* chase one another up towards the top of their compass; then the piccolo joins in with high trills, and all three come rushing downwards together.
B   For the *oboes*, showing a pair of them at their most soulful.

C The *clarinets* start playfully with gurgling little arpeggios, then have a moment of expressiveness before more arpeggios, now swooping across most of the instrument's compass.

D The *bassoons* start off with a pompous, faintly sinister march; then the first bassoon shows that he can play warmly and expressively too before the march resumes.

E The most brilliant and dashing of the variations, in the rhythm of a Polish dance, the polacca: the *violins* scurry up to a high note, then play emphatic chords followed by rich, swooning phrases, the firsts and seconds overlapping.

F A little slower, for the *violas*, a long, rather plaintive line.

G A gentle, caressing line, in syncopated rhythms, for the *cellos*.

H The *double basses* climb, as if step by step, to the top of their compass; then they declaim a melody up there – and climb down again.

I Against a soft string accompaniment, the *harp* plays lush chords and arpeggios.

J A series of calls on the *horns*, to remind us that these are hunting instruments: first up, to a series of rich chords, then down again.

K The *trumpets* chatter away, busily and nervously.

L Now the heavy brass enters: first the *trombones*, with an imposing melody, which the *tuba* echoes rather lower; finally the trombones and tuba seem to get into an argument, but manage to end in agreement.

M The percussion instruments take turns here. 1, the *timpani* (you can hear three distinct tones); 2, the deep-sounding (but unpitched) *bass drum* with the crashing *cymbals*; 3, the jangling *tambourine* and tinkling *triangle*; 4, the rattle of the *side drum* and the clop of the *Chinese woodblock*; 5, the *xylophone*; 6, the sharp clipping sound of the *castanets* and the soft boom of the *gong*; 7, the crack of the *whip*; and then all play at once.

Finally the orchestra is put together again in a fugue (see p. 67), the instruments entering in turn in the order we have just heard them. We start at the top, with the piccolo alone (ex. ii); it is joined first by the flutes, then the oboes, the clarinets and the bassoons. Now the woodwinds step into the background while the strings take their turn: violins (firsts and seconds), violas, cellos and double basses, followed by the harp. Next the brass enters, led by the horns and trumpets, followed by trombones and tuba; and finally the percussion join in. Lastly, while the upper instruments continue their games with the fugue subject, the first trombone and the horns, supported by the low brass, strings and bassoons, play the original variation theme at slower speed; the trumpets add their brilliance to bring the work to a vigorous and emphatic end.

ex. i

ex. ii

(fugue subject: given here
in its main key, D major)

ments of various sizes. In the next century, however, the clarinet came to be the leading band instrument because of its stronger tone and its superiority for playing on the march. It has retained that position.

In the modern wind or military band the clarinets play a central role, akin to that of the violins in the orchestra. A large band may include 10 or 12 clarinets, along with other woodwinds (piccolo, flutes, oboes, high-pitched clarinets, bassoons, saxophones) and a substantial body of brass (cornets, trumpet, horns, euphonium, trombones and tubas) as well as percussion and sometimes bass strings (cellos, double basses). Brass bands, popular in industrial societies in the nineteenth and twentieth centuries, are largely based on cornets and various sizes of tuba.

Another important large ensemble is the jazz band. Jazz is commonly played by small groups, for example, a clarinet, a trumpet, a trombone, a saxophone, and a rhythm section with piano, string bass (double bass) and percussion including drums. In the big-band days, however, there might be as many as four or five each of saxophones (with the same players doubling clarinets if needed), trumpets and trombones, with piano, guitar, string bass and drums.

Chamber ensembles

Composers have written music for numerous different combinations of instruments. But there are some standard groups that work particularly well and for which large and attractive repertories have been created. These are itemized in the table. Chamber music was originally intended for performance not in concert halls but in chambers, or rooms in a house; works of this kind are written in such a way that they are to be played with just one player to each part.

group	instruments
Trio sonata	2 violins (or recorders, flutes, oboes, or 1 violin and 1 flute etc) and continuo
String trio	violin, viola, cello
String quartet	2 violins, viola, cello
String quintet	string quartet + an extra viola or cello
Piano trio	piano, violin, cello
Piano quartet	piano, violin, viola, cello
Piano quintet	piano, 2 violins, viola, cello
Violin sonata	violin, piano
Cello sonata	cello, piano
Wind quintet	flute, oboe, clarinet, bassoon, horn

30 Nuremberg town musicians playing three shawms and a sackbut; drawing, c1660, artist unknown, Stadtbibliothek, Nuremberg.

Chapter III

The Structures of Music

Every piece of music, from the simplest song to the most elaborate symphony, needs to have some kind of organization, or form, if it is to be coherent to the listener. In music – as in the other arts – form has to do with the arrangement of the various elements. From the listener's point of view, it has chiefly to do with recognizing. It is by hearing something that you have heard before, and recognizing it, that you can perceive a piece as something more than a continuing, blurred series of unrelated sounds.

In the first part of this chapter we shall consider some of the ways in which composers have organized their music, which elements they have used, and how they have used them. In the second we shall look at the genres, or types, of music – the symphony, the quartet, the oratorio and so on – in terms of their structure and their history, noting which composers have particularly contributed to each genre.

Musical form

The most basic elements in the organization of Western music are melody and key. It is fairly obvious that the easiest thing to recognize is a melody that one has recently heard, and composers have always used melodic recurrence as a means of giving shape and artistic unity to a composition. A structural unit in a piece of music, however, may be much smaller than an entire melody. It may be a *phrase*, of perhaps six or seven notes, or even a *motif* (or a *figure*), of two or three, which the composer uses persistently so that it imprints itself firmly on the hearer's mind and gives the piece a sense of unity. The term *theme* is often used for a musical idea on which a work is based; it implies something longer than a motif, forming a unit in itself, but capable, like a motif, of giving rise to some kind of musical "argument" or working-out.

Phrase, motif, theme

These various structural units are used by composers to clarify, or articulate, the design of their work at different levels. For example, a movement lasting 15 minutes may have three main sections, each about five minutes long, the last of them beginning like the first and the middle one beginning with an altered version of the same material. At a more detailed level of structure, each section may consist of several melodies with linking sections in between; at a still deeper level there may be motifs in some of the melodies that are also heard in the accompaniments and linking passages. Much of that general description fits closely the first movement of what is possibly the best-known of all symphonies, Beethoven's Fifth, in which the four-note rhythmic motif that is the basis of the opening statement underlies the music of the entire movement; sometimes it supplies the main material, sometimes it is tucked away in accompaniment – though it always makes its presence felt.

Melodic devices as such are only one part of the composer's organizational armory. The Beethoven example shows that the rhythmic element may be more important than the purely melodic; his four-note figure starts as in ex. III.1a but is still unmistakable even when it recurs in such different forms as those in exx. 1b or c.

ex. III.1

Key

Second in importance to melody is key. As we saw in Chapter I, most Western music has a strong gravitational pull towards a tonal center: we talk of a Symphony in D, or a Concerto in B♭ minor, when the music feels as though it has a natural tendency to end on (respectively) a chord of D major or one of B♭ minor. We have seen, too, that composers cause their music to modulate, or change key, in the course of a movement, usually to one or more of the keys nearly related to the principal one of the movement – that is, to keys which have many notes in common with the principal key (see p. 26). A piece in C major normally modulates first of all to G major, which as we saw on p. 25 uses the same tones as C major bar one (F♯ instead of F); an analogous relationship applies, of course, in any other key. Examples of this modulation can be seen in two of the melodies discussed in Chapter I, *The Star-Spangled Banner* and *Heidenröslein* (see pp. 22–3); one goes from C to G, the other from G to D. A listener with even fairly modest experience soon recognizes that particular modulation and what it signifies in the design of a piece. He also soon comes to recognize the points at which a piece returns to its home key, which have an even greater structural meaning.

Composers developed subtle ways of handling modulation to convey structural meaning – for example, by modulating to very remote keys to create a sense of distance from the home key, or by changing key rapidly to bemuse the listener. They could, further, couple key and melody to powerful effect. In the main Classical type of form, usually known as "sonata form" (see p. 64), composers generally – at a point about two-thirds or three-quarters through a movement – moved to the home key and at the same time reintroduced the opening theme. This "double return" creates a moment of particular force in the structure. This could be emphasized by harmonic means: Mozart, in particular, had a way of reducing the harmonic interest just before this point in order to stress its drama – the mountain peak seems the higher because the surrounding countryside is so flat.

Harmony and cadence

There are other ways in which harmony is used in the structure of a movement. Composers of the Baroque period, for example, often based an entire movement on a fixed, recurring pattern of harmonies (much like twentieth-century jazz, with its spontaneously improvised melody and rhythm but pre-arranged harmonic sequence). In the Baroque period, movements were often constructed over a repeating bass-line; this is called a "ground bass" (because the bass serves as the ground on which the piece is built); it is more fully discussed below, p. 66.

There are numerous other kinds of compositional device by which a composer can manipulate the structure of a movement (or indeed a whole series of movements). The use of cadences – punctuation points, or resting points – can mark out the formal outlines of a movement for the listener. If the composer wishes, on the other hand, he can avoid them and create (as we saw on p. 28 that Wagner did in his mature operas) a continuously flowing texture in which the listener's expectation of a moment of repose is constantly frustrated, with an ebb and flow of tension that itself is a controlling element in the form of the music.

Cantus firmus

Most of the formal devices mentioned above belong to the Baroque, Classical and Romantic periods, and to a lesser extent to the twentieth century. In the Middle Ages and the Renaissance (that is, up to about 1600), the chief organizational device was the *cantus firmus* (Latin for "fixed song" or "fixed melody"). Here the composer would base his piece on a particular melody, which might be sung or played in long notes by one voice or instrument while the others sang free, faster-moving parts around it; or the melody might be worked into the texture in another way, or it might simply be sung in elaborated form. In some medieval music, the fixed melody might be repeated several times over, in a recurring rhythmic pattern: this, called *isorhythm* (see p. 96), gave the piece a certain unity. The fixed melody would normally be taken from the traditional repertory of chant, or *plainsong*, drawn up by the church (see p. 89), in which each melody is associated with a particular part of the liturgy (the prescribed form of church service); the music would thus contain an element familiar to the congregation. Later, after the Reformation, the Lutheran church in Germany built up a similar repertory of familiar hymn-tunes, called *chorales*, which composers could use as a basis for such works as cantatas and organ preludes. Some of these were adapted from popular songs of the time, just as were some of the melodies that Catholic composers of the Renaissance had used as the basis of Mass settings or motets (like *L'homme armé*, p. 22). Sacred or secular, from liturgical chant or popular song, the purpose was the same: to provide an element familiar to the listener, and to give the composer a foundation for his piece.

Plainsong

Chorales

There is an analogy to this in twentieth-century music. When, in the early years of the century, many composers felt that the traditional tonal system could no longer serve as a structural element, it became necessary to devise new methods of formal control. One of the most important of these is the 12-tone system established by Schoenberg (see p. 430), in which a "series", consisting of the 12 tones of the chromatic scale arranged in a specific, fixed order, which remains unchanged for the entire work, is the basic formal unit (ex. III.2 shows the series from Schoenberg's

ex. III.2

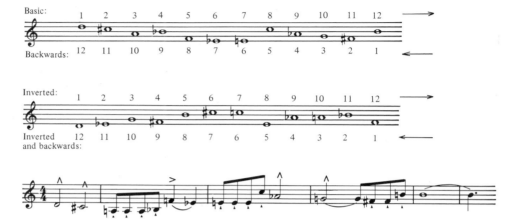

String Quartet no. 4, and the opening melody based on it). It can be used harmonically as well as melodically (that is, with the tones heard simultaneously, in chords, as well as successively, as a melody); each tone can be used at any level of pitch, high or low; the whole series can be transposed (that is, it can start on any tone, as long as its interval structure is kept the same); and it can be played not only in its basic form but also upside-down, backwards, or both. This kind of principle of serial organization of pitch was later applied also to elements other than pitch, such as rhythmic values and dynamic levels.

It is, of course, very hard to recognize a melody that is played backwards (even upside-down is difficult, and both upside-down and backwards is virtually impossible). Schoenberg's aim was not principally to provide something that the listener could readily grasp but to give the composer a disciplined basis for composition. It is characteristic of the time and place in which Schoenberg and his colleagues worked – post-Freudian Vienna, with its interest in the hidden workings of the human psyche – that they were concerned, too, with providing an inner, underlying unity to their music, whether or not it happened to be perceptible to the hearer.

The main forms

Here, however, our concern is perceptible musical form, the structure of a piece of music as it can be grasped by the listener and be an aid to understanding. In the chapters that follow, where we shall be looking at composers and their music in a historical context, and examining a selection of their music, the ways in which the music is organized will frequently be discussed. This discussion will often involve the use of special terms to describe particular procedures; and we shall now look at these terms and outline their meaning as regards the arrangement of the elements of music.

Binary

Binary form means simply two-part form. The term can be applied to anything from a short melody (a folksong, a hymn-tune) to an extended movement, as long as it consists of two sections that in some sense balance each other. Among the simplest examples are songs in which each verse ends with a chorus, like the *Battle Hymn of the Republic* or the *Skye Boat Song*. In music of the Renaissance and Baroque periods, dances were often written in binary form; and in the collections of idealized dances – that is, pieces in dance rhythm written to be listened to, not danced to – that became popular in the Baroque, binary form was increasingly used. Some of its most highly developed examples come in the harpsichord suites of J. S. Bach. These movements, often quite lengthy, tend to follow a regular pattern in key and melody:

$$
\begin{array}{llcll}
\text{melody} & A & B & : \| : A & B \\
\text{key} & T & D & : \| : D & T
\end{array}
$$

A – opening theme   *B* – closing theme
T – tonic (or home) key   D – dominant (or complementary) key

Each half of such a movement is repeated, and the listener is always aware of the fresh beginning – with the opening theme heard in a new key (sometimes in a different form, too, for Bach often turned it upside-down) – at the start of the second half. In some examples, the closing theme (*B*) consists of merely a few notes leading to the cadence; in others it can be several measures long. Another Baroque composer to use this form was Domenico Scarlatti, who wrote more than 550 sonatas for the harpsichord, most of them consisting of a single binary-form movement. In his sonatas, as in Bach's dances, the second part of the movement is often rather longer than the first and, while in the first part the music normally goes straight from the tonic key to the dominant (or relative major, if the music is in a minor key), in the second it might touch on a number of nearby keys.

Ternary

Ternary form means three-part form, on the pattern *A–B–A* (that is, the third part is identical with, or at least very similar to, the first). This is again a form found in folksongs and hymns, even in children's songs like *Twinkle, twinkle, little star*; another example is *Drink to me only*. The idea of repeating the first part of a piece after a different section has been heard is, of course, an obvious one, and ternary form has a long history. Composers of cantatas, operas and other vocal forms in the Baroque period wrote many ternary songs or arias: this form is known as the "da capo aria" ("da capo" means "from the head", indicating that the performer should go back to the beginning). In these, the virtuoso singer would decorate the repeated section with trills and other rapid passages. The minuet-and-trio movements – usually the third – of Classical symphonies and chamber works are ternary, in that the minuet is repeated after the trio. Sometimes a minuet or a trio is itself ternary, consisting of (say) eight measures (*A*, then repeated), a further 16 measures (*B*), and then *A* again. A minuet-and-trio could in effect be ternary within ternary, thus:

$$
\begin{array}{lll}
A & B & A \\
aba & cdc & aba
\end{array}
$$

The key structure in a ternary movement is usually "closed": that is, each section begins and ends in the same key.

Rondo

Rondo form is a natural extension of ternary. It is a form in which the main section recurs two or more times; its plan, at its simplest, is *A–B–A–C–A* (longer examples can be shown *A–B–A–C–A–D–A* or *A–B–A–C–A–B'–A* (with *B'* a variant of *B*). This form goes back to the seventeenth century, where it was particularly favored by the harpsichord composers working in France; one of the last, and the finest, of them was François Couperin, in the early years of the eighteenth. His character pieces might typically have a main section of eight measures and two or three episodes (the in-between *B, C* or *D* sections) of eight to twelve. Composers of the Classical period – Haydn, Mozart and Beethoven – used rondo form on a much larger scale, usually as the last movement in a sonata, chamber work or orchestral piece; in fact, the term "rondo" became so closely identified with finales that composers often wrote "rondo" above a finale even when the movement was not in rondo form, particularly if it was fairly light in character. A characteristic of rondo form is that the recurrences of the *A* section are in the home key; the episodes are normally in nearby keys, such as the dominant or the relative minor/major. (Beethoven occasionally has the rondo theme return in a different key, but that was always with the purpose of creating an effect of disorientation for the listener.) Here are diagrams of typical rondo movements:

1 melody *A B A C A*
    key T D T M T

2 melody *A B A C A B' A*
    key T D T S T T

3 melody *A B A C A D A*
            aba   *a*   *a*   *aba*
    key T D T M T S T

(in the plan above the rondo theme is itself ternary but is heard in full only twice)

M – relative minor   S – subdominant

Sonata form

Sonata form is the most important form of the Classical and Romantic periods. It came into being soon after the middle of the eighteenth century and remained in use at least to the middle of the twentieth, with various modifications. What we call "sonata form" is as much a style, or a way of thinking, as a structure. It evolved to accommodate the musical idioms of its time, as all musical forms have done; its basic ground-plan is not a mold into which the composer pours his ideas, adapting them to fit a pre-existing model, but a natural outcome of the character of the ideas themselves. A sonata-form movement falls into three main sections: Exposition, Development and Recapitulation. This is the ground-plan:

Exposition	Development	Recapitulation
A B	*A/B*	*A B*
T D	various	T T

Plate 3 *Opposite* Caccia *Tosto che l'alba* (see p. 99), with a portrait thought to represent the composer Gherardello da Firenze. *Squarcialupi Codex*, Florence, 1415–19. Biblioteca Medicea Laurenziana, Florence.

There may be an introduction to start with and a coda to end with, but these do not affect the basic outline or the principles of the movement's structure.

The *exposition* "exposes", or lays out, the thematic material of the movement. This divides into two groups of themes, *A* and *B*, or two *subjects*, as they are sometimes called. Depending upon the scale of the movement – and movements in sonata form can last anything between one minute and half-an-hour – each subject may be simply one melody or a group of melodies, or an assemblage of motifs with

very little melodic character at all. Several examples of sonata form are discussed later in this book, with detailed listening notes; in each the treatment and approach to the nature of the subject matter is quite different (they are Haydn, Symphony no. 104, p. 236; Beethoven, Symphony no. 3, p. 268; Schubert, String Quintet in C, p. 297; Brahms, Symphony no. 1, p. 361; and Tchaikovsky, Symphony no. 4, p. 372). The one thing common to all of them is that the first-subject material is in the main key of the work and the second is in a complementary key: normally the dominant, in a major-key work, or the relative major, in a minor-key one. There may be contrast between the themes themselves (some composers tended to use brisk, "masculine" themes in the first subject and gentler, more lyrical, "feminine" ones in the second); but there is always contrast between the keys of the two groups.

The exposition normally ends in the secondary key, and the *development* follows. This generally uses material from the exposition (it may equally be first-subject or second-subject material, or both), and "develops" it. There is no set procedure. Themes may be broken up into fragments, and used as material for dialogue; they may be treated contrapuntally; phrases from them may be repeated at different pitches; they may be used as starting-points for new ideas. The music is likely to range into different keys, perhaps even quite distant ones. Often the development section provides a climax of activity and excitement.

It may, however, be the arrival of the *recapitulation* that forms the principal climax, with the "double return" to the home key and the music that began the movement. The essential feature of the recapitulation is that, within it, the second-subject material returns, now in the home key. By doing so, it resolves the tension that has been set up by its original presentation, in the exposition, in a key other than the home one. The experienced listener is made aware of the sense of homecoming that this embodies, and realizes that the end of the movement cannot be far off. In an extended movement – the first one of Beethoven's Third Symphony is a good example – there is often a substantial coda (or tailpiece), which helps provide a proper feeling of finality.

The principle behind sonata form – the presentation of material in two keys, and the resolution of the resulting tension by the re-presentation of the secondary-key material in the primary key – runs through many other musical forms in the Classical and the Romantic periods. One important example of this is sonata-rondo form, of which the plan shown as (2) on p. 64 is an example. There the *B* material is presented first in the dominant and second in the home key; if the second and fourth appearances of the *A* material were omitted (and composers did sometimes omit one or the other), and if the *C* material were akin to a development, the plan would correspond exactly to that of sonata form. Another variant plan, somewhere between sonata and rondo, takes this form:

material *A B A C B′ A*   V – various
    key T D T V T T

Ritornello

Another form to which the sonata-form principle came to be applied is ritornello form, the standard form of Baroque concerto first movements. This has something in common with rondo in that it is based on a recurring theme. Here, however, the theme does not always recur in the home key; in fact – as in sonata form – its appearance in the home key signals that the end of the movement is close. Here is a typical plan:

orchestra or solo O   S   O'   S   O'   S   O
       key T T–D D D–M M M–T T

O – orchestra   T – tonic key
 S – solo   D – dominant
                     M – relative minor or other key

In this scheme, the orchestra opens and closes the movement with complete statements of its main material, called the "ritornello" (O); it has partial statements of the ritornello (O') in the course of the movement. The soloist has three main sections to play, and in these the music is likely to change key. The soloist's material may derive from the ritornello theme, and it often calls for virtuoso skills. (Examples of ritornello form discussed later in this book are Vivaldi's Concerto op. 3 no. 6, p. 180, and Bach's Brandenburg Concerto no. 4, p. 190.) This basic formal design served late Baroque composers for their opera and cantata arias as well as concerto movements. During the Classical period, ritornello form was enlarged by the inclusion of second-subject material, both in the opening ritornello and in the first solo section; here the secondary material reappears in the home key at the end of the movement, as in sonata form (for a sonata-ritornello movement, the first movement of Mozart's Piano Concerto in G, see Listening Note, p. 252).

Variation, ground bass

Variation form has been used in all periods of music. The principle behind it is simple: first state a theme, then embellish it and elaborate it in various ways. The idea of varying a theme goes back, as we have seen, to the Middle Ages: several of the ways in which music was built around a plainsong amount to variation technique. Variation form was popular in music of the Renaissance; the English composer William Byrd, for example, wrote variations on well-known melodies for the virginals. In the Baroque era, the Lutheran composers of northern Europe found ways of varying chorale melodies for organ; Bach contributed notably to that repertory (see pp. 160, 199). Another type of variation movement much used at this period was the ground bass, where a bass pattern is repeated with different music heard above it. There were a number of standard ground-bass patterns that composers used, often with particular associations – for example, the descending four-note bass shown in ex. III.3a was used for scenes of lamentation in operas, or for mournful music generally, and the one in ex. 3b was linked with dance music (this is the bass for the well-known *Greensleeves* melody; its first part is also the bass to the tune *What shall we do with a drunken sailor*). A more chromatic version of ex. 3a serves as the ground bass for Dido's lament in Purcell's opera *Dido and Aeneas* (see Listening Note, p. 165). Purcell and Bach were the two greatest masters of the ground-bass form. Bach's contributions include a remarkable movement for violin alone (a *chaconne*, using a dance rhythm traditionally associated with a ground bass) and his *Goldberg Variations* for harpsichord, his longest instrumental work (it can take an hour and a half to perform), in which each of the 30 variations – although

ex. III.3

they differ greatly in texture, pace and expressive character – is built on the same bass pattern.

In the Classical period, composers preferred the purely melodic type of variation. Mozart, for example, wrote several sets for the piano, which gave scope for his virtuosity both as composer and pianist. Usually the first two or three variations in a set are quite simple and stay close to the theme, which the listener can readily follow; later ones become increasingly complex and increasingly distant from the original melody (in our Haydn example – Listening Note, p. 240 – the theme itself hardly changes, but is repeated with different music around it). Beethoven carried this principle further and Brahms further still; their variations become more like miniature developments of motifs in the theme than mere melodic elaborations. Both these men, and some of their contemporaries in the late Classical and the Romantic periods, wrote most of their variations for piano, but there are many large-scale sets of variations in chamber works and in orchestral music. The finale of Beethoven's Choral Symphony (no. 9) is an extended set of variations; so is the finale of Brahms's last symphony (no. 4), which revives the Baroque ground-bass principle. A particularly interesting set of orchestral variations written at the end of the nineteenth century is Elgar's *Enigma Variations* in which each variation is designed to portray the character of one of Elgar's friends. Composers often wrote their own themes for treatment in variation form, but sometimes used well-known, existing ones or borrowed them from other composers. Brahms, for instance, wrote sets of variations on themes by Handel, Schumann and Paganini (and the Paganini theme he chose was also used by many other composers, including Paganini himself, Liszt and Rachmaninov). In the twentieth century variation form has been used in fairly traditional ways by such composers as Britten (see Listening Note, p. 56) and Copland, while Schoenberg and Webern have adapted its techniques to their less traditional idioms.

Fugue

Fugue, it has been said, is not a form but a texture. In a sense that is true. Yet there exist many pieces that can be described as fugues and have certain features in common. The fugue of Bach's time represents a late flowering of the techniques used by the polyphonic composers of the sixteenth century, the first golden age of polyphony. So it may be useful to outline these techniques and the repertory to which they gave rise.

The basic principle of sixteenth-century polyphony is that the voices sing, in succession, the same music to the same words; as they sing at different pitch, one hears each musical phrase several times over, at various levels, as for example at the opening of Palestrina's *Missa brevis* (see Listening Note, p. 122). The voices seem to imitate one another; this style, as we have seen (p. 30), is often called "imitative counterpoint". The same style was generally used in music of this period and the early Baroque for instrumental ensemble (under such titles as canzona, fantasy or ricercare). The word fugue – from the Latin *fuga*, meaning flight or pursuit – was applied to certain types of movement of this kind and later became standard.

Many keyboard composers of the seventeenth century wrote fugues, for harpsichord or organ, among them Frescobaldi in Italy, Froberger and Buxtehude in Germany. But the most inventive and most original of fugues are those by Bach. He wrote many for organ and even more for harpsichord, including two books with preludes, one in each of the major and minor keys (24 in each book: the set is always known as the "48").

31 Opening of the Fugue in C minor by J. S. Bach from *Das wohltemperirte Clavier*, book 1, 1722, autograph manuscript. Deutsche Staatsbibliothek, Berlin.

There are certain procedures that Bach and other composers generally followed in their fugues. A fugue begins, normally, with an exposition, in which its *subject* – the theme on which the entire piece is based – is heard, successively, in all the voices (the term *voice* is used, in instrumental music as well as vocal, for the contrapuntal strands of a composition; Bach's harpsichord fugues are mostly in three or four voices). As each voice enters, the texture grows fuller, and the exposition ends with a cadence, generally in the main key. In the remainder of the fugue, the subject is likely to be heard several more times, in any of the voices, and in any related key. In between the appearances of the subject there will be passages, generally quite brief, called *episodes*, which are usually related to the subject in some way.

Composers liked to use various ingenious contrapuntal devices in their fugues: sometimes, for example, the subject might be heard at half speed (or even double speed), and – this was popular, as effective in building a climax – there might be telescoped entries of the subject, giving the impression of the voices eagerly crowding in on one another (this is called *stretto*). Towards the end of the fugue, there is usually a decisive-sounding entry of the subject in the home key, giving an air of finality. Perhaps the central feature of fugue is the sense of dialogue between voices; the voice that first enters after the subject is heard is said to perform the *answer*, in imitation (not usually quite exact) of the subject – the word is significant.

Bach used fugue not only in his keyboard music (see Listening Note, p. 193, for one from the "48") but also in his chamber and orchestral music (see Listening Note, p. 190, for an example from a concerto); he also wrote fugal choruses in his vocal works, like his cantatas and, notably, in his Mass in B minor. But the most famous exponent of the choral fugue was his contemporary, Handel, who in his oratorios (dramatic works on biblical stories) used his theatrical sense to telling effect. While Bach was concerned with the intellectual aspects of fugue composition, Handel viewed fugue as just one way of creating a strong dramatic effect. He used fugue more freely than Bach did, often breaking off the counterpoint to make way for a vigorous rhythmic passage or a striking harmonic one (for a choral fugue from one of his oratorios, see Listening Note, p. 216). After the time of Bach and Handel, fugue was less a part of the standard musical language, but composers long continued to use it in church music and in other contexts for special effect – for example, to round off a set of variations (as in Britten's *Young Person's Guide to the Orchestra*: see Listening Note, p. 56).

Genres

Orchestral music
Symphony

The most important type of orchestral music is generally acknowledged to be the symphony. The word itself simply means "sounding together". Orchestral symphonies were first composed in the early part of the eighteenth century, when public concerts began. Initially, the short orchestral pieces called overtures, designed to begin opera performances, were used as orchestral items in concerts. Often they were in three distinct sections, or movements, the first and last of them fast in speed, the middle one slow. That is the form of the earliest symphonies; later it became usual to add an extra movement, in the triple meter of the most popular dance of the time, the minuet, between the slow movement and the final one.

The Austrian composer Joseph Haydn is often called the father of the symphony. He wrote more than 100 during the second half of the eighteenth century. Many others were also composing such works, but the body of symphonies that he created, especially those written at the end of his life for performance in Paris and London, represents a foundation for the genre (see Listening Note, p. 236). During the same period, Mozart wrote some 50 symphonies. The mature symphonies of these two men take some 25 to 30 minutes in performance. The next generation is represented by Beethoven, who expanded the form, producing works up to 45 minutes in length (see Listening Note, p. 268); his last symphony, his ninth, calls for a chorus as well as an orchestra and is more than an hour long. In these Classical symphonies, the first movement – which sometimes has a slow introductory section – is normally in sonata form, and is the intellectual core of the work. Usually the slow movement too is in sonata form, though Haydn often favored variations. The minuet, as we have seen, is normally ternary. The finale is usually in sonata or sonata-rondo form; in early examples, it is often a short and lightweight movement, but composers later came to feel the need of something that could better balance the first movement and supplied music of more substance. They also replaced the courtly minuet with the much livelier scherzo.

The days when composers wrote 100, or even 50, symphonies passed with the eighteenth century. The weightier works of the nineteenth were not of a kind that could be turned out by the dozen; each was an individual utterance, not an evening's disposable entertainment for a petty princeling, as Haydn's were. Beethoven's nine came to be regarded as a magic number that no one until recently dared exceed. Schubert completed seven; Schumann wrote four, one of them called the "Spring", another the "Rhenish", because of their sources of inspiration. Beethoven's "Pastoral" had already suggested that a symphony could be other than "absolute music" – that is, music without reference to anything outside itself (the "Pastoral" reflects his feelings about the countryside). Berlioz, in France, went further; his best-known symphony, the *Fantastic*, is sub-titled "Episodes in the Life of an Artist" and has a theme running through its five movements that represents his beloved and what happens to her (see p. 326).

The idea of writing symphonies with a story, or "program", attracted several composers, and inevitably drove them away from the traditional four-movement pattern, which was however maintained by such men as Brahms, Tchaikovsky and Dvořák (see Listening Notes, pp. 361 and 372). In the hands of Bruckner and Mahler, the symphony again expanded, to an hour or more. Bruckner maintained the four-movement pattern but Mahler, whose symphonies mostly involve vocal movements (the "meaning" of the work is so explicit as to demand verbal expression), freely varied the number. Each wrote nine symphonies. Sibelius wrote seven, the last of them in a single, highly concentrated movement. Stravinsky's two mature symphonies stand slightly apart from the central symphonic tradition (see Listening Note, p. 443). The finest body of traditional twentieth-century symphonies comes from Shostakovich, who wrote 15: some are part-programmatic, some involve singing, but all have something of the seriousness of purpose that has long been part of the symphony. With the abandonment of the traditions of tonality in the present century, the symphony, which normally depends on key contrast as a prop of its structure, has ceased to be as central as it once was. But composers still often regard the form as the ultimately testing orchestral one.

Symphonic poem

The line to which Berlioz's *Fantastic Symphony* belongs turned into a separate outgrowth, the symphonic poem or tone-poem. Liszt wrote several such pieces, expressing in most of them his reactions to literary or artistic works: *Hamlet*, for example, is an evocation of the Shakespeare character, though one passage describes Ophelia. Several Czech and Russian composers used the genre (Mussorgsky, for instance, in his *St John's Night on the Bare Mountain*), but its leading exponent was Richard Strauss, who wrote several of a very vivid kind, sometimes telling stories in music that can be brilliantly descriptive (see Listening Note, p. 400).

Overture

Closely related to the symphonic poem in the nineteenth century is the overture. In the early eighteenth century there were two types of overture, the Italian, with its fast–slow–fast structure, which as we have seen gave rise to the symphony, and the French, which consists of a slowish movement in jerky rhythms followed by a fugue and sometimes a dance movement. Both were originally designed as theater music, to open the evening, but after about 1800 composers tended to write overtures for concert use. These are usually like miniature symphonic poems. A good example is Mendelssohn's overture to *A Midsummer Night's Dream*, which was inspired by Shakespeare's play but not designed to be performed with it; the music clearly depicts elements in the play. His *Hebrides* overture however was inspired by the island scenery off the west coast of Scotland. Many other composers, like Brahms (*Tragic Overture*) and Tchaikovsky (*Romeo and Juliet*), have written concert overtures, usually in one movement (often in sonata form); these and overtures from operas are performed in the concert hall.

Concerto

The other large-scale orchestral form, besides the symphony, is the concerto. This began, in the seventeenth century, as a composition in which a small group of players or singers was set against a much larger group. It developed into the solo concerto and the concerto grosso of the early eighteenth century. The Italian composer Vivaldi was one of its leading figures; he composed several hundred concertos, many for a solo instrument (usually the violin) and orchestra. Some, for two or more soloists, belong to the concerto grosso type. Bach wrote early examples of the keyboard concerto, for harpsichord and orchestra; both he and Handel (who wrote organ concertos) also composed fine sets of works of the concerto grosso type. Some are in three movements (fast–slow–fast), the usual pattern followed by Vivaldi, but Handel's often have four or five. Ritornello form is normal for the fast movements.

The Classical period saw the expansion of the concerto by the use of a

32 BBC Symphony Orchestra at the Royal Festival Hall, London.

combination of ritornello and sonata forms. Its leading exponent was Mozart, whose 21 concertos for piano and orchestra are among his happiest works (see Listening Note, p. 252). With the nineteenth century, the concerto increasingly became a vehicle for the virtuoso – first in Beethoven's often stormy concertos for the piano, then in those of Liszt, Schumann, Brahms and Tchaikovsky. The violin concerto too flourished in this period: there are splendid examples by Beethoven, Mendelssohn, Brahms and Tchaikovsky. The fine comradely balance of Mozart's concertos is replaced by a sense of the lone soloist striving to hold his own against the full weight of the orchestra, an exciting contest although we know he is always bound to win, whether it is a thundering piano or a gently poetic violin. There are also examples for cello and a few for wind instruments. Almost all concertos are in three movements, on the fast–slow–fast pattern. The tradition has continued into the present century with works by Bartók, Berg, Prokofiev and Shostakovich; each has written concertos for violin and for piano while Bartók wrote a concerto for orchestra (see Listening Note, p. 452) in which the concerto form and spirit are evident but there is no single soloist.

Chamber music

Chamber music, though nowadays played at many concerts and recitals, and much recorded, was originally not intended to be listened to at all (the term means "room music"). It was composed simply for the pleasure of those who played it. In the early seventeenth century, the chief chamber music forms were for groups, or consorts, often of viols or recorders. The repertory consisted of arrangements of songs and of fantasias and canzonas (or similarly titled works), usually in a contrapuntal style or using dance rhythms. Another term often used was *sonata*, which means simply a piece to be sounded (that is, "played" – as opposed to a cantata, one to be sung). We have already met this term in the context of sonata form – which acquired its name as this structure was the one commonly used in sonatas of the late eighteenth century, the Classical period. Taken by itself, the term signifies an instrumental composition, either for keyboard alone (the piano sonata) or for an ensemble.

Trio sonata

It was first regularly used for the trio sonata, a genre that came into existence in the early seventeenth century, at the advent of the violin. Generally for two melody instruments (like violins, recorders, flutes, oboes, even cornetts) and continuo, it had two streams of development: the church sonata, primarily contrapuntal and in four movements, slow–fast–slow–fast, and the chamber sonata, which consisted of a group of movements in dance rhythm. The leading composer here was Corelli; Handel and Bach also used the form. These composers also wrote sonatas for one instrument and continuo, a type particularly cultivated by virtuoso performers as it gave them the opportunity to display their technical brilliance.

Violin sonata

These forms fell out of use with the changes of style in the eighteenth century. With the coming of the piano as the main domestic instrument, the leading chamber music form was for a time the piano sonata with violin accompaniment. Mozart wrote some 30 works of this kind; in his late ones the violin part is more prominent and by Beethoven's time the form had turned into the sonata for violin and piano, a type used by most leading composers of the nineteenth and twentieth centuries, among them Schubert, Brahms and Debussy. Instruments other than the violin were used in sonatas with piano, above all the cello (by Beethoven and Brahms, again) but also wind instruments such as the clarinet. In the early twentieth century Paul Hindemith even went as far as writing a series of sonatas for every main orchestral instrument with piano – including even the double bass, the english horn and the tuba.

Ensembles with piano

Related to the sonata for one instrument and piano are the forms known as the piano trio, piano quartet and piano quintet, for piano with two, three and four string instruments (see p. 58). These all came into existence during the late years of the eighteenth century. The piano trio (piano, violin, cello) was a favorite of the main Classical composers – Haydn wrote about 30, Mozart and Beethoven each half a dozen. Schubert and Mendelssohn each wrote two fine examples, and Brahms also contributed (in·addition he wrote trios using the clarinet and cello, as Beethoven had done, and horn and violin). Haydn and Mozart used three-movement form (fast–slow–fast) as a rule, as they also did in their sonatas; the piano trio was like a piano sonata with two accompanying instruments. Later composers, writing as much for concert use as for amateurs, favored the full four-movement form used in symphonies: fast–slow–minuet/scherzo–fast.

The same movement patterns were used in piano quartets and quintets, though the number of these is smaller. Mozart and Beethoven each wrote quartets, but their only quintets with piano are for the exceptional combination of oboe, clarinet, bassoon, horn and piano. Schumann and Brahms produced fine examples of each; so did the French composer Fauré.

String quartet

The most important of all the chamber music forms was the string quartet, for two violins, viola and cello. Haydn occupies the same central position in its early development as he does in that of the symphony. He wrote his first string quartets in the 1750s, his last in 1802; there are about 70 altogether, containing much of his most subtle and refined music. He had great influence on Mozart (24 years his junior), who composed 26 string quartets and indeed dedicated six of the finest of them to Haydn. All these are four-movement works, usually fast–slow–minuet–fast, though sometimes the minuet is placed second and the slow movement third. Sonata form is virtually always used in the first movement, and often in the slow movement and the finale (the latter is often a sonata-rondo). Variation form works well for the string quartet combination and composers often used it, generally for

33 Title-page of Corelli's *Sonate à tre* op.3 (1689), with the arms of Francis II of Modena to whom the collection is dedicated.

slow movements or finales – rarely in a first movement, where the intellectual "arguing" nature of sonata form seems to be needed in this genre, always regarded as a serious and intimate one designed for a knowledgeable audience.

Beethoven wrote 17 string quartets, much expanding the form – from the 25-minute scale of the Haydn–Mozart era to 40 minutes or more. The searching, profoundly original quartets of his last years mostly abandon the four-movement pattern; one has as many as seven, played without a break. That is exceptional; the composers of the next generations nearly always wrote four-movement quartets. Almost all the major composers used the form: Schubert, Mendelssohn, Schumann, Brahms, Dvořák, Verdi, Tchaikovsky, Debussy, Schoenberg, Bartók, Shostakovich, to name a few of the most important. Its central classical tradition was enlarged by the delicate, French-style textures of Debussy, and Bartók's powerful, dynamic writing and folksong-based rhythms.

34 Amadeus Quartet: (*left to right*) Norbert Brainin, Siegmund Nissel, Peter Schidlof and Martin Lovett.

Other string ensembles

Works for string trio, quintet, sextet or even octet follow essentially the same history as the string quartet but with different textures. There are string trios by Mozart, Beethoven and Schubert, but for nineteenth-century composers the trio sound was too thin and it was not until the twentieth, with Hindemith, Schoenberg and Webern, that the form was again seriously used. The string quintet has a richer history. Boccherini, an Italian contemporary of Haydn's, was the first prolific user of the form: he wrote over 100 (as well as a similar number of quartets), mostly for two violins, viola and two cellos. Mozart wrote six quintets – two are among his very finest works – with a viola rather than a cello as the extra instrument; Schubert's single quintet, one of his supreme achievements, has two cellos (and a resulting fulness of sound). Mendelssohn, Brahms and Dvořák are others to have written string quintets; Brahms, with his love of thick, rich textures, wrote two sextets for two each of violins, violas and cellos, and Mendelssohn wrote an octet (four violins, two each of violas and cellos).

Mixed ensembles

Less central to the repertory are the miscellaneous works that have been written for wind instruments. A quantity of flute quartets (flute, violin, viola and cello) comes from the late eighteenth century; but the clarinet's particular beauty of tone and ability to blend with strings drew fine quintets from Mozart, Weber and Brahms. Mixed groups (clarinet, bassoon, horn and strings) are used in the Septet of Beethoven and the Octet of Schubert, following an eighteenth-century "divertimento" tradition of lightweight chamber music. For wind instruments alone there is a considerable eighteenth-century repertory of serenade-type music for the band ensembles of the time, for example two each of oboes, clarinets, bassoons and horns; Mozart, Haydn and Beethoven wrote for such groups. Later, the wind quintet (flute, oboe, clarinet, bassoon and horn) was popular with minor composers and with twentieth-century French ones.

Keyboard music

The traditions of keyboard music go back at least to the early Renaissance. Most of the music from this time was intended for church use, and is built around traditional church melodies, but from the sixteenth century there are also dances and arrangements of popular songs and sacred pieces. This music was designed to be played on any instrument that was available – the organ (especially for sacred pieces) and the harpsichord or virginals (especially for dance music). The large

English virginal repertory of the late sixteenth century and the early seventeenth includes dances, song arrangements, sets of variations, contrapuntal pieces and "genre" pieces – music intended to reflect a mood, the character of a person, or something of the kind (closely akin to genre painting of the time).

There were four main kinds of keyboard work in the seventeenth century. First, the contrapuntal piece – called capriccio, canzona or ricercare, most commonly – which was often preceded by a piece in a brilliant style, which might be called toccata or prelude (to reach its height in the preludes and fugues of J. S. Bach). Such pieces were normally for organ or harpsichord. Second, the genre piece, which became a French specialty, and was handled with particular refinement by Bach's contemporary François Couperin. Third, the dance suite. Dances had often been performed in pairs (usually slow–fast); in this period it became usual to group them in sets of four or five, often Allemande–Courante–Sarabande–Gigue (in effect, moderate–fast–slow–fast), with an extra one or two (minuet, gavotte or bourrée, for example) after the sarabande (for particulars of these dances, see Glossary). Bach, Handel and Couperin are among those who wrote suites – as these collections are called – for the harpsichord. Fourth was the chorale prelude. This was a form for church use in Lutheran Germany in which, as we saw on p. 61, a well-known hymn melody is used as the basis of a piece for organ: it might be decorated, or worked into the texture of the music, or heard in slow notes against other music, or used as the basis for a fugue (for an example, see p. 200).

Piano sonata

The word "sonata" began to be used in solo keyboard music at the end of the seventeenth century for free pieces that do not belong in any of these groups. The leading composer of sonatas for harpsichord was Domenico Scarlatti, who wrote a vast number of single-movement pieces, some of them in a bold and brilliant style,

35   Wind Band of the Prince of Oettingen-Wallerstein: silhouette on gold ground, 1791. Schloss Harburg.

36 The Salle Pleyel, Paris, where Chopin often played: engraving from *L'Illustration* (9 June 1855).

in the second quarter of the eighteenth century. Soon after that, the multi-movement sonata became the chief genre of keyboard music: central figures in its establishment were Bach's sons, Carl Philipp Emanuel, working in Germany, and Johann Christian, in London. Haydn wrote more than 50 piano sonatas, Mozart nearly 20, Beethoven 32. The large majority of these are in the usual three-movement form, fast–slow–fast, the first movement in sonata form, the slow usually in some kind of ternary (it may also be in sonata form, though often a shorter version of it with the development curtailed or omitted), and the finale in rondo or sonata-rondo. Variation form is sometimes used, too, more often for the slow movement or finale than for the first movement.

19th-century genres

Of nineteenth-century composers, Schubert wrote several sonatas for piano; Chopin wrote three, and so did Brahms. But extended, abstract instrumental forms did not appeal strongly to composers of this time and the sonata was not central to the great tradition of Romantic piano music. Schubert, for example, wrote pieces that he called "impromptu" or "moment musical". Mendelssohn called his pieces "Songs without Words". Schumann used literary titles or ones that made some allusion outside music for most of his – "Butterflies", for example, or "Carnival Jest in Vienna". Chopin wrote many of his in the dance forms of his native Poland, like the mazurka or polonaise, and he also used the waltz, the study (or *étude*: these are designed to highlight some aspect of piano technique) and the nocturne or night-piece, in which he created a dreamy, romantic atmosphere. Liszt covered everything: there are dances, abstract pieces, atmospheric ones, literary ones (based on Petrarch sonnets, for example) and a huge, one-movement sonata. Brahms, more austere and traditional, used titles like intermezzo or capriccio; he also wrote sonatas and large-scale sets of variations, in the Beethoven tradition.

Several twentieth-century composers turned back to the sonata, notably two Russians, Scriabin (who wrote ten, as well as numerous preludes, "poems" and other pieces) and Prokofiev (who completed eight). The tradition of pieces designed to conjure up an atmosphere suited the two great French masters of the piano, Debussy and Ravel; the same applies to their successor, Messiaen, whose works chiefly evoke religious images or the world of birdsong. But it does not apply to Boulez, whose three sonatas are extended, intellectual works, of impeccable logic. The piano works of Schoenberg are simply "pieces", as too are those of Stockhausen. Bartók also composed one sonata but numerous small pieces, many of them folksong-based and many educational in purpose.

Sacred vocal music
Mass

The central form of sacred music, since the fifteenth century, has been the Mass of the Roman Catholic church. Its early development and its structure are discussed in the next chapter (pp. 88–90). Its basic five-movement form – Kyrie, Gloria, Credo, Sanctus (with Benedictus) and Agnus Dei – was used by all the great composers of the polyphonic era, for example Dufay, Josquin, Palestrina, Lassus and Byrd, and their Mass settings are broadly speaking their most substantial works (for one by Palestrina, see Listening Note, p. 122). As we saw earlier, most composers of this period built their Mass settings around a *cantus firmus*, a fixed melody which ran through the work in some way and helped give it unity.

The tradition of the polyphonic Mass setting came to an end around 1600; settings continued to be composed, but now using instruments and solo as well as choral singing. The Mass flourished again as a musical genre in Italy and particularly southern Germany and Austria during the eighteenth century. Haydn and Mozart composed several settings, for soloists, chorus and orchestra; Beethoven wrote two, the second (the *Missa solemnis*) on a huge scale that makes it impossible for liturgical use but a profoundly moving evening in the concert hall. That this should be so – and the situation has continued, in that few composers of distinction since the eighteenth century have written Mass settings for use in church – is a commentary on the church, society and music in recent times; but there have been some valuable concert settings of the Mass, for example Stravinsky's.

Requiem

A special kind of Mass is the *Requiem*, a Mass for the dead. The tradition of musical settings goes back to around 1500, but the form was not of great importance. It became more so in the late eighteenth century, the time of Mozart's famous *Requiem*, which he left unfinished when he died. A highly dramatic view of death, typical of the nineteenth century, is shown in the colossal scale of Berlioz's *Requiem* and the passion and fire-and-brimstone of Verdi's; others of their contemporaries (Liszt, Dvořák) produced notable settings, as especially did Fauré, who wrote a touching, gentle work. Brahms's *German Requiem* is not a true Requiem but a setting of German texts from the Bible relating to death and consolation. Britten's *War Requiem* intersperses the Latin text with bitter war poems in English.

Motet, anthem, church cantata

Equal in importance to the Mass as a sacred musical form is the motet. Its history begins in the thirteenth century, when words (*mots* in French: hence the name) were added to musical phrases previously sung without text. These developed into separate compositions, in which two or three voices took part, often singing different though related texts, sometimes in different languages (see p. 96). By the fifteenth century the motet had become a polyphonic setting of a Latin religious text, at first usually for three voices, later for four, five or more. The choice of text depended on the place the piece was to occupy in the liturgy. Sometimes a *cantus firmus* served as basis. In the sixteenth century the imitative style of polyphony was

37 Mass scene, probably at the court of Philip the Good of Burgundy, miniature from *Miracles of Our Lady*, Flemish, 1456, Bibliothèque Nationale, Paris.

increasingly used, for example in the music of Josquin, Lassus (see Listening Note, p. 120) and Palestrina (indeed this is sometimes called the "motet style"). Later in the century a more dramatic style, with contrasts of sound and texture, and instrumental accompaniment, was applied to the motet by composers such as the Gabrielis and Monteverdi.

With the Reformation, the motet was superseded in England by the English-language anthem, used by such composers as Byrd and Gibbons and, later, Purcell. It has a continuing history in Britain and America. In Lutheran Germany the term motet was maintained, and so was the general form, except that a chorale would be used rather than plainsong as *cantus firmus*; a leading seventeenth-century composer

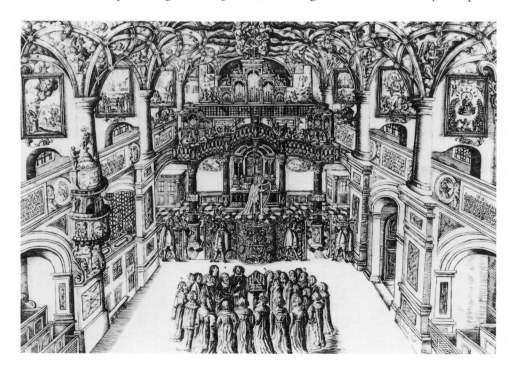

38 Schütz directing the Dresden Hofkapelle in the palace chapel: engraving from *Geistreiches Gesangbuch* (1676) by his pupil Christoph Bernard (the chapel is shown after its restoration in 1662, by which time Schütz was no longer Kapellmeister).

was Schütz, a pupil of Giovanni Gabrieli who followed Italian developments in style. Bach, in the early eighteenth, wrote six motets in a rich, elaborate style, for voices with only an instrumental bass. More important are his sacred cantatas. The word "cantata" does not strictly mean a sacred work but is always used in that sense for the Lutheran church works of which Bach's – some 200 have come down to us – represent the highest achievement. Intended for devotional use at Sunday and festival services, though not actually a part of the liturgy, they typically consist of an opening chorus, two or three arias (or a duet in place of one), and a closing chorale, all linked by recitative (see p. 82 for a fuller discussion). In France, a special tradition of ceremonial motet developed in the late seventeenth century at the court of Louis XIV, where Lully and his followers wrote works with large-scale choruses and expressive solos. The motet has had no continuous history since the eighteenth century; there are miscellaneous examples, by Mozart and others, but no established tradition.

Passion

An important part of the church liturgy has been the telling of the story of the crucifixion each Easter. Musical settings of the Passion were often used. In the Renaissance, there were settings in which the words of the narrator or Evangelist and the secondary characters were chanted, and those of Christ and the people sung in polyphony; other settings treated the whole polyphonically. In the seventeenth century, Schütz wrote Passions in which the narration and the words of the characters are sung to an unaccompanied line, and the words of groups are sung by choruses. There are fine settings of the Passion from the early eighteenth century, by Bach and his German contemporaries such as Handel and Telemann. Bach's, the supreme examples, are constructed of narrative (sung in recitative mainly by the Evangelist, with contributions from other characters, including Christ), with arias of religious contemplation, vigorous choruses from the populace and other participant groups, chorales (for the congregation) and large-scale choruses at crucial points to give shape and grandeur to the whole. Some Passion settings have been composed since, and a few have been affecting, but none approaches the power of the two of Bach's that have come down to us.

The telling of religious stories in music has not been confined to the Passion. In the Middle Ages, dramas on religious themes were often enacted in churches with appropriate chanted music. It was at the end of the Renaissance, with the Counter-Reformation, that an important new form arose called the oratorio. The word means "prayer hall" and oratorios were designed to be performed in such rooms – not as a part of the liturgy but as a "spiritual exercise". The early examples, from around 1600, embody the telling of the story in a speech-like musical setting (or recitative), with songs from the principal characters in the drama and short choruses (the "characters" may be abstract, like "Goodness" or "Temptation", for many of these are moral tales in which evil is overcome by religious virtue).

Oratorio

The oratorio originated in Rome, and its earliest master was Carissimi, in the mid-seventeenth century, who wrote works based on biblical stories with important parts for the chorus. His style was carried to France by Charpentier, but it was through Handel – who visited Italy as a young man and came into contact with Italian traditions – that the oratorio truly flowered. In England, during the 1730s and 40s, he devised a new style of dramatic oratorio with arias, recitatives and choruses that drew on English traditions of choral singing, and created a set of masterpieces (such as *Saul*, *Messiah* and *Judas Maccabaeus*: see Listening Note, p. 216, for an example) that represent the peak of the genre. These were not acted but performed in concerts, as were the later oratorios of Haydn, Mendelssohn and Elgar, who were all much influenced by Handel.

Secular vocal music

The most basic of musical activities is singing. Every era has had its own ways of expressing itself in song, and here we shall refer to the principal ones of distinctive character.

The earliest repertories of solo song are those created by the minstrels of the twelfth and thirteenth centuries, like the troubadours of southern France; their songs deal almost exclusively with idealized love for an unattainable beloved (see Listening Note, p. 92). Their musical forms follow those of the poetry they set, and these continued to be used well into the Renaissance, as different classes of the polyphonic *chanson*. This term, which is simply the French for "song", designates a

Chanson

large and varied repertory of the fifteenth and sixteenth centuries, mostly for three voices – though there are reasons to think that such pieces may often have been performed by one voice with two instruments or two voices with one instrument. In the fourteenth century, the leading composer was Machaut; important composers of the polyphonic *chanson* over the next two centuries include Dufay, Ockeghem, Josquin and Lassus (see Listening Notes, pp. 111 and 116).

Madrigal

The Italian counterpart of this French and Netherlandish form was the madrigal. The term was first used for a fourteenth-century form, normally for two voices, of which Landini was a leading exponent. It applies more importantly to a large repertory of the sixteenth and early seventeenth centuries, covering music for any number of voices from one to eight or even ten, but most commonly four or five. It found its poetic inspiration in the verse of the fourteenth-century poet Petrarch, and musically it took as its starting-point a slightly earlier form, the *frottola*, a lightweight type of four-voice song.

The madrigal at its height, in the middle and late sixteenth century, embodied imitative counterpoint but also a great variety of texture, with sensitive and often intense expression of the words. Leading composers of this time were Palestrina, Lassus and Andrea Gabrieli. At the end of the century the style became more elaborate and dramatic, with much stress on color; Marenzio (see Listening Note, p. 128), Monteverdi and Gesualdo are the most important composers of this late period in the madrigal's history. The form traveled abroad, most notably to England, where it found exponents in Byrd, Morley and (of the later generation) Weelkes (see Listening Note, p. 135). The dance-type madrigal, the *balletto* or ballett, was particularly favored in England.

Ayre

Another form of song, for one voice with lute or viols, was popular in England: the ayre (or air), cultivated particularly by John Dowland (see Listening Note, p. 139). The French had an equivalent to this in their *air de cour*, or "courtly air". The Italian equivalent is "aria", which is the standard term in Italy for song.

Aria

The aria was the main unit in such larger vocal compositions as the cantata or the opera. It could take various forms in the seventeenth century; there were arias on ground basses, arias in strophic form (that is, with several identical verses), arias of an A–B–B′ pattern, and by the end of the century A–B–A. This last, the *da capo* aria, was of special importance in the first half of the eighteenth century and was the chief form used by Bach in his cantatas and Handel in his operas. It normally followed ritornello form. With the expansion of musical forms in the latter half of the eighteenth century, arias needed to be curtailed, and the repeat of the A section was

39 "Go christall teares" by John Dowland from his *First Book of Songes or Ayres* (1597). The voice parts are arranged in "table-book" format, so that the piece can be sung as a madrigal by four singers seated round a table; or it can be sung as an ayre by the *cantus* singer with the lute accompaniment notated in the *cantus* tablature (see p. 14).

reduced to a part-repeat. This soon led to arias taking a sonata-form pattern. A new, more dramatic aria type arose, in which there were two sections, the first slow, the second fast. This, at first used only for the most important arias, became a standard type in operas of the nineteenth century, often with an interruption from another character or the chorus to motivate it. Later, however, aria patterns are dictated to such an extent by the dramatic situation for which the music is designed that standard patterns virtually disappear.

Arias represent the chief opportunities in an opera or any other extended vocal work for the strong expression of individual emotion. Many situations give rise to joint expressions of emotion by two people – most often, of course, lovers, but also (for example) father and child or conqueror and conquered. In such situations the composer will normally provide a duet, in form like an aria for two people, who may sing separately, together or (usually) both. Scenes for three, four or more people are not uncommon, where they all sing together: there are for example

Ensembles

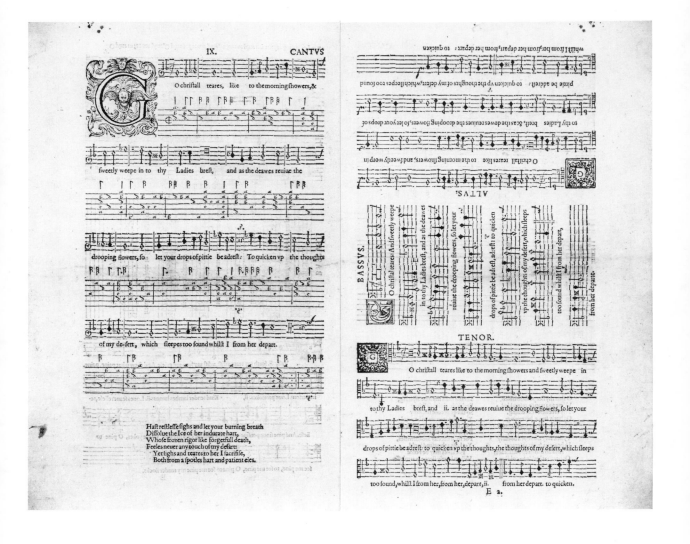

famous quartets in Beethoven's opera *Fidelio* and Verdi's *Rigoletto*, a fine trio and sextet in Mozart's *Marriage of Figaro* (see Listening Note, p. 249), and a septet of great beauty in Berlioz's *The Trojans*.

These larger ensembles generally take a form similar to those of arias in operas of the same period, though obviously their schemes are in some measure dictated by the complicated problem of expressing different kinds of emotion simultaneously. Often such ensembles embody dramatic action in a way that arias rarely do, especially in act finales. But the chief action in an opera tends to occur between, rather than during, the lyrical sections, in the narrative or dialogue parts, called recitative. Here the words are sung in a manner best described as conversational, which can be rapid (especially in comic opera) and very lightly accompanied, or can be very much heightened by a musical setting that exaggerates the inflections of speech, to convey strong feeling. Recitative was originally an Italian invention, and works most effectively in the Italian language; but it has been adapted in various ways to fit the needs of other tongues.

Recitative

Cantata

Outside the opera house, the principal Italian vocal form is the cantata. The term, as we have seen, is a very general one; but in the seventeenth and eighteenth centuries it had a fairly well defined meaning, of a composition for one or two voices and continuo, possibly with another instrument (or even a body of instruments). Typically, an Italian cantata of this time – such as those written by Alessandro Scarlatti or Handel – would consist of two or three arias each preceded by a recitative, though there are longer ones in which, for example, two singers have alternate arias and finally join in a duet. The theme of almost all these works is love and its betrayal.

In Germany, the great age of song came in the nineteenth century. German and Austrian composers had written music for voice with accompaniment before then, but it was with the flowering of German literature in the Classical and Romantic eras that composers found high inspiration in poetry and created the genre known as the *Lied* (German for song: plural *Lieder*). The beginnings of this tradition are seen in the songs of Mozart and Beethoven, but it is with Schubert that a new balance is found between words and music, a new absorption into the music of the sense of the words. Schubert wrote over 600 songs, some of them in sequences or cycles that relate a story – an adventure of the soul rather than the body. The tradition was continued by Schumann, Brahms and Wolf, and on into the present century by Strauss and Mahler. The body of song created in the *Lied* tradition, like that of the Italian madrigal three centuries before, represents one of the richest products of human sensibility.

The *Lied* tradition is closely linked with the actual sound of the German language. But there are parallels elsewhere, notably in France, with the *mélodies* of such composers as Fauré, Debussy and Poulenc, and in Russia, with the songs of Mussorgsky in particular. England too had a flowering of song, in the early twentieth century (represented by Vaughan Williams and Britten).

Lied

Dramatic music
Opera

The central form of dramatic music is of course opera. An opera is a drama set to music, for performance on stage, normally with orchestral accompaniment. It may be entirely sung, or there may be sections of spoken dialogue.

Opera as we know it came into existence around 1600, in the courts of north Italy, as an entertainment for a small, aristocratic audience. The first public opera

40 *Orpheus in the Underworld before Pluto and Persephone*: pen and ink drawing with wash by John Michael Rysbrack (1694–1770). Private collection. The Orpheus legend was a popular subject for opera composers.

house was opened, in Venice, in 1637. The leading composers of this early period were Monteverdi and Cavalli, in whose operas musically heightened speech is used for the dialogue, while the characters express their emotions in music of a more lyrical kind. There are also choruses (in a madrigal-influenced style) and interludes (in some cases dances) for the orchestra.

In the seventeenth century, Rome (where some operas on sacred topics were given) and Naples were important opera centers along with Venice; Alessandro Scarlatti was a leading figure in both cities. In Paris, Lully established French opera, influenced by the strong theater traditions of that country, the French love of dance and Louis XIV's fondness for lavish spectacle. A German opera house was opened in Hamburg, and in London some opera was given in English, but over much of Europe Italian opera was dominant throughout the early eighteenth century. Most early opera is based on plots drawn from classical mythology or history, re-interpreted in the spirit of the time.

Opera developed a number of clear-cut patterns in the early eighteenth century. In Italy, *opera seria* (serious opera) became standardized as a succession of arias linked by narrative recitative; it always dealt with heroic topics, with a *castrato* hero and a soprano *prima donna* (first lady). Earlier, serious operas had often included comic scenes for the everyday characters; now a type of opera that was purely comic (*opera buffa*) began to be composed, in a faster-moving, less exalted style, treating ordinary people and their doings rather than godly or heroic ones. The Italians continued to use recitative for the dialogue, but that did not work well with other languages. In Germany, the standard comic form was the *Singspiel*, rather like a play with songs; a similar type grew in England, with spoken dialogue. England also had ballad opera, in which the popular tunes of the day were given new words and sung by actors. In both Germany and England, however, Italian opera had a firm foothold: at the main court and public opera houses, serious operas were usually given in Italian (for example Handel's in London). France alone maintained a serious tradition (to which Rameau notably contributed) in the native tongue alongside a more popular type, *opéra comique*, which developed at the lively, open-air street theaters and included spoken dialogue.

The dominance of the singers (and audiences worshipped them then just as much as they do now) led to vocal brilliance being rated above dramatic expression. Led mainly by Gluck, whose *Orfeo* was first given in Vienna in 1762, some composers and the poets who wrote their texts, or librettos, "reformed" opera by giving greater stress to the drama and its expression. During the later eighteenth century, serious opera took in the ensembles (duets, quartets and so on) that had so successfully enlivened comic opera, and comic opera took in semi-serious characters. Mozart's operas, the greatest of the time, illustrate the effects of this fruitful mingling; he also composed two German operas, comic works of the *Singspiel* type but with rich and well developed music.

The Romantic era saw Germany taking a central role, with Weber as the most important early Romantic composer; Wagner was at the climax of the era. In his large-scale works all the arts come together; his operas have a continuous musical texture, without the traditional breaks between aria (for expression of emotion) and recitative (for narrative or conversation). His tradition was carried into the twentieth century by Richard Strauss. Meanwhile, in Italy, the early part of the century had been dominated by the comic genius of Rossini; later, Verdi, with his powerful handling of drama and his appealing use of the human voice, emerged as a figure comparable in stature with Wagner – and more widely admired because of the directness of his music.

In all the many rivalries that run through the history of opera – Gluck *v*. the old, Italian vocal tradition, Wagner *v*. Verdi – there is an element of words *v*. music, or dramatic integrity *v*. music. It need not be a real conflict, as Mozart for one proved; but opera reformers like Gluck and Wagner have always wanted to get away from what has seemed to them the artificial aspects of opera with clearly defined arias in which musical considerations seem to override dramatic ones. Any approach may succeed if executed with sufficient genius.

France, in the post-Revolution era, produced a type of "grand opera" on national, political or religious themes; Rossini and Verdi contributed to this repertory, in French, but the only native Frenchman of true importance was Berlioz. Later in the century the other, spoken-dialogue tradition gave rise to Bizet's *Carmen* (perhaps the most popular opera ever) and also successful, somewhat sentimental works by Gounod and Massenet. A Russian school arose, too, producing the grandly epic works of Mussorgsky as well as the more conventionally romantic operas of Tchaikovsky.

Italian opera was led into the twentieth century by Puccini, who added to the

Verdian tradition more of naturalism and more of sentimentality. Newer ideas came from France, with Debussy's sole but highly influential opera, *Pelléas et Mélisande*, a symbolist work in which the characters scarcely express their emotions but the orchestral music constantly hints at them. By contrast, the early operas of Richard Strauss and those of Schoenberg and Berg favor a powerful, even violent, emotional expression. There is also an element of naturalism in Berg's, as in the operas of Janáček, Prokofiev and Britten; their operas deal not with the acts of kings or heroes but with the troubles that beset ordinary men and women in their daily lives. These and most other opera composers of recent decades have used a continuous musical texture with moments where the characters can express themselves more expansively than in mere dialogue, yet without formal arias. An exception is Stravinsky, who for his most extended and important opera, *The Rake's Progress*, deliberately returned to a more conventional eighteenth-century style (for a subject from that period) – and likewise a formal, rhetorical style for his "opera-oratorio" *Oedipus rex* based on Greek tragedy. Several recent composers, however, have felt that the formal world created by the traditions of opera was anyway unsuited to the needs of musical theater today and have tried to develop musical drama away from the opera house – in the concert hall, on television, in churches and elsewhere.

An important development took place in the later nineteenth century with the growth, as a virtually separate form, of *operetta* – light opera, intended for a large, less intellectual audience. With Johann Strauss in Vienna, Jacques Offenbach in Paris and Arthur Sullivan in London (to name only three leading figures), this soon became a popular genre, treating amorous and sentimental topics, often with a touch of satire and parody. (There was a local counterpart in Spain and Latin America, the *zarzuela*.) It led to the musical comedy (or simply "musical"), a form that flourished chiefly on Broadway in New York and in the West End of London in its early days and became in the early twentieth century a vigorous expression of American popular culture (see Chapter XI).

Incidental music

Music has of course been used theatrically in contexts other than opera. Many plays demand the use of incidental music, to help set the atmosphere for particular scenes, to provide interludes, and for occasional songs, choruses or dances. Shakespeare's plays, for example, include sets of verses designed for singing, and these have been set many times over. Of all incidental theater music, the illustrative pieces written by Mendelssohn to *A Midsummer Night's Dream* (including a nocturne, a fairy scherzo and the wedding march) are the most famous.

Dance

Music for dance also has long traditions. Many operas include ballet sequences; in French ones particularly these may be long and important, from the time of Lully and Rameau to the nineteenth century. Sometimes they are simply diversions (or *divertissements*), sometimes they are central to the action. Like opera, ballet underwent "reform" in the mid-eighteenth century, moving from what was a primarily decorative art to a more expressive, representational one (Gluck had a share in this, akin to his role in opera reform). The Romantic ballet tradition of the nineteenth century culminated in the three great Tchaikovsky works, *Swan Lake*, *Sleeping Beauty* and *Nutcracker*, each a full evening in the theater. This classical tradition was continued in the twentieth by the dance impresario Diaghilev, who did much to revitalize the art and create a newly unified medium by bringing together leading composers, scenic artists and choreographers; his work gave rise to

41 Vaslav Nijinsky as the Faun in the ballet he choreographed on Debussy's *L'après-midi d'un faune* for the Ballets Russes, Théâtre du Châtelet, Paris, 1912: drawing by Valentine Gross after designs by Léon Bakst.

much new music, above all by Stravinsky, the greatest ballet composer of the period. Meanwhile, the American dancer Isadora Duncan had been revolutionizing the approach to dance in her free representation of intense feeling and her free choice of music: she even danced to Beethoven symphonies and operatic music by Wagner. The American John Cage has been the leading composer in recent times in the field of experimental dance.

Chapter IV

The Middle Ages

The history of music begins at the time when primitive Man found that he could sing or make noises by banging objects together or blowing through animal bones. These early manifestations of the human need for music are not, however, our concern here. The history of the music of our own, Western culture – which we should remember is only one of many, by no means the oldest, and only in recent times the most various and complex – may more reasonably be regarded as beginning with the cultures in which ours has roots, such as the Jewish, the Greek and the Roman. We know, from (for example) the Bible, with its numerous references to instruments and singing, and from the visual record of pottery, sculpture and painting, that music played an important part in the life of these peoples. But we have very little idea of what their music sounded like. We know something about their instruments but almost nothing for certain about what they played on them. There are no written musical notations that we can read and fully understand; and, with the so-called Dark Ages intervening, there is no historical continuity between ancient Greece or Rome and the Europe of the Middle Ages in which our present musical culture has its true beginnings.

Practically speaking, then, musical history must begin for us around the sixth century AD, when the traditional repertory of church chant, normally passed on orally from one generation to the next, began to be set down and codified. It would be misleading if, through the limitations of our knowledge, the impression were to be given that all music was church music. Rather, all *notated* music at this time was church music: monks were almost the only people who could read or write. We may be sure that even at this date there was music at courts – they were soon to be central to musical culture outside the church, for example the glittering court in the twelfth century of Eleanor of Aquitaine, where the tradition of courtly love-song especially flourished – and in the homes of noble families generally. Humbler people, too, must have sung in their homes, at work and convivially. But it is with the music of the church that our survey must begin – music that needs to be understood as emanating from the great Gothic cathedrals and the ancient monasteries of Europe, and to be read from the hand-copied books used at religious services in these establishments – or, more rarely, from the superb illuminated manuscripts that were prepared as records or as lavish gifts to kings, popes or princes.

42 Drawings contrasting "holy" and "worldly" music from a Psalter, possibly from Rheims, 12th century. St John's College, Cambridge.

Music of the church

The earliest Western music we are likely to encounter today dates from the Middle Ages. From its earliest years the Christian church has had a place for music and, although its function has varied, its presence is an almost constant factor.

By the beginning of the eleventh century, the form of the church service – celebrating the feasts of the church year, the saints' days and other liturgical occasions – had become more or less standardized in western Europe, though there was regional and local variation. Throughout the Christian world the centerpiece

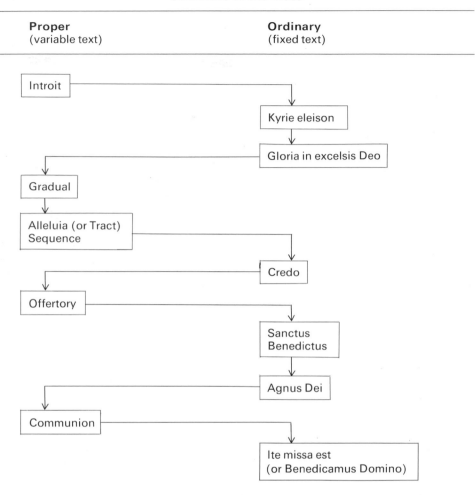

Structure of the Mass

Proper (variable text)	Ordinary (fixed text)
Introit	
	Kyrie eleison
	Gloria in excelsis Deo
Gradual	
Alleluia (or Tract) Sequence	
	Credo
Offertory	
	Sanctus Benedictus
	Agnus Dei
Communion	
	Ite missa est (or Benedicamus Domino)

43 St Gregory, the pope responsible for the categorizing of plainchant, and scribes: ivory book cover, 10th century. Kunsthistorisches Museum, Vienna.

of the liturgy was (and remains) the Mass. This ritual re-enactment of the Last Supper was designed to inspire people with the immutable certainty that the spiritual world offered, in contrast to the less certain circumstances of the everyday world in which they lived. Although the Latin text of the Mass was not accessible to most people, those without sufficient education to follow it would be familiar with the ritual and, if they attended a large church, would be affected by the pomp and ceremony of the liturgical celebration and the splendor of its music.

The earliest music in the medieval church was plainsong, or plainchant, sometimes known as "Gregorian" chant through its association with Pope Gregory I (590–604), during whose reign chants used in the Western churches were collected and categorized. For High Mass much of the text would be chanted to music. Some sections, forming the "Ordinary", always had the same words on every occasion; others, the "Proper", used different texts according to the feasts of the church year and the demands of the local liturgy. The table above shows how some of these sections might relate in a typical celebration of the Mass (spoken text would intervene between these chanted sections).

Plainsong is a single line of text and melody, sung either by the priest or by several voices of the choir in unison, or by priest and choir in alternation. It has a smoothly flowing, undulating line, often following the rhythm of the text, and falls naturally into separate phrases, with breaks for "punctuation", rather like spoken prose. Some chants have only one note for each text syllable ("syllabic chant"); others have more than one note, and sometimes extended groups, to each syllable ("melismatic chant"). The Gradual chant *Protector noster* shows both types (the opening is given in ex. IV.1). Its mood of calm assurance, common to much

ex. IV.1

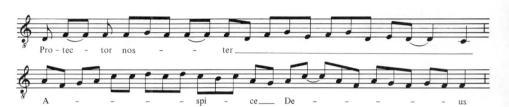

plainsong, reflects the quiet, unquestioning confidence that medieval people had in their religion. Plainsong melodies are classified according to mode (the particular pattern of tones and semitones used within an octave; see p. 26). The church modes were of fundamental importance to medieval composers.

The plainsong melodies used in medieval churches and monasteries were first passed down orally from one generation to the next, differing in detail in different communities; they only gradually took on a more or less standard, traditional form that could be notated. Early plainsong notation is known as "neumatic" – each note or group of notes was indicated by a "neume", or sloping sign, written above the appropriate text syllable. There was no music staff; only the direction of the neume and its position relative to its neighbors showed the shape of the melody. At the beginning of the thirteenth century a more precise staff notation, using square note-shapes on a staff, was developed. This could convey different rhythmic values within the melody, and is still used in the liturgical books of the Catholic church.

A vast body of plainsong – over 3000 melodies, each with its own significance in the liturgy – survives, and has long played an important part in church music. Chant has, moreover, been so greatly revered as a fixed point of reference that, besides being sung in its own right, it has formed the basis of much of the religious music composed during the medieval and Renaissance periods in Europe – as we shall see.

Secular song

Music-making in the Middle Ages was by no means confined to the church. From the end of the eleventh century secular music enjoyed something of a golden age, of around 200 years, among minstrels who traveled between the feudal courts of Europe. At different times and places they were referred to by different names – goliards, jongleurs, scops, gleemen, troubadours, trouvères, minnesinger – but all were united in one particular: the expression through words and music of the ideal of "courtly love". Their love-lyrics, which often idolized women as beautiful and unattainable, illustrate a side of medieval life that was in direct antithesis to the

44 Musicians round the Fountain of Youth, singing and playing (clockwise) S-shaped trumpet, three shawms, pipe and tabor, lute: miniature from the *Garden of Delights* by Cristoforo de Predis (or School), north Italian, before 1470. Biblioteca Estense, Modena.

austere spirituality of the chanting monks who were their contemporaries.

Among the exponents of this great flowering of secular song, the best known today are the troubadours, virtuoso poet-musicians who were active mainly in Provence, in southern France. They wrote their own poetry, not in Latin but in the vernacular (known in Provence as *langue d'oc*), set it to music and performed it as entertainment at all levels of society, either unaccompanied or accompanying themselves on instruments such as the harp, lute or fiddle.

Given the ravages of time and war, and the fact that the transmission of their music must have been mainly oral, it is remarkable that we have not only the names of many of these musicians – among the most famous are Marcabru (*fl* 1128–50), Bernart de Ventadorn (*d. c*1195), Guiraut Riquier (*c*1230–*c*1300), Adam de la Halle (*c*1250–*c*1290) – but also some of their compositions. These are among the earliest composers known by name. Although they came from a variety of social backgrounds, trouvères (from northern France) and troubadours in particular were often men of high birth – esquires, knights, even kings (for example Thibaut IV,

45 Singers accompanying themselves on psaltery and mandora: miniature from *The Romance of King Meliadus* written for Louis II, titular king of Naples, c1352–62. British Library, London.

King of Navarre). The musical forms they used take their names from contemporary poetic forms – *rotrouenge*, *lai*, *ballade*, *rondeau* and *virelai*; the last three of these, together with the secular motet, were to become the principal secular vocal forms of fourteenth- and fifteenth-century music.

The songs of the troubadours and trouvères range widely in style and mood: some delicate and restrained, some unadorned and syllabic, some rhythmic and dance-like (these often in triple time). They are usually easy to listen to and directly appealing; and they are highly evocative of the age of chivalry and courtly love. *Chanterai por mon corage* by Guiot de Dijon, who lived at the turn of the thirteenth century, reflects the atmosphere of the crusades to the Holy Land (Guiot himself, a trouvère and a native of Burgundy, went on crusade) (see Listening Note IV.A).

Listening Note IV.A

Guiot de Dijon: *Chanterai por mon corage* (c.1189)

Chanterai por mon corage	I shall sing to cheer my spirit
Que je vueil reconforter,	which I want to comfort,
Qu'avecques mon grant domage	so that with my great grief
Ne quier morir ne foler,	I may not die or go mad.
Quant de la terre sauvage	From the cruel land
Ne voi mes nul retorner	I see no one returning
Ou cil est qui rassoage	Where he is who soothes
Mes maus quant g'en oi parler.	my heart when I hear him spoken of.
Dex, quant crïeront 'Outree',	God! when they cry 'Outree',
Sire, aid és au pelerin	Lord, help the pilgrim
Par cui sui espaventee,	for whom I am so afraid,
Car felon sont Sarazin.	for the Saracens are evil.

This song from the time of the third crusade (1189) has three verses; we hear the first and the repeated refrain. The words express the grief and anxiety of a woman whose lover has gone on a crusade to the land of the Saracen, from which few men return. The solo soprano voice is "shadowed" – not supported by harmony – by a group of instruments (flute, lute, bass rebec and harp). The flute plays the melody given in ex. i; the voice then enters and sings the simple tune, altered slightly from line to line. It is decorated in different ways in successive verses, which are separated by the refrain reiterating the singer's fears.

ex. i

Early polyphony

So far all the music we have looked at has been "monophonic" (from the Greek, meaning "single-sounded"): that is, consisting of a single line of melody. The late Middle Ages saw a development that now seems to have been the most far-reaching in the history of Western music. At a time when the visual arts were beginning to be concerned with depth and perspective, the more learned of musicians – generally the highly educated clerics and the scholars attached to the more sophisticated ecclesiastical centers of Europe – began to have similar ideas, combining two or more melodic lines simultaneously to give "depth" to the music. This style of composition became known as "polyphonic" (from the Greek, "many-sounded").

At first there were only two melodic lines, both based on plainsong, moving in exactly the same rhythm and in parallel, one a 4th or a 5th below the other; later, a third or fourth voice was introduced, positioned an octave below or above the first or second. This rather severe style of early polyphony was known as *organum*; the earliest surviving examples are found in a large "handbook" or manual called *Musica enchiriadis*, which dates from around the year 900 (ex. IV.2*a*).

In the late eleventh century and the twelfth, musicians began to elaborate on this simple style of *organum* by giving the basic plainsong melody to the lower voice in long, held notes while a second voice above had a freely flowing, "melismatic" line in shorter note values (ex. 2*b*). The lower, principal voice was called the tenor (from the Latin *tenere*, "to hold"). The church apparently encouraged the use of *organum* in its services, as long as elaboration did not obscure the meaning of the liturgical text.

Léonin, Pérotin

It was natural that the cathedral of Notre Dame in Paris, one of the leading ecclesiastical centers of northern Europe, should be in the forefront of musical development at this time. In the late twelfth century a large group of musicians seems to have gathered there, including two whose names we know, Léonin

ex. IV.2

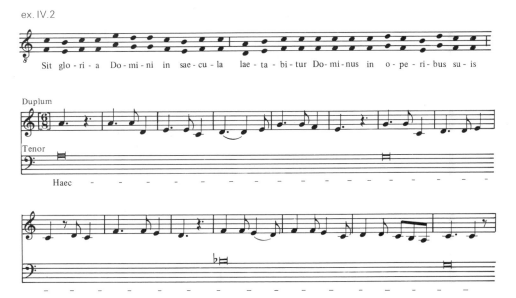

Sit glo - ri - a Do - mi - ni in sae - cu - la lae - ta - bi - tur Do - mi - nus in o - pe - ri - bus su - is

Duplum

Tenor

Haec -

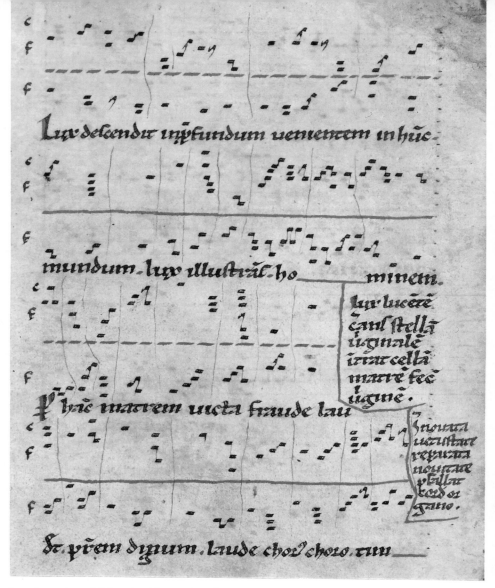

46 Organum "Lux descendit" from a 12th-century manuscript from St Martial. British Library, London.

(c1163–90) and Pérotin (fl 1200), who may have held official appointments in the cathedral. Their music is preserved in an enormous volume of *organum* for two voices, the *Magnus liber organi* ("Great book of organum"), thought to have been compiled by Léonin and revised by Pérotin. Léonin apparently wrote mainly for two voices, but Pérotin's music was more developed, even more adventurous, often using three or four voices, well-defined rhythms and shorter melismas. His *Viderunt omnes* illustrates this style (see Listening Note IV.B).

Organum illustrates the twofold importance of plainsong in medieval composition: the long tenor notes of the chant, though usually too drawn out to be easily audible as a melody, provide a foundation which is both structural, allowing the composer to devise more inventive upper parts above, and spiritual, acting as a symbolic reminder of the music's liturgical meaning. These two functions can be observed to some degree in most of the sacred music of the medieval and Renaissance periods that relies to any degree on chant. The most effective music that emanated from Notre Dame, as from Europe's other great ecclesiastical centers, was

Listening Note IV.B

Pérotin: *Viderunt omnes* (?1198), opening

Viderunt [omnes fines terrae salutare Dei nostri]   [All the ends of the earth] shall see [the salvation of our God]

In this monumental *organum*, probably written for Christmas 1198, four voices are used to create a rich fabric of sound. The organ has long, sustained notes, derived from plainsong, against which the voices weave an inventive counterpoint in short notes in a variety of almost dance-like rhythms. The upper voices often move in parallel 4ths and sometimes seem to echo one another. The time-scale of the piece is enormous: each syllable of the text is treated at great length. In this extract we can hear elaboration of the three opening syllables "Vi-de-runt". The sections of music for each syllable are self-contained and separated by short breaks.

of a piece with the Gothic architecture that surrounded it – soaring, magnificent and resonant – and it laid the foundation of a polyphonic style whose flowering was to last some 400 years.

The motet

Much medieval music is characterized by the same combination of "fixity" and "freedom" as appears in *organum*. Fixity is often present in the form of plainsong,

47 Illustration from a 12th-century Italian Exultet Roll. British Library, London. The text (chanted by the deacon) is upside-down relative to the illustrations, enabling those in front of the lectern to see the themes described as the manuscript unrolls.

48 Procession of the Blessed (with a positive organ): detail from a Last Judgment scene over the west door of León Cathedral, Spain, 13th century.

Plate 5 Church service: miniature from a Book of Hours, Paris, 15th century (for Mass music see p. 77). British Library, London.

usually in the tenor, which determines the structure and acts as a reference point for the other voices, while freedom is reflected in those other parts that are freshly composed and which may even have a different text (or texts) from the liturgical tenor chant.

During the thirteenth century the most important new form, distinguished by this joint reliance on fixity and freedom, was the motet. It is perhaps indicative of a general growing interest in the temporal world that both sacred and secular motets were composed, and that sacred and secular texts could even be used in the same piece. For example, a traditional Latin liturgical text in one part might be combined with a French secular poem in another, while the tenor retained the notes and Latin text of a plainsong melody (the *cantus firmus*, or "fixed song"). The term "motet" itself probably derives from the French *mot*, "word", which may refer to the added texts in the upper parts. By the end of the thirteenth century the *cantus firmus* motet had become a sophisticated and complex form, testing the skills and inventiveness of composers to the full. Most of the pieces that survive from this period are for three voices and are by anonymous composers of the Notre Dame school, Pérotin's successors.

Ars Nova

Vitry

Music theorists of the early fourteenth century described this thirteenth-century music as "Ars Antiqua" ("the old art"), for early in the century a new style, which they called "Ars Nova", was gaining currency. Its leader was the French composer and theorist Philippe de Vitry (1291–1361). Although he was employed by the church – he held several appointments in French towns and in 1351 was made Bishop of Meaux – Vitry was particularly active in a secular sphere. As a young man he studied at the Sorbonne in Paris and later served as secretary and adviser to several French kings, fighting as a soldier and traveling as a diplomat to other European courts.

Philippe de Vitry was highly regarded by his contemporaries in intellectual and musical circles, in particular for the famous work attributed to him, a treatise on music entitled *Ars nova*, which outlined the principles of the new style. During the previous century most "measured" music (as opposed to plainsong, which was "unmeasured") had been in triple meter, which was called *tempus perfectum* (medieval theorists, who were mystics as well as musicians, held 3 – the number of the Trinity – to be "perfect"). In his treatise Vitry observed that by the early fourteenth century duple meter had become acceptable. He also discussed isorhythm, the structural device in music whereby rhythmic patterns and units of melody were repeated in the course of a composition; and he codified the expanded rhythmic and metrical practices of his day in a system of "rhythmic modes".

Besides all his other activities, Vitry still found time to compose a dozen or so polyphonic motets, mainly for three voices. Much of their fascination lies in their successful combination of the medieval principles of fixity and freedom. His *Impudenter circumivi*/*Virtutibus*, for example, achieves an impressive musical effect within a strict rhythmical and metrical framework.

ant. Placebo domino. ps.
llexi quoniam ex
audiet dominus: vo
cem orationis mee.

Machaut

The most representative figure of the fourteenth century is Guillaume de Machaut (*d*1377). Statesman, cleric and poet as well as composer, he spent much of his life in the service of the nobility. Born around 1300, probably in Reims, he was secretary to John of Luxembourg, King of Bohemia, for nearly 20 years and probably traveled widely with him in Europe. In about 1340 Machaut returned to Reims as a canon of several major French churches; after King John's death at the Battle of Crécy in 1346, he served various members of the nobility, including Jean, Duke of Berry, and the future King Charles V. Machaut was highly regarded by his patrons as both poet and musician, and for them he supervised the preparation of his works in several beautifully illuminated manuscripts, which present a broad selection of his music unique for a composer of the Middle Ages.

Like that of many great composers, Machaut's music looks both backwards, to the thirteenth century and the age of chivalry, and forwards, to the fifteenth century

---

Guillaume de Machaut   Works
born ?Reims, *c*1300; *died* ?Reims, 1377

Sacred music Messe de Nostre Dame; 2 motets
Secular music 21 motets; over 115 French songs (ballades, rondeaux, virelais) for 2–4 voices – Ma fin est mon commencement; French virelais, lais for solo voice

---

and the early Renaissance. Among his wide-ranging output of religious and secular pieces, some early medieval forms such as the isorhythmic motet and the *lai* and *virelai* for solo voice figure strongly. But Machaut was also a progressive: he wrote extensively in the Ars Nova manner expounded by Vitry and other theorists, and was one of the first to produce polyphonic settings of secular poetry in traditional *formes fixes* (some 70 *ballades* and *rondeaux*) and to write a significant amount of polyphony for four voices instead of the more usual three. In addition, Machaut was the earliest composer by whom there survives a complete polyphonic setting of the Mass Ordinary. Previously, as we have seen, the texts of the Mass were chanted monophonically; the polyphonic Mass was a form that was to be central to liturgical music in the fifteenth century.

Machaut's *Messe de Nostre Dame*, his only extant setting of the Mass text, cannot be securely dated; but it is a work of great sophistication and skill and may well be a product of his maturity. It is for four voices. Four of its six movements (Kyrie, Sanctus, Agnus Dei and Ite missa est) use isorhythm and have a plainsong *cantus firmus* in the tenor voice, which serves as a framework and as a unifying element for the cycle. The movements also have melodic links. Before each movement of the Mass, one voice gives out the plainsong phrase on which the *cantus firmus* is based; then the other voices enter with the composed polyphony. In the Kyrie (see Listening Note IV.C) the flowing contrapuntal lines, with long melismatic phrases on extended vowel sounds, make the tenor *cantus firmus* barely audible. The Gloria and Credo are rather different: they are in a simpler, note-against-note style, which helps clarify the words of these longer, more involved texts – audibility of the words was a particular concern of the church authorities at this time.

Like other settings of the Mass Ordinary, Machaut's Mass was intended to play a functional part in celebrating the liturgy. It was performed, and can best be appreciated, not as a succession of six polyphonic movements (as on most

Plate 6 *Basse danse,* accompanied by musicians in a gallery, at the Burgundian court (see p. 109): miniature from the *Chronique d'Angleterre* by Jean de Waurin, 1470. Österreichische Nationalbibliothek, Vienna.

Listening Note IV.C

Machaut: *Messe de Nostre Dame* (?1364), Kyrie I

Kyrie eleison   Lord, have mercy upon us

The Kyrie, the opening movement of the Mass, is in three sections, symbolizing the holy Trinity and following the structure of the plainsong on which it is based. This melody (ex. i) is heard in a middle voice, called the "tenor". Against that slow-moving part, the upper voices – sung by tenors, in the modern sense of the word – weave a polyphonic texture in free rhythm, often with momentary breaks. The original notation of a work such as this does not give precise instructions to the performers, and needs to be interpreted. In the present performance, the high tenor voice at the top of the texture is supported by a recorder and a fiddle, the second voice by a harp and a reed organ, the third (the one singing the plainsong) by a small organ and a large fiddle, the lowest by a lute and a dulzian (a double-reed instrument of low pitch, like a soft-toned bassoon).

ex. i

commercial recordings) but with the polyphonic Ordinary movements interspersed with the chants of the Mass Proper appropriate to a specific feast in the church year (see table, p. 89). If we can imagine ourselves listening to the Mass beneath the lofty echoing arches of a great Gothic cathedral, like Reims, it is easy to see how this contrast between the modesty of plainsong and the elaborate grandeur of four-part polyphony can make a most powerful impression.

While Machaut's Mass summarizes many of the features of the Ars Nova, his shorter secular works provide more concise illustrations of his own particular qualities. The *rondeau* for three voices *Ma fin est mon commencement* ("My end is my beginning"), in which one upper voice sings a backwards version of the music sung by the other and the lowest voice is palindromic, shows his technical ingenuity; the conservative isorhythmic motets and monophonic *lais* show his gift for melodic invention; and the *ballades*, with their variety and their rhythmic vitality, show his concern as a poet for the relationship between words and music.

Machaut's music hints at a smoothness and sweetness, brought about by his use of consonant intervals between the voices, that is lacking in earlier medieval music. It begins to show a glimmer of the same ideals that inspired the works of fourteenth-century Italian painters like Giotto – religious symbolism gradually giving place to a more worldly expression of human feelings. This increased interest in secularization of the arts may have been related to the series of disasters that rocked Europe's foundations during the fourteenth century: the battle over papal authority that led to the papal schism and the "Babylonian captivity" in Avignon; the terrible suffering caused by the plague of 1348; the growing discord between church and state; and the squabbles between the states themselves, particularly among the city-states of Italy. Yet at the same time there was great artistic activity in secular Italy. It

49 Guillaume de Machaut: miniature from a French manuscript, 14th century. Bibliothèque Nationale, Paris.

was the era of Petrarch and Boccaccio, and as secular literature flourished so did secular music.

Secular polyphony

Italian polyphony of this period is vigorous and lively. Much of it reflects the pastoral, often lighthearted mood of its texts; favorite forms were the madrigal, the *ballata* and the *caccia*, all based on poetic forms. The *caccia* (or "chase") involves close musical imitation between the upper voices, as in a round or canon. One voice begins the tune and, a moment later, the second voice follows with the same music while the first continues, setting up a "chase". Usually a third voice, lower in pitch, sings a slower-moving line, taking no part in the chase. Unlike sacred music based on chant, this type of secular composition gives the important melodic material to the upper voice or voices, while the lower adopts a subsidiary role.

Listening Note IV.D

Landini: *Ecco la primavera* (late 14th century)

Ecco la primavera	Spring is here
Che'l cor fa rallegrare,	And it fills the heart with joy.
Temp'è d'annamorare	Now is the time to fall in love
E star con lieta cera.	And to be happy.
No'vegiam l'aria e'l tempo	We see the air and the fine weather
Che pur chiam' allegrezza.	Which also call us to be happy.
In questo vago tempo	In this sweet time
Ogni cosa ha vaghezza.	Everything is so beautiful.
L'erbe con gran freschezza	Fresh green grass
E fior' copron i prati,	And flowers cover the meadows,
E gli alberi adornati	And the trees are adorned
Sono in simil manera.	In the same way.
Ecco la primavera . . .	Spring is here . . .

This piece is a *ballata* or dance-song, a type popular from the thirteenth century to the fifteenth; Landini wrote almost 100 of them. It begins, in this performance, with percussion instruments setting the rhythm; then wind instruments give out the melody, which is taken up by the two voices (ex. i) while the percussion continue to give rhythmic support. Typically, the song is in triple meter. There are three verses, the first of them repeated at the end; each has the same music.

ex. i

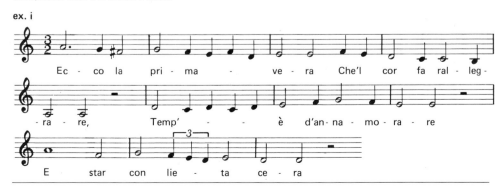

Landini

The greatest Italian composer of this period was Francesco Landini (*c*1325–1397). Blind from childhood, he learned to play several instruments, to sing and to write poetry. He spent most of his life in Florence and took part in the main philosophical and religious disputations of his day. He was renowned both as an organist and organ builder and as an intellectual. Most of his compositions are polyphonic *ballate*

Francesco Landini	Works
born ?Florence, *c*1325; *died* Florence, 1397	
Secular music 90 ballate for 2 voices – Ecco la primavera; 42 ballate for 3 voices; 9 madrigals	

for two or three voices. Many are simple, syllabic, dance-like settings, such as *Ecco la primavera*, a joyous welcoming of spring (see Listening Note IV.D); others are more complex, but all show his great melodic gift.

Ciconia

Another important composer of the time was Johannes Ciconia (*c*1335–1411). Although he was born in Liège, then in France, he spent many years in northern Italy, at first traveling in the service of Cardinal Albornoz and later holding an appointment at Padua Cathedral. Most of his secular works, madrigals and *ballate*, set Italian rather than French texts. In his dozen or so Latin motets for two, three or four voices, some of them written to commemorate historical events or to celebrate the fortunes of his patrons, Ciconia combined the complications of the late French Ars Nova style with the more directly expressive Italian style.

50 Minstrels at a wedding feast, with nakers, two shawms, bagpipe, two trumpets, fiddle, and portative organ, miniature from the *Thebiad of Statius*. Italian, *c*1380–90. Chester Beatty Library, Dublin.

51 Tombstone of Francesco Landini. S Lorenzo, Florence.

Instrumental music

We have seen how poet-minstrels like the troubadours might accompany themselves on plucked string instruments like the lute and harp, improvising instrumental melodies to complement and enhance their vocal lines; bowed string instruments like the fiddle were also common. Wind instruments probably included flutes, recorders, shawms (precursors of the modern oboe, with a double reed) and trumpets, and there was a whole battery of percussion instruments – cymbals, bells, triangles and all manner of drums. Although we do not know exactly how and when these instruments were used – composers rarely specified roles for individual instruments – they probably both accompanied and substituted for voices in secular polyphony and were used in dancing. The color and rhythmic vitality of much medieval secular music is enhanced by the judicious use of instruments.

Sacred music was more limited in this respect. Probably the only instrument allowed to participate in church services was the organ, though others might have been admitted for civic festivals and processions that were not primarily liturgical. Small, portable (or "portative") organs, which could be slung from a player's shoulders, seem to have been as common as the large, permanent structures that were built into medieval churches.

England

Little is known of earlier medieval music in England; but that country had a special claim to fame in the thirteenth century. There survives in one manuscript an anonymous *rota*, or canon, dating from about 1250, entitled *Sumer is icumen in*, which represents the earliest known example anywhere in Europe of polyphony for six voices. The freshness and vitality of this piece (the opening of the first voice is shown in ex. IV.3) is typical of much thirteenth- and fourteenth-century English music which, like Italian, was euphonious and surprisingly "harmonic" in conception, with much use of smooth progressions and the intervals of a 6th and a 3rd between voices. By the time of England's greatest medieval composer, John Dunstable, the foundations of an English style had been firmly laid.

Dunstable

Little is known of Dunstable's life. Born around 1390, he may have been attached to Hereford Cathedral for some years, and it is possible that he was in the service of the Duke of Bedford when the latter was Henry V's regent in France (1422–35). He

ex. IV.3

Su - mer is   i - cu - men in,   Lhu - de sing cu - cu,   Gro-weth sed and blo-weth med, And

springth the w - de Sing   cu - cu

died in 1453. Dunstable's music was certainly known on the continent, for he was highly praised in France and many of his compositions appear in Italian manuscripts. They are chiefly polyphonic music for the Mass, mostly for three or four voices, and a few secular songs.

Dunstable's music has many features typical of the English music of his time. Particularly attractive to contemporary and later continental composers was the sonority of texture resulting from his frequent juxtaposition of 6ths and 3rds between voices, instead of the more common, "open"-sounding 4ths, 5ths and octaves. There is also a greater feeling for chords and chordal progression – a concern for vertical (harmonic) as well as horizontal (melodic) logic – as well as a

---

John Dunstable   Works
*born c*1390; *died* ?London, 1453

Sacred music 2 Masses; Mass movements; over 40 motets and other settings of sacred Latin texts – Veni Sancte Spiritus; Quam pulchra es

Secular music French and English songs for 2–3 voices – O rosa bella

---

Listening Note IV.E

Dunstable: *O rosa bella* (early/mid-15th century)

O rosa bella, o dolce anima mia,	O lovely rose, o my sweet soul,
non mi lassar morire in cortesia.	let me not die in courtly love.
Ay lasso mi dolente dezo finire	Alas! must I end up being hurt by you,
per ben servire, e lialmente amare.	when I have served and loved you loyally.
O dio d'amore che pena e questa amare	O god of love, what pain this love is
vedi ch'io moro tutt'hora per sta giudea.	See how I am forever dying because of this faithless woman.
Soccoremi ormai del mio languire	Save me now from my suffering
cor del corpo mio non mi lassar morire.	Heart of my body, let me not die.

This late example of a *ballata*-type piece illustrates the smooth, sweet English style in which Dunstable was the leading composer. It is for three voices; in this performance viols are also used, emphasizing the mellifluous character of the writing. In the first verse, one voice is accompanied by two viols; later, all three voices sing together. Note the imitation at the opening (ex. i). The gentle, undulating lines, their tendency to move in parallel, the consonant harmonies, the occasional imitation between voices and the way the music leads towards clear cadences: all these are pointers towards the new manner of the Renaissance. There are four verses, all to the same music.

ex. i

52 Emperor Maximilian I attending Mass at Augsburg: woodcut, c1518, by Hans Weiditz.

greater equality among the voices and freer treatment of the traditional *cantus firmus* lines.

One of the more striking features of the best of Dunstable's music is its lyrical freshness, airiness and sheer "singability". The text settings are often clearly syllabic, as in his song *O rosa bella* (see Listening Note IV.E), a largely chordal setting where the chordal writing and the treatment of musical and textual accents contribute to a particular sweet, mellifluous effect.

Distinctive though these features are, some derive from earlier, often non-liturgical traditions, and some of Dunstable's longer motets use medieval isorhythm in different voices. Dunstable's greatness lies in his ability to fuse such austere techniques with a freer, more flexible approach to their conventions and with fresh, lyrical melody. Contemporary continental writers admired his English style, "contenance angloise", and he was an important influence on many continental composers of the fifteenth century. Indeed, Dunstable stands astride our historical boundaries, with one foot in the Middle Ages and the other in a new age – the Renaissance.

Chapter V

The Renaissance

Introduction

The period traditionally known as the Renaissance – the term means "rebirth" –
extends from around the middle of the fifteenth century until the last years of the
sixteenth. At the time, artists, thinkers, writers and musicians all felt that some kind
of corner had been turned, that the darkness and the dogmatisms of the Middle
Ages were passing, that a new era in the history of Man and his awareness was
dawning. This new era found much of its inspiration in the ancient classics and their
values: hence the idea of rebirth. Such values were particularly focused on human
beings, their individuality and their emotions, as opposed to the medieval
preoccupation with the mystical and the divine; the concept of "humanism" and its
link with the study of ancient Greece and Rome is central to the thinking of the
Renaissance. "Academies" began to be founded at which intellectual noblemen
gathered to discuss the classics and their implications for the arts of the time. The
first was in Florence in 1470; 80 years later, some 200 were in existence all over Italy.

The visual arts

The Renaissance was essentially an Italian movement, at least in its origins. It
produced a uniquely marvelous crop of painters and sculptors in that country –
Piero della Francesca, Bellini, Mantegna, Perugino, Botticelli, Leonardo da Vinci,
Michelangelo, Giorgione, Raphael, Titian, Tintoretto. In music there is nothing
quite of that order; there were few Italian composers of significance until Palestrina,
though the Italian courts, centers of artistic patronage, drew an immensely talented
collection of composers from the north (mainly from north-east France and from
Flanders, present-day Belgium). Their music shows a change of approach, as
compared with the previous generation's, analogous to that of Renaissance art.
There, the stiff, mystical, abstract and highly stylized postures of the Middle Ages
began to be superseded by natural, flowing ones, which allow human beings to be
seen feeling ordinary human emotions; a man or a woman can be an object of
interest in himself or herself, not merely in relation to the divine.

Such a change is not of course sudden; in painting it is already hinted at in the
work of Giotto (*c*1266–1337) and his contemporaries, as it is in the writings of Dante
(1265–1321) and, in the next generation, Petrarch and Boccaccio. But the change
was not consistent or universal at that early date, and in music (although parallels
might be seen in the work of such men as Landini or Dunstable) it is only with the

generation of composers active in the late fifteenth century that such a "humanistic" element is regularly found.

In painting, part of this quality is related to the development of the art of perspective; Renaissance pictures, speaking in general terms, have a sense of depth (only the tentative beginnings of this can be seen in medieval ones) and thus a realistic way of relating a person to his or her context. At just the same time, a way of giving music an audible depth was developing. While the medieval composer was content to depend upon such rigid devices as isorhythm – which provides a convenient mechanical framework but has little meaning for the listener beyond that – the Renaissance composer worked in a different way, composing the voice-parts in careful relation to one another, and with lines of a more supple character, so as to provide a succession of harmonies. This quickly led to the lowest voice having a slightly different status (and accordingly a slightly different style) from the others: here are the very beginnings of Western harmony, or sense of perspective in music. (It is, by the way, intriguing to note that some 450 years later composers abandoned the traditional ways of handling harmony just as artists were abandoning perspective.) Further, to give their pieces some degree of internal unity, they tended to assign the same musical phrases to each voice, normally in such a way that each sang the same phrase of music to a particular group of words. The voices enter successively with the same musical phrase, so that the polyphony becomes increasingly rich and interwoven: this "imitative" technique is the classical style of the Renaissance – and eventually it was to lead to the fugues of Bach.

Harmony and polyphony

53 Three shawms and a slide trumpet accompanying dancers: detail from the Adimari wedding cassone, Italian, c1450: Galleria dell'Accademia, Florence.

Humanism

The new emphasis on the human being was part of a general move towards the secular as opposed to the sacred, which had dominated life for so long. Power moved in the same direction, away from the church towards kings and princes. These, notably in the city-states of north Italy, were often men of high education and enlightenment, for example in Florence, where the Medici family held sway, or Ferrara, ruled by the Este. Such people were eager to display their power, wealth and taste in lavish entertainments. At their courts secular forms like the madrigal especially flourished, and at Florence in particular the *intermedio*, a mixed entertainment of dance, music of various kinds and poetry, was cultivated. At Rome, under the pope, church music remained central, as it also did at Venice, under civic rule. North of the Alps too there was a strong move towards the secular, notably in England where Henry VIII threw off papal influence; he and later Elizabeth I were important patrons of music, as was Francis I in France. Burgundy, now a part of France but then an independent country which included areas of what are now the Low Countries, had one of the most brilliant of all the courts of the fifteenth century, but its separate history came to an end in 1477.

The Reformation

The biggest change of all during this period, however, originated in Germany. This was the Reformation. It began as an attempt to rid the Catholic church of corruption and abuse and to "rationalize" religious practice by allowing every man and woman the right to worship in his or her own language. It caused bloodshed and destruction on a vast scale, over many decades, though in the light of history we can see it as an inevitable development of the Renaissance and its modes of thought. Its leader was Martin Luther (1483–1546). To him music was a vital part of worship, and although he greatly admired the Latin works of such composers as Josquin he realized that ordinary people's involvement in religion would be deepened were they allowed to participate in services rather than listen passively to Latin chant from the clergy and, in the larger churches, Latin polyphony from the choir.

Luther established a repertory of hymns, or "chorales" (so called because they

54 Frontispiece to Antico's collection *Frottole intabulate da sonar organi* (1517).

55 Facing pages from the *Chansonnier Cordeforme*, Savoy, before 1477. Bibliothèque Nationale, Paris. Among the anonymous French and Italian secular pieces, music by Dufay, Busnois, Ockeghem and Binchois has been identified.

were to be sung chorally), sometimes drawing on well-known songs, which would be familiar to his congregations, and sometimes composing new melodies himself; among his own compositions is *Ein feste Burg* ("A stronghold sure"), often called the battle-song of the Reformation (see pp. 186 and 199–202). In the reformed church the chorale largely came to take the place that plainsong had traditionally occupied in the Catholic church, as a basis for newly composed works.

The Lutheran reforms had great influence in Germany, especially the northern and eastern parts, and in Scandinavia. Another reformer, Jean Calvin (1509–64), was more influential in his native France, Switzerland, the Low Countries and Scotland; he was less interested in music than was Luther and advocated the use of psalms in austere, unaccompanied versions. In England too the church was reformed, under Henry VIII, and an Anglican church established with congregational participation and use of the English language.

The Counter-Reformation

The Catholic church was bound to react to the spread of the Reformation, which by the middle of the sixteenth century had created a huge schism. What is called the Counter-Reformation began in the 1540s: a move by the Catholic church to rid itself of malpractices and to encourage greater piety among the people, involving a revival of Catholic principles and their application in a carefully monitored, disciplined way. Music and its use in the church were among the topics discussed in the series of meetings held at Trent, northern Italy, between 1545 and 1563. The

56 Engraving from the title-page of the Spanish composer Francisco Guerrero's *Missarum liber secundus* ("Second book of Masses', 1582): a typical illustration of the Counter-Reformation period.

Council of Trent expressed concern over the use of secular melodies in church (for example as *cantus firmi* in Mass settings: see p. 61) and the weakening of the traditions of plainsong, and objected to over-elaborate polyphony that might obscure the liturgical words; virtuoso singing in particular was deplored, and so was the use of instruments other than the organ. In countering Luther and his reforms, the Council were in fact compelled to tread a similar path.

The net result was not only music of a new simplicity; the music of the Counter-Reformation is in fact marked by its fervor, its emotional content and its feeling of mysticism. Its greatest composer was certainly Palestrina, but the colorful polychoral and ensemble music of the two Gabrielis, Andrea and Giovanni, from Venice, is imbued with the Counter-Reformation spirit, and so is much music from Spain. The staunch Catholicism of that powerful country, whose empire included most of what is now Belgium, put it in the forefront of the fight against the Reformation.

Printing

It is difficult to imagine how the Reformation could have made any real progress without the invention of printing. Printing was invented (in the West) in the mid-fifteenth century; music printing began in about 1473 and in the last quarter of the century many liturgical music books, for the singing of chant, were produced from woodblocks, carved and inked. It was in 1501 that the first polyphonic music was printed, by Ottaviano Petrucci of Venice, using movable type; this was an anthology mainly of chansons by French and Flemish composers. It must have been a success, to judge by his reprints and his further publications. His methods were quickly copied elsewhere – in Germany, France and England, and in other Italian cities. Until this time, music had circulated only in manuscript, a laborious and costly process; now it became available to a much wider public. The international exchange of ideas that was now possible was important to the dissemination of Renaissance culture.

Petrucci and his followers printed music of all sorts: polyphony, both sacred and secular, instrumental music (including tablatures for the lute – that is, music that tells you not what notes to sound but where to put your fingers for the right ones), and, in the "reformed" countries, hymn books and psalm collections.

This new spread of music and ideas – supported by the idea of "Renaissance man", interested and skilled in all the arts and sciences – made it possible for music-making to become popular among the higher social classes in the sixteenth century. People learned to read music, to sing and to play instruments, and a new demand arose for any kind of music that could be performed in the home by a small number of modestly capable musicians. This demand was chiefly met by the new forms of secular song: the madrigal in Italy, and later in England and other parts of northern Europe, in France the chanson, in Germany the polyphonic Lied. The singing of madrigals and similar works came to be regarded as a pleasant domestic pastime. With one voice to a part, it offered an intimate form of music-making – primarily to entertain the performers themselves, and perhaps a few guests, but not a formal audience. The time of the public concert was still a long way off; and we understand music of the Renaissance best if we listen to it with an understanding of the kinds of role in society that it was originally intended to play.

The Franco-Flemish composers

At the court of Burgundy, a rich and splendid cultural environment was nurtured by the patronage of Philip the Good, third in a succession of four ruling dukes (the others were Philip the Bold, John the Fearless and Charles the Bold). By the time of Charles the Bold's death in 1477 the Burgundian ruling family was famed for both its political successes and the artistic brilliance of its court, and it attracted some of the greatest artists and musicians of the period.

Dufay

Among the composers of the "Burgundian school" was Guillaume Dufay (c1400–1474), the most significant figure of the period. Born in the region of Cambrai in northern France, he spent several years in Italy (in Rimini, Bologna, Savoy and Rome, where he sang in the papal chapel) and traveled extensively. He was thus well placed to achieve a fusion of the late medieval style of his native France and the early Italian Renaissance style, with its literary and humanist associations. His 200 or so surviving works include a number of complete polyphonic settings of the Mass ordinary, individual Mass movements and other liturgical settings, motets, and many secular songs, mainly with French texts.

To appreciate the true spirit of Dufay's music we have to try to view it as if looking forward from an earlier medieval period instead of looking back at it from the later Renaissance. Perhaps its most striking feature is its relative straightforwardness as compared with the complexities of some of the late Gothic music that preceded it. Dufay's music lacks no technical sophistication, but many of his works first impress the listener for their predominantly melodic character.

The *cantus firmus* of his Mass *Se la face ay pale*, for example, is not a piece of plainsong but derives from one of the voices of a secular chanson which Dufay had composed some 20 years earlier. The use of a secular *cantus firmus* in a sacred work became common in the fifteenth century and gives an idea of the degree of "secularization" of liturgical music at this period.

Here the *cantus firmus* appears in the tenor part throughout each movement, acting as a unifying element. The melody remains virtually unchanged, though its note-values are lengthened or shortened according to the metrical and rhythmic demands of each movement. Of the other three voices, the top one (*discantus*) is predominantly melodic and tuneful; the falling scale figure which opens the Kyrie serves as a motto theme, a common device in Masses of the period. Contrast is achieved in several ways, for example by changes of meter and by lightening of the texture – sometimes two of the voices drop out for extended passages, leaving the

---

Guillaume Dufay	Life

*c*1400	born in or near Cambrai
1409	choirboy at Cambrai Cathedral
1413–14	clerk at Cambrai Cathedral
*c*1420	in the service of the Malatesta family, Pesaro
1426–7	Cambrai
1428	singer in the papal choir, Rome; established as one of the leading musicians in Europe; developed ties with important courts in northern Italy
1434	*maître de chapelle* at Savoy court
1436	motet performed at the dedication of the dome of Florence Cathedral; canon at Cambrai Cathedral
1437	Este court, Ferrara
1451–8	Savoy chapel
1458	settled in Cambrai; beginning of period of pre-eminence
1474	died in Cambrai, 27 November

Guillaume Dufay	Works

Sacred vocal music 8 Masses – Se la face ay pale; Ave regina caelorum; Mass movements; over 20 motets; hymns

Secular vocal music over 80 chansons (rondeaux, ballades, virelais) for 3 voices – Ce moys de may

others to sing in duet fashion, overlapping and imitating each other. This too was common in fifteenth-century Masses. The skillful construction of the Mass *Se la face ay pale* around its *cantus-firmus* tenor is a fine technical achievement, yet it is barely discernible to the listener who is much more aware of the elegance of the melodies, the sonority of its harmonies and the smoothness of its textures.

Dufay's genius reached its height in sacred music, but he was also one of the greatest composers of polyphonic chansons in the fifteenth century. His 80 or so surviving songs range widely and show a new, flexible attitude to the standard

---

Listening Note V.A

Dufay: *Ce moys de may* (c.1440)

Ce moys de may soyons lies et joyeux
Et de nos cuers ostons merancolye;
　Chantons, dansons et menons chiere lye,
　por despiter ces felons envieux.

Plus c'onques mais chascuns soit curieux
De bien servir sa maistresse jolye:
Ce moys de may soyons lies et joyeux
Et de nos cuers ostons merancolye.

Car la saison semont tous amoureux
A ce faire, pourtant n'y fallons mye.
　Carissimi! Dufaÿ vous en prye
　Et Perinet dira de mieux en mieux:

Ce moys de may soyons lies et joyeux
Et de nos cuers ostons merancolye;
　Chantons, dansons et menons chiere lye,
　por despiter ces felons envieux.

This month of May let us be happy and joyous
And banish melancholy from our hearts.
　Let us sing, dance and make merry,
　To spite these base, envious creatures.

Let each one try more than ever
To serve his fair mistress well:
This month of May let us be happy and joyous
And banish melancholy from our hearts.

For the season bids all lovers
To do so, therefore let us not fail.
　Dear ones! Dufay begs you thus
　And Perinet will speak better and better.

This month of May let us be happy and joyous
And banish melancholy from our hearts;
　Let us sing, dance and make merry
　To spite these base, envious creatures.

This is a three-voice *chanson* of the mid-fifteenth century. The main melody is sung by the voice that is generally on top (ex. i); however, the second voice – called *contratenor* ("against tenor") – often overlaps with it, but also sometimes dips down below the voice that is usually lowest, the tenor. Composers of the time wrote the melody first, then the tenor, and last the *contratenor*, to fill in the harmony. The jaunty, teasing rhythms of *Ce moys de may* – which is rhythmically one of the liveliest of all *chansons* – capture the spirit of the words. Note how the musical setting reflects the rhyme scheme of the verse: the first group of four lines rhymes *a–b–b–a*, as do the third and fourth groups, but the second is *a–b–a–b*. The music of each *a–b* pair is the same, as is that of each *b–a* pair, so that the musical form is *A–B–A–A–A–B–A–B*. There is a short instrumental introduction, played here by a fiddle, harp and a type of medieval guitar, heard before each four-line group.

ex. i

---

medieval song forms like the *rondeau* and the *ballade*. Most of Dufay's chansons are early works; some can be dated precisely because they are linked with political or social events. His range of expression was wide, and his techniques varied according to the words of each song and the purpose for which it was composed. For example, *Resveillés vous*, a *ballade*, was written in 1423 for the marriage at Rimini of Carlo Malatesta to a niece of the pope; the style is florid, and the refrain text is designed to glorify Malatesta ("Charles gentil, qu'on dit de Maleteste": "Fair Charles, called Malatesta"). In an altogether different style is *Adieu ces bons vins de Lannoys*, a nostalgic *rondeau* that seems to reflect Dufay's own sorrow on leaving the area (and the wines) of Laon, in northern France, in 1426. *Ce moys de may* ("This month of May"), also a *rondeau*, shows Dufay in a more energetic and carefree vein of invention (see Listening Note V.A). Some of the music of *Ce moys de may* has no written text under the notes, which suggests that instruments were intended to play with some or all of the voice-parts. The instruments used in chansons might have included wind (recorders, shawms, crumhorns, sackbuts), plucked and bowed strings (viols, fiddles, lutes) and percussion (drums, tambourines).

Dufay's greatness lies in the wide scope and consistent high quality of his output, which sums up the compositional styles of his time and reflects the increasing flexibility with which medieval forms were being handled. Related to this flexibility, and perhaps also to a growing secularization, is the personal stamp found on some of his music, a feature rare in the medieval period but commoner in the years to come. At its most literal it is seen in the text of the last stanza of *Ce moys de may*, where the composer has introduced his own name into the song text. A more interesting example (because it also makes a musical point) is in the solemn four-voice motet *Ave regina caelorum*. Here Dufay uses the same unusual device, interrupting the traditional text of the motet in order to name himself and ask forgiveness for his transgressions in a moving, chromatic passage (ex. V.1).

This passage must have had a special significance for him, since he was to use it again in the last movement of his last Mass, *Ave regina caelorum* (based on the motet's *cantus firmus*); we know from his will that Dufay intended the motet to be sung at his deathbed. It is a rare coincidence of textual and musical expressiveness – while the text makes its point, the music creates an unmistakable mood of penitence. This

57 Dufay (with a portative organ) and Binchois (with a harp): miniature from *Champion des Dames* by Martin le Franc, French, 15th century. Bibliothèque Nationale, Paris.

ex. V.1

("Have pity on the pleading Dufay")

early example of "mood painting" is a supreme instance of the tempering of austere medieval traditions with Renaissance humanism.

Binchois

As a chanson composer Dufay was perhaps equaled by his contemporary Gilles de Bins, known as Binchois (c1400–1460). Though Franco-Flemish rather than Burgundian by birth, Binchois spent about 30 years in the service of Philip the Good of Burgundy. He is best known for his many chansons, which reflect popular taste more than Dufay's – simple and tuneful *rondeaux*, more often for three voices than for four, with the main melodic interest in the top voice. The lively *Filles à marier*, exhorting young girls not to allow themselves to be shackled by marriage, is a typical example. Like Dufay, Binchois was highly regarded by his contemporaries, though his range was not so great. A famous fifteenth-century miniature in Martin Le Franc's poem *Le champion des dames* (c1440, dedicated to Philip the Good of Burgundy), which praises Dufay and Binchois among others, shows the two together: Dufay stands close to a small organ, while Binchois rests his hand on a harp, instruments which might represent sacred and secular music and thus indicate symbolically the two men's differing emphases.

Ockeghem

Of the generation after Dufay and Binchois, the chief figure is Johannes Ockeghem (d1497), another Franco-Fleming. He may have been taught by Binchois himself, but that is not certain. Ockeghem was employed as a singer at Antwerp Cathedral and first served Charles I, Duke of Bourbon, whose court was at Moulins. He was later a singer and then head of the chapel to three successive kings of France, Charles VII, Louis XI and Charles VIII. He traveled relatively little, spending most of his time at court in Paris, though he visited Spain (on a diplomatic mission), Bruges and Cambrai, in northern France, where he stayed with Dufay. Ockeghem was widely praised both for his splendid bass voice and for his compositions, and after his death he was much lamented by poets and fellow musicians alike (see p. 116).

Ockeghem is renowned for his ingenious use of canon – exact imitation between voices – in his Masses and motets, and he seems to have been fascinated by intricate contrapuntal devices. His *Missa cuiusvi toni*, for example, can be sung in any of four modes, and his *Missa prolationum* involves a tremendously complicated series of canons and metrical effects. But he also had a special gift for long, expressive melody, with phrases in different voices overlapping to avoid cadences and to achieve a continuous fabric of sound – a technique of construction that differed from the shorter phrasing used by Dufay and Binchois but was later to become standard practice.

Johannes Ockeghem *born c*1410; *died* ?Tours, 1497	Works

Sacred vocal music 10 Masses – Missa cuiusvi toni; Missa prolationum; Requiem; Mass movements; 10 motets
Secular vocal music over 20 chansons

Another forward-looking element of Ockeghem's style is the greater equality he gives to the voices, extending the lower ones into a deeper register than had previously been common. He also shows a hint of interest in word-painting (musical illustration of the text), sometimes in a literal sense, such as using an ascending scale for the words "et ascendit in caelo" ("and he ascended into Heaven"), at others creating a musical mood to reflect the textual one. This was to become one of the most significant features of later Renaissance music.

Among the many other composers from northern Europe active in the late fifteenth century, the most important were Antoine Busnois (*c*1430–1492), who worked at the Burgundian court and is particularly remembered for his chansons, and Jacob Obrecht (*c*1450–1505) from the Netherlands, an extremely prolific and technically gifted composer of Masses who was among the most highly regarded musicians of the period.

Josquin

Ockeghem's pupils may have included the man who was to become the great composer of the early Renaissance: Josquin Desprez (*c*1440–1521). Josquin was a Frenchman who spent most of his adult life in Italy, first as a singer at Milan Cathedral and then in the service of the powerful Sforza family, rulers of Milan. He later sang in the papal choir in Rome, and then served Duke Ercole I in Ferrara, in northern Italy, before returning to France as a canon of the collegiate church of Condé-sur-l'Escaut, where he died.

Before he left the north Josquin composed in a reserved, sober style, like Ockeghem and his predecessors. But his experiences in Italy brought him into contact with a more fluent and flexible style, influenced by lighter secular forms; the music from these middle and later periods of his life is generally regarded as his finest. He was extremely prolific and very wide-ranging. Though Masses form a large part of his output, he also wrote over 80 polyphonic motets and about 70 secular songs (mostly to French texts).

The motet gave Josquin the best opportunities to exercise his individuality; its form was more flexible than that of the Mass, and the larger variety of available texts admitted almost as wide a range of moods as the chanson had earlier done. The motet *Ave Maria . . . virgo serena* for four voices, a prayer to the Virgin, provides a good introduction to his music and shows how an apparently simple style can conceal a wealth of ingenuity. The part-writing is predominantly imitative, but the ordinary listener is barely aware of such technicalities, for they never interfere with

58 Ockeghem (presumed to be the figure with glasses) among singers at a lectern: miniature from a manuscript dating from about 20 years after the composer's death. Bibliothèque Nationale, Paris.

the impression of flowing, mellifluous lines, transparent textures and sonorous harmonies. The mood, reflecting that of the text, is of perfect calm.

There are several reasons why Josquin's motet sounds so different from the motets of the fourteenth century. The melodies are more flowing and wider-ranging, free of the formulaic patterns of plainsong. The rhythms are more varied, less restricted by meter and by such devices as isorhythm. The harmony is richer, intervals are more sonorous and chord progressions move more naturally. Imitation has become an important structural feature and its smooth progress is often arrested by chordal sections where the voices move together. Dissonance has now gained an expressive value of its own and contributes greatly to the effect.

The most significant difference between Josquin's music and that of the Middle Ages is in general approach: Josquin is the first great composer to attempt to express emotion in music in any consistent way. In all but the most sophisticated of churches and chapels of this time, sacred music still meant monophonic music; polyphony was relatively new. The harnessing of the technical complexities of counterpoint preoccupied late medieval composers – an objective that went hand in hand with the intellectual spirit of the period. If we listen to almost any medieval motet without reading the text, we are hard pressed to tell from the music alone whether the piece is narrative or reflective, whether its subject is penitence or rejoicing, where the significant points in the text occur, whether it closes optimistically or gloomily. But Josquin was the first to explore the new humanistic Renaissance attitude – not only to religious expression but to man's whole approach to his relationship with the outside world. This becomes clearer on a better acquaintance with Josquin's music and is typified by his *chanson Nymphes des bois*, a deeply felt lament on the death of Ockeghem (see Listening Note V.B). It is this indefinable expressive quality in Josquin's music that places him unchallenged at the pinnacle of the early Renaissance.

59 Josquin Desprez: woodcut from *Opus chronographicum* (1611) by Petrus Opmeer.

Josquin Desprez		Life
*c*1440	born in north France	
1459–72	singer at Milan Cathedral	
1474	singer at Sforza family private chapel, Milan	
1476–9	in the service of Cardinal Ascanio Sforza, Rome	
1486–99	singer in the papal choir, Rome	
1499–1503	France	
1503–4	director of music to Duke Ercole I, Ferrara	
1504	canon of the collegiate church of Condé-sur-L'Escaut	
1521	died in Condé, 27 August	

Josquin Desprez	Works
Sacred vocal music 20 Masses – Missa pange lingua; Mass movements; over 80 motets – Ave Maria . . . virgo serena	
*Secular vocal music c*70 chansons – Nymphes des bois	

Listening Note V.B

Josquin Desprez: *Nymphes des bois* (1497)

Nymphes des bois, déesses des fontaines,	Nymphs of the woods, goddesses of the fountains,
Chantres expers de toutes nations,	fine singers of all the nations,
Changez voz voix fort clères et haultaines	change your strong, clear, high voices
En cris tranchantz et lamentations.	into searing cries and lamentations.
Car d'Atropos les molestations	For the ravages of Atropos
Vostre Okeghem par sa rigueur attrappe	Have cruelly ensnared your Ockeghem,
Le vray trésoir de musicque et chief d'oeuvre,	the true treasure and supreme master of music,
Qui de trépas désormais plus n'eschappe,	who can no longer escape death,
Dont grant doumaige est que la terre coeuvre.	and who, alas, is covered by the earth.
Acoutrez vous d'abitz de deuil:	Dress yourselves in clothes of mourning,
Josquin, Brumel, Pirchon, Compère	Josquin, Brumel, Pierchon, Compère
Et plorez grosses larmes de oeil:	And let your eyes weep copious tears:
Perdu avez vostre bon père.	for you have lost a good father.
Requiescat in pace. Amen.	May he rest in peace. Amen.

(one voice sings the following throughout)

Requiem aeternam dona ei Domine	Eternal rest give to him, O Lord:
et lux perpetua luceat ei.	and let perpetual light shine upon him.

This *chanson* is a lament on the death of the composer Ockeghem. Josquin made its funerary nature clear to both performers and listeners: to performers, by writing it in old-fashioned black notation; to listeners, by using a plainsong *cantus firmus* which would instantly be recognized as the ''Requiem aeternam'' from the Mass for the Dead (ex. i shows the melody line above the plainsong). Using a *cantus firmus* in a *chanson* was a reversion to an older manner, but in any case Josquin seems here to be using this older manner in deference to Ockeghem: in the first part of the *chanson* the range of the lines is narrow, there are long melismas, and the cadences are merged into the musical fabric rather than (as in most of Josquin's music) helping to articulate its structure. The second section is more what one would expect from Josquin, with its shorter phrases and more clearly marked cadences. The sadness that pervades the piece comes from the choice of mode, with its ''minor-key'' feeling; but the shape of the lines – the way they arch upwards and fall back – also plays a part. This is typical of the expressive quality of Josquin's music.

ex. i

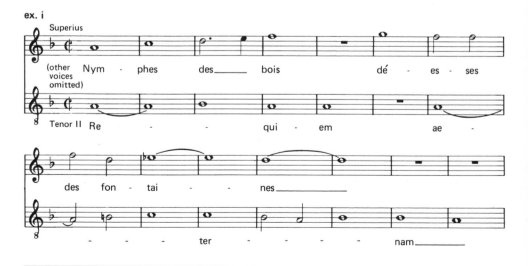

Isaac

The most interesting of Josquin's contemporaries was probably Heinrich Isaac (*c*1450–1517). Born in Flanders, he spent much of his life traveling through Europe, and after about ten years at the brilliant court of Lorenzo de' Medici in Florence he was appointed court composer to the Emperor Maximilian I in Vienna and Innsbruck, a post flexible enough to allow him to travel throughout the empire and to spend further years in Florence, where he was particularly popular.

Isaac composed nearly 40 Mass Ordinaries, over 50 motets and nearly 100 secular songs and instrumental pieces. His most famous work is the *Choralis constantinus* ("Choirbook of Konstanz"), a three-volume collection of nearly 100 polyphonic

60 Opening of Josquin's *Nymphes des bois* ("La déploration de Johan. Ockeghem"), showing the superius and contratenor parts, with the Requiem text in the tenor. Biblioteca Medicea Laurenziana, Florence.

settings of complete Mass Propers for all the Sundays and many of the feast days of the church year. It was commissioned in 1508 by the cathedral at Konstanz, where Isaac was then living, and it is a monument of its kind, demonstrating all the current techniques of Mass and motet composition.

Isaac's secular pieces include polyphonic songs in French, German and Italian. The Italian ones are in the *frottola* form for three or four voices, with clear-cut phrases, often with a text of a rather trivial nature. Other *frottola* composers include the Italians Bartolomeo Tromboncino (*c*1470–*c*1535) and Marchetto Cara (*c*1470–*c*1525), who both worked at the brilliant court of the gifted musician and patroness Isabella d'Este (1474–1539) at Mantua, in northern Italy.

Janequin

The lightness and simplicity of the Italian *frottola* were shared by the French *chanson* of the same period; it commonly had dance-like rhythms and the part-writing was chordal as often as it was contrapuntal. Among the leading *chanson* composers in the first half of the sixteenth century was the Frenchman Clément Janequin (*c*1485–1558). Although he spent much of his life in the service of the church, his sacred music is overshadowed by his secular, which includes over 250 *chansons*. Their texts are often quite passionate, telling of unrequited love, but some describe a historical scene or current event, with word-painting to reflect the vivid realism of the texts. Popular examples of this kind are *Le chant des oiseaux* and *La guerre*. *Le chant des oiseaux* is a sort of ornithological anthology: realistic vocal imitation of birdsongs. *La guerre* is a battle-piece, probably written to celebrate a French victory of 1515, and includes vocal imitation of calls to battle, cannon-fire and trumpet fanfares. Many of Janequin's *chansons* are simple, cheerful settings, often suggesting folk music in their direct manner and high spirits.

Janequin's French contemporaries included Claudin de Sermisy (*c*1490–1562), whose *chansons* are generally less extrovert and have a delicate charm. Flemish composers such as Adrian Willaert and Jacques Arcadelt also took up the French *chanson*, but they were more deeply involved in the early development of the Italian madrigal, an essentially polyphonic genre that was to prove even more influential than the *chanson*, as we shall see.

Lassus

The greatest composer that northern Europe produced at this time spent most of his adult life in southern Europe. Orlande (or Roland) de Lassus, or Orlando di Lasso as he was known in Italy, was born in 1532 in the Franco-Flemish town of Mons in Hainaut, an area that had produced a number of famous musicians. As a boy he is thought to have been a fine singer; there is even a tale that he was three times kidnapped for the sake of his beautiful voice. From about the age of 12 he was in Italy, first at the Mantuan court, then in Naples and Florence, and finally in Rome, where he was in charge of the music at the church of St John Lateran when he was only 21. After a short stay in Antwerp, in 1556 he joined the musical establishment of Duke Albrecht V of Bavaria in Munich and soon took over the ducal chapel, where he remained for more than 30 years. He died in 1594.

Lassus continued to visit Italy throughout his life, and his fame as a composer spread rapidly, not least because his output was so immense: over 2000 works, including Masses, Passions, hymns, over 500 motets, and over 400 secular pieces with Italian, French and German texts – an enormous achievement for a man who died in his early 60s. Many of his works were published during his lifetime, and he was highly regarded among his contemporaries.

Orlande de Lassus	Life

1532	born in Mons
1544	entered the service of Ferrante Gonzaga and traveled with him to Mantua and Sicily
1547–9	Milan
1550	entered the service of Constantino Castrioto, Naples
c1551	Archbishop of Florence's household, in Rome
1553	*maestro di cappella* of St John Lateran, Rome
1554	Mons
1555	Antwerp; supervised publication of early madrigals and motets
1556	singer in Duke Albrecht of Bavaria's chapel, Munich
1558	married Regina Wäckinger
1563	*maestro di cappella* of the Bavarian court, for which he provided numerous sacred works; continued making journeys to European musical centers to recruit singers; international reputation firmly established
1574	made a Knight of the Golden Spur by the pope
1574–9	journeys to Vienna and Italy; *Patrocinium musices*, five volumes of sacred music, published
1594	died in Munich, 14 June

Orlande de Lassus	Works

Sacred vocal music c70 Masses; 4 Passions; c100 Magnificat settings; over 500 motets – Alma redemptoris mater, Prophetiae sibyllarum; Magnus opus musicum; Penitential psalms; Lamentations; hymns

Secular vocal music c200 Italian madrigals and villanellas for 4–6 voices; c140 chansons for 4–8 voices; c90 lieder for 3–8 voices

Probably the most cosmopolitan and versatile composer of the later Renaissance, Lassus combined the features of several national styles to achieve a blend of the best of each: the beauty and expressiveness of Italian melody, the charm and elegance of French text-setting, and the solidity and richness of Flemish and German polyphony. But like all the best composers he had something of his own to add – a vivid imagination, with which he made dramatic and emotional musical responses to the words. That is particularly evident in his motets, where he set an enormous variety of texts. His cycle of 12 short motets entitled *Prophetiae sibyllarum* ("Prophecies of the sibyls") was a product of his adventurous youth: in setting the cryptic statements of these legendary prophetesses he plumbed expressive depths and created, through a striking use of chromaticism, an individual, highly colored style. A typical example is his eight-part motet *Alma redemptoris mater* ("Gracious mother of the Redeemer", see Listening Note V.C).

Lassus was a true man of the Renaissance, whose court appointment and European travels ensured that he was very much of the world. His secular pieces show his varied tastes. As well as spiritual and devotional madrigals, he set

61 Orlande de Lassus: engraving, 16th century.

Listening Note V.C

Lassus: *Alma redemptoris mater*

Alma redemptoris mater,	Gracious mother of the redeemer,
quae pervia coeli porta manes,	who stands at the doors of heaven,
Et stella maris, succurre cadenti	star of the sea, aid the falling,
surgere qui curat populo:	the people who struggle to rise:
Tu quae genuisti, natura mirante,	You who gave birth, by wonder of nature,
tuum sanctum genitorem:	to the Lord almighty,
Virgo prius et posterius,	eternal virgin,
Gabrielis ab ore sumens illud:	who received from the lips of Gabriel that greeting:
Ave, peccatorum miserere.	have mercy on our sins.

This brief motet, composed during Lassus's period at Munich and published in the large collection of his works issued by his sons after his death, is in eight voices – two four-part choirs, singing on the recording (as originally intended) from opposite sides, to give a spatial effect. A prayer to the Virgin Mary, it is typical of Lassus's fervent style, with its rich sound, its stately harmonic movement, the sense of the inner voices intertwining and echoing one another, the occasional highlighting of important words with dissonances, and the quiet, rapt moment as a tenor sings the words "Virgo prius et posterius" ("Virgin, first and last"): all these demonstrate the intensely devotional, almost mystical atmosphere of the church music of the Counter-Reformation. One needs to imagine such a piece sung by a small but skilled choir in a small side-chapel of a dark Catholic church, the air heavy with incense, the walls lavishly ornamented with Renaissance works of art and images dedicated to the Virgin.

lighthearted pastorals and racy ditties in several languages, including rumbustious German drinking-songs, which show yet another side of his personality. His versatility, his humanity and the expressive range covered in his exceptionally large output mark him as one of the most significant figures of the period.

Italy

Palestrina

Among the composers of church music working at the time of the Council of Trent was Giovanni Pierluigi da Palestrina (c1525–1594). He was so well attuned to the spirit of the Counter-Reformation that his music has traditionally been revered as the summit of sixteenth-century polyphony. He took his name from his likely birthplace, Palestrina, a small town near Rome, and his entire life was devoted to the service of the greatest churches of the city – S. Maria Maggiore, St John Lateran and St Peter's.

Palestrina owed his early success to the Bishop of Palestrina, Cardinal Giovanni Maria del Monte, who on his election in 1550 as Pope Julius III asked the composer to accompany him to Rome. Palestrina never enjoyed quite the same favor under subsequent popes, but always seems to have been comfortably placed, at the head of one or other division of the papal chapel. By his mid-30s he had earned a remarkable reputation as a composer and music director. Though attempts were made to entice him elsewhere, for example, Vienna and Mantua, he never left Rome.

Like his great contemporary Lassus, Palestrina was extremely prolific. He wrote many secular pieces, but his ecclesiastical appointments concentrated his main

62 Title-page of
Palestrina's *Missarum liber
primus* ("First book of
Masses", 1554), showing
the composer handing his
work to Pope Julius III.

Listening Note V.D

Palestrina: *Missa brevis* (1570), Kyrie

Kyrie eleison.	Lord have mercy.
Christe eleison.	Christ have mercy.
Kyrie eleison.	Lord have mercy.

This is a classic example of the Renaissance style of imitative polyphony. Each of the three short sections that make up the Kyrie is based on a single phrase, which can be heard virtually all the time in one or other of the four voices. Ex. i shows the first Kyrie in full, with each imitative phrase indicated (*x*: the imitation is 9 to 12 tones long); note that while the intervals between the tones do not vary, the speed does (twice, in the faster-moving version, marked *x'*, the imitation persists for only three tones). In the Christe, note that in ex. ii, the opening, the first five tones are exactly imitated but the alto voice moves slightly faster. In the second Kyrie, the voices enter in ascending order (see ex. iii); once all have begun, the bass sings the opening phrase of two measures five times over, each one step lower in pitch than the one before.

ex. i

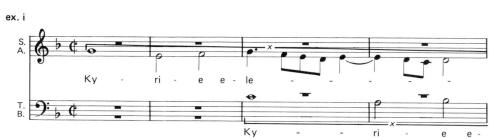

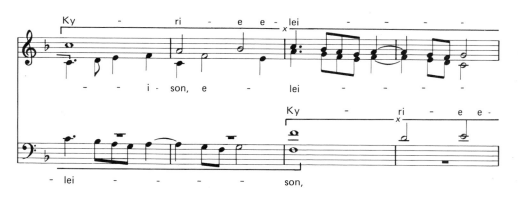

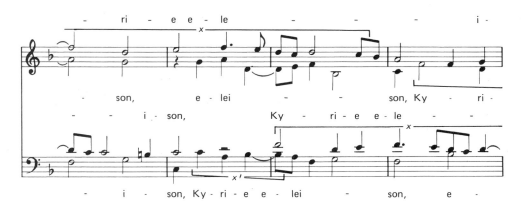

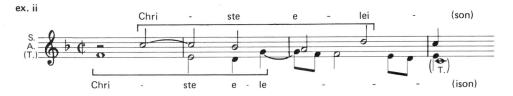

ex. ii

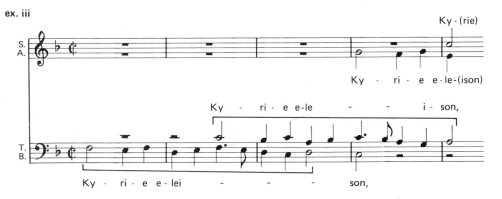

ex. iii

(note that the word "eleison" is usually sung with its first syllable elided with the last of "Kyrie", and that the "ei" is sometimes set as one syllable and sometimes as two)

energies on church music and he produced over 100 Masses (more than any other composer of the period), nearly 400 motets and many other sacred works.

Palestrina's Masses embrace all the current types of Mass composition. Many are "parody" Masses, which make use of existing pieces by other composers (or by himself), usually motets, interpolated into the structure of the Mass – at that period a standard method. Other Masses are based on a *cantus firmus*, usually plainsong (as had been common in the early Renaissance), though there are a few examples of secular tunes. Still others are freely composed, without reference to pre-existing music; it is in that category that the four-voice *Missa brevis* ("Short Mass") of 1570 belongs (see Listening Note V.D). The brevity of the work makes it readily approachable by a listener unprepared for the elaborate, technically complex contrapuntal style of much late Renaissance music; the writing is still imitative (the alto's opening phrase is taken up by the other voices in turn) but the interplay of voices is always clear to the ear.

The almost legendary reverence in which Palestrina was held began during his lifetime. Much of his music was published and widely diffused during the second

Giovanni Pierluigi da Palestrina	Life

*c*1525	born, probably at Palestrina, near Rome
1537	choirboy at S Maria Maggiore, Rome
1544	organist at the cathedral at S Agapito, Palestrina
1547	married Lucrezia Gori
1551	*maestro* of the Cappella Giulia, the musical establishment of St Peter's, Rome
1555	singer in the Sistine Chapel; *maestro di cappella* of St John Lateran, Rome
1561–71	*maestro di cappella* of S Maria Maggiore; period of growing reputation and influence
1564	appointed by Cardinal Ippolito d'Este to take charge of music at his villa in Tivoli, near Rome, during the summer
1566–71	music teacher at Roman Seminary; publication of important collections of motets and Masses
1571	*maestro* of the Cappella Giulia
1572–80	plague in Rome: wife and several close relatives died
1577	asked to revise books of plainsong following guidelines laid down by the Council of Trent
1581	married Virginia Dormoli
1594	died in Rome, 2 February

Giovanni Pierluigi da Palestrina	Works

Sacred vocal music over 100 Masses – Missa Papae Marcelli; Missa brevis; 375 motets – Stabat mater; 35 Magnificat settings; 68 offertories; Lamentations, litanies, sacred madrigals, hymns

Secular vocal music c140 madrigals

half of the century, and so great was his reputation within the church that in 1577 he was asked to revise the main source-books of plainsong in accordance with the guidelines laid down by the Council of Trent – a task he never in fact finished. His most famous Mass, the *Missa Papae Marcelli* ("Mass for Pope Marcellus"), may have been written to show that the Council of Trent requirements were not necessarily incompatible with beautiful polyphony in the traditional mold.

Unlike Lassus, Palestrina was basically conservative in his musical outlook; his constant proximity to the center of the Counter-Reformation meant that he was more restricted in the music he wrote and less free to experiment. But this seems to have suited him well. Rather than attempt new methods he refined the existing ones, and in doing so produced some of the most glorious sacred music of the period, characterized by a perfect technique and a noble mode of expression. Palestrina was the ultimate master of the "imitative style", which forms the backbone of sixteenth-century polyphony and is probably the single most characteristic feature of Renaissance music. At the same time, stepwise (conjunct) melody is essential to Palestrina's style: his lines have no awkward leaps, no feeling of imbalance. Every dissonance is prepared and resolved according to the rules governing smooth harmonic progression. There are few full cadences; instead, the phrases tend to overlap to form a "seamless" texture, in which the equality of voices and their mutual balance give the music a sense of perfect proportion. It is through this beautifully restrained yet expressive style that Palestrina has come to be regarded as the classic model of Renaissance polyphony.

During the early sixteenth century a number of northern composers were working in Italy; they included Jacques Arcadelt (c1505–1568), a Netherlander who was in charge of the papal chapel in Rome, and Adrian Willaert, who worked at St Mark's Cathedral in Venice. The northerners brought with them the French *chanson*, whose influence on the early madrigal can be seen in the latter's simple polyphony, clear-cut phrases and melodic writing. It was one of Willaert's Flemish pupils, however, Cipriano de Rore (1516–65), his successor at St Mark's, who introduced a greater lyricism to the madrigal, began to treat the voices more equally, and used more word-painting than had been common. It was this last feature that characterized the later Italian madrigal, at the courts of north Italy especially. But first we should touch on the directions music was taking in one of Italy's richest centers, Venice.

The Gabrielis

Venice, a trading city under an elected ruler rather than a princely family, reached the height of its prosperity in the sixteenth century. It acquired a musical tradition of a sumptuousness to match its wealth, artistic richness and love of pomp. The city's basilica, St Mark's, was the center of its ceremonial life and its musical life too. An eminent Netherlander, Adrian Willaert (c1490–1562), became head of music there in 1527; among the first Italians to hold important posts at St Mark's at this time were Andrea Gabrieli (c1510–1586) and his nephew Giovanni Gabrieli (c1555–1612).

Andrea was a prolific composer of sacred music and of madrigals. His madrigals are lighter in manner than most of those of his contemporaries, less intense and less contrapuntal. In his sacred music he developed an individual style to suit the needs of St Mark's for ceremonial music, and he was quick to see the special possibilities offered by the cathedral's architecture: he sometimes divided up his players and

Giovanni Gabrieli   Works
born Venice, *c*1555; *died* Venice, 1612

Sacred vocal music Symphoniae sacrae (1597, 1615) : mass movements; *c*100 motets – In ecclesiis

Instrumental music Canzoni e sonate (1615) ; canzonas, ricercares, fugues, toccatas for wind ensemble

Secular vocal music c30 madrigals

Listening Note V.E

Giovanni Gabrieli: *Canzon XIII* (1597), septimi e octavi toni

This canzona was included in Gabrieli's 1597 publication, *Sacrae symphoniae*. The "septimi e octavi toni" of the title refers to the mode in which it is written. It is typical of the antiphonal music favored in Venice, with "choirs" of instruments playing from different galleries. Here there are choirs of cornetts and sackbuts (trombones) to the left and right, while in the center is a softer-toned group consisting of string instruments and dulzian (akin to a bassoon). The piece begins with a short passage for all the instruments together; but most of it is in the form of a three-way dialogue, between the two "brass" groups and the third. Sometimes one choir simply echoes another (though the time-span between original and echo varies); but often one answers another in true dialogue, carrying the music forward as if in discussion; and sometimes all join together for a rich-sounding passage, in which imitative writing within the texture can be heard. Some of the musical ideas are brief, others are much longer. Towards the end the music heard in the first solo sections recurs. There is some brilliant ornamental writing, principally for the leaders of each group.

---

singers into groups, stationing them in different galleries, so that the listener would hear music from a variety of directions. This *cori spezzati* ("spaced choirs") technique was not exclusive to St Mark's or to Venice, but developed there in response to the cathedral's design, the Venetian love of the grandiose, and the genius of Andrea Gabrieli.

Giovanni Gabrieli followed up his uncle's work. In 1587 he published a volume called *Concerti*, "containing church music, madrigals and other works" by himself and Andrea, mainly for opposing groups of singers and players. This was the earliest use of the word "concerto". Giovanni used dialogue techniques with greater freedom and variety than had his uncle, and with more specific and more colorful instrumental writing, as well as a more intense and dissonant style.

The Venetian love of color belongs to music as well as painting. A work like Giovanni Gabrieli's *Canzon XIII* from a collection published in 1597 (see Listening Note V.E), shows him setting three contrasting ensembles against one another, sometimes in echo, sometimes in dialogue, and sometimes combining in rich counterpoint. In fact, in some respects he belongs – as we shall see in the next chapter – as much to the Baroque era as to the Renaissance, with his emphasis, especially in the works of his last years, on contrast of various sorts and his development of the concerto-like (or *concertato*) style.

Marenzio   Luca Marenzio (*c*1553–1599) is the chief figure in the later history of the Italian madrigal. He was closely associated with a number of cardinals and wealthy patrons in Rome and traveled to other Italian cities. His madrigals cover a wide variety of

Luca Marenzio   Works
born near Brescia, 1553 or 1554; *died* Rome, 1599

Secular vocal music c500 madrigals for 4–6 voices – Dolorosi martir, Io partirò; c80 villanellas

Sacred vocal music c75 motets

subjects and set both older and contemporary texts. The best of them combine the features of the earlier madrigal with his individual manner for text-setting by word-painting, the most notable element of his music. The images of Renaissance poetry inspired him to match in music not only the general mood of a poem but also specific words or ideas, with striking melodic twists and highly colored harmonies.

He was at his most characteristic in somber, dark-toned pieces, and he seemed to favor the richness of texture offered by five voices. In *Dolorosi martir*, a lament for the loss of a lover, a striking chromatic chord and dramatic change of style intensifies the emotion of the phrase "Misero piango" ("I lament in wretchedness"; ex. V.2). Similarly, a violent wrench in the harmony marks the expressive climax of *Io partirò* ("I shall depart"; see Listening Note V.F). Often an object or idea described in the text is reflected in the actual physical shape of the melodic line: an ascending scale may illustrate upward flight, short phrases punctuated by rests describe breathlessness or excitement, a falling semitone depicts swooning or death. Though these devices became the stock-in-trade of many late Italian madrigalists, Marenzio handled them with a sensitivity lacking in his less talented contemporaries.

ex. V.2

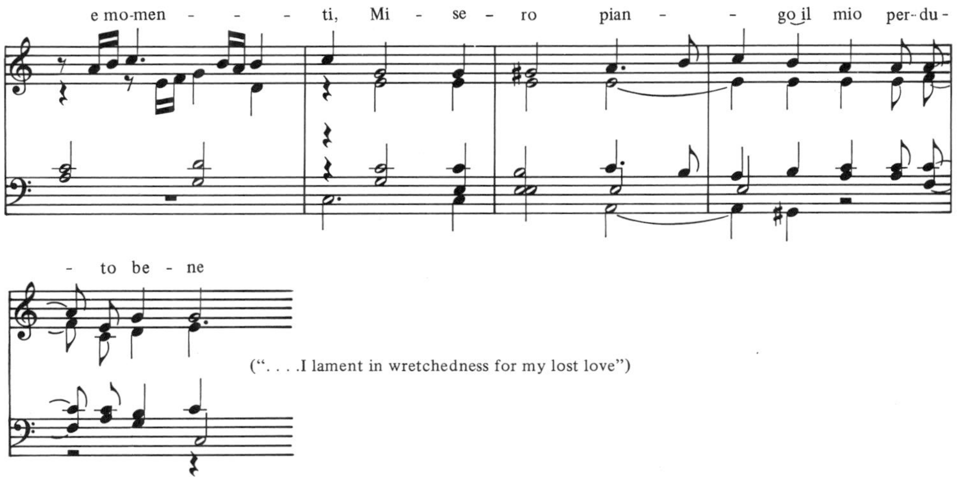

("....I lament in wretchedness for my lost love")

Gesualdo

A composer comparable to Marenzio in the striking use of chromaticism was Carlo Gesualdo (c1560–1613), Prince of Venosa. A highly original amateur musician, he has achieved fame as much for having had his wife and her lover murdered when he discovered their liaison as for his music. The unexpected harmonies in his madrigals (and to a lesser extent his sacred works) result from the unorthodox juxtaposition of

---

Listening Note V.F

Marenzio: *I must depart all hapless* (1581)

I must depart all hapless,
But leave to you my careful heart oppressed,
So that if I live heartless,
Love doth a work miraculous and blessed,
But so great pains assail me,
That sure ere it be long my life will fail me.

This madrigal was composed to Italian words (beginning "Io partirò", "I shall depart") and published in Marenzio's second collection of five-voice madrigals in 1581. Seven years later, it was included in the English publication *Musica transalpina*, a book of Italian madrigals in English translation; it is the English text we hear. There is still imitative counterpoint here, but much less strictly used, with echoes (often inexact ones) rather than true imitation; the stress is as much on the harmony as on the counterpoint. The second and (first time) the fourth lines are sung in straight harmonization rather than in imitative style. The climax to the piece, in the emotional line "But so great pains assail me", is purely harmonic, with a sharp chromatic twist on the word "pains". All this is typical of the north Italian madrigal of this period, the 1580s, with its delight in strongly expressive effect, matching the exaggerated emotion of the words.

---

apparently unrelated chords. Gesualdo's highly original musical language was entirely text-oriented. He responded dramatically to key words, especially those concerned with pain or grief. Though Gesualdo's style has aroused the interest of a number of twentieth-century composers (notably Stravinsky, who made arrangements of some of the madrigals), it bore no real fruit after Gesualdo's own time. It was too personal to attract inheritors, and it died with him.

Spain

If Italy was the cradle of the Counter-Reformation, Spain was the nursery, for it was there above all that religious indoctrination was strongest. The Inquisition raged against heretics (that is, non-Catholics, be they Protestants, Jews or Moors), while the founding of the religious society of the Jesuits in 1534 by the Spaniard Ignatius Loyola, and of several new monastic houses such as Ávila, created an atmosphere of spiritual persuasion that pervaded all walks of life.

Victoria

The greatest Spanish composer of the sixteenth century was Tomás Luis de Victoria (1548–1611). He was born in Ávila and as a boy sang in the cathedral choir. When

Plate 7 Musicians with viols, cittern and ?lute: detail of a painted frieze, *c*1585, in the Great Chamber of Gilling Castle, Yorkshire (see p. 136).

Tomás Luis de Victoria	Works
born Ávila, 1548; *died* Madrid, 1611	

Sacred vocal music over 20 Masses; 18 Magnificat settings; Music for Holy Week (1585): 2 Passions, Lamentations, responsories; *c*50 motets – O magnum mysterium, O vos omnes, O quam gloriosum

his voice broke he went to Rome to study at the Collegio Germanico, a Jesuit institution founded by Loyola, and he remained in the city for some 20 years, holding appointments at various churches and religious institutions. He must have become acquainted with Palestrina and may even have been his pupil. In the 1580s, after becoming a priest, he returned to Spain and spent the rest of his life peacefully in Madrid, first as composer and organist to members of the royal household and then as chaplain at a convent.

Like Palestrina, Victoria concentrated on sacred music, but to the total exclusion of secular. His 20 or so Masses are mostly of the "parody" type and were all published during his lifetime. His style, like Palestrina's, is essentially serious, but his mode of expression is more dramatic. He often makes quite emotional musical responses to his texts. His melodies range more widely and his rhythms are freer. Some people find his music mystical, almost ecstatic, perhaps reflecting the intense religious atmosphere of Counter-Reformation Spain. A number of works for eight voices divided into two choirs, and for 12 voices in three choirs (the psalm setting and parody Mass *Laetatus sum*), show Victoria's interest in polychoral writing.

England

The end of the sixteenth century in Italy witnessed the decline of the madrigal, essentially a Renaissance genre, in favor of a new style of song composition which properly belongs to the period we call "Baroque". But the madrigal was not yet dead. Individual pieces had reached England by about 1570, and the genre was taken up enthusiastically there by professionals and amateurs alike. Printed anthologies of madrigals by Italian composers were circulated in England with translated texts (*Musica transalpina*, 1588; *Italian Madrigalls Englished*, 1590), and soon English composers began to write their own, for there was a wealth of English poetry to draw on. The Elizabethan age set great store by literary and musical accomplishment, and in an environment where domestic music-making flourished (as in Italy) the madrigal was bound to thrive.

Byrd

The greatest English composer of the sixteenth century was William Byrd (1543–1623). The range, versatility and outstanding quality of his work set him above his English contemporaries and successors; he is often referred to as the English counterpart of Palestrina and Lassus. He was the last great English composer of Catholic church music and the first of the "golden" Elizabethan age of secular and instrumental music.

Byrd was appointed organist of Lincoln Cathedral at the age of 19 or 20, and remained there for about ten years. The post must have provided a firm grounding in Anglican church music, for in 1570 he was able to join the Chapel Royal as a singer and soon afterwards became its organist, a post he at first shared with his predecessor Thomas Tallis (c1505–1585). Tallis and Byrd must have worked closely together, for in 1575 they were granted a valuable royal monopoly on music printing in England and on the issue of printed manuscript paper.

Byrd remained in court service all his life. After the Catholicism that prevailed during the reign of Mary Tudor (1553–8, the period of Byrd's upbringing), England returned to Protestantism under Elizabeth and many Catholics feared

Plate 8 Trio of voice, lute and keyless flute (the music has been identified as the *chanson Joyssance vous donneray* by Sermisy, see p. 118): *The Concert*, painting, 16th century, by the "Master of the Female Half-Lengths". Schloss Rohrau, Vienna.

William Byrd	Life

1543	born, probably in Lincoln
1563	organist and master of the choristers at Lincoln Cathedral
1570	appointed singer in the Chapel Royal but did not go to London for two years
1572	organist (with Thomas Tallis) of the Chapel Royal
1575	granted, with Tallis, a royal monopoly on music printing; *Cantiones sacrae*
c1580	absent from London in Harlington during period of persecution of Roman Catholics
1585	Tallis died, leaving Byrd the printing patent
1588	*Psalmes, Sonets and Songs*
1593	moved to Stondon Massey, Essex
1623	died at Stondon Massey, 4 July

persecution. The queen seems to have tolerated Byrd's Catholic sympathies, however, for he is not known to have suffered for them. He was able to write music for both churches, including three sublime Latin Masses and a large number of Proper motets for the celebration of the Office. For the Anglican church he wrote Services (that is, polyphonic settings of the *Magnificat* and *Nunc dimittis*, *Venite*, *Te Deum*, *Jubilate* etc) and anthems (the English equivalent of motets), usually accompanied by the organ or other instruments, sometimes with solo vocal parts. The anthem was a peculiarly English genre which flourished in the early years of the seventeenth century.

Byrd's restraint and expressiveness as a composer of sacred music are shown at their finest in his short four-part motet *Ave verum corpus*, published in the first volume of his motet collection entitled *Gradualia* (1605). There is a simple beauty about the gentle chording of the voices, a rich warmth in the phrases as the opening notes of a phrase in one voice are taken up by the others (see Listening Note V.G).

Byrd excelled in elegiac music, but it would be a mistake to imagine that he wrote only gloomy works. As he grew older he seems to have become more cheerful; both his Latin and his Anglican music include marvelously joyful pieces, like the three-voice setting of *Haec dies*, with its buoyant opening and lively part-writing, and the exuberant six-part anthem *Sing joyfully*, where the overlapping voice-parts ring out like glorious peals of bells.

In his secular music too Byrd encompassed a wide range of texts and moods. Though he issued no volumes of madrigals he did publish two volumes of *Psalmes, Songs and Sonets* (1588 and 1611) and one of *Songs of Sundrie Natures* (1589), whose titles convey the miscellany of their contents. Some of the polyphonic songs here are madrigalian in their subject matter, but few approach the text imagery of Byrd's Italian contemporaries or, indeed, of his English successors such as Thomas Morley. Byrd's most productive years came before the Italian madrigal had taken a hold in England. Instead, he cultivated intricate, flowing counterpoint in his songs, as in some of his church music, in a style that he had inherited from earlier English composers such as Tallis and John Taverner (c1490–1545).

The closest Byrd got to the madrigal proper is probably *This sweet and merry*

ex. V.3

month of May, which appeared first in the anthology *Italian Madrigalls Englished* (it was of course an exception to the title) and subsequently in Byrd's own 1611 volume of *Psalmes, Songs and Sonets*. Even this piece is restrained compared with similar pieces by his successors, such as Morley's *Now is the month of maying* (see p. 133); but the exchange of imitative motifs, for example at the words "birds do sing and beasts do play" (ex. V.3: note figures *x* and *y*), is typical, as is the later change to triple meter and to a homophonic dance-like section for just a few measures. The sixth and seventh lines greet "Eliza" (that is, Queen Elizabeth), like many a piece published in the reign of that enlightened and music-loving monarch.

Byrd also excelled in instrumental music, both for solo keyboard instruments and for ensemble. Many of the keyboard pieces, intended for harpsichord, virginals, spinet or organ, are dance movements (e.g. pairings of pavan and galliard; see p. 136) or arrangements of popular tunes or vocal pieces. Their main interest lies in the imaginative way Byrd developed sets of "variations" on each tune, by dividing long notes into shorter ones, by changing the meter or the rhythmic detail, or by moving the tune from one level in the contrapuntal texture to another. His unending inventiveness in keyboard variations and pieces for five-part instrumental "consort" shows how a composer can use his imagination even within the strict framework of a pre-existing melody.

Many of Byrd's keyboard pieces are in the fine music manuscripts of the period: *My Ladye Nevells Booke*, devoted exclusively to Byrd and written in an exquisitely beautiful hand by the singer and composer John Baldwin in about 1591; and the enormous Fitzwilliam Virginal Book, an anthology copied by Francis Tregian, a Catholic recusant imprisoned for his beliefs in the early 1600s. Other Byrd

---

Listening Note V.G

Byrd: *Ave verum corpus* (1605)

Ave verum corpus natum	Hail, true body, born
de Maria vergine:	of the virgin Mary:
Vere passum, immolatum	who truly suffered and died
in cruce pro homine:	on the cross for mankind:
Cuius latus perforatum	from whose pierced side
unda fluxit sanguine:	water flowed with blood:
Esto nobis praegustatum	be a consolation to us
in mortis examine.	at our last hour.
O dulcis, o pie, o Iesu fili Mariae	O sweet one, O pious one, O Jesus, son of Mary,
miserere mei. Amen.	have mercy upon me. Amen.

This motet, published in a collection of 1605, has always been one of Byrd's most popular and admired works. For four voices, it shows his expressive technique used fully (though without the freedom or extravagance that might be applied in a madrigal) to treat a text about which Byrd, as a staunch Catholic, must have had strong emotional feelings. His style is very free compared with the orthodox imitative polyphony of, for example, the Palestrina *Missa brevis* (V.D). Rather, he makes his effects with telling harmony – at the very opening, for example, where the conjunction of a G♯ and a G♮ (in different voices: see ex. i, where these tones are marked x) produces an arresting and poignant effect – heard again at "O dulcis, o pie" (ex. ii). This harmonic device, known as a "false relation", was especially favored by the English composers of this time. There is, later, a little imitative writing, to the words "miserere mei", but even this is unorthodox; Palestrina's imitation is almost always at simple intervals, like the octave, the 4th or the 5th, while Byrd's may be at any pitch, so lending the imitated phrase different color and meaning.

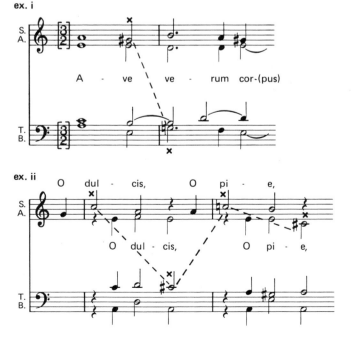

ex. iii

| William Byrd | Works |

Sacred choral music Cantiones (with Tallis, 1575); Cantiones sacrae (1589, 1591); Gradualia (1605, 1607); 3 Masses; Mass movements; Services – Short Service, Great Service; anthems; motets – Ave verum corpus; Anglican liturgical settings

Vocal chamber music Psalmes, Sonets and Songs (1588); Songs of Sundrie Natures (1589); Psalmes, Songs and Sonnets (1611)

Instrumental music fantasias and In Nomines for viol consort

Keyboard music fantasias, variations, dances, grounds for virginals

keyboard pieces were published in *Parthenia* (1612–13), a famous engraved anthology of keyboard music, the first to be printed in England.

Byrd's other music includes consort songs (solo songs accompanied by an instrumental ensemble, or consort, usually of viols), a peculiarly English genre, as well as consort music for viols alone, mostly elaborate contrapuntal fantasias and dance movements. His reputation during his lifetime was remarkable: he was described as "Father of British Music", justified by his fertile imagination and by the consistently high quality of his music.

The English madrigalists

It was left to Byrd's successors to carry the English madrigal to its high peak. There was no shortage of composers able and willing to do so: by the end of the sixteenth century there was a whole school of English madrigalists, amateurs and professionals, talented and not so talented. While the public demand was there, new pieces continued to appear in a veritable fever of production.

Among the related forms was the "ballett", also of Italian origin – a light, dance-like piece, less sophisticated than the madrigal proper, in repeating verses and often with a "fa-la" refrain. Thomas Morley (*c*1557–1602) and Thomas Weelkes (*c*1575–1623) were its chief exponents. Morley was a particularly interesting figure, a teacher, theorist and intellectual, as well as a popular composer; it was he who really laid the foundations of the English madrigal school. His lively ballett *Now is the month of maying* provides a foil to Byrd's "May" madrigal discussed earlier: here dance rhythms provide the inspiration for the piece, which has a tidy, strophic structure and repeated refrain. Byrd's madrigal is through-composed and more contrapuntal, and on another plane of seriousness. Neither is "better": they merely illustrate a difference in approach (ex. V.4).

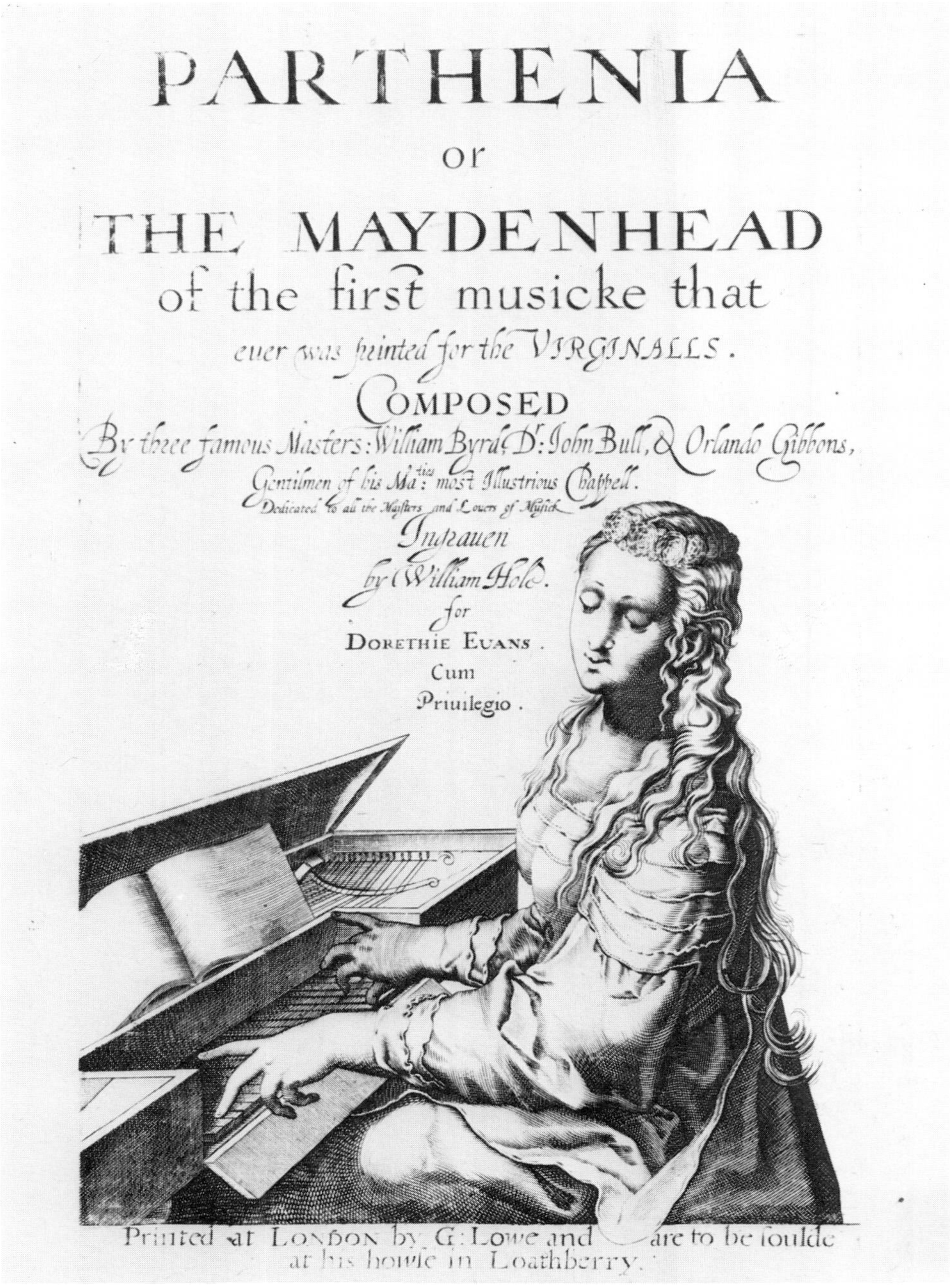

PARTHENIA
or
THE MAYDENHEAD
of the first musicke that
euer was printed for the VIRGINALLS.
COMPOSED
By three famous Masters: William Byrd D: John Bull, & Orlando Gibbons,
Gentilmen of his Ma:ties most Illustrious Chappell.
Dedicated to all the Masters and Lovers of Musick
Ingrauen
by William Hole.
for
Dorethie Euans.
Cum
Priuilegio.
Printed at London by G: Lowe and are to be soulde
at his howse in Loathberry.

63 Title-page of *Parthenia* (1612/13), a collection of English virginal music containing works by Byrd, Bull and Gibbons.

In 1601 Morley edited a volume of madrigals, *The Triumphs of Oriana*, compiled in honor of the queen ("Oriana" herself). Most of the leading madrigalists of the day contributed, each setting the words "Long live fair Oriana" as a refrain. It provides an interesting survey of the English madrigal at the end of the sixteenth century; but even this apparently most English of publications was inspired by an Italian anthology of 1592, *I trionfi di Dori*.

Thomas Weelkes wrote some bold and original madrigals, very Italianate in their

ex. V.4

approach to word-painting: *As Vesta was from Latmos hill descending* is a good example (see Listening Note V.H); he wrote many fine anthems too. His contemporary John Wilbye (1574–1638) was a madrigalist of particular refinement whose music is superbly crafted. His second book of madrigals (1609) includes such well-known pieces as *Sweet honey-sucking bees*, a gem of pictorial imagery, and the intensely beautiful six-voice setting *Draw on, sweet night*, one of the finest of English madrigals.

Listening Note V.H

Weelkes: *As Vesta was from Latmos hill descending* (1601)

As Vesta was from Latmos hill descending,
she spied a maiden queen the same ascending,
attended on by all the shepherds swain,
to whom Diana's darlings came running down amain.

First two by two, then three by three together,
leaving their goddess all alone, hasted thither,
and mingling with the shepherds of her train
with mirthful tunes her presence entertain.
   Then sang the shepherds and nymphs of Diana,
    Long live fair Oriana!

Thomas Weelkes's contribution to *The Triumphs of Oriana* was this colorful madrigal, for six voices. It shows how the word-painting of which the composers (Italian no less than English) of this period were so fond could be used with charm and ingenuity, along with other devices, to make an attractive effect. In the first line, the word "hill" is treated in a series of upward phrases, then neatly turned downwards for a cadence on "descending". The next line counters this with a series of imitations on an upward phrase at "ascending". "Attended on by all" is a straightforward harmonic passage, sung by all the voices; "Came running down amain" is of course a series of rapid, downward-running phrases. The "two by two" and "three by three" lines are sung, respectively, by the voices in pairs and in threes, with all six at "together"; and the "goddess all alone" is represented by a momentary solo voice. The line with "mingling" is full of overlapping counterpoints, that with "mirthful tunes" more obviously melodic. Then the literal, picturesque approach gives way to a rich polyphonic climax as all six voices weave in celebration of "fair Oriana", the maiden queen, Elizabeth I of England.

Ensemble music

As in the Middle Ages, instruments during the Renaissance took various roles. They were originally used functionally, to accompany voices or, in domestic music-making, to take a voice part; some madrigal publications were issued as "for voyces or violls". Many instrumental adaptations exist of chansons and madrigals. The instruments used would normally be viols or recorders, of various sizes, grouped in "consorts" or families. The commonest viols, for example, were the treble, the tenor and bass (held between the knees, like a cello). At first, such ensembles rarely played anything other than arrangements of vocal pieces; later, instrumental consort music was composed, by Byrd and his successors, notably Orlando Gibbons (1583–1625); these were often contrapuntal pieces entitled "fantasia" in England, "canzona" or "ricercar" in Italy and Germany. There was also much dance music for ensemble. Such pieces might be for "whole consort" (all viols, or all recorders) or "broken consort" (a mixture of string and wind instruments).

The relatively soft-toned instruments, and the lute, were sometimes described as *bas* ("low" or "soft"), while the strident ones were classified as *haut* ("high" or "loud"). The latter included wind instruments such as the cornett, trumpet, shawm (precursor of the modern oboe) and sackbut (an early trombone) as well as percussion. They were suitable for playing outdoors, to accompany dancing or in processions or in elaborate church ceremonial, as practiced by the Gabrielis in Venice, for example; these roles helped instrumental music gain independence from vocal. Dance music was soon being composed specifically for instruments, both solo and ensemble. Popular dances were the pavan (a slow, stately dance in duple time), which was often followed by a galliard (in a livelier triple time) and a passamezzo (an Italian duple-time dance, slightly faster than the pavan).

64 Wind band with treble and two tenor shawms, cornett, trombone and curtal: detail of the painting *Procession of the Religious Orders of Antwerp on the Feast Day of the Rosary*, 1616, by Denis van Alsloot. Museo del Prado, Madrid.

**Keyboard
music**

In the earlier Renaissance there was little distinction between music for keyboard instruments with plucked strings, such as the harpsichord or spinet, and that written for the organ, in spite of their differing capabilities. For example, a note played on the organ can be sustained for as long as the air is supplied to the pipe; but plucked string instruments have virtually no sustaining power. It may be easier to play faster music more satisfactorily on a plucked-string instrument than on the organ, and on the clavichord (where the strings are struck) some variation in volume can be achieved by touch.

When vocal music was transcribed for domestic keyboard instruments, compensation had to be made for the lack of sustaining power. Composers would avoid long notes, dividing them into a number of shorter ones, almost in a decorative fashion. This device was similar to the technique of writing variations on an existing theme, as practiced by Byrd. Between them, these features helped establish an independent style of keyboard writing distinct from vocal style.

The greatest keyboard composer in the late sixteenth century was an Englishman, John Bull (1562–1628), a virtuoso player who developed a distinctive style of writing with rapid scale passages, broken-chord figuration and brilliant ornamentation (see Listening Note V.I). Ex. V.5 shows how he might take a simple tune (*a*) at the beginning of a keyboard piece and transform it entirely through a technique of variation to produce an elaboration of it (*b*). Titles like "Fantasia" and "Canzona"

ex. V.5

Listening Note V.I

Bull: *Coranto "Alarm"*

This brief piece illustrates the dance music of the late Renaissance and the English keyboard style. The word "Coranto" is an English adaptation of the dance type known in Italy as the "Corrente" and in France as the "Courante". It is a triple-meter dance, sometimes with the groups of three paired, so producing the effect of groups of six with a subsidiary accent. If we imagine it in units of six, there are eight in the first half here (with a turn to the relative major, B♭, from the main key, G – minor as well as major – halfway through) and twelve plus a cadence in the second (with a hint of F major before it settles into G). Each half is repeated; the beginning of the second has figures suggesting a trumpet call, perhaps a call to arms, which accounts for the title of the piece. The work does not show the virtuoso technique for which Bull above all was famous among the English virginal composers, but does use their idiomatic keyboard style, with free part-writing and occasional imitation between the hands as well as lively ornamentation.

---

became common for keyboard pieces, as well as more fanciful ones associated with a particular acquaintance or patron (e.g. *My Lady Carey's Dompe*; "dump" was a title sometimes given to a solemn, sober piece in memory of someone). By the end of the sixteenth century keyboard music had come into its own; in the seventeenth it more than fulfilled its promise.

Lute music

Like the keyboard, the lute only gradually gained its independence from its traditional accompanying role. But by the end of the sixteenth century pieces for solo lute were being composed and published in a style of their own. There was a special emphasis on fantasias and sets of variations.

The lute was also used to accompany consort songs, such as those by Byrd and his successors, and it was partly from these that another distinctive English song form – the ayre – developed, which took over from the madrigal in popularity at the beginning of the seventeenth century; there was an equivalent French one, the *air de cour* ("courtly song"). Unlike the madrigal, with its equal and usually imitative voices, the ayre had its chief melodic interest in the top line. But it could be performed by several voices (accompanied or unaccompanied) or, more commonly, as a lute-song with a solo voice taking the top line and a lute supplying the lower parts, possibly with a viol reinforcing the bass.

Dowland

The ayre's greatest exponent was John Dowland (1563–1626). His extensive travels in Europe earned him a number of important court appointments and brought him international fame as composer and as virtuoso singer and lutenist. He was famous enough for many of his works to be printed and sold in cities such as Paris, Antwerp and Leipzig, the publishing centers of northern Europe. As a composer, he set some 70 pieces for solo lute and several sacred or devotional texts, as well as more than 80 ayres for voice and lute. His *First Book of Songes or Ayres of Foure Partes* (1597) was immensely popular, no doubt partly because the ayre could be adapted to whatever performing resources the amateur had at his disposal.

Dowland's ayres illustrate his ability to match in music the mood and emotion of a poetic text. He was undoubtedly at his best when in somber mood, as in *In darknesse let mee dwell*, with its passionate intensity, dramatic word-painting (e.g. at "hellish jarring sounds"), uneasy rhythms and colorful dissonances, in the wonderfully expressive *Flow my teares*, which became particularly well known in its

John Dowland	Works
born ?London, 1563; *died* London, 1626	

Secular vocal music over 800 ayres for voice and lute – In darknesse let mee dwell, Flow my teares, Fine knacks for ladies; I must complain

Instrumental music Lachrimae for viol consort and lute (1605); fantasias, pavans, galliards, almains, jigs for solo lute

Sacred vocal music psalms and spiritual songs

arrangement for solo lute under the title *Lachrimae* (Latin for "tears"), and in the gently elegiac lover's plaint *I must complain* (see Listening Note V.J). Dowland also wrote in a lighter vein, as in the jaunty, ballett-like *Fine knacks for ladies*, but here he was rivaled by others, notably the famous Elizabethan poet-musician Thomas Campion (1567–1620) whose lute-songs (e.g. *Never weather-beaten sail*), though less passionate than Dowland's, were no less well crafted and have an appealing charm.

The lute-song was a specialized English genre. It represented the last flowering of the Renaissance in England, and when it was at its height, at the turn of the century, new and far-reaching musical developments were taking place in Italy. These innovations are traditionally and conveniently regarded as heralding a new musical era: the Baroque.

Listening Note V.J

John Dowland: *I must complain* (1603)

I must complain, yet do enjoy my love,
  She is too fair, too rich in beauty's parts.
Thence is my grief: for Nature, while she strove
  With all her graces and divinest arts
To form her too too beautiful of hue,
She had no leisure left to make her true.

Should I aggrieved then wish she were less fair?
  That were repugnant to my own desires.
She is admired; new suitors still repair
  That kindles daily love's forgetful fires.
Rest, jealous thoughts, and thus resolve at last:
She hath more beauty than becomes the chaste.

This song comes from Dowland's third collection of songs, published as *The Third and Last Booke of Songs or Aires* in 1603. The words are by the poet and composer Thomas Campion (who also set them). Dowland's setting shows his characteristic vein of melancholy, with its gentle, arching lines and its tendency to drop back into a minor key – and even when the key is major there is a sense of false consolation. The accompaniment is played on a lute, with the bass line reinforced by a bass viol. The song is in G minor; it pauses (at "in beauty's parts", in the first verse) first in D, then (at "beautiful of hue") on the dominant of the home key, leading to the final line which is partly set in a contrasting rhythm to stress the poet's conclusion – "She had no leisure left to make her true" and "She hath more beauty than becomes the chaste".

Chapter VI

The Baroque Era

The word
"Baroque"

By the "Baroque" era, musicians generally understand the period from roughly 1600 to 1750 – beginning with Monteverdi, ending with Bach and Handel. The word is in fact little more than a convenient label for a period that has a certain degree of underlying unity because of its techniques and its approach to musical expression. "Baroque" comes from the French, and, further back, from a Portuguese term (*barroco*) for a misshapen pearl. It seems to have been used at first in the discussion of art and architecture, mainly by writers at the end of the period itself and usually in a negative, critical way, implying something that was clumsy, strange and overblown. Musicians adopted it, generally in the sense of confused, over-elaborate and harsh; the generation that followed the Baroque era, as we shall see in the next chapter, were eager to simplify and regularize the language of music and regarded the style of their immediate forebears as extravagant and irregular. Thus the word came into use, both in art criticism and music criticism, for the products of the seventeenth century and the early eighteenth. Nowadays, with the broader historical view that we have gained through the lapse of time, we apply the term to this period without any of its original disapproving implications of the clumsy or the rough: though the notions of extravagance and some kinds of irregularity, at least as compared with the music of the periods just before and just after, still have meaning.

The Renaissance, in its arts, emphasized clarity, unity and proportion. But as the sixteenth century moved towards its close, the representation of emotion came to be seen as increasingly important: for serenity and perfection of form have been overtaken by the urgency of the expression of feeling. In the visual arts this is seen in the forceful, dramatically colored paintings of Caravaggio (1573–1619). We have already seen its beginnings in music, in the madrigals of Marenzio and Gesualdo or the ayres of Dowland; the next generation was to carry it much further.

To create these strong effects, it was necessary to develop a new musical style. The smooth polyphony of the Renaissance was not, generally speaking, adaptable to a set of priorities so different from those of the era in which it had arisen. One of the most important creations of the Baroque was the concept of contrast. Renaissance music is typified by its flowing, interweaving lines, most commonly four or five in number, each of them singing (or playing) music that moved at roughly the same pace. Textures of that kind became increasingly rare in the years after 1600, and when they were used it was almost exclusively in the realm of

Contrast

church music – naturally the most conservative area because it was tied to traditional, unchanging liturgical patterns.

Contrast could exist on various planes: loud and soft; one color and another; solo and tutti; high and low; fast and slow (this could occur in two main ways, either a fast-moving part against a slow-moving one, or a fast section against a slow one). All these, and others, had their place in the musical schemes of the new Baroque era. Many of them are represented in the music of the important transitional composer, the Venetian Giovanni Gabrieli, whose interest in contrast we noted on p. 126. Numerous composers used the *concerto* or *concertante* style (meaning a style with a marked contrasting element), the essence of which was a texture that varied, sometimes with solo voice or voices, sometimes with larger groups; it was mostly applied to sacred music, particularly motets.

The most striking, most violent contrasts, however, were those in the new genre that we call "monody". This means a kind of solo song, with a vocal line that may be very florid and a slow-moving accompaniment for an instrument of the lute type or a harpsichord. The most important exponent of this genre (and to some extent its creator, in his epoch-making publication *Le nuove musiche* – "The new music" – of 1602) was the composer and singer Giulio Caccini (*c*1545–1618). The vocal line, taking its cue from the meaning of the words, could vary greatly in pace and in texture, from the simple to the highly embellished; this further contrasted with the

65 Stage design by Francesco Galli-Bibiena (1659–1737) for an unknown *opera seria*. Museo Nacional de Arte Antiga, Lisbon.

static line played by the accompanying instrument. Caccini had been a member of the group of musicians, intellectuals and noblemen of Florence (the "Camerata") who had met during the 1570s and 80s with the idea of re-creating what they took to be the ancient Greek ideal of expressing in music the "affect" (or emotional character) of the words; the style of monody follows up the thinking of that group.

Continuo

The word "accompany", used above, does not appear in the discussion of mainstream Renaissance music: as a concept, it belongs to the Baroque – it implies, of course, a difference in status between instrumental parts. And in fact the most important unifying feature of all Baroque music is the characteristic accompanying part, the basso continuo (or simply continuo). The continuo player, at a keyboard instrument (like the harpsichord or the organ) or a plucked string instrument (like the lute or guitar), was given a bass line, above which figures were usually written to indicate what additional notes he should play to fill in the harmony. Often there were two continuo players, one playing the written line on a sustaining instrument, like the cello, viol or bassoon, the other also supplying the harmony. The kind of texture that the use of continuo implies – a top, melodic line for a voice or instrument, a bottom line for a bass instrument, and a harmonic filling to the sandwich – is typical of the Baroque; often, just as typically, there might be two upper lines, perhaps for a pair of singers or (in a trio sonata) a pair of violins. The use of this kind of pattern, and especially the almost invariable presence of the continuo line, shows how important and how central to the idiom of Baroque music was the idea of a bass line that generated harmony. This was not a sudden development; throughout the sixteenth century there had been a tendency for the bottom line of the music to become distinct from the other strands of the polyphony. Only with the new Baroque idioms was this distinction fully recognized.

Harmony, cadence, rhythm

Along with these changes came other, related ones. With the abandonment of polyphony (or, more exactly, its relegation to the status of an old-fashioned method, to be used almost exclusively in certain types of church music), a new way of constructing movements was needed; and the emphasis on harmony led naturally towards the use of harmonic goals as stopping-points in a piece of music. These stopping-points, or cadences, would be arrived at by a sequence of harmonies of some standardized kind. Linked with these harmonic developments are rhythmic ones. In vocal music, the need to reflect the sense of the words meant that the music was obliged to follow, or even exaggerate, natural speech rhythms. In instrumental music (and some kinds of vocal piece, choral ones especially), dance rhythms came to be used. The bass patterns associated with the regular rhythms of dance music hastened the development of a sense of key, of the music's gravitational pull towards particular notes. At the same time, new instruments were developing that accelerated these processes, the most important being the violin family. While the viol had a tone well adapted to polyphonic clarity but was weak in rhythmic impetus, the violin with its clearly defined attack and its capacity for brilliant effect was suited to music in dance rhythms and to sonatas of a virtuosity comparable with that of the singers of monody. The interchange of vocal and instrumental idioms was a typical Baroque device; it may seem strange that the Baroque should have created these different idioms only to exchange them in its search for novelty and effect.

Passion and grandeur

It is the pursuit of striking effect, above all, that marks out the Baroque era from those immediately before and after. Composers aimed to move the passions (or the "affections", to use the word favored at the time), and not just instantaneously: they tried to sustain the "affect" of a movement – that is, the prevailing emotion that it expressed – throughout its length. The idea of exciting appropriate emotion was, moreover, closely attuned to the spirit of the Counter-Reformation. There are parallels to be seen between music and the other arts. The Baroque emotional extravagance that we find in the grandiose motets of Italy and the other Catholic countries in the early sixteenth century, some of them with multiple choirs and bold harmonic effects, may be seen as analogous to, for example, the new architecture of Rome: this was the period when the huge, overwhelming square and cathedral of St Peter's were built, and also the main part of the cathedral of St John Lateran. Like the giant Salzburg Cathedral across the Alps, these are designed – in a sense that no Renaissance one was – to make the mere human being who entered them feel puny beside these grand creations that embodied divine mysteries. Similarly, the decorated lines of the music have much in common with the florid ornament found in such buildings with their elaborate statuary – in Rome particularly, where the sculptor Gianlorenzo Bernini (1598–1680) enriched the new churches and public buildings. Further north, it was rather different, for this exuberant spirit was alien to Protestantism: the churches and the music alike are more sober. But the new mercantile spirit encouraged by the reformed faiths found musical outlets too, in the civic musical patronage of the north German cities like Hamburg and Leipzig,

66 Second day of the *divertissements* celebrating Louis XIV's conquest of the Franche-Comté, held in a garden salon specially created at the palace of Versailles, 1674: engraving after Israel Sylvestre.

Seconde Journée
Concerts de musique, sous une feüillée
faite en forme de Salon, ornée de fleurs, dans
le Jardin de Trianon.

Dies Secundus.
Varij musicorum concentus sub frondea
concameratione, floribus intertexta,
In hortis a Trianone dictis.

67 String orchestra playing in Westminster Hall during the banquet celebrating the Coronation of James II on 23 April 1685: engraving from the *History of the Coronation of James II* (1687), by Francis Sandford.

for example. It was mainly in the northern lands that a middle-class concert life arose towards the end of the seventeenth century – and in the eighteenth it was the middle classes who lent support to Bach's concerts in Leipzig, where his concertos were first heard, and to Handel's oratorio performances in London.

Patronage

Courts, however, remained important centers of musical patronage, along with the church. In Italy, it was the Gonzaga family, the rulers of Mantua, who employed Monteverdi before he worked for the church in Venice; and it was the great Venetian noble families who opened the earliest opera house to a wider public. Composers like Alessandro Scarlatti, Corelli and Handel were supported by the princely families around Rome. Germany suffered the Thirty Years' War in the early seventeenth century; after it, in 1648, the country was divided into numerous dukedoms, marquisates and the like, as well as some "free cities" (governed by city fathers) and church lands (governed by bishops): many of them had their own courts, with musical establishments headed by a *Kapellmeister* or "chapelmaster" whose duties included the organization of a choir and instrumental ensemble to provide music for worship and for entertainment. In France and England, with a central court, musical patronage was based firmly in Paris and London and there was relatively little musical activity elsewhere, except in the larger noble and ecclesiastical establishments, until the rise of the bourgeois groups towards the end of the seventeenth century.

Opera

One of the first creations of the Baroque period was opera. It arose in the first place out of the desire of the Florentine Camerata to re-create the ancient Greek drama with music, though it has other ancestors too, for example the lavish court entertainments of the time (*intermedi*) that used music, dance, drama and speech. The earliest operas were given as court entertainments, but by 1637 there were opera houses open to the public in Venice, and other Italian cities soon followed, notably Rome (where many of the earlier musical dramas were on sacred topics) and Naples. Most performances were given under the patronage of local noblemen. Around the middle of the seventeenth century, Italian opera was carried abroad, to Paris and Vienna in particular. The first German opera house opened in Hamburg in 1678, under civic patronage. It was royal patronage that promoted opera in Paris, at much the same date. England was a little later; opera there enjoyed royal support but essentially it was run as a commercial enterprise by various groups of noblemen.

Monteverdi

The early years

The first operas were written by Peri and Caccini; but the first great operas were written by Claudio Monteverdi. Monteverdi, born in 1567 in Cremona, the main Italian center of violin-making, has been described as a revolutionary and "the creator of modern music"; in that he represented human emotion in music with a new force and richness there is some truth in it. He was only 17 when his first musical publication was issued. By the early 1590s he had an appointment at Mantua, playing the violin or viol in the duke's group of musicians. At the court, the *maestro di cappella* ("master of the chapel") was Giaches de Wert (1535–96), a leading madrigal composer; Monteverdi had hoped to succeed to the post on Wert's death, but did not do so for another five years.

Monteverdi's madrigals up to this date follow, broadly, the prevailing trends, moving away from the Renaissance pattern of continuous polyphony and laying more stress on expressing the text – sometimes by matching its extravagance of sense or image with an equivalent musical extravagance (like a harsh discord or an abrupt leap), sometimes simply following its natural verbal rhythm, much as the

Claudio Monteverdi	Life
1567	born in Cremona, 15 May
1587	first book of madrigals published
c1591	string player at the Gonzaga court in Mantua
1600	reputation as a composer firmly established
1601	appointed *maestro di cappella* at Mantua
1607	*Orfeo* produced in Mantua; his wife, Claudia, died
1608	*Arianna*; returned to Cremona in a depressed state and tried to leave service of the Gonzagas
1610	*Vespers* published; began writing sacred music
1613	*maestro di cappella* of St Mark's, Venice; began reorganizing musical establishment there
1619	seventh book of madrigals published, including works in more modern style
1620–25	period of opera composition
1630–31	plague in Venice
1632	took holy orders
1638	*Madrigals of Love and War* (eighth book) published
1640	*The Return of Ulysses to his Country*
1642	*The Coronation of Poppaea*
1643	died in Venice, 29 November

Claudio Monteverdi	Works

Operas Orfeo (1607), Arianna (1608, music lost except for lament), Il ritorno d'Ulisse in patria (The return of Ulysses to his country, 1640), L'incoronazione di Poppea (The coronation of Poppaea, 1642)

Madrigals Book 1 for 5 voices (1587); Book 2 for 5 voices (1590); Book 3 for 5 voices (1592); Book 4 for 5 voices (1603) [Si ch'io vorrei morire]; Book 5 for 5 voices and continuo (1605); Book 6 for 7 voices and continuo (1614) [Lamento d'Arianna (1614)]; Book 7 for 1–6 voices and instruments (1619); Book 8, ''Madrigals of Love and War'', for 1–8 voices and instruments (1638) [Il combattimento di Tancredi e Clorinda (1624)]; Book 9 for 2–3 voices and continuo (1651)

Other secular vocal music 15 scherzi musicali for 3 voices (1607); 10 scherzi musicali for 1–2 voices and instruments (1632); canzonettas

Sacred vocal music Vespers (1610); Masses, psalms

monody composers did. With his fourth and fifth collections (1603–5) he went much further towards an expressive and free style. In polyphonic writing, the words were often unclear to the listener, because the different voices were singing different syllables at the same time. Here, Monteverdi takes care to avoid that, using a new recitative-like technique, preferring group dialogue to continuous imitative writing, and elaborating on crucial phrases in the text by treating them with imaginative freedom. He also made much greater use of dissonance, as an expressive device, than his predecessors had done, and freely varied the pace at which the music moved in order to strengthen the concentration of emotion at particular points. Not all of this was new: composers like Gesualdo and Marenzio had worked along similar lines. But the imagination and sensitivity that Monteverdi brought to these processes gave them new meaning.

"Orfeo"

The year 1607 saw the performance in Mantua of Monteverdi's opera *Orfeo*. It was given, probably at the court, by one of the learned "academies" – groups of intellectuals, amateurs and artists, characteristic of Italian life at this period. Its theme is the popular one of Orpheus's journey to the underworld to rescue his beloved, Eurydice; this offers a great opportunity for a demonstration of the power of music to move the passions, for in its central scene it is with his singing and his playing that Orpheus procures her release. *Orfeo* is the earliest opera regularly performed in opera houses today. It combines several features of the music of the time in a powerful way. The choruses are closely akin to the new madrigal style. The main part of the action is carried out in an expressive dialogue, not unlike monody, but treated with a freedom that enabled Monteverdi to mirror the sense of the words – for example by using harsh discords or unexpected leaps to heighten an expression of grief, or varying the pace or the texture to reflect the urgency with which the characters express themselves. One telling moment comes in the scene where Orpheus is joyously singing of his marriage, when the tragic news arrives of Eurydice's death: flowing, dance-like rhythms and lyrical lines give way to a halting recitative accompanied with jarring dissonances (see Listening Note VI.A). Orpheus's great plea to Charon to admit him to the underworld is set to richly ornamented music, supported first with two violins, then two cornetts (wooden trumpet-type instruments) and finally the harp.

Such variety of instruments was in itself unusual. This has been called the first modern use of the orchestra; that is an exaggeration, but certainly Monteverdi was aiming at something significantly new. He listed in the front of his score the instruments he required – two harpsichords, two small wooden organs and a reed organ, a harp, two large lutes, three bass viols, ten violins and two small violins, two instruments like small double basses, four each of trumpets and trombones, two cornetts and two recorders. Then, at various points in the score, he indicated which ones he required to play, choosing the color to suit the expression of words and music. *Orfeo*, which also includes instrumental dances, must have had an overwhelming effect, with its variety of resource and its intensity of expression. It is still very much in the late Renaissance tradition of courtly entertainments, however; not until the coming of the public opera houses do we find operas treating human characters in a fully human way.

Soon after the performances of *Orfeo*, Monteverdi must himself have longed for the powers of an Orpheus, for his wife Claudia, mother of his three children, died. It is appropriate that his next opera, *Arianna*, should have as its emotional focal point a great lament. In fact, only the lament survives; the rest of the music is lost. This

---

Listening Note VI.A

Monteverdi: *Orfeo* (1607), Act 2, excerpt

Dramatic context: Orpheus is celebrating, with his friends the shepherds, his marriage to Eurydice, whom he has long loved.

The music: A dance is heard on the strings (Monteverdi directs that it be played on violins and a bass string instrument, with accompaniment on plucked strings). This music occurs four times; in between, and following the final appearance, Orpheus sings a four-verse song, also in dance rhythm (ex.i). At the end, the music becomes slower, as a shepherd greets Orpheus on this happy day. Then suddenly the serene and cheerful tone of the music – it has all been in major keys, with smooth lines and harmonies – is broken as a foreign note is heard in the orchestra and the voice of a messenger is heard ringing out (ex. ii): "Ahi, caso acerbo!" ("Oh, bitter event!"): the music turns to the key of A minor, with strange and harsh dissonances. "What mournful sound disturbs our happiness?", asks a shepherd. The messenger tells the news, in a narrative style, but with expressive dissonances in the supporting harmony; at the actual news of Eurydice's death there are sharp harmonic twists – the messenger singing in E major, Orpheus responding in G minor (ex. iii): Monteverdi's intention of violence and disorientation is unmistakable.

68 Title-page of Monteverdi's *Orfeo* (Venice, 1609).

ORPHEUS

Vi ricorda, o boschi ambrosi,
De' miei lungh'aspri tormenti
quando i sassi ai miei lamenti
rispondean fatti pietosi?

Dite all'hor non vi sembrai
più d'ogn'altro sconsolato?
Hor fortuna ha stil cangiato
et ha volto in festa i guai.

Vissi già mesto e dolente,
hor gioisco e quegli affanni
che sofferti ho per tant'anni
fan più caro il ben presente.

Sol per te bella Euridice,
benedico il mio tormento,
dopo il duol si è più contento
dopo il mal si è più felice.

Do you remember, O shady woods,
my long and bitter torments,
when the rocks to my laments
took pity and responded?

Tell me, did I not then seem
more inconsolable than any other?
Now fortune has changed
and has turned my woes into joys.

I have lived with sadness and grief;
Now I rejoice, and those sorrows
that I suffered for so many years
make my present joy the more dear.

For you alone, fair Eurydice,
I bless my former torments;
after grief one is the more content,
after suffering one is the more happy.

	SHEPHERD
Mira, Orfeo, che d'ogni intorno	Wonder, Orpheus, that all around you
ride il bosco e ride il prato.	the woods and the meadows join in laughter.
Segui pur col plettr'aurato	Continue with your golden plectrum
d'addolcir l'aria in si beato giorno.	to sweeten the air on so blessed a day.
	MESSENGER
Ahi! caso acerbo!	Oh, bitter event!
Ahi! fat'empio e crudele!	Oh, impious and cruel fate!
Ahi! stelle ingiuriose!	Oh, unjust stars!
Ahi! ciel'avaro!	Oh, avaricious heaven!
	SHEPHERD
Qual suon dolente il lieto dì perturba?	What mournful sound disturbs our happiness?
	MESSENGER
Lassa dunque debb'io	I am wretched, for now I must,
mentre Orfeo con sue note il ciel consola	while Orpheus with his tones consoles the heavens,
con le parole mie passargli il core.	pierce his heart with my words.
	SHEPHERD
Questa è Silvia gentile,	This is the lovely Sylvia,
dolcissima compagna	the sweetest companion
della bell'Euridice. O quanto e in vista	of the beautiful Eurydice. Oh, how her face
dolorosa; hor che sia? Deh, sommi dei	is sad; what has befallen? O mighty gods,
non torcete da noi benigno il guardo.	do not turn your kindly glances away from us.
	MESSENGER
Pastor, lasciate il canto,	Shepherd, cease your singing,
ch'ogni nostra allegrezza in doglia è volta.	all our happiness is turned to grief.
	ORPHEUS
D'onde vieni? ove vai? Ninfa, che porti?	Where do you come from? where are you going? Nymph, what do you bear?
	MESSENGER
A te ne vengo Orfeo	To you I come, Orpheus,
messagera infelice	unhappy messenger,
di caso più infelice e più funesto.	of a matter most unhappy and most terrible.
	ORPHEUS
Ohimè, che odo?	Alas! what do I hear?
	MESSENGER
La tua diletta sposa è morta.	Your beloved wife is dead.
	ORPHEUS
Ohimè.	Alas!

ex. i

lament won Monteverdi still greater fame for its passionate expression of grief, and it was also published in the form of a madrigal. Later in the year of the work's performance (1608) Monteverdi sought to retire from the service of the Gonzaga family, apparently because of depression and overwork; he was refused. But then, in 1612, his employer died, and the new duke released several of his employees, Monteverdi among them. After a spell in his native Cremona, he was invited to Venice, the richest and most independent city of Italy, to be considered for the important post of *maestro di cappella*; he went, was offered the post, and accepted it.

Venice

One reason for the invitation to Monteverdi may have been that he was already known as a skillful and original composer of church music. In 1610 he had published a collection of music for the Vespers service; it was printed in Venice, dedicated to the pope. Probably it was based on music he had used in Mantua. Here again Monteverdi draws on a variety of new techniques to give the work greater impact: and this was all the more revolutionary in that these techniques came from a world of emotional and dramatic music and were not in the accepted church manner. He reserved his most conservative writing for the Mass setting in the collection; this is in the traditional imitative style, carefully and elaborately worked and full of contrapuntal artifice. The treatment is austere, with no madrigal-like illustrative word-setting. This style Monteverdi called the *prima prattica* ("first practice"); the new style he called *seconda prattica* ("second practice"). The psalm settings vary. Some use a contrapuntal style with plainsong running through, some a style with contrasting choirs, some the free madrigal manner he had developed. In all of them he contrasts one verse with another by varying the setting. It is in the motet movements that Monteverdi moves fully to *seconda prattica*, using a free, ornamental melodic line with the same kinds of expressive dissonance and color that he called upon in his operas. Monteverdi's *Vespers* – his most important work for the church (he wrote many more motets and other single works) – decisively brought Baroque expressive principles into the realm of sacred music.

At St Mark's, Venice, Monteverdi's first task was to reorganize what had become an inefficient, ill-managed music establishment. He engaged new, younger musicians, improved the pay, and brought the music library up to date. He was appreciated and his salary was raised. He worked additionally for other institutions in Venice and elsewhere (including Mantua, where a ballet of his was given in 1616). He also wrote operas and other dramatic pieces for performances in houses or palaces in Venice and Parma; none of his operas of this time, however, survives. Venice suffered from an epidemic of the plague in 1630–31; when it passed, Monteverdi wrote a Mass in thanksgiving. A little later, he took holy orders.

Monteverdi turned back to the madrigal in his early Venetian years. The sixth book (1614) includes two long laments, one of them based on the *Arianna* lament: his feeling for the effect on the listener of harsh, unexpected dissonance gives his laments an often heart-rending force. The seventh book, five years later, has a much wider range of types, from monodies to duets (some of his most attractive and tuneful pieces) and works for larger groups with instrumental support – melody instruments as well as the continuo he had used since the fifth book. An eighth book, which came out in 1638, is divided between *canti guerrieri* ("songs of war") and *canti amorosi* ("songs of love"). The "songs of war" reflect Monteverdi's theories about the "humors" – linked with early medical ideas, too – and their representation in music; they use what Monteverdi called the *stile concitato* ("agitated style"), with rapid repeated notes, or fanfare-like patterns, often for several singers together, producing a vigorous, aggressive effect (ex. VI.1). The battles mentioned in the texts, however, are not always real; often they are symbolic of love and amorous conquest. These theories, even if curious, lead to some of Monteverdi's most intense and passionate music; they never prevented him from paralleling in his music the inner sense of the words. In these works, and a further collection issued after his death, the old concept of the polyphonic madrigal gives way to a much freer kind of composition, of any length and for any performers, vocal or instrumental. The eighth book even includes a ballet from his

ex. VI.1

I sing of the raging and warlike Mars.

ex. VI.2

a.

Ne - ro - ne, Ne - ro - ne em - - pio Ne - ro - ne, Ne-

- ro - ne, o Di - o, Di - o, ma - ri - to be-stem - mia - to per sem - pre ma-le-

- det - to dai cor do - gli mie - i do-ve hoi mè_____ do-ve se - i?

Wicked Nero, oh god, accursed husband, for ever damned by the pain in my heart.

b.

Sen-to un cer - to non so che, che mi piz-zi - ca e di - let - ta, dim-mi tu che co - sa e-gli è

da-mi-gel - la a - mo - ro - set - ta. Ti fa - rei ti di - rei ti di - rei

ti_ fa - rei ma non so_ quel ch'io vor-re - i, ma non so_ quel ch'io_____ vor-re - i.

I feel an indefinable something which pierces and delights me: tell me what it is, loving damsel. I would do it, I would say it, but I do not know what I want.

Mantua days and a stage entertainment, *Il combattimento di Tancredi e Clorinda* ("The combat of Tancred and Clorinda"), which significantly tells of a fight between a crusader and his lover, disguised as a man, giving opportunity for music in both the warlike and (as, at the end, Clorinda dies) the amorous vein.

Last years

In his last years Monteverdi turned to opera again. As we have seen, the first Venetian opera houses opened in 1637, and he composed, it seems, three operas for them before his death in 1643. One is lost and there are doubts about whether all the music in the others is in fact his. The last is *L'incoronazione di Poppea* ("The Coronation of Poppaea", 1642), on the story of the Roman emperor Nero and his lover Poppaea. It is presented as a story about the power of love – Nero's, illicit though it is, for Poppaea – and how it transforms people's lives. Love triumphs over morality, and, with Monteverdi's music to support it, the listener is bound to be won over and to believe that the values of love override all others. Once again, Monteverdi harnesses a wide range of styles to drive home his expressive points. Nero and Poppaea sing amorous duets, in the manner of those in some of the madrigal collections. Octavia, the empress whom Nero renounces in Poppaea's favor, sings in the style of the monodists, using Monteverdi's full resource of dissonance to convey her bitterness and grief (ex. VI.2*a*). The servants take semi-comic roles, to provide relief: they sing frivolous ditties about their love, in the manner of Monteverdi's light, miniature madrigals or *Scherzi musicali* (ex. 2*b*). There is even a madrigal-like number when the friends of the philosopher Seneca, told by Nero to kill himself, beg him not to die. In the theater, the opera is effective not only because of the armory of musical resource that Monteverdi uses but above all because it is true to life: there are not, as in the earlier, mythological operas, characters that are wholly good or wholly evil, but rather a selection of human beings, all good in some ways and flawed in others, and victims of forces they cannot control. Monteverdi's great achievement, here as in his other music, is to realize so powerfully the underlying emotions.

Early and middle Baroque in Italy

Monteverdi's entire output consists of vocal music, secular or sacred; except within vocal works, he composed not a single piece for instruments. Yet he lived in the period when the violin was coming to the fore as the principal instrument for ensemble music (its strong rhythmic character was especially well suited to the dance patterns that predominated), while the organ, harpsichord and lute were given new scope by the stylistic freedoms of the Baroque.

Frescobaldi

The greatest keyboard composer of the day, and as near as there was to a keyboard counterpart to Monteverdi, was Girolamo Frescobaldi. He was born in Ferrara in 1583 and spent his working life in Rome apart from six years in Florence. From 1608 until his death in 1643 he was organist of St Peter's. He had an unrivaled reputation: he was called a "giant among organists", lauded for his skill and agility, and regarded as a model for performers and composers alike.

Frescobaldi composed in all the main forms of his time: there are complex, elaborately worked contrapuntal ricercares, canzonas (often in the form of increasingly brilliant variations), dances, fantasies and capriccios, and toccatas. These last particularly represent the Baroque element of rhetorical intensity, with their bold virtuoso ornamentation over a series of harmonies. Here we see the Baroque love of dramatic effect, of the grandiose and the overwhelming. Unlike the keyboard music of the previous generation, with its regular patterns, Frescobaldi's makes its effects with the unexpected, in harmony or in figuration, or in the complexity of his counterpoint, which can dazzle and confuse the ear.

Much of Frescobaldi's music was published, and it exerted a long and deep influence. Bach, in north Germany, was studying it almost a century later; and an English eighteenth-century historian, Charles Burney, called Frescobaldi the father of modern organ style.

Cavalli

In the field of opera, Monteverdi's natural successor was Francesco Cavalli. Born in 1602, he became a choirboy at St Mark's, Venice, in 1616, when Monteverdi was in charge of the music there; possibly he was a pupil of Monteverdi's. At the end of the elder man's life Cavalli served as his deputy. During the 1640s and 1650s Cavalli was the most prominent opera composer in Venice, and indeed in all Italy – he wrote operas too for Naples, Milan and Florence. In 1660 he was even invited to France, to perform operas in Paris: the principal event, a performance of *Ercole amante* ("Hercules the lover"), at Louis XIV's marriage festivities, was a mixed success because the acoustics of the theater made it almost impossible to hear the music. Back in Venice, he became *maestro di cappella* at St Mark's in 1668; by this time his operas were less in demand, and he published a collection of Vespers music. He died in 1676, recognized as the leading vocal composer of his day.

Cavalli, with his rival Antonio Cesti (1623–69), represents the next stage after Monteverdi in the development of Italian opera. His music is smoother, less intense, less violent than Monteverdi's. His lines are more consciously shaped and more graceful, moving fluidly between speech-like recitative, lyrical recitative and aria. The extremes that were so important to Monteverdi for passionate expression are already softened in the music of Cavalli, who was more concerned with writing effectively for the human voice. Cavalli's arias – nearly always in triple time – can be seen as the beginning of the *bel canto* ("beautiful singing") tradition that was to dominate Italian opera for centuries. He responded particularly well to pathos;

ex. VI.3

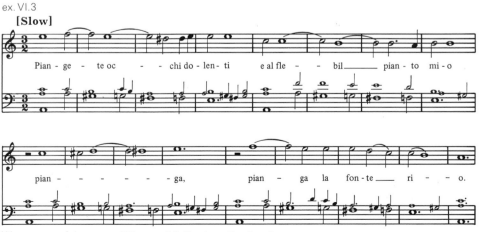

Weep, mournful eyes, and like my plaintive tears the river flows.

most of his operas include laments, which make their effect not by sharp discords or violent leaps, like Monteverdi's, but by the eloquence of their melodies, as in ex. VI.3, from *Egisto* (1643), his most popular work. He was also adept at comic scenes for the servants, like Monteverdi's shown in ex. 2*b* above.

Carissimi

While Venice was the principal operatic center during much of the seventeenth century, Rome, as the home of the Catholic church, was naturally the center of sacred music. At the beginning of the century sacred musical dramas had been given there. They were akin to operas on religious topics, for example *Rappresentazione di anima, et di corpo* ("Representation of the body, and of the soul") by Emilio de' Cavalieri (1600), or *Sant'Alessio* by Stefano Landi (*c*1631). Giacomo Carissimi was born in Rome in 1605, was choirboy and organist at the Tivoli Cathedral and later *maestro di cappella* at the Jesuit College. He composed numerous motets and other sacred works, and many cantatas for voice and continuo. But it is chiefly for his oratorios, composed for performance at the Oratorio of the Most Holy Cross, that he is remembered. In them he used the same means that Monteverdi did in his operas: vivid recitative, with dissonances to heighten the expression at crucial points, flowing arias, and ensembles. His works, called oratorios after the name of the building where they were performed, related biblical stories (for example those of Jephtha and the Judgment of Solomon), with a different singer taking the role of each character and a narrator to tell the story; particularly important was the chorus, which offers moral commentary on the story or takes a narrative part. Carissimi used Monteverdi's "agitated style" in his choruses, often writing rapid repeated chords in decisive rhythmic patterns – Monteverdi had always written such passages for solo voices in his madrigals, but Carissimi had the advantage of a full chorus and a church acoustic and was able to produce striking dramatic effects. Carissimi's importance lies in his application of the new methods, the Monteverdian *seconda prattica*, to religious topics and his establishment in Rome of an oratorio style as dramatic in its way as the style used in the opera houses. He died in 1674, but his influence was wide and long – it extended to Germany, to France (where Charpentier was probably his pupil) and even to England (for Handel later drew on his effects).

Northern Europe: early–middle Baroque

Schütz

If any composer can be regarded as the north European counterpart to Monteverdi, it is Heinrich Schütz. Like Monteverdi, he wrote nothing but vocal music, though in Schütz's case the sacred far predominated over the secular. This to some extent reflects the differences between German and Italian musical life and circumstances; for during much of Schütz's lifetime Germany, as we have seen, was riven by the Thirty Years War, her courts were impoverished, and in times of stress religious observation and consolation were a good deal more important than secular entertainment.

Schütz was born in Saxony in 1585. When he was 13, the ruler of Hesse-Kassel, the Landgrave Moritz, stayed at the inn owned by the Schütz family, heard the boy sing, and invited him to join his choir at the Kassel court; later Schütz studied law at university. Then the Landgrave offered him the opportunity to go to Italy to study with Giovanni Gabrieli. He went in 1609, and soon became a favorite pupil –

Heinrich Schütz   Works
born Saxony, 1585; *died* Dresden, 1672

Passions St Matthew (1666), St Luke (1666), St John (1666)
Oratorios Christmas Oratorio (1664); Seven Words from Christ on the Cross (1657);
Resurrection oratorios
Collections of motets Cantiones sacrae (1625); Symphoniae sacrae (1629, 1647,
1650); Geistliche Concerte (1636, 1639)
Psalm settings Psalmen Davids (1619, 1628)
Operas Dafne (1627)
Secular vocal music Italian madrigals (1611)

Gabrieli, when he died in 1612, left him a ring. Schütz returned to Germany the
next year and worked initially at the Kassel court. Then he was "borrowed" by the
more powerful ruler of Saxony, the Elector Johann Georg. Eventually Moritz had
to release Schütz to Johann Georg's court at Dresden where he became *Kapellmeister*
in 1618 or 1619. His job involved providing music for major ceremonies, religious
or secular, and supervising the musical establishment, which was the largest in
Protestant Germany.

Schütz remained in the service of the Dresden court for the rest of his working
life, though he had several spells away – he went to Venice in 1628–9, where he met
Monteverdi, twice stayed in Copenhagen to work at the Danish court, and several
times visited other German courts. His life, however, was unhappy. On a personal
plane, he lost his wife after six years of marriage, and his two daughters both died
before he did. On a professional plane, he had terrible difficulties because of the
impoverishment of the Dresden court caused by the war and its aftermath; many of
his musicians were dismissed, and those that remained were not paid. In 1635 he
tried to move permanently to Denmark; in 1645 he unsuccessfully sought to retire
from routine duties. He tried several times to retire as his working conditions were
so wretched; his repeated requests were ignored, though he was allowed extended
periods out of Dresden. Not until 1657, when he was over 70, was he released from
daily responsibilities. But he continued composing, and some of his most original
works date from his very last years. In 1670 he commissioned from one of his pupils
a motet for his own funeral, and two years later he died.

Schütz's first published work was a book of Italian madrigals, a product of his
studies with Gabrieli; they are a little old-fashioned compared with Monteverdi's
works of the time, being unaccompanied, but show a Baroque feeling for the
expressive use of dissonance. Later he was to compose at least two operas – the first
German opera, *Dafne*, in 1627, and a setting of the story of Orpheus in 1638; both
are now lost. Otherwise virtually his entire output is sacred. He made less use of the
chorale repertory than most German Protestant composers. His contemporaries,
like J. H. Schein (1586–1630) and Samuel Scheidt (1587–1654), tended to weave
these familiar hymn-tunes into their compositions. Schütz mostly preferred to
compose freely. He wrote numerous psalm settings, some very simple, some
intensely elaborate; he wrote many motets, some of which he called "sacred
symphonies" or "little sacred concertos"; and he wrote works for the major seasons
of the church year, like settings of the Christmas story and the Passion.

In some respects Schütz was quite conservative; many of his motets are in the older polyphonic manner, though they usually have features that show their composer to be familiar with a more modern approach, for example in their variety of pace or their striking treatment of crucial words. Often Schütz used a simple style because, in the straitened circumstances of the chapels for which he was composing, he had limited performers at his command. It also seems that the austerity of the times during the later part of the war and after it was reflected in the character of the music he produced, at least for choir; his solo writing still shows the expressiveness and drama of the monody composers.

Two works, typical in different ways, and from different times of Schütz's life, might usefully be compared. The motet *Veni, sancte Spiritus* ("Come, holy Spirit") was written in his early Dresden days, when the multi-choir music he had heard in Venice during Gabrieli's time was still in his memory, and the Italian use of contrast – in pace, texture, color and rhythm – was new and exciting to him. The work is laid out for four "choirs":

I   2 sopranos; bassoon
II   Bass; 2 cornetts
III 2 tenors; 3 trombones
IV   Alto and tenor; flute, violin, bass viol (with organ continuo)

It begins with Choir I in three-voice imitative counterpoint (ex. VI.4*a*), not the smooth counterpoint of the Renaissance composers but something more vigorous and arresting. Then Choir II gives out the next verse, using a different working of the same material – but now, instead of two high voices and one low instrument, it is set for one low voice and two high instruments. The third verse calls on Choir III; the counterpoint, though based on the same material, is fuller and richer, and the music is lower pitched (ex. 4*b*). The fourth verse, for Choir IV, is another five-voice working, softer in tone, higher in pitch (ex. 4*c*). The fifth, "O lux beatissima" ("O wonderful light"), is a grand, solemn tutti to begin with, a marvelously striking

ex. VI.4

Come, Holy Spirit/Greatest comfort/rest from labor.

effect; then there is free writing, with the tonal groups mixed and contrasted; and finally another tutti, sustained to the end.

The richness and elaboration of this work contrast remarkably with the darkness and severity of others of his pieces, and with none more strongly than the Passion settings of his old age. The *St Matthew Passion* begins and ends with brief four-voice choruses, in a simple manner, with little counterpoint. The main story is narrated, in the traditional way, by a singer (the Evangelist), here unaccompanied and with the pitches specified but not the rhythms, to allow for a natural speech–rhythm (ex. VI.5a); the music for the other characters (Christ, Peter etc) is written in the same way. There are brief choruses for the people, usually in an imitative style which represents quite naturally the clamor of a crowd or a smaller group (like priests or soldiers) (see ex. 5b). Passion music is, of course, somber by nature and purpose, but Schütz's takes this to a higher degree of gravity. He fittingly represents the dark times in which he lived, and has fairly been called the first great German composer.

ex. VI.5

a And they paid him 30 pieces of silver. And from that moment he sought an opportunity to betray him. Now on the first day of unleavened bread the disciples came to Jesus, saying:
b "Where will you have us prepare for you to eat the Passover?"

Plate 9 *Opposite*
Musicians playing the flute
and the lute in a
polyphonic chanson (see
p. 136): detail from the
painting *The Prodigal Son
among the Courtesans*.
16th century, artist
unknown. Musée
Carnavalet, Paris.

Schütz had a reputation as an organist, but as far as we know he wrote no music for his instrument, or indeed for any other instrument. Yet northern Europe in the seventeenth century was a productive region as far as instrumental music was concerned, keyboard music in particular. In the Netherlands there was an elder contemporary of Schütz's, Jan Pieterszoon Sweelinck (1562–1621), composer of brilliant toccatas and fantasias and of variations that followed up the traditions of the English virginalists. In middle Germany there was Johann Jacob Froberger (1616–67), a pupil of Frescobaldi who did much towards the development of the dance suite for harpsichord, and Johann Pachelbel (1653–1706), whose organ music, especially his chorale settings, had considerable influence.

Buxtehude

The most wide-ranging among the northern keyboard composers is Dietrich Buxtehude (c1637–1707), who worked in north Germany and regarded himself as Danish. Buxtehude spent eight years as organist in Helsingør (the Elsinore of Shakespeare's *Hamlet*) and in 1668 became organist of St Mary's, Lübeck – an important post in a "free", Hanseatic city, ruled (like Hamburg) not by a local princeling but by the city fathers. Soon after taking up his post, he revived an old practice of giving public concerts in the church (*Abendmusik*, "Evening music"); these were widely admired, and when Bach was a young man at Arnstadt he walked hundreds of miles to hear some of them and in particular to hear Buxtehude play the organ.

Buxtehude wrote some oratorios for the *Abendmusik* at Lübeck (these are now lost) as well as many cantatas and arias. He also wrote chamber music. But it is his organ music for which he is mainly remembered. About half of it consists of chorale preludes, works in which a familiar Lutheran hymn is used in some way – it might be as an inner voice around which the other voices weave counterpoints, or there

69 Musical scene
including (*left to right*) the
musicians Johann Theile,
Johann Adam Reincken,
and Dietrich Buxtehude:
painting, 1674, by
Johannes Voorhout.
Museum für
Hamburgische Geschichte,
Hamburg.

may be imitative passages based on each line of the melody, or (and this is the most common) the chorale may be presented in a richly ornamented form, as a florid melody, yet immediately recognizable to his congregation (see ex. VI.6). The other half consists of toccatas and fugues, often in a very brilliant, improvisatory style, with vivid passages contrasting with sustained ones, in the opening sections and well-worked fugues. No composer had a greater influence on the organ music of Bach.

ex. VI.6

England

The flowering of music in Elizabethan and early Jacobean England (that is, in the late sixteenth century and the early seventeenth), in the madrigal, the lute ayre, sacred music, keyboard music and music for instrumental consort, lent the country a natural resistance to the extremes of the Italian Baroque; also against it were the undemonstrative English temperament and the Puritan tendencies of the times. The situation in the world of architecture was similar: the true Baroque spirit is rare in England, though it is to be found in St Paul's Cathedral, built by Sir Christopher Wren in London at the end of the seventeenth century in deliberate imitation of Italian churches, or in the flamboyant Blenheim Palace, built near Oxford for the Churchill family in the early eighteenth by Sir John Vanbrugh. In music, English equivalents began to develop of the new Italian genres and styles. The monodic song, whose mannered diction was anyway ill-suited to the English language, found a parallel in the florid type of song of the first half of the century; the *concertante* motet of the Italians is paralleled by the verse anthem of the Anglican church, in which solo verses generally alternate with full passages for the whole choir. Opera was particularly slow to take root, but at court and later in the public theaters a mixed type developed, called "masque", owing more to French courtly entertainments than to Italian opera, including poetry, music, dance and lavish settings. These came to a decisive end – like the king himself – in the Commonwealth period from 1642; court and cathedral appointments for musicians were abolished and theatrical events discouraged. The monarchy was however restored in 1660, the year after Purcell was born.

Plate 10 Costumes by Bernardo Buontalenti for gods and planetary signs in the *intermedi* performed at the celebrations for the wedding of Fernando de Medici and Christine of Lorraine, Florence, 1589 (see pp. 106, 144). Biblioteca Nazionale, Florence.

Purcell

Henry Purcell is one of that small group of enormously talented composers, including Mozart and Schubert, who developed rapidly and died young. He was trained first as a choirboy in the Chapel Royal (the king's musical establishment) in London; a song was published as his when he was a boy of eight. At 15 he was appointed to tune the organ at Westminster Abbey; at 18 he was appointed a composer to the royal band; and at 20 he became organist of Westminster Abbey – his former teacher, John Blow, the leading English church composer of the time, seems to have stood down in Purcell's favor. In 1682 he also became a Chapel Royal organist. He had begun in 1680 supplying music for use in the London theaters, and from then on divided his time between religious music and theatrical, writing songs, chamber music and keyboard pieces too. He died at the age of 36, in 1695, recognized and mourned as a great composer.

Henry Purcell	Life
1659	born in southern England
1660s	chorister in the Chapel Royal
1674–8	organ tuner at Westminster Abbey, London
1677	composer to the royal band
1679	organist of Westminster Abbey
1680	fantasias for strings published; composed first "welcome" song and first music for the theater
1682	organist of the Chapel Royal
1683	organ maker and master of the king's instruments
1685	anthem *My heart is inditing* composed for James II's coronation
1689	*Dido and Aeneas* performed in Chelsea
1695	died in London, 21 November

Purcell was a highly original composer too. His command of melody was exceptional for its freedom, its readiness to take its rhythm and shape from the sound and sense of the words he was setting; harmonically, he was unusually enterprising, with free treatment of dissonance especially to underline a crucial word.

Among his earliest works are a group of pieces that he called "fantasias" – music for string instruments, probably viols, and belonging to a particularly English tradition. Composed around 1680, they are probably the last such works; as we have seen (p. 133), the generation of Byrd and Gibbons had worked in this form, and John Jenkins (1592–1678) and especially the eccentric Matthew Locke (c1622–1677) had brought it up to Purcell's time. The style of Purcell's fantasias is essentially that of the Renaissance polyphonists, but made much more instrumental and with bolder rhythms and harmonies, as ex. VI.7a shows. The changes of key, and the melodic intervals, would have been impossible to a composer of even half a century earlier; and the expressive manner, with contrasts of speed allowing for vivacious music to be set against music that is clearly grave in mood (sometimes with chromatic inflections of a kind associated with mournful feeling – see ex. 7b), is clearly of a later age. Purcell's other important ensemble works are his trio sonatas. He published 12 of these in 1683, for the more modern combination of two violins,

Henry Purcell

Opera Dido and Aeneas (1689)

Other music for the stage 5 semi-operas – King Arthur (1691), The Fairy Queen (1692), The Indian Queen (1695); incidental music and songs for plays

Secular choral music court odes – Come, ye sons of art, away (for Mary II's birthday, 1694); odes for St Cecilia's Day – Hail, bright Cecilia (1692); welcome songs – Sound the trumpet (for James II, 1687)

Sacred choral music c55 verse anthems, c16 full anthems; Te Deum and Jubilate (1694); services

Instrumental music fantasias for strings – Fantasia upon One Note (c1680), 9 fantasias (1680); Sonatas in 3 Parts (1683); Sonatas in 4 Parts (1697); March and Canzona for 4 slide trumpets (for Mary II's funeral, 1695); overture, In Nomines

Keyboard music suites, marches, grounds, hornpipes, dances for harpsichord
Songs   *Vocal duets*

70 Henry Purcell: portrait, 1695, attributed to John Clostermann. National Portrait Gallery, London.

ex. VI.7
a. Fantasia No.9

b. Fantasia No.1

bass viol and harpsichord or organ; a further set was issued by his widow after his death. Purcell said that he composed them "in imitation of the most fam'd Italian masters", and although some passages are very like those in the fantasias many others use a more brilliant and up-to-date violin style and the general feeling of the music is more harmonic or "vertical".

In the field of sacred music, Purcell was working in a long and conservative tradition. His anthems (he wrote about 65) are mostly in the verse anthem form, and the most characteristic are those that also call for orchestra (the Chapel Royal had a string group from 1662 to 1688). Here Purcell tends towards the Italian concertante style. The individuality of his contribution lies mainly in the rhythmic life and harmonic boldness of his finest examples, and in the way in which he widened the expressive resources of English church music by using the same kinds of device as in theatrical works. The opening of the anthem *Plung'd in the confines of despair*, for example, shows chromatic lines and harmonies expressing the despair of the lost soul (ex. VI.8).

ex. VI.8

As a composer of dramatic music Purcell was particularly gifted. Had he lived longer he might have created a tradition of English opera that could have resisted the international prestige of Italian opera (which, as we shall see, was to be the ruling form in the London musical theater). As it was, he wrote a great many incidental songs and dances to be given in plays, one true opera and a handful of "semi-operas". These last, which include *The Fairy Queen*, based on an adaptation of

Shakespeare's *A Midsummer Night's Dream*, are extended entertainments, mainly spoken drama but with musical sections of some substance at several points. In *The Fairy Queen* for example each of the five acts ends with a group of songs and choruses, some of them with dances. The music is thinly justified by the action. These works have proved difficult to revive because the quality of the original dramas is mostly quite low and their subjects are of little appeal, and also because the expense of putting on works with complete companies of both actors and singers is prohibitively costly. But some revivals have shown that the form works well in the theater, with the musical sections resolving the tensions of the drama.

Purcell's one true opera was composed not for the professionals of the London theaters but for a girls' school. This is the miniature masterpiece *Dido and Aeneas* (1689), which relates the story of Aeneas, fleeing from the destruction of Troy, falling in love with Queen Dido of Carthage and then having to leave her when the gods summon him to Italy (his mission is to found a new Troy, which is to be Rome). The music depicts Dido's court at Carthage, a hunt, a covey of witches and a sailors' scene; there are choruses, dances, recitatives and a variety of songs, several of them using ground bass (see p. 66), a favorite scheme of Purcell's and one he handled with particular art. The opera's climax is tragic – Dido's proud dismissal of her lover and her death, which follows her famous lament (see Listening Note VI.B).

Purcell's range was wide. He composed everything from bawdy catches to impassioned prayers, intimate chamber music to ceremonial court odes, fresh melodies and dances to elegiac laments. It is perhaps in the expression of the darker

---

Listening Note VI.B

Purcell: *Dido and Aeneas* (1689), Act 3, "When I am laid in earth"

Dramatic context: Dido, Queen of Carthage, has declared that she loves Aeneas, the Trojan prince who escaped the sack of Troy, and they have married; but the very next day Aeneas is summoned to Italy to fulfill his destiny as the founder of a new Troy (it is to be Rome). He has to leave his new bride, "One night enjoy'd, the next forsook". Dido, deserted and humiliated, looks forward to death in this famous lament.

The music: Like many Baroque laments, this song is constructed on a ground bass (see p. 66). The phrase shown in ex. i is repeated throughout; its falling chromatic scale, from G to D, is a traditional elegiac device, and here its effect is much strengthened by the free rhythms of the vocal line, which Purcell wrote in such a way that it often cuts across the five-measure phrases of the bass line. First the bass is heard alone, then twice to the first three lines of the text (the break comes actually during the word "create"); those two appearances are repeated, and then the last line is set, twice over, against two further statements of the bass (the break during "forget"). In the orchestral epilogue, the way the bass chromaticisms are taken up by the violins poignantly suggests the universal mourning at Dido's death.

When I am laid in earth,
May my wrongs create
No trouble in thy breast;
Remember me, but ah! forget my fate.

(words by Nahum Tate)

ex. i

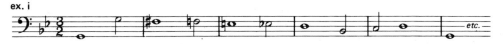

moods, grief, pathos and despair, that he proved himself even in so brief a life the greatest English composer of the Baroque and perhaps of any era.

France

The connections between France and Italy were historically strong. Two French kings had married ladies of the important Medici family from Florence, and these queens had imported Italian artists of various sorts to Paris; it was through this influence that ballet became popular in Paris at the end of the sixteenth century and that the new recitative style arrived (with a visit from Caccini) in the early seventeenth. Italian opera was introduced in the middle of the seventeenth century, with limited success (in spite of Cavalli's visit in 1660); the time was ripe for the establishment of French opera, for the devising of a style that took account of the French taste for dramatic entertainment, including ballet and giving due weight to the traditions of French declamation. The man who accomplished that, paradoxically, was an Italian.

Lully

Giovanni Battista Lulli was the son of a Florentine miller; he went to Paris in 1646, when he was not yet 14, as Jean-Baptiste Lully, working as a boy attendant to a noblewoman at court. He became a skilled violinist, guitarist, harpsichordist and dancer, and it was in that last capacity that he met the young king, Louis XIV. His fame grew rapidly and he advanced from one post to another – royal composer of instrumental music (1653), director of the small royal orchestra (by 1656: he made them into a high-precision group), ballet composer (by 1657), joint superintendent of music and chamber composer (1661), music master to the royal family (1662). Ten years later he had consolidated his position by obtaining the sole rights over all dramatic performances with singing. His musical absolutism was on a par with the king's political absolutism.

Lully attained this position more by clever manipulation than by musical skills. But he did create a new French dramatic musical style. He wrote mainly ballets at first, including songs that embody an adaptation of Italian affective recitative to the French language – which lacks the accentuation system of Italian (and most other languages) and thus falls less naturally into regular metric patterns. Lully's recitative is constantly changing in meter. In the late 1660s and early 1670s he wrote mainly ballet comedies, working with the well-known dramatist Molière; from then on, up to his death in 1687 (he died from blood poisoning after striking a toe with the stick he used for directing performances), he concentrated on classical tragedies, working with such distinguished dramatists as Quinault and Corneille. In all these works the music seems, compared with its Italian counterpart, constrained by the rhythms of the language and its vowel sounds (which give little scope for florid

Jean-Baptiste Lully	Works
born Florence, 1632; *died* Paris, 1687	

Operas (16) Cadmus et Hermione (1673), Alceste (1674), Armide (1686)
Comedy ballets (14) L'amour médecin (1665), Le bourgeois gentilhomme (1670)
Sacred choral music Te Deum; motets
Ballets and dance music

71 Scene from Lully's
opera *Phaëton*, first
performed at Versailles on
9 January 1683: pen and
wash drawing, school of
Berain. Bibliothèque de
l'Opéra, Paris.

singing). But there are also dance scenes and choruses, and the acts generally end
with a *divertissement*, a decorative scene often only marginally relevant to the main
action. Possibly Lully tailored the new French operatic form as much to his own
abilities, or their limitations, as to the French taste; but it worked, and the traditions
he laid down lasted long after his death and continued to influence the patterns of
French opera for two hundred years or more.

Lully held no official appointment in the royal chapel, but he wrote a certain amount of sacred music, especially motets of a ceremonial kind which seem to praise the magnificence of Louis XIV (whose supposed virtues were hinted at in the heroes of his operas) just as much as that of God. The chief church composers of Lully's time and the years following were Marc-Antoine Charpentier (c1648–1704), who studied in Italy, brought the dramatic oratorio style to France, and composed numerous Masses, motets and other church works that show his rich command of harmony; and Michel Richard de Lalande (1657–1726), who held various appointments in the royal chapel and as court chamber composer and wrote more than 70 large-scale motets, for performance at Versailles, which were long admired for their grace and their "nobility of expression".

Couperin

The most important and most gifted French composer during the first three decades of the eighteenth century was François Couperin. He was born in Paris in 1668, into a family of organists and harpsichordists; his uncle Louis (c1626–1661) had been particularly eminent as a harpsichord composer. When he was 25, François was appointed a royal organist, and soon was in demand in court circles as a teacher; later he was also harpsichordist in the royal chamber music. He died in 1733.

Couperin composed organ music and other pieces for the church, but his greatness lies in his perfection of the French chamber and harpsichord music idioms. His chamber works consist of several sonatas, among the earliest works written in France under that title, for two violins (or wind instruments) and continuo, in which he tried to bridge the gulf between the French and Italian traditions. The Italian sonata composers tended to write in a more brilliant and forceful manner, more rhythmic in impetus, more contrapuntal, than the French, who were chiefly concerned with dance-like rhythms and delicately ornamented lines. Couperin's

72 Musicians playing in the fourth chamber of the Queen's apartments at Versailles: engraving (1696) by Trouvain.

73 Part of the Table of Ornaments from Couperin's *Pièces de clavecin . . . premier livre* (1713).

sonatas, especially his later ones, include French-style dance movements but also Italianate fugal ones, in most of which there is however a French fineness of detail. He even wrote a pair of sonatas in honor of Lully and Corelli, twin masters of the French and Italian styles, and in some of the movements portrayed in picturesque terms the reception of the composers into Parnassus (or heaven). The Corelli work was published in a volume entitled *Les goûts-réünis* ("The styles reunited"). Couperin's other chamber works include a set of *Concerts royaux*, music written for the Sunday afternoon concerts that he directed before Louis XIV, and pieces for the bass viol, for the French had cultivated a special, sophisticated tradition of solo viol

François Couperin   Works
born Paris, 1668; *died* Paris, 1733

Keyboard music (*c*225 pieces) Pièces de clavecin, book 1, ordres 1–5 (1713), book
2, ordres 6–12 (1717), book 3, ordres 13–19 (1722), book 4, ordres 20–27 (1730);
L'art de toucher le clavecin (The art of playing the harpsichord, 1716)

Chamber music Concerts royaux (1722); Les goûts réünis (1724); Les nations
(1726); pieces for bass viol

Sacred vocal music Leçons de ténèbres (*c*1715); motets, versets

Organ music   *Songs*

ex. VI.9

playing long after that instrument had given way to the cello elsewhere.

As a harpsichord composer Couperin was unrivaled. He wrote some 225 pieces,
grouped in suites or "ordres" according to key and, to some extent, mood. Each has
a title: it might be a name of some particular person, or a state of mind, or a familiar
institution, or a natural phenomenon like a plant or animal, or indeed anything else.
A few simply have dance titles. The pieces are in a sense little portraits, though it
would be wrong to take their "meanings" too seriously. A few depict Couperin's
fellow musicians or his pupils. Mainly intended for amateurs, these pieces are not
generally difficult to play, although they do demand a sure command of
harpsichord ornamentation – ex. VI.9 shows how Couperin notated the music and
how the player was expected to perform it. This ornamentation may be seen as
analogous to the florid Rococo decoration of French art and furniture of the Louis
XIV period and the Regency that followed; and Couperin himself may best be
compared to Jean-Antoine Watteau (1684–1721) for the refinement of his art and
the expression of serious emotion behind a highly polished surface. Many of the
pieces are charming, even frivolous, and some are gracefully pictorial; but many,
too, are pathetic, grave, mysterious or noble.

Rameau   Lully's greatest successor as a dramatic composer was Jean-Philippe Rameau. Born
in Dijon, in Burgundy, in 1683, Rameau began his career as an organist and theorist.
He held posts in various cities (and briefly in Paris) as a young man, and settled in

Paris only in 1722–3 where he soon published collections of harpsichord music and theoretical books that earned him a reputation as an original and controversial thinker. As a composer, his ambitions lay in the theater. Not until he was 50 did he make his début there, when his opera *Hippolyte et Aricie* was given at the Paris Opéra. This work belongs to the Lullian genre of *tragédie lyrique*; Rameau went on to write several more, and he also composed in the other French theatrical forms, in particular the *opéra-ballet* (which is little more than a series of *divertissements* loosely strung together, with dance playing a large part). For the remainder of his life Rameau divided his energies between theoretical musical studies and composing for the stage. When he died, at the age of 81 in 1764, his last opera was in rehearsal. But he is said to have cared more about his theories than his compositions, for he was eager to interpret music in line with the rationalist, scientific outlook of his time. His theories were widely criticized. So was his music: initially his operas were attacked for their departures from the Lullian style, which was regarded as classical and immutable; later they were compared, often unfavorably, with the comic operas that visiting Italian troupes were giving in Paris.

Jean-Philippe Rameau   Works
born Dijon, 1683; *died* Paris, 1764

Operas (*c*30) Hippolyte et Aricie (1733), Les Indes galantes (1735), Castor et Pollux (1737)
Keyboard music 65 pieces for harpsichord
Chamber music 5 pieces for harpsichord and 2 instruments (1741)
Sacred choral music motets
Cantatas

Although he wrote many further operas, Rameau did not surpass his achievement in *Hippolyte et Aricie*. Following the usual French pattern, it is a five-act opera with a prologue; it is based on classical mythology, and further, Rameau's librettist drew on a play by Racine which would also have been familiar to his audiences. The prologue is allegorical, about a dispute between Diana (goddess of chastity) and Cupid (god of love), which Jupiter settles in Love's favor: this bears only indirectly on the rest of the opera. The main plot is concerned with the adulterous love of Phaedra, second wife of King Theseus, for his son Hippolytus, who in turn loves Aricia. There are the traditional *divertissements*: in the third act, for example, Theseus is welcomed home by singing and dancing from a troupe of sailors, and a troupe of hunters in the fourth offers entertainment to Hippolytus and Aricia. But in the second act the dance is better integrated into the action, for it is performed by infernal spirits during an expedition by Theseus into the underworld.

Unlike Italian opera of the time, in which there is a clear break between recitative (where the action takes place) and aria (where a character expresses his or her feelings), French opera has a relatively continuous texture. The recitative imitates the rise and fall of speech, but in a formal, declamatory manner, while the arias are usually brief and rarely lyrical in character, with no vocal roulades or florid writing and little repetition of words.

Rameau is at his most powerful in scenes like the one following Hippolytus's death, which gives scope for the expression of strong feeling; his style, in which –

ex. VI.10

Listening Note VI.C

Rameau: *Hippolyte et Aricie* (1733), closing scene of Act 4

Dramatic context: While Theseus, King of Athens, is away, his wife Phaedra has fallen in love with Hippolytus, Theseus's son by a previous marriage. Hippolytus, who anyway loves Aricia, rejects Phaedra, who asks him to kill her and seizes his sword; as he snatches it back Theseus returns. Phaedra allows him to think that Hippolytus was forcing his attentions on her (which Hippolytus is too honorable to deny); accordingly, Theseus asks his father, Neptune, god of the seas, to punish Hippolytus. Hippolytus is (apparently) killed by a sea-monster sent by Neptune.

The music: In this scene, where Phaedra enters to learn that through her deception she has caused the death of the man she loved, her tragedy and guilt are conveyed in declamation of a kind parallel to that of the French classical theater; Rameau's recitative is flexible in meter, following the natural rhythm of the words and heightening their emotion by adapting in music the natural rise and fall of the speaking voice. The scene is in three sections. Mm. 1–26: Phaedra enters and learns the situation from the hunters, who witnessed Hippolytus's disappearance in his fight with the monster; she sings in straightforward recitative. Mm. 26–48: Now Phaedra gives vent to her feelings; the claps of thunder that she hears and the shaking of the earth that she feels are represented by the orchestra, and her vocal line is freer and more vivid. Mm. 49–77: here she returns to a more formal declamatory manner of recitative as she addresses the gods.

PHAEDRA

mm.

1 Quelle plainte en ces lieux m'appelle?   What complaint calls me to this place?

CHORUS
(huntsmen and huntswomen)

3 Hippolyte n'est plus.   Hippolytus is no more.

PHAEDRA

5 Il n'est plus! ô douleur mortelle!   He is no more! oh mortal grief!

CHORUS

7 O regrets superflus!   O vain regrets!

PHAEDRA

8 Quel sort l'a fait tomber dans la nuit éternelle?   What fate made him fall into eternal night?

CHORUS

10 Un monstre furieux, sorti du sein des flots,   A raging monster, rising from the depths of the waves,

Vient de nous ravir ce héros.   Has just snatched the hero from us.

PHAEDRA

17 Non, sa mort est mon seul ouvrage.   No, his death is caused by me alone.
Dans les Enfers c'est par moi qu'il descend.   It is because of me that he is descending into the underworld.

Neptune de Thésée a cru venger l'outrage.   Neptune thought he would avenge Theseus's wrong.

J'ai versé le sang innocent.   I have shed innocent blood.

26 Qu'ai-je fait? Quels remords!   What have I done? What remorse?
Ciel! J'entends le tonnerre.   Heavens! I hear thunder.
Quel bruit! quels terribles éclats!   What noise! what terrible thunderclaps!
Fuyons! où me cacher?   I must flee! where shall I hide?
Je sens trembler la terre.   I feel the earth shake.
Les Enfers s'ouvrent sous mes pas.   Hell gapes beneath me.
Tous les dieux, conjurés   All the gods, conspiring
Pour me livrer la guerre,   To wage war on me,
Arment leurs redoutables bras.   Arm their redoubtable hands.

49 Dieux cruels, vengeurs implacables!   Cruel gods, implacable avengers!
Suspendez un courroux qui me glace d'effroi!   Hold back your wrath which freezes me with terror!

58 Ah! si vous êtes équitables,   Ah! if you are fair,
Ne tonnez pas encore sur moi!   Thunder on me no longer!
La gloire d'un héros que l'injustice opprime,   The glory of a hero oppressed by injustice,
Vous demande un juste secours.   Demands due relief from you.

68 Laissez-moi révéler à l'auteur de ses jours   Let me reveal to his progenitor
Et son innocence et mon crime!   Both his innocence and my guilt!

CHORUS

72 O remords superflus! Hippolyte n'est plus!   O vain remorse! Hippolytus is no more!

(words by Simon-Joseph Pellegrin)

following his own theories – a dissonance should sound on every chord, if possible, except the tonic of the home key, lends itself to the expression of anguish (see Listening Note VI.C). By contrast, the other most striking feature of any Rameau opera is the dance music. He applied to the established dance rhythms of French music a remarkable originality – of line, of harmony, of orchestration; these pieces are sometimes quirky and angular, sometimes warm and sensuous, always in some way piquant and emotionally suggestive. The very first dance in Act 1, for the priestesses of Diana, is typical in its hint of sadness beneath the gentle surface (ex. VI.10).

Rameau's later musical tragedies, apart perhaps from *Castor et Pollux* (his second, 1737), suffer from inferior librettos and rarely achieve the dramatic force of *Hippolyte et Aricie*. The dances retain their sparkle, but the characters rarely have much depth. Nevertheless, Rameau's operas continued the tradition established by Lully and without them the synthesis of Gluck's operas of the 1760s and 1770s (see p. 223) would hardly have been possible.

74 Interior of the Teatro Regio, Turin, during a performance of Francesco Feo's opera *Arsace*: painting, 1740, by Pietro Domenico Olivero. Museo Civico d'Arte Antico, Turin.

The Italian late Baroque

If the early and middle Baroque in Italy were times of experimentation and novelty, followed by consolidation, the late Baroque was a time of ripening and fulfillment, of firmly established forms that encouraged composers in the invention of new ideas. We may see Alessandro Scarlatti as the chief representative of opera and cantata as the middle Baroque moves to the late, and Pergolesi as representative of opera at the close of the Baroque and the dawn of the next era; while in the instrumental field Corelli stands for the establishment of the late Baroque ideal and Vivaldi and Domenico Scarlatti its final phase.

Alessandro Scarlatti

One of the most prolific composers of the era was Alessandro Scarlatti. Born in Palermo in 1660, he went to Rome as a boy and may have studied briefly with Carissimi; he was not yet 20 when his first opera was given there. He held a post as director of music to the exiled Swedish Queen Christina and had connections with several of the leading musical patrons in the city. In 1684 he moved (possibly because of a family scandal) to Naples, where he became *maestro di cappella* to the viceroy; he remained there for 18 years, composing operas at a phenomenal pace – he claimed that an opera of 1705 was his 88th stage work (only about half that number are known) – and was busy too writing cantatas, oratorios and other pieces. Dissatisfied with Naples, where the demands of his position were heavy, he left in 1702, spending some time at Rome and Venice; but he returned in 1708, and apart from a further spell in Rome stayed in Naples until his death in 1725.

Scarlatti wrote some 600 cantatas, mostly for solo voice and continuo. The totally free, monody-style setting of the time of Caccini and his followers had now passed; Scarlatti and his contemporaries used a more organized design, usually alternating recitative and aria, on some such pattern as *R–A–R–A*, *A–R–A–R–A* or *R–A–R–A–R–A*, and often there would also be a section in arioso style – that is, something between recitative and lyrical aria, suitable to accommodate the expression of strong emotion. Most cantatas dealt with the unrequited love of a shepherd for a shepherdess (or vice-versa), so that the music would express such feelings as love and yearning, jealousy and forgiveness.

The move towards more regular patterns is even more marked in operas of the time. In an early Scarlatti opera there may be as many as 60 arias, all quite brief, with recitative in between and occasional ensemble items (usually at the ends of acts). Some of the arias are in a simple *A–B* form, or sometimes *A–B–B'* (*B'* being *B* slightly modified); but these increasingly gave way to the *A–B–A* design which by the 1690s was standard. This pattern allowed for longer arias, better developed and

---

Alessandro Scarlatti   Works
born Palermo, 1660; *died* Naples, 1725

Operas (*c*50 surviving) La Teodora augusta (1692), Il Mitridate Eupatore (1707)
Sacred choral music c35 oratorios, c85 motets, Masses
Secular vocal music c600 cantatas for voice and continuo, madrigals
Instrumental music   *Keyboard music*

so better able to convey serious emotion; it also permitted the virtuoso singer, who was becoming increasingly important as opera was heard more often and in more cities, to show his abilities in the repeat of the *A* section by adding expressive embellishment. As the individual arias increased in length, so the number of them in an opera decreased.

The trends that we find in Scarlatti's operas can be seen in the works of other composers. Scarlatti, however, was the most gifted of his time, with a particularly graceful vein of melody and sensitivity to words; and pathetic emotion always drew from him an expressively shaded line. He was important in the development of the opera overture, which in Monteverdi's day had been little more than a short, arresting piece but which now grew into something more substantial. By the 1690s it normally consisted of three short movements, fast–slow–fast; this was eventually to lead to the symphony of the Classical period.

Scarlatti is often counted as founder of the "Neapolitan School", the group of opera composers in Naples who dominated the development of opera in the early

75 Interior of a typical Venetian theater in the 18th century: engraving from the satire *I viaggi d'Enrico Wanton* (1749) by Zaccaria Seriman.

part of the eighteenth century. Almost all his operas are serious; the best-known writer of comic opera was Giovanni Battista Pergolesi (1710–36), famous above all for *La serva padrona* (1733), a spirited piece with a charm and sentiment typical of the Neapolitans and looking ahead to the next, early Classical generation.

Corelli

In the realm of instrumental music, Arcangelo Corelli had an importance akin to Alessandro Scarlatti's and a reputation unrivaled in his time. Born near Bologna in 1653, he went to study in that city in 1666 and to Rome nine years later, where he quickly became prominent among local violinists and played for the leading musical patrons. He was employed by two cardinals from noble families, Pamphili and Ottoboni, led one of the opera orchestras, and in 1706 became a member of the select Arcadian Academy. He spent his final years preparing his last works for publication, and died in 1713.

He published, essentially, just six sets of works: his op. 1 and op. 3 are church sonatas, his op. 2 and op. 4 are chamber sonatas, his op. 5 is a set of violin solo sonatas, and his op. 6 a set of concertos. Each publication contains 12 separate works. The church sonatas are distinguished from the chamber ones – all are for two violins and continuo – by the fact that the former use abstract movement-types, normally including at least one fugal movement, while the latter are in dance rhythms. The establishment of the slow–fast–slow–fast movement pattern for church sonatas was largely due to Corelli.

Corelli's was long and widely regarded as a model of style, for its purity and formal balance; his works were republished many times over and retained a place in concert programs, especially in England, for more than a century after his death. The trio sonatas strike a classical balance between the instruments and obtain much of their musical momentum through the management of discord – the listener's expectation of the resolution helps propel the music onwards. His smooth and graceful melodic style is evident particularly in the slow movements of the op. 5 sonatas for violin and continuo; these works also show the measure of his virtuosity, in the movements where the solo violin pretends to play a fugue in several voices, using multiple stopping, and in the brilliant, dashing "perpetuum mobile" movements and the gigues. The concertos are for two violins and cello with a larger string body; in style they are like trio sonatas in which some of the music is played solo and some by a full string orchestra. There are no solo concertos, though the first violin sometimes dominates and in one or two movements has almost a solo role. They are old-fashioned in form compared with the concertos of Vivaldi and others; but their dignity, integrity and melodic charm (typified by the famous Christmas Concerto, op. 6 no. 8) lend them a certain timeless quality.

Vivaldi

While Corelli represents the conservative development of the late Baroque concerto, Antonio Vivaldi represents its progressive development. His concertos, which number about 500, are one of the peaks of the Italian Baroque. Vivaldi was born in Venice in 1678, the son of a violinist. He was an unhealthy child, with some kind of chest trouble, probably asthma, to judge by later reports of his health. He was trained for the priesthood and was ordained in 1703, though on grounds of health he was soon granted dispensation from saying Mass. Meanwhile he had become a skilled violinist and sometimes deputized for his father in the orchestra at St Mark's. It was in the year of his ordination, 1703, that he obtained his first musical appointment, as master of the violin at one of the Venetian orphanages, the

76 Pupils of the Ospedale della Pietà, Venice, playing their violins in the organ gallery. Museo Correr, Venice.

Ospedale della Pietà (the Hospital of Piety). This institution, one of four for which Venice was famous, took in orphaned, abandoned or poor girls and educated them, and in particular trained them in music if they showed any aptitude. The Pietà orchestra was well known for its virtuosity; several visitors to Venice reported on its concerts, during which the girls were discreetly shielded from the audience's view to avoid any impropriety. Vivaldi worked at the Pietà, with brief breaks, for some 15 years, during which time he wrote many of his concertos and some sacred music for the Pietà girls; the wide range of instruments for which he composed reflects the girls' abilities. His reputation grew, in Italy and abroad: he had some of his best concertos published, was sought out by visitors and received commissions to write concertos for performance elsewhere, for example at the court in Dresden.

Vivaldi's father was involved in the business of opera-house management, and it was probably this connection that led Vivaldi himself into the world of opera – both its composition and its management. Beginning in 1713, he wrote some 40 operas, several for performance in Venice but many for other cities in north Italy as well as Rome and Prague. This involved him in much travel and lengthy spells away from Venice, during which he kept in contact with the Pietà and even sent concertos by post, but after about 1718 he was officially employed there only in the period 1735–8; the appointment was discontinued because of Vivaldi's continual absences (he was in Amsterdam in early 1738, directing performances at a theater's centenary celebration). He undertook another journey in 1740, probably to Austria, where the singer, Anna Giraud, with whom he lived had lately been; he died in Vienna, apparently in poverty, in the summer of 1741. He was little mourned, even in Venice: he had been a difficult man, vain and avaricious – but he left a deep mark on the history of music.

Antonio Vivaldi   Works
born Venice, 1678; *died* Vienna, 1741

Concertos (*c*500) *c*230 violin concertos, *c*70 orchestral concertos, *c*80 double and triple concertos – L'estro armonico, op. 3 (1712); La stravaganza, op. 4 (*c*1713); Il cimento dell'armonia e dell'inventione concerti, op. 8 (*c*1725) [Le quattro stagioni, "The four seasons"]; *c*100 bassoon, cello, oboe and flute concertos

Operas (over 45) Orlando finto pazzo (1714), Giustino (1724), Griselda (1735)

Sacred choral music 3 oratorios – Juditha triumphans (1716); Mass movements – Glorias; psalm settings, motets

Chamber music Il pastor fido, op. 13 (The faithful shepherd, *c*1737: sonatas for 5 instruments and continuo); violin sonatas, cello sonatas; trio sonatas; chamber concertos

Secular vocal music *c*40 solo cantatas

As an opera composer Vivaldi is of modest importance. He used the standard forms of his day, and the music has some vitality if not much warmth, perhaps because he wrote for voices in a rather instrumental manner. His church music at its best has great vigor and, like the opera airs, betrays the influence of the instrumental concerto; a notable piece is the *Gloria* in D.

It is as an instrumental composer, particularly of concertos, that Vivaldi was – and is today – chiefly famous. Of his 500, close on half are for solo violin; over 100 are for solo bassoon, cello, oboe or flute, and about 150 have multiple soloists or are "orchestral concertos" (i.e. have no solo parts). A few are chamber concertos, without orchestra. The music itself is marked by its sheer energy, its driving momentum and its strongly rhythmic character; it is clearly the work of a violinist, drawing its figuration from what is possible and effective on a violin. His opening themes are nearly always direct and memorable, and their memorability is important because their recurrences need to be instantly recognized if the form of the movement is to be grasped. He also made much use of sequences – that is, repeating the same pattern at different pitches; in his inferior concertos (and for a composer who wrote so many there are bound to be weaker examples) the use of sequence can be dull and mechanical instead of generating tension, as it does in the better works. The Violin Concerto in A minor, no. 6 of the set he published in 1712 as his op. 3, *L'estro armonico* ("Musical fancy"), shows Vivaldi's vigorous style at its best, and illustrates well too his handling of ritornello form, which he normally used for the outer movements of his concertos (see Listening Note VI.D).

Vivaldi wrote a number of "programmatic" concertos – works that tell a story in

---

Listening Note VI.D

Vivaldi: *Violin Concerto* in A minor, op. 3 no. 6 (1712)
solo violin; strings (1st and 2nd violins, viola, cello, violone), continuo

1st movement (Allegro): Ritornello form, a
The movement begins (mm. 1–12) with a complete statement of the ritornello theme, which has two principal ideas, one based on repeated tones (ex. i), the other on arpeggio patterns (ex. ii). The first solo passage begins as ex. i, but soon the violin steers the music in a different direction and to the key of C, the relative major. After a brief orchestral reminder of the ritornello theme, back in a, the violin resumes with faster-moving music; this leads to a cadence in the dominant, e, where the main central ritornello starts (it is a shortened version of mm. 1–12). In the next solo (the third), the violin – using ideas derived from ex. i – leads through various keys, ending in the home key of a, where there is a decisive cadence. Now the final ritornello begins, with ex. i; but after a moment the violin interrupts with fast passage-work. The orchestra resumes, and again the violin intervenes, this time quite briefly; and then the orchestra completes the ex. ii section of the ritornello theme to bring the movement to an end. The vigorous, pounding rhythms of the orchestral music and the mixture in the solo part between rapid movement and large leaps (the solo following the central ritornello) are typical of late Baroque Italian concertos and Vivaldi in particular; also Vivaldian are the many sequences and the interruptions to the final ritornello.

2nd movement (Largo), d: solo violin in free, florid style, accompanied by violins and violas

3rd movement (Presto), a: Ritornello form

ex. i

ex. ii

their music, or at least carry some meaning outside the music itself. There is for example *La notte* ("The night"), with dark and sinister effects (this is a bassoon concerto); there is *Il gardellino* ("The Goldfinch"), a flute concerto, with bird effects; there is *La tempesta di mare* ("The storm at sea"); and, more vaguely as regards a meaning to be expressed in music, there is *Il sospetto* ("The suspicion"). The most famous of his concertos of this type is the group *The Four Seasons*, which Vivaldi included in a set he published in about 1725 as op. 8, with the fanciful title *Il cimento dell'armonia e dell'inventione* ("The contest between harmony and invention"). These go further than the others in that their music represents specific phenomena associated with each season – birdsong in the spring, for example, summer thunderstorms, harvesting in the fall, shivering and skating in winter. Yet the basis of the concerto form remains unchanged, for it is in the solo music (these are violin concertos) that Vivaldi generally depicts the changing events in the story he is telling, using the tutti either not at all or to depict a recurring element, for example the torpor created by the heat of summer. The same applies to the slow movements, which as in most of Vivaldi's concertos are generally a simple melody with light orchestral accompaniment; though in the Summer concerto distant thunder is heard and in Spring the soloist represents a sleeping goatherd, the viola the barks of his dog, and the orchestral violins presumably the rustling leaves. Vivaldi published with the concertos a set of sonnets outlining the events they portray.

Vivaldi's gifts had a certain brilliance and waywardness. They were not wide in range: his achievement was modest outside the concerto, and even within it the expressive scope is not large. Yet he brought to the concerto a new tone of passion, a new vigor, a new awareness of instrumental color and of how to exploit it. The freshness and clarity of his invention made his concertos attractive and influential: many other composers imitated and learned from them, the greatest of them being Bach.

Domenico Scarlatti

Domenico Scarlatti, a son of Alessandro, is another composer whose influence and indeed his importance are confined to a single form. He was born in Naples in 1685, the same year as Bach and Handel, spent some time in Venice and Rome, then went in 1719 to Portugal where he worked in the royal chapel in Lisbon until 1728. Finally, when the Portuguese princess married the Spanish crown prince, he left for Madrid, remaining there until his death in 1757.

In Italy, under the watchful eye of a domineering father, Scarlatti composed in the standard vocal forms, in which he produced little music nowadays considered worth a place in the repertory. We do not know what he composed in Lisbon because virtually all the music in the libraries there was destroyed in the earthquake of 1755. In Madrid he seems to have devoted himself to sonatas for the harpsichord,

Domenico Scarlatti	Works
born Naples, 1685; *died* Madrid, 1757	

Keyboard music c550 harpsichord sonatas
Sacred choral music Stabat mater; oratorios, cantatas, Mass movements
Instrumental music sinfonias, sonatas
Operas   *Secular vocal music*

of which he composed about 550, each a one-movement piece in binary form.

These sonatas are unlike any music that any other composer was writing at the time. They demand great brilliance on the performer's part: the music ranges across the whole keyboard, often moving very rapidly, with spectacular arpeggio figuration; other devices like hand-crossing, quick repeated notes, fast scale passages and so on abound and add to the dazzling effect. Scarlatti was clearly influenced by the sounds of Spanish music: sometimes guitar-like strumming is heard, and Spanish dance rhythms creep into some of the sonatas. Another feature, perhaps to be linked with guitar music, is the repetition, many times over, of a brief phrase, producing an almost nagging effect, like a cat worrying a mouse by teasing it in a variety of ways before making a decisive move. Scarlatti's tendency to shift between major and minor is another Spanish feature. His love of dissonance on the harpsichord, of the jangling sound that the instrument can make in full chords including dissonant notes, gives his music a special color; sometimes this is obtained by the use of "crushed notes", or acciaccaturas, struck with the chord but instantly released and thus adding bite.

Much about Scarlatti remains mysterious. Did he really write all his best music in his last 20 years? – if so, why did he mature so late? Are his sonatas intended to be played singly or in pairs, as their arrangement in the surviving manuscripts hints? Were some of the pieces intended not for the harpsichord but for the new piano (his princess employer owned several)? These are intriguing questions; most curious of all is the existence of a composer who, isolated from the mainstream of European musical life, created a form and a style all his own in Spain or Portugal.

Late Baroque Germany

In the late Baroque period Germany produced two of the greatest of all musical geniuses. They had careers as different as can be imagined: the one as a local organist, the other as an international opera composer. Before moving on to them, however, we should glance briefly at the man who, in their day, was considered their equal or indeed superior.

Telemann

Georg Philipp Telemann, born in 1681, was the most prolific composer of his age and pursued a career of apparently incessant activity. At the age of 12 he started writing his first opera and in his teens he composed music for religious plays at school. He gave up music when he went to study law at university, in Leipzig, but when his gifts were discovered he was commissioned to write a cantata every two weeks for the principal church in the city, and when he was 21 he became head of the local musical society and of the opera house. Three years later he was in Sorau (now in Poland) directing the music for the Count of Promnitz, and around 1708 he moved to Eisenach, leading the court orchestra and writing cantatas and instrumental music. In 1712 he went to Frankfurt as city music director. Finally, in 1721, he settled in Hamburg, one of the most prosperous of the German cities, where his job included the supervision of the music at the city's five main churches. A special attraction of Hamburg was that it possessed a well-established opera house.

The Hamburg post was well suited to Telemann's abilities. He was a composer of astonishing fluency and the task of writing two cantatas each week, along with extra ones for special occasions, a Passion setting each Easter and various ceremonial music, proved so easily within his capacities that in his spare time he could direct the local musical society and take part in operatic activities – in fact he was musical director of the Hamburg Opera from 1722 until it closed in 1738. The city authorities at first objected to his doing so much, but when he asked to leave to take up a similar appointment in Leipzig they quickly swallowed their objections and increased his salary. Meanwhile he composed new chamber works and was busily involved in music publishing, generally engraving the printing plates himself. His activity declined somewhat after 1740, when he was approaching 60, but that was largely because he chose to concern himself mainly (that is, besides the activities demanded by his job) with music theory and education – he was eager to cut through some of the academic ideas about the study of music and to make the art more accessible. Then, in his mid-70s, Telemann embarked upon the composition of oratorios, a genre that had previously little interested him; possibly he was affected by the example of his friend Handel who also turned to oratorio relatively late in life. Telemann's other achievements included the foundation and editing of a musical periodical and the championing of a composer's legal and financial rights in his own music, rights which we now take for granted but which in his day were by no means fully acknowledged. He died in 1767, composing to the end of his life.

Telemann was regarded in his day as a "progressive" composer, one who was moving away from the elaborate flowering of counterpoint of the late Baroque towards a more melodic idiom. In tune with his general musical philosophy, his music emphasizes the light, the graceful, the tuneful; rhythms are direct and symmetrical, accompaniments slender and unobtrusive. He had a wide range of style: his concertos are Italianate in manner, if without the fierce rhythmic drive of a Vivaldi, his orchestral suites are French in their overtures and dances (he visited Paris in 1737–8 and wrote French-style quartets, too), and he also wrote movements that drew on the folk music of Poland and Moravia (now part of Czechoslovakia). Whichever style he used, however, his own personal manner comes through, with its cheerful, shapely, conversational expression. His best-known works are those in his three collections entitled *Musique de table* ("Table music"), published in 1733 ostensibly as background music for eating but intended for more general use. Each set includes an overture in the French style, an Italian concerto, and chamber works including a quartet, a trio sonata and a solo sonata. Quartets were rare in the Baroque idiom and Telemann devised a way of writing involving much instrumental dialogue, for example where one instrument would give out a melody with continuo accompaniment and the other two would, as it were, comment on it. He had an astute command of instrumental style and color and wrote effectively for a variety of combinations.

Of Telemann's vocal works, only a few have survived, though the quantity is still large. He wrote fluently for the voice, and could illustrate a text in a direct and appealing way, as for example in his oratorio *Die Tageszeiten* ("The times of day") with its portrayals of sunrise and night. He wrote an early comic opera, *Pimpinone* (1725), similar in style to Pergolesi's *La serva padrona* but anticipating it by eight years. A composer as prolific as Telemann cannot pause long to think about each work, and when dealing with the big topics of life his music, compared with that of the greatest composers of the time, may appear a shade urbane and superficial, beautifully written and accomplished though it always is.

Bach

Between the middle of the sixteenth century and the middle of the nineteenth there were more than 80 musicians in Germany who bore the name of Bach. The ancestry of most of them can be traced back to a Veit Bach, who settled in central Germany around the 1540s, having come originally from what is now central or eastern Czechoslovakia; he was a baker by trade but also played a lute-like instrument. Seven generations later, eight Bachs were active as professional musicians, mostly church organists. The last two, one of them a grandson of J. S. Bach, died in 1845 and 1846. The area in which they chiefly lived was Thuringia, a reasonably prosperous rural part of central Germany, firmly Lutheran in faith, governed in small regions by dukes. Musical life flourished, at the courts of the local potentates and in civic institutions – the churches, first, but also the local town bands of *Stadtpfeifer* ("town pipers"). The greatest member of the family, Johann Sebastian Bach, was born on 21 March 1685, the son of a town musician of Eisenach (trumpeter and director of the town band) who himself was the son of a town musician of nearby Erfurt and Arnstadt.

Johann Sebastian Bach	Life
1685	born in Eisenach, 21 March
1700	chorister at St Michael, Lüneburg
1703	organist at the New Church, Arnstadt
1705–6	visited Lübeck to hear Buxtehude
1707	organist at St Blasius, Mühlhausen; married Maria Barbara Bach
1708	court organist in Weimar; prolific output of organ works
1713	*Konzertmeister* at Weimar court, responsible for providing a new cantata every four weeks
1717	*Kapellmeister* to Prince Leopold in Cöthen; many instrumental works, including Brandenburg Concertos, violin concertos, sonatas and keyboard music
1720	Maria Barbara Bach died
1721	married Anna Magdalena Wilcken
1723	*Kantor* of St Thomas's School, Leipzig, supplying cantata for the main city churches each Sunday
1727	*St Matthew Passion*
1729	director of the *collegium musicum* in Leipzig
1741	Berlin and Dresden; *Goldberg Variations*
*c*1745	*The Art of Fugue*
1747	visited Frederick the Great's court in Berlin; *Musical Offering*
1749	B minor Mass
1750	died in Leipzig, 28 July

Early years

J. S. Bach began his schooling in Eisenach, but when he was nine his mother and father died within a few months and he went to Ohrdruf, where his elder brother was organist, attending a particularly enlightened school there until he was 15. Then he went north to Lüneburg to a boarding school, free to needy boys with good voices; there he probably met Georg Böhm, one of the finest organists in north Germany, and he traveled to Hamburg to hear J. A. Reincken, the senior and

Johann Sebastian Bach   Works

Sacred choral music St John Passion (1724); St Matthew Passion (1727);
Christmas Oratorio (1734); Mass, b (1749); Magnificat, D (1723); over 200 church
cantatas – no. 80, Ein feste Burg ist unser Gott (*c*1744), no. 140, Wachet auf (1731);
motets – Singet dem Herrn (1727), Jesu meine Freude (?1723); chorales, sacred
songs, arias

Secular vocal music over 30 cantatas – no. 211, "Coffee Cantata" (*c*1735); no. 212,
"Peasant Cantata" (1742)

Orchestral music Brandenburg Concertos nos. 1–6 (1721); 4 orchestral suites – C
(*c*1725), b (*c*1731), D (*c*1731), D (1725); harpsichord concertos; sinfonias

Chamber music 6 sonatas and partitas for solo violin (1720); 6 sonatas for violin and
harpsichord (1723); 6 suites for solo cello (*c*1720); Musikalisches Opfer (Musical
offering, 1747); flute sonatas, trio sonatas

Keyboard music Chromatic fantasia and fugue, d (*c*1720); Das wohltemperirte
Clavier (The well-tempered keyboard), "48" (1722, 1742); 6 English Suites
(*c*1724); 6 French Suites (*c*1724); 6 Partitas (1731); Italian Concerto (1735);
French Overture (1735); Goldberg Variations (1741); Die Kunst der Fuge (The art
of fugue, *c*1745); inventions, suites, dances, toccatas, fugues, capriccios

Organ music over 600 chorale preludes; concertos, preludes, fugues, toccatas,
fantasias, sonatas

most brilliant organist of the region.

In 1702 Bach left Lüneburg. Appointments as organist at this time were normally
open to competition: Bach applied for one at Sangerhausen, won, and was offered
the post, but the local duke intervened and appointed an older man. Bach soon
found a position at Weimar, as "lackey-musician" at the secondary court there (this
was a junior post, as a servant with some musical duties). After a few months he
obtained an appointment more fitted to his abilities, as organist of the New Church
in Arnstadt; this was a minor church, the third in importance there. Bach did not
stay long and does not seem to have been particularly content in Arnstadt. Once, in
the company of his second cousin Barbara Catharina, he was involved in a fight
after insulting a bassoonist; he was reprimanded and was also told that his work was
unsatisfactory – apparently he got on badly with the students in the choir and failed
to rehearse them properly. Soon after this he was granted leave to go to Lübeck –
some 250 miles away, a journey he made on foot – to hear Buxtehude play; he
overstayed by almost three months, probably so that he could hear some
Abendmusik performances (see p. 160) and possibly so that he could inquire about
succeeding the 68-year-old Buxtehude. Again he was in trouble on his return, not
only for his long absence but also for his still unsatisfactory work; the authorities
now also complained that he introduced strange notes and elaborations into the
hymns, making them difficult for the congregation to follow. And he was in
trouble for bringing a young woman into the church.

Not surprisingly, Bach was soon looking elsewhere for a post, and in the spring
of 1707 he successfully undertook a trial for the organistship of the St Blasius
Church at Mühlhausen, about 35 miles away. He took up the appointment during
the summer, and in the fall he was married, to his second cousin Maria Barbara
Bach. But his stay at Mühlhausen was short: Bach found little encouragement
because the pastor was a strict Pietist who objected to any but the simplest music in
church. The congregation too was conservative. Again, this was no place for a

young musician whose brain and fingers teemed with new and imaginative ideas. So when he received an invitation to become court organist at Weimar, the following summer, he at once accepted – and, as he had done at Arnstadt, handed his old position to another member of the Bach family. He retained his connection with Mühlhausen; by now he was an authority on organs and he was asked to see through the rebuilding that he had initiated of the St Blasius instrument.

Weimar and Cöthen

Weimar had an unusual court regime, being jointly ruled by a senior and a junior duke. Bach had previously been employed by the junior; now he was working for the senior, Duke Wilhelm Ernst, and in a much more important capacity. Moreover, the duke admired his playing, and seems to have encouraged him in composition. Many of Bach's organ works were written at Weimar, including most of those in the prelude-and-fugue (or toccata-and-fugue) category, in which a fairly free and often brilliant first section is followed by a fugue, along the Buxtehude model, as well as chorale preludes, where a familiar chorale melody would be woven into the musical texture. One chorale prelude of the Weimar period is based on *Ein feste Burg* (ex. VI.11*a*; see also p. 107 and pp. 199–201). The opening of the prelude (ex. 11*b*) shows a typically original treatment: it starts with the chorale melody in the left hand, slightly elaborated and then running off into lively sixteenths; the right hand responds with a speeded-up version of the second line before giving out the first at slower speed, while the left takes up the fast version of the second. The Arnstadt fathers may not have liked Bach's elaborations on hymns, but clearly the Weimar duke relished the ingenuity of his art, especially as his settings of these chorales so often mirror faithfully the sense of the words associated with them.

Bach was at Weimar until 1717. During his years there six children were born to him and his wife, including two who were to become composers, Wilhelm Friedemann (born in 1712) and Carl Philipp Emanuel (born in 1714 – see p. 227). Professionally, he was active in teaching and in organ and harpsichord construction and repairs. In 1713 he applied for a post as organist at Halle, and was duly offered the position; but the duke, when he was told, gave Bach a salary increase and promoted him to *Konzertmeister*, with the task of providing a new cantata every four weeks. Soon after, however, something seems to have gone wrong. From 1716 there are few cantatas, and none from 1717. At the end of 1716 the old *Kapellmeister* died, and perhaps Bach expected to be promoted again to the senior post; but he heard that the duke was looking elsewhere (the post was offered to Telemann, who declined). So Bach sought a similar position, and was offered one by Prince Leopold of Cöthen. He applied in such strong terms for his release that the duke sent him to prison for four weeks and then dismissed him.

Bach must have been glad to move. At Weimar his employer was a strict disciplinarian who imposed puritanical standards on his employees; at Cöthen, Prince Leopold, a younger man, was a keen music-lover, a good amateur player himself, and a kind employer and good friend to Bach. By faith he was Calvinist, which meant that music played a very small part in worship; Bach wrote a few cantatas for special occasions but his chief duty was to provide music for his employer's entertainment and perhaps participation. Bach's life seems to have been active and varied: he was in demand for testing new organs, he had trips to Berlin to buy a new harpsichord, and he was one of the small group of musicians (some five out of a payroll of 15) who accompanied Prince Leopold when he went to take the

ex. VI.11

waters at a fashionable spa in Bohemia. It was during the second of such visits, in 1720, that tragedy struck the Bach family: he came back to find his wife, Maria Barbara, dead and buried. She was only 36, and left a family of four (two had died in infancy), aged eleven, nine, six and five. At the end of 1721, Bach remarried: his new wife, Anna Magdalena, was a singer at the court (or became one on her marriage), and like his first wife came from local musical stock – her father was a court trumpeter at nearby Weissenfels. She was only 20; Bach was 36. The marriage seems to have been happy, to judge by the tales of domestic music-making and the books he compiled for her of simple and tuneful keyboard pieces – and it was certainly fruitful, for she bore him no fewer than 13 children, of whom six grew to maturity and two achieved fame as composers (Johann Christoph Friedrich, born in 1732, and Johann Christian, born in 1735 – see p. 228).

In the month of Bach's marriage, his employer was also married. Leopold's new wife, unhappily, did not share his love for music, and from this time on Bach found his position at the court decreasing in importance. Bach had earlier considered leaving Cöthen: in 1720 he had applied for an important post as organist in Hamburg, had played in the city (delighting Reincken, the 97-year-old organist of St Catherine's Church there, with his command of the traditional technique of improvising on a chorale melody), and had been offered the position; but he declined, possibly because a hefty donation to the church funds seems to have been expected of him. A new opportunity came up in 1722, and closer at hand, in Leipzig, the largest city near the region where Bach had lived and worked. This was the post of *Kantor* of St Thomas's School, which carried with it the city directorship of music. The duties were heavy, but the prestige was high and the salary good. The *Kantor* was required to take general responsibility for music in the city's four principal churches, in two of which (St Thomas's and St Nicholas's) regular cantata performances with orchestra and choir were the rule; he also had to supervise other civic musical activities, compose music for special occasions like weddings or funerals as well as regular Sunday services, select the choirs and train the senior one

77　Johann Sebastian Bach: replica, 1748, by Elias Gottlob Haussman of his portrait, 1746, showing the composer holding a copy of his six-part canon BWV 1076. Princeton University Library.

78　Performance of church music, probably under the direction of Johann Kuhnau, Kantor of the Thomaskirche, Leipzig: frontispiece and title-page from *Unfehlbare Engelfreude* (1710).

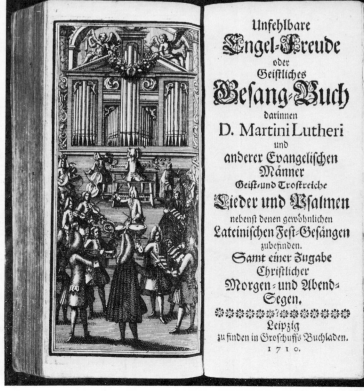

himself, and teach music at the school. (The teaching of Latin, a further requirement, was waived.) Other distinguished musicians applied for this post, and it was first offered to Telemann, who, however, was persuaded to remain in his Hamburg position (see p. 183). The second choice was J. C. Graupner, *Kapellmeister* at Darmstadt and a former pupil at St Thomas's; but he too withdrew when the Darmstadt authorities pressed him, with a salary increase, to stay there. The third choice was Bach.

The instrumental music

Before we follow Bach to Leipzig, it will be as well to look at some of the music he wrote at Cöthen; most of his chamber and orchestral works belong to the Cöthen years, as well as much of his harpsichord music. Of all these the best known are the Brandenburg Concertos, so called because Bach presented a manuscript of these six works to the Margrave of Brandenburg, who heard him play and asked to have some of his music. It is unlikely that Bach composed them specially; probably they are among the works he had written for the Cöthen players.

During his Weimar years, Bach had become interested in the current styles of Italian instrumental music and had made arrangements, for solo harpsichord or organ, of orchestral concertos, chiefly by Vivaldi and other Venetian composers. His own concertos are to some extent modeled on these: he used the Vivaldian type of ritornello form (see p. 180), though he liked – in accordance with the German tradition – textures rather fuller and more contrapuntal than Vivaldi's. He also followed German tradition in another way; while Vivaldi's published concertos (the only ones Bach had access to) were for strings, Bach liked to use wind instruments. He obviously enjoyed experimenting with instrumental combinations, as the layout of the Brandenburg Concertos shows:

no.	solo group (concertino)	tutti group (ripieno)
1	violin, 3 oboes, bassoon, 2 horns	strings, continuo
2	trumpet, recorder, oboe, violin	strings, continuo
3	3 violins, 3 violas, 3 cellos	the same used in unison, continuo
4	violin, 2 recorders	strings, continuo
5	violin, flute, harpsichord	strings, continuo
6	2 violas, cello	the violas used in unison, 2 bass viols, continuo

The schemes for all the concertos are unusual. The first two are the most colorful, with their wind groups: in no. 1 some of Bach's musical ideas are so devised that dialogues between the horns, the woodwinds and the strings help carry the music forward, while in no. 2 he secures variety by pairing the soloists in all the possible combinations. No. 3 departs in another way, by treating the groups of three (violins, violas, cellos) as solo players, each with different music to play, in the solo sections but having them play the same music, in unison, in the tutti ones; the contrast in texture is thus between emphatic tuttis and gentle, multi-strand music in the solo episodes. No. 6 works on a similar principle, and draws a special character from the absence of violins, so that its colors are dusky and veiled. No. 5 represents another important departure. Usually the role of the keyboard in orchestral or chamber music was to play a filling-in continuo part, but here the harpsichord is one of the solo team (at least in the solo sections; in the tuttis it reverts to supplying continuo harmony). It even has a lengthy cadenza before the final tutti of the first movement. This work is one of the very earliest keyboard concertos. No. 4 is

Listening Note VI.E

Bach: *Brandenburg Concerto no. 4* in G (1721)
solo violin, two recorders
1st and 2nd violins, viola, cello, violone, harpsichord

1st movement (Allegro): Ritornello form

The opening ritornello is unusually long (83 mm.), and in it the idea at the beginning (ex. i) is heard three times. Between the first and second times, there is passage-work on the material on ex. ii, in the third on ex. iii; its second appearance is the dominant, D.

The first solo section begins with passage-work for the solo violin, with occasional reminders of ex. i from the recorders; the music moves to D, but then, with references to ex. ii (violin) and ex. iii (recorders), quickly slips into e, the relative minor, for the ritornello that follows. The second solo begins with the two recorders (playing ex. iii material) and continuo; then the violin joins in with very rapid and brilliant scale writing. The music passes through a to C, where there is a short ritornello.

In the next solo, the violin plays 16ths throughout, sometimes in dialogue with the orchestra violins, sometimes with reminders from the recorders of ex. i. The short ritornello that follows is based on the first appearance of ex. ii material at the opening.

The next solo (the fourth) starts with the recorders in dialogue, soon joined by the orchestral violins (ex. iii material) with a steady stream of 16ths from the violin. The orchestra joins in to round off the music in b.

But the emphasis on b is at once strongly contradicted, as the music even more emphatically turns to G: and a complete, final statement of the opening ritornello ends the movement.

A feature of this movement is the lack of clear-cut divisions of the kind that the Vivaldi concerto movement discussed in Listening Note VI.D shows; the music of the solos often builds up gradually into the tuttis. Another feature is the closely worked thematic detail: virtually all the figuration is derived from the patterns seen in exx. i, ii and iii.

ex. i

ex. ii

ex. iii

2nd movement (Andante): free form, based on echo principle (see ex. iv); the solo group (violin, recorders) echoes phrases heard on the full orchestra, first two-measure phrases, then one-measure, and later just the final measure of a longer phrase. Some landmarks: m. 18, cadence in e; m. 28, cadence in a, followed by faster-moving solo recorder phrases; m. 38, beginning of chromatic passage, with cadence in b, m. 45; m. 55, lower instruments prominent, taking up main theme; m. 61, passage for soloists; mm. 70–71, final cadence, in b, leading direct to . . .

3rd movement (Presto): Ritornello-fugue
Although fundamentally in ritornello form, like the first movement and most other concerto movements of the period, this one is also fugal. The ritornello sections correspond roughly with the sections of a fugue in which the subject is heard, the solo sections with the episodes. Mm. 1–41 constitute the opening ritornello: the fugue subject (ex. v) is heard in turn on the viola, the second violin, the first violin with the soloist, the bass instruments and the two recorders, who also have an extra statement of it to round the section off.
In the first solo (mm. 41–66), the solo violin plays continuous 8th-notes while the recorders carry on a dialogue based on the subject. The music moves to D, the dominant, for the next ritornello, in which the subject is heard on the basses and then on the first violins; it changes key, ending in e. Again the solo violin leads off the ensuing section (mm. 87–126) with passage-work of increasing brilliance (ex. v can sometimes be heard in the background, on the orchestral violins) – there are arpeggios, then scale passages, then rapid bowing across the strings. The third ritornello begins when the orchestral violins join with the soloist on his reaching the subject – which is heard in quick succession on the recorders and the basses. It begins in e and ends in b; then (m. 152) the next episode starts, mainly for the recorders with continuo accompaniment, leading the music through G to C, where there is a brief ritornello with three entries of the subject. A few measures for the three soloists lead to another short ritornello, this time back in G; the soloists resume, but soon (m. 212) the basses come in, decisively, with ex. v – and there is now an air of emphasis that makes it clear that the end of the movement is close. There is a dramatic, rhetorical passage, then two last entries (basses, then recorders), and the movement is over.

ex. iv

almost a violin concerto; the two recorders have solo parts though of a Grade B kind compared with the violin's virtuoso, Grade A one. As in Vivaldi's concertos, there are divisions between solo and tutti sections; but the textures are much fuller, and the material is used more economically and more rigorously to provide stronger unity and logic (see Listening Note VI.E).

Bach used designs similar to the fugal ritornello type of the Brandenburg Concerto no. 4 finale in another group of works from the Cöthen period, the four "orchestral suites", as they are usually called. (The word "orchestra" may be misleading; the ensemble Bach used and expected, as we have seen from the size of the Cöthen establishment, was small – normally just one string player to a part, or at most two or three, so that none of the Brandenburg Concertos needs more than 13 players.) These suites are in the French style, with overtures in the abrupt, arresting, jerky rhythms that the French favored in their theater music; then follows a fugal movement with ritornello features, and after that a series of dances (minuets, gavottes, bourrées etc). These are among Bach's most cheerful and tuneful works; one has a solo part for flute, and two gain a touch of ceremonial splendor from the use of three trumpets and a pair of drums.

For Bach's fugal writing at its most varied, however, we may turn to another important work of the Cöthen years. Around 1722, he began to compose a series of preludes and fugues for the harpsichord or clavichord, one in each of the 24 keys, major and minor. He called this *The Well-Tempered Keyboard*, for it was partly designed to demonstrate that an instrument could be tuned to play effectively in every key. (Because of a number of physical and mathematical factors, it is impossible to tune an instrument with all the main intervals sounding smooth and sweet. A century before Bach, the favored systems produced excellent results in a very few keys, and acute discomfort in the rest; in Bach's time new forms of compromise were being devised to accommodate the wider range of keys that was needed. Nowadays we use "equal temperament", in which no interval is perfect but each is equally compromised, as the kind of music we create demands.)

These 24 preludes and fugues eventually, by 1742, became what all musicians call the "48", for Bach later wrote a second set. The preludes are movements of various kinds – some are brilliant display pieces, others are lyrical and aria-like, while yet others are contrapuntal or involve the working out of some pattern of keyboard figuration. The fugues are regarded as embodying the richest array of fugal techniques ever assembled, and in them Bach shows, again, that fugue is not – despite all the disciplines it involves – a mechanically applicable process but a live artistic creation where the treatment is dictated by the nature of the material. Some are highly complex in their form and development; no. 2 in C minor from Book I is an example of a direct and logical handling of fugal writing (see Listening Note VI.F).

Bach wrote other kinds of keyboard music at this period. There are the

Plate 11 *Opposite Parnassus* by Andrea Mantegna (*c*1431–1506), one of the paintings acquired for Isabella d'Este's studiolo at Mantua. Musée du Louvre, Paris. A Renaissance view of the Classical era. Parnassus was the home of the nine Muses who fostered the arts.

Listening Note VI.F

Bach: *48 Preludes and Fugues, I* (1722), Prelude and Fugue in C minor

This prelude and fugue come from Book I of Bach's collection of preludes and fugues in all the keys. The prelude is of the "toccata" type, a piece designed to demonstrate the abilities

of a player and the capacities of his instrument in music that is often rapid and virtuoso in style. Here Bach takes a pattern of notes (ex. i) and keeps close to it during most of the piece, using the pattern within changing harmonies (the harmonic scheme of the first seven measures is shown in ex. ii). At the end, the pattern gives way (without disappearing altogether) and there are a few measures of brilliant, dramatic writing to round the piece off. The fugue is in three "voices" – that is, in three clearly defined contrapuntal lines (which for convenience we may call soprano, alto and bass, though they do not conform to vocal pitch ranges). They enter in the order A, S, B; in this particular fugue, when any voice is assigned the subject (ex. iii), the other two (once they have entered) are assigned material that goes satisfactorily against it. When, for example, the Bass (B) enters with the subject (S), the soprano (S) has the first countersubject (C1) and the alto (A) the second (C2). The chart below shows how the material is divided between the voices on each recurrence of the subject. The subject is two measures long: the measures not accounted for in the chart are occupied with episodes, all quite closely derived from material in the subject or the first countersubject, sometimes with running scales in one voice (B, mm. 9–11; S, mm. 13–14; B, mm. 22–6).

m.	1	3	7	11	15	20	26	29
S	–	S	C1	S	C1	S	C2	S
A	S	C1	C2	C2	S	C1	C1	–
B	–	–	S	C1	C2	C2	S	–
key	c	g	c	E♭	g	c	c	c

ex. i

ex. ii

ex. iii

Countersubject 1

S.

Countersubject 2

A.

Subject

B.

Plate 12 Consort of viols at the court of Duke August the Younger: detail of the portrait *Duke August and Family*, c1645, by Albert Freyse. Landesmuseum, Brunswick. For German courts, see p. 144.

notebooks of simple pieces for his eldest son and his new wife; there are what he called "inventions" and "sinfonias" (exercises, in composition and performance, in the interchange of material between the hands, to help the player to gain independence of hand action); and two fine books of dance suites, known as the English Suites (which have long, concerto-like preludes as well as dances) and the French Suites. Each suite has the four basic dances (Allemande, Courante, Sarabande, Gigue) with an extra one between the last pair.

Before we pass on from the Cöthen years, the chamber music that Bach wrote there should be mentioned, in particular those works in which he attempted something new. His interest in the role of the harpsichord, which we have noted in Brandenburg Concerto no. 5, extended to its use in chamber groups. Traditionally, the harpsichord had been used merely to supply the continuo harmonies; but in the six sonatas for violin that he wrote at Cöthen he assigned it an obligatory, fully written-out right-hand part, sometimes accompanying but usually playing music essential to the texture. He thus turned the violin sonata from a two-voice medium with supporting harmony into a three-voice, or a free multi-voice, one. This is typical of his interest in enriching musical textures. The other notably original contribution came in the sonatas or suites for solo violin and cello – he wrote six such works for each instrument, with no accompanying part, but managing the distribution of notes in such a way as to imply harmony. This may seem to be the opposite of textural enrichment, yet paradoxically it is not, for the listener is invited to hear in his mind many notes that are barely touched or even merely hinted at, so that there is never an impression of a sparse or thin texture to the music.

Leipzig

Bach moved to Leipzig in May 1723. He must have been pleased to do so. In this thriving commercial city he would be the employee not of a private patron, who could act on whim, but the civic and church authorities; further, his sons could attend the St Thomas's School and be sure of obtaining a sound education. And the musical duties offered altogether more of a challenge than he had faced in his earlier posts.

He set to work in methodical fashion. He had to supply cantatas for performance each Sunday, and seems to have decided to build up a new repertory. Starting in June 1723, in his first year Bach composed a complete cycle of cantatas (about 60, allowing for feast days as well); in his second year he produced another complete cycle. He embarked on a third, which he took two years to complete. Then followed a fourth, in 1728–9 – though we cannot be certain about this as only a handful of the cantatas composed after 1727 have survived. There is evidence that he wrote a fifth cycle during the 1730s and 1740s.

Bach was, then, astonishingly industrious. Soon after he arrived in Leipzig he applied to the university for the restitution of a traditional right of the holder of his post to direct the music at certain services there; a dispute ensued, and a compromise was reached. This was only one of numerous quarrels in which Bach was involved. He was constantly alert for any infringement of his rights or privileges – for example in 1728, when a church official claimed the right to select some service music and Bach protested (in vain) that the choice ought to be his. Later, he was often at odds with the headmaster of St Thomas's School, for example over his neglect of teaching or his absence without permission (he still made many journeys to report on organs, and paid visits to nearby courts on special occasions). The headmaster appointed in the 1730s was an educational reformer whose academic ideals created conflicts with Bach who was eager to use the brightest boys for musical activities. But even before that time Bach, discontent with the musical resources assigned to him, had drawn up a strongly worded memorandum in which he set out the requirements for "a well-regulated church music".

In spite of the heavy responsibilities he carried at St Thomas's and the other churches, Bach found time to pursue other musical activities. Music was his preoccupation at home as well as at work: there were musical evenings at home (he noted, in 1730, that his family could provide a vocal and instrumental ensemble) and he must have expended much of his spare time on his sons' musical education. He did much other private teaching, especially in the 1740s; several of the best German organists and composers of the next generation were his pupils. He wrote a number of works with a particular eye to their usefulness for instruction, among them the second set of 24 preludes and fugues in all the keys and four books entitled *Clavier-Übung* ("Keyboard Exercise"), including organ chorale preludes and dance suites and variations for the harpsichord. One especially interesting collection forms the third book: here Bach contrasts the Italian and the French styles, publishing side by side an "Overture in the French Manner" and a "Concerto in the Italian Style". The French work consists of an overture in the dramatic, jerky rhythms of the kind Lully used, followed by a fugue and a series of characteristic French dances; the Italian one uses concerto form in its first and last movements, with "solo" and "tutti" passages distinguished as in orchestral concertos but here simply by contrasting weights of texture and different kinds of thematic materials. Bach's

79 Thomaskirche and Thomasschule (center), Leipzig: engraving (*c*1735) by J. G. Schreiber.

clear aim was to set down these two national styles in such a way as to make their differences clear to the student. In all this, his music never merely imitates that of composers from other countries; it always sounds his own, and sounds German.

Another important side activity of Bach's was his organization of the local musical society (or *collegium musicum*, to use the Latin term favored in Germany). He took up the directorship in 1729, when his period of intensive cantata composition was finishing. The society gave concerts weekly during its seasons – in a coffee-house in the winter, a coffee-garden in the summer. Bach revived his Cöthen repertory of instrumental music, and supplemented it with new harpsichord concertos and other music for small orchestra. The concerto for harpsichord was a novel idea; never before had the solo role in a concerto been given to a keyboard instrument (remarkably, at just the same time, Handel – far away in London – was beginning to compose concertos for organ: see p. 213). Most of Bach's harpsichord concertos, perhaps all of them, are adaptations of works originally written as violin concertos: Bach ingeniously rewrote passages that were designed to be effective on a string instrument to make them sound well on the harpsichord, and he added left-hand parts to enrich the texture. He also wrote multiple concertos – two for two harpsichords, two for three, and one (arranged from a Vivaldi four-violin concerto) for four. It must have been difficult to get four harpsichords and four harpsichordists together in a coffee-house music room, with an orchestra, but Bach's delight in rich textures and unusual instrumental effects justified it. In fact, the four (or three, in the triple concertos) rarely play together in counterpoint; more often the music falls into patterns of dialogue, using the kinds of symmetry of which Bach was so fond. He also performed other composers' music at these concerts – suites by his cousin Johann Ludwig Bach, for example, and pieces by the many musicians who visited Leipzig or passed through. He remained in charge of the *collegium musicum* up to 1741 (with a break in 1737–9), when the owner of the coffee-house died; it ceased activities soon after.

The Leipzig sacred music

Bach's central work, however, for the remainder of his life, was in the church and especially in the provision of music for St Thomas's. One of the first works he had performed on his arrival was the *St John Passion* – that is, a musical setting of the Passion story as related by St John. He followed this up a few years later, in 1727, with the *St Matthew Passion*, a longer work (it takes around three hours to perform) and one of his greatest achievements. By Bach's time, a full-length Passion setting involved a narrator (or Evangelist), singers to take the roles of Christ, Pilate, Peter and the other participants, and a chorus to represent the crowd; the Evangelist would tell the story, in lightly accompanied recitative, and the other characters would play their own parts. The story was however frequently interrupted, for hymns (chorales) to be sung by the congregation at appropriate reflective moments, and for arias of meditation on the religious message of the events described. In his two settings, Bach also framed the entire work with large-scale, contemplative choruses.

The Passion form offered him great scope. Much of the recitative is plainly set, the line following the natural rhythm and the rise and fall of the words; but where events of special force or poignancy are described Bach would alter the pace or give an unexpected twist to the line or the harmony (see ex. VI.12a). In the chorales he supplied harmony that reinforced the sense of the words, often, for example, adding a dissonance or a chromaticism for a word or phrase of emotional significance (see

ex. VI.12

a.

(the vocal rhythms are slightly modified from
the German original to accommodate
the English words)

c.

(other instruments with the voices)

ex. 12*b*). Dramatic power comes particularly in the crowd choruses, where the clamor of the mob is represented in overlapping counterpoint, for example where the people proclaim that Christ is worthy of death (ex. 12*c*); and the ugliness of mob emotion is conveyed in the chorus where his crucifixion is demanded, with its harsh, misshapen lines (ex. 12*d*). Bach's finest music in the *St Matthew Passion*, however, is found in the arias, where the powerful emotion aroused by the events portrayed is dissolved and raised to a higher level in the lyrical lines and expressive harmony; and also in the great choruses at the beginning, the middle and the end of the work, in which moderately slow music, in large-scale ritornello forms planned with clear and satisfying symmetries, raises the whole Passion on to a plane of collective, communal experience through the involvement of the chorus.

Bach wrote three Passion settings (St Matthew, St John and St Mark, the last of which is mostly lost) for Good Friday performances. His basic work for St Thomas's was the production of a weekly cantata, as we have seen, and probably he wrote as many as 300 altogether. They are composed, usually, for a small choir (Bach liked to have around 12 singers), with solos for two or three choir members, and an orchestra of strings and organ with up to half a dozen wind instruments. An average cantata lasts between 20 and 25 minutes; a few, for special occasions, may be up to 45 minutes long. The congregation would normally join in the singing of the final chorale, which would have words appropriate to the day in the church year for which the cantata was designed. This would, typically, follow an opening chorus and a couple of arias.

The text for the day, and meditations on it by the poet who supplied the words for the composer, made the cantata unified as a religious entity. Sometimes Bach and his contemporaries reinforced that unity with a musical one, derived from the chorale melody linked with the text; in the cantatas of 1724–5, particularly, Bach wove the chorale melodies into his music – since these, and the words that belonged with them, were familiar to his congregation, this helped hold their interest and remind them of the religious message. We may look at this process in one of the finest of his cantatas, *Ein feste Burg* (no. 80), using the famous Reformation chorale (see p. 107) and designed for the Reformation Festival, an important event in the Lutheran church year.

Here the chorale (ex. VI.13*a*) is used in almost every movement. To begin with,

ex. VI.13

there is a large-scale chorus, which like many Bach choruses starts fugally (ex. 13*b*). The fugue subject, however, is a variant of the chorale melody (as the upward note-stems in ex. 13*c* show); what is more, at the first climax of the fugue, when all the voices have entered with the subject, it is heard again, proclaimed with due grandeur in slower-moving notes by a high, ringing trumpet with a pair of oboes (ex. 13*d*). Then the fugue resumes, with the second line of the chorale melody now worked into the texture, and again proclaimed by the trumpet. The same procedure continues, so that the whole chorale is absorbed within the fugue and sounded on the trumpet.

Next comes a duet for soprano and bass, with a busy violin part and continuo support. While the bass sings a new, free line, the soprano counterpoints it with a fresh variant of the chorale (ex. 13*e*). After a recitative for bass and a brief soprano aria, there is a chorus in which the chorale is treated in a new way. There is an allusion to it at the beginning (ex. 13*f*), and then the chorus enters and sings the chorale in unison, in a different rhythm and against a rich orchestral fabric (ex. 13*g*). The cantata ends with a tenor recitative, a duet for alto and tenor – and a final statement of the chorale, in which the congregation could join, set in four-part harmony.

Last years

Bach traveled a certain amount during his Leipzig years, often to inspect organs, sometimes to perform; he several times went to Dresden, where he held a title as Court Composer. In 1741 he went there to present one of his patrons with a new work, the *Goldberg Variations* (named after the young harpsichordist, probably a pupil of Bach's, whom the patron is said to have employed). This, which Bach later published as the fourth and last book in his *Clavier-Übung*, is his longest and most demanding harpsichord work; it uses traditional variation form but in a new way, with only the bass pattern of the melody stated at the opening being used and with 30 variations which in turn dazzle by their virtuosity, move by their depth of expression and fascinate by their contrapuntal elaboration. The set is like a summation of the musical forms that Bach had used throughout his life in his harpsichord music – French overture, fugue, invention, dance movements and so on, all linked by what is in effect a ground bass.

There is reason to think that Bach, in several of his late works, was setting down a lifetime's experience in composition, almost as if he were preparing a musical testament of an era. Another journey he made in 1741 was to Berlin, probably to his son Carl Philipp Emanuel, now court harpsichordist there. A visit to Berlin six years later proved particularly important. His son's employer, Frederick the Great of Prussia, admired his learned art and invited him to improvise at the piano a fugue on a theme by Frederick himself (he was a skilled flutist and a composer). Bach did so, and promised to publish the fugue; but when he got home to Leipzig he decided to go further than that and offer the king a musical collection built around his theme. This he called *Musical Offering*. It includes not only a written-out version of the improvised fugue but also a larger fugue, for six voices (playable on the organ), a series of canons of different kinds, and a trio sonata for flute, violin and continuo – this sonata, some of it in a distinctly more modern style than the rest, was clearly intended to please the flute-playing king, the more so because he worked the royal theme into it (ex. VI.14). The theme is ingeniously used, especially in the canons; in some it is in canon with itself, in others it accompanies a canon on fresh material. Here again we see Bach, in his last years, anxious to enshrine his art.

ex. VI.14

In fugue composition, too, Bach left a monument. He wrote, probably in the early 1740s, a work that he called *The Art of Fugue*. It has fugues of all sorts: simple, inverted, double, triple and quadruple, in the French style, and "mirror-wise" – this last meaning a fugue in which all the music could be played inverted (high notes for low ones, upwards-moving phrases for downwards, etc), a tremendous *tour de force* of technique for a composer (ex. VI.15*b* shows a passage in original and mirror forms). For this work Bach provided his own theme (ex. 15*a*), not unlike the king's, but somewhat more flexible and better adapted to the smooth textures that Bach used here. In this rather austere, abstract work it could well be that Bach was setting down models of his fugal art, for a generation that no longer cherished it.

The work we call the B minor Mass may belong to the same category. Bach wrote a "Missa" (the shorter, Lutheran Mass) in 1733, dedicating it to the Dresden court. This consists of a Kyrie and Gloria, the first two movements of the traditional Roman Catholic Mass. It was not until the late 1740s that he enlarged the work into a full Roman Catholic Mass, which he did by composing two new movements and adapting a number of others from cantatas and similar works. The B minor Mass was never performed by Bach, nor intended for performance, and it again seems that in putting it together he was satisfying his desire to create a model example of this ancient and traditional form. In this work, as in the other late compositions of the same sort, he used a wide variety of forms and techniques, some of them belonging to earlier eras. Sometimes he worked old plainsong melodies into the texture, as was done in medieval and Renaissance music; there are also plain fugal movements without independent orchestral accompaniment, of a kind long outdated in the 1740s.

ex. VI,.15

The music on the two lower staves is a 'mirror' reflection of that on the two upper, voice by voice
(as shown by the dotted lines on the first two tones of each entry)

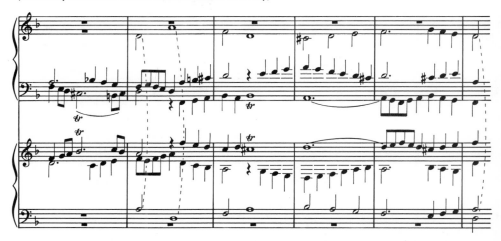

Bach was in fact regarded in his day as an old-fashioned composer, and properly so. He was not "old-fashioned" because he was out of touch with new currents of musical thought; on the contrary, he was familiar with the works of men like Telemann, Hasse (the leading opera composer at Dresden), Pergolesi and of course Vivaldi. He simply chose a more conservative path. He was criticized for his methods – for example, writing music too intricate in line and counterpoint to be "natural" (which to the new theorists of the mid-eighteenth century meant tuneful and lightly accompanied), and asking voices to sing lines as complicated as those he could play on the keyboard (there is some truth in that). When he died in the summer of 1750, after a year of uncertain health and finally blindness, he could look back on the music he had created and see in it a comprehensive summary of the musical art of the Baroque period, drawn together with an unparalleled inventiveness and intellectual concentration.

Handel

The other great composer of the late Baroque period, George Frideric Handel, was born in a neighboring province of Germany within four weeks of J. S. Bach, into the same religious faith and a similar social background. But while Bach remained in central Germany, and continued composing in the manner traditional to his background, Handel traveled widely and made his career far away from his homeland – and his music reflects his cosmopolitan life and the taste of the wider public for whom he composed.

Early years: Germany and Italy

Handel was born in the Saxon town of Halle in 1685. His father, a barber-surgeon, discouraged his musical leanings; he presumably wanted his son to enter a profession less hazardous and more respected, and directed him towards the law. As a boy, Handel had to pursue music surreptitiously; he is said to have sneaked a clavichord into an attic where he could practice unheard. But when the family visited the nearby court at Weissenfels, where his father was court surgeon, the duke heard Handel playing the organ and advised his father to let him study music. Handel's house stood close by the city's main Lutheran church, and the boy became

George Frideric Handel		Life
1685	born in Halle, 23 February	
1694	pupil of Zachow at the Church of Our Lady, Halle	
1702	law student at Halle University; organist of the Calvinist cathedral	
1703	violinist and harpsichordist in Hamburg opera orchestra	
1705	*Almira* (Hamburg)	
1706–9	Italy: Florence, Rome and Venice; contact with the Scarlattis and Corelli; oratorios, operas, many cantatas	
1710	*Kapellmeister* to the Elector of Hanover; first visit to London	
1711	*Rinaldo* (London); Hanover	
1712	settled in London	
1717	*Water Music*; director of music to Earl of Carnarvon (later Duke of Chandos) at Cannons, near London	
1718	*Acis and Galatea*	
1719	visit to Germany to recruit singers for the Royal Academy of Music, of which he was musical director	
1723	composer to the Chapel Royal	
1724	*Julius Caesar*	
1726	naturalized English	
1727	anthems for George II's coronation, including *Zadok the Priest*	
1729	second Royal Academy established after collapse of first; to Italy to recruit singers	
1733	first organ concertos	
1735	first Lent series of oratorios in London; *Alcina*	
1737	collapse of Handel's opera company (and its rival, the Opera of the Nobility); Handel ill	
1739	*Saul, Israel in Egypt*; composed 12 Grand Concertos, op. 6	
1742	*Messiah* (Dublin)	
1752	*Jephtha*; deterioration of eyesight leading to virtual blindness in two years	
1759	died in London, 13 April	

George Frideric Handel   Works

Operas (over 40) Almira (1705), Rinaldo (1711), Giulio Cesare (1724), Rodelinda (1725), Orlando (1732), Ariodante (1735), Alcina (1735), Serse (1738)

Oratorios (over 30) Acis and Galatea (1718), Athalia (1733), Alexander's Feast (1736), Saul (1739), Israel in Egypt (1739), Messiah (1742), Samson (1743), Semele (1744), Belshazzar (1745), Judas Maccabaeus (1747), Solomon (1749), Jephtha (1752)

Other sacred vocal music 11 Chandos anthems; 4 coronation anthems; Utrecht Te Deum and Jubilate (1713); Latin church music – Dixit Dominus (1707)

Secular vocal music over 100 Italian cantatas; trios, duets, songs

Orchestral music Water Music (1717); 6 Concerti grossi, op. 3 (1734); 12 Grand Concertos, op. 6 (1740); Music for Royal Fireworks (1749); organ concertos; suites, overtures, dance movements

Chamber music trio sonatas; sonatas for recorder, flute, oboe, violin

Keyboard music harpsichord suites, dance movements, chaconnes, airs, preludes, fugues

a pupil of Zachow, the organist there, under whom he made rapid progress both as composer and as player (of the violin as well as keyboard instruments). When he was 17 he entered the university, and he also took a temporary post as organist of the Calvinist cathedral.

A year later, he left Halle and went to Hamburg, a busy commercial center with a lively musical life and an opera house. It was at the opera house that he found employment, as a second violinist and later as harpsichordist; and he made friends with Johann Mattheson (1681–1764), later an eminent composer and theorist. He and Mattheson went to Lübeck in 1703 to hear Buxtehude (as Bach did later: see p. 160) and they evidently considered applying to succeed him, being put off, however, by the obligation to marry Buxtehude's daughter. Handel, it seems, was already wedded to an operatic career. His first opera, *Almira*, was given at the beginning of 1705 (he was still not quite 20) and his second a few weeks later. The first was a success, the second a failure.

Handel composed two further operas for Hamburg, but by the time they were given, in 1708, he had left the city. There was only one place that an ambitious young composer keen on opera could study: Italy. He was in fact invited there by a prince of the Medici family, from Florence, and it is to that city that he went at the end of 1706. He spent more than three years in Italy, dividing his time between Florence, Rome and Venice, with a journey to Naples. Opera was now forbidden at Rome, by papal decree; but a number of cardinals and princes in or near the city were noted patrons and at least four of these men commissioned music from Handel or employed him. He wrote two oratorios there, one a moral tale about abstract virtues, the other a setting of the Resurrection story which was spectacularly performed on a stage. He also wrote numerous cantatas – not sacred works, like Bach's, but mostly pieces some ten minutes long for solo voice and continuo consisting of two songs (usually about unrequited love) each preceded by a recitative. Handel quickly developed a new vein of melody suited to the Italian language, thus acquiring the experience he needed to be a success in the opera house. These fluent, graceful pieces offer the earliest evidence of the great melodist that

Handel was to be. It was in Rome, too, that he composed a group of works for the church, writing in Latin for the Roman Catholic liturgy. His brilliant *Dixit Dominus*, written in 1707, shows with its broad lines, its striking and picturesque choral effects and its vigorous, punched-out rhythms that he was already a masterly composer for chorus.

As an opera composer, he had two notable successes: in Florence, probably at the end of 1707, and in Venice, in winter 1709–10, when his *Agrippina* was so well received that it was given 27 times in all, an exceptionally high number.

In Italy Handel met many of the leading composers of the day, among them Corelli, the Scarlattis, father and son, and Vivaldi. He is said to have engaged in competition with Domenico Scarlatti, whom he far surpassed on the organ though on the harpsichord they were adjudged equals. He was much influenced in his composition by some of these men, in particular Alessandro Scarlatti, whose warm, flowing melodic style was to be his model. He also met potential patrons, among them several Englishmen who pressed him to go to London; but the invitation he accepted was from the Elector of Hanover, and when in 1710 he left Italy it was to the north German city of Hanover he went, where he was appointed *Kapellmeister* at the electoral court.

London: the early years

One of Handel's conditions of acceptance of the post at Hanover was that he should immediately take a year's leave for a visit to England. The Elector of Hanover was in fact the heir to the English throne, then occupied by the aging Queen Anne; possibly there was an understanding that Handel would eventually work for him when he came to London. Handel spent his first visit to the English capital in establishing a position for himself there. London had a flourishing theatrical life, but opera was not yet a regular part of it; a few English operas had been given, and some in Italian, with mixed success. English connoisseurs of music were realizing that if they wanted to hear the kinds of singing that they had heard in Italy and in some German cities there would have to be an Italian opera house in London. So they set about founding one. It still exists.

At the beginning of 1711, then, Handel composed the first Italian opera written specially for London, *Rinaldo*. It was a huge success, but it also started a controversy – for while the audiences were delighted with the singing, the music itself and the theatrical effects (which included not only ingenious machinery for scene transformations and the release of live sparrows for a woodland episode), some London intellectuals were contemptuous of the effects and scorned the idea of opera in Italian, sung by castratos before an English-speaking audience.

Handel went back to Hanover in the summer, and remained there for more than a year, occupied with composing duets for Princess Caroline and some instrumental music, and with learning English. By the fall of 1712 he was back in London, having been allowed leave "for a reasonable time". In effect, he stayed for the rest of his life. He lived at first at the house of Lord Burlington, a noted patron of the arts, where he met many of the leading literary men in London; while he was there he composed four more operas. He began to establish himself at the English court, composing a *Te Deum* and *Jubilate* for performance at St Paul's Cathedral in celebration of the Peace of Utrecht and an ode in honor of Queen Anne's birthday. That was in 1713, in which year the queen awarded him a generous salary. The following year, however, she died, and the Elector of Hanover – Handel's employer – came to London as the new king, George I. Stories have been told of how Handel, embarrassed at having overstayed his leave from Hanover, sought to restore his favor with George I by arranging a serenade for him at a water-party on the Thames. The tale is unlikely, for within days of his arrival in England George had heard music by Handel and had doubled his salary; probably Handel was never truly out of royal favor. But the music for a water-party – one is known to have taken place in 1717 – survives and is among the most popular of his works. The *Water Music* is in three sections: one in F, using horns along with the strings and oboes; one in D, with trumpets; and one in G, mainly in a more chamber-music-like style, using flutes. One might guess that the royal barges went up-river to the F major music, that the king dined to the pieces in G, and that he returned downstream to Westminster to the ringing trumpets in D. The music borrows from the grand ceremonial style that was particularly favored in France, and consists mainly of dances. An exception is the fanfare-like movement designed to show off the horns and the way they could ring across the water.

About 1717 Handel took a position as resident composer at the country house, just outside London, of the Earl of Carnarvon (later Duke of Chandos), a newly rich nobleman with a small musical establishment. Handel remained at this house, Cannons, until about 1720, and composed both sacred and dramatic music there. The main sacred works are the 11 "Chandos anthems", pieces very much in the Purcellian tradition but with an Italianate melodic style that is expressive and colorful: they reflect the confident, worldly attitudes of the Anglican church of the time. The two dramatic works, however, proved to be of greater importance. One of them, a setting of the biblical story of Esther, was in effect Handel's first English oratorio. The other was *Acis and Galatea*, a miniature opera on the mythological tale of the love of the shepherd Acis for the nymph-goddess Galatea and the jealous intervention of the giant Polyphemus who slays Acis. Probably composed for a handful of singers and a tiny orchestra, for performance on the terrace of a country mansion with gardens, woods and lakes nearby, it has a grace and freshness all its own. Although the artificial pastoral convention is used, the emotions expressed are real and powerful. The first half chiefly consists of love-songs for Acis and Galatea themselves, in Handel's fluent, sensuous melodic style and with some happy touches of nature imagery; Acis's "Love in her eyes sits playing" (see Listening Note VI.G) is typical of his gently amorous manner. The second half moves on to tragedy, but not without humor: the grotesque Polyphemus sings his famous serenade to Galatea's beauty, "O ruddier than the cherry", to the accompaniment of a small, high-pitched recorder. The climax comes in Galatea's final song, over Acis's body, where in sublime music she uses her godlike powers to turn him into a spring so that he will live for ever; the soft, throbbing accompaniment of recorders and low violins at the same time conveys the tenderness of her emotions and the flow of the "crystal flood" that Acis has become.

The opera ventures

Up to this time, operatic life in London had been haphazard and poorly run. A group of noblemen now decided to put it on a firmer basis and founded an organization to finance and regularize the hiring of theaters, players, singers, scene designers, composers and so on, and to raise money by selling subscriptions for seats. It was called the Royal Academy of Music; the king's patronage meant that "Royal" could be used. Handel, appointed musical director, went off in 1719 to the main courts and opera centers of Europe to hear singers and engage those he wanted. In 1720 the Academy opened; Handel's *Radamisto* was its second opera,

80 Handel: marble statue, 1738, by Louis François Roubiliac, commissioned for Vauxhall Gardens. Victoria and Albert Museum, London.

Listening Note VI.G

Handel: *Acis and Galatea* (1718), "Love in her eyes sits playing"

Dramatic context: The first act of the masque *Acis and Galatea* treats the idyllic, pastoral love of the shepherd Acis and the nymph Galatea; the second deals with the intrusion of the giant Polyphemus who kills Acis. "Love in her eyes sits playing" is sung by Acis in Act 1.

Love in her eyes sits playing,
And sheds delicious death;
Love on her lips is straying,
And warbling in her breath!
  Love on her breast sits panting,
  And swells with soft desire;
  No grace, no charm is wanting,
  To set the heart on fire.
Love in her eyes . . . etc.

(words probably by John Gay, or Alexander Pope)

The music: This song (Larghetto, E♭) is for tenor voice with oboe, strings and continuo. It is in *da capo* form: that is, the first part – here a setting of the first four lines of the text – is repeated in full after the second. There is first a short orchestral preface, the melody of which is echoed by the singer on his entry (m. 7). The lilting rhythm and graceful line are characteristic of the amorous "pastoral" tradition to which *Acis and Galatea* belongs. The tenor rounds off his first solo with an elegant cadence ("warbling in her breath") in the dominant, B♭. The orchestra reminds us of the opening phrase, bringing the music back to E♭; after that, there is a continuous vocal line – note the occasional echoing phrase from the oboe, the pause on "death", the little roulade on "breath" – to the final cadence. In the second section, the orchestra is silent, apart from the supporting continuo instruments; the music, beginning in c and ending in g (a typical scheme), uses and extends material from the first section. Then the first section is repeated; in this context the singer is free to add, if he wishes, some elaboration or decoration of the melodic line to enhance its appeal and expressiveness.

---

performed at the King's Theatre to great applause.

The main triumphs of the Academy were still to come, however. For the second season, some of the singers Handel had hired in 1719 arrived, notably the superb castrato Senesino; his powerful alto voice made him the ideal singer of the big heroic roles. Another composer, Giovanni Bononcini (1670–1747), was enlisted to help supply new operas, which he did at least as successfully as Handel himself. Then in 1723 a new soprano, Francesca Cuzzoni, arrived; her brilliant singing created a sensation. In 1724 and 1725 Handel composed some of his finest operatic music, particularly in *Giulio Cesare* and *Rodelinda*.

We may pause to look at the former – an opera about Julius Caesar and his doings in Egypt – as an example of late Baroque serious opera. Like most of its kind, it is constructed almost entirely of arias, with recitatives between them. The dramatic action takes place in the recitatives, and in the arias the characters sing of their emotions. Most of the arias are in *da capo* form, in which the opening section is repeated after a short middle section (*A–B–A*); and at the end of each aria the character who has sung it goes off the stage – partly so that he can be applauded without disturbing the action and partly because his aria is a musical and dramatic climax to the scene. In *Giulio Cesare*, there are six main characters: Julius Caesar himself (taken by a male alto, Senesino), the Egyptian Queen, Cleopatra (soprano, Cuzzoni), Ptolemy, Cleopatra's brother, and as King of Egypt her rival (another

81 Scene from Handel's *Flavio*, believed to show Gaetano Berenstadt (*right*), Senesino (*left*) and Cuzzoni: engraving by J. Vanderbank.

male alto), Cornelia, the widow of Caesar's former Roman enemy Pompey (contralto), and her son Sextus (male soprano), and the Egyptian general Achillas (bass – the bass voice was usually reserved to military men). The plot is involved: briefly, it deals with the rivalries of Cleopatra and Ptolemy for the Egyptian throne and their courting of Caesar's help – Ptolemy by treacherously murdering Caesar's Roman rival (whose widow he then pursues) and Cleopatra by attempting to ensnare him with her beauty.

The music is carefully planned to preserve the relative status of the cast members; the table below shows the quantity assigned to each. It is also designed to show the qualities of character of those they are portraying. The simplest is Achillas, a bluff soldier, direct in expression over his actions, whether military or amorous (for he too is drawn to Cornelia). Ptolemy's cruel, vengeful, unscrupulous disposition is artfully conveyed, nowhere more tellingly than in the orchestral prelude to his final aria where the eccentric line (ex. VI.16a) seems to signify his deviousness. Cornelia typifies the virtues of a wife of ancient Rome, loyal to her husband's memory, Sextus the virtues of a loyal son whose one thought is of revenge. The most complex characters are Caesar and Cleopatra themselves. Caesar starts with a song of triumph on landing in Egypt, continues with an outburst of fury at Ptolemy's outrage and his assumption that he could gain favor by killing a Roman (ex. 16b: music of this kind, sung at high pitch but with a man's lungs and chest cavity, could

ex. VI.16

b You are impious, I tell you; flee from my sight, you are all cruelty.
c You are my star, dear hope.

d I shall bewail my fate, so cruel and so harsh, as long as there is life in my breast.

have immense force; a contemporary described Senesino as "thundering out" his music). His Roman nobility is conveyed in a somber scene where he stands by the urn containing Pompey's ashes and pays tribute to his former enemy. The cautious, wily military man is portrayed in another aria, where on meeting Ptolemy he compares himself to the huntsman who goes silent and concealed – a part in the orchestra for horn, the instrument of the hunt, drives the point home, and represents another typical piece of imagery of the kind composers used to add variety and color. His later arias further enlarge the character – there is a fiery, warlike song when he finds himself betrayed and trapped, a plea for comfort in his grief at supposedly losing his beloved and a song of triumph in the end (for all ends well in an eighteenth-century serious opera, and Caesar and Cleopatra are united: this is not of course historically true).

character	arias	shorter items	duets
Caesar	8	2	1
Cleopatra	8	1	1
Sextus	5	—	1
Cornelia	3	2	1
Ptolemy	3	1	—
Achillas	3	—	—

No less rich is Handel's drawing of Cleopatra's character in his music. She begins with a spirited, kittenish group of arias, showing her as an ambitious young woman (ex. 16*c* shows the opening of the third of them). She begins Act 2 by attempting, in disguise as a serving-maid, to seduce Caesar, and shows here a voluptuous side to her personality, which Handel stresses by providing an exceptionally rich accompaniment, with a harp, a theorbo (a large lute) and a viol to add density and color to the orchestra of strings, oboes and bassoon. Now, with the onset of love, she becomes an emotionally more powerful character, and when she believes

Caesar to have been killed she mourns him eloquently (ex. 16*d*). Later, imprisoned by her brother, she mourns her fate in truly tragic terms, and here Handel uses the *da capo* aria in an unusual way, making the middle section an outburst of rage and determination. Her last aria, when she is freed by Caesar and pledged to him, recalls the style of the earlier ones but with a new breadth to convey her growth of stature.

Not all of Handel's operas are musically as rich or dramatically as convincing as *Giulio Cesare*. The Royal Academy continued putting them on, but it also continued steadily to lose money, and in 1728 it collapsed. There had been errors of judgment, for example the hiring of another soprano, Faustina Bordoni, which led to the forming of factions and eventually an undignified fight on the stage between the two ladies. Meanwhile, Handel had been active in other spheres: in 1723 he was appointed composer of the Chapel Royal, and he wrote four anthems for the coronation of George II in Westminster Abbey in 1727 (one, *Zadok the Priest*, has been performed at every British coronation since). That year he became a naturalized English subject.

Opera however remained in the forefront of his mind. Handel and the Academy theater manager decided to put on operas themselves, and after another continental trip to find singers they were ready to start at the end of 1729. Their success was limited. Several operas failed, and the singers did not much please the audiences. Soon a rival opera organization, known as the Opera of the Nobility (it was run by a group of noblemen), was set up; from 1733 London, which could not support one opera company, was asked to support two. Not surprisingly, both collapsed, in 1737; by then Handel had composed no fewer than 13 new operas since the closing of the Academy, including some of his finest – notable are *Orlando* and *Alcina*, not on heroic themes like the Academy ones but based on tales of magic, with their basis in medieval literature rather than ancient history or mythology. Handel's interest in opera – or perhaps his confidence in the possibility of pursuing it successfully – seems to have faded during the 1730s, and after four more he finally abandoned the form in 1741. By then he had a good idea of the new directions his creative career was taking.

The move to oratorio

Back in 1718, as we saw, Handel had written two dramatic works to English words. The occasion for them had passed in the 1720s and they had been put aside. But in 1732 *Esther* was privately performed, by friends of Handel's, at a London tavern. Then another group, unconnected with Handel, advertised a performance; without a copyright law, Handel could not prevent it, but he could – and did – retaliate, by giving a performance himself, adding extra music so that his version would seem to be the most up-to-date and authoritative. The Bishop of London, however, forbade him to have the story acted on the stage. A little later, the same happened with *Acis and Galatea* – a performance by rivals, a retaliation by Handel with extra music but no stage action.

The success of these works gave Handel new ideas about his future. In 1733 he performed a new oratorio, *Deborah*, after the biblical story, during Lent, when operas were not allowed; that summer, in Oxford, he gave *Acis and Galatea* and another new oratorio, *Athalia*. In Lent 1735 he held an oratorio season in London, and during the intermissions he played organ concertos – an entirely new genre in which, during the 1730s and 40s, Handel (and then a few other composers in England) created a repertory. Handel's own concertos are notable for their brilliance and grandeur, and his performances helped attract audiences.

During the late 1730s, as Handel's interest in opera waned, he turned increasingly to other large-scale vocal forms. There is an ode in honor of music, to words by Dryden, *Alexander's Feast*, two more oratorios, the dramatic *Saul* and the choral epic *Israel in Egypt*, and in 1740 a Milton setting *L'Allegro ed il Penseroso* ("The cheerful man and the thoughtful man"). They met with only mixed success. Handel also wrote a quantity of instrumental works around this time; some of his earlier ones had been collected and issued in print by the leading London publisher, John Walsh, and now Handel added his finest ones, a set of 12 concertos for strings, op. 6, written in the first place for use at his oratorio concerts. These and Bach's Brandenburg Concertos stand as twin peaks of the Baroque concerto repertory. Handel's are not as consistent in form or style as Bach's, nor as carefully worked out; he composed in broader strokes and depended more on the striking quality of his ideas, his melodic gift and the sheer originality and variety of the music. Some of the concertos have dance movements, some have elaborate fugues, some have large-scale ritornello movements, some are not much more than exquisite melodies with accompaniment.

In 1741, Handel was invited to visit Dublin and give concerts in aid of charities there. He accepted, and set about preparing two new works. One was what he called a "Sacred Oratorio", better known as *Messiah*; the other was *Samson*, based on verse by Milton. He arrived there in November, and gave two concert series with great success. The climax was the first performance, on 13 April 1742, of *Messiah*. The hall was full; the ladies had been asked to wear dresses without hoops, and the gentlemen to abandon their swords, so that more people could be admitted.

82 Opening of the aria "Ev'ry valley" from the autograph of Handel's *Messiah*, 1741. British Library, London.

A reporter wrote that "words are wanting to express the exquisite delight it afforded to the admiring crouded audience. The sublime, the grand, and the tender, adapted to the most elevated, majestick and moving words, conspired to transport and charm the ravished heart and ear".

Messiah (not *The Messiah*) has become not only the most famous and most loved of Handel's works but also the most famous and most loved of choral works in the English-speaking world. Handel was at his most inspired when composing it during six weeks in the summer of 1741. He discovered fresh stimulus in the familiar biblical words that his friend Charles Jennens had put together for him, and recalled not only the traditions of German Passion music in which he had been brought up but also the melodic grace of his Italian settings (some of the choruses use music he had first composed as Italian love duets) and the grand choral effects that he had inherited from the English tradition through Purcell. Handel's theatrical sense is present in *Messiah* too, in the music announcing the birth of Christ (with the distant trumpets and the effect as of a choir of angels), in the drama of the Passion music, above all in the grandeur of the most famous number, the Hallelujah chorus: here Handel said that, while composing it, he saw "the great God himself upon his throne, and all his company of angels" (see Listening Note VI.H).

Back in London, Handel now seems to have had a clear picture of his future activities. Opera was now behind him; his main occupation was to give seasons of oratorios and similar works at Covent Garden theater. He was composing now not primarily for the small, aristocratic class with inherited wealth, land and titles, but for a more broadly based middle-class public as well who, created by the new commercial and industrial activity that had already made London the biggest, busiest and most prosperous city in the world, were keen to share the cultural pleasures of the upper classes but were also touched by the religious spirit of the times and thus wanted "improvement" from their pleasures as well as diversion.

Handel gave his new *Samson* (he had not performed it in Dublin) in Lent 1743, with great success; *Messiah*, which followed, was a failure – the singing of biblical words in a theater offended many people and the work became popular in London only when, in 1750, Handel gave performances of it in a chapel for charity. The oratorio seasons continued. At some, Handel experimented – in 1744 he gave *Semele*, not an oratorio but more like an opera, based on an erotic story from classical mythology, set in English with oratorio-like choruses and with no acting. It was a failure; the new audiences found none of the moral uplift they were seeking. The same happened the following season with *Hercules*, another classical drama. These two are among Handel's finest works, the former for its portrayal of sensuous love (the well-known "Where'er you walk" comes from it), the latter for its powerful treatment of jealousy. Neither was liked in Handel's time and only recently have they come to be appreciated.

The oratorios chiefly admired in Handel's own day include, besides *Saul* and *Samson*, *Judas Maccabaeus* – a rousing, warlike piece that caught the national mood at the time of the 1745 Jacobite rising. Among the others is the particularly splendid *Solomon*, distinguished for its lavish writing both for the chorus and for instruments, and the single oratorio on a Christian theme, *Theodora*, which was indifferently received. Handel, famous for his dry wit, said to friends who commiserated with him on the empty house, "Never mind; the music will sound the better".

Each of the oratorios relates, in musical-dramatic terms, a story, usually a well-known Bible one. Each of the singers plays a particular character: in *Saul*, for

Listening Note VI.H

Handel: *Messiah* (1742), Hallelujah Chorus

Hallelujah! Hallelujah!
For the Lord God omnipotent reigneth
The Kingdom of this world is become
    the Kingdom of Our Lord
And of his Christ.
And he shall reign for ever and ever
King of Kings and Lord of Lords
And he shall reign for ever and ever
Hallelujah! Hallelujah!

This chorus, the most famous piece Handel wrote, ends the second of the three parts of his oratorio *Messiah*. His vigorous and triumphal choral style is demonstrated in the music of the opening, the repeated, emphatic Hallelujahs (ex. i). A new idea is introduced to the words "for the Lord omnipotent reigneth" (ex. ii) and this is worked in counterpoint against the cries of "Hallelujah".

This music reaches a cadence, in the home key of D; a quieter section of choral harmony ("The kingdom of this world") begins, but it is not quieter for long. Then there is a fugal setting of the words "and he shall reign for ever and ever" (ex. iii). But Handel rarely persisted with fugue in exultant or dramatic passages, and here he heightens the drama by having the top voices rise gradually up the scale, sustaining each tone ("King of Kings and Lord of Lords") while the lower ones pound away at "for ever and ever, Hallelujah". All this material is worked together to provide a climax, with the trumpets in the orchestra becoming increasingly prominent as the affirmation of faith is powerfully driven home.

ex. i

ex. ii

ex. iii

example, the Jewish king himself is a bass, his son Jonathan a tenor and David an alto. The chorus may assume different roles: sometimes they represent an army or a populace, sometimes they simply provide an external observer's commentary on events. In *Belshazzar* they start as a chorus of Babylonians, on their second appearance offer a general comment, on their third are captive Jews, and later take the part of the Persian army. Handel was careful in such situations to provide different kinds of music to indicate the character of the different groups. In *Theodora*, for example, the Romans have tuneful, rhythmic choruses while the Christians have grave contrapuntal ones. But many of the choruses culminate in the praise of God in a brilliant, exuberant vein, clearly influenced by the ceremonial Anglican church music of the time. As in the operas, the main action is in the recitatives, which here are of course in English (the new audience expected the words to be comprehensible, in their own tongue), and the arias express the characters' emotions. Although the oratorios were never acted on the stage, here too Handel thought in dramatic terms; the printed books of words in which the original audience could follow the performances even included stage directions.

The last of Handel's biblical oratorios was *Jephtha*, written in 1751. As he composed it his eyesight began to fail; at one point in the score, at the chorus "How dark, O Lord, are thy decrees, All hid from mortal sight", he noted in the margin that he had to break off owing to the failure of his eyes. He was able to resume, but by 1753 he was virtually blind; he continued to attend performances, and even managed to play organ concertos – at first he relied on his memory, but later had to improvise the solo sections, indicating to the orchestra when they should enter.

There are a number of enigmas surrounding Handel. One concerns his personal life. He never married, though he is said to have had some love affairs with women musicians; no word of scandal, however, in an age of gossip, has come down to us. Another, more troublesome, concerns his "borrowings". He often re-used music from an early work in a later one; *Rinaldo*, for example, hastily written when he first went to London, incorporates items from his Italian compositions. But he also used other composers' music – pieces by Keiser, Muffat, Telemann, even much older men like Carissimi, and countless others. Usually he adapted and rewrote what he used, nearly always improving it and stamping his own character upon it. He "borrowed" music frequently, extensively, and throughout his life; sometimes he bought music from abroad and within months of receiving it was using ideas from it in his own works. That there was deception in all this, and some kind of moral flaw, is clear; yet the individuality, the grandeur and the honesty that shine through his music provide their own answer.

At any rate, Handel was much esteemed by those who knew him. He was a quick-tempered man, but keenly witty, "impetuous, rough, and peremptory in his manners and conversation, but totally devoid of ill-nature or malevolence", wrote a contemporary. He had a gluttonous appetite. He played in private concerts, at the homes of patrons, in his young days, but gradually withdrew into a life of more privacy. He practiced the harpsichord a great deal; it is said that the keys of his instrument were worn hollow. He had friends, and sometimes visited them in the country; his London ones were mostly of the upper-middle class rather than his fellow musicians. He attended church regularly in his later years, going to St George's, Hanover Square, from his house nearby in Brook Street (which still stands). He died in April 1759, aged 74. Three thousand Londoners attended his funeral; he was buried in Westminster Abbey.

Chapter VII

The Classical Era

Classicism

"Classical" is a misused word. Even when it is used properly, it has several different though related meanings. Its chief misuse, these days, is when "classical music" is opposed to "popular music"; there it is intended to include all kinds of "serious" music, irrespective of when or for what purpose they were composed. Here we use the term mainly to denote the music of the period that runs roughly from 1750 to the death of Beethoven in 1827.

Why *classical*? That word, strictly, applies to the ancient Greeks and Romans, to "classical antiquity", the two great Western civilizations of early times. Many eras since then have looked back at "the ancients" and tried to borrow what is best about their cultures. They did so, as we have seen, in the Renaissance, and then again at the beginning of the Baroque period. But it was the mid-eighteenth century that truly began to rediscover classical antiquity, especially through archeology, and to build up a new picture of its simplicity, its grandeur, its serenity, its strength, its grace, all typified in the newly found and freshly excavated temples of Greece and southern Italy. The remains of Pompeii, for example, were found in 1748: artists drew them; engravers copied them, for wider circulation; theorists worked out the principles along which they were designed. Historians and estheticians – the most famous was the German J. J. Winckelmann (1717–68) – studied and praised the works of classical antiquity and put them forward as models for their own times. Creative artists quickly followed: Sir Joshua Reynolds (1723–92), for example, stressed that the highest achievement in painting depended on the use of Greek or Roman subjects and their representation of heroic or suffering humanity, a principle also followed notably by Jacques-Louis David (1748–1825), the official artist of the French Revolution, in his heroic paintings. Sculptors too, like Antonio Canova (1757–1822), used classical statues as the basis for their figures of modern men and women. Classical history, mythology and philosophy came to be increasingly influential, as the opera plots favored at this time show with their settings in ancient times and their identification with the ancient virtues.

Borrowing from the association of merit with the ancient civilizations, people have always regarded the word "classical" as implying a model of excellence. To say that something is "a classic" suggests, whether it be a poem or an automobile, that it is a superior example of its kind, still praised, admired and suitable to be considered a model. We also tend to use the word to imply something about design, for example in the expression "classical proportions", which means proportions that possess a natural balance, without extravagance or special originality, but following an accepted principle of rightness. It is the acceptance of such principles of "just proportion" and natural balance that marks out an important distinguishing feature of music of the Classical period. This was a time when virtually all composers pursued the same basic ideas as to how music should be constructed: the idea of balance between keys, to give the listener a clear sense of where the music was going, and between sections, so that the listener was always correctly oriented within a piece and had a good idea of what to expect of it. Composers could be original less by varying the systems of composition or the outlines within which they worked than by the ingenuity and the enterprise they could exercise to charm or surprise the listener.

It may be said that there was no "Classical period" in music, only a "Classical style", the one in which Haydn, Mozart and Beethoven wrote their masterpieces. In terms of "models of excellence", that is partly true. Yet the styles used by those

83 St Michael's Square, Vienna, with the Burgtheater (right foreground) and Spanish Riding School behind it: engraving (1783) by C. Schütz.

three men were not created by them alone; others writing at the same time composed in basically the same manner, and all drew on the same traditions. We shall now examine some of the ways in which the Classical style differs from that of the late Baroque, that used by Bach and Handel.

Rococo, galant

There are a number of intermediate stages between the Baroque and the Classical. As with the term "Baroque" itself, music historians have drawn on other disciplines for words to describe them. One such is "Rococo", a term that art historians have used particularly of French decorative work of the late seventeenth and early eighteenth centuries. In French architecture of that time, the strong, severe lines came to be broken or softened by shell-work (*rocaille* in French), and there developed a newly picturesque, elegant, fanciful style. Like all aspects of French culture and taste, this style traveled rapidly across Europe; it was particularly favored in southern Germany and Austria. It is always dangerous to try to draw close parallels between music and other arts, but (as we saw in the last chapter's discussion of Couperin, for example, p. 168) there was in music a similar breaking down of larger lines and a growing interest in graceful, detailed elaboration; it also manifested itself, though differently and somewhat later, in Germany, Austria and Italy (where the gentle melodies of the Neapolitan composers typically represent it). The Rococo, though not a central development in music history, represents a symptom of the breakdown of the severe grandeur of the Baroque, a breakdown that was essential if a new style was to replace it.

Another term from France, *galant*, has wider implications in the growth of the Classical style. It means "gallant", at its simplest; but its meaning in the arts was richer than that. It implied, first, the idea of pleasure, of a fairly straightforward, undemanding kind: sensuous pleasure, quite apart from moral uplift or deeper artistic satisfaction. It also implied a certain elegance and worldliness. Musically it carried a range of meanings. First, it meant a flowing melodic style, free of the complexities of counterpoint; for a *galant* melody to be heard to maximum advantage it would normally be lightly accompanied, generally by a continuo instrument (like the harpsichord) with a static or slow-moving bass line that did nothing to draw attention away from the melody. The ideal medium for *galant* melody was the singing voice, in a cantata or an operatic song (preferably on an amorous text); the composer would construct it in simple, regular phrases, answering one another in an agreeably predictable fashion, and the singer would shade the line expressively. Another popular medium was the flute (as opposed to the more old-fashioned and austere recorder), which was specially esteemed for its capacity for elegant and tender shading. The term *galant* could also imply the use of dance rhythms (the extra dance movements that Bach and others included in their keyboard suites were known as "galanteries"); it often signified the use of a number of stereotyped melodic phrases, akin to graceful bows or curtseys (see ex. VII.1), and always a fairly small scale.

ex. VII.1

The term *galant* came into use, applied to music, soon after the year 1700. The style it described began to gain currency in the 1720s but came to be the prevalent one only around the middle of the century, as the generation of Bach and Handel and their contemporaries disappeared and a new one assumed importance. By then, the driving bass lines of the Baroque masters, which could impart so much vitality to a piece, were giving way to ones that moved more slowly and merely served to support what went on above them. The Baroque preference for fugal texture was giving way to one in which the top line came an easy first, with the bass second and the middle ones nowhere. The long and generally quite irregular phrases of Baroque music gave way to shorter ones, usually in two- or four-measure patterns, in which the listener could sense the outcome as he heard the beginning.

The Enlightenment

What were the reasons for these changes in the language of music? A major one is that the climate of thought was changing, with what is called the Enlightenment. The early part of the eighteenth century saw important changes in philosophy, in the wake of the scientific discoveries of Isaac Newton in England and René Descartes in France: rationalism and humanitarian ideals came to the fore, mysticism and superstition faded. The idea of extending culture to the ordinary man and woman – that is, to the middle classes as well as the nobility to whom it had exclusively belonged in the past – was one of the goals of the Enlightenment: human life should be enriched by the arts. Thus we find, in the early eighteenth century, forms of opera arising that were given not only in foreign languages and private theaters but in native languages and in public. In France, the genre known as "opéra comique", in which songs were interspersed with spoken dialogue in simple stories about common folk, got decisively under way in the middle 1720s at the Paris "fair theaters", appealing to a public far wider than could ever have ventured into the court Opéra. In England, while Italian opera entertained the London aristocratic audiences, a middle-class public enjoyed, especially from the 1730s, lightweight operas with spoken dialogue, composed in a simple and tuneful style; these were performed not just in London but all over the country. In Germany, English operas of this kind, translated and given in Berlin and Hamburg around the

84 Song "The Absent Lover" from *The Musical Entertainer* (1737–9) by George Bickham.

middle of the century, provoked the development of the native German form, the *Singspiel*. And in Italy, new forms of comic opera appeared in the early part of the century, often in local dialects, in Naples, Venice and other centers, appealing with their popular subject-matter and their catchy melodies to a public that found the behavior of the classical and mythological figures of serious opera incomprehensible and their music boring.

Opera was only one of the media that showed this spread of culture. It was in these years that music publishing became a substantial industry, enabling ordinary people to buy music and sing or play it at home – on the instruments which, with the development of new manufacturing techniques, they could now afford. It became an important social accomplishment for a young woman, especially, to play the harpsichord or the piano; the flute and the violin, the other favored amateur instruments, remained on the whole male preserves. Numerous home tutors were published for these instruments in the eighteenth century. Composers, writing music for home consumption, were eager to make it easy enough to play yet interesting enough to play with taste and elegance; this was a factor in the shift, discussed above, towards a more regular melodic style. The amateur was also much encouraged to sing the music he or she might have heard at public entertainments: books of "favorite songs" from the newest operas (in London also those sung at the famous outdoor pleasure gardens) were printed and sold while they were fresh in the audience's memories.

It was not only opera that was attracting new listeners. It was in the eighteenth century that concert life began as we know it. In earlier times instrumental music was chiefly intended for performance at court or for groups of gentleman amateurs to play in their homes. Now a new phenomenon arose. Groups of people, often of both amateurs and professionals, got together to give concerts for their own pleasure (or for their living) and for the pleasure of others who came to hear them. In larger cities, where more professionals were to be found, orchestral concerts were regularly given. London and Paris led, and others were quick to follow. The concerts of court orchestras were often opened to a paying public. During the late eighteenth century in particular, concert life developed rapidly; traveling virtuosos went from city to city, organizing concerts in each, while local musicians of repute often gave annual "benefit concerts" (from which they retained the takings). The orchestra as an entity began to take firm shape. The concept of a public that came to concerts to listen was a novel one, demanding a novel approach to composition; it was more than ever necessary for a piece of music to have a logical and clearly perceptible shape, so that it would grasp and hold the listener's attention and interest. Composers rose to this challenge: above all, the three great men of the era, Haydn, Mozart and Beethoven.

Opera

The one genre of music that, in the middle of the eighteenth century, was regarded as supreme across Europe was Italian opera. There were opera houses in all the great cities of Italy. But there were more north of the Alps where Italian opera was given: in Vienna, for example, at many German courts (like those in Munich, Stuttgart, Dresden and Berlin), and in London; even as far afield as Warsaw, Stockholm and St Petersburg (now Leningrad) the fashion for this most polished and sophisticated form of art was admired and occasionally indulged. Paris, with its French-language traditions of theater and opera, tried to resist it, but there too supporters of Italian opera proclaimed its superiority to the native product.

In the last chapter, looking at the music of such men as Alessandro Scarlatti, Pergolesi and Handel, we saw the kind of opera that was generally performed. This, *opera seria*, enjoyed a rich flowering around the mid-eighteenth century, especially with composers like Johann Adolf Hasse (1699–1783, a German who worked in Naples, Venice, Dresden and Vienna), Nicolò Jommelli (1714–74, active in Stuttgart, Naples and north Italy) and Tommaso Traetta (1727–79, active throughout Italy). These and many others, usually setting librettos written with supreme elegance and professionalism by the priest and poet Pietro Metastasio (1698–1782), the leading librettist of the day, brought to opera the new and graceful melodic style of *galant* music. Their operas consisted almost exclusively of arias (in which a character expressed his feelings) linked by recitatives (in which the action of the drama took place). In an age when beautiful and athletic singing was much prized, and singers commanded fees equivalent to those of today's pop stars, composers were ready to supply the music that the singers wanted.

Gluck

It is in the "reform" of this kind of opera that Christoph Willibald Gluck was particularly important. Gluck was born in south Germany, near the present Czech border, in 1714; he studied in Prague (the nearest large city), then Vienna (capital of the Austro-Hungarian Empire) and finally in Italy. He worked in Italy, then briefly in London, but mainly in Vienna; there he moved in intellectual circles where dissatisfaction was felt with existing art forms – characteristic of Enlightenment thinking, reflecting the desire to portray emotion more simply, more truthfully, and in a manner more meaningful to the person of feeling and sensibility. In London, Gluck had seen the actor David Garrick, famous for his capacity to move the emotions of his audiences. In Vienna he met the ballet choreographer Angiolini, who was eager to promote the "action ballet" as opposed to the older decorative dance, and the poet Raniero de Calzabigi, who believed that opera should be built around the natural expression of human emotions rather than the heroics of the Metastasio tradition. Also in Vienna, through court circles, he came into contact with French musical-dramatic traditions.

Gluck, then, almost seems to have been selected by destiny to draw together these threads and produce a new kind of opera to reflect the changing times. And in fact his own musical gifts – their limitations, too – pointed him in the same direction. He was not a fluent melodist or a wide-ranging harmonist, but had a gift for creating a strong atmosphere by simple means. His first "reform" work was a ballet, *Don Juan* (1761). The next year came his opera *Orfeo ed Euridice*, a new treatment of the story of Orpheus's recovery of his dead wife, Eurydice, from Hades by the power of his music and his subsequent loss of her when compelled, in spite of the gods' edict, to

Christoph Willibald Gluck		Works
born Erasbach, 1714; *died* Vienna, 1787		

Operas (over 40) Artaserse (1741), Orfeo ed Euridice (1762; rev. 1774 as Orphée et Euridice), La rencontre imprévue (1764), Alceste (1767; rev. in French 1776), Paride ed Elena (1770), Iphigénie en Aulide (1774), Armide (1777), Iphigénie en Tauride (1779)

Ballets Don Juan (1761)

Songs	*Sacred vocal music*	*Chamber music*

85 Frontispiece to the first edition of Gluck's *Orfeo ed Euridice* (Paris, 1764).

Plate 13 *Opposite Florentine Court Musicians*: painting by Anton Domenico Gabbiani (1652–1726). Palazzo Pitti, Florence. A sonata for violin and harpsichord (see pp. 72, 142).

look back at her. (In this version she is restored a second time; the eighteenth century, believing that virtue must not go unrewarded, abhorred unhappy endings.)

Orfeo, then, differs from most operas of its time in a number of important ways. First, it avoids what was then the usual type of plot, with dynastic rivalries, amorous misunderstandings, disguises and so on in favor of a simple, familiar tale of all-consuming love. Secondly, it has no *da capo* arias with elaborate writing for the voice; instead there are arias of unusually varied lengths whose scale and design are

dictated by nothing other than the needs of the situation. Thirdly, the old pattern of alternate recitative and aria, with sharp breaks between them in the musical texture, is dropped in favor of a continuous sequence of linked numbers, always with orchestral support (avoiding the unnaturalness of the change of texture when recitative had only harpsichord accompaniment). Fourthly, a central role is assigned to the chorus – as mourners, as Furies, as Blessed Spirits – stressing the collective nature of human emotion. The opera begins with mourners around Eurydice's tomb, and continues with Orpheus singing a series of short verses, increasingly impassioned, interspersed by outbursts in orchestrally-accompanied recitative; nothing could be more distant from the usual operatic opening. Then the second act is devoted entirely to Orpheus's visit to Hades, his progressive taming of the Furies by his pleas, and his taking Eurydice away (the contrast between the dark, pounding, minor-key music for Hades and the soft, gentle sounds for the Elysian Fields is a stroke of genius). In Act 3, Eurydice implores him to look back on her, and as he gives way and does so she falls lifeless, at which he sings Gluck's most famous song, "Che farò senza Euridice" ("What shall I do without Eurydice"); the gods eventually restore her, and their reunion is celebrated in a ballet and chorus.

Gluck wrote more "reform" operas, including *Alceste* (1767; his and Calzabigi's reform principles are expounded in a preface to the score) and, in Paris, *Iphigénie en Tauride* (1779) – for, having changed the course of opera in central Europe, he resolved to do the same in the European intellectual capital, where he gave new, French versions of *Orfeo* and *Alceste* and four further operas. He succeeded. Gluck was not the only reformer, nor even the first (Jommelli and Traetta, for example, had attempted similar reforms); but he stands alone in his capacity to represent, in intense and poignant form, the emotions of suffering humans in the tales of classical mythology, using only the simplest means. Gluck died in 1787, universally revered; he influenced those around him, including Mozart, but it was not until the time of Berlioz and Wagner that he had true successors.

Stamitz

From time to time, the accidents of history have a profound effect on the arts. In 1742 Carl Theodor became hereditary ruler (or Elector) of the Palatinate, a province in south-west Germany whose center was Mannheim. He was rich, and his passion was music. He engaged a young violinist of Bohemian descent, Johann Stamitz (1717–57); to judge by the rapid rise in his salary, Stamitz served well, and in 1745–6 he became concertmaster and in 1750 director of the instrumental music. Seven years later he died, not yet 40. But he had laid at Mannheim the foundations of an orchestral tradition that was to influence the greatest composers of the day and the central orchestral genre, the symphony.

The Mannheim School

Stamitz composed more than 50 symphonies, and in them developed new styles of using instruments, treating strings and winds in quite different ways (Baroque composers gave them virtually the same kinds of music to play). He often had the winds sustain the harmony while the strings carried the melodic interest, and in tuttis sometimes gave the melodic line to the basses below vigorous tremolandos for the violins. His handling of dynamic effects was newly enterprising. Others, notably Jommelli, had used the *crescendo*, but Stamitz developed a kind of orchestral *crescendo* so thrilling to contemporary audiences that (according to one writer) they would rise in their seats as the music grew louder. He developed the "Mannheim rocket", a rapid phrase, and the "Mannheim sigh", an expressive falling one. His

Plate 14 *The Death of Dido*: painting by Guercino (1591–1666) (see p. 165). Galleria Spada, Rome.

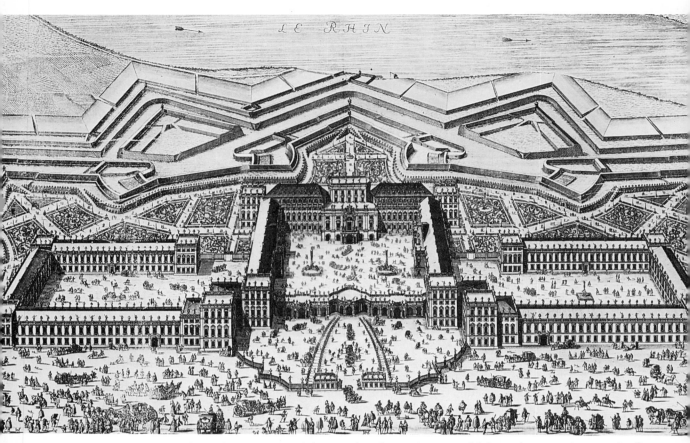

LE RHIN

86 The electoral palace at Mannheim: engraving (1725) after the drawing by the architect Jean Clemens de Froimont.

fiery fast music and his tender slow pieces could have been written only for a virtuoso orchestra. A commentator dubbed the Mannheim band "an army of generals", and indeed almost all its members, mostly from Bohemia, were gifted composers; they wrote music for themselves, and knew precisely how to exploit their special abilities to create new, bold effects. "No orchestra in the world", wrote a contemporary, "has ever excelled the Mannheim one. Its *forte* is a thunderclap, its *crescendo* a cataract, its *diminuendo* a crystal stream babbling into the distance, its *piano* a breath of spring." The players carried their methods to Paris, where many of them regularly appeared, and others came to hear them in Mannheim; and the standards and the style came, due to Stamitz's genius as organizer, composer and disciplinarian, to influence the whole of European music.

Bach's sons

Four of Johann Sebastian Bach's six sons achieved fame as musicians. The richest in natural gifts was said to be Wilhelm Friedemann (1710–84), the eldest; he held an important post as church organist in Halle, in Saxony, but seems to have been difficult and unsettled and never fully developed his talent. Third of the four was Johann Christoph Friedrich (1732–95), who exercised his pleasant but modest abilities as a composer at the small court at Bückeburg. The two who were prolific and internationally esteemed were Carl Philipp Emanuel (1713–88), the outstanding North German composer of his time, and Johann Christian (1735–82), who traveled south to Italy, then made his career in London.

C. P. E. Bach

C. P. E. Bach did not have to go far for his musical training. He learned composition and keyboard playing from his father and attended the school, where his father taught, at St Thomas's Church in Leipzig. He went on to university, at Leipzig and then Frankfurt an der Oder, as a law student (a general education, not vocational training). In 1738 he was invited by the Prussian crown prince, Frederick, to join the distinguished group of musicians he was assembling near Berlin. Frederick, who played the flute, had drawn together some of the leading musicians in Germany, among them the flutist, composer and teacher J. J. Quantz. In 1740 Frederick became emperor and C. P. E. Bach moved into Berlin as court keyboard player; his duties included accompanying the flute solos played by Frederick the Great himself. But his prestige at court was small, and so was his salary. He tried to find posts elsewhere but succeeded only in 1768 when he was appointed, on Telemann's death, as director of music at the five principal churches in Hamburg and *Kantor* (in effect chief music teacher) at a school there. Hamburg was not only a "free city", with no governing court; it was also a leading intellectual center where Bach could mix with poets, writers, university professors and philosophers. In Berlin he had composed chiefly for the keyboard; here he had to devote much of his energy to church music, though he continued to produce instrumental works, keyboard and orchestral.

Carl Philipp Emanuel Bach	Works
born Weimar, 1714; *died* Hamburg, 1788	

Keyboard music sonatas, fantasias, rondos, sonatinas, minuets, fugues
Orchestral music concertos and sonatinas for harpsichord; symphonies
Chamber music trio sonatas, sonatas for wind and strings
Choral music   *Songs*

C. P. E. Bach was also a great theorist. His *Essay on the True Art of Playing Keyboard Instruments* (1753) not only deals with technical questions, like fingering, ornamentation and accompaniment, but treats at length esthetic matters, and especially his main concern: expressiveness. He was the central figure in the creation of the North German *empfindsamer Stil*, best translated as "highly sensitive style", in which the transmission of strong, definable emotion is all-important. His most characteristic music is found in the keyboard sonatas, best played not on the harpsichord, with its even dynamics, but on the more sensitive clavichord, which allowed fine gradations of tone, or the early piano. His style is often rhetorical, with sudden pauses, sudden flurries, sudden changes of key, and in general much original and arresting writing. One of his fantasias – a typical form for him, with the freedom it implies – is said to represent Hamlet's famous soliloquy. If some of his music seems disjointed by comparison with the more orderly output of his contemporaries, that is because he emphasized strength of expression above all else. The opening of his Rondo in E♭ (ex. VII.2) shows some of his characteristics: the emotional "leaning" appoggiaturas (like the first note in m. 2), the expressive chromatic notes (mm. 6 and 22, for example) and the abrupt changes in dynamics.

Outside keyboard music, C. P. E. Bach was less influential. His keyboard works were quickly published and widely circulated, which most of his others were not.

ex. VII.2

Much of his church music was hastily put together, in response to the heavy demands of his Hamburg post, from earlier works. But his many concertos and his symphonies include music of power and intensity, often unconventional (for example, he disliked breaks in a piece, so sometimes ran movements together in dramatic ways) and full of unexpected effects; there is a fiery quality about them, often with rapid scales or arpeggios and instruments dashing from one end of their compass to the other, that typifies the earnestness of North German music of this generation. People of a deeply serious temperament, partly molded by their staunch Lutheranism, they could not fall in readily with the *galant* frivolities favored further south; with the learned counterpoint of J. S. Bach's era a thing of the past, it is in this fire and intensity, and above all in the *empfindsamer Stil*, that we find the North Germans' interpretation of the early Classical style.

J. C. Bach

J. S. Bach's youngest son was something of a renegade. Born in 1735, he was not yet 15 when his father died; he went to Berlin and continued his music studies with his half-brother Carl Philipp Emanuel. Then his life took a sharply different course.

Around 1754, he went to Italy to pursue his studies; by 1757 he was a Roman Catholic, and after another three years he was appointed an organist of Milan Cathedral. Then he departed still further from the Bach family traditions by entering the world of opera. His first opera was given in Turin in 1760; others followed in Naples. Then he was invited to London to take charge of opera performances; he accepted, and went in the summer of 1762. His operatic career there was patchy, but he settled in London where, apart from journeys to Mannheim and Paris to give new operas, he spent the rest of his short life. He was music master to Queen Charlotte and for a time a fashionable teacher; he was an early exponent of the new pianoforte; and with another German immigrant (C. F. Abel, whom he may have known from his childhood) he ran an important concert series. Later his fortunes declined, and he died in 1782.

87 Scene from Rousseau's *Le devin du village* ("The village soothsayer"), first performed at Fontaine-bleau on 18 October 1752: engraving by P. A. Martini after J. M. Moreau. Rousseau's light opera had much influence on the development of the French *opéra comique*.

Johann Christian Bach   Works
born Leipzig, 1735; *died* London, 1782

Orchestral music symphonies, overtures, symphonies for double orchestra, piano
concertos
Chamber music Six Quintets, op. 11 (1774) for flute, oboe, violin, viola and
continuo; quartets, trios
Keyboard music sonatas
Operas (10 Italian, 1 French)   *Sacred choral music*   *Cantatas*

J. C. Bach combined a solid German technique with a command of the graceful melodic style and the formal clarity of Italian music. His operas follow the older Italian traditions, with florid, tuneful arias, often richly scored for the orchestra, but little drama of the Gluckian kind; in fact, when he was involved in putting on Gluck's *Orfeo* in London, he diluted its "reform" quality by adding traditional numbers of his own, as the local taste required. His keyboard music is less adventurous than that of his brother, but is more neatly composed and better suited to the amateur players for whom it was mainly intended. Where C. P. E. Bach is passionate, J.C. is polished and urbane, with clear, "singing" melodies, deft accompaniments and shapely musical forms. His chamber music too is gracefully written; outstanding is a set of six quintets for flute, oboe, violin, viola and continuo, where the melodies are artfully devised for dialogue between groups of instruments; this kind of civilized conversation between instruments is characteristic of *galant* music at its finest.

J. C. Bach's orchestral music too represents a highpoint, notably in the warm, graceful expressive manner of his slow movements. He favored the three-movement Italian symphony form, but with a stronger content than his Italian contemporaries provided in their symphonies, which were often little more than collections of musical clichés. Bach made a point of well-defined contrasts, perhaps between a strong opening motif and a lively continuation, or between a martial first theme and a lyrical, "feminine" second. Three of his finest symphonies are designed for a double orchestra, with a smaller group (strings and flutes) contrasting – ideally in space as well as color – with the main body (strings, oboes, bassoons, horns). His music brings together the best features of the German and Italian traditions and achieves real vitality and refinement while unashamedly serving the needs of the society for which it was intended. It is not surprising that J. C. Bach's music was especially attractive to Mozart.

Haydn

When Joseph Haydn was born, in 1732, J. S. Bach had just composed his *St Matthew Passion*; Handel's *Messiah* was still ten years off. When he died, in 1809, Beethoven had written his Fifth Symphony. His long life thus covers a vast series of changes in musical style. What is more, he himself was central to those changes, and was recognized as such by his contemporaries. It would be wrong to regard Haydn as a revolutionary, certainly as an intentional one; the changes he instituted arose not from a conscious desire for change but from a wish to supply the kinds of music society demanded of him – whether it be the princely family, the Esterházys, who employed him during most of his working life, or the public, in Vienna, London

Franz Joseph Haydn	Life
1732	born in Rohrau, Lower Austria, 31 March
1740–49	choirboy at St Stephen's Cathedral, Vienna
1750–55	freelance teacher and musician in Vienna
1755–9	study with Nicola Porpora; period of great musical development and contact with prominent musicians and patrons
1759	*Kapellmeister* to Count Morzin; instrumental and keyboard works
1760	married Maria Keller
1761	appointed to the service of Prince Paul Anton Esterházy at Eisenstadt
1766	*Kapellmeister* of Prince Nikolaus Esterházy's musical establishment at the new palace at Esterháza; beginning of prolific output of church music, opera, symphonies, baryton music, string quartets, piano sonatas
1768–72	"Sturm und Drang" ("Storm and Stress") period of expressive, passionate minor-key instrumental works
1775–85	concentration on operas
1781	commissions from publishers; String Quartets op. 33 composed "in a new and original manner"
1785	Paris symphonies; beginning of friendship with Mozart
1791	returned to Vienna after Prince Nikolaus Esterházy's death
1791–2	first visit to London, with the concert manager J.P. Salomon; Symphonies nos. 93–8 performed
1792	took Beethoven as pupil in Vienna; String Quartets opp.71 and 74
1794–5	second visit to London; Symphonies nos. 99–104 performed
1795	*Kapellmeister* to the younger Prince Nikolaus Esterházy, composing a Mass each year for Eisenstadt
1798	*The Creation*
1801	*The Seasons*
1803	last public appearance
1809	died in Vienna, 31 May

and elsewhere, who bought his music and went to his concerts. In exercising his skill and his ingenuity to answer these needs, he devised many new ways of putting music together and delighting his hearers.

Early years

Haydn was born in Rohrau, a village in Lower Austria. His father, a cartwright, was fond of music. The boy had a good voice, and at the age of eight joined the choir of St Stephen's Cathedral in Vienna. He remained there some nine years, acquiring sufficient musical skills to scrape a modest living when he left by giving lessons, playing the violin or the organ in church or serenade orchestras, and accompanying. It was through accompanying for the Italian composer Nicola Porpora that he learned much about singing and the Italian language, and came into contact with some of the leading figures in Viennese musical life; Porpora also gave him instruction in composition. His first appointment, around 1759, was as music director to Count Morzin. During these early years he composed a few sacred works, keyboard pieces (some in the manner of C. P. E. Bach), and many divertimentos – pieces for various combinations of instruments, usually intended to

Franz Joseph Haydn	Works

Symphonies no. 6, "Le matin", D (?1761); no. 7, "Le midi", C (1761); no. 8, "Le soir", G (?1761); no. 22, "The Philosopher", E♭ (1764); no. 45, "Farewell", f♯ (1772); no. 49, "La passione", f (1786); no. 73, "La chasse", D (?1781); nos. 82–7, Paris Symphonies; no. 92, "Oxford", G (1789); nos. 93–104, London Symphonies: no. 94, "Surprise", G (1791), no. 100, "Military", G (1794), no. 101, "Clock", D (1794), no. 103, "Drum Roll', E♭ (1795), no. 104, "London", D (1795)

Other orchestral music violin and cello concertos; divertimentos, cassations, dances, marches

Chamber music c70 string quartets – op. 20 nos. 1–6 (1772); op. 33 nos. 1–6 (1781); op. 50 nos. 1–6 (1787); op. 54 nos. 1–3 (1788); op. 55 nos. 1–3 (1788); op. 64 nos. 1–6 (1790); op. 71 nos. 1–3 (1793); op. 74 nos. 1–3 (1793); op. 76 nos. 1–6 (1797); op. 77 nos. 1–2 (1799); op. 103 (1803, unfinished); 32 piano trios; string trios, baryton trios

Operas (c11) Il mondo della luna (1777), L'isola disabitata (1779), La fedeltà premiata (1780)

Oratorios Die sieben letzten Worte (The seven last words, 1796), Die Schöpfung (The creation, 1798), Die Jahreszeiten (The seasons, 1801)

Choral music 14 Masses; sacred and secular works

Keyboard music 52 sonatas; variations

Vocal music solo cantatas, vocal quartets and trios, canzonettas, arrangements of British folksongs, canons

provide more or less easygoing pleasure for listeners and performers. Probably his earliest string quartets date from the period with Morzin or just before.

Esterházy Kapellmeister

In 1761 Haydn was appointed to the service of the Esterházy family. The Esterházys were Hungarians (though Germanized) with long traditions of artistic patronage. They owned a castle in Eisenstadt, not far from Vienna, and in the 1760s built a new palace on the Neusiedler lake (just within present-day Hungary), called Eszterháza, in which there was an opera house. Haydn was initially subordinate to a senior *Kapellmeister* but in 1766 assumed charge of the prince's musical establishment, which then included some 15 musicians; he was required to compose exclusively for his employer and to take charge of the music library and the instruments.

Haydn's post was a demanding one. He was expected to compose in a wide range of media, and in quantity – there even survives a letter reprimanding him in which he was "urgently enjoined to apply himself to composition more diligently". His music in the late 1760s and early 1770s includes symphonies, divertimentos, much chamber music, many pieces for the baryton (the viol-like instrument which Prince Nikolaus Esterházy himself played), operas and church music. Haydn later said of his music of this time: "I was away from the world, there was no one nearby to confuse or disturb me, and I was forced to become original".

The least original works are the divertimentos, the baryton music (though Haydn was unendingly ingenious in devising music for the prince's limited abilities) and the vocal items. Church music, designed to fit an ancient liturgy, was almost inevitably conservative in style, while the operas of this period, mostly based on plots by the popular Venetian dramatist Carlo Goldoni, tend to follow stock comic patterns and though full of attractive music they are rarely very dramatic or of much expressive depth.

The string quartets

Haydn reserved his most striking and original ideas for his chamber works, especially his string quartets, and his symphonies. The string quartet was regarded as the form for the connoisseur; it was designed for the amateur groups of music-lovers who gathered regularly to savor this particular repertory. Haydn's string quartets were not written exclusively for Prince Esterházy but (with the prince's permission) for printing and publication in Vienna, where they could (and did) enlarge his reputation. He completed a set of six, probably in 1770, then embarked on another set, which he finished the next year; a third followed the year after. Each set, traditionally, consisted of six works, the standard publisher's package and a convenient quantity of music for an evening of amateur music-making.

These three sets – numbered (for the publishers' convenience rather than as a record of Haydn's output) opp. 9, 17 and 20 – established the four-movement pattern, with quick outer movements and a slow movement and a minuet in between. They also show a remarkable series of changes in Haydn's musical thinking. Op. 9 radiates the confidence of a composer full of strong, new ideas about how to make a piece interesting – there are ingenious accompaniment textures, sudden changes of pace and style in the melodic first violin part, some strikingly spacious first movements, much fire, many strokes of wit. In the next set this rampaging vitality is not so much tamed as disciplined; each work is more purposefully organized and holds better together.

This process is carried further in op. 20; moreover, the range and depth of the music are significantly enlarged as Haydn's command increases. The ideas are more fully worked, the moods more strongly defined and sustained, the scale of imagination is larger. Each work has a marked character – the third, for example, is a fiery piece in G minor, full of abrupt, unexpected turns of phrase, while the sixth is a relatively light, cheerful, witty piece in the warm, open-sounding key of A major. The most original are no. 2, with its exploration of textures (it starts with a high cello solo) and a dramatic slow movement, and no. 5. This last is another minor-key

ex. VII.3

a.

b.

work, whose new spaciousness is clear from its very first measures (ex. VII.3*a*), with their slow-moving harmony. In a typical piece of "development" Haydn later twists this idea in new directions (ex. 3*b*), using subtle changes in an idea already familiar to the listener to carry the music forward, to expand it, to challenge the mind by drawing from it new expressive meanings. There follows an intense minuet, far from the traditional courtly dance in its minor-key hints of darkness, and a gently pastoral slow movement where the first violinist is assigned a florid, decorative line, weaving above the main melody. The last movement is a fugue. Haydn, like some other Austrian composers of this time, revived this Baroque form to provide a new kind of finale, exploiting the string quartet as four equal voices and offering a way of writing a fairly weighty movement in a different style; it was more an experiment than a departure.

"Storm and Stress"

We have noted that op. 20 no. 5 is in a minor key. A large proportion – of the order of 95% – of works composed in the third quarter of the eighteenth century were in major keys; the minor was used exceptionally, generally for music of a passionate, angry or sometimes sad character. Haydn composed many symphonies, probably 30 or 40, for the entertainment of the Esterházy family during the 1760s; one, perhaps two, are in minor keys. Of those he wrote in the early 1770s, almost half are minor. Much German art – literature, drama, painting – was affected during the 1760s and 1770s by what is called the *Sturm und Drang* ("Storm and Stress") movement, and the Haydn symphonies with numbers in the 40s, or even from 39 to 52, show him departing from the idea of an elegant, tasteful piece of entertainment music written to charm his patrons in favor of music that embodied urgency and strong emotional feeling. The slow movements are slower and more intense (Adagio instead of the usual Andante), the rhythms less regular, the lines less smooth, and there are sudden changes of pace. The opening of Symphony no. 44 in E minor shows something of this (ex. VII.4).

ex. VII.4

From the mid-1770s, however, Haydn seems to have drawn away from this style. Possibly his employer found it uncongenial; perhaps it was anyway a passing phase. In any case, it was opera that chiefly occupied him in the ten years from 1775: not only composing but also arranging, planning the repertory and directing the performances. He wrote more comic operas, but also serious ones; for all the beauty of their music, stage performances tend to show that they lack some vital ingredient as regards dramatic vitality and feeling for character. The symphonies of this period are traditional, expansive, cheerful works, less personal than those preceding; but there is an important set of string quartets, op. 33 (1781), which Haydn himself advertised as composed "in a new and special manner" – this may concern the style of instrumental writing, with its use of dialogue, but more likely refers to the rather lighter and more polished character of the works.

International figure

In these years Haydn's reputation had been steadily widening. His music had been carried by the activities of international music publishers – who in the days before copyright laws could "pirate" and print any foreign publication they thought they could sell, without payment to its composer – to the areas served from London, Paris, Amsterdam, Berlin and Leipzig as well as Vienna. From Spain came a request for a church work, for Passion week; from Italy, the King of Naples commissioned concertos for a kind of hurdy-gurdy; from Paris, one of the greatest musical centers, came an invitation to compose six symphonies – to which Haydn responded with nos. 82–7, works of a new originality and brilliance. But the most important contact was with London. He had earlier declined an invitation to the English capital, but had sold music to publishers there; this time a leading violinist and concert promoter from the city, J. P. Salomon, on hearing of Nikolaus Esterházy's death in 1790 and realizing that Haydn would be free, went to Vienna and collected him.

This was a great adventure for Haydn, now approaching 60. London was a famous center for commerce, industry and the arts, and was the largest city in the world, offering rewards like no other. He was well treated during his two long visits: received at court, rapturously applauded at his concerts, richly entertained, greeted with warmth by his fellow-musicians, honored with an Oxford doctorate of music, taken to choral performances on a scale he had never imagined. And he fell deeply in love with Rebecca Schroeter, the widow of a musician (he had left his wife, a shrewish woman with whom he had never been happy, in Austria).

The London symphonies

For his London concerts Haydn composed 12 symphonies, his greatest achievement in orchestral music. They include works that have since earned themselves nicknames – the "Surprise", with its loud chord to arouse anyone who might doze; the "Clock", with its ticking figure in the slow movement; the "Drum Roll", called after its unusual opening; and the "Miracle", so called because miraculously no one was hurt when at its première a chandelier fell on the audience seats, as all the audience had rushed forward to applaud. The last of the symphonies (for no good reason) is known as the "London", no. 104 in D; it has some features that show the directions in which Haydn's music had moved (see Listening Note VII.A).

It begins, like many of his mature symphonies, with a short introduction – slow music, designed to set the atmosphere for a work of substance; the main rhythmic figure of this introduction, interestingly, uses the characteristic jerky motion of the Baroque French overture, also designed to arrest the listener's attention. The main Allegro section starts with a typical Haydn theme, sounding direct enough but full of potential for development. In a sonata-form movement of this sort, a second subject may offer thematic contrast. Some composers maximized that contrast (as Mozart often did), but others minimized it; Haydn, in the interest of a tight, unified structure for his movements, often almost eliminated it. His procedure here is typical: the first eight measures of the second subject are the same as those of the first, though the second phrase moves in a different direction. The unity of the thinking behind the movement is clear and striking. This kind of tautness of design

---

Listening Note VII.A

Haydn: *Symphony no. 104* in D (1975)
2 flutes, 2 oboes, 2 clarinets, 2 bassoons
2 horns, 2 trumpets; timpani
1st and 2nd violins, violas, cellos, double basses

1st movement: Adagio—Allegro
The movement is in sonata form, with a slow introduction. The introduction (Adagio) begins in d, with a fanfare-like figure using dotted rhythms; full orchestra alternates with quieter sections for strings with one or two woodwinds. The music trails off softly, leading to the main Allegro.
Exposition (mm. 17–123) The main theme of the movement (ex. i) is heard on the violins; it consists of two 8m. phrases. The energetic tutti that follows – which uses figure x from ex. i – leads to the dominant key, A, and after the cadence (m. 64) the main second-subject material is heard. This – typically for the mature Haydn – is close to the first-subject material, but moves off in a different direction. A busy tutti ensues, followed by a quieter section with a theme of its own (ex. ii: it refers, however, to x) and a short tutti ends the exposition.
Development (mm. 124–92) Figure y from ex. i provides the main material at the start – first for strings, then with flute and oboe, then in a tutti, where z from ex. ii reappears. The music ranges through various keys, of which e is the most persistent; it comes back to D for the ...
Recapitulation (mm. 193–294) This follows the Exposition (with some changes in the deployment of the orchestra) up to halfway through the first tutti, where it now remains in the home key and there is an emphatic tutti based on y (echoed, wittily, by the strings). The second-subject material is treated much more briefly this time, with more dialogue in the

orchestra. Ex. ii duly reappears, unchanged except in key and orchestral detail; the final tutti strongly reaffirms the home key of D.

2nd movement (Andante): Ternary form (A–B–A': A' is a variation on A, B partly a development), G

3rd movement (Menuett: Allegro): Ternary form (with each section itself ternary), D–B♭–D

4th movement (Spiritoso): Sonata form, D

88 Joseph Haydn: portrait, 1791, by John Hoppner. Royal Collection, London.

enabled composers – Haydn himself, but especially the next generation and most of all Beethoven – to write more extended works that retained their structural wholeness.

Another design Haydn particularly liked was variation form, because it lent itself to the kinds of continuous development process that he wanted. Many of his slow movements are in some sort of variation pattern, often double, with two ideas alternately varied: *A-B-A'-B'-A''* is a scheme he favored. The London Symphony Andante is similar, *A-B-A'*, but made the more concentrated by the *B* section itself being something between a variation and a development of *A*. The finale is another elaborately worked structure, for all its carefree air and its themes hinting at folk music (complete with a bagpipe-like drone bass).

Haydn returned from London to Vienna a happy man – and a rich one. After a career as a provincial *Kapellmeister* to an aristocratic patron, he had become an international celebrity, applauded by connoisseurs and fêted by royalty. He was a simple enough man to take enormous pleasure in his new status as the greatest living composer, at a time when social change had not only raised the standing of the creative artist but also ensured that he could reap the proper financial rewards. The London visits also profoundly influenced the music he was still to write.

| The final years | Between the two journeys to London, Haydn spent a year and a half in Vienna (1792–3). His new reputation had as yet made little impact on the Viennese, and he spent much of his time preparing new works for the second visit. Among them are six string quartets; Salomon's concert programs were not purely orchestral, as orchestral concerts are today, but also included songs, concertos, sometimes keyboard music, and usually chamber works. String quartets, formerly exclusive to the connoisseur's salon, were now given in the concert room. It is instructive to see how this affected Haydn's style. Most of his earlier quartets begin softly, with the statement of a theme; but the quartets of this group, opp. 71 and 74, and most of his later ones, start with a loud, arresting gesture – essential to quieten the hubbub of a talkative audience. |

Haydn had composed several sets of quartets since op. 33. There had been two groups each of six in the late 1780s, and the masterly op. 64 set in 1790, essentially intimate works in the true chamber-music tradition. In the op. 71 and 74 group the style is more brilliant, with a good deal of virtuoso writing for Salomon's violin and fuller, more sonorous textures. This more "public" quartet style remained with Haydn in the works of his last years back in Vienna. He was to compose only eight more complete quartets: six (op. 76) in 1797, a further two of what was to have been another six (op. 77) in 1799, and then another half-quartet in 1803 which he was too weak and weary to finish. The new self-confidence can be seen in the extraordinary variousness of these quartets. Some are serious and tightly argued, some lyrical, some playful. One of the most popular is op. 76 no. 3, the most famous part of which is its second movement, a set of variations on the "Emperor's Hymn" that Haydn had composed as an Austrian national anthem (see Listening Note VII.B).

The last years of Haydn's creative life, however, were spent primarily on vocal music rather than instrumental. Hearing large choirs in London singing the music of Handel had filled him with awe, and had inspired him, as a deeply religious man, with a desire to write sacred choral music. Providentially, the opportunities came. The new Esterházy prince, Nikolaus the younger, asked Haydn to resume charge of his musical establishment, but with lighter responsibilities. Haydn agreed. His chief

89 Fanfare to the special performance of Haydn's *The Creation* given in the hall of the Old University, Vienna, on 27 March 1808 to mark the composer's 76th birthday (he is seated center foreground): copy of a miniature by Balthasar Wigand, painted on a box-cover (now lost). Historisches Museum der Stadt Wien.

duty was to write a new Mass for performance in celebration of the princess's name-day; he wrote six such works in the seven years 1796–1802. He had written Mass settings before, though none since 1782. Now he carried the Austrian Mass tradition to a noble climax by integrating its conservative manner with a symphonic concentration and unity – most of the movements have the clear, strong structure that Haydn, with his experience of composing symphonies, had at his command. The six late Masses have half-jokingly been called "Haydn's greatest symphonies".

While he was working on them, Haydn was also writing two extended choral works more directly related to his experience in England. These were oratorios, composed not for church performance for private patrons but for large-scale concert performance before a wide public. Haydn had composed oratorios before, but these were quite different, emphasizing the chorus rather than the soloists and thus turning the work towards the character of a collective religious celebration. One was *The Creation* (1798), where he set a German version of a text originally written for setting in English; the other was *The Seasons* (1801), to a German version of verse by a Scotsman in which the bounties of Nature as provided by God are lauded.

If there is a single work that summarizes Haydn the man and Haydn the composer, it is *The Creation*. Musically, it embraces his mature symphonic style, but it draws too on Viennese traditions and on English, Handelian ones. And the music wonderfully reflects Haydn's grandeur and simplicity of spirit. There are joyous choruses, like "The heavens are telling the glory of God", which ends the first part,

Listening Note VII.B

Haydn: *String Quartet in C*, op. 76 no. 3 (1797)
2 violins, viola, cello

1st movement (Allegro): Sonata form, C

2nd movement (Poco Adagio): theme and variations, G
This movement consists of a statement of a theme, 20 mm. long, followed by four variations. The statement (ex. i) is by the first violin, harmonized by the other instruments. These variations are unusual in that the theme itself is unchanged but its setting is different each time. In the first (ex. ii shows the opening two measures), the second violin plays the theme while the first has 16th-notes around it. In the second, the theme is on the cello, with the first violin playing in syncopated rhythms (i.e. its accents are not on the main beat: ex. iii). When the viola takes the melody, in the third variation, the other instruments weave quite elaborate counterpoints around it (ex. iv). Finally, the melody is back in the first violin, with an enriched, often chromatic accompaniment (ex. v).

3rd movement (Menuett: Allegro): C
Classical string quartet minuet movements are normally in ternary form, Minuet–Trio–Minuet. Sometimes the minuet and the trio themselves are ternary, too (an *A* section, a *B* section and a return of the *A*); the present example however is more like sonata form in miniature. The first section (ex. vi) moves from C major to its dominant, G, where a new phrase is heard (m. 12) and a cadence reached (after 20 mm.); then all this is repeated. After a further 12 mm. (based on the opening figure: see ex. vi, *x*), there is a slightly expanded ''recapitulation'', in which the music remains in the home key of C; then the new phrase is heard in C. That entire section is repeated too.
The trio, in a, follows a similar pattern, its first phrase (only 8 mm.) ending with a cadence in the dominant, e; then there is a free, development-like section (in which the music moves to the major key, A, with a poetic and gentle effect), after which it comes back to a and the opening strain – now modified so as not to modulate to e but to remain in a.
After the trio, the minuet is heard again (normally without repeats).

4th movement (Presto): Sonata form, c – C.

ex. i

in which the creation of the earth is related; the chorus is used to tremendous effect at such moments as "And there was light", with a radiant, hugely affirmative chord to the final word. Then there are songs to describe, poetically as well as pictorially, the rolling of the sea, the flowering of the meadows, the flight of birds. In the second part, the creation of living creatures is described, often with illustrative music whose imitations of nature are both appealing and amusing, as Haydn certainly intended – the cooing dove, the leaping lion, the creeping worm. In the third and final part Adam and Eve are heard, celebrating the world and their mutual love. So *The Creation* treats of many topics close to Haydn's heart. Appropriately, it was the last work he heard, at a concert in March 1808; little more than a year later, Napoleon's armies were bombarding Vienna, and indeed Napoleon had posted a guard of honor outside Haydn's house by the time the aged composer died, on 31 May 1809. After his death he was rightly honored as the principal creator of the Classical style.

Mozart

Haydn's greatest contemporary, and the other master of the mature Classical style, was Wolfgang Amadeus Mozart, born at Salzburg in 1756. Both were Austrians; yet their careers were quite unlike, and their music, though clearly of the same era, is remarkably different in character. Born 24 years after Haydn, and dying 18 years before him, Mozart composed a lesser quantity of music, but he excelled in every sphere – opera, sacred music, the concerto, the symphony, chamber music.

The child prodigy

Wolfgang's father, Leopold Mozart, was a composer and violinist, and author of an important book about violin playing. By the time Wolfgang was four he could play the harpsichord; when he was five he was composing. Before his sixth birthday his father took him from their home city of Salzburg to ·play at the court of the Elector of Bavaria in Munich. Soon Leopold abandoned composition to devote himself to fostering "the miracle that God let be born in Salzburg" (as he put it). The next years were spent in traveling the breadth of Europe to exhibit the boy's genius: several times to Vienna, and as far afield as Paris, London and Amsterdam, as well as to every musical center in southern and western Germany. Leopold saw it as his ordained task to show his child to the world, and was not averse to any financial rewards for doing so. Mozart was put to various tests, like playing the harpsichord with a cloth covering his hands (so that he could not see the keys) or improvising on themes supplied to him. In 1770, he was taken by his father to Italy, the home of opera; he heard operas by leading composers, took lessons from the most famous teacher of the day, played at concerts and wrote operas for production, at Milan, the first when he was only 14. He twice returned in the next few years.

When Mozart came back to Salzburg from his last Italian journey, early in 1773, he was just 17. His compositions were already voluminous. There were sacred works, including four settings of the Mass. There were several dramatic works, among them two full-scale operas for Italy and shorter ones composed in Salzburg. There were more than 30 symphonies, mostly pieces about ten minutes long, and about a dozen lighter orchestral works (serenades or divertimentos, intended as background music for festivities). And there were pieces for harpsichord. Mozart's father had given him composition lessons, but the quick, impressionable boy had learned mainly by listening to other composers' music and imitating the things he liked. For example, the symphonies he wrote during his years in London (1764–5) copy features of the symphonies by J. C. Bach that he heard there, while the Italian

Wolfgang Amadeus Mozart	Life

1756	born in Salzburg, 27 January
1761	first public appearance; taken by his father, Leopold, to Munich; beginning of career as child prodigy touring European musical centers (Paris 1763, 1765; London 1764–5) playing the harpsichord
1770–73	three journeys to Italy; *Lucio Silla* (Milan 1772)
1773	Vienna; contact with Haydn's music; composed first works that hold a place in the repertory, instrumental music and sacred works for Prince-Archbishop of Salzburg
1775–7	concertmaster in Salzburg; first piano sonatas and concertos
1777–8	visits to Munich, Mannheim, Paris, seeking a post; Symphony no. 31 for Concert Spirituel, Paris
1779	court organist in Salzburg; cosmopolitan orchestral works
1781	*Idomeneo* (Munich); resigned from Salzburg court service; beginning of career in Vienna, playing, teaching and composing for piano
1782	*The Abduction from the Seraglio* (Vienna); married Constanze Weber
1783	concentration on vocal, contrapuntal and wind music; six string quartets dedicated to Haydn
1784	became a freemason
1784–6	highpoint of acclaim in Vienna; 12 mature piano concertos
1786	*The Marriage of Figaro* (Vienna)
1787	*Don Giovanni* (Prague); Leopold Mozart died
1788	court chamber musician in Vienna; Symphonies nos. 39, 40 and 41 ("Jupiter")
1790	*Così fan tutte* (Vienna)
1791	*The Magic Flute* (Vienna), *La clemenza di Tito* (Prague); died in Vienna, 5 December

symphonies of 1770 use the kinds of theme and orchestral texture favored by the Italian composers of the day. Later in 1773, Mozart spent ten weeks in Vienna, where his father sought a post for him; there he came into contact with Haydn's latest music, and the string quartets and symphonies of that summer and the following months show him adopting some of Haydn's techniques.

Most of the music Mozart had so far written, though astonishing for its fluency and inventiveness, is relatively conventional. His earliest pieces regularly played today belong to the end of 1773 and early 1774. Outstanding are two symphonies, one in G minor, K183 (Mozart's works are identified with "K" numbers, indicating their place in the chronological catalog by Köchel) and one in A, K201. The G minor work departs sharply from the traditional pattern of tuneful, graceful, entertaining music with its urgent and agitated tone (ex. VII.5). Even the last movement, which in most symphonies of this time is a cheerful, high-spirited piece, remains taut and impassioned. This is partly a result of Mozart's choice of a minor key. As we have seen (p. 65), the contrasting, second-subject music in a minor-key work was usually in the major and to most people's ears the change represents a brightening or softening of the mood; but when, as in both the fast movements here, the music associated with that brightening or softening later comes back, to

ex. VII.5

ex. VII.6

Wolfgang Amadeus Mozart   Works

Operas Idomeneo (1781), Die Entführung aus dem Serail (The abduction from the Seraglio, 1782), Le nozze di Figaro (The marriage of Figaro, 1786), Don Giovanni (1787), Così fan tutte (1790), Die Zauberflöte (The magic flute, 1791), La clemenza di Tito (1791)

Symphonies no. 31, "Paris", D (1778); no. 35, "Haffner", D (1782); no. 36, "Linz", C (1783); no. 38, "Prague", D (1786); no. 39, E♭ (1788); no. 40, g (1788); no. 41, "Jupiter", C (1788)

Concertos piano concertos – no. 15, B♭, K450 (1784); no. 17, G, K453 (1784); no. 18, B♭, K456 (1784); no. 19, F, K459 (1784); no. 20, d, K466 (1785); no. 21, C, K467 (1785); no. 22, E♭, K482 (1785); no. 23, A, K488 (1786); no. 24, c, K491 (1786); no. 25, C, K503 (1786); no. 26, "Coronation", D, K537 (1788); no. 27, B♭, K595 (1791); 5 violin concertos; Sinfonia concertante for violin and viola, K364 (1779); concertos for bassoon, clarinet, flute, flute and harp, oboe

Other orchestral music serenades – Serenata notturna, K239 (1776), "Haffner", K250 (1776); Eine kleine Nachtmusik, K525 (1787); divertimentos, cassations, dances

Choral music 18 Masses – no. 16, "Coronation" (1779), no. 18, c (1783, unfinished); Requiem (1791, unfinished); Exsultate jubilate (1773); oratorios, short sacred works

Chamber music 23 string quartets – "Haydn Quartets" (1783–5) – G, K387, d, K421; "Dissonance", C, K465 (1785); "Prussian Quartets" (1789–90); 6 string quintets – C, K515 (1787), g, K516 (1787); clarinet quintet, flute quartets, piano quartets, piano trios, string trios, piano and violin sonatas

Piano music 17 sonatas; rondos, variations, fantasias, works for piano duet and 2 pianos

Vocal music concert arias for voice and orchestra; songs for voice and piano

---

end the movement, in the minor, the effect is of darkness and seriousness firmly restored. The work in A major stands out in other ways. It begins softly, with a gentle and subtle idea (scarcely a theme) that Mozart then reworks in a full orchestral passage (ex. VII.6); there is a leisurely, graceful slow movement and, after a minuet, a finale that takes the traditional gigue-like rhythm of last movements but with its vigorous gestures and its question-and-answer phrases sustains a high tension. Mozart was turning from a gifted child into a composer of high imagination and originality.

Early maturity

By this time, Leopold Mozart was seeking a post for his son – in Germany, in Italy, in Vienna. He himself was an employee of the Prince-Archbishop of Salzburg, who in effect ruled the region and who, in the usual way, employed a "chapel" of instrumentalists and singers to supply music, for worship in the cathedral and entertainment at his palace. Wolfgang, when he was only 13, had been taken on as concertmaster, at first unpaid. But provincial Salzburg, Leopold felt, was no place for his son. He could earn a decent living in a court post, but there were slender opportunities to prosper through writing operas or playing before rich and noble patrons. Moreover, with the recent death of the old archbishop and the appointment of a less easygoing successor in Count Hieronymus Colloredo, Leopold recognized that opportunities to take leave to compose or perform elsewhere were likely to be restricted.

However, none of Leopold's approaches bore fruit. Wolfgang was a difficult person to employ – too young for a senior post, too accomplished for a junior one, and always apt to disturb the smooth running of a musical establishment because of his obvious superior abilities and his likely need for long periods of leave. So there was no choice but to remain at Salzburg and to produce the kinds of music required. The years 1773–7 saw him particularly occupied with church music and lighter orchestral music – serenades for celebrations at the university or among local families. There were also concertos, among them several for violin (Mozart may have played some of these himself: he was a capable violinist as well as a superb pianist) and four for piano, of which the last, K271, was written for a visiting virtuoso and hints at the great things he was later to do in this genre.

In 1777, the Mozarts' patience with Salzburg ran out, and Leopold sent his son away to find worthy employment. He went to Munich, where he was refused a post; to Mannheim, where he was told there was no vacancy; and to Paris, where he met tragedy as well as failure, when his mother, who had traveled with him, died. Mozart disliked the French and was suspicious of their behavior towards him, and his music made no strong impression. He may have been offered a post, but if so he refused it. It is fascinating to see, in the symphony he wrote for the leading Paris concert organization, how he adapted his style to the local taste. The Paris orchestra, probably the finest in Europe, prided itself on its violins' vigorous and precise attack. Mozart, knowing his symphony would make a good effect if he exploited that, began it with a brilliant, dashing scale. Throughout the symphony he used a showy orchestral style of a kind he had never attempted before – there are sudden dynamic contrasts, difficult and exposed passages, powerful tuttis, and in the finale a wittily hushed beginning that delighted its first audience.

While Mozart was in Paris his father, seeing the hopelessness of his quest for a better job, arranged for him to return to Salzburg with a more senior concertmaster's position. This he unenthusiastically accepted; he disliked Salzburg's provincialism, felt he was undervalued there, and was frustrated by the limited opportunities. So for most of 1779–80 he was back in his native city writing church music as well as orchestral works that reflected what he had learned in Mannheim and Paris. Then, in late 1780, he was invited to Munich to compose an opera for the court theater. The archbishop let him go and he enjoyed a great success with one of his noblest works, *Idomeneo*, a serious opera on a theme from Greek mythology. He was still in Munich when an instruction arrived from Salzburg: the archbishop was about to visit Vienna, and Mozart should go there to attend on him. Mozart duly went. This was a turning-point. After consorting with noblemen in Munich and playing in Vienna before the emperor himself, he found himself placed among the valets and the cooks at the archbishop's table. Moreover, the archbishop refused him permission to play in other noblemen's houses to which he had been invited. Angry and insulted, Mozart complained and asked for his discharge; at first it was refused, but eventually he was released, as he wrote, "with a kick on my arse . . . by order of our worthy Prince-Archbishop".

The early Viennese years

During these weeks in Vienna, Mozart had investigated the possibility of earning a living there, by teaching, playing and composing and perhaps later with a court appointment. Vienna, Mozart once wrote, was "the land of the piano", and he quickly set about establishing himself as a pianist. He wrote and published piano sonatas and piano and violin sonatas, following these with three concertos. He took on several pupils; as each normally had a daily lesson, Mozart was assured of a regular income. In 1782 he had a new German opera, *Die Entführung aus dem Serail* ("The Abduction from the Harem"), performed; during that year he was married, to Constanze Weber, with whose elder sister, a singer, he had fallen in love at Mannheim five years before.

But the new compositions about which Mozart cared most were six string quartets. They would make him little money, but quartets were for connoisseurs, and he was eager to show a mastery of the genre akin to that of Haydn – to whom, as supreme master of the string quartet, he gracefully dedicated them on publication (rather than to a rich patron who would pay him for the dedication). Mozart composed them slowly, over more than two years: partly because there was no urgency, but partly because their composition posed new challenges, in particular the development of a style and manner that was exclusively appropriate to the ensemble of two violins, viola and cello. Mozart was not willing simply to write a melody, a bass and filling-in parts; the music had to be conceived in terms specific to the string quartet.

90 Wolfgang Amadeus Mozart: silverpoint drawing, 1789, by Doris Stock (the original was destroyed in World War II).

The opening measures of the first of the group, K387 (ex. VII.7), show something of how he did this as well as illustrating other points in his style. It begins in rich four-part harmony (mm. 1–4), then moves into dialogue, with the same phrase three times over on different instruments leading to a cadence, not in the home key of G but E minor, leaving a sense of the unfinished; a decorated version of the same phrase (m. 9) rounds off the musical sentence. Next the second violin plays the opening phrase, interrupted by the first with the same phrase, leading (m. 13) to dialogue on a five-note figure from it, guiding the music towards D with a chromatic descent in the first violin (m. 16) answered by chromatic ascents from the other instruments; this echoes a phrase heard earlier (m. 4) – almost everything here, in fact, derives from the opening statement. There are other Mozart fingerprints: the chromaticisms, to intensify the impact of the music; the dialogue phrases of mm. 5–7, again adding intensity and surprising the listener with their different twists; and the use of counterpoint, to make the music, yet again, more intense by ensuring that it has life not only on the surface but at every level (mm. 16–18 show how the involvement of all the instruments can make the climax the more telling). The quartet is in the usual four movements: there is a minuet, a grave but eloquent Andante making much use of the kinds of instrumental interchange we have just seen, and a finale which like the Haydn op. 20 no. 5 (see p. 233) uses fugal writing, though within a conventional sonata-form movement.

Mozart's early Viennese years produced several works with leanings towards fugal writing. This is partly because his interest in earlier music, including that of Bach and Handel, had been aroused by contact with the Viennese nobleman and diplomat Baron van Swieten, one of the few music-lovers of the time to take older music seriously. Mozart directed concerts at the baron's house at which older music was played and later arranged Handel works for these revivals, "improving" them (as he felt) by adding parts for instruments that Handel did not use. (Nowadays this seems to us akin to painting over Renaissance pictures in brighter, more varied colors, but in Mozart's time few people appreciated the integrity of earlier art – as witness the rewritten Shakespeare texts of the eighteenth century.) Old-fashioned counterpoint can be heard, for example, in the Mass in C minor that Mozart began in 1782–3 (but never finished); in church music it always had a place. It also unexpectedly comes in a serenade for wind instruments. The wind serenade or

ex. VII.7

Listening Note VII.C

Mozart: *The Marriage of Figaro* (1786), Act 1, Terzetto

Singers: Count Almaviva (baritone), Don Basilio (tenor), Susanna (soprano)

Dramatic context: Count Almaviva has been trying to seduce his wife's maid-servant, Susanna, who is engaged to his valet, Figaro. He has come to her room to make an assignation; when he arrived, she was (innocently) with the page, Cherubino, who has been in trouble with the Count because of his amorousness. Cherubino hid behind a chair – and when the Count heard Don Basilio (a cleric and music-master) approaching he concealed himself behind the same chair while Cherubino slipped round and sat on it, covering himself with a dress that was draped over it. But in conversation with Susanna Basilio makes remarks about Cherubino's adoration of the Countess, and this – for the Count is a fiercely jealous man – provokes him into revealing himself.

The music: This terzetto (a word used for a trio for voices) shows how the sonata-form type of structure could be used in vocal music. The arrangement of thematic material and keys is exactly like that of an instrument sonata-form movement, with ex. i as the first subject and ex. iii as the second; mm. 1–57 correspond to an exposition, 57–146 to a development and 147–222 to a recapitulation. But the nature of the material, and the ways in which it recurs, are so managed as to give extra force and subtlety to the drama. Note, for example, how ex. i comes at each assertion of authoritarian anger from the Count; how ex. iii's appearance in m. 70 is in the same sense as its original one; and how ex. ii is used with irony – the hint is there first time (m. 16), comes again at his hypocritical disavowal of malice (m. 85), and finally, after the Count has used the same music while discovering Cherubino, with the sharpest irony in m. 175.

		mm.	key	
COUNT				
Cosa sento! tosto andate, E scacciate il seduttor.	What do I hear? Go at once and send the seducer away.	4	B♭	ex. i: the Count expresses his anger
BASILIO				
In mal punto son qui giunto, Perdonate, o mio signor.	I have come at a bad moment; Forgive me, my lord.	16	B♭	ex. ii: Basilio (with a hint of irony and malice)
SUSANNA (*almost fainting*)				
Che ruina, me meschina! Son oppressa dal dolor.	Unfortunate me, I'm ruined! I am cast down with misery.	23	b♭–f	shift to minor at Susanna's anxiety
COUNT, BASILIO (*supporting her*)				
Ah già svien la poverina! Come oh dio! le batte il cor!	Ah, the poor girl is fainting! Good heavens, how her heart beats!	43	F	ex. iii: expression of sympathy
BASILIO		57		
Pian pianin su questo seggio.	Gently to this chair.	59	F	Close of section; modulating section begins

SUSANNA (*reviving*)

Dove sono! cosa veggio!	Where am I? what is happening?	62		
Che insolenza, andate fuor.	How dare you! let me go!	66	g	Susanna's anger at being handled – and guided to the occupied chair

COUNT

Siamo qui per aiutarti,	We are only helping you;	70	Eb	ex. iii; note expression similar to m. 43
Non turbarti, oh mio tesor.	Do not be disturbed, my treasure.			

BASILIO

Siamo qui per aiutarvi,	We are only helping you;			
È sicuro il vostro onor.	your honor is safe.			
Ah del paggio quel che ho detto	What I said about the page	85	Eb–	ex. ii
Era solo un mio sospetto!	was no more than my suspicion!		Bb	

SUSANNA

È un'insidia, una perfidia,	It's a trap and a falsehood;	92	Bb	
Non credete all'impostor.	Don't believe this deceiver.			

COUNT

Parta parta il damerino!	This little beau must go away!	101	Bb	ex. i: the Count's anger

SUSANNA, BASILIO

Poverino!	Poor boy!	104		

COUNT (*ironically*)

Poverino!	Poor boy!	110		
Ma da me sorpreso ancor.	But I've found him out again.			

SUSANNA, BASILIO

Come! Che!	How so? what?	116		

COUNT

Da tua cugina	At your cousin's place	121	Bb	recitative-like section for the narrative
L'uscio ier trovai rinchiuso,	I found the door locked;			
Picchio, m'apre Barbarina	I knocked, and Barbarina let me in,			
Paurosa fuor dell'uso.	looking unusually flustered.			
Io dal muso insospettito,	My suspicions aroused,			
Guardo, cerco in ogni sito,	I looked, I searched everywhere,			
Ed alzando pian pianino	And lifting very gently	129	Bb	ex. ii
Il tappetto al tavolino	the cloth from the table			
Vedo il paggio . . .	there I saw the page! . . .			

(*he illustrates this with the dress on the chair, discovering the page*)		139		note how *x* (ex. ii) turns upward as the page is discovered
Ah! cosa veggio!	Ah, what do I see?	141		

SUSANNA

Ah! crude stelle!	Oh, cruel heavens!	143		

BASILIO (*laughing*)

Ah! meglio ancora!	Oh, better still!	145		

COUNT

Onestissima signora!	You most virtuous lady!	147	Bb	ex. i: the Count's anger again, now quiet and menacing
Or capisco come va!	Now I understand how things are!			

SUSANNA

Accader non può di peggio;	Nothing worse could happen;			
Giusti dei! che mai sarà!	Great heavens! whatever next?			

BASILIO

		168	Bb	part of ex. iii
Così fan tutte le belle;	All the women are the same;			
Non c'è alcuna novità!	There's nothing new about it!			
Ah del paggio quel che ho detto	What I said about the page	175	Bb	ex. ii, reflecting Basilio's irony
Era solo un mio sospetto!	was no more than my suspicion!			

91 Scene from
Beaumarchais' comedy *Le
mariage de Figaro* (1784):
engraving by J. B. Leinard
after Jacques P. J. de
Saint-Quentin. (This is the
scene represented in
Mozart's opera, in the Act I
terzetto: Listening Note
VII.C).

divertimento was a light form; Mozart had written several such pieces in Salzburg,
normally for open-air performance by two each of oboes, bassoons and horns (a
standard military band ensemble, also used for marches and the like). He composed
three wind works in the early Viennese years, of which the most remarkable is K388
in C minor, for eight instruments (clarinets as well as oboes, bassoons and horns).
The hearers must have been surprised at a serenade of such vigor and passion, and in
a minor key, with its warmly expressive slow movement set between a first
movement and a minuet of exceptional tension and dissonance, followed by a
variation finale that exploits the instruments' color, technique and expression.

Listening Note VII.D

Mozart: *Piano Concerto in G* K453 (1784)
solo piano
flute, 2 oboes, 2 bassoons, 2 horns
1st and 2nd violins, violas, cellos, double basses

1st movement (Allegro): Sonata-ritornello form, G
Opening ritornello (mm. 1–74)   The main theme (ex. i) appears at once on the violins, with
comments from flute and oboe. A short tutti follows, which fades (note the bassoon and
flute) into a new, gently lyrical theme (ex. ii), heard first on violins, then echoed on
woodwinds. There is an abrupt key change, to E♭, but not for long, and the music moves
back to G for a brief violin theme and a very brief tutti.
Solo exposition (74–170)   Now the piano enters, at first with its version of ex. i; after some
bravura passages, and a modulation to D, the dominant, it states a new theme (ex. iii) – a
theme which is never played by the orchestra and is very much the soloist's preserve.
However, the music soon moves into piano passage-work, against a background of

woodwind in dialogue; this leads to the bassoon and flute (now bassoon and oboe) phrases heard earlier, and to a restatement – now in D (it was in G, the home key, before), of ex. ii, with the piano echoed by the woodwinds this time. More solo bravura leads to a decisive cadence, in D.

Central section (mm. 171–226)　There is a short tutti (based on material heard in earlier tuttis) and then a free section where the pianist ranges wide up and down the keyboard, with woodwinds in support and strings sustaining the harmony; the music goes far afield in key, but returns (m. 203) to e (the relative minor of G), and thence to the home key for the . . .

Recapitulation (mm. 227–349)　Ex. i is heard in the orchestra, as at the beginning of the concerto, though the piano soon intervenes; then ex. iii and ex. ii recur, as in the solo exposition, though with many minor differences, especially in scoring. After more bravura passages, the abrupt E♭ modulation recurs, heralding the solo cadenza – the moment where traditionally the soloist can take off on his or her own, in freely improvised music, though as Mozart himself left attractive cadenzas for this concerto (he composed them for a pupil) most pianists use these. When the cadenza finishes, there is a final tutti, using material from earlier ones.

2nd movement (Andante): Sonata-ritornello form, C

3rd movement (Allegretto): Theme and variations, G

The piano concertos

Mozart's middle years in Vienna reached a climax in the piano concertos of 1784–6. This was the time when the Viennese public recognized and admired his genius as composer and pianist and readily flocked to his concerts, which he gave during Lent, when the theaters were closed. In the 12 piano concertos of these years he greatly enlarged the concept of the concerto. This, as we have seen, was originally a Baroque form, in which solo episodes alternated with orchestral ritornellos. In tune with the thinking of his time, Mozart added to this a Classical-style, sonata-form contrast of keys and thematic material; others, like J. C. Bach and to some extent Haydn, worked along similar lines, but only Mozart achieved a satisfying balance of elements, including of course the soloist's virtuosity. He did this, at least at first, less by using the kinds of concentration we saw in the string quartet than by allowing themes to multiply; they are linked either by brilliant passage-work (scales, arpeggios etc) or, for the larger ones, by orchestral tuttis. The relationship between piano and orchestra is very subtle. The orchestra states some of the themes, and provides accompaniment and punctuation; the piano re-interprets some of the orchestra's themes, ventures some of its own, occasionally accompanies the orchestra's leading wind players, has opportunities to show its brilliance and thus its right to a special position, and brings the movement to a climax in a solo cadenza. Typical of the concertos of 1784 is K453 in G, composed for one of Mozart's pupils, Barbara Ployer, with its lyrical themes, its clear-cut form, its attractive writing for wind instruments and its fluent virtuoso passages (see Listening Note VII.D). For the slow movement the piano has music that is florid, dramatic and rich in expression, often elaborating ideas already heard in the orchestra; in the finale piano and orchestra share evenly in the interest in a witty set of variations. No two of Mozart's concertos follow exactly the same scheme. In the later ones he tended to move away from the multiplicity of lyrical themes towards shorter, more motif-like ideas, and this led to music more strongly unified. The two mature concertos in C, K467 (1785) and 503 (1786), exemplify this; the former is also famous for the poetic eloquence of its slow movement with its soaring piano lines, its throbbing orchestral accompaniment and its disturbingly dissonant harmonies. Also in this later group are Mozart's two minor-key concertos (D minor, K466; C minor, K491), which are among his supreme achievements; both begin with material that is essentially orchestral in style, which the pianist cannot take up – so in each case the solo entry begins with a new, lyrical theme of particular pathos and gentle beauty. The C minor work especially is outstanding for the wind writing in its slow movement and for its inventive variation finale. There is an analogy between the piano soloist in a concerto and the singer of an operatic aria; it is no coincidence that Mozart excelled in writing for both. It is from this time that Mozart's most famous operas come: *The Marriage of Figaro*, first given in Vienna in 1786, and *Don Giovanni*, given the following year in Prague.

The mature instrumental music

Before we look at Mozart's ultimate achievement, as an opera composer, we should survey his mature instrumental music and look more closely at some of it. He wrote in every medium: piano sonatas, some striking and adventurous, others primarily teaching pieces; piano and violin sonatas, where he shifted the balance from its traditional emphasis on the piano (with the violin merely accompanying) towards one in which both instruments had full expressive rein, as well as piano trios and larger works; string quartets (though he never surpassed the achievement of the set dedicated to Haydn) and string quintets; more concertos, including a fine one for clarinet; and symphonies.

The string quintet was a genre uncommon in Mozart's day, but he seems to have been specially drawn to it. He wrote two – K515 in C and 516 in G minor – in the spring of 1787, then two more in 1790–91. In K515 and 516, which represent a peak in his chamber music, he drew richly on the opportunities that the extra instrument (a second viola) provided for different kinds of symmetry of texture (the opening bars, ex. VII.8, show one, the first violin in dialogue with the cello with the middle instruments supplying the harmony). The C major quintet, his most spacious chamber work, unfolds in leisurely fashion, allowing for a new richness in its sound, its motivic working, its range of key in the first movement; its slow movement is like an operatic love-duet for violin and viola, while the finale mixes counterpoint and wit as no composer had done before. Even more esteemed, perhaps, is the G minor work, for its poignancy and depth of feeling. About the time he was writing these works Mozart heard that his father, back in Salzburg, was dying.

Mozart wrote few symphonies in his mature years, mainly because piano concertos served better for his public appearances in Vienna. In 1786, however, he composed one for a visit to Prague, and in the summer of 1788 he produced three. The last two, K550 and 551, are in G minor and C, like the quintets, and bear a similar relationship. The G minor work at once declares its originality in the grace and restrained passion of its opening theme, with its throbbing viola accompani-

ex. VII.8

Plate 15 *Opposite Jupiter and Semele*: painting, 1722–3, by William Kent (see p. 215). Ceiling of the King's Drawing Room, Kensington Palace, London.

ex. VII.9

ment (ex. VII.9); its first three notes (x) underlie the entire first movement, sometimes carrying its main argument, sometimes lurking inside the orchestral texture, but always lending a certain nervous tension. That tension, or urgency, is brought to the surface in the last movement, fiery music which in the central development undergoes a vigorous, almost harsh contrapuntal treatment. But the finest manifestation of counterpoint in Mozart's symphonic music comes in the C major work. This, called the "Jupiter", stands in a tradition of ceremonial music in C major, as the presence of trumpets and drums in the orchestra and the military rhythms attest. For the finale Mozart reverted to the kind of movement he had used in the string quartet K387 – a sonata-type movement infused with fugue; the themes, short and motivic, are designed for treatment in combination. There are several fugal sections but only at the very end of the movement does Mozart show his full hand and combine all the material, drawing the music together in a coda of unique power: a fitting culmination to his symphonic output.

At the time of his last symphonies Mozart was 33. His Viennese career had begun to turn sour; he was no longer in demand as a pianist, and although he now had a court appointment it was a minor one with fairly modest rewards. Mozart and his family never starved, and probably could always afford a servant and a carriage of their own; but they had periods of financial difficulty and Mozart was obliged to borrow, in spite of the successes he enjoyed right up to the end of his life as an opera composer. His last year, 1791, was particularly active: during the summer he wrote two operas, one for a popular Viennese theater, the other for performance at Prague during coronation celebrations. Prague was a city Mozart liked; his operas had been warmly received there. But the new work, *La clemenza di Tito*, was only moderately successful in September 1791. Mozart returned to Vienna, where at the end of the month *The Magic Flute* was first given – to increasing applause during October. Meanwhile, he worked on a *Requiem*, which had been requested from him in mysterious circumstances (it was commissioned by a nobleman who wanted to pass it off as his own); later it was said that Mozart thought he was composing it for himself. For in November he became unwell, and after a three-week feverish illness that defied the doctors, and still defies definite diagnosis (it was not poisoning, as has been suggested), he died on 5 December.

The operas

Mozart composed happily and eagerly for every medium, but it was in opera that his chief passion lay. He wrote a school opera, in Latin, when he was 11, and a full-

Plate 16 *Madame Henriette Playing a Bass Viol*: painting by Jean Marc Nattier (1685–1766). Musée de Versailles. Madame Henriette was the daughter of Louis XV. For the French viol tradition, see p. 169.

scale comic opera when he was 12. His first great opera was *Idomeneo*, written for the Munich court when he was 25; that was followed by his German opera for Vienna the next year. The operas, however, which have always stood firmly in the public taste are three: *The Marriage of Figaro*, *Don Giovanni* and *The Magic Flute*.

Like Shakespeare's comedies, Mozart's comic operas (as all these three are) are not simply funny. We have seen (pp. 223–5) what Gluck did for serious opera; Mozart did something parallel for comic opera by infusing it with a new humanity and depth of feeling. There were numerous operas in the middle and late eighteenth century about noblemen with too eager an eye for country girls, and in all of them the nobleman is frustrated and virtue triumphs. That happens, too, in *The Marriage of Figaro* (or *Le nozze di Figaro* – it was composed in Italian), but with a difference. For the characters Mozart drew, with the help of his clever librettist Lorenzo da Ponte, and the French playwright Beaumarchais on whose drama it was based, are not the pasteboard caricatures generally found in the theater but recognizable human beings. Mozart's music gives them life. The songs for Count Almaviva and his neglected wife, for example, are distinct in tone from those for their servants, Figaro and Susanna (the Countess's maid, whom the Count desires); the music tells the listener of their social backgrounds and of the sexual tensions that provide the opera's mainspring; and the music for the adolescent page, Cherubino, portrays his youthful, all-embracing sexuality as words cannot. We hear, in the music for the Count, his urgent passion for Susanna and his fury at the idea that his own servant might enjoy privileges from which he is excluded. We hear Figaro's cynicism regarding women when he thinks Susanna faithless; and we hear her relishing the thought of joy in her beloved's arms. Mozart's music does not, like that of most

92 Stage design by G. Fuentes for the 1799 Frankfurt production of Mozart's opera *La clemenza di Tito*. Institut für Theaterwissenschaft, University of Cologne.

93 Opening of Bartolo's aria in Act 1 scene iii from the autograph of Mozart's opera *Le nozze di Figaro*, completed 29 April 1786. Deutsche Staatsbiiliothek, Berlin.

Italian operas of the time, simply present lively tunes with light accompaniments; the melodic line, the suggestive harmony, the rich orchestration carry messages about the emotion behind the words. As in most comic operas, the action is carried forward in the recitatives and the ensembles; the arias are moments of repose, where a character expresses his or her reactions to the situation. Mozart's ensembles are especially ingenious; the long, elaborate act finales, divided into sections as the nature of the action changes (and each section possesses the integrity of a symphonic movement), succeed in propelling the plot forward and sustaining the tension. (See Listening Note VII.C, p. 249.)

The Marriage of Figaro was successful in Vienna and Prague, and it was for the latter city that Mozart, again with Da Ponte, wrote *Don Giovanni*. This too deals with the tensions of class and sex: Giovanni is a Spanish nobleman with an insatiable desire for sexual conquests. Ultimately he is consigned to eternal damnation, in a great scene where the statue of a man he has murdered (the man was defending his daughter's honor) comes to sup with him and drags him, unrepenting, down to the flames of hell; this scene drew from Mozart a noble, inexorable setting in D minor. The score is fascinating, too, for its portrayal of Giovanni's victims (or intended ones) – the peasant girl Zerlina, with her simple, pretty tunefulness; Donna Elvira, whom he has betrayed, and whose venom towards him is faintly flavored with the comic, since a scorned woman pursuing her former lover cannot escape concealed laughter; and Donna Anna, the proud young woman whose father he killed and whose passion for vengeance underlies the opera. The contrasting character sketches of Giovanni and his servant Leporello again show Mozart's musical representation of social class. Though still a comic opera, *Don Giovanni* touches on serious issues; but Leporello's presence, and his common-man's comments, wry or facetious, ensure that we do not treat it as tragedy. The last of Mozart's Da Ponte operas, *Così fan tutte* (1790), is an elegant but heartfelt comedy about infidelity.

Italian was the language preferred for operas at the court theater in Vienna. Outside court circles, however, German was spoken, and an opera for middle-class audiences had to be in that language. Mozart, happy to write in his native tongue, was pleased to accept in 1791 an invitation to collaborate with the theater manager and actor, Emanuel Schikaneder, on a pantomime-like German opera. Since 1784 Mozart had been a freemason, as was Schikaneder, and the text and music of *The Magic Flute* (*Die Zauberflöte*) incorporate much masonic symbolism. It starts like a traditional fairy-tale with a heroic prince (Tamino) attempting to rescue a beautiful princess (Pamina) from the clutches of a wicked magician (Sarastro); but it soon becomes clear that Sarastro represents the forces of light and Pamina's mother, the Queen of Night, those of darkness. *The Magic Flute* may have a trite and silly libretto. But it is artfully designed to provide many different kinds of music: the Queen of Night's angrily glittering coloratura; Sarastro's and his priests' noble utterances; the popular ditties for the bird-catcher Papageno (sung by Schikaneder) who accompanies Tamino on his quest; the tense trios for the Queen's Ladies and the serene ones for the three Boys or Genii who support Tamino; and the music for Tamino and Pamina themselves, which is direct and intimate as the music of Mozart's Italian operas is not. This is a philosophical opera, about two people's lofty quest for realization and ideal union; with this is contrasted Papageno and his role as a child of nature. The sublimity of the music with which Mozart clothed *The Magic Flute* shows him unmistakably as a true man of the Age of Enlightenment.

Other opera composers

The Magic Flute is a *Singspiel*, a German-language opera with spoken dialogue – indeed it is the supreme example of the genre. As we have seen (p. 221), each of the main European countries had its own kind of light musical theater, of which the *Singspiel* was the German one; Haydn also wrote some *Singspiels*, and so did many other composers, including another Viennese, Carl Ditters von Dittersdorf (1739–99), and a leading German figure, Johann Adam Hiller (1728–1804). Most of these works are simple in style, almost like spoken plays with songs. English operas of the time, which were composed in large numbers by such men as Charles Dibdin (1745–1814) and William Shield (1748–1829), are similar. In both these countries, but even more so in France, light opera reflected contemporary social criticism, with its emphasis on the bourgeois values (duty, honesty, kindness, innocence) as against aristocratic unscrupulousness or heartlessness. *Opéra comique* was finding the middle course its audiences wanted between, on the one hand, the coarse, often bawdy fair entertainment in which it had originated, and on the other the more pretentious forms of opera still favored at court and by the aristocracy. Its leading exponents were A. E. M. Grétry (1741–1813), noted for his fluent melodic style and his gentle, very French, expressive charm, and F. A. D. Philidor (1726–95 – even more famous as the leading chess player of the time). Only in Italy was there no opera with spoken dialogue; because of the language's capacity for rapid and rhythmic speech and its musical rise and fall, recitative could serve as well in comedy as in serious opera. Italian comic opera, which (as we saw, p. 222) began in Naples early in the century and spread northwards to Rome, Venice, and even across the Alps to the other countries where Italians worked, before the middle of the century, had roots in the Italian theater or *commedia dell'arte*; in the last quarter of the century its leading exponent was Domenico Cimarosa (1749–1801), a Neapolitan whose career took him to all the main centers in Italy and then to Russia, where he was briefly court composer to Catherine the Great at St Petersburg (now Leningrad). His most famous comic opera, *Il matrimonio segreto* ("The secret marriage"), was given in Vienna in 1792, with such success that the emperor demanded an immediate repeat performance – the only known encore of an entire opera.

Cimarosa was not the only Italian comic opera composer of distinction. There was Baldassare Galuppi (1706–85), whose tuneful settings of the texts of the comic dramatist Carlo Goldoni (1707–93) dominated the Venetian theater; there was Niccolò Piccinni (1728–1800), whose vein of sentiment, heard in *La buona figliuola* (1760, a version of Richardson's novel *Pamela*), won him special fame; and, comparable in popularity with Cimarosa, there was Giovanni Paisiello (1740–1816), whose vivacious *Barber of Seville* (1783) was so much a classic that it was thought impertinent of Rossini to set the same story in 1816.

Italian was the language of court opera, and much public opera too, across most of Europe; so it was natural that Italian composers should occupy important positions in the courts and the musical life of many countries – Germany and Austria, England, Spain and Portugal, and even France, in spite of the strength of native traditions. Italian instrumentalists, too, were prominent, like Nardini in Stuttgart or Giardini in London. These were violinists, continuing the strong Baroque tradition.

Boccherini

Luigi Boccherini, born in Lucca in 1743, was a cellist. As a young man he had three spells playing in Vienna (capital of the empire to which most of Italy belonged), took part in what were probably the earliest public string quartet performances (Milan, 1765), and achieved international fame with his appearances in Paris in 1768. He was invited to Madrid, where in 1770 he was appointed composer to the prince, Don Luis. He spent the rest of his life in Spain, working for various other patrons after Luis's death in 1785, notably the King of Prussia, Friedrich Wilhelm II, in Berlin, a keen amateur cellist for whom he could supply chamber works with attractive and interesting parts for the cello. Later, circumstances were difficult for him, and he had to eke out his slender pension by arranging his music for the increasingly popular guitar. He died in 1805.

Boccherini was a composer of highly individual gifts, which his isolation in Spain from the mainstream of European musical thinking encouraged him to develop. Like Domenico Scarlatti, he often reproduced in his music hints of Spanish folk idioms, like the thrumming of guitars, the syncopated rhythms, the languid phrasing. He was chiefly a composer of chamber music; he wrote more than a hundred string quintets (mostly for two violins, viola and two cellos), almost as many string quartets, and numerous trios and other chamber pieces. As a cellist himself, he often called upon that instrument to play rapidly and brilliantly, sometimes soaring eloquently to the top of its compass. Such writing could never have fitted into the compositions of Haydn or Mozart, who thought more in terms of ensemble than of individual effect. But it was typical of Boccherini. He admired Haydn, but lacked the Austrian composer's feeling for formal integrity. Instead, he aimed for rich and varied textures, and cultivated a gentle, suave melodic style, often ornate and fine in detail. He wrote symphonies, and concertos for his own instrument; but it is above all in the string quintets and quartets that the individual warmth and grace of his music are to be found.

Clementi

Among Boccherini's friends and colleagues was the Austrian–French composer Ignace Pleyel (1757–1831), a pupil of Haydn who settled in Paris as a music publisher and instrument manufacturer. He was one of several enterprising musicians of the time who combined the creative and commercial sides of music. Of these the most eminent was Muzio Clementi, born in Rome in 1752. He was taken to England at the age of about 15, studied diligently for seven years, then began to develop a reputation as a harpsichordist and soon embarked on a performing career. In 1781 he was in Vienna, where he competed with Mozart before the emperor – Mozart thought Clementi "a mere mechanicus", but Clementi, more generous, said that he had never before heard anyone play with such spirit or grace as Mozart. He returned to London, and spent much time there during the rest of his life, playing, composing, publishing and supervising the making of pianos; he continued to travel a good deal, partly to perform but increasingly to pursue his business interests. He retired to the country in 1830 and died two years later.

Most of Clementi's compositions are for the piano, the instrument he played and helped develop. His early music is in a direct, harpsichord-like style. But he soon began to exploit the new pianoforte with its capacity for brilliant effects and rhetorical writing – in this he ran parallel to, perhaps in advance of, Beethoven – and his late music even suggests Chopin in the elaboration of its lines and textures. (Clementi's pupil, the Irishman John Field, 1782–1837, was the true creator of the nocturne style that Chopin later invested with such richness of expression.) Known towards the end of his life as "father of the pianoforte", Clementi was a great innovator rather than a great composer and his chief importance lies in the way that he laid the foundations of the piano style of the next generation.

Beethoven

It was with the explosion of the genius of Ludwig van Beethoven, at the turn of the century, that the classical era reached both a climax and a dissolution. "Explosion" is the word: for Beethoven's music embodied a new dynamism and power which not only demanded that it be listened to in different ways but also symbolized the changing role of the composer in society – no longer its servant, required meekly to meet its needs, but its visionary, its hero-figure.

Youth

Beethoven was born in Bonn, on the Rhine, in western Germany. At the court there of the Electors of Cologne, his grandfather had briefly been in charge of the musical establishment and his father was a tenor singer when, at the end of 1770, Ludwig was born. Discovering that he was exceptionally talented in music, his father wanted him to be a child prodigy, a second Mozart, and compelled him to practice long hours; he played in public when he was eight, but his precocity was not of the order of Mozart's. He had instruction on the piano, the organ and the violin, and when he was about ten he began more serious studies, including composition, with C. G. Neefe, the Bonn court organist. At 13 he had a post as assistant organist, and four years later he was sent to Vienna to study. There he probably had some lessons with Mozart; but the trip was brief as Beethoven was summoned home to see his dying mother. In 1789 he assumed the responsibility of managing the family, for his father was a heavy drinker. His main court duty was to play the viola in the chapel and theater orchestras. But Bonn was too small a town for a developing composer; soon after Haydn passed through on his journey from London to Vienna, in 1792, Beethoven was sent to the Austrian capital to study under him.

The lessons were not particularly successful; Beethoven afterwards said that Haydn took little trouble over him, and though Haydn esteemed the younger man

Ludwig van Beethoven	Life

1770	born in Bonn, baptized 17 December
1792	studied with Haydn in Vienna
1795	public début as pianist and composer in Vienna
1799	publication of Piano Sonata no. 8 in c, op. 13 ("Pathétique")
1800–02	deterioration of hearing and period of depression
1802	Heiligenstadt Testament, October
1803	beginning of heroic "middle period"; Eroica Symphony
1805	*Fidelio*
1806–8	prolific composition, mostly large-scale instrumental works, including Symphonies nos. 5 and 6 ("Pastoral") and "Razumovsky" Quartets
1812	letter to the "Eternal Beloved"; beginning of "silent period"
1813	beginning of "final period"
1814	highpoint of popular acclaim in Vienna; last public appearance as a pianist
1815	appointed guardian of nephew Karl
1818	Piano Sonata no. 29 in B flat op. 106 ("Hammerklavier") completed
1820–23	compositional activity: late piano sonatas, "Diabelli" Variations
1823	*Missa solemnis* completed, Symphony no. 9 ("Choral") begun
1825–6	concentration on string quartets
1827	died in Vienna, 26 March

he seems to have been unsympathetic to his musical ideas. When Haydn went back to England, Beethoven took the opportunity to turn to J. G. Albrechtsberger, a diligent, methodical teacher. Meanwhile, he was beginning to establish himself as a pianist, playing in the salon concerts organized by noblemen in their houses and making his Viennese public début early in 1795 in one of his concertos. About this time his first important publications were issued: three piano trios op. 1 and three piano sonatas op. 2. As a pianist Beethoven, according to reports of the time, had immense fire, brilliance and fantasy, as well as depth of feeling. In no other musical medium could he be so bold or so wholly himself. In these early years, it is in his piano music that he was most free and most imaginative. The first movement of his first published sonata, in the "stormy" key of F minor (ex. VII.10), shows at once the new urgency of voice – in the impetuous opening, in the insistent way that figures (*x, y*) are repeated to press towards a climax, and in the tension created by accented notes (mm. 22, 23) and the undercurrent of movement (mm. 20 onwards). It is easy to see how different an impression Beethoven was trying to make here from Mozart or Haydn: the assertiveness, the aggression of the unruly young man from the provinces is far from the graceful entertainment offered by the preceding generation.

Ludwig van Beethoven   Works

Symphonies no. 1, C (1800); no. 2, D (1802); no. 3, "Eroica", E♭ (1803); no. 4, B♭ (1806); no. 5, c (1808); no. 6, "Pastoral", F (1808); no. 7, A (1812); no. 8, F (1812); no. 9, "Choral", d (1824)

Concertos 5 piano concertos – no. 4, G (1806), no. 5, "Emperor", E♭ (1809); Violin Concerto, D (1806); Triple Concerto for piano, violin and cello, C (1804)

Overtures and incidental music Coriolan (1807); Leonore Overtures nos. 1, 2 and 3 (1805–6); Egmont (1810)

Opera Fidelio (1805, rev. 1806, 1814)

Choral music Mass in D (Missa solemnis, 1819–23)

Piano music 32 sonatas – no. 8, "Pathétique", c, op. 13 (1799), no. 14, "Moonlight", c♯, op. 27 no. 2 (1801), no. 21, "Waldstein", C, op. 53 (1804), no. 23, "Appassionata", f (1805), no. 26, "Les adieux", E♭, op. 81a (1810), no. 29, "Hammerklavier", B♭, op. 106 (1818); 33 Variations on a Waltz by Diabelli, op. 120 (1823); variations, bagatelles

String quartets op. 18 nos. 1–6 (1798–1800); op. 59 nos. 1–3, "Razumovsky Quartets" (1806); op. 74, "Harp" (1809); op. 95 (1810); op. 127 (1824); op. 132 (1825); op. 130 (1826); op. 133, "Grosse Fuge" (1826); op. 131 (1826); op. 135 (1826)

Other chamber music piano trios – op. 97, "Archduke" (1811); string quintets; piano quintet; sonatas for piano and violin – op. 24, "Spring" (1801), op. 47, "Kreutzer" (1803); Octet for wind instruments (1793)

Songs An die ferne Geliebte ("To the distant beloved"), song cycle for tenor and piano (1816); Scottish songs

In his early Viennese days, Beethoven lived on a salary from his Bonn employer, and was accommodated in the establishments of various noble patrons, for example Prince Lichnowsky. It was with Lichnowsky that in 1796 he embarked on his first concert tour, to Prague, Dresden and Berlin. And Lichnowsky was the dedicatee of one of Beethoven's most striking works, the Piano Sonata in C minor op. 13, always known as the *Pathétique*, marked by its somber first-movement introduction which later recurs to dramatic effect in the course of a fiery movement. C minor was a key Beethoven favored a good deal, at this time and later, for serious, dark-toned utterances. One of the trios of his op. 1 was in that key; Haydn, on seeing it, had counseled Beethoven against publishing such a piece, for he found music of this temper alien. There is a C minor work in the set of string quartets Beethoven wrote – emulating Haydn and Mozart, but also competing with them – in the last years of the century. His first two symphonies date from 1800 and 1802, but the passionate tone of his other early works is muted here; he was not yet so fully in command of orchestral writing that he could embody his most original thoughts in such works. It is still the piano sonatas that contain the most striking ideas. There is something original in every one of the 17 he composed up to 1802 – examples (besides the one quoted above and the *Pathétique*) are op. 10 no. 3, where the first and last movements show Beethoven building large structures from motifs of just a few notes, with a slow movement profoundly dark-toned, dissonant and pathetic ("portraying a sad state of mind, with every shade of melancholy", said Beethoven of it); while op. 26 embodies a remarkable funeral march, and op. 27 no. 2 is the famous *Moonlight*, whose gently romantic reflectiveness brings a whole new world of feeling into the ambit of the sonata.

ex. VII.10   **Allegro**

The "heroic" period

Beethoven's creative life has traditionally been divided into three periods: his youth and early manhood, with his establishment as a major composer (1770–1802); his middle life (1803–12), in which he handled all musical forms with full command and produced many of his most famous works; and his final period (1813–27), when the personal stresses he underwent are reflected first in the small number of works he produced and second in their intensely serious, often very intimate character. This division makes good sense and relates convincingly with the times of change, or of personal crisis, in Beethoven's life.

During 1802 Beethoven went through some kind of profound depression. It was probably in 1796 that he first became aware that his ears had become less keen; by 1800 he was aware not only that his hearing was impaired but also that the condition was worsening and was unlikely to be arrested, still less cured. To Beethoven the composer, it was not a catastrophe. As a gifted and thoroughly trained musician, with a perfect "inner ear", he could hear music, even complicated music, by looking at it, and could write down the ideas that came into his head. (He had never composed at the piano, but rather at his desk, jotting down his ideas in piecemeal, sketchy form, then working at them to give them shape and meaning.) To Beethoven the pianist, it was a disaster: any ideas of a career as a virtuoso, traveling Europe to the applause of music-lovers, would have to be abandoned. So would piano teaching (an important source of income); so would conducting his own music. And to Beethoven the social man, deafness was a catastrophe. He wrote to a friend, in 1801, that he was "living a miserable life. For almost two years I have ceased attending social functions, simply because I cannot say to people 'I am deaf'". His ability to communicate freely with his fellow men – and with women – was appallingly damaged; he could never hope for a normal social life. As time went on, he became more and more turned in on himself, unable to share his thoughts and his problems with others, growing steadily more odd, more eccentric, probably more aggressive. This was a long, gradual process; in 1802 he still had several years of concert-giving ahead of him and his social life was not yet a total void. But in October that year, when he was in a village called Heiligenstadt outside Vienna, he wrote a strange document (the "Heiligenstadt Testament"): a kind of will, addressed to his two brothers, Carl and Johann (born 1774 and 1776), it describes his bitter unhappiness over his affliction in terms suggesting that he thought death was near.

Beethoven, however, came through this depression with his determination strengthened. He wrote, more than once, of "seizing Fate by the throat" and of the

94 Ludwig van Beethoven: pencil drawing, c1818, by Carl Friedrich August von Kloeber. Beethovenhaus, Bonn.

impossibility "of leaving this world before I have produced all the works that I feel the urge to write". This new resolution, this readiness to fight back against cruel adversity, is echoed in the "heroic" character of his music of the ensuing years. While nearly all Beethoven's music so far had been "absolute" (that is, had no extra-musical content), now he wrote large works that carry implications about his attitudes to life. There is, for example, his oratorio *Christ on the Mount of Olives*, of 1803, in which there is clearly some identification between Christ's suffering and that of Beethoven himself. In the opera *Fidelio* (or *Leonore*, as it was at first called), of 1804–5, other aspects of Beethoven's suffering and aspirations are dealt with, as we shall see. The most obvious product of his "heroic" phase, however, is the *Eroica* Symphony.

The *Eroica*, Beethoven's third symphony, was written in the summer of 1803. At first Beethoven called it "Bonaparte": it was intended as a tribute to Napoleon, the hero of revolutionary France. But the following spring the news arrived that Napoleon had proclaimed himself emperor; Beethoven, angry and disillusioned at what he saw as a betrayal, ripped the title-page bearing the dedication off the score, tore it in half, and wrote on the symphony: "Heroic Symphony, composed to celebrate the memory of a great man". The most obvious difference between the *Eroica* and any earlier symphony – by Beethoven or anyone else – is that it is on a much enlarged scale. A late Haydn symphony takes 25 minutes to perform; the *Eroica* takes 45. Yet, paradoxically, it does not have long themes – quite the contrary, for its themes are little more than motifs of a few notes, particularly in the great first movement (see Listening Note VII.E). The principal idea is simply based on the chord of E♭ major; second-subject material is made up of a series of ideas, none of them exactly a "theme", held together by their sheer power and momentum. Most remarkable of all is the development, in which most of the exposition ideas are thoroughly worked over, often in complex combinations or in alternation, and then the music seems to twist in wilful, perverse directions, landing on a huge, devastating discord, several times repeated: after which, as if chastened, it quietens and a new lyrical theme is heard, in a distant key.

That alarming climax and its softening, and the music that then hesitantly and mysteriously leads back to the recapitulation, provides one of the noblest yet most disturbing passages in Beethoven. The symphony continues in this exalted vein. The slow movement is a somber yet heroic funeral march, with a middle section that in its expressive oboe theme adds sentiment to the mourning. The third is a Scherzo; Haydn, years before, had talked of the need to invent a new kind of minuet, and Beethoven's need to express something less graceful and more violent had led him to this much more rapid triple-meter movement. The finale follows a variations pattern, one that was increasingly to suit his way of thinking. This one is on a theme that he also used in a ballet and a piano work. Its peculiarity lies in the way that Beethoven presents its bass (ex. VII.11) before the theme itself. At first there is humor in the idea and its presentation, but as the movement proceeds it

ex. VII.11

Listening Note VII.E

Beethoven: *Symphony no. 3* in E♭, *Eroica*, op. 55 (1803)
2 flutes, 2 oboes, 2 clarinets, 2 bassoons
3 horns, 2 trumpets; timpani
1st and 2nd violins, violas, cellos, double basses

1st movement (Allegro con brio): Sonata form, E♭
Exposition (mm. 1–148)   Two explosive chords: and the main theme of the movement (ex. i) is heard on the cellos, repeated on winds; there is an orchestral crescendo and it is heard again more emphatically – but there is a sudden twist and the music is in the dominant key, B♭, for the second subject. The second subject in this movement is not a single theme, but a collection of short ideas: first, a dialogue around a three-note phrase (ex. ii), then a rising scale in the woodwinds (ex. iii) – which is carried upwards into a powerful, turbulent tutti by the violins (ex. iv); after that comes a sustained theme with repeated notes and changing harmonies (ex. v), from which another crescendo leads to a tutti, ending with emphatic chords and then a lyrical line for violins and flute. At the very end of the exposition (which Beethoven directed to be repeated, though this is not often done), ex. i is heard.
Development (mm. 148–397)   The music shifts to c, and then to C, where ex. ii is set against the rising scales heard earlier. Then ex. i returns in the cellos and double basses, successively in c, c♯ and then d, where an angry tutti bursts out, using ex. iv (with an ex. i derivative, ex. vi, in quieter interludes). This carries the music on through g, c, f and b♭ to A♭, where the music linking ex. ii and rising scales is heard again. Now, however, it gives rise to a passage like a fugue opening; this, and recollections of first-subject linking material, lead the music to a huge climax, a series of crashing, dissonant chords. This breaks off, and out of it comes a new, lyrical theme (ex. vii), in the distant key of e, heard first on the oboes and then (in a) on the flutes. But now ex. i asserts itself again, in C, and although ex. vii is heard again (clarinets, e♭) there is a clear feeling that the music is on its way towards the home key and the recapitulation. It still takes some time to get there: there is a tutti, with ex. i material weaving through it, then sustained wind chords with the strings hinting at ex. i, then string tremolandos – through which, as if impatient, a horn softly plays ex. i, and at last we arrive at the . . .
Recapitulation (mm. 398–551)   Ex. i is heard on the cellos; but then the music takes an unexpected turn to F (ex. i on the horn) and then another to D♭ (ex. i on the flute) before it settles in the home key. The music is adjusted so that it remains in E♭ for the second-subject material, which follows in the succession as before.
Coda (mm. 551–691)   A movement on so large a scale needs to be well rounded off, and the coda here – as in other large-scale works of Beethoven and later composers – is almost like a second development section. It starts with ex. i in D♭ and then in C, moving on into f, where ex. vii is drawn into the musical argument. Then a long crescendo – related to the one that ended the development – leads to a lyrical statement of ex. i on horns, then violins, then more emphatically on the bass instruments (with the rhythm of ex. iv prominent above) and finally on trumpets and horns. Ex. iii is briefly recalled just before the end.

2nd movement (Funeral march, Adagio): Ternary form, c–C–c.
3rd movement (Scherzo, Allegro vivace): Extended ternary form (A–B–A–B–A), E♭
4th movement (Allegro molto): Variation form, E♭

ex. i

ex. ii

ex. iii
(woodwind)

ex. iv
(violins)

ex. v
(woodwinds)

ex. vi   (violins)

see ex. i

ex. vii
(oboe)

gains in drama and force, to reach a noble, intense slow variation close to the end and a jubilant final climax. No early listener to this work could doubt that in it Beethoven was redefining the nature of the symphony.

He continued to do so. No. 4 is relatively orthodox, but the next two each break new ground. No. 5, in C minor, begins with the famous motif of ex. VII.12a, with its menacing nature, said to represent "Fate knocking at the door". It is made the more menacing by its persistence: this motif appears throughout the movement, in one form or another, driving along the stormy tuttis, introducing the second subject (the introductory horn call provides the outline of the lyrical idea that follows, so that the movement's entire material is tightly held together: see ex. 12b). The second movement is in variation form: like several of Haydn's slow movement variations, it varies two themes in alternation – it is no accident that the rhythm of the second corresponds with the rhythm that dominates the first movement.

ex. VII.12

With the third movement, a dark-toned Scherzo, the link is more explicit, for after a *pianissimo* opening statement the horns suddenly burst in, *fortissimo*, with ex. 12c. The movement becomes more sinister, with this rhythm reduced to an uneasy mutter, then to a background rumble: but then the finale breaks in. C minor changes to C major; the slender, ghostly orchestration gives way to a blazing, triumphant sound, enriched by three trombones in the middle, a piccolo at the top and a double bassoon at the bottom, as well as bass drum, cymbals and triangle, and the menace of the four-note rhythm is transformed into jubilation (ex. 12d).

In discussing the symphonies of Haydn and Mozart, it is never possible to talk so specifically, or with such certainty, about the emotions that the music is intended to evoke. Here there can be no doubt. Beethoven's Fifth Symphony begins with a threat, explicit in the music's insistent rhythms and tone; it ends with a triumph, darkness defeated by light. It is a typical product of Beethoven's heroic phase, and we can scarcely fail to see the work as representing, in Beethoven's mind, his own conquering of the forces of adversity by which he felt he was beset.

The Sixth Symphony is also representative music, but in a quite different sense; and it further tells us something important about Beethoven the man. He called it "Pastoral Symphony". It is about the countryside – or, rather, about Beethoven's reactions to the countryside. There are five movements instead of the normal four, the extra one being made necessary by Beethoven's plan for the symphony: I, Awakening of happy feelings on arriving in the country; II, By the brookside; III, Peasants' merrymaking; IV, Thunderstorm; V, Shepherds' song of thanksgiving after the storm. In a famous remark, Beethoven said that the symphony was "more the expression of feeling than painting". Although the third movement is akin to a peasants' dance (with hints of the bagpipes) and the fourth contains representations of rumbling thunder, Beethoven did not intend us to listen to the music as a

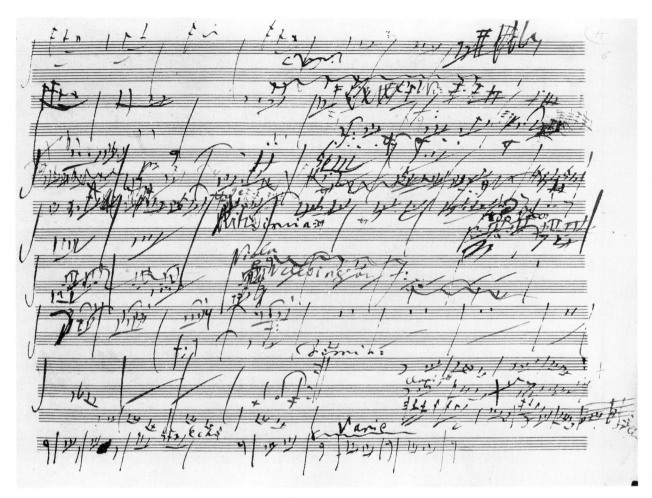

95 Autograph sketches for Beethoven's Symphony no. 6 in F ("Pastoral"), 1808. British Library, London.

depiction of events. What the *Pastoral* Symphony makes clear is that Beethoven loved nature and the countryside. He lived in a large city, but went each spring and summer to stay in some nearby spa or small town and to take country walks. In his time, natural rural beauty was only just beginning to be admired; the previous generation, the age of landscape gardening, had held that unruly nature could be bettered by human art.

Like the *Eroica*, the Fifth and the *Pastoral* are large-scale symphonies, taking around 40 minutes in performance; the scope of Beethoven's ideas and the elaboration of their working-out demanded an expanded time-scale compared with what had served for Haydn or Mozart. The same applies to Beethoven's chamber music. His op. 18 string quartets were on the traditional Classical scale, about 25 minutes long. His op. 59 string quartets, of 1806, have a time-span akin to those of the symphonies. There are three of them, dedicated to the Russian ambassador in Vienna, Count Razumovsky (hence their nickname, the "Razumovsky Quartets"); in his honor each was to include a Russian folk melody. In the first, the folk melody heralds the finale as it succeeds the Adagio; in the second, it provides the trio of the Scherzo. No one has found a Russian folk melody in no. 3: probably Beethoven settled for a movement (the Andante) in a melancholy idiom, with short, repeated phrases in what he took to be a Russian manner.

The first of the quartets is the most striking and the most characteristic of Beethoven's expansive middle-period style. The grandeur of its opening at once proclaims its breadth of conception (ex. VII.13a). The fact that the harmony does not change for six and a half measures, and then not again for eleven and a half, while an extended melody (often seeming to contradict the harmony) is outlined on the cello and then the first violin, establishes the amplitude of the music in the hearer's mind. Further, the opening melody contains the seeds from which the rest of the movement's material derives, sometimes directly but more often through

ex. VII.13

Plate 17 *Opposite Concert at Schloss Ismaning*: detail of a painting (1731) by Peter Jakob Horemans. Bayerisches Nationalmuseum, Munich. The players are performing music such as Telemann's *Musique de Table* (p. 183).

Plate 18 *Overleaf* The palace of Eszterháza (the garden front; the opera house is just visible on the left): painting, 1780, by Bartolomeo Gaetano Pesci (see p. 232). Országos Müemléki Felügyelöség, Budapest.

subtle links of shape or pattern. Most obvious is the rising four-note figure (x) at the beginning, which lends its shape to several later ideas (sometimes moving down rather than up, but the derivation is unmistakable: see ex. 13b, for example); but the cello figure (y) in mm. 2–3 is equally germinal (see exx. 13c and d). These examples demonstrate how Beethoven could hold an extended movement together as an artistic unity.

The quartet continues with a Scherzo and an Adagio molto e mesto ("Very slow and sad"). In the sketchbook Beethoven used when putting this movement together there is a jotting about "a willow or acacia tree over my brother's grave"; his brothers were in fact both alive and well, but clearly he was thinking in elegiac terms when he was writing this movement. Its appoggiatura-type dissonances (ex. VII.14: each is marked +) had long been the traditional way of expressing grief

ex. VII.14

or yearning, and here, as in the funeral march of the *Eroica*, the darker, despairing expression is relieved by gentler, singing, almost hymn-like major-key passages. Yet this is certainly one of the most intensely felt movements in Beethoven's middle-period music, demanding great concentration from players and listeners alike until the moment when the Russian folk melody steals in, lightens the mood, and draws the work to a joyous, exuberant conclusion – as we have seen, this was becoming a pattern for Beethoven, symbolizing triumph over adversity. It was now as applicable to the string quartet as to the more public symphony – only lately had string quartets, long intended for the private pleasure of four players in a drawing-room, become fare for public concerts, and Beethoven was one of those who adapted its style in accordance with social need.

Opera

By the early years of the new century, Beethoven was widely recognized – not only in his home city of Vienna – as a leading composer, a highly original one whose latest works were eagerly awaited by connoisseurs and the public and were competed for by music publishers. With an annuity guaranteed by Prince Lichnowsky he could live in reasonable comfort. He was now anxious to prove himself in a new sphere: opera, which offered a composer the richest rewards, both material and in reputation. An opportunity came in 1803, and Beethoven started work; but the opera-house manager (Emanuel Schikaneder, who had put on Mozart's *Magic Flute*) lost his job and plans were abandoned. The next year he had an invitation to write an opera for the Theater an der Wien. He cast around for a plot and libretto; only a topic close to his heart, he felt, could draw from him music that embodied his deepest feelings. He did not have to look far. Since the French Revolution, many operas had been written that appealed to a love of freedom and hatred of tyranny; many were "rescue operas", having as their climax the last-minute rescue from death of the hero or heroine. Several of the kind had been given in Vienna. A literary friend of Beethoven's, Joseph von Sonnleithner, prepared for

Plate 19 *Concert in a Venetian Palace*: painting, 18th-century, artist unknown. Casa Goldoni, Venice. An early orchestra (p. 55).

96 Scene from Beethoven's opera *Fidelio*, in the revival staged at the Kärntnertor Theater, Vienna, in 1814: engraving from the *Wiener Hoftheater Almanach* (1815).

him a libretto using a French story, by J. N. Bouilly, allegedly based on an actual incident: it was called *Léonore ou L'amour conjugal* ("Leonore, or Married Love"). Beethoven worked at the opera, to be called *Fidelio*, during much of 1804 and 1805. It is a tale of political oppression, set in a grim prison where the freedom-loving Florestan has been kept in a dungeon for two years by the district governor, Pizarro; his wife Leonore, disguised as a young man (Fidelio), takes a job at the prison, where the jailer's daughter Marzelline falls in love with "him". In the end, Leonore prevents Pizarro from killing her husband by throwing herself between them – and at that instant a fanfare is heard proclaiming the arrival of the Minister of

State to inspect the prison and liberate those unjustly detained.

Beethoven had immense trouble composing the work. When it was first performed, late in 1805, it was a failure – though that was partly because it was given before an audience largely of French officers (Napoleon's army had conquered Vienna a week before). Beethoven's friends told him that it was too long and began too slowly; he shortened it radically, and it had two performances, but then Beethoven quarreled with the theater authorities and withdrew it. He did not revive it again until 1814, when he had made extensive further changes. The opera begins like a cheerful German *Singspiel*, and only towards the end of the first act (in the earlier versions, the second) do Beethoven's individuality and nobility of manner assert themselves – in the great song where Leonore, learning Pizarro's intentions, summons up hope and strength to fight them. The act ends with a chorus for the prisoners, allowed out of their cells to see the light and breathe the air. The second act is largely set in Florestan's dungeon, as he lies wretched and half-starved; its climax is his rescue by Leonore and their rapturous, exalted duet, "O namenlose Freude" ("O joy beyond words").

Comparisons between the 1805 original and the 1814 version are fascinating for what they tell us about Beethoven's development and his changing view of the work (and indeed of life in general). In the later version the cheerful beginning is shortened. Leonore has a new, intensely dramatic opening to her aria. Florestan is given a new ending to his prison aria, in which he feverishly sees a vision of Leonore; and after the rescue a long recitative, in which Florestan and Leonore hesitantly begin to converse after two years apart, is removed in the 1814 version. Such changes tend to make the opera less the story of two particular people and more a generalized tale about abstract good and evil; the characters may emerge less individually, but its moral force is greatly increased.

One reason why Beethoven found the subject of *Fidelio* so attractive is that it dealt with freedom and justice. Another is that it dealt with a heroic theme and triumph over adversity. A third is that it dealt with marriage. Beethoven longed to marry; at the time he was composing *Fidelio*, in fact, he was deeply in love with Josephine von Brunsvik. Like his earlier love, in 1801, for Countess Giulietta Guicciardi, it came to nothing. In both cases the young ladies were Beethoven's pupils; in both, the barriers of social class proved unsurmountable. In any case, we cannot know whether the young ladies reciprocated Beethoven's passion. Possibly Beethoven never found a woman who could match his lofty image; and we may anyway doubt whether a man so violent in his feelings, so absorbed in his art, so unruly and quarrelsome in his relations with those around him, was capable of engaging in a stable relationship.

But he continued, it seems, to hope. A document, as strange as the Heiligenstadt Testament, has come down to us: a letter, written in the summer of 1812 and addressed to the "Eternally Beloved". It is a passionate love letter, expressing a desire for total union yet also expressing resignation at its impossibility; it speaks of mutual fidelity, of the pain of enforced separation, of hopes for a life together. It is hard to know what it means. The weight of evidence points to its having been addressed to Antonie Brentano, a Viennese aristocrat married to a Frankfurt businessman – they and their ten-year-old daughter had known Beethoven for two years, and we know that she admired him. But there is little reason to think that she and Beethoven had a love affair or even contemplated living together; in fact we do not even know whether the letter was actually sent. It could well have been the product of an intense private fantasy about marriage to an ideal, but safely unattainable, woman.

The last period

The year 1812 – critical in European history, with Napoleon's defeat in Russia – was a turning-point in Beethoven's life. In the preceding years he had composed much of the music by which he is chiefly remembered: the fourth to eighth symphonies, the fourth and fifth piano concertos (the latter, the "Emperor", one of his grandest conceptions, with the piano's heroic strivings and commanding assertions), the supremely lyrical violin concerto, a Mass, songs, chamber music, several fine piano sonatas including the great *Appassionata*. In 1808 he had considered becoming musical director at the court in Kassel of the King of Westphalia; but he was not eager to leave a busy capital city for a small, provincial one and when three of his Viennese admirers banded together to provide him with a guaranteed income he was glad to be able to stay. His career as a pianist was now finished. He played his last public concerto in 1808; when he appeared at a charity concert in 1814 he could not hear himself play, and banged in the loud passages while in the soft ones he played so delicately that the notes did not sound.

The years following 1812 have been called his silent years: first, because he composed relatively little; secondly, because he was more than ever cut off from the world by his deafness and became increasingly morose, suspicious and quarrelsome. He drove away all but his most tolerant friends with his aggressive behavior, was unable to keep servants, and lived in perpetual confusion, even squalor. From 1815 onwards he had another great worry: his nephew Karl, son of his brother Carl Caspar (who died that year). Beethoven thought the boy's mother a bad influence and fought with her in the courts to be appointed guardian – he succeeded, but as guardian he was inevitably a failure, and Karl grew up an unhappy and wild young man who felt little of the gratitude or affection that his uncle demanded.

The trials, social and personal, that Beethoven underwent seem to have a clear reflection in his music. For one thing, his deafness prevented his hearing new works by other men, so his own idiom, instead of altering as the years passed, stayed basically the same, only growing more refined and concentrated. His interest in variation form becomes less a matter of elaborating a theme than of probing into it and discovering new layers of meaning. Several of Beethoven's late piano sonatas – he wrote three in 1814–18, three more in 1820–22 – include variation movements of this kind, but the most striking of his piano variations is the set on a waltz of Diabelli. The publisher Diabelli sent several Austrian composers a trivial little waltz theme, asking each to write one variation on it so that he could publish a collective set. Beethoven, it seems, became intrigued by the theme and sent Diabelli 33 variations of intense complexity and technical difficulty in which the waltz theme is far transcended by the boldness and imagination of his ideas.

Another form that increasingly fascinated Beethoven at this time was fugue. In earlier works, like the *Eroica*, he had sometimes used fugue in his development sections. Now he did so more often, and at greater length, for example in the late piano sonatas. Fugue, like variation, gave him a framework for the persistent treatment of a musical idea; in the finale of the op. 106 sonata, in particular, he wrestles endlessly and furiously with what is already a strange theme, turning it upside-down and inside-out. Its angry contortions seem to mirror Beethoven's restless, impassioned personality and the "distressful circumstances" under which, he later said, it was composed.

The final works   The great climaxes to his life's work, however, were still to come: they consist of two choral works and a group of string quartets. One of the choral works was a Mass, begun for performance at the ceremony in which one of his oldest and most trusted friends and patrons, the Archduke Rudolph of Austria, was to be enthroned as an archbishop. Unfortunately it was not finished in time. The other was a choral symphony. In 1817, he had accepted an invitation to write two symphonies for the Philharmonic Society of London and to go there to direct them. He did not do so, but the invitation drew him back to symphonic composition.

In the Choral Symphony, no. 9, many of the trends in Beethoven's compositional thinking were drawn together. The first movement carries to a new extreme the concept of the generating motif: the "theme" at the opening (ex. VII.15), essentially a two-note figure, is the germ from which much of this long

ex. VII.15

and powerful movement springs, and its derivatives are worked out plainly and openly so that the listener can hear them grow. The main idea of the second movement, a scherzo, is treated in a fugue exposition. The third is an extended double-variation slow movement (the kind favored by Haydn: see p. 236), on the pattern *A-B-A'-B'-A"* – though the *A"* section is as long as the rest of the movement and embodies several freely worked-out variations. This movement draws on a vein of intense lyricism characteristic of Beethoven's late music. The final movement sees Beethoven for once making the meaning of an instrumental work articulate. Many earlier finales, as we have seen, carried strong hints of extra-musical meaning (like the triumph of the Fifth). But here Beethoven actually provides a verbal text and introduces a chorus and soloists to join in the expression of feelings about humanity and universal brotherhood: in this he echoed the composers of post-Revolution France. The words are from Schiller's *Ode to Joy*,

ex. VII.16

ex. VII.17

Assai sostenuto [slow, sustained]

which Beethoven had long admired and had considered setting as early as 1793.

The movement is a huge set of variations. In its introduction, the earlier movements of the symphony are recalled: then comes the famous "Joy" theme (ex. VII.16*a*) – first on cellos and double-basses alone, next in fuller orchestral settings. Then the movement seems to begin over again, and a bass singer, after declaiming "O friends, not such sounds as these; let us strike up more pleasing ones, full of joy!", sings the "Joy" theme. Thereafter the theme appears in different guises to parallel the sense of the words – military, for example, when the tenor sings of marching to victory over sorrow or tyranny (ex. 16*b*). A new theme, introduced to the words "O you millions, I embrace you", is combined with the "Joy" theme in an exultant double fugue for the chorus (ex. 16*c*). This long movement, nearly half-an-hour's music, is one of the most difficult and strenuous ever composed: intentionally so, for the sense of striving and effort is an essential part of the message of the music.

Beethoven finished work on the Choral Symphony early in 1824; in May it had its first performance – he was too deaf to conduct (two years earlier he had had to give up an attempt to conduct *Fidelio*) and, at the end, sat in utter absorption until a friend tugged his sleeve and told him that the audience were applauding wildly. Afterwards he gave a dinner party for the conductor, the concertmaster Schuppanzigh and his own assistant Schindler, which ended in disaster as Beethoven virtually accused them all of cheating him of money due from the performance. He was as difficult and quarrelsome as ever.

In 1823 Beethoven had accepted a commission from Prince Golitsïn, of St Petersburg, for some string quartets, a form he had not considered since 1810. With the Choral Symphony premières behind him, he set seriously to work on these, designing them for the quartet led by Schuppanzigh. They occupied him for the rest of his creative life and form a personal, intimate counterpart to the public statements of the Choral Symphony and the Mass for Archduke Rudolph. Golitsïn had asked for three works; when he had written three, Beethoven still had more to say, and produced another two. The three central ones, traditionally numbered opp. 132, 130 and 131 (in that order of composition), are on a new plane of spiritual depth, as is borne home to the listener in the often strange but exalted nature of their ideas, the abruptness of their contrasts, their passion, their emotional intensity. Take for example the opening of the A minor quartet op. 132 (ex. VII.17): it begins with a series of "imitations" of the soft, slow-moving cello phrase *a* (which reappears later in this quartet, and in others), rudely interrupted by the first violin's dashing off in sixteenths (*b*) and then the important cello phrase *c*, which is taken up by the violin and prolonged to make what is to be the movement's main idea – and this in turn is interrupted by an explosive, disruptive unison which, however, yields to a measure of Adagio, then another dash by the violin and a return to the main theme. The music is eventful, restless and challenging in a new way; and the diverse ideas thrown up in these opening measures are treated later in the movement, followed up, developed and welded into a powerful unity, so that the confusing opening comes to make sense. The slow movement reflects the fact that Beethoven was ill during the work's composition: he headed it "Sacred song of thanks to the divinity on convalescence, in the Lydian mode". By using the old Lydian church mode Beethoven intentionally gave the music a certain feeling of antiquity and remoteness from ordinary human experience; and his treatment also gives it the sound of a chorale prelude, as if a solemn hymn is being sung in the slow passages in half-notes. The chorale-like music is presented with two variations, into which small motifs are woven with increasing elaboration; in between come sections marked "Feeling new strength", which portray a revival of vigor and warmth.

In opp. 130 and 131 Beethoven further extended the language of the string quartet. Op. 130, where again the first movement material is presented in diverse scraps, has six movements, including two slow movements of an intense, ethereal beauty that surpasses anything else in Beethoven. For its finale Beethoven originally wrote a huge fugue, long, harsh and immensely demanding, to listener and player alike; his publisher persuaded him, however, to replace it with a simpler movement as the quartet was too long and too difficult. Op. 131 is in seven movements, though they are played continuously and, since they have material in common, seem to form a unity. The first is a slow, sublime fugue, the fourth a complex set of variations.

Beethoven finished his last quartet in the fall of 1826. During the preceding summer he had been profoundly disturbed when his nephew Karl, with whom he had so turbulent a relationship, tried to commit suicide; soon after, it was arranged that Karl would join the army. Beethoven and his nephew went, in the meantime, to spend some weeks at the country home of Johann van Beethoven, the composer's second brother. He returned, in haste (after a quarrel, apparently), in December, and was immediately taken ill. The doctors could do little but relieve the symptoms; everyone knew he was dying, and he was sent gifts, among them money from the London Philharmonic Society and wine from one of his publishers. On 26 March 1827, he died, during a thunderstorm; his last action was to raise a clenched fist. Some 10,000 came to mourn at his funeral: he had lived into the age – indeed had helped create it – when the artist was the property of mankind at large.

Chapter VIII

The Romantic Era

Romantic art

Unlike the terms "Baroque" and "Classical", which have little use in ordinary conversation or writing, "Romantic" is a word full of meanings in everyday use. Dictionaries define it as to do with romance, imagination, the strange, the picturesque, the fantastic. In the arts, it is similarly applied – to literature, painting or music in which fantasy and imagination are in their own right more important than such classical features as balance, symmetry and wholeness. Because the Romantic era succeeded the Classical one, roughly at the turn of the eighteenth century, it is usual, and convenient, to define the characteristics of Romantic art and especially music by comparison with those of the art of the Classical period.

The most obvious difference between Classical music and Romantic music is usually expressed as one of precedence: in the Classical world, form and order come first, in the Romantic, expressive content does. A Classical piece of music, broadly speaking, has a clear-cut structure which the hearer is intended to perceive (at some level of awareness) as an important part of the musical experience, indeed as its basis, within which the emotion generated by any incident takes its place. By contrast, a Romantic piece depends on strong emotional expression, which may be generated by some subtlety or richness of harmony or color, by some dramatic juncture, or a variety of other means; and this is more important to the impact of the work than is its form. While the form of the Classical work was a natural outcome of the material of which it was composed, a way of giving it logic and order and balance, Romantic artists tended to accept the form as an entity in itself and to fill out the traditional Classical patterns with ideas ever more arresting, attractive and laden with emotion, or to vary them as the spirit moved.

The Classical age, then, was one – as we have seen – of orderliness, of serenity, taking its models from the ancient cultures of Greece and Rome; it is no coincidence that the plots of serious operas were taken from classical mythology and history, which stressed the virtues admired in the eighteenth century. That period was called the Age of Reason, or the Enlightenment. In *The Magic Flute*, the three temples that lead to a symbolic heaven are labeled "Wisdom", "Nature" and "Reason"; there is no worshipping Fantasy or Imagination. Yet even during the eighteenth century some disquiet spirits had rebelled against the prevalence of the rational and the well-proportioned: this disquiet manifested itself in the German "Storm and Stress" movement, in England in "gothick" architecture which attempted to re-create medieval styles (and along with them a sense of mystery), and in all Europe an

97 Walpurgis Night scene from Delacroix's illustrated edition (1828) of Goethe's *Faust*.

interest in the Orient, with its exotic and fascinating remoteness.

By the turn of the century the lure of the Middle Ages, and things associated with that period, was rapidly gaining ground. Now opera plots were often drawn from medieval history or legend, or from such works as the Waverley novels of Sir Walter Scott (1771–1832) which aimed to recapture an age of chivalry and high romance. Mysticism, the demonic, the supernatural: all these, which had no place in the rationalist schemes of the eighteenth century, began to reassert themselves as a part of human experience.

The most famous and most influential manifestation of these interests is in the *Faust* of the great German writer Johann Wolfgang von Goethe (1749–1832) – in Faust's compact with the devil in his search for immortality and for sensual experience with an idealized woman. Numerous composers wrote works around Faust, Mephistopheles and Gretchen; some also treated the more philosophical second part of Goethe's great work. In the graphic arts similar interest in the dark, nightmarish side of human experience is seen in the works of such men as Francisco Goya (1746–1828), John Henry Fuseli (1741–1825) and William Blake (1757–1827); in music, examples of their strong expression are Schubert's song *The Erl-king*, where a boy's soul is snatched away by an evil spirit during a ride through a forest, or the Wolf's Glen scene in Weber's *Der Freischütz*, where magic bullets are cast with the devil's aid, or the Witches' Sabbath in Berlioz's *Fantastic Symphony* with its shrieks and its ominous sounding of the "Dies irae" ("Day of Wrath") plainsong.

Religion and politics, too, form a part of this picture. Catholicism, as the faith of the Middle Ages, underwent a new revival; its music, departing from the decorative Rococo that in effect Mozart and Haydn had been content with, acquired a new solemnity and plainness – the restoration of polyphony and plainsong were widely encouraged, and the church music of the Renaissance began to be seriously studied and even used as a model.

Social change

Socially, this was a time of rapid change. With the American Revolution of 1776, a colony for the first time proclaimed its independence from its rulers: this was the first of a series of momentous events. The French Revolution, in 1789, had seen the near-extinction of the ruling classes in France; all the other crowned and noble heads of Europe were trembling. The Napoleonic Wars which raged from the late 1790s up to 1815 created confusion and poverty; meanwhile, the Industrial Revolution was fast gaining momentum and the shape of society was undergoing fundamental and permanent changes, with great cities growing up (often with appalling living and working conditions) and the countryside becoming depopulated. Political or social oppression became a subject susceptible to treatment through artistic protest; obvious examples are found in the poetry of William Blake (who writes of the "dark, satanic mills") and in his paintings of industrial desolation. In music, as we have already seen, Beethoven could hymn the brotherhood of man in his Choral Symphony (a type of work which owes its existence to the massive choral "revolutionary hymns" created in the wake of the French Revolution) and for his only opera set a plot concerned with freeing an innocent man from wrongful oppression. Other composers had earlier set the *Fidelio* story, which is only one (if the greatest by far) in a whole tradition of "rescue operas", coming in the first place from France but traversing much of Europe – except those places where a conservative and oppressive monarchy could still suppress such subversive ideas. Other kinds of political theme, often of an epic, historical character involving the oppression of national or religious groups, gained favor, especially in France, where massive spectacles, made possible by advances in theater design and lighting, were especially admired.

Escapism and Nature

Another aspect of Romanticism involved the use of art to escape from the increasingly unpleasant realities of life. One of the precursors of Romanticism, the German writer W. H. Wackenroder (1773–98), talked of the "wonder of music" as the "land of faith ... where all our doubts and sufferings are lost in a resounding ocean". Nature herself offered one escape route. The eighteenth century had paid homage to Nature, but chiefly packaged into beautifully laid-out landscapes,

98 *Winter*: oil painting, 1808, by Caspar David Friedrich (original destroyed). Neue Pinakothek, Munich.

improved by Man from a crude and imperfect original, where idyllic scenes could be relished. Raw Nature was admired rather less: when Dr Samuel Johnson traveled to the Scottish Highlands he took good care to draw the carriage blinds as he was disturbed by the prospect of the hills. The nineteenth century however saw Nature as a huge and mysterious force, beside which Man shrank into insignificance. The paintings of Caspar David Friedrich (1774–1840) illustrate powerfully the impact of Nature on Man, often portraying a solitary man standing in awe or fascination at some wild scene of mists, rocks, turbulent waves or gaunt trees (which sometimes looked as if struck by lightning). A musical analogy might be the storm movement in Beethoven's *Pastoral Symphony* or the country scene in Berlioz's *Fantastic Symphony*. The poetry of William Wordsworth (1770–1850) also talks of Man's relation to Nature and its ability to exalt him or fill him with awe.

Haydn and Mozart did not, of course, portray Nature in their music (except in Haydn's direct imitations, in his late oratorios, *The Creation* and *The Seasons*). Beethoven did; so did Mendelssohn, for example in his *Hebrides* Overture (where the music unmistakably symbolizes the waves of the Scottish coastal waters) and his *Italian Symphony*; so did Schumann in his *Spring Symphony* and Liszt in his symphonic poems, to cite only a few. Here we find music used to draw pictures, sometimes to depict events (as we shall see, in Liszt's case especially). Or, it may be argued, music does not draw or depict but conveys the same emotion as do the pictures or the events themselves. The same kinds of analogy came to exist between music and the literary arts; no longer is a song simply a poem set to music but, in the hands of a Schubert or a Schumann, a distillation of the emotion referred to in the words. This alliance between the arts is particularly characteristic of the Romantic era, and it found its ultimate expression in the "total art work" (*Gesamtkunstwerk*) conception of the mature operas of Richard Wagner, in which music, words, scenery and stage movement combine in a single whole – or at least that was Wagner's objective. This represented the highest ideal of the Romantics, the all-embracing, transcendent artistic experience: its culmination in acts of love and of death, in *Tristan und Isolde*, carries Romanticism to its farthest point, indeed to the farthest points of life itself.

Yet the huge scale of Wagner's operas represents only one side of the Romantic spirit. In the early days of Romanticism, especially, the emphasis is not on the large but the small. Beethoven, the last great classicist and a "pre-Romantic", wrote large-scale music; but the next generation were essentially miniaturists. Schubert's large structures are not always secure; his spirit is conveyed more essentially in his short songs or piano pieces. The greatest poet of the piano, Frédéric Chopin, created miniatures – waltzes, Polish mazurkas, atmospheric night-pieces that he called "nocturnes" – which catch a fleeting series of emotions in a brief time-span. The nature of the music written by these men, and others, rules out extended works; the expression of the moment is too pungent to be accommodated within a large-scale structure.

The music of Chopin and Liszt raises another issue central to the Romantics: technical virtuosity. Virtuosos had of course long been admired; Bach and Mozart, and many earlier men, were performers of dazzling skill. But now virtuosity attained new dimensions; what in an earlier age might have been thought tasteless and lacking in musical substance became attractive to audiences. Players technically as accomplished as Chopin or Liszt, but not their equals as musicians, toured Europe and America and filled the concert halls. One of particular fame was the Italian violinist, Nicolò Paganini (1782–1840), whose cadaverous appearance and phenomenal technical skill led those who heard him to suspect some sinister alliance with the devil. The audiences were larger, and drawn from a wider range of social groups, than those of the eighteenth century; larger concert rooms – necessary economically – had to accommodate performances less intimate, less refined, more arresting and more immediately appealing than those that had satisfied the previous generation, when art was the preserve of the connoisseur.

Naturally enough, it is to this age that the concept of "artist as hero" belongs. We have already seen the beginnings of it with Beethoven. While a man like Haydn was content to accept the status of a servant – he would not have thought of questioning it – the Romantic composer viewed himself quite differently. He was not simply supplying a commodity to his employer; he was a creator of something valuable and permanent. Haydn would not have expected his symphonies to outlive him; he wrote them by the hundred and regarded them as expendable, to be surpassed and superseded by those of the next generation. During Haydn's lifetime, however, the idea of preserving and even performing the music of the past began to gain currency, and to Beethoven and the Romantics composition was for posterity. The creative artist was now the visionary – compare any eighteenth-century composer portrait with the famous one of Chopin by Eugène Delacroix (1798–1863), expressing his agonized, Romantic genius – and he saw himself as the equal of any man. When, in the middle of the nineteenth century, Liszt came to Weimar, in central Germany, to work for the duke, it was as a friend and an honored guest, not as an employee to write music to order. In this new context, it is not surprising that the Romantic composer set a great deal more store than the Classical on originality. The Classicist was generally content to conform with existing standards and models; the Romantic was always under pressure to assert his individuality.

As we look in more detail at the main Romantic composers and their music, we shall see various patterns emerge. Among the musical genres they used are most of those of the Classical era. The symphony becomes larger as composers strive to embody within this chief orchestral genre the widest possible range of expression. The concerto becomes increasingly a vehicle for virtuosity, and one in which the "heroic" soloist may battle, symbolically, against the world (the orchestra) – and triumph. Not surprisingly the most characteristic orchestral form of the new era is the symphonic poem, in which the music tells a story, or at least parallels its emotions: Liszt, influenced by Berlioz, is the central figure in this development. Chamber music, moving from the drawing-room to the concert hall, acquires a more public character. Piano music moves away from the abstract sonata towards the genre piece (designed to capture a particular emotion or atmosphere) and the idealized dance. Opera takes different directions in different countries, but everywhere it deals with big issues, like the destiny of Man or the destiny of nations. The most characteristic new genre of the Romantic era is the solo song with piano, as cultivated in the German-speaking countries (and accordingly known as the *Lied*). Its first great master was Franz Schubert.

99 Nicolò Paganini: ink and wash drawing by Edwin Landseer (1802–73). Private collection.

Schubert

If, as the saying goes, "those whom the gods love die young", Schubert was even more divinely beloved than Mozart; Mozart died at 35, Schubert at 31. Like the elder master, Schubert, with his prodigious natural gift and his wide range of feeling, seems to have reached even at that modest age a kind of maturity that escapes many who live far longer.

Franz Schubert		Life
1797	born in Vienna, 31 January	
1808	choirboy in the imperial chapel, Vienna	
1810	studied with Antonio Salieri	
1814	*Gretchen at the Spinning Wheel*	
1815	schoolmaster; prolific output, especially of songs; *The Erlking*	
1816	abandoned teaching; organized first "Schubertiads", evenings with close friends to perform his music	
1818	music master to the children of Count Johann Esterházy, Zseliz; first public concert	
1818	Vienna; reputation increased and circle of friends widened; *Erlking* published	
1822	*Wanderer* Fantasia, "Unfinished" Symphony	
1823	first period of serious illness; *The Beautiful Maid of the Mill*	
1824	Octet, *Death and the Maiden* Quartet, A minor Quartet	
1825	"Schubertiads" resumed; "Great" C major Symphony	
1827	*Winter's Journey*; torchbearer at Beethoven's funeral	
1828	three piano sonatas, string quintet; died in Vienna, 19 November	

Franz Peter Schubert was a Viennese by birth, unlike the other three "Viennese Classicists" (he is often counted as a fourth but in reality he more properly belongs to the Romantic age). He was only a first-generation Viennese: his father had been born in Moravia (now a part of Czechoslovakia), his mother in Silesia (now part German, part Polish). Vienna, capital of the empire that ruled most of central Europe, was a magnet to people from the nearby countryside. Born in 1797, Schubert was the youngest of the four surviving children, all sons, of the marriage. His father, a schoolmaster, taught him the violin, his eldest brother the piano; but he soon overtook them both and was sent to the local organist – who quickly gave him up as he already seemed to know all the organist could teach him. When he was 11 he became a choirboy in the imperial chapel, which involved his attending the city college, a leading boarding school where music was an important part of the course. Schubert soon became concertmaster of the orchestra, sometimes directing it, and came under the tuition of the court music director, Antonio Salieri, a former colleague of Mozart's who years before had given lessons to the young Beethoven.

Schubert did well in all subjects at school, but in music he shone brilliantly. Already he was composing, songs and instrumental pieces, including string quartets in which he played with his father and brothers (his mother died in 1812). He produced numerous composition exercises and songs in 1813, and also his First Symphony and an attempt at an opera. Later that year he left school, and embarked upon training for the career his father had planned for him, as a teacher. He continued to compose fluently and enthusiastically, and from 1814 date his first Mass setting and a fine string quartet. But more important were his songs, one in particular. Schubert had read Goethe's *Faust*, and was attracted by the scene where Gretchen, at the spinning-wheel, is thinking about a lover. Written when he was 17, *Gretchen at the Spinning-Wheel* already shows the special qualities that mark out Schubert as a songwriter – the ability to depict poetically in his music something

Franz Schubert

Works

Songs song cycles – Die schöne Müllerin (The beautiful maid of the mill, 1823), Winterreise (Winter's journey, 1827), Schwanengesang (Swansong, 1828); *c*600 others – Gretchen am Spinnrade (Gretchen at the Spinning Wheel, 1814), Heidenröslein (Little rose on the heath, 1815), Erlkönig (The Erlking, 1815), Der Wanderer (1816), Der Tod und das Mädchen (Death and the maiden, 1817), An die Musik (To music, 1817), Die Forelle (The trout, *c*1817), Der Hirt auf dem Felsen (The shepherd on the rock, 1828), with clarinet

Orchestral music symphonies – no. 5, B♭ (1816), no. 8, ''Unfinished'', b (1822), no. 9, ''Great'', C (*c*1825); overtures

Chamber music 15 string quartets – a (1824), ''Death and the Maiden'', d (1824); String quintet, C (1828); Piano quintet, ''The trout'', A (1819); Octet for clarinet, bassoon, horn, 2 violins, viola, cello and double bass (1824); piano trios, violin sonatas and sonatinas

Piano music 21 sonatas – c (1828), A (1828), B♭ (1828); Wanderer Fantasia, C (1822); Moments musicaux (1828); impromptus, dances; piano duets – Sonata, ''Grand duo'', C (1824), Fantasia, f (1828), variations, marches

Operas Alfonso und Estrella (1822), Fierabras (1823)

Incidental music Rosamunde (1823)

Sacred choral music 7 Masses; *c*30 other works

Partsongs

non-musical, the spinning of the wheel, and to couple with this the expression of the words, so that the wheel itself seems to carry and partake in the expression of Gretchen's unhappiness (ex. VIII.1: note the chromatic inflexion of the measure shown separately).

In 1815, the 18-year-old Schubert became a schoolmaster. He continued to compose, and at great speed. That year saw the composition of almost 150 songs, as well as two symphonies, piano music, two Mass settings and four small-scale operas with spoken dialogue (none of them achieved a performance until long after his death, but clearly he was eager to practice dramatic composition). Of the songs, several are to texts by Goethe, by the great classical poet Friedrich von Schiller (1759–1805) and by the pseudo-medieval Scottish poet known as Ossian whose tales of the romantic north fascinated many musicians (he was not actually medieval but a contemporary writing in a mock-ancient manner).

The greatest song of this year was the Goethe setting *The Erlking* (see p. 282). It is a song of the ballad type, telling a story rather than portraying a mood: a father is carrying his son on horseback through a forest, trying to ward off the evil spirit (the Erlking) who appears to the fevered child and eventually kills him. The pounding piano accompaniment symbolizes first the horse's hooves, but also the intense agitation felt by father and son, while the fiercely dissonant harmony depicts the tragic events and especially the boy's terror. Schubert's friend Josef von Spaun later

ex. VIII.1   **[Not too fast]**

Plate 20 *Opposite* Gluck
and his wife Marianne (see
p. 223): portrait by Krafft.
Historisches Museum der
Stadt Wien.

told how, visiting Schubert, he found him reading the Goethe poem in high excitement, how he composed the song at great speed and how friends were immediately gathered to hear it – which they did with astonishment and enthusiasm. One can sense that it was composed at white heat; its vivid, passionate expression, its feeling of alarm and horror at the confrontation of the innocent child with death and the supernatural, sound a new note in music, different from anything of Mozart or even Beethoven. This is music of the new, Romantic age.

Schubert had always enjoyed music-making in the family home. Now, by 1816, he was building up a circle of friends of his own, young men like Spaun or the law student Franz von Schober, who took part in "Schubertiads", evenings of performing Schubert's newest music. It was partly for these gatherings of middle-class, artistically aware, enthusiastic young people that Schubert composed. But gradually his reputation widened: a well-known opera baritone, J. M. Vogl, began to sing Schubert's songs, with the composer accompanying, in drawing-room recitals during 1817 and the next year one of his songs was published. He had a break from teaching in 1816–17 but then returned to the family home and resumed, giving up finally only in summer 1818 when he accepted a post as music master in the family of Count Johann Esterházy (relatives of Haydn's former patrons).

1816 was another amazingly prolific year, again with song at the forefront of his output, though there were also sonatas for violin and piano and the Fifth Symphony, a work of particular charm and warmth of feeling; if it lacks the formal coherence of Haydn, Mozart or Beethoven, it has no pretensions to being for public performance (it was designed for a private orchestra which had grown out of the family quartet). 1817 was productive too, with a sudden burst of interest in the

100 *Schubert evening at
the home of Joseph von
Spaun*: sepia drawing by
Moritz von Schwind
(1804–71). Historisches
Museum der Stadt Wien.
Schubert is at the piano,
with the singer Vogl on his
right, and von Spaun on
his left.

piano sonata, another symphony, a couple of lightweight overtures in the manner of Rossini (then extremely popular in Vienna) and of course many songs. Among these are three favorites: the gently grave *To Music*, a setting of words by Schober in praise of the art of music, lovingly and subtly composed in such a way that the "art of music" – a graceful melody and some characteristically expressive harmony – makes the point on its own behalf; the somber *Death and the Maiden*, akin in topic to *The Erlking* but making its effect more simply and darkly as Death invites the Maiden to sleep in his arms; and *The Trout*, where against a lyrical voice melody, a piano figure represents the glittering fish darting in the stream. This song uses one of Schubert's typical methods in making its point. It is a "modified strophic" song (a strophic one being in several verses to the same music). Schubert often set out as if to write a simple strophic one, then, coming to its emotional climax in the final verse, changed the music at that point so as to arrest the listener's attention by its unexpectedness and at the same time to color the crucial words more sharply. Indeed there is reason to think that one of the factors that dictated Schubert's choice of verses to set was that an opportunity for this treatment presented itself. He read a great deal of poetry seeking suitable material for setting; he set many fine poets, but also some indifferent ones, for a good song – as he proved – can be made out of quite ordinary verse if its images and structure lend themselves to musical treatment.

The middle years

Back in Vienna at the end of 1818, Schubert took rooms with his friend the poet Johann Mayrhofer. This began a period that was happy and productive and saw his reputation steadily increase. He composed a couple of theater works – a spoken play with songs and incidental music for a drama; neither was of high quality but both helped bring his name to notice. Another work was heard at a private concert in the home of a leading patron, the father of a friend of Schubert's. In the summer Schubert went to Steyr, 90 miles west of Vienna, with Vogl, and was commissioned to write a piano quintet – this was the "Trout" quintet, of which the fourth movement is a happy set of variations on the song. The whole work is permeated with its spirit, captured in the ebullient melodies, the beguiling harmonies and the easily brilliant piano writing – which is often high-pitched and quick-moving, adding a glitter to the textures.

His circle of friends continued to widen: it came to include poets, court officials, singers, the dramatist Franz Grillparzer and the painter Moritz von Schwind who left us a famous depiction of a Schubertiad. Some of Schubert's friends got together to have *The Erlking* and others of his songs published; curiously, the Viennese publishers were slow to take up Schubert's music, probably because he had no real reputation as a concert performer. He spent some of the summer of 1821 in a holiday party with friends outside Vienna and part of the fall with Schober at a castle in St Pölten, where he went for the peace and quiet he needed to write an opera. This was *Alfonso und Estrella*, of which Schober wrote the words; it is full of colorful and attractive music, but the plot is not strong and the work as a whole lacks a sense of theatrical pace – Schubert was inclined to treat each number in his normal, songwriter's style of rich lyricism, and to think too little about the relationship of one to another, so that the whole seems like a succession of beautiful songs without any real development of action or character. The work was anyway left unperformed until a quarter of a century after Schubert's death; Vogl was too critical of the text to recommend it, and the opera promoters could make more money out of Rossini than by putting on a piece by a little-known local composer.

Plate 21 *Top left* Vauxhall Gardens, the most famous of the London pleasure-gardens (see p. 222): watercolour, 1784, by Thomas Rowlandson. Victoria and Albert Museum, London.

Plate 22 *Left* Rehearsal for a sacred cantata (p. 79): gouache, c1775, artist unknown, in a family album. Germanisches Nationalmuseum, Nuremberg.

101 Franz Schubert:
pencil drawing by Moritz
von Schwind (1804–71).
Private collection.

The great outpouring of songs of 1815, 1816 and 1817 had now slowed to a trickle. Only about 15 date from 1818; in 1819 he wrote about double that number, and each of the next three years saw the composition of around 15 to 20. He was now putting more of his personality and his intellectual and emotional concentration into instrumental music. Two works from the end of 1822 demonstrate this in particular: the *Wanderer* Fantasia for piano and the Unfinished Symphony. Schubert already had behind him about a dozen piano sonatas, numerous dances and other shorter pieces, as well as piano duets (well suited to his convivial musical evenings). This Fantasia is however something new: it attempts something that composers had scarcely done before, nor even thought of the need or desirability for doing. Virtually the whole four-movement work is organized around the same theme. It is stated emphatically at the opening (ex. VIII.2a); the contrasting lyrical idea or "second subject" that follows preserves the rhythm and the idea of repeating a phrase one step higher (ex. 2b). It is not a conventional second subject, though at first it seems like one (if in a distant key rather than the expected G major); the movement is not in the traditional sonata-form pattern. There is in fact a secondary "second subject", which takes as its starting-point the three-note figure x from ex. 2b, shown in ex. 2c. The slow movement, which follows without a break, gives the work its name: it is based on a song, *The Wanderer*, composed six years before – and yet its opening seems to be based on the same idea as the first movement, or at least the same rhythm (ex. 2d). In the song, this music comes to the words "The sun bathes me in cold, the blood dries up". The Adagio gives way to a Scherzo, whose opening, principal theme is a more distant derivative but still a clear one of the theme heard at the start (ex. 2e); and the later contrasting theme (ex. 2f) equally clearly comes from ex. 2b. The finale – or one can think of it as a continuation of the first movement after a long interruption – begins fugally (ex. 2g). This transformation of themes, where the same musical idea is made to acquire a range of different expressive senses, was later to be pursued by such men as Liszt, Berlioz and Wagner. Schubert's idea was chiefly to find a way of bringing unity to an extended work, a matter that seems to have troubled him, for with his strong lyrical and harmonic gifts the passing events in his music are of such striking character that they are liable to undermine unity and continuity.

The other remarkable work of late 1822 was the famous Unfinished Symphony. It is unlike any earlier symphony in its profoundly poetic manner, its mystery and its pathos, as the dark-colored opening shows with its hushed cellos and basses, then throbbing strings over which oboe and clarinet in a strange unison float their theme. Later there is "symphonic argument" of a more usual, Beethovenian kind, but the atmosphere of the work as a whole is that of its opening measures, and the slow movement that follows does nothing to contradict that. Schubert started to sketch a third movement, but got no further. Why did he not finish what was potentially so great a work? We do not know; perhaps he put it aside because he had no need of a symphony at the moment, then later could not recapture its expressive world. In fact, he probably gave the manuscript to his friends the Hüttenbrenner brothers in 1823 (possibly to discharge some sort of obligation to them) – it remained in Anselm Hüttenbrenner's possession until 1865 and had its first hearing 33 years after Schubert's death. He never heard it himself.

There may be other, more tragic factors behind his turning away from this symphony, for at the end of 1822 a catastrophe occurred in Schubert's life. There is evidence that he sometimes visited prostitutes (sexual activity with girls of his own

ex. VIII.2

class was then out of the question). He now contracted syphilis. There were many treatments for this disease and a number of supposed cures (because certain symptoms disappeared), but its nature was not fully understood. The progress of the disease, and the treatments he underwent, are easy to follow in the light of his friends' surviving comments on his health over the next few years; for the rest of his life he suffered various uncomfortable and often embarrassing symptoms. The disease moved fast, and it was of syphilis (not typhus or typhoid fever, as some books say) that he died. The compositions of his remaining years, 1823–8, have to be seen in the light of his awareness of his illness and the suffering he underwent, and it may be that it was some mental association between the composition of the Unfinished·Symphony and the contraction of this terrible illness that made it impossible for a man of such sensitive temperament to return to the work.

The late years   The year 1823 began with Schubert's return from his rooms in Schober's house to the family home. The *Wanderer* Fantasia was published early in the year, and Schubert sold several collections of songs to Viennese publishing firms; his reputation was now sufficient to attract publishers' interest. He turned again to dramatic music, writing a short operetta in the early spring and a more ambitious serious opera, *Fierabras*, across the summer; typical of its time, it has a medieval setting, and there are fine, characteristic pages in it although its dramatic vitality is too limited for successful performance in a theater. Both this and the operetta remained unheard, again, until after Schubert's death.

Schubert was out of Vienna during the summer, at Steyr and Linz (where he was made an honorary member of the musical society). During the fall he was ill again – possibly he was in hospital in November – but able to work, and the chief product of the late part of the year was the song cycle *Die schöne Müllerin* ("The beautiful maid of the mill"). This is a collection of 20 songs telling, often by symbolizing human emotion in terms of nature, a story in which the poet (and thus the singer) is protagonist: he arrives at the mill, falls in love with the mill-girl, enjoys happiness with her, feels anger and jealousy when she turns to another man, and dies. The bubbling of the brook is heard in many of the songs and there is much other nature imagery, designed to reflect the emotion expressed in the words. The choice of topic, with resignation and bitterness at the end, seems appropriate to Schubert's state of mind; though this kind of expression – love and despair, mirrored through Nature – is in any case typical of early Romantic art.

Other compositions of 1823 were some fine incidental music for a feeble play called *Rosamunde* and a small group of songs to words by Friedrich Rückert. The next year was virtually blank as far as song is concerned, but it saw Schubert return to chamber music after a gap of several years. First came an octet for wind and strings, a happy work in six movements, in the tradition of Beethoven's similar septet and, looking further back, of the late eighteenth-century divertimento. It was commissioned by a count who played the clarinet. There were also two string quartets, in A minor and D minor. The A minor work is predominantly lyrical, with hints too of the elegiac and the mysterious; its slow movement is a set of variations on a theme Schubert had used in the *Rosamunde* music. The D minor, altogether more fiery, pushes the medium of the string quartet towards richer, almost orchestral sonorities. It begins with a dramatic gesture (ex. VIII.3*a*), from which the descending triplet (*x*) becomes the chief material of the movement – some of the ways in which Schubert uses it to maintain the tension and to propel the

ex. VIII.3

music forward by using it in dialogue may be seen in ex. 3*b*. Another feature of Schubert's mature style is his use of accompaniment figures, which may be simple or elaborate but always hold together a sustained passage and usually have a poetic content of their own. In ex. 3*c*, the melodic interest is in the second violin and the cello parts, with the viola providing the main harmonic filling-in; but the first violin has a delicate figure (derived from the passage immediately before) which adds a gloss and richness to the texture.

These examples come from the first movement, the most dramatic and fully developed. The second, a set of variations on a theme and a set of harmonies from Schubert's *Death and the Maiden* song, is one of his most imaginative creations. Its five variations begin with an improvisatory flight by the first violin and continue with a poetic cello solo with a soaring, sustained line. Next is an angry-sounding variation with fierce accents, and fourth a gently expressive one turning to the major key; the fifth is the dramatic climax – it starts like a minor-key version of the fourth but gradually acquires more force until the upper three instruments are hammering out sixteenths above a wilful bass from the cello; this subsides into a coda which, as if weary of struggle, returns to the opening theme, now more gentle and in the major mode. A Scherzo follows, and a long, vigorous finale, which leaps along in gigue-like rhythms, its energies only momentarily subdued for a richly sonorous contrasting theme.

These three masterpieces were written early in 1824; for spring and summer Schubert went once again to the Esterházy family in Hungary. His original circle of friends in Vienna had dwindled, and for more than one reason he was inclined to sigh for happier, more innocent days. Back in Vienna, he went early in 1825 to live near to Schwind, now his closest friend; a new group formed, and Schubertiads resumed. Meanwhile, more of his music was being performed elsewhere and more was reaching print.

He spent much of the 1825 summer in Upper Austria. It was probably at this time that he composed his last and greatest symphony, known as the "Great C major" (it is usually called no. 9, sometimes no. 7; in fact, counting only the complete symphonies and the Unfinished, it should be no. 8). It is on a large scale; all its ideas are extended and fully worked out. The Andante introduction, with its solitary horn melody, sounds a Romantic voice; a distant horn conjures up favorite Romantic images. But the main part of the movement is more classical – much more so than the Unfinished – in its orderly statements and repetitions, and in the expressive blandness of the material itself, which is better designed for symphonic argument than most of Schubert's ideas. There are moments of Romantic mystery, too. In the first-movement exposition the music, where it might be expected to settle into the dominant key, G major, dips into remote E♭, and the sound of soft trombones – instruments used mainly for their effectiveness in loud music – playing a broad melody that gradually seems to guide the music back where it ought to be, is one of the most imaginative strokes in symphonic music.

The rest of the symphony is on a correspondingly large scale. The Andante is a continuous outpouring of melody, first a plaintive one in A minor on the oboe, later a warm, major-key one on strings, echoed by winds: the themes develop, in their way – not an argued, Beethovenian way but an extension of the themes themselves. When the oboe resumes the opening melody, it is enhanced by a delicate, characteristic accompanying figure. There is an energetic Scherzo and a long and brilliant finale whose grandeur and sweep and bold, original strokes are comparable with those of the first movement and provide a proper balance to it.

This great symphony, unhappily, is another work that Schubert himself never heard. Probably he had intended it for the Vienna Philharmonic Society, but it lay unknown in the possession of Schubert's brother Ferdinand until 1837, when Robert Schumann found it; the first performance, in which passages were omitted because of the work's length, was conducted by Mendelssohn two years later.

Schubert was back in Vienna by October 1825. More publications appeared, particularly of piano music, in 1826, and his name was gradually becoming better known – though his application for a post in the emperor's musical establishment was turned down. It was not a prolific time for composition, but he wrote nearly 20 songs in the year and a very fine string quartet, a work of some violence with its rapid changes of mood, its tense tremolos, its abrupt changes of key and its ferocious accents. There is almost a sense of personal pain and anger behind this remarkable, deeply original music.

A similar pain runs through Schubert's main composition of 1827, the song cycle

Winterreise ("Winter's Journey"). The poems, like those of *Die schöne Müllerin*, are the work of Wilhelm Müller, no great poet but one whose flowing words, attractive imagery and shapely structures made them ideal for Schubert. As in the earlier cycle, the poems tell, largely through analogies with Nature, of desolation and longing; sometimes they refer to rejection in love, to bitter loneliness, to happy memories that have grown sad in recollection, to solitude and misery in a world where everyone else is joyous, to aimless wandering through cold and dark, and ultimately to death. The music itself is austere; most of the songs are in minor keys, many are slow, and the old warmth and harmonic richness are rare. It is not surprising that Schubert's friends were disturbed at this gloom; they feared for his state of mind – it is hard to imagine anyone's composing such music unless it arose from personal experience of the emotions depicted.

Half the *Winterreise* songs were written in early 1827 (when, incidentally, Schubert was a torch-bearer at Beethoven's funeral); the others were written in the fall. In between, he had two trips outside Vienna. Although his illness continued to trouble him a good deal, composition continued, sometimes at a rapid pace. To late 1827 and early 1828 belong the two fine piano trios, of which the one in B♭ stands out for its vitality and lyrical warmth. There are also several short piano pieces, mostly lacking the purposefulness of sonata movements but attractive and relaxed in mood; he had them published under the titles *Impromptu* and *Moment musical*.

1828, then, began promisingly. Schubert must have been heartened when, in March, a concert exclusively of his music – the only one he gave – took place in an inn owned by the Philharmonic Society and brought him some useful income. His publishing plans went forward. He composed a new Mass and a group of songs (later to be gathered together under the title "Swansong"); he also worked on a new symphony. In September he moved to lodgings with his brother, and within a few weeks produced four major instrumental works – three piano sonatas and a string quintet.

We have seen that Schubert's command of musical design was not as strong as Beethoven's. But a work like the Piano Sonata in B♭ of September 1828, the last and grandest of these three, shows a powerful structure of its kind. It is not comparable with Beethoven's partly because Schubert's objectives were quite different from the elder composer's. His gifts, his musical personality, were of another kind – gentler, more lyrical, more concerned with harmonic effect and the quality of piano texture. His piano music achieved a climax of greatness in these last three sonatas of the late summer of 1828. His chamber music too reached new heights with the String Quintet in C written at much the same time. For this work Schubert specified an ensemble consisting of string quartet plus an extra cello instead of the usual extra viola (as in Mozart's quintets); this allows for greater enrichment of the sound and for the possibility of a low-pitched bass line continuing even when the first cello is playing in its high, tenor register. As in the B♭ sonata, the music is full of lyrical, expansive melodies, subtle and emotionally suggestive turns of harmony, and original effects of musical texture (see Listening Note VIII.A).

This first movement is one of Schubert's great achievements as a lyrical yet symphonic composer. In the equally remarkable slow movement, one of the texture patterns of the B♭ sonata – a harmonized melody in the middle register, accompanied above and below – is taken further. Ex.VIII.4*a* shows the opening, with the main melody in the second violin, the bass in the second cello, an

Listening Note VIII.A

Schubert: *String Quintet in C* D956 (1828)

2 violins, viola, 2 cellos

1st movement (Allegro ma non troppo): Sonata form, C

Exposition (mm. 1–154)   The music begins slowly, with soft, glowing chords and a theme that only gradually seems to take shape. But its melodic line (ex. i) serves as a bass, for the two cellos together, in the stormy tutti that follows. This comes to a close with a cadence on G, and the key poetically shifts to E♭ where a new, lyrical theme (ex. ii) is stated – first by the two cellos, with the other instruments accompanying, then by the two violins. The theme itself goes from E♭ to G, the key we expect at this point, and when the violins have reached G the first embarks on a new idea (subtly linked with ex. ii); it is echoed two measures later and one octave lower by the viola, with accompaniment figures on the other instruments (see ex. iii). This spacious passage eventually comes to a climax, with a phrase (ex. iv) that is used for dialogue in the section that follows. A new theme (ex. v) heralds the end of the exposition, and the music becomes harmonically more static. (Schubert indicated a repeat of the exposition, but this is not often observed.)

Development (mm. 155–266)   The material chiefly developed comes from ex. ii (figure *x*) and ex. v (figure *y*). Using these, the music ranges far afield in key – to A, f♯ and c♯, then to the major of c♯ (that is, D♭) and back again through c♯ to E. During this, the first violin sings a high, deeply poetic line while the viola and first cello pursue ideas derived from *y*. A large section (the one moving from f♯ to E) is repeated, identically, one step lower – that is, from e to D. The music then switches to d and to more intense activity: the viola follows the first violin in quick, triplet movement, the second violin follows the second cello in a more energetic line derived from *y*. The music finds its way back to C; there is a moment of violence, but calm soon arrives and we are back at the . . .

Recapitulation (mm. 267–414)   The slow-moving ex. i is now accompanied by extra movement, first in the violins, later in the cellos. Schubert takes us to F for the restatement of ex. i in the bass. This enables him to recapitulate, from that point onwards, almost identically (as he usually prefers, unlike the previous generation of Viennese composers). The second-subject material thus begins in A♭ and reaches the home key of C for the ensuing section.

Coda (mm. 414–45)   The music of the recapitulation draws to a halt, and suddenly we are back with the slow, soft chords from the beginning of the movement. But the calmness is brief, indeed illusory, as the cellos burst in with a violent, explosive *fortissimo*; a moment later the violins do the same, in the remote key of b♭. This dark mood, however, seems to burn itself out, and finally a sort of calm returns, based on the figure *x* material used in the development, and with only the occasional chromatic note and a sense of nostalgia for the innocence of the opening to darken it.

2nd movement (Adagio): Ternary form, E—f—E
3rd movement (Scherzo: Presto): Ternary form, C—f—C
4th movement (Allegretto): Sonata form, C

ex. i

ex. ii

ex. iii

ex. iv

ex. v

ornamental accompaniment in the first violin. Ex. 4*b* shows the same passage as it appears in the recapitulatory section, with the accompaniment assuming a new expressive life of its own. This flowering is provoked by the middle section – perhaps the stormiest, indeed blackest music that Schubert ever wrote, full of angry, dissonant harmonies, supported by tremolos and dislocated rhythms, and in the distant key of F minor. Here the darkest moods of *Winterreise* are expressed in instrumental terms. Then, in the middle of the hectic, ebullient Scherzo comes a trio section which, instead of the conventional lyrical contrast, offers slow, bleak music, again in remote F minor. The finale is outwardly happier, but (typically) makes much of major/minor alternation, tingeing the music with darkness.

There was reason for darkness, and Schubert probably knew it. He went for a brief walking tour in October 1828, about the time he was working on the quintet, but was weak and exhausted. Curiously, he arranged to take counterpoint lessons

ex. VIII.4

from a well-known Viennese music theorist during November, and even wrote some exercises; possibly he wanted to follow up the canonic writing of the quintet but felt technically ill-equipped. In fact, it seems that he never took the lessons; during November he was increasingly weak, often unable to eat, barely able to correct the proofs of the second part of *Winterreise*. Schubert's own wintry journey was over: he died on 19 November 1828. Grillparzer's famous epitaph – "The Art of Music here entombs a rich possession but even finer hopes" – is appropriate enough for a genius who died at 31; but it is typical of its times in failing to recognize that this man's genius did in fact reach full maturity, and that the legacy of his last few years places him among the very greatest of masters.

Early Romanticism in Germany

Schubert has been called a "Romantic Classicist", and the combination term is a fair one, for his art, however deeply imbued with Romantic attitudes to life, is still rooted in the musical traditions of Haydn, Mozart and Beethoven. There were others in Germany who show a similar mixture in different forms and proportions, for example the pianist-composer J. N. Hummel (1778–1837), a pupil of Mozart's who extended an essentially Mozartian style with Romantic harmony and brilliance, and Louis Spohr (1784–1859), who also started from a Mozartian language and extended it chiefly through expressive chromatic harmony, color and virtuosity (he was a violinist, and also probably the first man regularly to conduct an orchestra with a baton). Neither of these fully embraced a Romantic attitude to his art; the first to do so in Germany was Weber.

Weber

Carl Maria von Weber was born in 1786, in north Germany, into a family of musicians; Mozart's wife, Constanze, was one of his cousins. He traveled much in his early years and his first main studies were in Salzburg, under Michael Haydn, Joseph's younger brother. He was not yet 12 when, in Munich, he wrote his first opera; his next had a performance, in the Saxon town of Freiberg, when he was just 14, and a third followed a year later. Before he was 18 he was appointed *Kapellmeister* at the theater in Breslau (now Wroclaw, Poland); he tried to institute reforms to improve the level of performances, but made enemies and had to resign. After a brief time at a nearby court he went in 1807 to the Stuttgart court, where he played the piano and wrote songs, chamber music and piano pieces; but in 1810 there was an unfortunate incident involving money – he does not seem to have behaved dishonestly – and he had to leave. His career reads like a German travelogue (he even thought of writing a musical travel guide to Germany): he went to Heidelberg, Darmstadt, Munich (where he wrote attractive concertos for clarinet and bassoon, and his comic opera *Abu Hassan* was well received), then on a concert tour with a clarinetist friend to Prague, Dresden, Weimar (where he met Goethe) and Berlin.

In 1813 his life became more stable when he was appointed *Kapellmeister* at the Prague opera house. Again he spent much of his energy on reform, but he also enlarged the repertory and began to write newspaper essays to attract audiences. Further, he fell in love with a singer, whom he was later to marry. All this time his health, never good, was deteriorating. In 1816 he left Prague and after further travels became royal *Kapellmeister* in Dresden. A staunch German nationalist, he had difficulties there as the Italian influence was traditionally strong; his plans to improve the German opera were often countered by the Italians. Meanwhile, he was at work on an opera for performance in Berlin, *Der Freischütz*; it was ready in mid-1820, and given a year later. It was a triumph. Weber eventually managed to

---

Carl Maria von Weber   Works
born Eutin, 1786; *died* London, 1826

Operas Der Freischütz (The freeshooter, 1821), Euryanthe (1823), Oberon (1826)
Orchestral music 2 piano concertos (1810, 1812); 2 clarinet concertos (1811); bassoon concerto (1811); Konzertstück for piano and orchestra (1821); overtures
Choral music 2 Masses (1818, 1819); 6 cantatas
Piano music Aufforderung zum Tanze (Invitation to the dance, 1819); 4 sonatas; variations, dances
Incidental music   Chamber music   Songs

102 The Wolf's Glen
scene from Weber's *Der
Freischütz*, in the 1822
Weimar production
designed by Carl Wilhelm
Holdermann: aquatint by
C. Lieber.

have it given at Dresden early in 1822. Soon after, it was given in Vienna, where he was commissioned to write another opera in the same manner. But he chose another, grander manner, less suited to his talents, for the new work, *Euryanthe*. He was back in Vienna (where he met Beethoven and Schubert) in late 1823; *Euryanthe*, handicapped by a poor libretto, had a mixed reception.

The strains of these years – he had worked endlessly and the rewards had been slender – had told on him; he had tuberculosis and realized he could not live long. Then an invitation came to write an opera for the 1825 season in London; the fee was large, and he accepted for his family's sake, although he knew that the journey could only accelerate his illness. This trip was postponed for a year; he left in February 1826, in feeble health. In London he was warmly welcomed, but grew increasingly weak. The new work, *Oberon*, was well received (although a piecemeal work, quite unlike the kind of opera Weber really believed in, and encumbered by an absurd plot). But his condition worsened and he died, far from his home and family, in June 1826.

Weber had great gifts and occupies a special place in the history of opera. He wrote melodies of an appealing charm, he had a rich command of orchestral color (as *Oberon* in particular shows), and he had a real sense of how to convey atmosphere and drama, one of his devices being the use of a special theme in connection with a character, which he would alter to convey that character's feelings or behavior. (This technique, as we shall see, was later developed by Wagner.) *Der Freischütz* – the title literally means "The Freeshooter" – is his only opera regularly performed nowadays. It is a tale of the supernatural, about a forester who sells his soul to the devil in order to obtain magic bullets, with which he can prove himself a marksman worthy of his beloved, the head ranger's daughter. The opera is full of typical early Romantic features: magic bullets, ominous dreams, a bridal bouquet that turns out mysteriously to be a funeral wreath, Nature (in the form of a forest) that both fascinates and alarms, comradely drinking-songs and hunting-songs, and of course the devil. For the convivial songs Weber uses the style, with a folk-music basis, favored by the many new choral societies that were coming into existence; these help give the opera its pronounced German flavor which so pleased the early audiences. But the most characteristic and most striking scene is the one in the Wolf's Glen where Max, the forester, makes his compact with the devil. Here Weber truly enlarges the vocabulary of music. As the scene opens, we hear soft trombones and low clarinets, a hushed *tremolando* on the strings, a chromatically wandering bass line, in sinister harmonies using chords that make the key feeling uncertain. Then there are shrieks on the woodwinds, shouts from an offstage, invisible chorus of spirits, a clock striking midnight, breathlessly quiet music alternating with violent outbursts, and a series of effects of increasing terror follow as the seven magic bullets are cast. The music is not just horrific; Weber was a real musical thinker and planner, and the scene has a structure, in terms of pace, key and motif, that makes it the more effective.

Weber also contributed significantly to piano music and the concerto, song and choral music. Not all his musical ideas are distinguished, but the best and most original were inspired by drama and his new and vigorous response to the stimuli of Romanticism give him a special importance. Weber was also the first composer to write serious music criticism, an activity that shows an awareness of musical issues and their relation to other aspects of life that it would be impossible to imagine in composers of a generation earlier. This selfconsciousness about the musician's role represents another aspect of the Romantic artist's attitudes to his art and society.

Mendelssohn

Weber conforms well to the traditional notion of the Romantic artist who struggles through poverty and incomplete recognition, and in the end dies of "consumption". Felix Mendelssohn, emphatically, does not. He was born in 1809, in Hamburg, into a well-to-do upper-middle-class Jewish family, with a well-established cultural and intellectual background. His grandfather, Moses Mendelssohn (1729–86), was an eminent philosopher and a literary man; his father was a banker. The family moved to Berlin in Felix's infancy, where he received a careful, thorough education and his precocious musical gifts were encouraged. He wrote six symphonies when he was 12 and a further seven over the next two years – works following the Classical style but with much spirit and individuality as well as great technical polish. There were also choral and piano works and early attempts at theater music. When he was only 12, he was taken to meet Goethe, and a warm friendship developed. At 16 he was taken to Paris, where the senior Italian

Felix Mendelssohn   Works
born Hamburg, 1809; *died* Leipzig, 1847

Orchestral music symphonies – no. 3, "Scottish" (1842), no. 4, "Italian" (1833),
no. 5, "Reformation" (1832); overtures – A Midsummer Night's Dream (1826),
Calm Sea and Prosperous Voyage (1828), The Hebrides [Fingal's Cave] (1830, rev.
1832), Ruy Blas (1839); piano concertos – no. 1, g (1831), no. 2, d (1837), Violin
Concerto, e (1844); 12 string symphonies

Oratorios St Paul (1836), Elijah (1846)

Chamber music Octet (1825); 6 string quartets; 2 string quintets; piano quartets,
cello sonatas, violin sonatas

Piano music Lieder ohne Worte (Songs without words), 8 vols. (1829–45); sonatas,
variations

Sacred choral music cantatas, motets, anthems, psalms

Organ music preludes and fugues

Songs   *Partsongs*   *Incidental music*

composer Luigi Cherubini (1760–1842), an opera composer much admired by
Beethoven, encouraged him to follow a musical career.

Few musicians up to this time had as full a grounding in literature and philosophy
as did Mendelssohn. His father's house was the meeting-place of influential writers
and thinkers. Lines from Goethe's *Faust* colored his Octet for strings, written when
he was 17; the scherzo of this vividly and richly scored work, Mendelssohn's first to

ex. VIII.5

have a firm place in the repertory today and remarkable for its masterly construction, was inspired by a scene involving fairy spirits. More fairies, Shakespeare's from *A Midsummer Night's Dream*, affected another work of this time, his overture for that play. Although in normal sonata form, it includes music descriptive of incidents or characters in the play – the soft wind chords at the beginning and end hint at the atmosphere of the woodlands where much of the action takes place (ex. VIII.5*a*), the rapid motion of the high violins unmistakably represents the fairies (ex. 5*b*), the "hee-haw" figure (ex. 5*c*) clearly mimics Bottom with an ass's head, while the expressive second subject stands for the youthful pairs of lovers (ex. 5*d*). The whole work is exquisitely scored, with novel and poetic effects; it captures, with astonishing truth, the spirit of Shakespeare's world.

Mendelssohn's chief teacher, when he was a boy, was the composer Zelter, who was also director of the well-known Berlin choral society, the Singakademie. There he had come across choral music by J. S. Bach, which was unfamiliar – at this time performers preferred more recent music and Bach's was largely forgotten. But Mendelssohn came across a copy of the *St Matthew Passion* and, realizing its greatness, asked Zelter if he could perform it; Zelter agreed, and in 1829, just over a century after its première, the work was revived for the first time since Bach's own performances. This historic occasion initiated the long-term revival of Bach's choral works.

Up to this time, Mendelssohn's travels had been mainly in Germany. Now he went further afield: first to London, where he was particularly well received, and on to Scotland, where he carefully noted his impressions (and made many attractive and accomplished drawings); then, in 1830, to Italy, including Venice, Rome and Naples, where again he stored his impressions. These journeys provided him with material for some of his finest works. The Scottish trip suggested to him musical ideas from which he composed a symphony and an overture, this last another inspired and atmospheric descriptive piece. In the Hebrides islands, off the Scottish coast, he had seen Fingal's Cave, and the swell of the waves on the rocky coastline – as well as their more violent buffeting of it in a storm – can be heard in the music: ex. VIII.6*a* stands for the smooth flow of the water, and a figure from it (*x*) is drawn

ex. VIII.6

from it and developed in a stormy passage (ex. 6*b*). Another musical element in this work, unrelated to Nature, has its source in Mendelssohn's poetic imagination – the distant fanfares of trumpets (or other instruments imitating them), hinting at some mysterious presence in the caves or behind the craggy rocks, especially where the instruments echo one another. In all this we see again that part of the Romantic spirit that concerns itself with the observation of Nature and Man's awe at her calm and her violence alike.

Having played a part in the revival of Bach, Mendelssohn now did the same for Handel, whose music had been kept alive in England but was little performed in Germany. In Düsseldorf, where he became city music director in 1833, he gave *Israel in Egypt* that year and several more oratorios in the two years following. In Düsseldorf he helped found a new theater and revived some of the greatest operas from Mozart's time onwards in fine performances. He wrote an oratorio himself, *St Paul*, which he conducted at a Düsseldorf festival in 1836.

To the early 1830s – when Mendelssohn was still in his own early 20s – belong many of his finest works. Among them is his *Italian Symphony*, written in 1832 shortly after his return from Italy and first performed in London the next year. It reflects the fascination that Italy, with its brilliant, clear skies, its warmth and its vitality has always held for artists, like Goethe and Handel, from the colder, cloudier north. The opening measures (ex. VIII.7a) catch this clarity and brilliance

ex. VIII.7

unmistakably, not only in the dashing, energetic line of the theme, heard on violins in octaves (and set off by a pizzicato chord akin to a shot from a starter's pistol), but also in the extraordinary boldness and originality of the accompaniment, rapid repeated notes on the flutes, clarinets, bassoons and horns. The music is always fluent and graceful, yet such was Mendelssohn's technique that he could also give it symphonic coherence; in the development section of the first movement, for example, a little motif (ex. 7b) is worked up into a lengthy, well-argued fugue, into which the first phrase of ex. 7a intrudes, first discreetly and then persistently, pressing the music to a climax, then subduing it and leading it to the recapitulation. The slow movement, said to draw its main theme from a Czech pilgrim song, is sometimes called a pilgrims' march. Here again Mendelssohn's ear for orchestral color produces remarkable results – the "march" theme, first heard on high violas, whose reediness is enhanced by an oboe and a bassoon, is then taken up by violins with a strange, wailing counterpoint on a pair of flutes, lending it a hint of mystery, like some ageless ritual procession. The third movement is closer to minuet than scherzo in its warmth and charm, with a suggestion of distant fairy horns in its middle section; the finale is a rapid movement in the manner of a saltarello, a dance from Naples.

In 1835 Mendelssohn became conductor of the orchestra of the Gewandhaus ("Cloth Hall") in Leipzig, a post he held for the rest of his life. He did much to raise the standard of the orchestra and improve its working conditions; he revived music by Bach and forgotten works by Mozart, he pressed the claims of Beethoven, still a modern composer (he gave the Ninth Symphony, the *Choral*, six times), and he introduced music by Weber and Schubert, including the "Great C major" Symphony, of which he conducted the première in 1839. He also gave new works by Schumann and directed "historical concerts", series which spanned from Bach to his own time. In the early 1840s he spent some time in Berlin, at the request of the new Prussian king, who wanted to reform the arts there; but circumstances were difficult and he had mixed success though it was for a Berlin performance at this time that he supplemented his *Midsummer Night's Dream* overture with music for other scenes of the play, including the most famous wedding march ever written. Mendelssohn was also taken away from Leipzig by repeated journeys to England, where he was immensely popular – he was friendly with Queen Victoria and her German consort, Prince Albert, and much loved by the choral societies which had come to occupy a large place in English musical life. It was for one of these that he composed his oratorio *Elijah*, essentially in the Handelian tradition though adapted to the musical style of the day; it had its first performance, with Mendelssohn conducting, at a festival in Birmingham in 1846, and was a huge success.

Leipzig, however, remained the center of his activities. In 1843 he founded there what was to be the most famous of all the European music conservatories of the time; in the second half of the century it was undisputedly the best place for musical study and especially attracted students from abroad, Britain, the USA and northern Europe in particular.

Among the compositions of these years are chamber works, including two piano trios (the one in D minor is the most sparkling and effective piece composed for the medium) and several string quartets, in which he tended to follow the Beethoven tradition, producing beautifully shaped works with some compelling Romantic coloring. But his finest achievement of this period was his Violin Concerto, written in 1844 for the leader of the Gewandhaus Orchestra, and the first of the great Romantic violin concertos. Here Mendelssohn's capacity for appealing, poetic writing found an ideal outlet in the sweet, refined voice of the violin which could draw lyrical and plaintive melodies above the sound of the full orchestra. His adaptation of traditional concerto form to the special lyrical character of the work is typical of his mastery: for example in the opening measures, where he dispenses with the orchestral prelude and simply supplies a gentle accompaniment for the violin theme, or in the new role he finds for the cadenza – formerly the climax at the end of the first movement, now a point of repose to provide a magical link between development and recapitulation. The slow movement is songlike, with a touch of the sentimentality characteristic of the time (present too in some of Mendelssohn's piano music, like the *Songs without Words*); in the finale, those fleet-footed fairies are back in a movement of spirit and brilliantly handled virtuosity.

Mendelssohn seemed, in the mid-1840s, to be at the highpoint of his career: in a secure and important post, admired and sought after by music lovers across Europe, looking to the future as head of a great educational institution, and happy in his family life (he had married, in 1837, the daughter of a Reformed Church minister – his own family had embraced Christianity in his childhood – and had five children). But perhaps there was some hidden flaw. The freshness of the works of his youth had gone, and for all his unrivaled technical command nothing had quite taken its place. When he returned home from his last English journey, in the spring of 1847, he heard of the death of his sister Fanny, who had always been particularly close to him. That summer he wrote a string quartet, a passionate work in the dark key of F minor. But he was unwell; in the fall he grew weak, and in November he died. It is curiously tempting to offer a Romantic interpretation and see his death as an answer to the dilemma of a prodigious genius that never quite discovered the inner resources needed for its fulfillment.

Schumann

If a single composer had to be chosen to represent the features of Romanticism, probably Robert Schumann would be the best choice. He was almost as much a

Robert Schumann	Life
1810	born in Zwickau, Saxony, 8 June
1828	law student at Leipzig University but neglected studies in favor of music and literature
1829	piano lessons with Friedrich Wieck; Heidelberg University
1830	lodged with the Wiecks in Leipzig
1831	"Abegg" Variations published
1832	first trouble with hand, prejudicing his career as a concert pianist
1834	founded *Neue Zeitschrift für Musik* which he edited for ten years
1835	*Carnaval*; first serious interest in Clara Wieck, Friedrich's daughter
1837–9	relationship with Clara interrupted by her long absences on concert tours with her father, who strongly opposed their marriage
1840	married Clara after court case; nearly 150 songs including *A Woman's Love and Life, A Poet's Love*
1841	orchestral music
1842	chamber music
1843	choral music
1844	toured Russia with Clara; moved to Dresden
1846	Clara gave first performance of Piano Concerto
1850	*Genoveva* (Leipzig); appointed musical director in Düsseldorf
1852	health deteriorated
1853	met Brahms
1854	attempted suicide; committed to asylum
1856	died in Endenich, near Bonn, 29 July

Robert Schumann	Works

Songs song cycles – Frauenliebe und -leben (A woman's love and life, 1840), Dichterliebe (A poet's love, 1840), Liederkreis, op. 24 (1840), op. 39; *c*275 others

Piano music "Abegg" Variations, op. 1 (1830); Papillons, op. 2 (1831); Davidsbündlertänze, op. 6 (1837); Carnaval, op. 9 (1835); Phantasiestücke, op. 12 (1837); Kinderszenen (Scenes from childhood), op. 15 (1838); Faschingsschwank aus Wien (Viennese carnival pranks), op. 26 (1840); Album für die Jugend (Album for the young), op. 68 (1848); 3 sonatas (1835, 1838, 1853)

Orchestral music symphonies – no. 1, "Spring", B♭ (1841), no. 2, C (1846), no. 3, "Rhenish", E♭ (1850), no. 4, d (1841, rev. 1851); Piano Concerto, a (1845); Konzertstück for 4 horns and orchestra (1849); Introduction and Allegro for piano and orchestra (1853)

Chamber music Piano Quintet, E♭ (1842); Piano Quartet, E♭ (1842); 3 string quartets (1842); piano trios, violin sonatas

Opera Genoveva (1850)

Choral music Das Paradies und die Peri (1843); Scenes from Faust (1853)

Incidental music Manfred (1849)

Partsongs   *Organ music*

literary man as a musician, and images from literature pervade his music; he was preoccupied with self-expression; he was a miniaturist with a strong lyrical and harmonic gift. And his own life embodied Romantic events in abundance.

He was born into a literary world. His father was a publisher, bookseller and writer, working in the Saxon town of Zwickau when, in 1810, Schumann was born. Stories of his early abilities focus more on the writing of poems and articles than on music, though as a boy he was an accomplished pianist. There are also tales of his early love affairs or at least enthusiasms; some too of his enthusiasm, apparently often satisfied, for champagne. His literary enthusiasm was above all for the writings of Jean Paul, as the novelist J. P. F. Richter (1763–1825), noted for his richly sentimental but humorous style, was known. In 1828 he went to Leipzig University to study law, but he spent his time in musical, social and literary activity and never attended a lecture. At this period he composed some piano music and songs; he also took piano lessons from an eminent teacher, Friedrich Wieck (1785– 1873), who had a nine-year-old daughter, Clara.

Schumann was not happy in Leipzig, and the next spring he moved to Heidelberg University, where a friend of his was a student and one of the law professors had written on musical esthetics. It was music he was studying (though not very methodically), rather than law, as had been intended; eventually he persuaded his mother, with a letter from Wieck to say that he could be a fine pianist if he would work hard at it, to permit him to turn to a musical career. He came back to Leipzig in the fall of 1830, to live in Wieck's house and study theory as well as the piano. Nothing, however, went quite according to plan. Wieck, anxious to foster his daughter's career as a child prodigy, was often away on extended tours. The theory lessons were slow to begin and quick to finish. And then Schumann had trouble with his right hand; almost certainly this was due to treatment he had been given for a syphilitic sore – probably he had contracted the disease in 1828 or 1829. His finger was permanently weakened and not fully controllable; a career as a virtuoso pianist was closed to him.

But composition could continue, and did. His first work to be published, a set of piano variations on the name of a girl acquaintance, Abegg (the theme uses the notes A, B, E, G, G), appeared in 1831; other piano works and a symphony movement date from this time. A similar idea runs through another, larger work, *Carnaval*. Here the "theme" is A, S, C, H (in German A, E♭ [Es], C, B, or A♭ [As], C, B: see ex. VIII.8). Asch was a Bohemian town from which Ernestine von Fricken, a 17-year-old pupil of Wieck's, came; Schumann and she had a love affair and contemplated marriage, but he abandoned her in favor of Clara Wieck, for his interest in Wieck's daughter took a new direction in 1835, when she was 16.

ex. VIII.8

By then, Schumann had embarked on a career in music journalism. In 1834 he had founded the *Neue Zeitschrift für Musik* ("The New Journal for Music"; it still exists); it was published twice weekly at first, then weekly, and Schumann was its editor and leading writer. He was not a balanced critic; his taste was very personal, and though he was quick to spot the talent of such men as Chopin and Brahms, and to praise the special genius of such men as Schubert (on whose "Great C major" he wrote a detailed essay) and Berlioz (whose *Fantastic Symphony* he likewise lauded), he also liked some trivial music and disliked some that we now see to be of high value. His writing however has great spirit and character, and he uttered many wise and penetrating remarks about the nature of music which, taken together, summarize the musical philosophy of Romanticism.

In his criticism, and in his music, Schumann often donned disguises: he wrote under various names, chiefly "Eusebius" and "Florestan" (modeled on characters in a Jean Paul novel), also "Master Raro" (originally a name for Wieck) and others. Eusebius represented the gentle, lyrical, contemplative side of his own character, Florestan the fiery, impetuous side. These names, and others, appear as movement titles in *Carnaval*; the opening measures of Eusebius and Florestan (ex. VIII.9) show

ex. VIII.9

the one dreamy, the other vigorous. Also in *Carnaval* are pieces after the *commedia dell'arte* characters Pierrot and Arlequin, and such others as "Coquette", "Papillons" (butterflies, a favorite image of Schumann's), "Chiarina" (his name for Clara), "Chopin" and "Paganini" (musical tributes to those men). This carnival-like parade of the characters in Schumann's life or imagination ends with a "March of the League of David against the Philistines" – the League of David being

Schumann and his friends fighting for true art against the anti-art philistines. This way of putting together an extended composition was typical of Schumann and his time: a collection of "characteristic pieces", each short and simple in form, allowing contrast in mood and texture, without putting strain on the composer as regards unifying the work or holding it together – in *Carnaval*, the last movement uses material from the first and thus acquires a sense of climax and finality.

Schumann continued composing for the piano; these next years produced sonatas as well as studies and character-pieces of different sorts, including *Davidsbündlertänze* ("Dances for the League of David"), *Kreisleriana*, fantasy pieces around the character of a mad *Kapellmeister* created by the Romantic writer E. T. A. Hoffmann, and the *Kinderszenen* ("Scenes from Childhood"), a series of musical nursery pictures for the delight of young pianists. But affairs of the heart dominated his life. Clara and he wanted to marry, but Clara's father would not hear of it; he took her away and forbade contact between them. Whether this was due to his uncertainties about Schumann's character or his knowledge of Schumann's disease is unsure; probably the former, as the long-term consequences of syphilis were little understood and Schumann seemed to be cured. However, in the summer of 1837 Clara communicated with him and formally agreed to their marriage, though her father continued to thwart it. They were often apart – Clara spent some time in Dresden, and Schumann had a period in Vienna in connection with the *Neue Zeitschrift*. He was often deeply depressed and close to suicide. But in May 1839 they took legal steps to make Wieck's consent unnecessary; not until September 1840, after Wieck had disgraced himself with violent outbursts in court, did they marry.

1839 had been a year of strain for Schumann and he had composed little. But 1840, when his and Clara's love was realized and consummated, was wonderfully creative – and in a medium he had neglected for more than ten years. It was natural at this juncture in his life that he should turn to song. He wrote almost 150 songs in

103 Robert and Clara Schumann: daguerreotype, 1850.

1840, including several collections ("Liederkreis") and two cycles: one, clearly provoked by his and Clara's situation, tells the story of "A Woman's Life and Love", through falling in love, marriage, motherhood and widowhood; the other, like Schubert's two great cycles, tells of a love that fails. This is *Dichterliebe* ("A Poet's Love"), to words by Heinrich Heine (1797–1856), with whose subtle, often pained poetry with several layers of meaning he felt a natural sympathy. *Dichterliebe* begins with the poet's declaration of love in springtime, moving on to Nature imagery with mention of nightingales' song and flowers, and paralleling the loved one with the image of the Virgin in Cologne Cathedral by the Rhine. But the love is rejected, and the second part of the cycle deals in the poet's exclusion from the joys of the nightingales and the flowers, from the company of happy people, as he dreams of loneliness on the mountainside and of awaking in his grave, and ultimately he talks of burying his love in a coffin. Schumann was less spontaneous a nature poet than Schubert; he concentrates more on the emotional focal point of a poem than on the details of the text. As a piano composer, he was used to conveying the full expressive content of a piece in his piano writing; he continued to do this in his songs. Many of the finest among them achieve their most powerful moments in a piano solo at the end (a postlude), where the voice has stopped and the emotion can be given full expression in the piano part. And often, during the body of a song, the voice and piano seem to share the expression, as in the opening song of *Dichterliebe* (see Listening Note VIII.B).

Schumann wrote further songs during the 1840s, but those of this first outpouring have a freshness and emotional impact that he scarcely matched later. From song he now moved to orchestral music, anxious to attempt the larger forms which until then had defeated him (he had tried to compose symphonies but had never completed one). Clara, perhaps unwisely, encouraged him. In the early days of 1841 he composed a symphony, which Mendelssohn conducted in March, with

---

Listening Note VIII.B

Schumann: *Dichterliebe* (1841), "Im wunderschönen Monat Mai"

Im wunderschönen Monat Mai,	In the most beautiful month of May,
als alle Knospen sprangen,	as all the buds were breaking,
da ist in meinem Herzen	there was in my heart
die Liebe aufgefangen.	the awakening of love.
Im wunderschönen Monat Mai,	In the most beautiful month of May,
als alle Vögel sangen,	as all the birds were singing,
da hab' ich ihr gestanden	then did I tell her
mein Sehnen und Verlangen.	of my longings and desires.

(words by Heinrich Heine)

Heine's poem is straightforward, telling of the coming of love in the springtime and paralleling it – typically for its time – with the blooming of Nature. Schumann's setting, however, is far from joyous. The key is f#, predominantly; the voice part alone begins (in each verse) in A – a key Schumann often used for springtime music – and ends in D. But essentially it is the piano, in its prelude (ex. i), its interlude and its postlude, that conveys the true sense, here as in all Schumann's songs; and it begins with dissonance and pathos (see ex. i) and ends the same way. Schumann is not writing about the coming of love but about the unhappy recollection of a love that has vanished. In the voice line, the expressive appoggiaturas (marked *x* in ex. ii) should be noted, hinting at sadness even to the word "wunderschön" – though on "Herzen" it is the more usual expressive emphasis. The upward curve of the line, from "da ist" to "aufgefangen", is characteristic in treating the surging emotions of new love.

ex. i   Slow, gentle

ex. ii

Im wun - der-schö-nen Mo - nat Mai,   als   al - le Knos -   pen

sprang - en   da ist   in mein - em Her - zen   die

Lie - be auf - ge - fang - en.

fair success; two more symphonic works followed, and, for Clara, a movement for piano and orchestra which later became the first movement of his Piano Concerto. Much of it is an orchestrally accompanied piano piece, though there are orchestral interludes and sometimes the piano accompanies an instrument from the orchestra – for example when the clarinet takes up the contemplative main theme (ex. VIII.10a) and steers it in a new direction (ex. 10b). The second and third movements of the concerto were written in 1845.

After the orchestral year, a year of chamber music. Married to a concert pianist, Schumann began to feel that he was living in her shadow, and sometimes decided to stay at home rather than travel with her. During such a spell in 1842 he turned to chamber music, and though he composed little when she was away (he was in a state of deep depression) he wrote, soon after her return, three string quartets and three works with piano, of which the Piano Quintet has always been a favorite for the freshness and the romantic warmth of its ideas and the vigor with which it is carried forward; it is essentially the work of a pianist-composer, with piano writing more interesting and effective than the writing for strings.

In the next year, Schumann turned to choral music, writing (among other works) a setting of parts of *Faust*. He went on a lengthy tour of Russia with Clara, during which he was again depressed, and he underwent some kind of breakdown that summer. In the fall he and Clara moved to Dresden. If the intention of the move was to minister to Schumann's health or to improve his professional life, it was unsuccessful. They spent five years in Dresden. Compositions of the period include songs and part-songs, chamber works, music for children and an opera, *Genoveva*. He had given up the editorship of the *Neue Zeitschrift* but his career as a performer had in no way advanced. So when in 1849 he was invited to take on the musical directorship of Düsseldorf he was bound to consider it, though he had hopes of a post in Dresden or Leipzig. It was in Leipzig, in June 1850, that *Genoveva* had its première, which was moderately successful – though the best performance,

ex. VIII.10

significantly, was the one Schumann did not himself conduct. The opera, with much beautiful music but little theatrical sense, is rarely heard nowadays.

Schumann and Clara moved to Düsseldorf in September. The early months there were prolific: he wrote his Cello Concerto (his idiom is happily suited to that instrument's natural eloquence), the noble *Rhenish Symphony*, with a movement inspired by the grandeur of Cologne Cathedral, which it splendidly conveys, and revised an earlier symphony to form the one we know as no. 4 in D minor – he thought of calling it a symphonic fantasy because of its free form, with interlinked movements. But the appointment did not work out well. Schumann's indifferent conducting meant that the orchestra and especially the chorus disliked performing under him. During 1852–3 his health and spirits deteriorated, and though he had another creative summer in 1853 and made a loyal new friend – a young man by the name of Brahms – it was becoming impossible for him to maintain his directorship.

At the beginning of 1854 Schumann, who all his life had dreaded going mad, began to have hallucinations. In February he attempted suicide by throwing himself in the Rhine; he was rescued and taken to an asylum. There he lived on for more than two years, having rational spells in which he could write letters and even do a little composition, but visits excited him and Clara was not permitted to come. His disease finally killed him in July 1856; undoubtedly it had affected his perceptions for years, possibly affecting his capacities as a conductor, certainly his compositional skills – or so it would seem, for the music of his last 12 or even 15 years lacks the personal stamp and assurance of much that had gone before. Schumann left much music that no one now thinks of performing, but at the opposite extreme stand his songs and his piano music in which the spirit of Romanticism is at its most appealing.

Romanticism outside Germany and Austria

The German-speaking countries were the homelands of early Romanticism in music; German nationalism in the late eighteenth century, German poetry, drama and legend (especially as interpreted by Goethe), and German love of the transcendental all went towards ensuring that. In Italy, as we shall see (p. 334), Romanticism took a different direction; in northern Europe, including England, it had no strong manifestation – there were no great Romantic composers. In the Slavonic countries it was slow to develop, partly because of the social backwardness of their institutions; when it did develop, as we shall see in Chapter IX, it did so powerfully and distinctively. Yet, for all Germany's pre-eminence, the world capital of Romanticism was Paris. Germany, still not a nation, had rival (indeed sometimes warring) capitals: Berlin in the north, Dresden (with nearby Leipzig) in the east, Düsseldorf in the west, Munich in the south – and in Austria there was Vienna. Accidents of history had made France more centralized, and Paris the largest and culturally the richest city on the European mainland. Its salons offered unequaled opportunity for aristocratic patronage, and it is to there that men like Chopin and Liszt naturally gravitated – as well as composers like the Italian Gaspare Spontini (1774–1851) and especially the German-born Giacomo Meyerbeer (1791–1864), leading figures in the spectacular *grand opéra* tradition that centered on the French capital.

Chopin

The greatest master of the Parisian salons in the early Romantic era was a Pole, by birth and by sentiment. The father of Frédéric (or Fryderyk) Chopin was in fact a Frenchman who had left France in 1787 to avoid army service; he took a Polish wife and settled in Warsaw a few months after the birth of their only son in 1810. Frédéric had a natural gift for the keyboard, improvising readily at the piano and composing dances in the familiar national rhythms; when he was only seven one of his polonaises was published. As a child he often played in aristocratic homes, and he took part in a public concert before his eighth birthday. While he was at school he took music lessons with the head of the Warsaw Conservatory, where on leaving he became a full-time student, taking a three-year course in theory and composition.

But Warsaw was too small and too provincial for a musician of Chopin's potential, as he must have realized when he heard such visiting artists as Paganini and Hummel (whose graceful piano style much influenced him). In 1829 he visited Berlin, and then Vienna, where he was well received. He returned to plan an extended concert tour, but there were delays, partly because of political unrest in Europe. Among his works of this time is a waltz, ex. VIII.11, which already shows the elegance of line and subtlety of harmony that were always to distinguish his music. At the time, however, he was above all celebrated in Warsaw for his treatment of national melodies and rhythms, and his absorption of Polish folk traditions into high art.

Chopin left for Vienna in the fall of 1830 and stayed there some months without particular success. In September 1831 he settled in Paris, where he quickly became established: he was taken up by patrons, was considered a fashionable teacher, and – being as polished a person as he was a musician – moved with ease in the world of the salons. A concert he gave in February 1832 was well received, but he made it clear that he did not seek a virtuoso's career, which would not only have made

104   Frédéric Chopin: detail of portrait, 1838, by Eugène Delacroix. Musée du Louvre, Paris.

Frédéric Chopin   Life

1810	born near Warsaw, 1 March
1818	first public appearance in Warsaw
1822–7	music lessons with the director of the Warsaw Conservatory
1827–9	student at the Warsaw Conservatory
1829	encouraged by noble families in Warsaw
1830	acclaimed in Vienna; toured Germany
1831	Paris
1832	reputation established in Paris after first public concert; became fashionable teacher, member of salon society, popular with noble Polish families, friendly with leading composers, writers and artists
1836	met George Sand; first signs of illness
1837	England
1838	Majorca with Sand and her children; worsening of illness; worked on 24 Preludes
1839	recovered at Sand's summer home at Nohant; B♭ minor Piano Sonata
1841–6	summers at Nohant
1847	liaison with Sand ended
1848	Paris Revolution; concert tour of England and Scotland; last public concert in London
1849	died in Paris, 17 October

---

heavy demands on him physically but would also have called for a more demonstrative, flamboyant approach to pianism. He gave, in fact, fewer than 30 public performances in his entire career; his delicate, veiled, finely detailed playing was heard to better advantage among connoisseurs in a private drawing-room.

Chopin quickly became accepted into the élite artistic society of Paris. His musician friends included Berlioz, Liszt, Meyerbeer and the Italian opera composer Bellini, whose graceful vocal style has its echoes in Chopin's music; he also came to know men like Alfred de Musset, Heine, Balzac and Delacroix, who painted his portrait. He mixed in Polish émigré circles, and may there have met the Countess Delfina Potocka, a notorious beauty; it has been said that they were lovers, but it is doubtful whether Chopin had real sexual interest in women.

Among his music of these early Paris years are numerous dances, studies,

---

Frédéric Chopin   Works

Piano music 3 sonatas – c, op. 4 (1828), b♭, op. 35 (1839), b, op. 58 (1844); 4 ballades – g, op. 23 (1835), F, op. 38 (1839), A♭, op. 47 (1841), f, op. 52 (1842); 24 Preludes, op. 28 (1839); Fantaisie-impromptu, c♯, op. 66 (1835); Barcarolle, F♯, op. 60 (1846); nocturnes, polonaises, rondos, scherzos, studies, waltzes, variations

Orchestral music (all with solo piano) piano concertos – no. 1, e (1830), no. 2, f (1830); Variations on "Là ci darem" (1827); Andante spianato and Grande polonaise (1831)

Chamber music Piano Trio (1829); Cello Sonata (1846)

Songs

ex. VIII.11

nocturnes and a ballade. For the dances – not intended for actual dancing – Chopin usually chose either the waltz or one of the Polish national types, mazurka or polonaise. Some of the mazurkas, especially, even though transferred from countryside to salon, capture the flavor of the folk-dance rhythm (see Listening

ex. VIII.12   **Vivace assai**

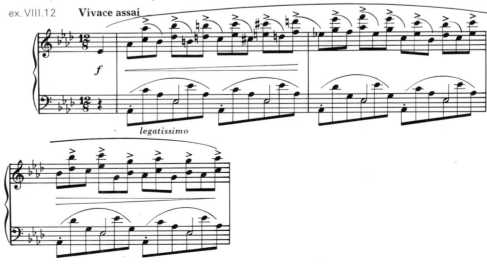

Listening Note VIII.C

Chopin: *Mazurka no. 45*, op. 67 no. 2 (1849)

This piano piece is written in ternary form, in g. The mazurka is a Polish country dance or song, in triple meter and usually with an accent on the second or third beat of the measure. There are various characteristic rhythmic patterns, one of which the present example follows closely; this has the accent shifting between the second and third beats, as can be seen from ex. i.

First section (mm. 1–16)   This consists of two eight-measure phrases (the first is shown in ex. i), of which the second follows the first for five measures and then reaches a more decisive cadence in g.

Second section (mm. 17–32)   The music now turns to B♭, the relative major. There are again two eight-measure phrases, the first moving (from its fifth measure) with a downward sequence through B♭, then A♭ to G♭ (though never settling in any of them), the second following the same pattern but then arriving at a clear-cut cadence in B♭. There follows, in mm. 33–40, a slightly mysterious linking passage for the right hand, unharmonized, leading to the . . .

Repeat of First section (mm. 41–56)   Identical with the first section.

ex. i

Note VIII.C). The studies (or *Etudes*, the familiar French title) show how real music can be made out of a technical piano-playing challenge; each piece deals with some specific issue, like dealing with complex patterns of accentuation across the main beat combined with sustaining particular left-hand notes (ex. VIII.12). These are generally brief pieces; the ballades are more extended. They take their name from a supposed narrative content; Chopin indicated that they are related to epic poems by a Polish writer in Paris, Mickiewicz, though it is uncertain how exact or how generalized that relationship is meant to be. In the ballades Chopin used broader themes, sometimes assigning to each a particular keyboard texture; the themes are not "developed" in the Beethovenian sense, which would be inappropriate to their lyrically expressive nature, but their recurrences, in part or complete and in the home key or a related one, make the formal outlines clear. This is a natural method of constructing a piece for a composer who, like Chopin, worked by improvising at the piano. Further, Chopin usually added an increasing element of virtuosity in the course of a piece, so making each recurrence more of a dramatic event.

It was in the nocturne that Chopin deployed piano texture most atmospherically. Here his model was the Irish composer and pianist John Field (1782–1837). Most composers for the early piano had exploited its capacity for technical brilliance, in which it outshone its predecessor the harpsichord. Field used a new delicacy of touch; he made the piano sing; and with his left hand he wove a soft texture, using the sustaining pedal to make important bass notes persist. Chopin (like others, including Friedrich Wieck) was impressed by the new expressive potential of Field's

ex. VIII.13

approach. With his superior imagination and technique, he was able to carry it still further; the range of accompaniment patterns is large, and each has its own poetic character. Most, like the one shown in ex. VIII.13, involve a singing, finely detailed melody above a gently moving bass part.

The main non-musical event in Chopin's life during the 1830s was his famous liaison with the novelist George Sand (her real name was Aurore Dudevant). When, through Liszt, they met in 1836, she was 32, legally separated from her husband, author of two novels which questioned existing social institutions (notably marriage), striking rather than beautiful, respected in literary circles for her intelligence and her progressive and fresh thinking. In the winter of 1838–9 Chopin left Paris with her and her two children for the Spanish Mediterranean island of Majorca. It was a mixed success. For much of their time they were in a disused convent in the hills above Palma, but conditions were primitive, it was damp, and Chopin had bronchitis, which must have accelerated the tuberculosis that eventually was to kill him. They returned and went to Sand's country home, where she nursed the weak Chopin back to health. They went back to Paris in October 1839, living close to one another but not together; each summer from 1841 to 1846 they went to Sand's country home. This highly ambiguous liaison, which ended in 1847 when Chopin became involved in her family quarrels, was a potent source of inspiration to him; much of his most deeply felt music dates from his years with her, and once they had parted he wrote scarcely another note.

Without Sand's careful nursing, his health began to fail. Circumstances were against him: the 1848 revolution in Paris left him without pupils or means of support. He accepted an invitation to London (he had been there before, in 1837), where he played at private concerts and was generously treated; he also went to Manchester and Scotland, staying near Edinburgh with his pupil and passionate admirer, Jane Stirling. He was back in Paris by the end of 1848, and grew steadily weaker. His sister came from Poland to care for him, and was with him when he died in October 1849.

Nearly all Chopin's music is for solo piano. There is a fine cello sonata from his late years, a piano trio, a handful of Polish songs; his orchestral works all have solo piano parts – the most important are the two concertos he wrote as a young man in Poland, though they are criticized, not unfairly, for weak orchestral writing. The works of his time with Sand include, besides the relatively small-scale mazurkas, waltzes and nocturnes, several larger items: three of the ballades, three scherzos, several polonaises (in which Chopin's feelings for his homeland draw from him some splendidly heroic music) and two sonatas. The scherzos include some of Chopin's most vivid and red-blooded music, fiery and fast-moving. The ballades combine lyricism and drama, as we have seen, and each has its climax of virtuosity. The two sonatas of his maturity, each in four movements, demand a new view of what a sonata is: there is no Beethovenian unity, though the B♭ minor work acquires coherence from having been composed around its slow movement, the famous funeral march (written two years before the other movements) – its dark colors cast a pall on the composition of the remaining part. The later sonata has much exalted invention and fantasy, and its outer movements show a true, sonata-like purposefulness. Chopin was above all a poet of the piano, and it is for that that we chiefly value him. But it would be wrong to underrate his range, which extends from the graceful to the grandiose, the tenderly poetic to the tempestuously passionate.

Liszt

The other great pianist-composer of the Romantic era, after Schumann and Chopin, is Franz Liszt: less fine a composer, arguably, but a musical thinker of much importance and a crucial figure in the history of musical Romanticism. Liszt was born in 1811, in Hungary, where his father was in the service of the Esterházy family, Haydn's patrons. Their native language was German rather than Hungarian. Liszt studied in Vienna with Czerny and Salieri, and gave his first concerts when he was 11. In 1823 the family moved to Paris, where Liszt quickly made his mark; he was still only 12 when he made his London début. By the time he was 16 he was a veteran touring virtuoso, and gave up traveling to teach, at the same time considering entering the priesthood. Meanwhile, he was moving in Parisian literary and artistic society – his friends included Heine, Victor Hugo and Berlioz, whose music he greatly admired; Chopin's friendship came a little later. In 1831 he heard Paganini and resolved to become his pianistic equivalent. He transcribed works by Berlioz and others for the piano; he always believed that any piece of music, for

Plate 23 *Opposite* The bassoonist Felix Reiner, a court musician (p. 222), and instruments: detail of a painting, 1774, by Peter Jakob Horemans. Bayerische Staats-gemäldesammlungen, Munich. For the bassoon, see p. 44.

Franz Liszt	Life
1811	born in Raiding, near Sopron, 22 October
1821	studied the piano with Carl Czerny and composition with Antonio Salieri in Vienna
1822	first public concert, in Vienna
1823	Paris; first tours as an acclaimed virtuoso pianist
1826	first important piano works
1827–30	contact with leading writers and artists in Paris; friendship with Berlioz
1831	deeply impressed by Paganini's violin playing and determined to emulate his virtuosity on the piano
1833	friendship with Chopin; first piano transcriptions
1835	teaching in Geneva; living with Countess Marie d'Agoult (they had three children)
1839	undertook to pay for Beethoven memorial in Bonn; beginning of years of travel throughout Europe and most brilliant period as a flamboyant virtuoso
1844	separated from the countess
1847	beginning of relationship with Princess Carolyne Sayn-Wittgenstein
1848–57	musical director to the Grand Duke of Weimar; made Weimar a leading musical center, conducting new orchestral works and operas, some by Wagner (now a close friend); many orchestral works
1858	resigned Weimar post
1861	Rome
1865	took minor holy orders; religious music
1869–85	divided time between Rome, Weimar and Budapest
1886	died in Bayreuth, 31 July

whatever medium it was written, could be performed on the piano just as effectively, and throughout his life he made transcriptions – sometimes he went further, writing fantasies on themes from popular operas, which made excellent recital material as the audiences could be expected to recognize the themes and to appreciate his brilliant reworkings of them. He was beginning to compose

Plate 24 *Left* Musicians playing the cello and square piano (see p. 222): detail of the painting *George, Third Earl Cowper and the Gore Family* by Johann Zoffany (1733–1810). Yale Center for British Art. The square piano was the most common domestic keyboard instrument in England and the US in the late eighteenth century.

Franz Liszt	Works

Orchestral music Faust Symphony (1854); Dante Symphony (1856); symphonic poems – Tasso (1849, rev. 1854); Les préludes (1854); Hunnenschlacht (The slaughter of the Huns, 1857); Hamlet (1858); piano concertos – no. 1, Eb (1849), no. 2, A (1849), Totentanz for piano and orchestra (1849)

Piano music Transcendental Studies (1851); Album d'un voyageur (Traveler's album), 3 books (1836); Années de pèlerinage (Years of pilgrimage), 3 books (1837–77); Six Consolations (1850); Sonata, b (1853); Mephisto Waltz no. 2 (1881); Hungarian Rhapsodies, ballades, studies; numerous transcriptions (music by Bach, Beethoven, Bellini, Berlioz, Schubert, Wagner etc)

Choral music St Elisabeth (1862); Christus (1867); Masses, psalms

Songs   *Secular choral music*

LISZT és a NŐK.

105 Liszt idolized by female admirers after a concert: caricature from *Bolond Istók* (25 March 1876).

significant original pieces, too, by the mid-1830s.

Liszt was a glamorous figure, intensely attractive to women. In 1834 he met the Countess Marie d'Agoult; they soon became lovers, and the next year they went to live in Switzerland, Liszt taking up a teaching post in Geneva. Later, they traveled – to Paris, to George Sand's country home, then in Italy, where Liszt found a powerful source of inspiration in Italian art. Their third child was born in Rome in May 1839. Liszt gave many concerts and composed prolifically for the piano; much of his music embodies his impressions of the places they visited, or the artistic associations of those places, for example "The Lake of Wallenstadt", "Sonnet 123 of Petrarch" and "The Fountains of the Villa d'Este". Many of the pieces are headed with verses of poetry, by Byron, Schiller, Michelangelo and others. He later collected these pieces as *Années de pèlerinage* ("Years of Pilgrimage"); some of the music is graphic, like the "Fountains" piece, where rapid, sweeping arpeggios suggest the flowing water, but most represent Liszt's own emotional reactions.

The ensuing years were Liszt's busiest. He had committed himself in 1839 to paying a large sum for a Beethoven memorial which had been threatened by lack of funds, and this meant that he had to resume a traveling virtuoso's career. In 1839–47 his program reads like a guide to European travel: he played not only across Germany and central Europe but as far afield as St Petersburg (Leningrad) and Moscow in the north-east, Constantinople (Istanbul) in the south-east, England and Scotland in the north-west, Spain and Portugal in the south-west. Everywhere he was marveled at, fêted and loved. He and the countess decided to separate in 1844, and in 1847 he established a new relationship with Princess Carolyne Sayn-Wittgenstein. It was she who persuaded him to give up a virtuoso's life, and he accordingly took up an appointment he had been granted in 1842 on an honorary basis, as music director to the Grand Duke of Weimar, who was eager to re-create the artistic prestige his city had enjoyed in Goethe's time.

The Weimar years were fruitful ones. Living there, with Princess Carolyne (her presence not officially acknowledged as she was not divorced from her husband), he had an orchestra and theater at his disposal. At the theater, he gave premières of several important operas, notably Wagner's *Tannhäuser*. With the orchestra, he could experiment. To these years belong not only many piano pieces and songs but virtually his whole orchestral output. This includes two piano concertos, 12 symphonic poems and two programmatic symphonies. The symphonic poems are based on ideas from art or literature: *Hamlet*, for example, was inspired by Shakespeare, *Tasso* by a Goethe play (and by Liszt's own knowledge of the Italian poet), *Hunnenschlacht* ("The Slaughter of the Huns") by a huge picture depicting a battle in early medieval times. The music is less narrative than expressive of the emotions aroused by the subject; normally there is no attempt actually to portray events, though the different themes may represent particular aspects of the subject of the work – in *Hamlet*, for example, there is a theme that can be identified with Ophelia, and the work ends with a funeral march.

The principles are carried further in Liszt's *Faust Symphony*, written in 1854. The first movement is headed "Faust", the second "Gretchen" and the third "Mephistopheles" – "three character studies after Goethe", he called it. But it is more than that, for the treatment of the themes and the ways they are related are linked to the Faust story; at its simplest, the Faust themes and the Gretchen ones intermingle, and the Faust themes are parodied in the Mephistopheles movement. This technique, akin to those Berlioz had used in his *Fantastic Symphony* (see p. 326) and to Wagner's, allows the music to express character development, perhaps even to tell a story in some modest degree. Ex. VIII.14 shows something of this. Ex. 14a is one of the main motifs associated with Faust, as it first appears. Exx. 14b, c and d show other forms in the first movement, 14e a more lyrical, amorous version in

ex. VIII.14

a. **Lento assai**
(ob.)

b. **Affettuoso**
(cl., hn.) *mf*

p

Gretchen's movement, 14*f* and *g* mocking ones in Mephistopheles's. Faust's other themes too are subjected to this kind of transformation.

Liszt, however, did not regard this as solely a dramatic technique, with meanings outside music. His greatest piano work, the Sonata in B minor, composed in 1852–3 and dedicated to Schumann, uses a similar method: its three movements, which are played continuously, are largely derived from a single main theme and its offshoots, so that the sonata has a powerful unity across its long time-span. The technique is basically similar to the one used by Schubert in his *Wanderer* Fantasia (see p. 290), though worked with greater intellectual sophistication.

Towards the end of the 1850s Liszt's position at Weimar grew more difficult, partly because there was a new Grand Duke whose interest in music was limited, partly because of Princess Carolyne, partly because Liszt's progressive musical tastes were not echoed by the court – especially his support of Wagner, who was in political disfavor. Liszt resigned in 1858 and finally left Weimar three years later, going to Rome, where his hopes of the princess's securing a divorce were disappointed. Rome, however, remained his base for the next eight years. His thoughts of entering the priesthood returned, and he took minor orders in the Roman Catholic church (though never actually became a priest). Not surprisingly, his music of this period reflects his increasing religious interests – oratorios, Mass settings and motets are among his works of the 1860s and 70s. He gave piano lessons, in Weimar and Budapest as well as Rome. He was estranged from Wagner for a time, because of Wagner's affair with Liszt's daughter Cosima (who was married to the pianist and conductor Hans von Bülow), but they were reconciled and were together in Venice shortly before Wagner's death there in early 1883. His travels continued to the end; in the spring of 1886 he was in London, where his oratorio *St Elisabeth* was performed and he was received by Queen Victoria. In the summer he was in Bayreuth, listening to Wagner operas; and it was there, at the end of July, that he died.

Liszt was a strange mixture: would-be priest, yet with a diabolic streak in his make-up and notorious for his countless illicit love affairs; a composer capable equally of exalted, noble invention and cheap effectiveness; a musician who lived by his virtuosity yet was also a searching, adventurous thinker with new ideas about the future of music. Some of those ideas he put into effect, in his notions of thematic transformation and, very strikingly, in the bold harmonies of the dark, austere piano works of his last years. If more important, ultimately, for his contributions to the art of music than for the music he actually composed, he remains one of the most fascinating of the Romantics.

Berlioz

Among the early Romantic masters the solitary Frenchman, Hector Berlioz, stands a little apart. He was no pianist, and no purveyor of piano miniatures, but a man with flair, grand ideas and a formidable sense of drama.

Berlioz was born in 1803, not far from Lyons. His father expected his son to follow him into the medical profession. But Hector, who played the flute and the guitar, and had jotted down a few compositions in his youth – a Paris publisher had

Hector Berlioz	Life
1803	born in La Côte-St-André, Isère, 11 December
1821–4	medical student in Paris; composition lessons with Jean Le Sueur
1826	entered Paris Conservatoire; first noteworthy compositions
1827	saw *Hamlet* in Paris and developed passion for Shakespeare and Harriet Smithson, the actress who played Ophelia
1831	to Rome after winning the Prix de Rome at the Conservatoire
1832	Paris
1833	married Harriet Smithson
1834–40	period of greatest works, including *Requiem*, *Romeo and Juliet*, *Summer nights*; active as a musical journalist
1841	beginning of decline in popularity in France
1842	first concert tour of Europe as a conductor
1844	separated from Harriet Smithson; beginning of increased concert-giving in Europe and of literary activity
1846	*The Damnation of Faust* performed in Paris and poorly received
1848	beginning of period of further tours and less concentrated composing
1852	Weimar with Liszt, who gave a Berlioz Week
1854	married Marie Recio, with whom he had been for 12 years
1856–8	work on *The Trojans*
1863	second part of *The Trojans* performed in Paris with limited success
1862	*Beatrice and Benedict*
1864	health deteriorating
1869	died in Paris, 8 March

Hector Berlioz Works

Operas Benvenuto Cellini (1838), Les troyens (1858), Béatrice et Bénédict (1862)
Orchestral symphonies – Symphonie fantastique (1830); Harold en Italie (1834),
Roméo et Juliette (1839); Grande symphonie funèbre et triomphale (1840);
overtures – Waverley (1828); Le roi Lear (1831); Le carnaval romain (1844)
Sacred choral music Grande messe des morts (Requiem) (1837); Te Deum (1849);
L'enfance du Christ (1854); motets
Secular choral music Lélio (1832); La damnation de Faust (1846)
Vocal music (solo voice with orchestra) La mort de Cléopâtre (1829); Les nuits d'été
(Summer nights, 1841)

even printed a song he had sent in – was bent on a musical career. He went, in 1821, to medical school in Paris, but found dissections and operations hateful to his sensibilities (the keenness of which he was at pains to stress when, years later, he wrote his memoirs). More to his taste were the opera performances he heard, especially those of works by Gluck, to whose music he was devoted. He continued medical studies up to 1824, half-heartedly, but also studied music under the composer Le Sueur and wrote an opera, a Mass and other works. The Mass, after an abortive attempt that only reinforced his father's opposition to a musical career, was performed, and Le Sueur encouraged him to pursue music. He did. His parents' financial support was now modest, and he scraped a living by writing, singing, teaching and anything else he could manage. He enrolled in 1826 at the Paris Conservatoire, and was now finding his voice as a composer – from this period an overture (*Waverley*, after Scott) and part of an opera survive.

In 1827 he went to the theater to hear *Hamlet*, in English (which he did not understand); he was profoundly impressed by the play – Shakespeare was to be a lifelong influence – and still more by the Irish actress playing Ophelia, Harriet Smithson, for whom he conceived a powerful romantic passion. He pursued her unremittingly, and it is the unruly love he felt for her that stands behind his first great work, the *Symphonie fantastique* ("Fantastic Symphony"). In fact, a rather more immediate love affair with a lively young piano teacher, Camille Moke, whom he nearly married, provided him with the perspective on his passion for Harriet Smithson which he needed to be able to write the symphony. Although Beethoven, whom Berlioz worshipped, was the model, little about the symphony is Beethovenian; it has five movements, and is built around a "program" which Berlioz distributed at performances.

The symphony portrays a musician who, in despair over a hopeless love, has taken opium and is in a feverish, dream-haunted sleep. First (the first movement: "Reveries, Passions"), he recalls the emptiness before he met his beloved – a slow introduction, passionate but unfocused and arbitrary, with climaxes that fade into nothing – and then the fierce love that she inspired in him. The beloved is represented by an *idée fixe*, a theme that recurs obsessively; ex. VIII.15a shows its plain form, in which it stands as the first subject of a sonata-form movement. Second, he is at a ball, graceful but later hectic – it is exquisitely scored, with only upper woodwinds, horns, strings and a pair of harps. But suddenly the music takes an unexpected change of key, and the beloved appears (ex. 15b), the theme transformed to fit in with the rhythm of the dance music; as the ball ends, she

ex. VIII.15

reappears distantly. The central movement represents a country scene – more literally treated than Beethoven's in the *Pastoral Symphony*, with shepherds' pipes, bird-calls and a drowsy languor. Then the music becomes turbulent, and the beloved's theme is heard (ex. 15c); finally there is distant thunder, Nature imagery symbolizing the unease. The fourth movement and the fifth call on the Romantic preoccupation with death and the supernatural. The composer dreams that he has killed his beloved and is being marched to the gallows (the ugliness of the occasion is stressed by the raucous brass instruments, with cornets and rasping, low-pitched trombones); the beloved's theme is heard as the guillotine blade falls. Then comes a Witches' Sabbath, in which the beloved takes part, her theme vulgarized and grotesque on a high-pitched clarinet (ex. 15d). The "Dies irae" sounds on bells, the clatter of skeletons is heard (violinists striking their strings with the wood part of the bow), and all moves to a hectic conclusion.

Shortly before the première of the *Fantastic Symphony*, Berlioz had been awarded the Prix de Rome, a scholarship to that city for a Conservatoire student (he had entered four times, had failed the previous year because his work was considered too original, so wrote a conventional piece that the examiners would be sure to like). He left for Rome after the première. But he was unsettled there, and almost returned to Paris, particularly as he heard nothing from Camille, to whom he was betrothed; then he heard that she was to marry someone else, and set off to kill her, her fiancé, her mother and himself – but thought better of it and went back. This inspired in him a sequel to the *Fantastic Symphony*, called *Lélio, or The Return to Life*; that work, and one song, were the sole products of a 15-month spell in Italy during which he concentrated more on absorbing atmosphere than on work.

Berlioz was back in Paris late in 1832, and at once gave a concert with the *Fantastic Symphony* and its new sequel; he arranged for Harriet Smithson to attend, and afterwards they were introduced. She could hardly fail to be impressed by the composer who had put his passion for her into this music; soon she reciprocated it, and they were married – contrary to the wise advice of friends and both families – the following fall. They were happy for a time, but by about 1840 had drifted apart. Meanwhile, however, Berlioz was busy both with composition and, to earn a living, journalism; he was a brilliant, witty, opinionated and colorful writer for the Parisian periodicals. Several important works belong to this period: the symphony *Harold in Italy*, based on Byron's epic poem *Childe Harold*, commissioned by Paganini and including a solo viola part for him (1834); the opera *Benvenuto Cellini*, at first turned down but given at the main Paris house, the Opéra, in 1838 – a highly original if patchy score, full of spirited ideas, which the conservative orchestra and singers could barely cope with and which was taken off after a mere three performances; and the *Grande Messe des Morts* (or *Requiem*), written to a government commission for performance in the large Invalides church.

The *Grande Messe* is on a huge scale; the French, at the time of the Revolution, had encouraged massive musical events to appeal to large, popular audiences. Berlioz's work belongs in that tradition. It calls for 16 timpani and brass bands in the four corners of the church, so that in the movement dealing with the last trumpet the listener hears music from all sides, sometimes in turn, sometimes all together. The work is not, however, mainly noisy; in some ways it is stark and austere, with

---

Listening Note VIII.D

Berlioz: Overture, *Roman Carnival* (1843)

2 flutes (1 flute, 1 piccolo), 2 oboes (1 oboe, 1 english horn), 2 clarinets, 2 bassoons
4 horns, 2 trumpets, 2 cornets, 3 trombones
timpani, cymbals, triangle, tambourines
1st and 2nd violins, violas, cellos, double basses

Allegro assai – Andante – Allegro vivace; A

The overture is a single movement with a slow introduction; there is also, however, a fast introduction to the slow introduction – a short section (18 mm.) designed to set the carnival mood. That is in the main key, A; the introduction proper (mm. 19–77) begins in C, with a solo for the english horn (ex. i), taken up (in E) by the violas, then by the violas and cellos followed one quarter-note later by the violins (now in A) with a rhythmic accompaniment on the brass. Soon swooping scales are heard on the woodwinds, heralding the main part of the overture – which is in an unorthodox form, akin to sonata, with a repeated exposition but an abbreviated recapitulation that omits reference to the first subject.

Exposition (mm. 78–158; 168–255)   The dashing first theme is announced by muted violins (ex. ii) with a scurrying little continuation phrase (ex. iii). Rapid repeated tones on the brass bring in the second subject, in E (ex. iv): this theme is already familiar – it is the music used to open the overture. After a brief link, based on ex. iv, this section is repeated, identical except that it is now more elaborately scored and the changes of key following ex. ii are now different.

Development (mm. 256–343)   This begins with a loud, argumentative tutti (note the violins' loud, persistent reiteration of the note E). The key changes to F for a quieter section where first the bassoons and then the trombones play a version of ex. i, the english horn theme from the introduction, while the violins keep the rhythm of the Allegro spinning along. There is a long crescendo, during which the music finds its way back to A major.

Recapitulation (mm. 344–55)   Simply a statement of ex. iv in the home key.

Coda (mm. 356–446)   A mock fugue, on ex. iv, begins in the lower strings; ex. i is again heard on the trombones, starting in E♭ but quickly working back to A. Then there is some discussion, for full orchestra, of ex. iii, followed by a curious few moments when the meter switches from 6/8 into 2/4, and then a brilliant climax, based on ex. iv, with blazing brass and dashing strings.

106 *A concert in the year 1846:* engraving by Cajetan after Geiger, based on Grandville's popular view of Berlioz's flamboyant conducting, with a vast orchestra and deafened audience.

thin textures, plain counterpoint, and in the Offertory (which greatly impressed Schumann) the chorus sing in unison on just two notes while the orchestra weaves an increasingly elaborate contrapuntal web. Another striking movement is the Sanctus, with its high, ethereal writing for violins and flutes.

This work was performed in 1837; the next year saw the failure of his *Benvenuto Cellini* at the Opéra – but he extracted from it one of his finest concert pieces, the overture *Roman Carnival* (see Listening Note VIII.D). Another government commission, the *Grande symphonie funèbre et triomphale* ("Great funereal and triumphant symphony"), written for a ceremony commemorating the tenth anniversary of the 1830 revolution, represents Berlioz's ceremonial side; the music itself is not his best, but the solemn martial tone and the "funeral oration" for solo trombone are like nothing else in his output. Between these two he wrote a "dramatic symphony" on the story of *Romeo and Juliet*. The Shakespeare play had always moved him intensely, especially because of its association with Harriet, and for his treatment of it as a kind of choral symphony he took a number of crucial scenes, sometimes setting the words, sometimes providing an instrumental representation. The Queen Mab scherzo has fairies even lighter and fleeter of foot than Mendelssohn's; the texture is like the finest threads of gossamer. Whether the work is successful, in terms of artistic coherence, is perhaps doubtful; but it is full of beautiful things that wonderfully capture the atmosphere of the play. Among the audience at the first performance, in 1839, was the young Richard Wagner, who was deeply impressed by the work and the artistic ideals behind it.

Berlioz had composed, over the years, a number of concert overtures; most are extremely brilliant, effective orchestral pieces, usually inspired by some literary work, for example Shakespeare's *King Lear*. Partly through these, his reputation had begun to travel abroad. Now, in the early 1840s, he wanted to travel abroad himself, the more so as his marriage to Harriet was showing signs of strain. His position in Parisian musical life was now acknowledged, but he still felt cynical towards the conservative musical establishment in the French capital. So in 1842 he embarked on the first of a series of concert journeys across Europe, taking with him a singer, Marie Recio, whose lover he had become; he and Harriet were to separate in 1844 and he married Marie ten years later, after Harriet's death. Marie sang in his concerts and for her he orchestrated songs from the *Nuits d'été* ("Summer Nights") series, delicate, refined and often exquisite pieces that he had composed in the 1830s with piano accompaniment.

Berlioz's early concert tours were to Germany, Belgium and the French provinces. Later he went as far afield as Russia, and several times to London. He found himself better appreciated abroad than at home; he was a celebrity and his new ideas were welcomed as they never had been in Paris. The point was driven home particularly strongly in 1846. Over the previous two years he had composed a major new work, based on Goethe's *Faust*: a "dramatic legend" called *La damnation de Faust*. Incorporating some music from his "Eight scenes from *Faust*" of the 1820s, it is for chorus, soloists and orchestra, and though it has been performed on the stage it is really a concert-room work. When he gave it in Paris in 1846 he was deeply hurt by the public indifference towards one of his most original and spectacular creations.

Berlioz treated *Faust* rather as he had *Romeo and Juliet*, taking from Goethe's original a selection of scenes that particularly appealed to him as material for musical treatment while preserving the broad dramatic design. The first section – simply because Berlioz wanted to include a popular Hungarian national march (he wrote some of the work in Hungary) – is set in that country; the second deals with Faust and Mephistopheles, with drinking scenes, scenes for soldiers and students, and a delicate, graceful sylphs' dance; the third centers on Marguerite (the French usage for Gretchen); and the last has as its climax Faust's consignment to Hell.

Like so many Romantic composers, Berlioz was inspired by the Faust story to some of his finest, most characteristic music. Its opening theme (ex. VIII.16*a*) is a typical Berlioz one, not only for its sense of ineffable longing but also for its curious implications of harmony and rhythm. Most melodies of the eighteenth and nineteenth centuries imply a movement of harmony in time, subject to certain conventions (or, to put it another way, they are conceived within some standard harmonic pattern); Berlioz's often do not. This has something to do with the influence on him of the French language and its flexible rhythmic structure; but more it is a matter of Berlioz's never having been a pianist and accustomed to the disciplines of harmony that are both trained into the piano learner and acquired under the pianist's exploring, creative fingers. Berlioz's explorations were in the mind, and show freedoms that had no place for men like Schumann or Chopin, as another melody from *Faust* shows, the Romance for the lonely Marguerite when her desire for Faust is aroused, with its haunting and unexpected touches (ex. 16*b*).

Poetic melodies like these represent one side of this work; others are found in the rousing march, the vivid choruses and ebullient songs, in the exquisite delicacy of the music for the sylphs and wills-o'-the wisp, and in the music of the extraordinary final scenes. Here Mephistopheles takes Faust on a Ride to the Abyss: we hear the

ex. VIII.16

(The burning flame of love consumes my fair days. Ah, my peace of mind has now gone for ever.)

insistent pounding of horses' hooves, peasants intoning prayers, the wails and shrieks of monsters, as the music strides hellbound with increasing momentum, leading to a Pandemonium scene where a chorus sings a made-up language appropriate to the inhabitants of hell – though finally Marguerite ascends to heaven to the sound of upper woodwinds, harps and violins. Berlioz was a master of orchestration (he wrote a standard nineteenth-century work on the subject) and *Faust* shows him at his most original and effective. And it shows him as the arch-Romantic, his music filled with images of Nature, the macabre and the supernatural, death and redemption, and love, both idealized and intensely erotic.

In 1848, the year that Europe (Paris included) was torn by revolution, Berlioz was in London, conducting operas – though the company ran into trouble and he was never paid – and establishing himself through concerts of his own music. In 1852 he was in Weimar, where Liszt put on a revised version of his *Benvenuto Cellini* and a Berlioz festival; the two composers exchanged dedications of their Faust works. *Cellini* failed in London the next year, but Berlioz had the satisfaction of conducting Beethoven's *Choral Symphony* and of meeting Wagner. In 1854 two very different – except in that both are unorthodox – works of a religious character were performed: his *Te Deum*, a ceremonial piece in the manner of the *Grande*

Messe des Morts, full of grand effects (some of them derived from the use of a children's choir of 600, an idea coming from his experience at St Paul's Cathedral, London, when he had heard a massed children's choir); and the gentle and charming oratorio *L'enfance du Christ* ("The Childhood of Christ").

As he grew older, the travels diminished. He continued to write about music – memoirs, travel tales and anecdotes as well as criticism and textbooks. Opera remained important to him, as a world he had never conquered yet vital to him because of his veneration of Gluck. Two operas belong to his late years. One, *Béatrice et Bénédict*, based on Shakespeare's *Much Ado about Nothing*, was in his own words "a caprice written with the point of a needle". The other, after the Latin poet Virgil, who for him stood next to Shakespeare, is his great epic *The Trojans*. It had a chequered history. He wrote it in 1856–8, for the Paris Lyric Theater (where he conducted a famous revival of Gluck's *Orfeo* in 1859); that theater refused it, and the Opéra took it on; then the Opéra too changed their minds and it was restored to the Lyric Theater. Next it was found too long, and only the last three acts ("The Trojans at Carthage") were given; the first part ("The Fall of Troy") was never staged in Berlioz's lifetime. The two parts were, astonishingly, given simultaneously in two different halls in 1879, then on successive evenings in 1890; but the work was not staged whole until 1957, in London.

The Trojans is Gluckian in its classical grandeur and its sense of tragic inevitability, and Meyerbeerian in its *grand-opéra* spectacle, with crowd scenes dealing with the fates of nations against which the loves and fears of individuals are set in high relief. We see Cassandra, the prophetess whose destiny it is to be disbelieved, warning the Trojans against the wooden horse, then the sack of Troy and the women's lamentations; in the second half, the Trojan prince Aeneas arrives at Carthage, and to some of Berlioz's most potently atmospheric love music he and Dido, the Carthaginian queen, fall in love – to be separated by the gods' decree that Aeneas go to Italy and found the city that will be Rome. This noble work, drawing together so many of the creative threads that run through Berlioz's life, embodies some of his richest ideas, worked out over a huge canvas, and there is a tragic irony in its failure to secure a performance in his own day.

In the 1860s Berlioz suffered from internal illness, and was much depressed by deaths in his family – Harriet had died in 1854 and Marie in 1862. He struck up a curious friendship at this time with a woman, by then an elderly widow, with whom he had been infatuated as a boy of 12. His Romantic quest for the unattainable was in a sense satisfied. In 1866–7 he undertook some final tours – to Vienna and (too arduous for him) Russia; he came home weakened, and in 1869 he died. No one did more than this most visionary of the Romantics to widen the scope of musical expression, equally in its means and in its wider objectives.

France after Berlioz

Before we turn to the very different world of Italian music, and thence to the three great figures who dominated the second half of the nineteenth century, we may look at the generation of French Romantics after Berlioz. Apart from César Franck (1822–90, born in what is now Belgium), none achieved much distinction in instrumental music: Franck wrote Lisztian symphonic poems, a fine Symphony in D minor, and pieces for piano and his own instrument, the organ. Charles Gounod (1818–93) also began as an organist and church musician, but his reputation was chiefly made in the opera house. Best known among his operas is one based on *Faust*; it may be criticized for treating Goethe's profound work as a peg for a tearful tale, but its lyrical expressiveness and its sense of the theatrically effective made it for many years the most loved of French operas. In that it was eventually displaced by Georges Bizet's *Carmen*: a failure on its first performance, in 1875 (just before Bizet's death, at the age of 36), but soon recognized as a masterpiece for its powerful portrayal of emotion (especially jealousy and female sexuality), its brilliantly colorful and varied score and its Spanish atmosphere. It brought to the lyric stage a new realism in its handling of passionate feeling.

Another prominent figure in French opera of this time was Jacques Offenbach (1819–80), a German Jew by birth who went to Paris and, unable to find anyone to stage his operas, founded his own company, the Bouffes Parisiens ("Parisian comics"), who gave short, light operas which mocked at the lax morals of the sophisticated Parisian society. His mordant wit and his sense of the absurd (having the Greek gods dance a can-can in his *Orpheus in the Underworld*, for example), treated in lively melody and piquant harmony, assured his success. He also wrote one serious work, *The Tales of Hoffmann* (unfinished at his death).

Offenbach's style of operetta was widely copied, adapted to the needs of different countries or cities. His most eminent follower was the Viennese waltz composer, Johann Strauss junior (1825–99), who somewhat softened the wit and sentimentalized the content and the musical style to meet Viennese tastes. His best-known operetta is *Die Fledermaus* ("The Bat", 1874). In England the leading figure was Arthur Sullivan (1842–1900), who with W. S. Gilbert created a repertory with a firm and lasting appeal to middle-class English-speaking audiences. The tradition traveled to the United States, too, but eventually took on a rather different form in the musical comedy (or simply the "musical").

Italy

The story of Italian music in the nineteenth century is essentially the story of opera, and the story of Italian opera is essentially the story of the music of four men: at the beginning of the century, Rossini; in the early Romantic years, the 1830s and 40s, Bellini and Donizetti; and thereafter Verdi.

Rossini

The life of Gioacchino Rossini is a spectacular success story, but with some shaded areas. He was born in Pesaro, on the Adriatic coast, in 1792 (on leap-year day). His main musical studies were in Bologna, a famous seat of learning in musical as in other subjects. He made his début as an opera composer in Venice, in 1810, with a one-act comic opera; a similar work two years later spread his reputation across half Italy. He next won his spurs at the most famous of Italian opera houses, La Scala, Milan, where he had a success with *La pietra del paragone* ("The Touchstone"), a full-length work. Then he went back to Venice for two more. In 16 months up to the beginning of 1813 he had written seven operas.

Within weeks another had followed: *Tancredi*, the first of his serious operas. The spirited comedy and gentle sentiment give way to a more lyrical and dramatic style. Rossini continued to pursue both. The next opera, *L'italiana in Algeri*, is totally, often absurdly comic, a tale about an Italian girl shipwrecked in Algiers who escapes the desires of the Bey by, with her lover, enrolling the Bey and his men in an imaginary brotherhood and making them helplessly drunk at its ceremonials.

Gioachino Rossini Works
born Pesaro, 1792; *died* Passy, 1868

Operas Tancredi (1813), L'italiana in Algeri (The Italian girl in Algiers, 1813), Il barbiere di Siviglia (The barber of Seville, 1816), La Cenerentola (Cinderella, 1817), Semiramide (1823), Le Comte Ory (1828), Guillaume Tell (1829)
Sacred choral music Petite messe solennelle (1864); Stabat mater (1841); Masses
Secular vocal music Les soirées musicales (Musical evenings, 1835); cantatas, choruses
Chamber music string sonatas

There are touching songs for the lovers, but the emphasis is firmly on the rapid comic songs and confused ensembles. Four further operas followed in the remainder of 1813–14.

All of Italy had by now capitulated to Rossini, except the most important southern center, Naples. For the leading opera house there, San Carlo, he wrote an opera in the fall of 1815 on the story of Queen Elizabeth of England. But before following up its success he had a period in Rome, with far-reaching consequences. First, he wrote a "semi-serious" opera for one theater. While it was still in preparation he arranged to write one for the rival house – a comic opera on a story that had been successful before, that of the *Barber of Seville*. The story, which treats the same characters (created by Beaumarchais) as Mozart's *Figaro*, had been set by Paisiello (see p. 260) back in 1784. Rossini's choice was risky but successful: not just for the Roman audiences of 1816 – in fact they did not much care for it – but for posterity. No comic opera has ever been as much loved or performed. Beethoven admired it; so did Verdi. The music sparkles from start to finish. The overture in fact is drawn from an earlier opera of Rossini's, as he had to fulfill his commission in great haste, but in its wicked high spirits it still fits the opera like a glove. The plot has many familiar ingredients – the old man who wants to marry his ward, the ardent "student" lover who turns out to be a nobleman, the comic old priest-cum-music-master, above all the eager and artful girl who contrives to get the right man in the end. And to this collection of characters Rossini brings music that not only makes us laugh – as in the brilliant "patter songs", where the syllables are articulated at a crazy speed, or the ensemble in the Act 1 finale, "Freddo ed immobile", where all stand frozen to the spot with astonishment as they sing – but also touches the listener, with its graceful and gentle sentiment (in the serenade for Count Almaviva, for instance), or sharply illuminates a character (in Rosina's song, which so deftly hints at her wiliness and her determination to get her way).

107 Rossini, caricatured by Mailly when the composer was 75, from *Le Hanneton* (4 July 1867).

This, however, was essentially a comic interlude for Rossini – it was, incidentally, followed up by another of almost equal quality the next year, when Rossini offered his charming and vivacious treatment of the Cinderella story, *La Cenerentola*. His main efforts went into serious works for Naples: an opera on the story of Othello, one on Armida, a sacred one on the biblical tale of Moses. In these, and particularly in *Semiramide* (Venice, 1823), Rossini gradually expanded his canvas. The scenes grow longer and more fully developed, the musical textures become more elaborate, with more ensembles and greater use of the chorus.

In 1822, the impresario of the Naples opera houses – whose mistress, the singer Isabella Colbran, Rossini married that year – put on a Rossini festival in Vienna; it was a huge success. The next year Rossini went to Paris and London, and in 1824 he settled in Paris. He became director of the Théâtre-Italien, where he put on operas of his own and by others. Two years later, he decided that it was at the Opéra itself that his real ambitions lay. At first he adapted earlier, Italian works to French texts and performing requirements, trimming off some of the vocal elaboration that suited Italian words and Italian tastes to produce a more austere and direct melodic line. Then he wrote two works in French: an *opéra comique*, *Le Comte Ory* (1828), and *Guillaume Tell* ("William Tell", 1829). This last, on a play by Schiller, is a grand historical epic, using the favored French features of ballet and spectacle yet much enriched by its ensembles and its elaborate orchestral writing. It has every claim to be regarded as his greatest work, but its length and its elaboration mean that it is rarely performed.

Rossini was 37 when *William Tell* was first given. It was his last opera. He needed no more money, for he had managed his finances cleverly; he had written an opera to satisfy his deepest artistic ambitions; and he had left a repertory that would leave laughter echoing round the world's opera houses for decades, even centuries. Why, he felt, should he compose more operas and open himself up to criticism for being "out of date"? He had plenty of laurels, and was ready to rest on them. So he retired. He wrote a little more music, some sacred, some instrumental. He lived for some time in Paris, then in Bologna (1837–55), where he was mostly in poor health, and finally back in Paris. He had separated from Colbran and from the 1830s was cared for by Olympe Pélissier, whom he married in 1846 on Colbran's death. In his last years, restored to Paris and to health, he lived an active social life and composed a little more (including some piano and vocal pieces that he called "Sins of Old Age"); he died, honored by a world grateful for what he had given it, in 1868.

Rossini lived through the early days, indeed the middle ones too, of Romanticism. Yet it is hard to see him as a true Romantic. Most of his operas deal with topics that were familiar on the stage in the Classical era, and there is nothing in his expressive world akin to, say, Weber's exploration of the supernatural, Schumann's literary and poetic inclination, or Berlioz's fevered imagination. *William Tell* treats a heroic and national subject, but its expression remains conservative in approach. Romanticism comes into Italian opera only with the next generation, and even then rather hesitantly.

Donizetti

Unlike his rival Vincenzo Bellini (1801–35), whose strength lay in exquisitely shapely vocal lines, Gaetano Donizetti was less the refined Romantic, more the sturdy, professional man of the theater whose job it was to supply a need. But he outlived Bellini by more than a decade and it was he above all who carried Italian opera into the era of full-blooded Romanticism. He was born in Bergamo, in north Italy, in 1797; he studied there and acquired a solid technique and sense of professionalism from an Italianized German, J. S. Mayr (1763–1845), an esteemed composer of opera. He had some operas given in north Italian centers, but his career proper began in Rome in 1822 when a notable success led to an invitation to Naples. There he wrote 22 operas over the next ten years, as well as almost half that number for other Italian cities. His reputation gradually grew, stimulated especially by the success in 1830 of his opera on Anne Boleyn (a wife of Henry VIII of England), given in Milan. He retained his connection with Naples, returning for a new opera about annually, but spent more time in north Italy and from 1835 in Paris, where he

settled in 1838 (his young wife had died the previous year). There he adapted and revived *Lucia di Lammermoor*, which had been a striking success at Naples in 1835 and is his finest work. His Parisian career was on the whole successful: *La favorite* was well received at the Opéra in 1840 and *Don Pasquale*, one of his liveliest comedies, delighted the Théâtre-Italien audiences three years later. By that time he had accepted a half-time post at the Austrian court, in Vienna. But his health grew poor and his behavior manic, and he died in Bergamo, of syphilis, in 1848.

Donizetti began his career as the natural successor to Rossini: a prolific composer ready to apply his skills to the creation of works that singers could effectively perform and audiences enjoy. Like Rossini, he was happy to adapt existing material to immediate requirements. His comedies take a step, if a small one, beyond Rossini's in their vein of touching sentiment; the lover's aria "Una furtiva lagrima" ("A furtive tear") in the charming *L'elisir d'amore* (Milan, 1832) brings true pathos into a comic situation. But it is in his masterful handling of big, complex dramatic scenes that Donizetti chiefly struck into new territory (territory later to be cultivated by Verdi). The confrontation of the rival queens in his opera on *Mary Stuart* (1835) – note the usual Romantic interest in historic subjects, set in the remote north – is one example. Another is the famous sextet in *Lucia di Lammermoor*, also a confrontation scene and also set in Scotland, in which the characters express their different reactions to the situation, sharing a sense of tension and foreboding. The foreboding soon proves justified: in the next act Lucy appears in her great Mad Scene, bespattered with blood, having killed her husband on their wedding-night, singing guilelessly in duet with a flute and weaving elaborate vocal roulades. Donizetti's ability to control dramatic tension, using line, harmony or color, was remarkable, and without him the greater achievement of Verdi would have been impossible.

The operatic masters: Verdi and Wagner

Two men dominated opera in the high Romantic era: an Italian, Giuseppe Verdi, and a German, Richard Wagner. Their styles, their methods, their philosophies, even their subject matter differed in almost every imaginable respect, and the differences typify national cultural differences at the deepest level. The operas of these two provide the backbone of the repertory of the world's opera houses, and what they have in common – a search for the profoundest and most telling expression of dramatic truth through music – is of far greater consequence than what separates them.

Giuseppe Verdi was born in October 1813, near Busseto in north Italy. As a young child he studied music locally; his main schooling was in Busseto, where he had the classical education normal for a middle-class child, and studied music under the church organist. When he was 18 he applied for admission to Milan Conservatory, but was refused: he was past the proper admission age and inadequate as pianist and in counterpoint. He studied in Milan nevertheless, then returned to Busseto in 1835 as town music-master; he was required to teach at the music school and to direct concerts. On the strength of his new appointment he could marry Margherita Barezzi, daughter of his patron. During these years he composed some sacred works, choruses and short orchestral pieces.

In 1839 Verdi felt ready to venture into a wider world; he resigned his post and

Verdi

Plate 28 *Left* Interior of La Scala, Milan: painting, c1830 (see pp. 334, 338). Museo Teatrale alla Scala, Milan.

Giuseppe Verdi   Life

1813	born in Roncole, near Busseto, 9 or 10 October
1832	study in Milan
1835	town music master in Busseto; married Margherita Barezzi
1839	Milan; *Oberto* given at La Scala; his wife and two children died; beginning of period of deep depression
1842	*Nabucco* (La Scala), established Verdi's international reputation; beginning of steady output of operas and travels throughout Europe to supervise productions
1847–9	Paris
1851	*Rigoletto*·(Venice)
1853	*Il trovatore* (Rome), *La traviata* (Venice)
1859	married Giuseppina Strepponi, with whom he had already had a long relationship
1860	entered parliament
1867	*Don Carlos* (Paris)
1871	*Aida* (Cairo)
1874	*Requiem* performed in Milan
1887	*Otello* (Milan)
1893	*Falstaff* (Milan)
1901	died in Milan, 27 January

---

moved to Milan. Later in the year his first opera, *Oberto*, was staged at La Scala. It was successful enough to interest the leading Italian publisher, Ricordi, and to induce the Scala director to commission further operas from him. His next, a comic work, was a failure. Verdi, whose two infant children and then his wife had just died, went into a depression and resolved to give up composing. He was nursed through it by the Scala director, who found a libretto, on the biblical story of Nebuchadnezzar, to fire him. The result, *Nabucco*, was a triumph when, in 1842, it reached the stage; within a few years it had carried his name to every important musical center in Europe, and then beyond, to America, south as well as north.

Now came what Verdi later called his years in the galleys: years of hard work and drudgery, when composing was a matter more of perspiration than inspiration. He wrote not only for Milan but for Rome, Naples, Venice, Florence and Trieste; there was also one opera for London (where he considered taking up a longer-term post)

Giuseppe Verdi   Works

Operas Oberto (1839), Nabucco (1842), Macbeth (1847, rev. 1865), Rigoletto (1851), Il trovatore (The troubadour, 1853), La traviata (The woman gone astray, 1853), Les vêpres siciliennes (The Sicilian vespers, 1855), Simon Boccanegra (1857), Un ballo in maschera (A masked ball, 1859), La forza del destino (The force of destiny, 1862), Don Carlos (1867), Aida (1871), Otello (1887), Falstaff (1893)

Sacred choral music Requiem (1874); Quattro pezzi sacri (1889–97)

Secular choral music songs

Chamber music String Quartet (1873)

ex. VIII.17

and an arrangement of an earlier one for Paris. Eight further operas date from the 1840s; much the finest is *Macbeth*, after Shakespeare (1847). The somber grandeur of the play appealed profoundly to Verdi, and he matches it in his score. The scenes for the witches and the assassins follow established Italian opera traditions, but elsewhere Verdi tried to key the music more closely to the dramatic action than he did in his more conventional works. Outstanding is the sleep-walking scene, where Lady Macbeth is haunted by the blood on her hands (metaphorically); although in the tradition of the *Lucia di Lammermoor* Mad Scene, Verdi avoids florid vocal writing, which would be quite unsuited to the topic and the setting, and has Lady Macbeth sing a taut vocal line under which the insistent orchestral figuration conveys her anxieties (ex. VIII.17).

One of the most moving scenes in *Macbeth* falls at the beginning of the last act, where a group of Scottish exiles, who have fled from Macbeth's oppression, are mourning their situation. There is a similar scene in *Nabucco*. When Verdi wrote music of this kind, with a patriotic message, he was really writing about the unhappy lot of the Italians, who had been under foreign – Austrian and Spanish – domination for centuries. Italy was at this time not a country but a geographical region, tied together by language and culture; the move towards union, the Risorgimento, grew stronger during these years and Verdi was deeply committed to it. When he wrote stirring music, it was understood by his audiences in Italy; and there are numerous scenes in these early operas which in some way appeal to this understanding, sometimes through an oblique remark, sometimes more openly.

The middle years

With the 1850s, Verdi reached a creative turning-point. Two of his finest and most admired operas come from this time: *Rigoletto* (1851) and *La traviata* (1853). The former, based on a Victor Hugo story, deals powerfully with a seamy side of life: its topics are abduction, seduction and murder, in a context of life in and around the Mantua court of the sixteenth century. The central character, Rigoletto, is a court jester who cruelly mocks the courtiers whom his Duke cuckolds. His own daughter is then abducted and presented to the Duke, and in the end she sacrifices her life for the Duke as she loves him. Verdi's strong and vivid score conjures up the atmosphere of the court at a ball, it touchingly sketches the character of the jester's daughter, and it forcefully portrays Rigoletto's thirst for vengeance. The topics treated in Verdi's music make demands quite different from those of earlier opera, and accordingly require a more direct, more earthy, less idealized musical language.

From the same period come *Il trovatore* – famous for its rousing melodies but less persuasive as a theatrical work – and *La traviata*. *La traviata* (literally, the title means "The woman gone astray") represents a side of Verdi, and a side of Romanticism, opposite from that displayed in *Rigoletto*. Based on a play by Dumas set in the "demi-monde" of Paris, it is concerned with true love, in a world where attachments were unofficial and medium-term; its denial as an act of self-sacrifice, and the heroine Violetta's death from consumption (tuberculosis). Here Verdi's triumph lies in the sensitive depiction of many different levels and shades of love, from the purely frivolous to the intense and impassioned. The opera ends with the lovers reunited but Violetta dying – and as she does, she hears (ethereally, on high violins) the music associated with their love and its beginnings: one of the most touching scenes in all opera.

Verdi's personal life was by this time on a more secure basis. In his early days in Milan he had been befriended by the soprano Giuseppina Strepponi; they met in

108 Costumes for the first production of Verdi's *Rigoletto* at the Teatro la Fenice, Venice, 11 March 1851.

Paris in 1847 and soon lived together. They did not marry for a while; when their conduct was questioned by gossips at Busseto Verdi wrote a firm letter to his former father-in-law rejecting anyone's right to call him or Strepponi to account – a characteristic reaction from a man of pride and sturdy independence. They finally married in 1859. Verdi was incidentally a non-believer and strongly opposed to what he saw as the oppressive influence of the church; some of this feeling comes through in his operas.

Verdi lived, of course, in oppressive times. When *Rigoletto* was given in Venice, it had to have an anonymous duke as its central figure, not (as in the Victor Hugo original) the King of France; for Rome, the *Macbeth* witches had to be gipsies; and later an opera involving the assassination of a Swedish king, *Un ballo in maschera* ("A Masked Ball"), had to be shifted to Boston and the king turned into a colonial governor. The censor took a stern view of the politically subversive.

Rigoletto was a huge success on its first performance; so was *Il trovatore*. *La traviata* failed initially, but Verdi made changes and it soon established itself. Then he was invited to write an opera for Paris, and went to live there for more than three years before the production of the new work, *The Sicilian Vespers*. He had numerous difficulties with the Paris Opéra and legal actions against other houses where unauthorized performances of his works were given. He left the city early in 1857. The contact with the French *grand opéra* tradition, however, had been fruitful, and the Italian operas of Verdi's next years are infused with *grand opéra* elements. The personal dramas of his earlier Italian operas no longer gave him the scope he wanted. *Simon Boccanegra*, composed for Venice in 1857, is a grandly somber piece, concerned with political power in medieval Genoa, the rivalries of the nobles and the plebeians, and a love affair that crosses those barriers. It was unsuccessful; nowadays it is often admired, less often performed. Next came *A Masked Ball*, written for Naples in 1858 and more Italian in its focus on personal drama and the incident surrounding it; it was however based on a *grand opéra* libretto (by Eugène Scribe, the acknowledged master of the genre). Verdi ran into trouble with the censors and refused to make all the changes they demanded; the Naples performance was canceled and the opera had its première at Rome the next year. Third in this group is *The Force of Destiny*, given at St Petersburg (Leningrad) in 1864: a fascinating but rambling opera, in which a tragic personal drama – an accidental killing and the vendetta that arises from it – is set against a rich pageant of military and monastic life. The plot is creaky, but the music is thrilling and varied.

Meanwhile, Verdi had become involved in real-life politics as well as stage ones. In 1860 Italy had thrown off most of her foreign oppressors and achieved nationhood; Verdi deeply admired the chief architect of these developments, Cavour, and agreed (though reluctantly) to enter the new parliament. After Cavour's death the next year, he rarely attended. In 1874 he was honored by election to the Senate.

Verdi had regarded himself as retired from composing from about 1860. Each opera composed thereafter was undertaken simply because he wanted, for one reason or another, to undertake it – for *The Force of Destiny* it was the trip to Russia, but for most it was the challenge of the subject. One particularly exciting challenge was offered by *Don Carlos*, a French *grand opéra* after the play by Schiller. This work touches on all the themes that had appealed to Verdi: nationhood (of Flanders, present Belgium, oppressed by her Spanish overlords and the Catholic church); the rival power of church and state (realized in the opera in a dark-toned duet for two basses, where the Grand Inquisitor tells King Philip II that he must sacrifice his own son); male courage and comradeship; the conflict of generations; and above all love, which has numerous cross-currents and complications. At the center of the opera there is a spectacular "auto-da-fé" scene in which heretics are burned by the Inquisition. The characters are no longer the pasteboard creatures who filled Verdi's

109 Verdi's *Don Carlos*: title-page of the first Paris edition, published by Escudier (1867).

earlier operas but real people coping with powerful internal conflicts: Carlos, prince of Spain, wanting to assert himself by bringing freedom to his father's subjects in Flanders, and in love with his father's young second wife; Queen Elisabeth, torn between duty to the husband she was compelled to wed and love for his son, whom she was originally to have married; and Philip himself, an old man haunted by the loss of his power, his tense relationship with the church and the alienation of those close to him. There is place in this rich and wide-ranging opera

110 Giuseppe Verdi: photograph.

for every kind of music that Verdi could write, and in it he extended himself further.

In one sense, he was over-extended: the opera went on far too long, and large sections had to be omitted before the first performance in 1867. When it came to be given in Italy in 1884 he revised it further, pruning it heavily and supplying new, more economically composed material. He habitually revised operas that seemed to him to need it: *Macbeth*, *Boccanegra* and *Force of Destiny* all underwent partial rewriting. But he was still writing new works too. Among these was *Aida*, first given at Cairo in 1871, soon after the opening of the Suez Canal. Here again we have the conflicts of country and love, for the Egyptian general Radames loves the Ethiopian Aida, daughter of his arch-enemy. The plot, however, is much simpler than that of *Don Carlos*. There are fewer events, fewer ornaments to the main line of the opera's action, fewer psychological complications: the result is that Verdi had greater freedom to clothe the plot in melodically expansive music. There is still room for spectacle, which indeed is necessary to provide a context large enough in scale for the personal drama. *Aida* emerges as a perfectly balanced and controlled Italian transformation of *grand opéra*.

Verdi's next major work was not an opera but a *Requiem*. This originated in a proposal he made in 1868, on Rossini's death, for a *Requiem* to commemorate him, to which several leading Italian composers would contribute movements. This never materialized, but in 1873 the Italian poet Alessandro Manzoni, whom Verdi revered, died; so Verdi used the movement he had written for a Rossini *Requiem* towards a new, complete one for Manzoni. Verdi's *Requiem* has been criticized as operatic in style; but the kind of music he wrote for the expression of strong emotion was inevitably operatic and the style finds a proper use here. And in a tribute to two Italian artists a distinctively Italian manner is scarcely out of place. The *Requiem* had its first performance at a Milan church in 1874. It was repeated at La Scala, and the next year Verdi took it to London, Paris and Vienna.

Last years

If his career as a composer had stopped with the *Requiem*, that might have seemed fitting. There was a precedent, in Mozart. Verdi had apparently retired; he conducted occasional performances, like an acclaimed *Aida* in Paris in 1880. He was close on 70. But his friends knew there was more music in him – none better than his publisher, Giulio Ricordi (who had only to gain from any reawakening of his creative urge); and it was Ricordi who hinted to him at the possibility of a Shakespeare opera, on *Othello*. Verdi had earlier considered and rejected *King Lear*; the problems of adaptation were too great. Now his friend the poet and composer Arrigo Boito (1842–1918) produced for him an *Othello* libretto, and he was duly tempted. He composed the work slowly, during 1884–5, and it was given at La Scala in 1887. It is Verdi's tragic masterpiece. Though still firmly within the tradition on which Verdi had always drawn, of operas built up of arias, duets and so on, *Otello* (to use its Italian title) has more continuity of texture than any earlier opera he had written. This is not simply a matter of Wagner's example – Wagner's mature operas are virtually seamless, as we shall see – but of Verdi himself wanting to move away from the traditional formality of arias sharply marked off from their neighboring items, except where the dramatic context makes it particularly natural. There are "set pieces" in *Otello*, but they arise in a properly and powerfully motivated way, and the surrounding musical texture is fluid, with the recitative-type dialogue (or monologue) newly flexible. Further, the orchestration and the harmony have a new subtlety and expressiveness.

This was still not the end. In 1889, when Verdi was 76, Boito again tempted him with a Shakespeare text, this time a comedy, a genre Verdi had not touched for more than 50 years, and in which his only previous effort had been a failure. Verdi took up the challenge and *Falstaff* duly came to the stage in 1893, the year he was 80. In method it is akin to *Otello*, but there is even less here of formal arias or ensembles and more of dialogue – conversation, exclamation, interjection, laughter. While *Otello* deals with fierce, large-scale emotions like love and hate and jealousy, here life is a frolic: the plot centers on a fat old man who likes to think he is still a dab hand at seduction, but all he achieves is a ducking in the river Thames and a drubbing from a troop of mock fairies in Windsor Forest. There are no real arias, except one for the "Fairy Queen", but the music bounds along at a great pace, little motifs flecking in and out of the gossamer orchestral texture, aria and recitative meeting at some middle point. This wonderfully benign, good-humored piece ends with a fugue – a form Verdi abhorred and could use only as a joke – on an Italian version of Shakespeare's "All the world's a stage": an appropriate ending for the greatest master of Italian opera.

It was very nearly the end for Verdi. He wrote a group of sacred choral pieces, partly experimental in nature, in his last years, completing them in 1897. That year Giuseppina died; Verdi himself lived on, in Milan, where he died at the beginning of 1901. At his burial there was national mourning.

Wagner

Richard Wagner was the greatest German opera composer of his day, the German counterpart to Verdi. He was not merely that. As no one had done before, he changed opera – not just opera, but music itself. Nor just music, but indeed art: the impact of this man, his creations and his thought, left the world a different place. He arouses men's passions, intellectual and emotional, as no artist had done before, nor any since. More has been written about him than any man besides Jesus Christ. He has been hailed as a high priest of a thousand philosophies, many of them mutually exclusive, even contradictory. His music is hated as much as it is worshipped. The only issue beyond dispute is his greatness.

Wagner was born in Leipzig on 22 May 1813. The first of many questions surrounding him concerns his paternity: was he the son of the police actuary Friedrich Wagner, his mother's husband, who died six months after his birth, or of the painter, actor and poet Ludwig Geyer, a close friend, whom she married soon after? The evidence is ambiguous; all we know is that Wagner was affected by the doubts over his origins. The family moved to Dresden, where Richard attended the leading church school; later he moved to Leipzig, going to St Thomas's School, where a century before Bach had taught. His interests at this time were ancient Greek tragedy, the theater (especially Shakespeare and Goethe) and above all music. He had taken lessons in harmony, piano and violin, and eagerly copied out music by Beethoven for study – the standard procedure when printed music was costly. He composed a number of pieces himself and had an overture played at a Leipzig concert. In 1831 he entered Leipzig University to study music, but his chief studies were under the Kantor at St Thomas's. The truth about these early years – and indeed about other parts of his life, too – is not always easy to establish. Wagner left a detailed autobiography, but when his information is checked against other sources it often proves to be wrong; he was inclined to angle the facts, or even alter them, to suit his purpose.

Richard Wagner	Life

1813	born in Leipzig, 22 May
1830	St Thomas's School, Leipzig
1831	Leipzig University
1834	musical director of theater company in Magdeburg
1836	*The Ban on Love* given in Magdeburg; married Minna Planer
1837	musical director of the theater in Riga
1839	Paris; contact with Meyerbeer
1842–3	*Rienzi* and *The Flying Dutchman* acclaimed in Dresden; appointed *Kapellmeister* to Saxon court in Dresden
1848	banned from Germany because of involvement in revolutionary politics; to Weimar (to see Liszt), Switzerland, Paris
1849	settled in Zurich
1850	*Lohengrin* (Weimar); *Opera and Drama*; *Ring* cycle started; began traveling widely as a conductor
1861	revised version of *Tannhäuser* given in Paris to hostile audience
1864	moved to Munich at the invitation of King Ludwig II of Bavaria; began affair with Liszt's daughter Cosima von Bülow
1865	*Tristan und Isolde* (Munich)
1866	set up house with Cosima at Tribschen, by Lake Lucerne
1868	*The Mastersingers of Nuremberg* (Munich)
1870	married Cosima; composed *Siegfried Idyll* for Cosima in gratitude for their son
1871	moved to Wahnfried, a house near Bayreuth
1874	*Ring* cycle completed
1876	first festival at Bayreuth where Wagner had designed an opera house for the *Ring*, which was given its first performance
1882	*Parsifal* (Bayreuth)
1883	died in Venice, 13 February

At the end of 1832, a symphony of Wagner's had performances in Prague and Leipzig. It was well received, but this was his last substantial instrumental work. That winter he wrote a libretto for an opera, started composing it, then scrapped it; he embarked on another, *Die Feen* ("The Fairies") at the beginning of 1833, and quickly completed it, but it remained unheard until after his death. His first opera to gain a hearing was his next, *Das Liebesverbot* ("The Ban on Love"), based on a Shakespeare comedy, which he conducted at Magdeburg in 1836. It had only a single performance; the company giving it, which Wagner had been conducting since 1834, dissolved before the planned second. A member of this company was Minna Planer, a soprano; Wagner fell passionately in love with her and followed her to Königsberg later in 1836. They were married in the fall. The marriage was not at first (nor indeed in the long run) a success, for Minna left him for another man for several months during 1837. That summer, however, he was appointed conductor at the theater in Riga on the Baltic, where she rejoined him. In 1839 he was not re-engaged; in any case, he wanted to go to Paris, for the opera on which he was now working, *Rienzi*, was in the *grand opéra* tradition. He and Minna had to

Richard Wagner	Works

Operas Das Liebesverbot (The ban on love, 1836), Rienzi (1842), Der fliegende Holländer (The flying Dutchman, 1843), Tannhäuser (1845, rev. 1861), Lohengrin (1850), Tristan und Isolde (1865), Die Meistersinger von Nürnberg (The mastersingers of Nuremberg, 1868); Der Ring des Nibelungen (The ring of the Nibelung, 1876): Das Rheingold (The Rhinegold, 1869), Die Walküre (The Valkyrie, 1870), Siegfried (1876), Götterdämmerung (Twilight of the gods, 1876); Parsifal (1882)

Orchestral music Siegfried Idyll (1870), Kaisermarsch (1871), Grosser Festmarsch (1876)

Songs Wesendonk-Lieder (1857–8)

Choral music   *Piano music*

stow away on a ship to evade their creditors; after a stormy journey by the Norwegian coast, they reached England, and then went on to France – by a coincidence, Wagner met Meyerbeer in Boulogne during the journey.

Paris and
Dresden

In Paris, Wagner scraped a living with hack-work for publishers and theaters. He was befriended by Meyerbeer and considerably influenced by the music of Berlioz. *Rienzi* was soon finished and a *Faust* overture composed; he also drafted a libretto on the legend of *The Flying Dutchman* – it was accepted by the Opéra, but for setting by another composer (he in fact went on to set it himself). With a recommendation from Meyerbeer, he submitted *Rienzi* to the Dresden Court Opera; it was accepted, and in 1842 Wagner left Paris for Dresden, where the opera had a triumphant première in October. Three months later *The Flying Dutchman* followed. While *Rienzi* is an enormously long, grandiose opera, set in medieval Rome, dealing with the rise and fall of a hero of the people, *The Flying Dutchman*, much shorter and more intense, treats a supernatural theme – the haunted Dutchman who sails the seas endlessly until redeemed by a woman's trusting love. A driving theme and a stormy orchestral texture are associated with the Dutchman, a gentler theme with Senta, who loves him and saves him; the ghostly music recalls that of Weber (whom Wagner greatly admired) in *Der Freischütz*, but the passion and the broad sweep of the music sound a new note. Wagner had originally set the story in Scotland, but to give it autobiographical significance changed it to Norway, relating it to his own sea journey from Riga.

After the success of *Rienzi*, Wagner had accepted the post of royal *Kapellmeister* at the Saxon court in Dresden, which happened to fall vacant. It suited his needs: the position gave him security, a place where his music could gain a hearing, and opportunities to exercise his organizational genius. Yet it was perhaps a curious position for a man with revolutionary leanings like Wagner's. He had for some time been associated with a group "Young Germany", a semi-revolutionary intellectual movement, and the reforms he wanted in the theater had broad social and political implications.

For the moment, however, Wagner kept clear of active politics. During the 1840s he wrote two more operas, *Tannhäuser* (1845) and *Lohengrin* (1847). The former is concerned with the triumph of a woman's Christian love over pagan sensuality – the theme of redemption again. The setting is medieval Germany. *Lohengrin*, which also has a medieval setting, is about a knight of the Holy Grail;

again a woman's love and faith (or in the end lack of them) are central. In both these operas Wagner begins to move away from the concept of opera as songs linked by narrative sections; there are still separate lyrical numbers, but the divisions are less sharp and the impression is of a more continuous texture. Much of the narrative music has a semi-melodic character and a supporting fabric of orchestral sound that helps convey its sense.

In 1848, Europe's year of revolution, Wagner was caught up in political activity. He was involved in revolutionary and anarchical propaganda, and although publicly he had supported the monarchy he firmly sided with the rebels when in 1849 Dresden was the scene of turmoil. To escape arrest he fled first to Weimar, where he sought Liszt's help, and then to Switzerland and safety. Germany was closed to him for 11 years. Soon he went to Paris, where he met and almost eloped with a young woman he had known from Dresden. Meanwhile, *Lohengrin* had its première in Weimar, under Liszt (Wagner could not attend); its limited success provoked Wagner into thinking more deeply about new forms of opera or musical theater. He wrote an important book on this topic, *Opera and Drama*, in 1850 – his basic statement about his view of the relationship of music and theater. Wagner was a prolific writer; over the years he had written numerous essays, criticisms, theoretical studies and polemical articles in musical and general periodicals, including studies of his own works and those of other composers (Beethoven's especially). One is called *The Artwork of the Future*; another, notorious one is his bitterly anti-semitic *Judaism in Music*, some of it a merciless attack on Meyerbeer.

The middle years

Wagner spent most of the 1850s in Switzerland, active in the musical life of Zürich but expending most of his energies on a new, great conception. This started as an opera based on the mythological story, from the Nordic and Germanic sagas, of the hero Siegfried. He started with the idea of an opera treating the story of Siegfried's death, but then prefaced it with another opera scenario, on the young Siegfried. These were to become *Götterdämmerung* ("The Twilight of the Gods") and *Siegfried*. Then he planned a third opera to precede these, telling an earlier part of the story, *Die Walküre* ("The Valkyrie"), and finally yet another, prefatory work, *Das Rheingold* ("The Rhinegold"). For each, he wrote first an outline in prose; then he wrote the poem, or libretto, as he expected to set it to music. Thus he wrote the text in reverse order (and of course he had to do much detailed revision of the sections written first); but he composed the music forwards, and more than 20 years elapsed between the first part of *Rheingold* (at the end of 1853) and the conclusion of *Götterdämmerung* (at the end of 1874).

Two other works, of more normal dimensions, were composed while this work, *The Ring of the Nibelung*, was in progress: *Tristan und Isolde* and *The Mastersingers of Nuremberg*. *Tristan*, written in 1857–9, was stimulated by a love affair he had with Mathilde Wesendonck, the wife of a silk merchant in Zürich who was one of Wagner's most generous patrons. Wagner set some of her poems to music, and clearly identified their illicit love with that of the lovers in this new work, the greatest of all love operas. He was part-way through the third of the *Ring* operas, *Siegfried*, when the need to write *Tristan* intervened. And before he had finished *Siegfried* he paused again, to write *The Mastersingers*. These pauses were not made purely for personal or artistic reasons: his publishers would not accept the *Ring* – its huge length made it commercially unattractive – but would pay him well for an opera of normal length. He was chronically in debt and needed the money.

There were other interruptions. In 1860, he was in Paris, spending many months on a revision of *Tannhäuser* to suit French tastes. When eventually the new version was performed, it was literally shouted down – not simply a matter of Wagner's music, but a political protest against the Austrians who had supported the performance. Still, Wagner's prestige was enhanced by his having the work given at the Opéra, and that led to the partial revocation of the ban on his entering Germany; it was totally revoked in 1862. In the same year Wagner and Minna finally parted. Wagner did a certain amount of traveling during this period, conducting concerts in London in the 1850s, Vienna and Russia in the early 1860s. But the crucial event of the early 1860s, the one that made possible the achievements of Wagner's late years, was the invitation from the young King Ludwig II of Bavaria to come to Munich. This inaugurated patronage from Ludwig on a scale that cleared Wagner's debts, provided him with a regular income, permitted him to compose the music he wanted to and eventually to found a festival for its performance under ideal circumstances.

Munich, Tribschen, Bayreuth

Wagner moved to Munich during the summer of 1864, having slipped out of Vienna earlier in the year to avoid imprisonment for debt. He was generously treated by Ludwig, but the Bavarian politicians mistrusted his influence at court and his freedom with Bavarian money (he was given a sumptuous house, and a new theater was to be built for him); moreover, he became the center of scandal when it was known that he was now having an affair with Cosima von Bülow, daughter of Liszt and wife of the conductor Hans von Bülow – whom Ludwig, at Wagner's request, had appointed to a post as royal musician. This may have begun the previous year; it had certainly done so by the summer of 1864, with Bülow's connivance. The next April, on the day that Bülow conducted the first rehearsal of *Tristan und Isolde*, their first child was born; she was christened Isolde. Wagner stood as godfather; her legitimacy had to be established because of public opinion and the risk of the scandal's compelling Ludwig to withdraw his support. *Tristan* was produced in June, but the singer of Tristan's role died and it had only four performances. At the end of the year, Ludwig was obliged to ask Wagner to leave Munich. Early in 1866 Wagner and Cosima set up house at Tribschen, by Lake Lucerne in Switzerland, though it was not for another two years that she finally came to live with him. Meanwhile, he completed *The Mastersingers*, which had its première in Munich in June 1868, with Wagner seated beside Ludwig in the royal box. His once-progressive political stance had now taken a sharp turn to the Right and towards a ferocious German nationalism.

Wagner remained at Tribschen until 1872. In 1870 he had married Cosima, whom Bülow had now divorced (Minna Wagner had died in 1866); by then she had borne him two more children. She devoted herself to him utterly, writing down his autobiography from his dictation and keeping detailed diaries of their daily life, as well as ministering to all his needs. He completed the third of the *Ring* operas, to which he had now returned, and the first two were given at Munich in 1869 and 1870. The fourth, *Twilight of the Gods*, was drafted early in 1872. By then, Wagner was hard at work on his plans for a new opera house, designed particularly for the *Ring*. This was to be at the small town of Bayreuth. Wagner and his friends devised numerous fund-raising schemes, but had little success, and it was only through Ludwig's intervention in 1874 that the plans could be carried through. At the end of that year the last of the *Ring* operas was completed.

111 Richard Wagner: photograph.

The first Bayreuth Festival took place in the summer of 1876. It was an artistic triumph, but a financial disaster, and once again it was the Bavarian treasury that bailed him out. Now Wagner started work on a new opera, a "sacred festival drama" to be called *Parsifal*; this occupied him up to the beginning of 1882 – he was working more slowly now, troubled by his health (he had heart trouble and other complaints), and had to devote some of his energies to money-raising. He also spent much time traveling in Italy in the early 1880s. *Parsifal* had its first performances at the 1882 Bayreuth Festival. Wagner went back to Italy, to recuperate after the arduous summer; he had decided to write no more operas but to return to the symphony. It was not to be: in February 1883, in Venice, he had a heart attack and died. A few days before, his father-in-law, Liszt, had visited him and had been seized by the idea of composing a piano piece about a funeral procession with a gondola. Wagner's body was conveyed by gondola to the railway station, then by train to Bayreuth, where he was buried in the garden of his house, Wahnfried.

Wagner's mature operas

We saw how, in *The Flying Dutchman, Tannhäuser* and *Lohengrin*, Wagner was beginning to move away from traditional conceptions of opera towards a new and powerful unity, mainly through the use of recurring themes with particular dramatic associations and a more continuous musical texture. These ideas are carried very much further in his mature operas – or music dramas, as he preferred to call them. The idea of recurring themes was not of course new. The seeds of it can even be found in Mozart; and several other composers used an already-heard theme later in an opera as a reminder of a person, an event or a state of mind – as we saw in *La traviata*, where Verdi's musical recall tells us that the dying Violetta is remembering her and Alfredo's early passion. Before that, Weber had used recurring ideas with sharper dramatic point: for example, themes heard in association with a particular character and re-heard to hint at his presence. The kind of thematic transformation used by Berlioz and Liszt, in orchestral music, is similar.

Wagner drew all these ideas together, and combined with them a Beethovenian sense of the way in which developing themes can support a large symphonic structure. He made the *leitmotif* ("leading motif") his basic way of linking music and drama. In his mature works, some kind of brief theme is associated with every significant idea in the drama: people, objects, thoughts, places, states of emotion

ex. VIII.18

a. the forging of the metal

b. the sword

c. the horn call

d. love theme

and so on. These ideas are of course related in character to what they portray, as some examples – taken from the *Ring*, which has over its four evenings a huge corpus of *leitmotif* material – can readily show (ex. VIII.18): these four ideas represent respectively the forging of metal, the brave idea of a sword to redeem the world, the hero Siegfried's horn-call and a love theme. These *leitmotifs* are not simply "labels", designed to draw attention to something that is happening on the stage. Often they stand for much larger concepts. Thus the *leitmotif* used for the ring – forged from gold from the Rhine, and capable of bestowing power on its possessor – has also been described as standing for the purpose of the psyche or the self, and the one used for Loge, the god of fire, can be interpreted as representing libido or primal energy from the unconscious. Then, further, a *leitmotif* may develop and change to signify development and change in what it stands for. For example, the joyous cry of "Rhinegold!" heard from the Rhinemaidens, custodians of the gold (ex. VIII.19*a*), acquires a dark flavor when the gold, stolen from them, is being forged (ex. 19*b*).

ex. VIII.19

The *leitmotif*, as Wagner used it, offers the composer great opportunities for the subtle treatment of ideas. It may, for example, be heard in the orchestra to represent an unspoken thought of a character on the stage; or it may tell the audience something unknown to those on the stage, like the identity of a disguised character or the motives behind some action. It may establish a connection with some earlier event. A number of *leitmotifs* may be combined to show links between ideas. Many of them are in any case thematically related where the ideas they stand for are connected. Sometimes the relationships become clear only as the music and the drama progress – ex. VIII.20, for example, shows a motif associated with passion and agitation which is clearly linked with the love theme of ex. 18*d*.

There are no "songs" in the *Ring*. The musical texture is made up of an enriched

ex. VIII.20

112 Wagner's
Götterdämmerung: stage
design by Joseph
Hoffmann for the first
performance, Bayreuth,
1876. Richard-Wagner-
Museum, Bayreuth.

narrative and dialogue (there are virtually no instances of two characters singing
simultaneously); the orchestra supplies a texture of commentary and explanation. It
has been said, only half-jokingly, that the entire action of the work could be
followed by listening to the orchestra alone, with the voices left out altogether. The
work is enormously long: *Rheingold* plays continuously for about two-and-a-half
hours, *Walküre* and *Siegfried* each around five hours (including intervals) and
Twilight of the Gods six hours. The network of *leitmotifs*, which multiplies as the
work proceeds, holds this structure together, and Wagner supports it in two main
ways: first, through his superb sense of theater, which enables him to give each act a
powerful shape; and second, through his clever building-in of musical recapitulations. In *Walküre*, for example, Wotan, chief of the gods, tells his daughter the
Valkyrie (warrior maiden) Brünnhilde of the events portrayed in *Rheingold*; in
Siegfried there is a "riddle scene" in which earlier events are discussed; and in
Twilight of the Gods there is a lengthy prologue in which the Norns (or Fates) discuss
what has happened in the world above, and a Funeral March for Siegfried in which
the events of his life are recalled. In all of these Wagner is able to draw together the
musical material associated with the events discussed. As the work proceeds – and
particularly in the last part of *Siegfried* and *Twilight of the Gods*, written after the
long break when Wagner composed other operas – the musical fabric becomes
thicker, but that makes good dramatic sense as the plot does so too.

The *Ring* is Wagner's greatest achievement; it has even been claimed, not
unreasonably, as the greatest achievement of Western culture, so huge is its scale, so
wide-ranging the issues it deals with, so profoundly unified is it on so many planes.
It is based on ancient sagas: Wagner believed, as others have done too, that the
truths embodied in myth have meanings far beyond any literal interpretation. The

story of the *Ring* is about gods, dwarves (Nibelungs), giants and humans; it has been read (and performed) as a manifesto for socialism, as a plea for a Nazi-like racialism, as a study of the workings of the human psyche, as a forecast of the fate of the world and humankind, as a parable about the new industrial society of Wagner's time. It is all of these, and much more too. It touches at some point on every kind of human relationship and on numerous moral and philosophical issues. It is inevitably the focus of all debate on Wagner's greatness and the meaning of his works.

It does not, however, embody all of Wagner. The other three operas of his full maturity each go uniquely far in a particular direction. *Parsifal*, in which acts akin to Holy Communion are portrayed on the stage, treats in a Christian context the theme of redemption which runs through all Wagner's works (the *Ring* included, for there Brünnhilde redeems the world with her immolation on Siegfried's funeral pyre and her restoration to the Rhine of the stolen gold). The theme of *Tristan und Isolde* is sexual love, expressed with the full force of the language Wagner was devising in the 1850s: the same narrative style as he used in the *Ring*, though here warmer and more lyrical, and the same large orchestra, though here treated in a richer and more sensuous way than in the more austere mythological saga.

Above all, Wagner here extended the expressive capacity of music by developing a style more chromatic than anyone had attempted before. Chromaticism, since the time of Monteverdi, Bach and Mozart, had been recognized as a means of heightening emotional expression. Then, it always operated within a clear sense of key, which it would contradict only momentarily; but with Wagner it was used so freely, and in so many simultaneous layers, that it loosened the sense of key or even broke it down altogether. This had long-term implications, as we shall see in later chapters; in *Tristan*, it led to a sense of instability, for as soon as the listener feels that

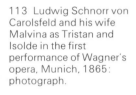

113 Ludwig Schnorr von Carolsfeld and his wife Malvina as Tristan and Isolde in the first performance of Wagner's opera, Munich, 1865: photograph.

Listening Note VIII.E

Wagner: *Tristan und Isolde* (1865), Prelude
3 flutes, 2 oboes, english horn, 2 clarinets, bass clarinet, 3 bassoons
4 horns, 3 trumpets, 3 trombones, tuba
timpani; harp
1st and 2nd violins, violas, cellos, double basses

The prelude to *Tristan und Isolde* sets the mood for the opera with its treatment of some of the main motifs, those which express the main theme of the work – passionate yet hopeless yearning. The most famous is the one heard at the opening, ex. i, representing the mutual longing of the lovers, Tristan and Isolde; the chord marked *x* is the so-called "Tristan chord" (difficult and ambiguous to analyse in terms of traditional harmony).

mm.

1–17	statement and repetition of ex. i; in mm. 14–15 its last two tones are repeated, then extended upwards (mm. 16–17).
17–42	a new theme, ex. ii, is stated on the cellos, with a continuation (ex. iii) that incorporates features of ex. i; then the cello theme is heard again on oboe, clarinets and horn (m. 32), and another figure (ex. iv) linking exx. i and iii is repeated.
42–62	the music becomes a little more animated, and soon another theme (again linked with all the earlier ones) is heard, ex. v, on the oboe and then clarinet. Ex. ii is now strongly developed in the woodwinds (mm. 51–4), after which the cello theme (ex. ii) is taken up by violins and cellos, then woodwinds, to a powerful climax (m. 62).
63–73	the violins play a series of lyrical phrases (ex. vi shows the first) in ascending sequence, the urgency gradually increasing.
74–83	the cello theme, ex. ii, returns on strings, then woodwinds, at the climax of the preceding section, and adds further to the passionate intensity of the music: the ultimate climax is at m. 83.
84–110	fragments of ex. ii are heard on the violins, and ex. i returns; then there is more dialogue around ex. iv; there are more recollections of the cello theme (mm. 96–8) before ex. i is heard on the english horn and oboe, and lastly, very softly, on the bass clarinet and clarinet. The cellos and double basses round off the prelude – and lead into the opera.

ex. i

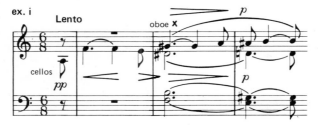

ex. ii

ex. iii

the music is moving in one direction, that direction is contradicted. There are similar procedures in the *Ring*, but they move more slowly and less restlessly. The particular melodic style of *Tristan* enhances the restlessness: the sense of passionate yearning that permeates the opera is conveyed partly through the chromatic dissonances and the way they demand to be resolved – the notes seem to press urgently onward, and often upward. The famous opening measures of the opera, with the enigmatic "Tristan" chord (as it is always known), have two notes (see Listening Note VIII.E ex.i) demanding to move upward in this way; later, Wagner uses this device in different instruments at the same time, not merely to make the effect the more strongly but also to give a sense of harmonically shifting sands. This applies above all to the second act of the opera, which is virtually a continuous love scene, touching on every emotion from the gentlest and tenderest to the most fiercely passionate. At the end of the work, Tristan dies, at the instant of reunion with Isolde; she then dies too, a "Love-Death", by his body – the ultimate, transcendental act of love being union in death.

Tristan, Isolde, Wotan, Brünnhilde, Siegfried: these are not people you meet every day. They are not meant to be "real" people at all, but ideal embodiments of human qualities. Wagner did however write one opera about real people, or more nearly real ones: *The Mastersingers of Nuremberg*. Here he abandoned myth in favor of history – German history, of course – setting the opera in the sixteenth century and in a famous center of Germanic art, one of the homes of the Mastersinger tradition of the Renaissance. The characters in this work, a comic opera though in its way deeply serious, are worthy citizens of Nuremberg, including one historical figure, the cobbler-musician Hans Sachs; another of them is in effect Wagner himself. The hero of this opera is Walther von Stolzing, a noble poet-musician who loves the daughter of a rich mastersinger and hopes to win her hand by victory in a song contest. At first he is derided for his strange song, which breaks all known rules, but ultimately he triumphs, helped by Sachs's explanation that art cannot be constrained by old rules and that true genius creates new ones; the analogy with Wagner's view of his role as extending through his genius the laws of music needs no emphasis.

The Mastersingers does not in fact follow *Tristan* into the world of harmonic complexity, nor does it follow the *Ring* into that of motivic elaboration. The work is distinguished by the constant warmth and good humor of its music, the expressiveness of its individual themes, and above all by the richness with which they are interwoven. Perhaps to some extent taking a cue from its setting in the sixteenth century, a great age of polyphony, *The Mastersingers* contains some of the most fluent and sumptuous polyphonic writing of the nineteenth century; and in it Wagner created some memorable characters, like Sachs the benign and generous cobbler, Beckmesser the foolish and pedantic town clerk (whom Wagner identified with his critics), and the lovers Walther and Eva. It may not be Wagner's greatest or most important work, but it shows his humor and humanity as no other work does, and the world would be a poorer place without it.

After Wagner

Wagner's impact on the art of music was such that no one could ignore him. Some conservative spirits stood aside, finding his music noisy, pretentious, dissonant and uncomfortably sensual – "the music of the future", to use Wagner's own, partly ironic term. Among composers, he had a number of direct followers, who attempted to apply his methods uncritically, for example Engelbert Humperdinck (1854–1921), composer of the children's opera *Hansel and Gretel* (1893). Others, like Richard Strauss, found their own language and dramatic approach by absorbing Wagnerian elements and retaining only what they needed of them. Even outside the German-speaking countries he was influential: it is at least arguable that Verdi's late works were affected by him, and although most French composers found "Wagnérisme" alien to their thinking the operas of Massenet and Debussy undeniably show his influence. In Germany and Austria the two most eminent of his followers were Hugo Wolf, in the field of song, and Anton Bruckner, in the symphony: these men's work will be considered, along with that of others of the post-Wagner generation, in the next chapter. Here it remains to consider one composer, 20 years younger than Wagner (and 11 younger than Bruckner), who was generally though in a sense misleadingly regarded as a rival or opponent of Wagner's, and who may be seen as a true heir to the tradition of Bach, Beethoven, Schubert and Schumann: Johannes Brahms.

Brahms

Johannes Brahms was born in Hamburg in 1833, the son of a double-bass player; his mother was older than his father by 17 years. His childhood studies were guided by his father, but at seven he started piano lessons under another teacher, made rapid progress, and in his early teens was sent to Eduard Marxsen, a leading Hamburg pianist and composer. To eke out the modest family income he was soon playing in taverns around the Hamburg dock area and making arrangements of music for the group in which his father played. At 15 he gave his first solo recital. In 1850 he met the Hungarian violinist Eduard Reményi. With him he went on a concert tour three years later during which he met the eminent violinist Joseph Joachim (1831–1907) and, at Weimar, Liszt – with whom, however, he felt himself out of sympathy. He also met Robert and Clara Schumann, in Düsseldorf; Schumann drew attention to him in an enthusiastic article. Soon after his return to Hamburg, Brahms heard of Schumann's breakdown and went to Düsseldorf and then Bonn to be near him – and near Clara, for whom he developed a romantic passion which remained with him, at a calmer level, all his life. Brahms never married. He had several romantic attachments but seems to have veered away if they threatened to become too close; his friendship for Clara, 14 years his senior, had a strong musical basis and he often invited her views on his new works.

Johannes Brahms	Life

1833	born in Hamburg, 7 May
1848	first piano recital; earned living playing in taverns etc
1850	concert tour with the violinist Reményi during which he met the violinist Joachim, who became a close friend, and Liszt
1853	met Schumann who proclaimed his genius in a periodical article
1854	to Bonn to see Clara Schumann, to whom he became passionately devoted; first piano works
1857	Hamburg; piano teacher and conductor of the court orchestra at Detmold
1859	founded and conducted ladies' choir in Hamburg
1860	signed a manifesto opposing the "new music" of Liszt
1863	conductor of the Vienna Singakademie
1864–71	freelance teacher in Hamburg; piano and chamber works, *German Requiem*
1872–5	conductor of Vienna Philharmonic concerts; *St Antony Variations*
1876	completed First Symphony, started in 1855
1877–9	Second Symphony, Violin Concerto
1879	awarded many honors; *Academic Festival Overture*
1881	rift in friendship with Joachim; offered Meiningen court orchestra to try out works
1883	Third Symphony
1885	Fourth Symphony
1891	met the clarinetist Richard Mühlfeld who inspired four works
1897	died in Vienna, 3 April

Brahms's main compositions in these years were principally for his own instrument, the piano. They include three substantial sonatas, of which the last, in F minor, shows, in its mixture of the passionate and the contemplative, and in its rich, often dark-toned textures, the direction his genius was taking. He also wrote some songs at this time. During the late 1850s he spent some months in each year at the small court at Detmold, where he could work with an orchestra. For this group he composed two light orchestral works which he called serenades; he did not yet feel ready to write anything as ambitious as a symphony. He tried embarking on one, but then decided to use the music in a two-piano sonata and finally in a piano concerto – this became the Piano Concerto in D minor, a work of extraordinary fire and originality, as its opening phrase (ex. VIII.21) shows: music that is in a sense clumsy yet derives from that clumsiness a power, almost a feeling of anger, that is new to music.

New it may have been, but still firmly in a tradition of purely musical expression: Brahms had no interest in changing the nature of expression in music, or lending it non-musical implications, as did Liszt, Berlioz and Wagner. Indeed he said so, in a famous manifesto that he and three others published in 1860 and which placed him decisively in a musically conservative camp. He was now living in Hamburg, where he held a post as conductor of a ladies' choir, but he was also active as a pianist-composer and traveled a good deal to play. Some important piano works belong to

ex. VIII.21

Johannes Brahms   Works

Orchestral music symphonies – no. 1, c (1857–8), no. 2, D (1877), no. 3, F (1883), no. 4, e (1885); piano concertos – no. 1, d (1858), no. 2, B♭ (1881); Violin Concerto (1878); Concerto for violin and cello (1887); Academic Festival Overture (1880); Tragic Overture (1881); St Antony Variations (1873); serenades

Chamber music 2 string sextets (1860, 1865); 2 string quintets (1882, 1890); 3 string quartets – c, a (1873), B♭ (1876); Piano Quintet, f (1864); 3 piano quartets (1861, 1862, 1875); 3 piano trios (1854, 1882, 1886); Clarinet Quintet (1891); violin sonatas

Piano music sonatas – no. 1, C (1853), no. 2, f♯ (1852), no. 3, f (1853); rhapsodies, intermezzos, ballades, capriccios, variations; piano duets – Liebeslieder Waltzes (1874, 1877); Hungarian Dances (1852–69)

Choral music Ein deutsches Requiem (A German Requiem, 1868); Alto Rhapsody (1869)

Songs Vier ernste Gesänge (Four serious songs, 1896); over 180 others

Partsongs   *Organ music*

this period, among them his *Variations on a Theme by Handel*, which continues the Beethoven variation tradition with its individually characterized series of variations, in a sequence that imposes a strong, broad shape to the work, with a powerful fugue forming a climax of complexity and virtuosity. Each variation follows the outline, melodic or harmonic, of the Handel theme, but each has a texture and rhythm of its own and several of them develop particular phrases from the theme, thus giving the music a symphonic quality and coherence.

Brahms had published a good deal of music by this date, but still, coming up to the age of 30, looked for wider recognition; and when he saw the post of conductor of the Hamburg Philharmonic concerts about to become vacant he hoped to succeed to it. But he was passed over. He had in fact left Hamburg shortly before, to make himself known in Vienna; now he decided to stay in the Austrian capital, where he accepted a post as director of the Singakademie in 1863. This was a choral society which often sang unaccompanied, and Brahms was accordingly drawn to study a repertory of earlier music. He remained only one season there, however; he could make a living by playing, and he also did some teaching.

He later considered the possibility of taking a formal appointment, but preferred to remain freelance except in the period 1872–5 when he conducted the Vienna Philharmonic Society concert series. For all that he really wanted to do was compose. Brahms was a slow and intensely self-critical composer; he consulted his friends, especially Joachim and Clara Schumann, about new works, and was always ready to revise them – he destroyed much that he wrote, held pieces back from publication, and was often indecisive, as with the D minor Piano Concerto, over the form a piece should take. In 1864, for example, he completed a Piano Quintet which he had started as a string quintet and then converted into a two-piano sonata before he settled on its final form.

During the late 1860s and the 1870s, then, Brahms was based in Vienna, with occasional journeys to lakeside holiday resorts, mainly in Switzerland, or to spas, where he could work in peace and comfort. There were concert tours, on which he played only his own music. His compositions of this time include piano and chamber works, and songs; but there was no orchestral music between 1860 and 1874, when he wrote the popular and attractive *St Antony Variations*. He still did not feel ready to undertake a symphony.

He did produce a major choral work, the *German Requiem*, in the late 1860s. He had begun work on it many years earlier (again unsure of just what form it should take), and took it up soon after his mother's death in 1865. It came before the public in piecemeal fashion – three movements in 1867, six the next year and the complete seven in 1869. It is not a traditional Roman Catholic *Requiem* for the dead but a series of settings of biblical texts, in German, that speak of death, mourning and comfort. It is predominantly slow in tempo and veiled in color. The first movement, in fact, is scored without violins; the words, "Blessed are they that mourn", are set with quiet restraint and tenderness. In the second, which has the somber gait of a funeral march although in triple meter, the main theme comes from sketches Brahms was making at the time of Schumann's death for an orchestral work; its concluding fugue reflects Brahms's interest in the choral music of Bach and Handel, which he admired and helped revive. There are two further fugal movements later in the work, one of them also incorporating a passage representing – not with musical imitation, but rather by conjuring up the emotions

ex. VIII.22

of terror – the last trumpet. But the message of comfort is always there; it is worth noting that the three movements that begin in the minor mode all end in the major, in light and reassurance instead of darkness and threat. The message of comfort is most plain in the fourth and fifth movements. The fifth – the one Brahms added after the first "complete" performance – is the only one with soprano solo, the words significantly including the passage "I will comfort you as one whom his own mother comforteth". But no less poetic is the choral setting in the fourth of "How lovely are thy dwellings", to a typically spacious Brahmsian theme (ex. VIII.22). It is worth noting the four-measure introduction on the flute, the same music as the sopranos then sing, though upside-down; this is a device of a kind Brahms often used to strengthen the unity of his music by relating one idea to another.

The first symphony

It was in 1876 that Brahms at last felt ready to give his first symphony to the world, which had been waiting for it impatiently. He had begun its composition as far back as 1855, but had moved even more slowly than usual, feeling conscious of the role that he had come to occupy in people's minds as heir to the Beethoven symphony tradition. He had to be sure to be worthy of so weighty a responsibility. He cast the work in the traditionally somber key of C minor, and began it with a slow introduction in which all the main ideas of the first movement are foreshadowed. This grand, solemn, uncompromising music contains figures which later acquire a sharper character when presented in faster tempo and in different combinations and relationships. Brahms was endlessly inventive in exploring the possibilities of even very simple ideas, and often built entire movements out of them; they may be turned upside-down, for example, interwoven or changed in pace. His broad scheme in this movement is very much like Beethoven's, and as in many of Beethoven's mature works there is further development of the ideas in a coda; Brahms, however, ends the movement on a note of contemplation rather than Beethovenian heroic triumph (see Listening Note VIII.F).

But the heroic triumph was there, even if the tragedy and the storms to be weathered were longer than Beethoven's and more obviously dark. Brahms's slow movement is a contemplative, lyrical interlude which ends with a solo violin adding a voice of special eloquence – a departure for a symphony, where so personal an expressive tone is rare and in a sense out of keeping with the mood of collective emotion that generally predominates. Instead of a scherzo, Brahms supplies a gentle-toned piece, mainly relaxed in mood; he preferred this kind of movement, often called an "intermezzo"-type, to a normal scherzo mainly because the long, sometimes violent music of his outer movements needed to be offset and a Beethoven-style scherzo would not have served.

Brahms begins his finale with music as grave and intense as that of the first movement, though now there are electrifying passages built of string pizzicatos, dramatically accelerating, that provide an air of excitement and expectation: and suddenly the C minor darkness gives way to C major, and a noble theme rings out on the horn, accompanied by shimmering strings and soft trombones, soon to be followed by a chorale-like idea on trombones and bassoons. But the great moment, in a sense the climax of the entire symphony, comes when the introduction draws to its close, the textures clear, and the theme at which the earlier music hinted finally appears – a gloriously long-breathed melody, sober yet full of nobility (ex. VIII.23).

Brahms's audiences had expected a symphony they might call "Beethoven's Tenth", and this clinched it, for the theme has an obvious resemblance to the one in

ex. VIII.23

the finale of Beethoven's Ninth (p. 277). But Brahms's treatment is altogether different from Beethoven's. The Beethoven finale is a massive set of variations, but Brahms's theme is unmistakably intended as the main idea of a sonata-form movement. Again, elements from the theme are used in a variety of senses, musically speaking, whose link provides an underlying unity; other themes too are handled in this manner, and Brahms's skill in making the same ideas appear in different guises and senses gives his music its tautness and strength of direction.

The completion and successful early performances of his symphony seem to have released something in Brahms: now he felt ready to fulfill his destiny as an orchestral composer. His Second Symphony, an altogether gentler and more relaxed work than his First, though no less rigorously put together, was written the following year, 1877, at a lakeside resort, and first performed at the end of the year by the Vienna Philharmonic. The next year, at the same resort, he wrote his Violin Concerto, for his friend Joachim: another extended and spacious work, it taxes the soloist severely (a "concerto *against* the violin", said Joachim), and in doing so it surpasses even the Beethoven concerto, on which it is to some extent modeled, in its heroic effect as the solo voice of the violin struggles against the orchestra.

One of the few privately organized orchestras surviving in Europe at this time was the modest-sized one (some 50 players) at the court of the Duke of Saxe-Meiningen. Its director was Hans von Bülow, who, since hearing Brahms's First Symphony – and since the time of his break with Wagner on personal grounds – had come to see Brahms as the true custodian of the tradition stemming from Beethoven (whom he venerated). He offered Brahms the use of the Meiningen orchestra to try out his works in progress, and Brahms eagerly accepted. That was

---

Listening Note VIII.F

Brahms: *Symphony no. 1 in C minor* op. 68 (1876), first movement
2 flutes, 2 oboes, 2 clarinets, 2 bassoons, double bassoon
2 horns, 2 trumpets; timpani
1st and 2nd violins, violas, cellos, double basses

1st movement (Un poco sostenuto – Allegro)
Introduction (mm. 1–37)   The music begins with the violins and cellos striving upwards, chromatically (ex. i), while the woodwinds, violas and horns state a downward-moving theme (ex. i: note figures *x* (both parts, 1 and 2), *y* and *z*. (These, typically for Brahms, may be used either way up: compare ex. i and ex. ii). Another idea is heard, on woodwinds and pizzicato strings (ex. iii); a third, based on *y* from ex. i, follows on the strings before ex. i

returns (in g). There is a short oboe solo, and soon the main part of the movement begins.

Exposition (mm. 38–190)   The main theme of the first subject is made up of the figures already heard, *x* and *y* (as shown in ex. ii). The continuation is ex. iv, a faster version of ex. iii. At the end of the tutti, the transition section – leading from the first-subject material to the second – begins; the lower strings have x^1, the woodwinds *y* (ex. v), but soon there is an exchange (strings on *y*, woodwinds on *x*). All this material continues to be heard in what follows, and particularly in the second-subject material, now in E♭, the relative major (see ex. vi), where the oboe and cello are prominent; but the oboe moves on to a new theme and then a dialogue with the clarinet – and in turn a version of this is shared by clarinet and horn. There is a big crescendo, built on *z* (*y* is also present). This tutti ends the exposition, which Brahms directed to be repeated (that is not always observed).

Development (mm. 189–339)   There is a short but turbulent tutti on *y*, then a quieter, sustained passage with solo flute and oboe. The music has moved through several keys, and pauses briefly in the home key of c before moving off to f for a development of *z*, the three-note figure. This leads into distant keys again, and culminates in emphatic dialogues between strings and winds, as if each is trying to dominate. But then the music settles back into c, and quietens, for a sustained passage based on x^1, heard mainly in the violins at first (against it woodwinds sometimes have descending 3rds, just as at the very opening – see ex. i); then the bass instruments take it up, *z* returns, and with x^2 leads the music to a powerful climax. There is a moment of wild modulation (with x^1 in the top of the orchestra and x^2 at the bottom), and we are back at the . . .

Recapitulation (mm. 339–458)   This follows the Exposition fairly closely, but the scoring is now enriched and the transition section is shortened, while the second-subject material is in C with hints of c.

Coda (mm. 458–511)   As the Recapitulation closes, the music erupts into another dialogue, now more violent, between strings and winds; it ends, explosively, and a quieter and more lyrical passage follows, based on x^1, in the violins. Now the music slows down (marked *Meno Allegro*) and the opening measures are recalled, now meditatively, even wearily, and the movement ends on a soft chord of C major.

2nd movement (Andante sostenuto), E: Ternary form
3rd movement (Un poco Allegretto), A♭: Ternary form
4th movement (Adagio – Allegro non troppo), c—C: Sonata form with slow introduction

in 1881, the year of his massive Second Piano Concerto. It encouraged Brahms still further to pursue orchestral composition. In 1883 he completed his Third Symphony, in 1885 his Fourth, working at them chiefly during the summers and usually by a lake or some other rural setting. The Fourth, which was to be his last, illustrates in its finale Brahms's application to his own music of a principle of form which he had met in his editorial work on the earlier composers he admired: the passacaglia. Here the music is held together by a theme constantly repeated. Brahms's theme, announced emphatically at the outset (ex. VIII.24a), is sometimes conventionally used in the bass (ex. 24b) and sometimes tucked away unobtrusively inside the melody and the harmony (as in ex. 24c). Even if it cannot always be heard, it provides a means for holding the music together, and the improvisatory melodic character of the movement is held constantly in check by the harmonic constraint of the pattern of notes woven into the music.

Brahms's next, and last, orchestral work followed in 1887. This was a double concerto for violin and cello. He had always loved the cello – in his first sextet for strings, written back in 1859–60, he had given it three of his most glorious themes,

ex. VIII.24

some soaring, some serene, and he also wrote two sonatas for the instrument. When he heard Dvořák's Cello Concerto he is said to have wished that he had composed such a work himself. Eventually he did, but he coupled the cello with a violin. In doing so he was partly making a peace offering to his old friend Joachim, from whom he had been estranged for some years after he had sided with Joachim's wife in a domestic dispute. The Double Concerto went some way towards healing the breach. Its first movement is in Brahms's most austere vein, but the slow middle movement is scored and harmonized with an almost luxuriant richness and the finale turns once again to the gipsy echoes from Brahms's youth.

Meanwhile, chamber music and songs had flowed steadily from Brahms's pen. His third and last violin sonata dates from 1888 and a string quintet – Brahms loved the richer textures that could be obtained from a group larger than the traditional string quartet – comes from 1890. About that time he heard the clarinetist Richard Mühlfeld play at Meiningen and was impelled to write a series of works for him, including a Clarinet Quintet (1891) in which Brahms revels in the variety of soft and rich colors in the ensemble of clarinet and strings. This is another highly organized work, in which themes are constantly being reshaped and given new meaning. In the slow movement, for instance, the simple and lyrical opening theme provides the basis for the vivid and impassioned flourishes – again recalling gipsy improvisations – in the contrasting section, and in the intermezzo-style third movement, the lyrical opening theme provides the outline from which the sprightly middle section takes off. This technique, so important a part of Brahms's musical thinking, is akin to that used in theme-and-variation movements, a type in which he excelled and of which the finale of the quintet supplies an outstanding example. The quintet ends with an especially ingenious and satisfying example of Brahms's way of transforming themes, for the final variation is in the rhythm of the quintet's first movement, and moreover its lines have something in common with that movement: so that when, as it ends, the opening music of the whole work is recalled, it arises naturally out of what has just been heard and the unity and integrity of the quintet become strikingly clear.

In these late years Brahms returned, after a gap of more than ten years, to piano music. He wrote four sets of pieces during 1892: short, independent pieces with titles like Intermezzo or Capriccio, some of them fiery and brilliant but mostly reflective, subtle and fanciful, and all written with the serene mastery of the mature composer. Virtually all his life Brahms had composed songs, up to 1886; and here too he turned back at the very end, writing in 1896 a set that he called *Four Serious Songs* – songs to biblical texts, concerned, as in the *German Requiem*, with death and consolation. These are somber music, dark-toned and powerful, written when he knew that death was near; his earlier songs are closer to the traditions of Schubert and Schumann, though with hints too of German folksong in many of them.

The *Four Serious Songs* were Brahms's last composition. He was only in his early 60s; but in spite of the universal recognition accorded to him in his late years – he had received various orders, and was offered the freedom of his native Hamburg, for example – he had suffered from the deaths of many friends. In 1896 he developed cancer of the liver; a cure at a spa did not help him, and next spring he died. Brahms was no revolutionary, and an innovator only in an unobtrusive way (though a way that was eventually to have a profound influence on later composers such as Schoenberg); his principles were classical, yet in his music a warm and truly Romantic spirit is unmistakable beneath the often gruff and austere surface.

Chapter IX

The Turn of the Century

The Romantic era is usually seen as continuing up to those critical years around 1910–13, just before the outbreak of World War I. But we do well to distinguish between its beginnings, in the hands of such men as Chopin, Schumann and Berlioz, and the post-Wagnerian period. The break is not, of course, sharp and clear; history does not usually fall conveniently for historians who want to draw lines. In the last chapter, however, we dealt principally with composers who preceded Wagner or stood apart from him (like Verdi and Brahms) because they had already found their own musical language before they felt Wagner's impact. Of the composers considered in the present chapter, virtually all were affected by Wagner, even those who consciously rejected him. These are men who were active chiefly between the 1870s and World War I, though some lived longer (Richard Strauss even beyond the end of World War II).

Essentially, this is the era when composers, in face of the breakdown of the traditional tonal system under the weight of Wagnerian chromaticism, sought new ways of developing the language of music. It was not, however, mainly because of Wagner that the composers of Russia and eastern Europe chose the directions they did. The middle of the nineteenth century was a time when the peoples of many European countries became increasingly aware of their national identity. Partly this was because of the growing interest in the past and in the meaning of national traditions. But it was also closely linked with current political developments, as the traditional rulers, princely and ecclesiastical, were forced to give way to more democratic forms of government and as groups bound by language and tradition threw off foreign domination. Belgium and the Netherlands (or Holland) became kingdoms in 1830, Italy in 1861, Germany an empire in 1871. Others, while remaining under foreign dominion, found a new awareness of their traditions: the Czechs and Hungarians, for example, began to cherish their folksong and literature although German was the language, generally speaking, of the ruling classes. In these countries and in Poland and Russia, the traditions of cultivated music were largely Italian and German, but now composers began to set words in the tongue spoken by the large majority of the people. It was natural that in doing so they should make efforts to incorporate features of their national folksong traditions – not only did such melodies fit with the rhythms and the rise and fall of the words, but they also had a familiarity that was bound to be appealing. Economic factors played a part: with the advance of industrialization, larger population centers were

Nationalism

beginning to develop, and from what had once been a rural peasant class a middle class was forming, ready to go to concerts and opera houses.

The composers of Russia – not all of them, for the greatest, Tchaikovsky, stood somewhat apart from this development – formed the most prominent and most deliberate group of nationalists, using folksong liberally in their music. This was a period when other arts, too, flowered in Russia, with the poet Pushkin at the beginning of the century and the writers Tolstoy, Chekhov and Dostoyevsky later. The Czechs called more on the rhythms of their native language than on folk melody; they had, as part of the Austro-Hungarian empire, deep roots in the Germanic (and Italianate) central European tradition. Northern Europe too had long had links with Germany, but Grieg was not the only composer to draw on local folk music. Spanish composers at the end of the century, like Albéniz, Granados and Turina, also drew strongly on their local traditions.

The increase in national consciousness was not confined to the periphery of Europe. Brahms, as we have seen, used German folksong, and Wagner was deeply aware of his identity as a German; Verdi was equally alive to his as an Italian. But in these countries, and in France, the traditions of art music were strong and individual enough for the use of folksong to be neither necessary nor manageable: composers' language was already marked by national taste and style, while folksong did not readily fit into the well-formed style that composers of these countries used. In Britain, the predominant taste was Germanic, though eventually a powerful folksong movement was to assert itself. In the United States, art music traditions, which essentially were imported from Europe, were very diverse though again mainly German. Louis Moreau Gottschalk (1829–69) drew on Afro-American and Hispanic elements, but the best-known American composer of the century, Edward MacDowell (1860–1908), was fully cosmopolitan in his musical language.

Exoticism

The use of national features could be something more than national assertion. The Russian composer Rimsky-Korsakov wrote a *Spanish Caprice*, using the colors and the rhythms of Spain, and a work called *Sheherazade* hinting at the music of the Middle East. This was part of a fairly widespread movement toward the mysterious and the exotic. Other composers looked beyond Europe: Debussy, for example, sought inspiration in the gamelan music and the gongs of Indonesia, which he heard at the Paris Exhibition of 1889, and wrote an Egyptian ballet (he also composed Spanish-colored music, like many Frenchmen, including Bizet before him and Ravel after), while Puccini looked still further afield – to Japan, China and the American Wild West – in search of new colors and ideas. There are parallels to this in the visual arts, for example in the inspiration sought by Paul Gauguin (1848–1903) in the South Pacific. Here there was also a clear element of escape from the sophistication and artificiality of Western society in favor of a "return to Nature", to which there could be no exact analogy in music although the composers who used folksong certainly had similar feelings. A close parallel at this period between music and painting, however, may be drawn between Debussy and the French

Impressionism, Symbolism

Impressionists, such as Claude Monet (1840–1926) and Camille Pissarro (1830–1903), in his use of washes of color and vague, suggestive harmony in place of clear-cut themes, and his reliance on dreaminess and sensory impression. Arguably he is even closer to the Symbolist school, including such painters as Gustave Moreau (1826–98), and the poet Stéphane Mallarmé (1842–98), the author of the poem that gave rise to his most famous work, *L'après-midi d'un faune*, but to see precise parallels between them is difficult.

Two other French writers, Honoré de Balzac (1799–1850) and Emile Zola (1840–1902), demand to be mentioned here, however, Balzac as the initiator of a new realism that arose out of Romanticism and Zola as perhaps its most powerful exponent. Balzac, more than anyone else, represents the reaction against the idealistic, imaginative, fantastic side of Romanticism. His closest equivalent in the visual arts was Gustave Courbet (1819–77). The realism of Bizet's *Carmen*, discussed in the last chapter (p. 334), provides a close musical parallel, closer than that of the operas of Massenet, who though a realist added a tinsel-like layer of Romantic decoration. Realism (*verismo* in Italian), which has strong political overtones in its readiness to face up to social evils (rife in these times, the heyday of industrialization) as well as psychological realities, can also be seen as part of the reaction against the exalted emotions of Verdi's operas and *grand opéra* generally, and against the unreality and loftiness (even if they are symbolic) of Wagner's world. It had a powerful influence on opera composers, especially Italian ones, who encountered it in the writings of the novelist Giovanni Verga (1840–1922).

The first important *verismo* composer was Pietro Mascagni (1863–1945), whose *Cavalleria rusticana* ("Country chivalry", 1889) tells an unvarnished tale of infidelity and revenge in a Sicilian village; a one-act work, it is usually coupled in the theater with *Pagliacci* ("Clowns", 1891) by Ruggero Leoncavallo (1858–1919), a similar tale in a context of a traveling theatrical troupe. Puccini is not generally regarded as a *verismo* composer, and certainly he is much more than that; but there are elements of the same kind of realism in his depiction of the life of impoverished artists in Paris in *La bohème* and in the wanton cruelties of *Tosca*. Several other Italians took similar paths; so did Germans and Frenchmen, but fewer of their operas are still performed (an exception is *Louise*, 1900, by Gustave Charpentier, 1860–1956). There are also strong realistic elements in some of the operas of Janáček.

Richard Strauss, however, the most important opera composer in central Europe in the early decades of the twentieth century, had little to do with realism, although the first two of his operas to have entered the repertory (*Salome*, 1905, and *Elektra*, 1909) embody brutality and lust of the kind that the *verismo* composers relished. They might perhaps be called psychological *verismo* operas in that they explore with an attempted realism some basic aspects of the human psyche, using for the purpose a biblical story (as interpreted by Oscar Wilde) and a classical one. This interest in underlying human motives may be seen as sharing something with the contemporary work of Sigmund Freud (1856–1939) – whose links with Mahler, whom he briefly treated, are possibly even stronger. Strauss moved away from the violence of these early operas, and from the ostentatious manner of his early symphonic poems, which carry the narrative aspects of Liszt's similar works very much further, using thematic transformation in a post-Wagnerian way, with a huge orchestra. After *Elektra*, he wrote *Der Rosenkavalier*, a large-scale work that deals with love-affairs in eighteenth-century Vienna, treated with wit and high sophistication. There are parallels here with the *fin de siècle* ("end of the era") decadence of the *art nouveau* movement and with the daring, sexually allusive drawings of Aubrey Beardsley (1872–98) – an art that plays with art.

Strauss nevertheless lies firmly in the central European tradition, for he was more *enfant terrible* than revolutionary (as he was long regarded). So too does Mahler who, for all the influence he had on the next generation, expanded the framework of the Romantic symphony, as Bruckner had done in the previous generation, not only, like Bruckner, to accommodate symphonic development on a Wagnerian

Realism

scale but also to express a wide range of extra-musical ideas – culminating, in the colossal Eighth Symphony, with philosophical concepts drawn from Part II of Goethe's *Faust*. This expansion of resources that we see in Bruckner, Strauss and Mahler is characteristic of the closing phase of an era. It is tempting, and only partly an over-simplification, to regard such works as the last desperate, passionate, dying cries of the central Romantic tradition.

Russian nationalism

Apart from the products of the eccentric genius Mikhail Glinka (1804–57), Russian music before the middle of the nineteenth century was a provincial affair. Then various factors combined to change matters. The conditions for music in Russia improved with the foundation of the Imperial Russian Music Society in 1859, the St Petersburg Conservatory in 1860 and the Moscow Conservatory in 1865. There was the stimulus of Berlioz's visit in 1867. There was also the arrival of diatonic harmony at a point where it could incorporate the modalities of Russian folk music and liturgical chant. And there was the emergence of a highly gifted generation of creative individuals, led by Modest Mussorgsky (1839–81), Mily Balakirev (1837–1910), Nikolay Rimsky-Korsakov (1844–1908), Alexander Borodin (1833–87) and Pyotr Tchaikovsky (1840–93).

Tchaikovsky

Pyotr Ilyich Tchaikovsky was born in 1840 in the Vyatka province, where his father was a mining engineer and factory manager. His mother had a French grandfather, but his attraction to things French has normally been connected not so much with this blood tie as with his having been taught by a French governess, Fanny Dürbach, engaged by the family between 1844 and 1848. In the latter year the Tchaikovskys moved to St Petersburg, where the future composer was educated at the School of Jurisprudence (1850–59). During this time, and particularly in the wake of his mother's death in 1854, he began to compose seriously, but on leaving the school he was obliged to take a post in the Ministry of Justice until in 1863 he became a full-time student again, now at the St Petersburg Conservatory, where his composition teacher was the young and energetic director Anton Rubinstein (1829–94).

Rubinstein soon became recognized as the opposite of Balakirev: cosmopolitan where the other was adamantly Russian, concerned for the standard genres more than for the picturesque symphonic poems that appealed to Balakirev, conservative in his musical tastes (their opposition was a reflection of that between Brahms and Wagner). The young Tchaikovsky was naturally influenced by Rubinstein's views, and effectively began his composing career with a symphony sub-titled "Winter Daydreams" (1866). But in the winter of 1867–8 he came into contact with Balakirev, who by this time was already at the head of a group of composers known as "The Five", the others being Mussorgsky, Rimsky-Korsakov, Borodin and César Cui (1835–1918). Recognizing Tchaikovsky's talent, Balakirev was eager to make him a sixth member of the circle, but two things prevented that. The first was geographical distance: the Five were based in St Petersburg, whereas Tchaikovsky was now teaching at the new conservatory in Moscow. The second was a natural solitariness on the part of Tchaikovsky, who seems already to have sensed that his homosexuality isolated him from his fellow men.

Nevertheless, Balakirev had considerable sway in encouraging nationalism in Tchaikovsky. That nationalist streak grew from its appearance in his opera *The Voyevoda* (1869) to its full expression in two later operas, *The Oprichnik* (1874) and *Vakula the Smith* (1876): *The Voyevoda* and *The Oprichnik*, which was almost a re-

---

Pyotr Ilyich Tchaikovsky   Life

1840	born in Kamsko-Votkinsk, Vyatka province, 7 May
1850–59	student at the School of Jurisprudence, St Petersburg
1859–63	clerk at the Ministry of Justice
1863–5	studied with Anton Rubinstein at the St Petersburg Conservatory
1866	professor of harmony at the Moscow Conservatory; First Symphony
1868	met Balakirev and his group of nationalist composers ("The Five") but did not join their circle
1870–74	nationalist compositions, especially operas, attract attention
1875	Piano Concerto no. 1
1876	began correspondence with Nadezhda von Meck, a wealthy widow who helped him financially
1877	married Antonina Milyukova but separated after a few weeks; emotional breakdown
1878	Fourth Symphony, *Eugene Onegin*, Violin Concerto; resigned from Moscow Conservatory; beginning of period of creative sterility but increasing popularity in Russia
1885	*Manfred* Symphony
1888–9	toured Europe as a conductor
1890	Nadezhda von Meck ends correspondence and allowance; beginning of deep depression
1891	USA
1893	Sixth ("Pathétique") Symphony; died (?suicide) in St Petersburg, 6 November

---

Pyotr Ilyich Tchaikovsky   Works

Operas The Voyevoda (1869), The Snow Maiden (1873), The Oprichnik (1874), Vakula the Smith (1876), Eugene Onegin (1879), Mazeppa (1884), The Queen of Spades (1890)

Ballets Swan Lake (1877), The Sleeping Beauty (1890), Nutcracker (1892)

Orchestral music symphonies – no. 1, "Winter Daydreams", g (1866), no. 2, "Little Russian", c (1872), no. 3, "Polish", D (1875), no. 4, f (1878), no. 5, e (1888), no. 6, "Pathétique", b (1893), Manfred (1885); piano concertos – no. 1, b♭ (1875); Violin Concerto (1878); Francesca da Rimini (1876); Hamlet (1888); overtures – Romeo and Juliet (1869), 1812 (1880); Italian Capriccio (1880); suites, variations

Chamber music Souvenir de Florence, string sextet (1890); string quartets; piano trio

Choral music cantatas, services

Piano music   *Songs*

write of the earlier score, were grand historical dramas, while *Vakula* was a fairy-tale fantasy. None of them is much performed now: indeed, of Tchaikovsky's ten operas only *Eugene Onegin* (1879) and *The Queen of Spades* (1890) are part of the repertory. However, the other early work written under Balakirev's influence was one of the most popular of concert pieces and Tchaikovsky's first mature achievement. It was the "fantasy overture" *Romeo and Juliet* (1869).

The theme of fatal love had an obvious personal significance to Tchaikovsky. It was one to which he returned in his later illustrative pieces with a literary basis: *Francesca da Rimini* (after Dante, 1876), *Manfred* (after Byron, 1885) and *Hamlet* (after Shakespeare, 1888). But equally characteristic is the musical style of *Romeo and Juliet*: its vivid orchestration, its frankly emotional themes and its adaptation of sonata form to justify and control a dramatic construction with two strongly characterized ideas in unlike keys (in this case B minor and D♭ major). Tchaikovsky's music does not belong in the Haydn-Beethoven-Brahms tradition of development, but his way of cross-cutting between his dissimilar themes, intensifying differences of tonality and texture, provides a new concept of development, just as his apotheoses are effective replacements for the more usual recapitulation. These are things that had been part of the symphonic poem or descriptive overture as it had been handled by Liszt and Berlioz. But *Romeo and Juliet* made them more violently effective, and also prepared the way for a reintegration of symphonic-poem techniques into the four-movement symphony without the programmatic support of, say, Berlioz's *Fantastic Symphony*.

Tchaikovsky first attempted this in his Second Symphony (1872), whose Ukrainian folksongs earned it the nickname "Little Russian", and then again in his Third (1875), called the "Polish". But both these works suggest he was suppressing his dramatic instincts (they come out in the strongly characterized middle movements), and his best orchestral piece of this period was one where drama could be a central part of the substance: his First Piano Concerto (1875). It is significant here that an obvious structural "fault" – the failure of the famous opening tune to reappear – has not held the work back, for the real function of the opening is not to state a theme but rather to propose a style, one in which piano and orchestra are rivals in emotional and dynamic power as each in turn takes on the responsibility of melodic outburst. Soon afterwards it was the rivalry of swans that occupied the composer in his first ballet, *Swan Lake* (1877), where he delighted in the

114 Characters from the first production of Tchaikovsky's ballet *Nutcracker* at the Maryinsky Theater, St Petersburg, 1892: photograph.

opportunity to write exquisitely illustrative music without thought of large-scale musical form. It was a fairy-tale musical world to which he was to return in two later full-length ballets, the magnificent *Sleeping Beauty* (1890) and his masterpiece of orchestral brilliance, *Nutcracker* (1892).

Meanwhile, in the real world Tchaikovsky's state was not so happy. He became convinced that marriage could release him from the homosexual inclinations about which he felt so guilty. When a certain Antonina Milyukova wrote to him in the spring of 1877 with a confession of love he was prepared to see where it might lead – especially when he thus found himself in much the same position as the hero of the opera he was just beginning, *Eugene Onegin*. Onegin repulsed his admirer and came to regret his folly; Tchaikovsky accepted the attentions of his Antonina, but the outcome was the same. The two were married on 18 July, less than three months after that first letter; by October they were permanently separated, after a summer which the composer had largely spent escaping from his new wife.

Tchaikovsky's emotional perturbation during this period of crisis is documented in the letters he wrote to his brother Modest and to his distant patron Nadezhda von Meck, who gave him financial and (by correspondence) moral support on condition they never meet. But the intensity of his feelings comes out as well in the music he was writing, above all in his Fourth Symphony (1878), in F minor.

If this symphony is unmistakably autobiographical, however, it documents not only Tchaikovsky's near-hysteria but also his artistic maturity. The first movement, in particular, shows his mastery of musical form as a vehicle for the dramatic confrontation of sharply featured yet still companionable themes. The device of the motto theme, which appears in all four movements to make it abundantly clear that the symphony is a single experience, was adapted from Berlioz's *Fantastic Symphony* and was common in late nineteenth-century music. Less common was the close derivation of other subjects from the motto theme. For example, the limping scale motif of the third and fourth measures of the motto theme becomes the starting-point for the first subject (see Listening Note IX.A).

Listening Note IX.A

Tchaikovsky: *Symphony no. 4* in F minor op. 36 (1877–8), first movement

2 flutes (and piccolo in later movts), 2 oboes, 2 clarinets, 2 bassoons
4 horns, 2 trumpets, 3 trombones, tuba; timpani (and bass drum, cymbals, triangle in 4th movt)
1st violins, 2nd violins, violas, cellos, double basses

The movement follows the standard sonata-form outlines but only partly uses the principles of the form.

Introduction (mm. 1–26) The motto theme (ex. i) is loudly announced by horns and bassoons, echoed by trumpets and woodwinds.

Exposition (mm. 27–193) In a moderate tempo, with a hint of waltz rhythm, the violins and cellos state the principal theme (ex. ii); it is taken up, extended and developed, used in dialogue, heard in the bass instruments, and finally presented in a fierce tutti. Solo clarinet and bassoon then lead to the second subject, centered on A♭ (minor rather than the expected major) but modulating widely. The first theme here is presented by woodwinds (clarinet, then flute and oboe, with comments from others), but also important is another theme heard against it, first on strings: ex. iii shows the two together. Now the music turns to B major and ex. iv is heard, in which an idea from ex. iii (*x*) is in dialogue with ex. ii material. This continues, mainly using first subject (ex. ii) ideas, towards a loud and sustained climax (note the new closing theme, heard on strings and then horns).

Development (mm. 193–283)   The motto theme bursts in on trumpets, echoed by horns and woodwinds. Now an extended development of ex. ii material begins, essentially in the form of a long crescendo; at its climax the motto theme, on trumpets, cuts through the texture, and this heralds the . . .

Recapitulation (mm. 283–355)   There is only a perfunctory statement of first-subject material, and that in D minor rather than the home key of F minor: but in view of the dramatic treatment of the first-subject themes in the development the omission is not surprising. So as soon as m. 294 the bassoon presents ex. iii, with other woodwinds, and the counter-theme comes on the horn. The exposition plan is closely followed. Moreover, with ex. ii appearing in D minor (Ab minor before), ex. iii comes in F major (B major before), bringing us back to the home key.

Coda (mm. 355–422)   As before, the motto theme interrupts; also as before there is a continuation based on the first subject. Now (m. 381) the tempo increases, and both the first subject and the motto theme are treated with growing drama. With a high, loud, searing statement of the first subject the movement hurries to its close.

2nd movement (Andantino): Ternary form, bb

3rd movement (Scherzo: Allegro): Ternary form (strings pizzicato throughout; trio sections for woodwind and brass groups), F

4th movement (Allegro): Rondo form, F

There can be little doubt that Tchaikovsky thought of his themes in terms of their expressive character. According to a program for the symphony which he sketched for Mme von Meck, the motto theme is the voice of fate, "which prevents the impulse to happiness from attaining its goal". The first subject represents the misery of the individual under this edict; the second finds him discovering solace in daydreams; and the third speaks of an imagined happiness. But always after this third subject, at the end of the exposition and again at the end of the recapitulation, the motto theme enters to give the lie to easy contentment. The effect of this the second time around is to leave the music open-ended: the coda, following in directions indicated by Beethoven and Berlioz, is now so much a second development that it seems to require a second recapitulation, and so the cycle might continue forever.

This provides a musical, as well as an expressive excuse for the recurrence of the fate motto in the subsequent movements, as if continuing unfinished business left over from the first. Both the middle movements are relatively lightweight, emotional and musical evasions. In the second movement, according to Tchaikovsky's program, the protagonist loses himself in nostalgia, and in the third he seeks oblivion in wine, though in both he is recalled by the summons of fate.

The finale is a recall to seriousness, and again Tchaikovsky makes an expressive point by clearly structural means, since the movement opens with a newly strengthened version of the opening of the scherzo. But Tchaikovsky's long-delayed answer to the contradictions of the first movement is not altogether convincing. One may doubt whether he really felt, as his program has it, that the fate-hounded individual might lose himself in peasant merrymaking, and his provision of a rondo on folktunes at this point is a reversion to the simpler world of the Second Symphony and not a release of the tensions built up in the carefully planned progress of the first movement.

Nevertheless, the finale may be authentic in expressing a raising of the composer's spirits. He completed the work, early in 1878, towards the end of a long stay in western Europe, where he had gone to get over his marriage. It was a productive holiday, for he also finished *Eugene Onegin* and saw the ballet *Sylvia*, of which the music by Léo Delibes (1836–91) greatly impressed him and left its mark on his own *Sleeping Beauty*. Moreover, towards the end of this period of escape, in the spring of 1878, he enjoyed the companionship of the handsome young violinist Josif Kotek (1855–85) in Switzerland, and wrote for him his Violin Concerto in D.

Tchaikovsky returned to Russia in April 1878 and in October resigned from the Moscow Conservatory, since he could now live on his allowance from Mme von Meck. His marriage was over (divorce followed in 1881 when Antonina obligingly produced an illegitimate child), and outwardly his life was peaceable. These were not, however, the conditions under which he had shown himself to work best, and for the next few years he produced relaxed suites instead of symphonies, grand epics (*The Maid of Orleans*, 1879, and *Mazeppa*, 1884) instead of strong, intimate dramas like *Onegin*.

The ending of this period of ease was announced by *Manfred* (1885), where Tchaikovsky again followed a plan of Balakirev's, this time for a four-movement symphony based on Byron's verse drama. No doubt he recognized himself in the hero, doomed to roam the mountains in a hopeless attempt to expiate nameless sins, and the symphony bears comparison, both in its structure and in its expressive character, with its F minor predecessor. So too, still more so, does the Fifth

Symphony in E minor (1888), where the problems of integrating a motto theme are overcome with complete confidence when the finale converts the motto from an anxious probing into a march of triumph. The opera *The Queen of Spades* (1890) is also about a man accursed by fate and cut off by his obsessional nature from any normal social life.

The suggestion in all these works – though not directly in his sumptuously escapist ballet *The Sleeping Beauty* – is that Tchaikovsky was not able to live at peace with himself in the way suggested by the works of the early 1880s, like the Serenade in C for strings. His Sixth Symphony in B minor (1893), for which his brother Modest suggested the descriptive title "Pathétique", makes this quite clear. Here he refused the lures of peasant jollity and the triumphal march accepted in the last two symphonies and instead made the finale a great Adagio, sinking into an inevitable depression. Once again his urge to ruthless self-disclosure produced a new kind of musical structure, for this was the first great symphony of the nineteenth century to end with a slow movement (later examples include Mahler's Third and Ninth).

Three days after the first performance of this symphony, which took place on 28 October 1893, Tchaikovsky – according to testimony smuggled out of Russia in recent years – was brought before a court of his peers from the School of Jurisprudence and accused of bringing the alma mater into disrepute by virtue of his homosexual proclivities; a nobleman had complained of his relationship with a nephew. The sentence of the court was that he should kill himself. Whether this is wholly true must remain uncertain. What we do know is that he died a week later, whether because he took arsenic in obedience to such a decree, or because (according to a traditional tale) he caught cholera from drinking untreated water, no one can be sure.

The Five

If despite their manifest differences Tchaikovsky can be compared with Tolstoy in conceiving his art in classical Western terms, the group known as "The Five" belong with Dostoyevsky as men rebelliously different, individual and Russian.

Balakirev

Mily Balakirev, with no advanced musical education himself, was suspicious of its value for others, and it pleased him that Borodin was an academic chemist, Rimsky-Korsakov an ex-sailor and Mussorgsky a minor civil servant, none of them with more musical training than any boy of their period and (upper or middle) class. Similarly, technique was regarded as a potential enemy to genuineness of expression, with the result that Mussorgsky and Borodin labored for years at operas they never completed (*Khovanshchina* and *Sorochintsy Fair*, and *Prince Igor*). The artist was to be a type familiar in Russian culture: less a highly accomplished craftsman (though paradoxically Rimsky was this above all) than a saint harrying himself to get every idea into its truthful shape.

Borodin, Cui, Mussorgsky and Rimsky-Korsakov met and began taking lessons with Balakirev in the late 1850s or early 1860s, and by 1867 were regarded as members of a group around Balakirev, when the critic Vladimir Stasov, a champion of their music, coined the nickname "The Mighty Handful" for them. This was the period when they were mighty indeed: the period of Balakirev's two orientally-colored masterpieces (*Islamey* for piano, *Tamara* for orchestra), of Rimsky's orchestral narratives *Sadko* (1867) and *Antar* (1868) and his opera *The Maid of Pskov* (1872), of Borodin's Second Symphony (1876) and *Prince Igor* project (begun in 1869), and of Mussorgsky's *Boris Godunov* (1872).

Mussorgsky

Boris Godunov alone – and it stands almost alone, as the one large-scale work he completed – would be enough to establish Modest Mussorgsky's place as the outstanding composer of this group. He was born on 21 March 1839 in Karevo (Pskov district), the son of a landed family, and educated at the Guards Cadet School in St Petersburg. Though he toyed with composition and was a polished pianist, there is no evidence that he regarded music with much seriousness until in 1857 he met the composer Dargomïzhsky (1813–69) and Cui, and then Balakirev, with whom he took lessons. The next summer he resigned his army commission, and a year later, in 1859, he paid a visit to Moscow, where he was powerfully struck by the remnants of ancient Russian culture (St Petersburg was more recent, an Enlightenment city). If this gave him an ideal of rude native strength, eventually realized in *Boris* and the finale of the piano suite *Pictures at an Exhibition* (1874), his progress towards that ideal was slow and uncertain, for in his works of the next few years there are strikingly individual creations, like the *Intermezzo symphonique in modo classico* for piano (1861) with its melody in Russian peasant style, as well as academic exercises and sentimental trivia. The inconsistency was to remain characteristic, as was the difficulty Mussorgsky experienced in finishing larger works. A symphony was planned in 1861–2, and a great deal of work, some of it rescued for *Boris*, went into a setting of Flaubert's novel *Salammbô* as grand opera (1863–6).

Partly the problem was one of time. The liberation of the serfs in 1861 reduced Mussorgsky's income from the family estate, and so he was obliged in 1863 to take a post in the government service. But there was also his drinking: he seems to have become intermittently alcoholic after the death of his mother in 1865. And there was the difficulty that he was in search of expressive means for which there were few precedents. On the one hand he was attracted to the art of old Russia, as represented musically in the chant of the Orthodox Church and in folksong. On the other, he was excited by Dargomïzhsky's exploration of musical realism: the capturing in song of quirks of speech and nuances of expression, without much care for melodic shapeliness, harmonic coherence or metrical stability.

In 1866 Mussorgsky began to achieve the naturalism he wanted in his songs, usually through the effect of placing each in the voice of an incisively sketched character, in a style of pungent irony. The song thus becomes like a miniature operatic scene. Many of Mussorgsky's greatest songs are contained in cycles that are almost intimate operas: *The Nursery* (1870), a sharply unsentimental view of childhood with words by the composer, *Sunless* (1874), using poems by his cousin

---

Modest Mussorgsky   Works
born Karevo, 1839; *died* St Petersburg, 1881

Operas Salammbô (1866), Boris Godunov (1869, 1872, rev. 1873), Khovanshchina (1880), Sorochintsy Fair (1880)

Orchestral music St John's Night on the Bare Mountain (1867)

Songs Song cycles – The Nursery (1870), Sunless (1874), Songs and Dances of Death (1877); c50 others – Mephistopheles' Song of the Flea (1879)

Piano music suites – Pictures at an Exhibition (1874); Intermezzo in modo classico (1861, orchestrated 1867)

Choral music

115 Chaliapin as Boris Godunov in Mussorgsky's opera: photograph.

Count Arseny Golenishchev-Kutuzov but painting a quite personal pessimism, and *Songs and Dances of Death* (1877), a sardonic collection also with words by Golenishchev-Kutuzov.

But the breakthrough of 1866 also cleared Mussorgsky's path to opera. In 1868 he quickly set the first act of Gogol's comedy *The Marriage*, which gave him the diverse peasant characters and the irony he had proved he could handle in his songs. However, he seems to have been put off this project by the poor reception it had at a private performance: even Dargomïzhsky, himself a stark realist, felt that realism had now gone too far. It is equally possible, though, that the pressure of a new opera – that was to be *Boris Godunov* – was responsible for the abandonment of *The Marriage*, for Mussorgsky's masterpiece was begun in the same year and, in its first version, finished the next. But it had to be several times revised, and was long best known in a version by Rimsky-Korsakov designed to increase its effectiveness. Nevertheless, *Boris Godunov* remains an eccentric opera – a study of the guilt-ridden tyrant tsar in separate frames of action and narrative rather than in any dramatic continuity – and a certain roughness and crudity of style do not seem out of place.

Boris's great monologues in the second act best show Mussorgsky's attention to verbal rhythm and meaning, as well as his readiness to depart from orthodoxy in creating expressive effects in the orchestra. The first two measures of ex. IX.1 are typical of much of the slower music of the opera in their monotone chanting reminiscent of ecclesiastical practice: the quicker songs tend instead to emulate the zest of folksongs. Also typical is the modal flavor, here that of an artificial mode in alternating major and minor 2nds (E♭–F–G♭–A♭–B♭♭–C♭–[C]–D), which may be supposed to account for the unconventional harmonies. The accentuation of the word "Tsars" shows another characteristic feature, for this single word not only causes Boris to rise to his highest pitch but also brings about a switch in the harmony and texture of the accompaniment. Finally, the highly chromatic figure that enters the orchestra at this point, in insidious, reedy tone, is a startling image of the tsar's guilt, his memory of the murder of the boy heir: the motif keeps opening out, fanwise, through a grating major 2nd (a symbol for blood too in Bartók's *Bluebeard's Castle*) to an unsettling diminished 7th chord.

Boris Godunov, based on Pushkin's play about the tsar who followed in the wake of Ivan the Terrible, provided Mussorgsky with opportunities for great splendor in his ancient Russian style, using the old modes and the sounds of great bells; it also gave him the chance to explore some highly contrasted varieties of musical character, from the saturnine, possessed tsar himself to his lively children (depicted with the fresh, keen, detached style of *The Nursery*), or from the solemnly chanting historian monk Pimen to the vulgar, folksong-singing pair of itinerant friars Varlaam and Missail. The Polish act adds two more types in the self-satisfied Marina and her wily, seductive Jesuit confessor, but the heart and the truth of the opera are contained in the seven scenes that Mussorgsky wrote first.

Even before the production of *Boris Godunov*, he had started work on another historical opera, *Khovanshchina*, but this was left unfinished, as was the comedy he was writing simultaneously, *Sorochintsy Fair*. One part of the latter was to have been a witches' sabbath using music he had originally conceived as a symphonic poem, *St John's Night on the Bare Mountain* (1867), and then redrafted for inclusion in an opera-ballet in collaboration with Rimsky-Korsakov, Borodin and Cui. Otherwise his only important later works were songs and *Pictures at an Exhibition*, where his

ex. IX.1

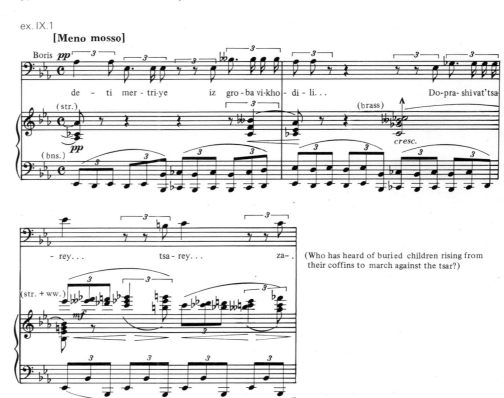

(Who has heard of buried children rising from
their coffins to march against the tsar?)

skills as a musical illustrator went into creating graphic equivalents for images in the paintings and drawings of his friend Victor Hartmann; the suite has several times been orchestrated, notably by Ravel. Mussorgsky's last years were ones of sporadic work on his two operas, interleaved with bouts of depression and alcoholism, though also with periods when he was able to function quite normally in society, even to the extent of accompanying a singer on a recital tour in 1879. He died in St Petersburg just a week after his 42nd birthday.

Borodin

Borodin's career was not unlike Mussorgsky's: although he composed two fine string quartets and two-and-a-half symphonies (no. 2 an expression of the principles of The Five in orchestral terms), his central work was an opera, *Prince Igor* – a grand historical pageant, full of exotic oriental touches, which it fell to Rimsky-Korsakov to edit and publish.

Rimsky-Korsakov

The two remaining members of The Five, Nikolay Rimsky-Korsakov and César Cui, were both much more productive, though slighter creative figures (Cui especially). Rimsky's *The Maid of Pskov* was in the historical genre favored by Mussorgsky and Borodin, but several of his other operas, including *Snow Maiden* (1881) and above all *The Golden Cockerel* (1907), were fantasies of magic and the supernatural that gave the excuse for the spectacular effects in which he excelled. Generally the more human characters in these operas are surrounded by music in folk style, while the magical elements are depicted in terms of chromaticism, often introduced by means of symmetrical divisions of the octave such as the whole-tone scale or the scale of alternating major and minor 2nds already encountered in *Boris Godunov*. In either case, Rimsky's orchestration is unusually varied and brilliant, as it is also in such orchestral works as *Sheherazade* (1888) and the *Spanish Caprice* (1887). His *Principles of Orchestration*, posthumously published in 1913, remains one of the standard texts on the subject and, taken with his music, suggests the influence he must have had on such pupils of his as Stravinsky and Prokofiev.

Later Russians

Apart from this heritage of orchestral splendor and modal usage passed on by Rimsky-Korsakov, the direct effect of The Five on subsequent composers was slight. Balakirev's later pupils were lesser composers like Anatoly Lyadov (1855–1914) and Sergey Lyapunov (1859–1924), while Tchaikovsky's pupil Sergey Taneyev (1856–1915) established at the Moscow Conservatory a definitely westward-looking, non-nationalist creative ideology. Taneyev was a composer of modesty and discretion who produced a distinguished body of chamber music including six string quartets, but his music has been overshadowed by that of two of his pupils, Sergey Rachmaninov (1873–1943) and Alexander Scriabin (1872–1915).

Both were outstanding pianists as well as composers, and both were admirers as much of Chopin as of Tchaikovsky, but otherwise they could not have been more different. Though he made some early ventures into opera, Rachmaninov worked largely in the standard genres of symphony, concerto, sonata, piano prelude and étude, while Scriabin gradually left behind conventional form as he left behind other musical conventions in his last years: the last five of his ten piano sonatas, for instance, are each in a single movement, and similarly his three symphonies of 1899–1904 had their successors in single-movement orchestral experiences, *The Poem of Ecstasy* (1908) and *Prometheus, Poem of Fire* (1910). Moreover, as these titles indicate, the later Scriabin was possessed with a vision of music as an agent of spiritual enlightenment, while Rachmaninov had no more pretensions for his art than that it should please and stir. This divergence is reflected again in Scriabin's progressive departure from major-minor tonality, while Rachmaninov, though he outlived his contemporary by nearly 30 years, remained resolutely a diatonic composer.

Rachmaninov

Sergey Rachmaninov was born in Semyonovo on 1 April 1873 into a family of failing fortunes. He studied at the conservatories in both St Petersburg and Moscow, graduating from the latter in 1892. He then started out on a career as a concert pianist while also composing freely: his popular Prelude in C♯ minor dates from the year of his graduation, his First Symphony from three years later. This period of confidence was brought to an end, however, by a calamitous performance of the symphony in 1897, after which he virtually abandoned composition until he produced his Second Piano Concerto (1901), whose immediate success restored his creative self-image. With its passionate and lyrical melodic style and its brilliant writing for the piano it has always been among the most popular of his works. More quickly followed, including two operas which he conducted during two seasons when he was conductor at the Bolshoy Theater in Moscow (1904–6). After this, disturbed by political conditions in Russia, he established a second home in Dresden, where he wrote his Second Symphony (1907) and his symphonic poem *The Isle of the Dead* (1909).

Also in 1909 he made his first tour of the USA and then returned to live in Russia. The next few years were ones of great compositional activity. Rachmaninov continued to add to his recital repertory, notably the two sets of *Etudes-tableaux*

Sergey Rachmaninov   Works
born Semyonovo, 1873; *died* Beverly Hills, 1943

Orchestral music piano concertos – no. 1, f♯ (1891), no. 2, c (1901), no. 3, d (1909), no. 4, g (1926); symphonies – no. 1, d (1895), no. 2, e (1907), no. 3, a (1936); The Isle of the Dead (1909); Rhapsody on a Theme of Paganini for piano and orchestra (1934); Symphonic Dances (1940)

Piano music sonatas – no. 1, d (1907), no. 2, b♭ (1913); Preludes, op. 23 (1903), op. 32 (1910); Etudes-tableaux, op. 33 (1911), op. 39 (1917); Variations on a Theme of Corelli (1931)

Choral music Liturgy of St John Chrysostom (1910); The Bells (1913)

Operas Aleko (1892), Francesca da Rimini (1905)

Songs Vocalise, op. 34 no. 14 (1912)

Chamber music Cello Sonata (1901); piano trios

(1911–17), but he also wrote a choral symphony after Poe, *The Bells* (1913), and two unaccompanied choral works for the Orthodox Church. In these he drew – as did Tchaikovsky in his liturgical music and Mussorgsky in *Boris Godunov* – on the fruits of a revival of orthodox music. From this he developed a church style in which his rich harmony does not carry the emotional melodic line so characteristic of his piano and orchestral music, which speaks expressively and formally of a yearning for the Westward-looking Russian romanticism that Tchaikovsky had brought to its peak a generation and more before.

After 1917, Rachmaninov's nostalgia was joined by a deep sense of dislocation from his homeland. He and his family left Russia within two months of the October Revolution and settled the next year in the USA. There, to make a living, he became a professional pianist, going on concert tours every season and also making records. Meanwhile, composition was quietly laid aside until in 1926 he wrote his Fourth Piano Concerto, a rambling work that underwent several phases of revision without being made the equal of the Second or the hugely demanding Third. It was followed, however, by a sequence of major works in which he reviewed his earlier style from an American standpoint of brilliance and detachment: the *Corelli Variations* for piano solo (1931), the *Paganini Rhapsody* for piano and orchestra (1934), the Third Symphony (1936) and the *Symphonic Dances* (1940). The last three works, performed for the first time by the Philadelphia Orchestra, were written with the precision of American orchestras in mind, while Rachmaninov's preference for variation structures in his late music also suggests a more objective manner than before. Sometimes, especially in the *Symphonic Dances*, the nostalgia becomes part of the musical substance, with themes from earlier works brought to an apotheosis: this happens in the *Dances* with a subject from the First Symphony and quotations too from one of his church works. Thereafter Rachmaninov wrote no more, and he died at his home in Beverly Hills in 1943.

East European nationalism

The assertion of national identity through music, and particularly by the use of traditional, folk elements in art music, became important in all the leading countries of eastern Europe during the later nineteenth century. In Poland, Stanislaw Moniuszko (1819–72) established a national opera tradition; his *Halka* (1848) and *The Haunted Manor* (1865) are still widely performed in that country. The next Polish composer of wider importance is Karol Szymanowski (1882–1937) who, much influenced by Scriabin, is notable for the opulent textures and harmonies of his symphonies and his violin concerto, though Polish coloring is felt in some of his piano music (naturally affected by Chopin). In Hungary, an opera tradition was begun by Ferenc Erkel (1810–93), whose *Bánk Bán* (1861) is a national classic. In Bohemia (now part of Czechoslovakia), closer to the older centers of European musical life (indeed including some of them), national aspirations asserted themselves particularly strongly just after the middle of the century – and in Smetana and Dvořák there were composers of international stature to exploit them.

Smetana

Bedřich Smetana was born in 1824 in the Bohemian town of Litomyšl, where his father, who played the violin, was a brewer. He never attended a conservatory and gained his musical education piecemeal, but was able to earn a living in Prague in the 1840s as a piano teacher while producing a large quantity of trivial piano music. It was not until after a meeting in 1858 with Liszt, one of his heroes, that he wrote his first important works, a set of three symphonic poems on historical figures and events. During this period he was conducting in Sweden, but in 1861 he returned to Prague and wrote an opera: in tune with the nationalist feelings of the time, he chose a theme from his country's history, *The Brandenburgers in Bohemia*. Smetana had been brought up as a German-speaker, and had first used Czech only in 1856; he now mastered his national language and used it for his opera. Given the mood of the time, the opera was assured success, and he swiftly followed it up with a spirited comedy of Bohemian peasant life, *The Bartered Bride*. This tuneful and appealing work is Smetana's only opera to hold a secure place in the international repertory today.

  Both these operas were produced at the Provisional Theater in 1866; in the same year, Smetana was appointed conductor at the theater. He composed two further nationalist operas in the ensuing years, *Dalibor* (given in 1868) and *Libuša*, not given until 1881, by which time Smetana had resigned his post because of deafness. From the 1870s date his cycle of six symphonic poems, *My Country*, based on the countryside, the history and the legends of Bohemia. The best known of these is *Vltava*, which traces in music the course of the country's main river. Smetana himself left an account of what the music represented: first a forest rill (represented on flutes, gently murmuring and gurgling: ex. IX.2*a*); then it grows into a mighty stream (a broad violin theme, with its roots in folk music: ex. 2*b*); next it moves through the forest, where sounds of the hunt are heard (fanfares on the winds), to a village where a wedding is being celebrated (with a dance, mixed march and polka); then the river is seen by moonlight (soft strings and woodwinds) with water nymphs dancing; eventually the river resumes its flow, passing stormily through rapids and finally streaming broadly and majestically on to Prague (a noble, crowning tutti, as the music at last moves from minor to major: ex. 2*c*).

ex. IX. 2

Meanwhile, Smetana's more personal thoughts went into his string quartet in E minor (1876), sub-titled "From my Life" and consisting of a musical autobiography in four movements. It begins with a sonata-form movement, bounded by questing music in E minor that represents, Smetana wrote, "the call of Fate to take up life's struggle". The scherzo is replaced by a Slavonic equivalent, a polka, in both peasant and ballroom forms: the composer discovers his sources in the villages while making his living in the salons of the aristocracy. The slow movement recalls "the happiness of my first love", and the finale, beginning as a rustic dance in E major, evidently recalls the equal happiness of discovering a folk-rooted style. But the dance breaks off, and Smetana introduces the whining high E that had racked his inner ear during his approaching deafness. Themes from the first movement and the finale reappear as if in recollection, and the work ends uneasily after its poignant intermingling of life with art. The illness (syphilis) that caused his deafness eventually killed him, in 1884; he received the funeral of a national hero.

Dvořák

By the time of Smetana's death, his example had been followed by others, notably Antonín Dvořák. Dvořák was born in 1841 in the village of Nelahozeves, where his father was a butcher. He studied at the organ school in Prague (the organ schools were centers of musical education in Bohemia, by no means solely for organists: Janáček attended the same institution 20 years later). Then he gained work as a viola player, being Smetana's principal in the orchestra of the Provisional Theater, where he played in the first performance of *The Bartered Bride* and in a concert conducted by Wagner. Smetana and Wagner were the main, and confusing, influences on his early music, though from the first he was intent on writing in the conventional genres of symphony and string quartet. His Third Symphony (1873) won an Austrian national prize and brought him to the notice of Brahms, whose

Antonín Dvořák	Life
1841	born in Nelahozeves, 8 September
1857	Prague Organ School
1863	viola player in Prague Provisional Theater Orchestra, from 1866 under Smetana
1873	married Anna Cermáková; organist of St Adalbert, Prague
1874	Third Symphony won Austrian National Prize
1878	Slavonic Dances published; encouragement from Brahms and first international recognition
1884	first of nine visits to England, where he became extremely popular and where several works (e.g. Eighth Symphony, *Requiem*) were first performed
1891	professor of composition at the Prague Conservatory; awarded many honors
1892–5	director of the National Conservatory of Music, New York; "New World" Symphony, "American" String Quartet, Cello Concerto
1895	director of the Prague Conservatory
1898	beginning of concentration on opera
1904	died in Prague, 1 May

DR. DVORAK'S GREAT SYMPHONY.

"From the New World" Heard for the First Time at the Philharmonic Rehearsal.

ABOUT THE SALIENT BEAUTIES.

First Movement the Most Tragic, Second the Most Beautiful, Third the Most Sprightly.

INSPIRED BY INDIAN MUSIC.

The Director of the National Conservatory Adds a Masterpiece to Musical Literature.

Dr. Antonin Dvorak, the famous Bohemian composer and director of the National Conservatory of Music, dowered American art with a great work yesterday, when his new symphony in E minor, "From the New World," was played at the second Philharmonic rehearsal in Carnegie Music Hall.

The day was an important one in the musical history of America. It witnessed the first public performance of a noble composition.

It saw a large audience of usually tranquil Americans enthusiastic to the point of frenzy over a musical work and applauding like the most excitable "Italianissimi" in the world.

The work was one of heroic proportions. And it was one cast in the art form which such poet-musicians as Beethoven, Schubert, Schumann, Mendelssohn, Brahms and many another "glorious one of the earth" has enriched with the most precious outwellings of his musical imagination.

And this new symphony by Dr. Antonin Dvorak is worthy to rank with the best creations of those musicians whom I have just mentioned.

Small wonder that the listeners were enthusiastic. The work appealed to their sense of the æsthetically beautiful by its wealth of tender, pathetic, fiery melody; by its rich harmonic clothing; by its delicate, sonorous, gorgeous, ever varying instrumentation.

And it appealed to the patriotic side of them.

For had not Dr. Dvorak been inspired by the impressions which this country had made upon him? Had he not translated these impressions into sounds, into music? Had they not been assured by the composer himself that the work was written under the direct influence of a serious study of the national music of the North American Indians? Therefore were they not justified in regarding this composition, the first fruits of

HERR ANTONIN DVORAK.

Antonín Dvořák	Works

Orchestral music symphonies – no. 1, c (1865), no. 2, B♭ (1865), no. 3, E♭ (1873), no. 4, d (1874), no. 5, F (1875), no. 6, D (1880), no. 7, d (1885), no. 8, G (1889), no. 9, "From the New World", e (1893); Slavonic Dances (1878, 1887); Slavonic Rhapsodies (1878); Symphonic Variations (1887); Nature, Life and Love (1892); Violin Concerto (1880); Cello Concerto (1895); symphonic poems

Operas The Jacobin (1897), Rusalka (1900)

Chamber music 14 string quartets – no. 12, "The American", F (1893), no. 13, G (1895), no. 14, A (1895); Piano Quintet, A (1887); piano trios – Dumky, op. 90 (1891); 3 string quintets; string sextet, piano quartet

Choral music Stabat mater (1877); St Ludmilla (1886); Mass (1887); Requiem (1890); Te Deum (1892); choral songs

Piano music Dumka (1876); Humoresques, op. 101 (1894); piano duets – Slavonic Dances (1878, 1886)

Songs

encouragement may well have contributed to his rapid creative development at this relatively late stage.

But the actual example of Brahms was important too. Dvořák dedicated a quartet to him, and made sure the outer movements were in orthodox sonata form, but like Smetana he introduced a polka instead of the usual scherzo. He also used Slavonic dance rhythms in his first mature symphony, no. 6 in D (1880), and in a string quartet, where the second movement is headed "Dumka" and the finale has the rhythm of the *skočna*, a Czech leaping dance. The *dumka* was a lament which Dvořák often interpreted as a melancholy song incorporating bright dance sections: this happens in the six *dumky* that make up his fine Piano Trio in E minor (1891). Another *dumka* appears among the 16 Slavonic Dances (1878 and 1886), which were published in orchestral and in piano duet versions and served to popularize Dvořák's music at this time of emergent mastery.

The proof that a Bohemian style could appeal outside central Europe came in 1884 when Dvořák conducted his music in London to immense acclaim. Commissions came for an oratorio for the Leeds Festival (*St Ludmilla*), a cantata for the Birmingham Festival (*The Specter's Bride*) and a new symphony for the Philharmonic Society of London (no. 7 in D minor). During the next few years he paid several visits to England, for the first performances of these and other works. Then in 1891 there came a request from further afield, when he was invited by Jeannette Thurber to direct the National Conservatory of Music in New York. He accepted the post, and, apart from one holiday at home, spent 1892–5 in the U.S.A.

While there he took an interest in the music of black Americans and Indians (Mrs Thurber was anxious he should write an opera on the subject of Hiawatha, but this came to nothing). Some of his American research went into the works he wrote, including his Ninth Symphony in E minor, "From the New World", and his F major string quartet, "American" (both 1893). However, what he extracted from his New World sources was a vein of pentatonic melody – that is, based (largely) on a five-note scale (rather like the black keys on a piano) – which is so widespread in folk music that it could equally have been east European. Dvořák dealt with this irregular element in his music by regularizing it and accommodating it within the diatonic system.

ex. IX.3

The main themes of the string quartet are strictly pentatonic; those of the "New World" symphony are slightly less so, but still bring a new idiom into the realm of symphonic music as the three main themes of the first movement demonstrate: ex. IX.3*a* shows a pentatonic scale, to which ex. 3*b*, heard on the horns to start the main part of the movement, nearly but not quite conforms; the first second-subject theme, ex. 3*c*, acquires its exotic flavor by quite different means (the narrow compass and the "folky" flattened 7th degree of the scale, marked *x*), though it becomes pentatonic in the version taken up by the strings (ex. 3*d*); and lastly the famous flute theme of the second subject (ex. 3*e*), which is close to pentatonic – close, too, to "Swing low, sweet chariot", which Dvořák must have met in America. The equally well-known theme of the slow movement, given out in the throaty, expressive tones of the english horn (ex. 3*f*), once more evokes the nostalgic world of the song of black Americans; but again his treatment presses it into the mold of the post-Brahmsian symphony.

He made this kind of theme very much his own. In the Cello Concerto that he wrote in his last months in New York, in 1895 – perhaps the finest of all concertos for that most eloquent instrument – several of the themes have this same pentatonic leaning, but the music is in the end as Brahmsian as anything Dvořák produced.

Back in Bohemia, Dvořák wrote two more quartets in 1895, his last chamber works; they were followed by a group of five symphonic poems. His final years were mostly devoted to opera, ranging from Bohemian folktale comedy to high

116 (*Opposite*) Part of an article on Dvořák's Symphony no. 9 in E minor ("From the New World") from the *New York Herald* (16 December 1893) after its first performance at the Carnegie Hall a few days earlier.

Wagnerian tragedy by way of the fairytale fantasy of his dramatic masterpiece, *Rusalka* (1900). He died in Prague in 1904.

Janáček

Dvořák's influence was deep on his Czech successors, so deep that even Leoš Janáček, born in the village of Hukvaldy, Moravia (now central Czechoslovakia), in 1854, composed in the Bohemian style of his elder contemporary for much of his life. His early music, however, is of slender value in comparison with the works he wrote in the last third of his life. Above all his last ten years were an extraordinarily productive period that saw the composition of four great operas, mostly on highly unconventional topics – *Katya Kabanova*, *The Cunning Little Vixen*, *The Makropoulos Case* and *From the House of the Dead* – as well as a Mass, a Sinfonietta, two string quartets and a few other works.

There were general musical reasons for this late flowering: one may be the influence of Stravinsky, though the no less important influence of Mussorgsky had of course long been felt. At the same time there was a personal reason: this was the intense emotion Janáček experienced when he conceived a strong attachment for a married woman, Kamila Stösslová, who was the imagined heroine of all his late operas. Then again, his late music can be seen as at last attaining the distinctive Moravian character he had been looking for all his life. In that respect it may be significant that, like Smetana, he wrote in his last years a chamber work looking back at his early life and musical formation, the wind sextet *Youth* (1924).

The Moravian quality of his music is on one level a matter of accentuation. He made notations of the rhythms and pitch inflections of people's speaking voices, and used the experience in creating, Mussorgsky-like, a great variety of operatic characters clearly distinguished from one another by their vocal behavior. It was, indeed, in an opera with a Moravian village setting, *Jenůfa* (1904), that he began to emerge as an independent composer, gradually leaving behind the jollification of *The Bartered Bride* and discovering a more realistic way of handling people in emotional conflict. To a listener from the USA or western Europe, used to the languages of a different, smoother rhythmic structure, Janáček's music often sounds jagged and violent; in the operas this is further stressed by his orchestral writing, where he often obtains harsh, strongly characterized effects by using instruments at the extremes of their compass.

In achieving this kind of realism, Janáček also learned from Moravian folk music, which encouraged him towards a style of short melodic phrases, baldly repeated or

---

Leoš Janáček   Works
born Hukvaldy, 1854; *died* Moravská Ostrava, 1928

Operas Jenůfa (1904), The Excursions of Mr Brouček (1920), Katya Kabanova (1921), The Cunning Little Vixen (1924), The Makropoulos Case (1926), From the House of the Dead (1928)

Choral music Mass (1908); Glagolitic Mass (1926); cantatas, male-voice choruses

Other vocal music The Diary of One who Disappeared (1919); songs

Orchestral music Taras Bulba (1918); Sinfonietta (1926)

Chamber music string quartets – no. 1, "Kreutzer Sonata" (1923), no. 2, "Intimate Letters" (1928); Youth, wind sextet (1924)

Piano music

117 Čapek's design for the lawyer's office in Janáček's opera *The Makropoulos Case*, first performed 18 December 1926. Moravské Muzeum, Brno. The opera was based on a play by the artist's brother.

juxtaposed in the building up of large structures, each phrase normally being identified with its own orchestral coloring. In instrumental works – the quartets and most particularly the Sinfonietta for orchestra – whole movements are constructed from repeated figures in this way, and the liturgical text of his Slavonic Mass makes possible similar kinds of repetitive structure.

In opera, however, Janáček uses his brevity as a means to color conversation. Long solo passages (or "arias") are rare. Instead, there is a quick crossfire of different characters, different kinds of music: the more diatonic for his heroines (especially Jenůfa, Katya and the Vixen), the more grating and angular for their antagonists. Where there are extended solos, as in *From the House of the Dead* (set in a prison camp), they take the form of narrations, in which the singer himself imitates a variety of different characters, thus creating operas within the opera.

Forms so based on contrast present problems of ending, which in most cases Janáček solved by finishing with an apotheosis: the animal opera *The Cunning Little Vixen*, the Sinfonietta and *From the House of the Dead* provide notable examples. The quartets, however, being more intimate expressions, are more open-ended. Janáček actually sub-titled the second of them "Intimate Letters" (by implication, letters to

Stösslová), which he breaks off suddenly, as if in mid-sentence; in the first quartet, named the "Kreutzer Sonata" (after Tolstoy's book condemning marriage as an impediment to love), he had left the movements hanging in the air. The quartets, too, display his abrupt contrasts no less violently than do the operas.

Rooted so deeply in Moravia, musically and personally, Janáček spent most of his life in the provincial capital of Brno, where he taught at the organ school and wrote acute, often fanciful articles for a local newspaper. Most of his extraordinary late music, however, was composed back in his home village, where he had bought a house in 1919, and he died in the nearby town of Moravská Ostrava in 1928.

Vienna

The Bohemia and Moravia of Smetana, Dvořák and Janáček was until 1918 part of the Habsburg empire, ruled from Vienna, and to some extent the very existence of a Czech national style depended on composers keeping their distance from so richly endowed a musical capital: Dvořák in particular was very conscious of that, and resisted commissions to write for Vienna. However, there was certainly no single Viennese style. Brahms was to be heard in the concert halls and the younger Johann Strauss in the ballrooms, but there were also others, whom the conservative Viennese public took less readily to their hearts: Bruckner, Wolf and Mahler.

Wolf

Hugo Wolf (1860–1903) made enemies through his work as a music critic. He was outspoken, and heaped praise on Wagner at the expense of Brahms. Not surprisingly, he was influenced by Wagner's harmony and declamatory style in the songs that form the great bulk of his output. But at the same time his penetrating search for character, for the particular "voice" of a song, for psychological insight, belongs very much in the Vienna of Freud. During the brief period of his greatest productivity, 1888–91, he worked at feverish pace: about 180 songs date from those years, divided into settings of Mörike, Goethe and Spanish and Italian poets in translation. Thereafter he wrote a second volume of Italian songs (1896) and an opera, *Der Corregidor* (1895), but these came in sudden, white-hot bursts of creative energy that interrupted a general torpor, which may be attributed to his syphilis. In the autumn of 1897 he lost his never steady hold on sanity, and he died in a sanatarium.

Bruckner

Anton Bruckner, also neglected and even despised in Vienna for his Wagnerism, drew something quite different from the master of Bayreuth: not the psychological recitative but the symphonic breadth. He also had a career very different from Wolf's. Born in 1824 in Ansfelden, near Linz, he was the son of a schoolmaster-organist and began by following his father's profession, notably at the monastery of St Florian near his home village. Then from 1855 to 1868 he was organist at Linz Cathedral. In his early years there he studied harmony and counterpoint by correspondence with the Viennese teacher Simon Sechter, and then had lessons locally, continuing these studies until he was 43. In 1863 he encountered Wagner's music through a performance of *Tannhäuser* in Linz, and soon afterwards began to write works that are characteristic: his First Symphony, in C minor, and large-scale Masses. All these works, however, were subsequently revised. Indeed, Bruckner all

Anton Bruckner   Works
born Ansfelden, near Linz, 1824; *died* Vienna, 1896

Symphonies "no. 0", d (*c*1864), no. 1, c (1866), no. 2, c (1872), no. 3, d (1877), no. 4, "Romantic", E♭ (1874, 1880), no. 5, B♭ (1876), no. 6, A (1881), no. 7, E (1883), no. 8, c (1887), no. 9, d (1896, unfinished)
Choral music Requiem (1849); Masses – no. 1, d (1864), no. 2, e, with woodwind and brass (1866), no. 3, f (1868); Te Deum (1884); cantatas, motets
Chamber music String Quintet, F (1879)

Organ music   *Piano music*   *Partsongs*   *Songs*

his life lacked confidence in his mastery and meekly accepted criticism, even the uncomprehending criticism that persuaded him to make wholesale, damaging cuts in his broad structures.

In 1868 he was appointed Sechter's successor at the Vienna Conservatory, where he remained to the end of his life with a dedicated band of disciples (including Mahler, who, however, never actually studied with him) while his music attracted scorn. Apart from his *Te Deum* (1884) and a few other choral works, he devoted himself to the symphony. Gradually he perfected his approach to the form. Beethoven's Ninth gave him the basic outline – a monumental opening movement, a profound Adagio, a driving scherzo in sonata form and a cumulative finale; Wagner provided the time-scale and some of the harmony. (He visited Wagner at Bayreuth in 1873, dedicating to him his Third Symphony, and in his later symphonies he added to his orchestra a quartet of Wagner tubas, the instruments Wagner had designed for the *Ring*.) But Schubert was his nearest predecessor in matters of form. His sonata allegros often have three groups of subject matter rather than two and, like Schubert's, tend to substitute repetition in a different key for development.

The result, however, is wholly original. Bruckner's long apprenticeship as a church musician, and his devotion to the Catholic faith, imprinted the ecclesiastical modes into his musical nature, and the individuality of his harmony often results from modal inflections. Similarly, his treatment of the orchestra in large homogeneous blocks suggests the work of an organist manipulating stops, though this style of instrumentation enabled him to achieve colossal effects with an orchestra of modest proportions for the period. Only in his Eighth Symphony, in C minor (1887), the last he completed, did he introduce a harp and expand the woodwind from double to triple; and nowhere did he use the unusual woodwinds (piccolo, english horn etc) or the additional percussion prized by Wagner, Mahler and Strauss.

His greatest originality lay in his conception of time. Long-held notes (often in the form of string *tremolandos*) and sequences of continuingly repeated figures create effects of stillness not otherwise to be found in Western music before Messiaen, and more generally his structures are static rather than dynamic. Where Brahms was making development more and more central to his music, Bruckner was insisting above all on statement, on the symphonic treatment of objects that are essentially stable. Sonata form is not, as in Beethoven and Brahms, a resolution of some conflict inherent in the opening material; instead it is the mold for a symmetrical movement from statement to changed statement and back to statement.

ex. IX.4

That sort of form suits the themes of great length and solidity that are most characteristic of Bruckner. The opening of the E major Seventh Symphony (ex. IX.4) is also characteristic in its unfolding of a long melody over a *tremolando* accompaniment – a reminiscence of Beethoven's Ninth Symphony, perhaps, affected also by the memory of Schubert's G major string quartet. The initial arpeggio, however, is majestically Brucknerian, and Brucknerian alone: where a Haydn arpeggio theme would be pressing forward towards some conflict, this one is like a slow inhalation, taking breath as it rises to the dominant. But the dominant turns out to be weak. In a passage where chromaticism is typically modal in its derivation, Bruckner arrives not in a normal B major but in a key of B with its second and third degrees flattened, recalling the Phrygian mode of Renaissance church music. Then the second limb of the theme, beginning with a change of scoring in the tenth measure, changes the falling 4th of the start into a falling augmented 4th or tritone, again a feature of the Phrygian mode. The tritone fall is heard three times at progressively higher levels before the theme at last settles in the area of the dominant. And so there is a symmetry in the theme of diatonic antecedent (E major arpeggio) followed by a chromatic-modal consequent, then chromatic-modal antecedent (measures 10–15) followed by diatonic consequent.

The symmetry of the whole movement is just as clear. In Bruckner's normal way, the exposition is long and straightforward, introducing three themes (the second is unstable in tonality, the third is in B minor). The "development" explores these themes in different keys, turning them upside down: the arpeggio motif from the first theme is used in B major, while the third theme is heard simultaneously in inverted and normal forms, in E minor: a common procedure in Bruckner – there is another example when the first theme returns in E major. In a sense this marks the start of the "recapitulation", but E major is only too briefly sustained and the reprise of the third theme is in G, not E; the movement does not follow the sonata-form principle, harmonically speaking. The full reinstatement of E major comes only in the last 31 of the movement's epic 443 measures, where the arpeggio motif, again in standard and inverted forms, plays over what is a massive decoration of the E major triad. This is not the affirmative arrival it might be in a Beethoven or Brahms symphony, but the completion of a giant arch, with a return to the open diatonicism with which the symphony began.

The whole work is an arch on a still greater scale, for at the end of the finale the arpeggio motif comes back again to add splendor to the concluding E major. But

Bruckner's next symphony, no. 8, goes further in the confirmation of unity, for there the ending of the last movement, over sustained triads of C major, brings back the principal themes not only of the opening Allegro but also of the Adagio and the Scherzo. It is for such feats of construction and symmetry, as well as for their aura of sanctity, that Bruckner's symphonies have been aptly compared with great medieval cathedrals.

The modal characteristics are of course a reminder of plainsong, and Bruckner's brass writing in particular often has the quality of a wordless chorale. Moreover, the purity of his style – its rooting in basic tonal elements (triad and arpeggio), its rhythmic plainness, its block-like use of the orchestra – contributes to a sense of objectivity, of personal emotion dissolved in an act of prayer and praise. There is also evidence of this in Bruckner's use in his symphonies of a style developed largely in sacred choral works, in his quotation from his choral works in his symphonies, and in his decision to dedicate his Ninth Symphony, whose finale he did not live to complete, "to the King of Kings, Our Lord". He died peacefully in Vienna in 1896.

Mahler

Mahler followed Bruckner in expanding the dimensions of the symphony so that a single work lasts for an hour or more, but his aims and methods were entirely different. Where Bruckner's symphonies are all interpretations of one ideal, Mahler's are diverse stages in a spiritual autobiography. Only three of his symphonies are, like all Bruckner's, four-movement cycles for orchestra (nos. 1, 6 and 9). The number of movements may be larger (five in nos. 2, 5, 7 and 10; six in no. 3) or smaller (two in no. 8). Equally common is Mahler's extension of the range

Gustav Mahler	Life
1860	born in Kalischt (now Kaliště), 7 July
1875–8	Vienna Conservatory
1880	*The Song of Sorrow*; conductor at Bad Hall summer theater
1881–3	conductor at Laibach and Olmütz
1883–5	opera conductor at Kassel; composed *Songs of a Wayfarer* after unhappy love affair
1885–6	conductor of German Opera, Prague
1886	conductor of New State Theater, Leipzig
1888	met Richard Strauss, who became a lifelong friend; conductor of the Budapest Royal Opera
1891–7	conductor at the Hamburg State Theater; Second, Third and Fourth Symphonies
1897	baptized Roman Catholic; conductor of the Vienna Court Opera and, with gifted colleagues, was responsible for one of its most brilliant decades
1902	married Alma Schindler; beginning of period of intense composition
1907	elder daughter died; Mahler diagnosed to have heart disease
1908	conductor of the Metropolitan Opera, New York, spending summers in Europe composing
1909	conductor of New York Philharmonic Orchestra; *The Song of the Earth*
1911	died in Vienna, 18 May

Gustav Mahler	Works

Symphonies no. 1, D (1888), no. 2, "Resurrection", c (1894), no. 3, d (1896), no. 4, G (1900), no. 5, c♯ (1902), no. 6, a (1904), no. 7, e (1905), no. 8, E♭ (1906), no. 9, D (1909), no. 10, f♯ (1910, unfinished)

Songs (with orchestra) song cycles – Lieder eines fahrenden Gesellen (Songs of a wayfarer, 1885), Kindertotenlieder (Songs for the death of children, 1904); Des Knaben Wunderhorn (Youth's Magic Horn, 1893–8); Das Lied von der Erde (The song of the earth, 1909)

Choral music Das klagende Lied (The song of sorrow, 1880)

of the symphony by adding voices: solo women's and choral voices in nos. 2–4 and a great mass of soloists and choirs in the symphonic oratorio that is no. 8, sometimes known as the "Symphony of a Thousand".

Gustav Mahler was born in 1860 in the Bohemian village of Kalischt. The family soon moved to the town of Iglau, where he came into contact with various kinds of music – military bands, folksongs, café music and salon pieces – storing up childhood memories that were to be revived in his symphonies. He also learned the piano and even started an opera, displaying enough talent to gain admission to the Vienna Conservatory, where he studied from 1875 to 1878. He then remained in Vienna, attending lectures at the university, working as a music teacher, and writing a cantata, *Das klagende Lied* (1880), which is immediately characteristic of the mature composer, even though composed when he was still in his late teens. The style of Romantic medievalism and nature-poetry comes from nineteenth-century German opera, and the harmonic language has the chromatic intensity of *Tristan*, then little more than a decade old. Mahler's use of the orchestra, however, is already independent, showing his preference for clear, sharp-edged textures in which threads of melody and accompaniment stand out starkly. Even the themes bear comparison with those of later works, as does the subject, which is death, with all its associations of sorrow, inevitability, absurdity and guilt.

By the time *Das klagende Lied* was completed Mahler had started work on an opera, but it was not staged and is now lost. He was never to write another, even though much of his life as a practical musician was spent in the opera house, for in 1880 he began a career as a conductor that led him to important posts in Prague, Leipzig, Budapest, Hamburg, Vienna and New York. He became one of the outstanding conductors of his day, unstinting in his demands on players and singers, but unstinting too in his demands on himself. He strove to achieve the most persuasive rendering of a work, even, he felt, if that meant making alterations to the text.

He took very much the same line with his own works. His First Symphony, in D, may have been begun as early as 1884 but was not definitively completed until the mid-1890s, when it had been reduced from five movements to four and changed from a symphonic poem into a work in the more traditional form. That it was first a symphonic poem suggests the importance of Richard Strauss to the young Mahler, less as an influence than as a champion, though very soon the two men were to be forced into the position of rivals for the torch of the great tradition. (Brahms, shortly before his death in 1897, is said to have remarked that it was Mahler, not Strauss as most people then thought, who marked the way forward.)

118 (*Opposite*) Mahler conducting: silhouettes by Otto Böhler.

Mahler's First Symphony uses themes from his song cycle of the same period *Lieder eines fahrenden Gesellen* ("Songs of a wayfarer"). This was something that Schubert had done in several of his later chamber works, but in Mahler's case the introduction of a song theme hints at a psychological program underlying the music, and in his next three symphonies such programs become quite explicit, since songs are included. The Second Symphony, in C minor moving to E♭ major (1895), has a mezzo-soprano song as penultimate movement and a choral finale; the Third, in D minor-major (1896), again has a solo song (for contralto) followed by a choral piece, but this time a purely orchestral finale takes over; and the Fourth, in G moving to E (1900), has just the song (for soprano) as finale.

All three works use texts from *Des Knaben Wunderhorn* ("The boy's magic horn"), a collection of folk poetry (and imitations of folk poetry) of the early nineteenth century. Mahler also made a number of independent settings of the *Wunderhorn* poems, whose naivety was a perfect vehicle for his music, so much more ironic, complex and inquisitive.

The Second and Third Symphonies use other verse too. The grand choral finale to no. 2 sets an ode on resurrection by Klopstock: a work that begins with a movement filled with doubt ends in gigantic optimism. The Third Symphony, according to its original program, is an ascent through the realms of existence. Its huge first movement, lasting for half an hour, is followed by five movements in which the composer listens in turn to meadow flowers (a delicate minuet), forest animals (a scherzo), the night (the contralto song, with words by Nietzsche), bells (with angel choirs of women and boys) and love (Adagio). The Fourth, of more normal dimensions, may be considered to make a similar climb, since it ends with the soprano singing of the delights of heaven.

While this work was in progress, Mahler was baptized into the Catholic church, though apparently for practical rather than religious reasons: his Jewishness was an obstacle to his gaining an appointment in Vienna, where he became director of the Court Opera later the same year.

In 1901 he married Alma Schindler (1879–1964), the daughter of a painter and later, after Mahler's death, the wife successively of an architect (Walter Gropius) and a novelist (Franz Werfel). Also in 1901 he embarked on a period of intense creativity, and though his conducting duties left him only the summers in which to compose, by 1905 he had completed three new symphonies: no. 5 in C♯ minor moving to D major, no. 6 in A minor and no. 7 in E minor moving to C major. Again there were associated volumes of songs: the *Kindertotenlieder*, setting five of the 400 or so poems that Friedrich Rückert wrote on the deaths of his two children, and another group of Five Rückert Songs, all set for voice and orchestra.

Much of this music – the symphonies as well as the songs – seems to convey Mahler's feeling of being pursued by fate, represented in the immense finale of the Sixth Symphony by the crushing blows of a hammer. In terms of his own life, however, the doom was prophetic rather than actual. At the Vienna Opera he was staging radically new productions designed by Alfred Roller, and he became the proud father of two daughters, born in 1902 and 1904. It was in 1907 that life caught up with his art. His elder daughter, like Rückert's children, died from illness, and he himself was diagnosed as having a heart condition.

In the fall of that year Mahler conducted his last operas in Vienna. Although his years at the Court Opera had been among the most distinguished in its history, they were not untroubled and his ideas often met with resistance. Meanwhile, he had been invited to conduct at the Metropolitan Opera in New York, which he did for two seasons, beginning in 1908 – though the outlook of the company, with its emphases on Italian opera and star singers, was alien to him. When in 1909 he was offered the conductorship of the New York Philharmonic, he accepted, resigning from the Metropolitan. He was to conduct only one complete season, for it was during his second that he contracted his last illness. Mahler introduced many new works to New York in the concerts he conducted with the orchestra (86 in all), but neither his programs nor his manner were popular with the orchestra or the public, and his departure was little regretted.

If Mahler's music of these later years – indeed of all periods – is unmistakably introspective, it appears to speak also of a wider impending tragedy: that of Imperial European culture, in which he had come to hold a prominent place at Vienna, and that of the musical language. For his confrontation with death, explicit in the *Kindertotenlieder* and implicit in the Sixth Symphony, is a confrontation too with the dissonance and chromaticism that were threatening the extinction of tonality – not only in Mahler's music but also at exactly the same time in Strauss's and Schoenberg's. His responses to the threat were manifold. Highly characteristic

119 "Longing for Happiness": section from the *Beethoven Frieze* by Gustav Klimt, first shown at the Secession's 1902 exhibition. Österreich-isches Galerie, Vienna. The figure of the knight (whose features resemble Mahler's) also appeared as Klimt's contribution to the volume of tributes to Mahler published by Paul Stefan in 1910.

is a tone of poignant nostalgia, present even in the music he was writing as a teenager, but focusing now on the remembrance of the lilting simplicity of the *ländler*, the country cousin of the Viennese waltz. Nostalgia in Mahler, however, is normally combined with a fierce irony, as in the Scherzo of the Fourth Symphony, a *ländler*, with its mistuned solo violin, or the parodies of *ländler*, waltz and march that flit across the nocturnal landscape of the Seventh Symphony. A more regretful sort of nostalgia is often connected with themes from the Rückert settings to which Mahler looks back in his slow movements, notably the Adagietto of the Fifth Symphony and the Andante of the Sixth, which both include motifs from the Rückert sets.

While slow movements and scherzos thus contemplate, from different standpoints, the purer lyricism and the easier diatonicism of an earlier age (specifically that of Schubert), the outer movements of Mahler's symphonies tackle the contemporary problems of an expanded tonality. A strong meter is often needed to guarantee forward motion, and in many cases Mahler recalls the military music of his boyhood: both the opening movement and the finale of the Sixth Symphony, for instance, are largely fixed to march rhythms. The main theme of the opening movement is typical in its urgent dynamism (ex. IX.5).

Listening Note IX.B

Mahler: *Das Lied von der Erde* (1908), "Der Trunkene im Frühling"

tenor solo
piccolo, 2 flutes, 2 oboes, E♭ clarinet, 2 B♭ clarinets, 2 bassoons, double bassoon
4 horns, trumpet; harp
1st violins, 2nd violins, violas, cellos, double basses

This is the fifth movement of a symphony consisting of six orchestral songs, alternately for tenor and contralto. All six have words from *Die chinesische Flöte* ("The Chinese Flute"), a volume of Chinese poetry adapted into German by Hans Bethge.

mm.	Der Trunkene im Frühling	The spring-time drunkard
1–16	Wenn nur ein Traum das Leben ist warum denn Müh' und Plag'!? Ich trinke, bis ich nicht mehr kann, den ganzen lieben Tag!	If life's only a dream why all this fuss and bother!? I drink till I'm full the livelong day!
17–30	Und wenn ich nicht mehr trinken kann, weil Kehl' and Seele voll, so taund' ich bis zu meiner Tür und schlafe wundervoll!	And when I can't take any more, when body and soul are full, I stagger back home and sleep like a top!
31–45	Was hör' ich beim Erwachen? Horch! Ein Vogel singt im Baum. Ich frag' ihn, ob schon Frühling sei.– Mir ist als wie im Traum.	What do I hear when I wake up? Hist! A bird sings from a tree. I ask him if it's springtime yet. To me it's like a dream.
45–63	Der Vogel zwitschert: Ja! Ja! Der Lenz ist da, sei kommen über Nacht! Aus tiefstem Schauen lauscht' ich auf,– der Vogel singt und lacht!	The bird twitters: yes, yes! Spring's here: it came overnight! I listened for it closely, the bird sings and laughs!
62–73	Ich fülle mir den Becher neu und leer' ihm bis zum Grund— und singe, bis der Mond erglänzt am schwarzen Firmament!	I fill my glass again and drink it to the dregs, and sing till the moon comes up in the black heavens!
74–89	Und wenn ich nicht mehr singen kann, so schlaf' ich wieder ein.– Was geht mich denn der Frühling an!? Lasst mich betrunken sein!	And when I can't sing any more, I go to sleep again. So what's the point of spring!? Just let me be drunk!

mm.	
1–16	This is the first stanza of the poem. Wind instruments open the song on the dominant of A major and then swerve up drunkenly to accommodate the tenor's entry in B♭. His second line introduces a highly important rhythmic motif (ex. i) and lands on A, but now the orchestra is in F major (ex. ii): the strings develop ex. i. Then, by way of G major, tenor and orchestra together climb back to A major, which is reached in a brilliant filling-out of the opening music.
17–30	The second stanza is a varied repeat of the first.
31–45	A slackening of tempo goes along with a harmonic uncertainty that is appropriate for the moment of the drunkard's awakening. On listening, though, he hears again the dominant of A major, and the solo violin recalls the earlier string theme, which is later taken up by the piccolo. When the orchestra is most firmly rooted in A major, the tenor line is at its most chromatic: this is his moment of questioning, marked *sinnend* ("pensively"). He ends again on a high A, but this time the orchestra is not with him: they have already moved towards F major for the next stanza.
45–63	The original tempo returns, but the previous stanza has introduced the idea of "dream" and all the parts are unfamiliar. The first line is lightly accompanied by violins, horn, oboe and piccolo, with a solo violin for the twittering bird. Then, when the tenor sings of spring, there is a new tonality: D♭ major, warmly orchestrated. The tempo slows again, and the music stays in the area of D♭ to the end: the tenor's usual final A is now a soft A♭.
62–73	As the drunkard fills his glass, the music slips into the bland normality of C major, when it reaches up again to A major at the end in the manner of the first two stanzas.
74–89	The final stanza is a further varied repeat of the first.

This fifth movement functions as a scherzo in the whole *Das Lied von der Erde*, which has the following plan:

I   Tenor solo: vigorous allegro
II Contralto solo: slow movement with chamber orchestration
III Tenor solo: moderately quick movement of light character
IV Contralto solo: lively movement
V   Tenor solo: quick comic movement
VI Contralto solo: long, slow finale.

ex. i

ex. ii

ex. IX.5

The wide leaps that become increasingly characteristic of Mahler's melody arise here in a series of upward strivings to counter the falling octave at the start of the theme. But the upward urges cannot reach firm ground in the way that the downward drop does. There is a strong tendency to fall away (m. 3) or to reach a diatonically favored note with effort from its semitone neighbor (mm. 4 and 5). Then, with a change of scoring from unison violins to woodwinds, the melody collapses.

This is quite evidently a dramatic as well as a musical subject. As such, it is embroiled in music of constant change, where its outline may be more or less distorted. Mahler still follows the outline of sonata form, but his music no more operates in a sonata manner than does Bruckner's, though the reasons for this are quite opposite. Where Bruckner's music is about statement and symmetry, Mahler's is all development and thrust, so that his recapitulations are usually much transformed or followed by new developments in a coda. The symphony takes on a narrative aspect, as it had for Berlioz and Tchaikovsky, but Mahler manages to do without a motto theme as his central character: instead there is a basic motivic connection among the themes of a symphony (in the case of the Sixth, *A–C–A*), and a powerful expressiveness that marks them all as autobiographical. One result of the narrative conception is what has been called "progressive tonality", and here again the contrast with Bruckner is interesting. Bruckner's music circles around a stable home key; Mahler's journeys in most cases from one to another, for emotional narratives cannot be expected to end where they began, unless they are narratives of obsession like the Sixth Symphony.

As narratives, Mahler's symphonies are filled with picturesque detail: the music of café and barracks, the sound of herdbells in the Alps (nos. 4 and 5), the serenades of guitar and mandolin (no. 7). His search for color, and at times for emphatic weight, produced a great enlargement of the orchestra, and though to some extent this was prompted by Strauss, Mahler's wider range of instruments generates an utterly different sound-world. Moreover, in his later works there is an increasing concentration on small groups, so that the large orchestra becomes a source of many different chamber ensembles: even the "Symphony of a Thousand" has its moments when the forces are measured rather in handfuls, particularly in the setting of the end of Goethe's *Faust* that forms its second part (the first is a vast choral hymn, *Veni Creator Spiritus*).

After this, fearing to embark on a Ninth Symphony, which had been for Bruckner and Beethoven their last, Mahler wrote a symphony in the disguise of an orchestral song cycle and called it *Das Lied von der Erde* (1909; see Listening Note IX.B). Setting Chinese poems in translation, the music has some naive Chinese color in its use of metal percussion and pentatonic motifs, but it is much more a work of European than oriental sensibility, not least in the long song of farewell with which it ends. The same atmosphere of melancholy departure then provided the emotional character for the whole of the Ninth Symphony (1909), though the unfinished Tenth (1910) would appear to have been working towards a much more positive close. Judgments have to be cautious, because Mahler left this work at quite an early stage of composition when he died, in Vienna, in the spring of 1911.

Strauss

Four years younger than Mahler, Richard Strauss also found himself very early as a composer, but unlike Mahler, whose genius was not fully and widely recognized until the 1960s, he enjoyed almost from the first a generous measure of public acclaim, so that for more than 60 years he was regarded as the outstanding German composer of the age. He was born in Munich in 1864, the son of the principal horn-player in the Court Orchestra. Encouraged by a musical, though musically conservative, family environment, he began to compose when he was six, and had lessons from musicians associated with his father's orchestra. He never attended a conservatory, though he did spend two terms at Munich University before the growing success of his music emboldened him to devote himself to composition.

At this time he veered towards the more classical stream in nineteenth-century music, represented by Mendelssohn and Brahms. But then, while embarking on his career as a conductor at Meiningen (1885–6) and Munich (1886–9 and 1894–8), he became a follower much more of Wagner and of Liszt. Symphonies and quartets were replaced in his output by symphonic poems, beginning with the "symphonic fantasy" *Aus Italien* ("From Italy", 1886) and continuing with seven more such works during the next dozen years. There was also a first opera, the Wagnerian *Guntram* (1893), but this was not a success, and Strauss's reputation became that of a composer of symphonic poems and of songs (he never wrote chamber music again).

The symphonic poems were played all over Europe and in the USA almost as soon as they were composed. They show Strauss's inventiveness as an orchestrator and his skill in the creation of musical narratives based on themes which combine strong character with an openness to variation. To some extent these were Mahler's strengths as well, but where Mahler's music all seems to be speaking of himself, Strauss was at his best when telling stories about others. Of course, when he is writing about imagined heroes in *Don Juan* (1889), *Macbeth* (1888), *Till Eulenspiegel* (1895) or *Don Quixote* (1898) he is writing about facets of himself, but the choice of a character gives his music an objectivity that is at the opposite extreme from Mahler's naked subjectivity.

Naturally the two composers had quite different approaches to musical form. Where Mahler's sonata movements push towards continuity, drawing the listener into the musical process, Strauss preferred rondo and variation forms in which elements of sectionality and repetition allow a more considered viewpoint. Mahler conveys experience, whereas Strauss encapsulates experience in an image.

The difference is apparent too in their use of illustrative detail. Mahler's café and mountain episodes are allusions in his subjective narration. But Strauss delighted in making self-sufficient musical pictures, such as the passage in *Don Quixote* where he depicts the bleating of sheep in discordant *tremolandos* on clarinets and brass. The same work also shows his ability, surpassing that of Liszt or Berlioz, to move his themes through a diversity of musical atmospheres while keeping them recognizable. The work is sub-titled "Fantastic Variations on a Theme of Knightly Character", and it is marked out as a set of symphonic variations, while being at the same time a cello concerto. *Don Juan* is a sonata-form movement, with episodes, *Till Eulenspiegel* a rondo. The latter, the last of his short tone-poems (the later ones are much longer, over half an hour), is arguably the most brilliant of all – Strauss readily identified with a hero always ready to cock a snook at authority (see Listening Note IX.C).

It was not a large step from these "theatrical" symphonic poems into opera, and after his autobiographical *Symphonia domestica* (1903) Strauss made that step definitively. Apart from his *Alpensinfonie* (1915) and two pieces with solo left-hand piano in the 1920s, he wrote nothing more of consequence for the orchestra until the 1940s. He also now wrote many fewer songs. Instead his main efforts went into opera, beginning with *Salome* (1905) and *Elektra* (1908), each of which is in a long single act and each of which projects a world of emotions at high pitch, backed by music of corresponding harmonic extremity. Setting Wilde's play on the biblical story of John the Baptist at the court of Herod, and then Hofmannsthal's drama on the hysteria and vengeance of Electra, Strauss showed himself the contemporary of Mahler in his highly complex, often virtually atonal harmony, as well as in his use of a large and richly variegated orchestra. It even seemed possible that after *Elektra* he would be obliged, like Schoenberg at precisely the same time, to relinquish tonality altogether.

Instead, he wrote *Der Rosenkavalier* ("The Cavalier of the Rose", 1911). This has sometimes been regarded as the gesture of a conservative, even as the escape-act of a musician unwilling to grapple with contemporary issues. However, the highly sophisticated, sentimental and humane comedy of *Der Rosenkavalier* is just as much a product of its time as Schoenberg's *Erwartung*. The latter's plunge into atonality is mirrored in Strauss's opera by a completely artificial diatonic masquerade in which the Vienna of Maria Theresa vibrates to the waltz rhythms of a century on. At the same time *Der Rosenkavalier* initiated one of the most fruitful partnerships in the history of opera, for now Strauss was fully collaborating with Hofmannsthal, not simply setting a pre-existing play of his. The combination of the highly cultivated Austrian poet and the practical, theater-bred Bavarian musician worked well. Though the two men irked each other at times, they went on from *Der*

Listening Note IX.C

Richard Strauss: *Till Eulenspiegels lustige Streiche* op. 28 (1894–5)

piccolo, 3 flutes, 3 oboes, english horn, clarinet in D, 2 clarinets in B♭, bass clarinet in B♭, 3 bassoons, double bassoon

4 horns in F (4 horns in D ad lib), 3 trumpets in F (3 trumpets in D ad lib), 3 trombones, tuba

timpani, triangle, cymbals, bass drum, side drum, large ratchet

16 1st violins, 16 2nd violins, 12 violas, 12 cellos, 8 double basses

The title is usually translated as "Till Eulenspiegel's Merry Pranks": the work is a tone poem on a satirical trickster of German legend. However, the illustrative aim is combined with purely musical intentions. Strauss himself, in his full version of the title, described the piece as being in rondo form, and there are some signs too of sonata structure, while the highly effective transformation of themes is obviously a supreme example of the art of variation.

1–5	The opening phrase (ex. i) seems to say "Once upon a time . . ."; but it is also to represent Till later on.
6–45	The horn announces a main motif for Till (ex. ii); it is taken up by other instruments, eventually the whole orchestra.
46–112	Another Till motif, based on ex. i, is heard on the high clarinet in D (ex. iii); possibly it represents Till's subversively witty nature, and its variability is in

	accord with his habit of escaping detection or punishment. The theme is developed and varied at some length.
113–78	A quiet passage where the first six notes of the theme are heard on basses and then flute, soon followed by a rapid upward clarinet scale, heralds an episode depicting Till riding into a busy market-place, overturning the stalls and putting the market women to flight, then riding off (the theme on trombones).
179–208	The rhythm changes for Till's second practical joke. Here he is disguised as a priest in a procession; the march-like theme is heard on bassoons and violas, but soon invaded by mocking derivations of ex. iii, and then are heard muted brass phrases and a violin downwards slide as he reveals himself.
209–303	Now Till is in amorous mood; both themes appear, smoother and sweeter than before. But he is rejected, and resolves to take vengeance on the world; the music becomes livelier and angry, with a heavy-footed, strongly marked version of ex. i (m. 271).
304–84	A group of solemn people, professors of some kind, approach; Till immediately starts to mock them (ex. iv, violins and horn). Fragments of Till themes mingle with those for the professors, and prevail over them.
385–428	The music becomes faster and more jolly for a moment, then mysteriously shadowy.
429–573	Till's horn theme (ex. ii) is stated again: this is akin to a recapitulation but the music continues to develop with increasing energy and high spirits towards a climax of outrageous defiance.
574–656	The brazen noise is halted, and a drum roll represents Till's being brought to trial: dark chords are heard in the orchestra, answered by Till's perky clarinet phrase (ex. iii) – this happens repeatedly, with increasing emphasis. He is sentenced, and executed (two heavy chords, trombones and other low instruments: his soul is heard taking flight). There is a brief epilogue, recalling the opening with affection, and finally eight high-spirited measures pay tribute to his merry roguery.

ex. i **Leisurely**

ex. ii

ex. iii **Very lively**

ex. iv

Richard Strauss	Life

1864	born in Munich, 11 June
1882	Munich University; Serenade for 13 wind instruments performed; beginning of period of prolific output
1885	assistant conductor of the Meiningen Orchestra; international recognition as a composer
1886–9	conductor at the Munich Court Opera
1889	Weimar; *Don Juan* established him as the most important young composer in Germany
1894	married Pauline de Ahna; conductor at Munich Court Opera
1895–8	prolific years, especially of orchestral music (including *Till Eulenspiegel, Thus spake Zarathustra, Don Quixote, A Hero's Life*); conducting tours of Europe
1898	conductor of the Royal Court Opera, Berlin; turned to opera composition
1905	*Salome* (Dresden) causes scandal
1904	conducted first performance of *Symphonia domestica* in New York
1909	*Elektra* (Dresden), the first of many successful collaborations with the librettist Hugo von Hofmannsthal
1911	*Der Rosenkavalier* (Dresden)
1919–24	director of the Vienna State Opera; output begins to diminish
1929	Hofmannsthal died
1933–5	appointed (without consultation) president of the Nazi state music bureau but removed for collaborating with a Jewish librettist
1942	*Capriccio* (Munich); beginning of period of concentration on instrumental works
1945	voluntary exile in Switzerland
1948	*Four Last Songs*
1949	died in Garmisch-Partenkirchen, 8 September

Rosenkavalier to create four more operas over the next two decades: *Ariadne auf Naxos, Die Frau ohne Schatten* ("The Woman without a Shadow"), *Die ägyptische Helena* and *Arabella*. The relationship ended only with Hofmannsthal's death in 1929.

These later Strauss–Hofmannsthal operas form a diverse group: two whimsical interpretations of Greek myth (*Ariadne* and *Helena*, neither attempting anything like the near-hysteria of *Elektra*), a symbolist fairytale (*Die Frau ohne Schatten*) and another sophisticated Viennese comedy (*Arabella*). Only *Ariadne* has gained a regular place in the repertory – not in its original version, when it was designed as half of a double bill with the seventeenth-century French playwright Molière's *Le bourgeois gentilhomme*, but in its revised state, replacing the Molière with a prologue introducing the "composer", singers and other artists of the entertainment to come. The contact with the seventeenth century seems to have spurred Strauss to anticipate neo-classicism in writing for a chamber orchestra of just 37 players, though it may be that he was impressed rather by Schoenberg's Chamber Symphony op. 9 than by any Baroque or Classical precedent: certainly the music is not neo-classical in style. The story of Ariadne and Bacchus – the opera within the

120 *The Stomach Dance* (or *Dance of the Seven Veils*): ink drawing, 1893, by Aubrey Beardsley, one of his illustrations to Oscar Wilde's *Salome*. Fogg Art Museum, Cambridge (Mass.).

opera – is a high-flown poetic exploration of love which is effectively deflated by the simultaneous presence of *commedia dell'arte* characters doing their act, while the prologue is the occasion for Strauss and Hofmannsthal to consider the practicalities of their art as preparations for the "opera" to get under way in a nobleman's house.

If *Ariadne auf Naxos* is an opera about opera, so also are two of Strauss's later works, *Intermezzo* (1924) and *Capriccio* (1942: his last opera – he had written four others since Hofmannsthal's death). *Intermezzo*, with a libretto by the composer himself, is a dramatization of his marital life as much as the *Symphonia domestica* had

Richard Strauss	Works

Operas Salome (1905), Elektra (1909), Der Rosenkavalier (The cavalier of the rose, 1911), Ariadne auf Naxos (1912), Die Frau ohne Schatten (The woman without a shadow, 1919), Intermezzo (1924), Arabella (1933), Capriccio (1942)

Orchestral music symphonic poems – Aus Italien (1886), Don Juan (1889), Till Eulenspiegels lustige Streiche (Till Eulenspiegel's merry pranks, 1895), Also sprach Zarathustra (Thus spake Zarathustra, 1896), Don Quixote (1897), Ein Heldenleben (A hero's life, 1898); Symphonia domestica (1903); Eine Alpensinfonie (1915); Metamorphosen for 23 strings (1945); horn concertos – no. 1, E♭ (1883), no. 2, E♭ (1942); Oboe Concerto (1945)

Choral music Deutsche motette (1913)

Songs Four Last Songs, with orchestra (1948); *c*200 others

Chamber music

Piano music

121 Richard Strauss's *Der Rosenkavalier*: stage design by Alfred Roller for Act 1 in the first performance, Dresden Court Opera, 26 January 1911.

been: a comedy of misunderstanding, jealousy and benign reconciliation, self-reflecting in that it puts the composer's persona on stage, but not troubling itself overmuch with his art. *Capriccio*, on the other hand, is an allegory of the longstanding dispute between words and music for primacy in opera. The Countess, the central character, is placed in the impossible position of having to choose between a poet and a composer as rivals for her affections, and at the end of a gentle, supremely accomplished and elegiac work her difficulty remains unresolved.

Strauss intended that *Capriccio* should be his last work: he was 78 when it was first performed, in Munich in 1942, at the turning point in World War II. Unlike many

122 Richard Strauss (*right*) with the librettist Hugo von Hofmannsthal, *c*1915: photograph.

of his colleagues, he remained in Germany after 1933, and even foolishly allowed his name to be used to add some spurious prestige to the Third Reich, though for most of the Hitler years he lived in retirement at his Bavarian home. Retirement from composition, however, was not so easy. He wrote no more operas, but returned to the forms and genres of his youth: a Second Horn Concerto (1942) joined the one he had written for his father in 1883, and in the same key of E♭. There were two other concertos for wind instruments, two works for a Mozartian serenade ensemble of winds and a largely proportioned movement for strings, *Metamorphosen* (1945), an elegy for the Germany that was being destroyed in the bombing raids on Dresden, Berlin and other cities. As if these works were somehow unofficial, coming after the main body of his music, Strauss gave them no opus numbers. He ended the sequence with the conscious farewell of the *Four Last Songs* for soprano and orchestra (1948), and died at his home in Garmisch in September 1949, before those songs had been heard.

Northern Europe

Strauss's near-contemporary Jean Sibelius (1865–1957) was responsible for the main Nordic extension of the symphonic tradition, following the Bohemian extension achieved in the previous generation by Smetana and Dvořák. He was not the first Scandinavian to make an international reputation: the Norwegian Edvard Grieg (1843–1907) had already established a reputation in Germany, England and the USA, chiefly through his piano miniatures, which drew on Norwegian folk traditions, but also for his atmospheric music for Ibsen's play *Peer Gynt* and his popular piano concerto, which was admired (and performed) by Liszt. Of Sibelius's contemporaries, the Swede Wilhelm Stenhammar (1871–1927) and the Dane Carl Nielsen (1865–1931) shared his devotion to the symphony; Nielsen in particular wrote symphonies of great force and individuality, with a Mahlerian chromatic style and a high degree of motivic unity, but distinguished chiefly for the driving rhythms and the tough, unpolished angular quality of his themes and harmonies.

Sibelius

Jean Sibelius was born in 1865 into a Finland that was part of the Russian empire and remained so until after the revolution of October 1917. His family belonged to the Swedish-speaking minority, but he went to a Finnish-speaking school in his home town of Hämeenlinna. While there he began to show aptitude as a violinist and composer, and his first hope in his youth was to become a violin virtuoso (his D minor Violin Concerto of 1903 was consciously created as a memorial to those lost hopes, and was his only concerto of any consequence). In 1885 he went to Helsinki to study law at the university, but gave up after a year in order to devote himself to composition studies with Martin Wegelius, followed by periods of further study in Berlin (1889–90) and Vienna (1890–1).

Up to this point he had composed mostly chamber music, but on his return to Helsinki he wrote a big choral symphony on stories from the *Kalevala*, the Finnish national epic: *Kullervo*, whose successful première in Helsinki in 1892 immediately established him as his country's leading composer. That position was his for the rest of his life, guaranteed in the earlier decades by a succession of symphonic poems on Finnish myths interspersed among the great pillars of his seven symphonies. The first two of these still contain some evidence of his admiration for Tchaikovsky, but the breadth of his melodies and the slow pace of his harmony have few parallels outside Bruckner. Where Bruckner's music is essentially stationary, however, Sibelius's grows by processes of organic development worked on the basic motifs, a technique utilized with full assurance for the first time in his Third Symphony, in C major (1907), a work of classical discipline and grace.

The Fourth Symphony (1911) shows this technique being employed most intensively, within a harmonic world as dissonant as that of the contemporary late works of Mahler. The central matter of the musical argument here, very simply, is

123 *Symposium*: group portrait, 1894, by Akseli Gallén-Kallela, with (*right to left*) Sibelius, the conductor Robert Kajanus, Oskar Merikanto and the artist. Private collection.

Jean Sibelius   Works
born Hämeenlinna, 1865; *died* Järvenpää, 1957

Orchestral music symphonies – no. 1, e (1899), no. 2, D (1902), no.3, C (1907),
no. 4, a (1911), no. 5, Eb (1915), no. 6, d (1923), no. 7, C (1924); tone poems – En
saga (1892), Finlandia (1899); Pohjola's Daughter (1906), Nightride and Sunrise
(1907), Tapiola (1926); Karelia Suite (1893); Violin Concerto (1903)

Incidental music The Tempest (1925)

Choral music Kullervo (1892); cantatas, partsongs

Chamber music String Quartet, "Voces intimae", d (1909); pieces for violin and
piano

Songs   *Piano music*

the tritone, that interval most at odds with the major-minor system. Almost
everything that happens in the work can be related very directly to this interval, and
the argument is continuous, despite the presentation of the music in four distinct
movements. Ex. IX.6*a–d*, representative moments from each of the movements,
may indicate how deeply the tritone is embedded in the melodic and harmonic
substance of the music.

The first two examples here suggest how pedal points (or sustained harmonies)
are as characteristic of Sibelius as of Bruckner. More purely typical of Sibelius is the
obstinacy with which the tritone is insisted upon in place of the more euphonious
major 3rd (first and second movements) or perfect 5th (third and fourth
movements). Moreover, the constant presence of the tritone binds the four
movements together to such an extent that the individuality of each is undermined.
The Fourth Symphony can be regarded as a slow introduction followed by a sonata
Allegro, a slow movement and an Allegro finale, but the movements sound rather
like different ways of dealing with the tritone of the opening, and any resemblance
to the normal structural models does not go very far. The second movement, for

ex. IX.6

a. **(Slow)**

b. **Allegro molto vivace**   c. **(Slow)**

d. **Allegro**

(○ – to be played as harmonic)

instance, has elements of a scherzo as well as sonata form, while at the same time it makes a transition from the quick music of its opening to the slow movement that follows.

Continuity of this sort is taken further in the Fifth Symphony, in the "heroic" key of E♭ major (1915), where the first movement transforms itself from a sonata Allegro into a quick scherzo, though the central slow movement and the triumphant finale complete a more normal design. The Sixth Symphony is once more in four movements, but the Seventh, in C (1924), is at last completely continuous and conveys an entire symphonic experience, with its elements of slow movement and scherzo, within a single movement. After this Sibelius wrote an incidental score for Shakespeare's *Tempest* (1925) and a final symphonic poem, *Tapiola* (1926), but then practically nothing for the remaining 30 years of his life.

There may well have been personal reasons for this creative silence. His heavy drinking, a problem since his student days, has sometimes been blamed. But it is equally possible that he had achieved his ideal of a seamless, all-embracing symphonic development in his Seventh Symphony and could conceive no way forward without repeating himself. There were rumors, and hints from the composer himself, of a near-complete Eighth Symphony in the 1930s, but whatever existed of this was destroyed. Sibelius meanwhile lived on, celebrated at home and abroad, and died at his house near Helsinki in 1957.

Elgar

The rise of Sibelius and Nielsen in the Nordic countries was paralleled by that of Elgar in England, in the same decade, the 1890s. Edward Elgar was born near Worcester in 1857, the son of a piano tuner and music retailer. He had no formal training in music, but from his mid-teens onwards was able to make a living as a violinist, organist, bassoonist, conductor and music teacher in and about Worcester. And all the time he was composing. Until 1890, when he was 33, he wrote little that is remarkable or even distinctive, but his firm conviction of his worth led him to move to London, to try his luck. He had some salon pieces published, including his *Salut d'amour*, but there was no interest in more ambitious works, and after little more than a year the Elgars returned to home ground, taking a house in Malvern.

During the next few years he gradually built the foundations of a personal style, deriving in equal measure from the symphonic Brahms and the more spiritual

---

Edward Elgar   Works
born Broadheath, near Worcester, 1857; *died* Worcester, 1934

Orchestral music symphonies – no. 1, A♭ (1908), no. 2, E♭ (1911); overtures – Froissart (1890), Cockaigne (1901); Wand of Youth Suites nos. 1–2 (1907–8); Variations on an Original Theme "Enigma" (1899); Pomp and Circumstance Marches (1901–7); Introduction and Allegro for strings (1905); Falstaff (1913); Violin Concerto (1910); Cello Concerto (1919)

Choral music The Dream of Gerontius (1900); The Apostles (1903); The Kingdom (1906)

Chamber music Violin Sonata (1918); String Quartet (1918); Piano Quintet (1919)

Songs Sea Pictures, with orchestra (1899); c45 for voice and piano

Piano music Salut d'amour (1888) [later orchestrated]

Incidental music   *Partsongs*   *Organ music*

Wagner, in a sequence of cantatas that enjoyed much success among the choral societies then abundant in England. One of them is *Caractacus*, which won him a commission to write an oratorio for the Birmingham Triennial Festival of 1900 (the festival for which Dvořák had written his *Requiem* nine years before). The resulting work was *The Dream of Gerontius* (1900), a setting for soloists, chorus and orchestra of Cardinal Newman's poem on death and transport to heaven. This, with the *Enigma Variations* for orchestra (1899), brought the long-hoped-for breakthrough. Within 18 months of its Birmingham première the oratorio had been heard in the USA and in Germany, where Elgar was congratulated by Strauss as "the first English progressivist"; the variations too were widely played.

These variations owe their nickname to the heading "Enigma" Elgar placed over his theme, which he remarked "went with" some other melody; the puzzle has never been satisfactorily resolved. After the theme come 14 variations which, in the manner of Brahms's *St Antony Variations*, form something akin to a condensed symphony: the ninth variation is a big slow movement and the last is headed "Finale". At the same time this is a set of character variations in the manner of Strauss's *Don Quixote*. The score is dedicated "to my friends pictured within", each variation being a portrait of someone from Elgar's circle, beginning with his wife and ending with himself. Ex. IX.7 shows the theme together with its transformations in the fourth variation (William Meath Baker, an abrupt country gentleman) and the ninth ("Nimrod", Elgar's nickname for his publisher Alfred Jaeger).

ex. IX.7

The theme itself is subtly constructed as a succession of variations on the same rhythmic figure, avoiding both a firm cadence and the strong beat until the final slip from B♭ into G major. It is an apt subject for variation, since its hesitancy allows resolution in different ways while its concluding harmonic shift is an invitation to continue. The hesitancy is most easily overcome, of course, simply by removing the rests and leaving the theme in 3/4, as in both the variations illustrated, but when the model is placed further in the background, other metrical possibilities become available, like the meandering 12/8 of the fifth variation. Equally various is the scoring of the work, for an orchestra that was moderate for its day – Elgar retained

124 Elgar conducting a recording session at the Gramophone Company's City Road studio, London, January 1914: photograph.

his allegiance to the orchestral sound of Brahms rather than that of Strauss.

During the next dozen years he composed copiously, within the style he had established of Brahmsian formal integrity spiced by Wagnerian chromaticism and by modalities that may have come from church music or folksong. There were two symphonies, a Violin Concerto and a radiant work for string quartet and string orchestra, the Introduction and Allegro. There were numerous songs and partsongs, and there were two more oratorios, *The Apostles* and *The Kingdom*. Elgar was heaped with honors, including a knighthood in 1904, and in 1912 he moved again to London, under very different circumstances from those of 1890. Little new, though, was now composed. The "symphonic study" *Falstaff*, a richly imagined portrait of the Shakespearean character and Elgar's most Straussian work, appeared in 1913. During the 1914–18 War he wrote a variety of patriotic and theatrical scores. Afterwards he turned to chamber music. But his eloquent Cello Concerto in E minor (1919), run through with nostalgic feeling for a past era, was a leave-taking; later projects, including a third symphony and an opera, appear to have made little progress.

As with Sibelius, there may have been personal reasons for his creative retirement: the death of his wife in 1920 has often been thought at least a contributing factor. But it seems that he recognized too the change in the temper of the age brought about by World War I. The culture that gave rise to the Romantic symphony had gone. Elgar returned to the rural midlands of his birth, but did not abandon musical activity, for he appeared frequently as a conductor of his music and recorded a large part of it: these recordings, with Strauss's, are the first in which a major composer has been able to leave an audible account of his intentions, and they reveal Elgar's view of his music as more incisive and leaner than in many later performances. He died in Worcester in 1934.

France

Elgar's creation of an English symphonic style was not matched by any similar development in France. Franck's influence was strong on works written in the 1880s and 1890s by Ernest Chausson (1855–99) and Paul Dukas (1865–1935), but then petered out as a deliberately anti-symphonic manner was developed by Claude Debussy. Meanwhile the areas of greatest achievement were opera and, particularly, song. Among opera composers, Jules Massenet (1842–1912) was the most popular, ranging wide between exotic *grand-opéra* spectacle and medieval religiosity to intimate dramas of sentiment: his two most admired works, *Manon* (1884) and *Werther* (1892: after Goethe – rather a long way after), are of this last type, for his chief gift lay in romantic action judiciously sweetened and colored by music. In the area of song the outstanding figures were Henri Duparc (1848–1933), who composed a tiny handful of exquisite songs, and Gabriel Fauré (1845–1924), a sensitive and graceful song-writer (notably in his settings of Verlaine) who also composed much fine piano and chamber music and a *Requiem* of exceptional gentleness and subtlety.

Debussy

Fauré's late development made him effectively a contemporary of Debussy, who also began to find himself through a response to the new poetry of the period: to Verlaine in many of his early songs and to Stéphane Mallarmé in his orchestral prelude to the poet's *L'après-midi d'un faune* ("The afternoon of a faun", 1894).

Claude Debussy, born at St Germain-en-Laye in 1862, studied as a pianist and composer at the Paris Conservatoire (1872–84). As winner of the Prix de Rome, he left the Conservatoire to spend two years in the Italian capital, but was unsettled there and returned with relief to Paris, where he lived for the rest of his life. Around this time his music began to acquire an individual, often modal character, as may be found in the first Verlaine settings and in the cantata for soprano, women's chorus and orchestra *La damoiselle élue* ("The chosen maiden", 1888), on a poem by Dante-Gabriel Rossetti. Visits to Bayreuth in 1888–9 and an encounter with Javanese music quickened his artistic progress. Only a very few works are fully Wagnerian; the point was rather that his first-hand experience of Wagner convinced him of the

Claude Debussy	Works

Orchestral music Prélude à "L'après-midi d'un faune" (Prelude to "The afternoon of a faun", 1894); Nocturnes (1899); La mer (The sea, 1905); Images (1912)

Operas Pelléas et Mélisande (1902)

Ballets Jeux (Games, 1913)

Piano music Suite, pour le piano (1901); Suite bergamasque (1905); Estampes (1903); Images (1905, 1907); Children's Corner (1908); Preludes, 2 books (1910, 1913); Studies (1915); two pianos – En blanc et noir (In white and black, 1915)

Chamber music String Quartet (1893); Cello Sonata (1915); Sonata for flute, viola and harp (1915); Violin Sonata (1917)

Incidental music Le martyre de St Sébastien (1911)

Songs Fêtes galantes (1891, 1904); Chansons de Bilitis (1898); c60 others

Choral music La demoiselle élue (The chosen maiden, 1888)

Claude Debussy	Life

1862	born in St Germain-en-Laye, 22 August
1872	entered the Paris Conservatoire to study the piano and (from 1880) composition
1880–81	summers in Russia as pianist to the family of Madame von Meck, Tchaikovsky's patron, with whom he toured Europe
1885	to Rome after winning the Prix de Rome at the Conservatoire
1887	Paris
1888	heard Wagner's music at Bayreuth
1889	impressed by Javanese music, heard at the World Exhibition in Paris
1890	beginning of "Bohemian" years and friendships with literary figures
1894	*Prelude to "The Afternoon of a Faun"*
1897	married Rosalie (Lily) Texier
1901	music critic of *La revue blanche*
1902	*Pelléas et Mélisande*; reputation as a composer established
1904	beginning of prolific period; left wife to live with Emma Bardac; Lily's attempted suicide caused scandal
1905	*La mer*; daughter born; growing international acclaim
1908	married Emma Bardac
1909	first signs of illness
1913	concentration on stage works and projects; *Jeux*
1914	depressed by illness and outbreak of war
1915	Studies for piano, *In White and Black*; two sonatas
1918	died in Paris, 25 March

need to approach music differently. In oriental art he found some clues towards a modal understanding of harmony, a delight in decoration and an avoidance of symphonic continuity. Occasionally the Eastern influence is admitted in a title, as in the piano *Pagodes* (1903), but in essence it pervades a good deal of his output.

Equally strong is Debussy's appeal to Greek culture. The search for a new esthetic freedom in an imaginative re-creation of the Orient or of ancient Greece was important to artists of all kinds in Paris in the 1890s and 1900s. It may be seen in the Symbolist poetry of Mallarmé and his imitators, in the novels of Debussy's friend Pierre Louÿs and in the paintings of Gustave Moreau and others; and it was this strand in French culture, rather than that represented by the Impressionist painters, to which Debussy most nearly belonged. There are parallels with the Im-

Listening Note IX.D

Debussy: *Prélude à "L'après-midi d'un faune"* (1894)
3 flutes, 2 oboes, english horn, 2 clarinets in A, 2 bassoons
4 horns, 2 harps, antique cymbals in E and B
1st violins, 2nd violins, violas, cellos, double basses

The work is based on the poem by Stéphane Mallarmé describing subtly and suggestively the amorous daydreams of a faun on a warm afternoon. On some levels there is a close fit between music and poem (for instance, Debussy wrote as many measures as Mallarmé had written lines), but in other respects the relationship is more one of evocation.

mm.

1–10	*Très modéré* ("very moderate"). Unaccompanied solo flute sounds the main theme (ex. i), echoed by horns with delicate orchestral accompaniment.
11–20	Repeat of ex. i with orchestral support, and with its latter, diatonic part generating interest from oboe and then tutti before dying away on clarinets.
21–30	Two short developments of ex. i, still on solo flute, both featuring harp arpeggios and both quickly subdued.
31–36	Variant of ex. i on clarinet initiating a move towards the middle section.
37–43	*En animant* ("becoming animated"). Further, diatonic variant of ex. i on solo oboe opens a middle section of clearer harmony and forward movement. The oboe's phrases are discussed in alternation by violins and woodwind.
44–50	*Toujours en animant* ("more animated"). Above process brought to a climax and then stilled.
51–4	*1er mouvement* ("original speed"). Activity begun again by solo clarinet echoing material from mm. 40ff.
55–78	*Même mouvement et très soutenu* ("the same speed, very sustained"). New theme in Db (ex. ii), only distantly related to what has gone before, is heard in quiet but full orchestration, and briefly developed before it too dissolves.
79–85	*Mouvement du début* ("speed of the opening"). Ex. 1 returns on flute, supported by rich string chord of E major and harp arpeggios. Oboe leads commentary afterwards (*Un peu plus animé*: "a little livelier").
86–93	Repeat of previous section, but with the theme now on solo oboe and at first in Eb. The harmony turns round to E major again during the commentary, led this time by english horn.
94–105	*Dans le 1er mouvement avec plus de langueur* ("at the original speed with more languor"). Confident repetition of ex. i on two flutes, leading into trails of triplets and then into a further statement of the theme on solo flute, from which solo oboe takes over.
106–10	*Très lent et très retenu* ("very slow and held back"). Final echo of ex. i from horns and low 2nd violins, followed by last enactment of the work's characteristic cadence from C♯ minor to E major.

ex. i   **Very moderate**

p doux et expressif

ex. ii   woodwinds

p   *mf*

pressionists: in the vagueness of his shapes, the subtlety of his coloring and the novelty of his forms. But his friendships were all with literary men rather than painters, and his works – particularly the many uncompleted stage projects and the smaller body of songs – testify to the importance of literature in his creative mind.

It was even a work of literature that released his first orchestral masterpiece, the *Prélude à "L'après-midi d'un faune"*. Mallarmé's poem concerns the erotic reverie of a faun, and Debussy's music adopts not only the poem's atmosphere but also its form, with lazily contemplative outer sections and a more active middle. As such it is not so much a prelude to the poem as a complete musical equivalent.

The first essential feature to be noted is the importance of instrumental color. The opening melody is unmistakably a theme for the flute, and it works effectively on other instruments (oboe and horns in the last part of the work) only if its rhythm and key are changed: in its original form it stays with its original instrument. The gentle loosening from key centers is also very Debussyan. The initial flute phrase falls through a tritone C♯–G and returns, marking out especially the Lydian or whole-tone scale G–A–B–C♯. Throughout Debussy's music the whole-tone scale is a prominent melodic and harmonic feature, permitting through its symmetry a rapid movement among distantly related keys (see Listening Note IX.D).

While working on the prelude Debussy composed his String Quartet in G minor (1893), which at first seems orthodox. It is in the traditional four movements and has elements of cyclic thematicism inherited from Franck, but the textures especially in the second movement are often based on ostinatos sounded across and against one another, suggesting a more direct influence of Eastern music than is normal in Debussy. Harmonically, although it is in G minor, it has modal coloring.

Debussy naturally returned to the old modes when his poetic reference was medieval (e.g. in the piano prelude *La cathédrale engloutie*, "The submerged cathedral", or the three choral songs on poems of the fifteenth-century nobleman Charles d'Orléans) and when it was Greek (e.g. in the song cycle *Chansons de Bilitis*). However, as the quartet shows, the modes were not used exclusively to evoke another time and another place. Rather they were natural allies, like the whole-tone scale, for a composer who worked largely with triadic harmonies while moving them with freedom from the rules of the diatonic system.

The achievement in this way of a new musical language caused Debussy some trouble. In the middle section of the prelude to *L'après-midi d'un faune* he had not been able to write quick music without some reversion to diatonic practice, and for several years afterwards he completed little. But then around the turn of the century he produced outstanding and fully accomplished works in every genre that interested him: song (the *Chansons de Bilitis*), orchestral music (the *Nocturnes*), piano music (the suite *Pour le piano*) and opera (*Pelléas et Mélisande*, 1902). Apart from the songs, all these works were a little time in the finishing. After this breakthrough, however, Debussy worked more quickly and confidently, producing the symphonic sketches *La mer* ("The sea", 1905) and the orchestral *Images* (1912), as well as an abundance of piano music, including two sets of *Images* (1905–7) and two sets of *Préludes* (1910–13).

Of the earlier group of works, the *Nocturnes* find Debussy closest to his painter contemporaries. The title is intended to refer not to Chopin but to Whistler, whose coloring of grays and highlights Debussy sought to re-create in music, in three movements depicting clouds, holiday festivities and sea enchantresses. On the other hand, *Pelléas et Mélisande*, his only completed opera, is necessarily a literary work. In it he set, without much alteration, a play by the Belgian Symbolist Maurice Maeterlinck, who was trying, through fairytale allegory and an extremely reticent kind of dialogue, to portray on stage the inner mysteries of his characters. Music can only assist in the projection of mental processes beyond words – Debussy's music above all, with its release from the logic of diatonic harmony and its suggestion of dream-states.

Like characters in a dream, the people of Debussy's opera belong in a world that is largely unexplained (their kingdom is "Allemonde", or all the world) and their

125 Golaud and Mélisande in a scene from the first production of Debussy's opera *Pelléas et Mélisande* at the Opéra-Comique, Paris, in 1902.

hopes, fears and motivations are only glancingly expressed. And so although the basic action of the piece is the most banal emotional triangle (Mélisande, married to Golaud, falls in love with his half-brother Pelléas; Golaud kills Pelléas; Mélisande dies as well), Maeterlinck's discretion and Debussy's obliqueness give it a haunting atmosphere entirely new to opera. It was a difficult work to follow. During the 16 years he lived after the first performance of *Pelléas* Debussy worked on a variety of theatrical ideas – most assiduously on a pair of pieces based on stories by Edgar Allan Poe – but nothing was finished.

Meanwhile the piano pieces of 1903–13 contain in miniature much that is most characteristic of Debussy and that had come to fruition while he worked on the opera: the use of the church modes and the whole-tone scale, a delicate flexibility of rhythm (already evident in ex. IX.D from the *Prélude à "L'après-midi d'un faune"*), a feeling for the resonating qualities of the instrument and a release from developmental form. Only *L'isle joyeuse*, one of his longest piano pieces, has some vestige of sonata form; other works are static in structure, either of ternary

(*A–B–A*) design or based on ostinato patterns.

Even the three substantial movements of *La mer* depart from convention, in ways suggested by their titles. The first, "From dawn to midday on the sea", is concerned with the growing clarity and power of its main theme, from complex textures where the strings may be divided into 15 parts to the forceful tuttis of the close. The last similarly uses vague and direct music, but now in alternation: it is a "Dialogue of the wind and the waves". In between, the "Play of the waves" is a scherzo where thematic outlines and instrumentation are subject to constant change, to create Debussy's ultimate achievement in free form. All the movements thus use the variability of the sea as a metaphor for music in perpetual motion. The analogy with watery movements is continued in some of the piano pieces that followed, such as *Reflets dans l'eau* ("Reflections in the water"), *Poissons d'or* ("Goldfish") or *Ondine*.

The orchestral *Images* do not at all make up a coherent cycle in the manner of *La mer*. "Ibéria", much the biggest of them, was composed first. It is a contribution not only to the large repertory of Spanish music by Frenchmen (Chabrier's *España* had started the trend in 1883) but also to Debussy's own catalogue of popular galas, observed with detachment and well defined – this is the manner of the central *Nocturne* and also of the piano prelude *Feux d'artifice* ("fireworks"). The other two *Images*, "Gigues" and "Rondes de printemps", are more abstracted in expression and are exercises in a favored technique of viewing a folktune through a haze of ostinatos and decorations. In "Gigues" the tune is associated with a solo oboe d'amore, but in "Rondes de printemps" the coloring is much more fluid, as in Debussy's last orchestral score, the ballet *Jeux* (1913).

This was one of several works for the theater that he produced during his last few years, while also continuing to work at the Poe operatic double bill. Apart from *Jeux*, written for the Diaghilev season that also included Stravinsky's sensational *The Rite of Spring*, there was an hour-long incidental score for a spectacular, wildly overblown "mystery" of religiosity and eroticism by the Italian writer Gabriele d'Annunzio (*Le martyre de Saint Sébastien*), an Egyptian ballet and a children's ballet. Over-pressed, and already suffering from the rectal cancer that was to kill him, Debussy sought the help of younger colleagues in orchestrating these works.

But *Jeux* was so new in conception, and orchestral color was so much a part of its substance, that Debussy could delegate no part of it. Like the centerpiece of *La mer*, but on a larger scale, it is music of perpetual change, worked on a few thematic suggestions that never appear twice in quite the same form. The tendency to complexity in the orchestral textures renders the ideas difficult to grasp and hold in the memory; the effect is of a continuous fluidity. In expressive terms, this is music where feeling is no less serious for being capricious. The scenario, originally choreographed by the great dancer Vaslav Nijinsky, concerned the flirtatious encounters and disagreements among a group of people playing tennis on a summer day, but for all their contemporary setting they are near relatives musically to the faun of Debussy's earlier score, which was also in the repertory of the Diaghilev company as a vehicle for Nijinsky.

Illness and the outbreak of war depressed Debussy's creativity, so that little was achieved in 1914, but the next year his compositional spirits were revived by a commission to edit Chopin's piano works, and he added to his own a set of 12 *Etudes*. These are a remarkable, and remarkably mixed, group. Most of them concentrate on some aspect of keyboard technique indicated by their titles ("For thirds", 'For repeated notes" etc), but they are also studies in compositional style.

Plate 29   *Opposite* Bizet's *Carmen*: stage design by Emile Bertin for Act 1 in the original production at the Opéra-Comique, 1875 (see p. 334). Bibliothèque de l'Opéra, Paris

"Carmen" 1er acte   E Bertin

"For opposing sonorities" is an unusual instance of free form springing from oppositions of clear and succinct musical ideas, rather than from the indefinite arabesques more normal in Debussy's music between *L'après-midi d'un faune* and *Jeux*. "For fourths", where the domination of 4ths produces an environment inhospitable to the tonal system, shows the same formal liberty. But perhaps most startling of all is the final "For chords", a study in clear-cut syncopation. Like other composers of his time, Debussy had been fascinated by ragtime, to which he had alluded in the "Golliwog's Cake-walk" from the piano suite *Children's Corner*. But here he reacted as well to a visitor from the opposite direction: Stravinsky, whose *Rite of Spring* had rather stolen the thunder of his *Jeux* in the 1913 ballet season.

Debussy's ability to respond further to Stravinsky was limited by his illness and by his consciousness of being a French artist – this prompted by wartime patriotism. His final project was a set of six sonatas for different ensembles, looking back to the chamber music of Couperin and Rameau, and proudly signed "Claude Debussy, musicien français". Only three were composed: one for cello and piano, one for flute, viola and harp and one for violin and piano. The Cello Sonata is a last essay in the style of sophisticated masquerade that Debussy had discovered in setting Verlaine a quarter-century before. He called it "Pierrot angry with the moon", and its quick changes of mood (emphatically avoiding anything like normal cello expressive writing) have the irony of a character study. In the trio sonata, by contrast, the character is that of his orchestral scores, for the flute, viola and harp provide a Debussy orchestra in microcosm, and the free interchange of thematic reminiscences is characteristic of his orchestral pieces. Finally, the Violin Sonata is fantastical in the manner of its cello companion, playing with a variety of poses including those of the gipsy virtuoso and the salon artist.

Debussy made his last public appearance in the première of the Violin Sonata, in Paris in May 1917, and wrote no more music; he died in Paris the following March.

Ravel

Maurice Ravel, born in the Pyrenees in 1875, took a quite different approach from Debussy. Trained as a pianist, he was impressed by the virtuosity and splendor of Liszt, who, much more than Debussy, is the main influence on his piano works *Jeux*

Maurice Ravel   Works
born Ciboure, Pyrenees, 1875; *died* Paris, 1937

Orchestral music Rapsodie espagnole (1908); La valse (1920); Boléro (1928); Piano Concerto for left hand (1930), Piano Concerto, G (1931)

Piano music Pavane pour une infante défunte (1899) [later orchestrated]; Jeux d'eau (1901); Sonatine (1905); Miroirs (1905); Gaspard de la nuit (1908); Valses nobles et sentimentales (1911) [later orchestrated]; Le tombeau de Couperin (1917)

Ballets Ma mère l'oye (Mother Goose, 1912); Daphnis et Chloé, 1912

Operas L'enfant et les sortilèges (The child and the spells, 1925)

Chamber music String Quartet (1903); Introduction and Allegro for harp, flute, clarinet and string quartet (1905); Piano Trio (1914); violin sonatas

Songs Shéhérazade, with orchestra (1903); Histoires naturelles (1906); Chants populaires (1910); c25 others

Choral music

Plate 30 *Left* Puccini's *Tosca*: scene by Hohenstein from Act 1 in the original production at the Teatro Costanzi, Rome, 1900 (see p. 420). Commemorative postcard.

d'eau (1901) and *Miroirs* (1905). Debussy's importance was rather to give him the elements of an orchestral style: his *Shéhérazade* for soprano and orchestra (1903) owes much to *Pelléas*, even though the longing for the East is expressed with a franker sensuousness than Debussy would have found delicate. Once Ravel had assimilated this influence, as he had by the time he wrote his orchestral *Rapsodie espagnole* ("Spanish Rhapsody", 1908), he was creating music quite different from Debussy's. Their use of modes and the whole-tone scale is still often similar, but Ravel's ideas tend to be more sharply etched, his textures to be utterly precise and his forms correspondingly clear, often with a great deal of repetition (this he carried to the ultimate in his famous *Boléro* of 1928, which goes on repeating the same tune in a continuous orchestral *crescendo*).

Ravel mastered the orchestra as a machine, fitting parts together in a way that made Stravinsky call him a "Swiss watchmaker". He made orchestral versions of most of his piano works (excluding the two Lisztian ones mentioned above), and also made the most commonly played orchestration of Mussorgsky's *Pictures at an Exhibition*. Bright and highly accomplished, his orchestration suggests a creative mind that thrived on artifice, and indeed Ravel enjoyed exploring in each work a particular musical character: the Hispanic, the childlike, the Baroque.

His Hispanic works include not only the *Rapsodie espagnole* and *Boléro* but also several songs and an opera, *L'heure espagnole* ("Spanish time", 1911), a farce of amorous intrigue set in a clockmaker's shop. His other opera, also in one act, is his most intensive exploration of childhood: *L'enfant et les sortilèges* (1925). This is a storybook fantasy, to a libretto by Colette, in which domestic objects – pieces of china, chairs, the fire and so on – come to life to alarm and chastise a naughty child, who is further scolded by the trees and animals of the garden until he redeems himself by showing kindness to one of them. The variety of unreal situations stimulated Ravel to characteristically exact and strange inventions in a style combining wistfulness with clarity. It was the style he had found earlier in his fairytale ballet *Ma mère l'oye* ("Mother Goose", 1911).

That work dates from his most productive period, when he also composed an hour-long ballet for Diaghilev, the ancient Greek story of *Daphnis et Chloé*; a set of post-Schubertian waltzes, and a song cycle to poems by Mallarmé accompanied by an exquisite ensemble of flutes, clarinets and piano quintet. At this time he was living in Paris, where he had been a student at the Conservatoire from 1889 to 1895; a man of independent means, he held no appointment, nor did he teach or perform much in public, except during a tour of the USA in 1927–8.

During World War I his rate of composition slowed down as he worked, through his piano suite *Le tombeau de Couperin*, to a neo-classical style of sparer texture and greater harmonic strain within models of form and phrasing inherited from the past. In the Mallarmé poems he had come near atonality (the scoring was a reaction to Schoenberg's *Pierrot lunaire*, see Chapter X), and though nowhere else in his music is a sense of key so weak, he moved away from the triads enriched with 7ths and 9ths that had been the basic elements of his harmonic language.

His first important works after *Le tombeau de Couperin* are chamber ones, for forces of purposely limited harmonic texture. But there were also larger works that combined the new, severe harmony with the old: *L'enfant et les sortilèges*, the macabre-seductive waltz fantasy *La valse* and two piano concertos, a grim and challenging one for left hand alone (1930) and a vibrant one in G major for two hands (1931). Some of these works take a topical interest in jazz.

Ravel's jazz coloring and his later harmony owe something to Stravinsky. During most of this period, from 1921 onwards, he lived outside Paris, but it was in the capital, in 1937, that he died – after five years of illness that had kept him from completing any new work.

Italy

The age of Debussy in France, Mahler in Austria and Elgar in England was in Italy the age of Puccini, whose operas dominated the Italian stage from the first production of his *Manon Lescaut* in 1893 to his death 30 years later.

Puccini

Giacomo Puccini was born in 1858 in Lucca, where his father was of the fourth generation of Puccinis to have served the republic and the church as composers. Giacomo, five when his father died, studied with other local teachers with a view to taking on the family responsibilities, but when he was 17 he saw *Aida* and determined to be an opera composer instead. He therefore went to the Milan Conservatory. In 1883 he finished his studies and wrote his first opera, on a tale of

126 Puccini (seated) with the librettist Luigi Illica, a few months before the composer's death: photograph.

Giacomo Puccini	Works
born Lucca, 1858; *died* Brussels, 1924	

Operas Le villi (1884), Edgar (1889), Manon Lescaut (1893), La bohème (1896), Tosca (1900), Madama Butterfly (1904), La fanciulla del West (The girl of the golden West, 1910), Il trittico (1918) [three one-act operas: Il tabarro (The cloak), Suor Angelica, Gianni Schicchi], Turandot (posthumous, 1926)

Choral music   *Instrumental music*   *Songs*

supernatural enchantment. It had some success when given in Milan in 1884, and on the strength of it the astute publisher Giulio Ricordi initiated an association of composer and publishing house that was to continue throughout Puccini's life. He then tried his hand, rather less successfully, at a tragic opera after an Alfred de Musset book.

He found the way forward pointed by his junior, Pietro Mascagni, whose one-act *Cavalleria rusticana* (1889) introduced a new kind of opera, dealing with contemporary life, including its more sordid side, in a naturalistic and full-bloodedly emotional way – what, as we have seen (p. 368), is called *verismo* opera. Puccini was not truly a *verismo* composer: his operas are not set in the (then) present; many have exotic locations; only a few have elements of the "realistic" world of feeling. But the heightened emotional condition of *verismo* opera is very much a feature of his works.

The first of his operas that shows the influence of the *verismo* school is *Manon Lescaut* (1893), the story of tragic love that Massenet had set nine years before. Here he proves himself a superior musician to any of his Italian contemporaries (and to Massenet) through his command of musical-dramatic resource: among all music of the period, only Mahler provides a parallel case of Wagnerian harmony being carried to such expressive extremes and of special instrumental effects being used to intensify the feeling. The work was a great success.

Puccini did well, however, not to attempt to repeat it. He now turned to something different. *La bohème* (1896), a tale of aspiring artists and their loves in the "bohemian" world of mid-century Paris, is an altogether softer, more sentimental piece, much of it in a light-hearted, conversational style, but with a deeply touching final scene where – as in Verdi's *La traviata* – a girl dies of tuberculosis, reconciled with her lover. Here Puccini used the pentatonic scale as a source of strikingly memorable orchestral ideas, and as a means for penetrating beneath the civilized surface of the major-minor system to a more raw, coarser musical and expressive world.

La bohème is Puccini's most popular opera, but his next two, *Tosca* and *Madama Butterfly*, run it close. *Tosca* (1900), set in reactionary Rome when the cause of freedom seemed to depend on the successes of Napoleon, attacks the emotions in its scene where the tenor hero is tortured by the police as information is extracted from his lover (the singer Tosca); Puccini's music seems almost to twist the thumbscrews. He was master at playing with the audience's emotions in such situations. Another spectacular scene in this opera ends the first act, where the police chief Scarpia is seen devising a scheme, during a church service, to force Tosca to become his lover; the conjunction of religious and sexual emotion is characteristic. Puccini's melodic style may be seen from the beginning of the tenor's aria in the last act, as he prepares to

ex. IX.8

Andante lento appassionato molto

face execution (ex. IX.8). The emotional force of the moment – the text is "Time has passed and I am in despair! and never have I so much loved life!" – is conveyed in the short, irregular phrases, and by the logic of the motivic structure (note the repetitions at different pitch for verbal repeats) that points up the rhythmic changes introduced to give a feeling of spontaneity.

Scenes like these show Puccini's remarkable sense of theater: a sense that is manifested in his command of color, motif (and especially its use for raising dramatic tension) and harmony. His use of pentatonic melody, as seen in the *Tosca* example, has no role in expressing location (perhaps it helps convey the intense, melancholy emotion that so often belongs to his characters), but it does do that in the ensuing works. *Madama Butterfly* (1904), set in Japan, incorporates some real Japanese melodies, but also has a good deal of pentatonic music to convey its oriental exoticism. Most of Puccini's heroines are "little women", who suffer and die for their true, limitless love. One such is Madam Butterfly, the Japanese girl duped by an American naval officer into marriage, then deserted; his capacity to compel the audience's emotions in sympathy with his heroines is particularly striking here. It happens again in his next opera, *La fanciulla del West* ("The Girl of the Golden West"), set in California in the gold rush; to Puccini the Far West was just as exotic as the Far East. His later operas, which include a "triptych" written for the Metropolitan in New York (and containing his only comedy, *Gianni Schicchi*, a slightly macabre piece set in medieval Florence) and *Turandot*, a savage drama set in China, show him enlarging his harmonic and orchestral style, influenced by Strauss and especially Debussy. But none of these has ever challenged in appeal the three operas – *La bohème*, *Tosca* and *Madama Butterfly* – that he composed around the turn of the century. He died in 1924, leaving *Turandot* unfinished.

Chapter X

Modern Times

The story of modern music begins, essentially, in the years leading up to World War I. These years saw the composition of numerous works firmly rooted in the past: there are the symphonies of Mahler, Sibelius and Elgar, or the operas of Strauss, Massenet and Puccini (discussed in the previous chapter). But they saw, too, a number of works, by younger men, that struck a new – and harsher – note. The most famous, or notorious, of them was Igor Stravinsky's *Rite of Spring*, which caused a riot on its first performance. There are also several by Arnold Schoenberg (piano pieces, chamber works, above all the pieces for speaker and chamber group called *Pierrot lunaire*) and his students Alban Berg and Anton Webern, and by Béla Bartók (the opera *Bluebeard's Castle*, the *Allegro barbaro* for piano).

Violence

These works – and there are many more by other composers – did not merely carry further the continuing processes of the breakdown of tonality and an increase in dissonance. There is in them a conscious, deliberate element of violence and distortion, a renunciation of traditional ideas of the beautiful and the expressive. Bartók's "barbaric" Allegro involves ferocious, ugly pounding of the keyboard. Stravinsky's ballet sets new levels in dissonance and rhythmic energy, of a "primitive", disorientating kind. Schoenberg's *Pierrot lunaire* inhabits a world of nightmare fantasy, macabre and absurd, with hints of cabaret music. The traditional bourgeois concertgoer was meant to be offended and disturbed from his complacency by works like these; and he duly was, just as the traditional bourgeois art-lover was infuriated by the art of the time.

This was a period when artists of all kinds were seeking to find a more truthful, more expressive way of treating the realities of human existence in the harsh, dissonant world of the twentieth century than a photographic realism could offer. Vincent van Gogh, back in the 1880s, had intentionally altered, even distorted, reality in line with his feelings. His methods were pursued by such Expressionist painters as Oskar Kokoschka (1886–1980) and Wassily Kandinsky (1866–1944) – Kandinsky's move towards abstraction invites analogy with Schoenberg's towards atonality. Equally an analogy may be drawn between Stravinsky and early Cubism, particularly as represented by Pablo Picasso (1881–1973), an artist with whom Stravinsky in fact collaborated. Another fascinating parallel with musical developments of the time is suggested by the prose of James Joyce (1882–1941), which relinquishes the traditional priority of meaning in favor of various kinds of patterning and allusion.

France – with Paris still the artistic capital of Europe, and the natural home for an expatriate Russian like Stravinsky – and the German-speaking countries, with their weight of tradition from the previous century, led in most of these new developments. But the wind of change was felt everywhere. In America, Charles Ives was composing pieces with irrational juxtapositions of musical ideas and deliberately distorted harmonies. Soon Edgard Varèse was to arrive in the country with his revolutionary ideas about musical sounds, partly based on the noise-world of an industrial, urbanized society. In Italy, the Futurists – a movement including visual and literary artists as well as musicians – were thinking along similar lines; one of this group of machine-age artists, Luigi Russolo (1885–1947), spent years devising an ingenious series of *intonarumori* (noise-intoners) – musically a dead end, but a symptom of the times nonetheless, comparable perhaps with Dadaism.

Atonality

With the total abandonment of tonality, as is found in the work of Schoenberg and his disciples during the first decade of the twentieth century, it became necessary to devise new methods of musical structure. In these "atonal" works, Schoenberg, Berg and Webern found themselves drawn – at a subconscious, creative level – to use complex forms of imitation between voices or instruments. It is out of this necessity and their reaction to it that Schoenberg's 12-tone system (see Chapter III, p. 62) began to be devised. It was codified in the mid-1920s, but was not widely used outside the circle of Schoenberg's direct influence for more than 20 years, and even then its use was not long sustained. It did however give rise to more complex forms of serialism: Schoenberg's method applies serial processes to pitch, but others later carried the principle further and applied it to such elements of music as rhythm, dynamics and tone-color. Pierre Boulez is among the one-time "total serialists".

Neo-classicism

At the end of his life Stravinsky, attracted by Webern's use of serialism, adopted it; but his earlier work, once past his strongly Russian phase (to which *The Rite of Spring* belongs), is primarily neo-classical. The term "neo-classicism" is used in music to describe those works of the first half of the twentieth century that look back beyond the Romantic era to the Classical, the Baroque or even earlier for inspiration or simply for technical procedures. Others besides Stravinsky, notably Prokofiev, have drawn on classical forms in their instrumental music; in opera Stravinsky's *The Rake's Progress*, with its strong Mozart echoes, is outstanding among neo-classical works. Paul Hindemith, whose music is notably tidy in its forms and techniques, and unromantic in feeling, has also often been called a neo-classicist. Another, of a rather different kind, was the Italian composer and pianist Ferruccio Busoni (1866–1924), who particularly sought inspiration in Bach, as his *Fantasia contrappuntistica* testifies.

There were other significant and widespread influences on music in the years around and after World War I. The folksong interests of the previous generation persisted, but had changed in focus. Men like Ralph Vaughan Williams in England and Béla Bartók in Hungary were collecting folksong on a methodical, scientific basis, using recording machines as well as pencil and paper. Bartók researched not only in his native country but in neighboring regions and even in Turkey and the Middle East. These men used folksong in their music, Bartók in particular in such a way as to reinvigorate it rhythmically after the sterile, sluggish, mechanical rhythms of some late Romantic music.

There was a social, or political, element in this too, aimed at bringing music out of the drawing-room, the salon and even the concert hall into a wider realm and giving it contact with and meaning to a broader and perhaps less sophisticated public. One of the ways of doing this was to introduce elements from the folk or traditional music of the people. In the USA, where folk-music traditions were relatively recent, composers like Aaron Copland and George Gershwin also drew on the important native jazz traditions. These traditions indeed influenced Europeans too, notably Stravinsky and Ravel.

The political events of the first half of the twentieth century had a good deal of influence on music. They always have, of course: composers in the employ of royal or noble patrons have naturally been expected to compose music to the greater glory – and the perpetuation in power – of their masters, and we should not expect a state to exercise any lesser rights over those it pays to provide its music. States can, however, change their attitudes, as Soviet Russia did in her early days. After the revolution in 1917, Stravinsky left Russia for good (apart from a brief visit as an honored guest at the end of his life). Prokofiev, also out of sympathy with the new regime – and fairly certain that it would be out of sympathy with him – left, though the pull of his native land later proved irresistible. Initially, the Soviet regime encouraged many sorts of experimental music; but later, with Stalin in charge and intellectuals increasingly under pressure, experimentation was strongly discouraged, the experimental composers were removed and their works banned. Music was required to be optimistic in spirit and readily appealing to large audiences, as well as encouraging self-sacrifice and effort on behalf of the community. Prokofiev and Shostakovich were, broadly, ready to accept these principles without regarding them as improper attacks on artistic freedom (which is always a relative concept); but they were often troubled by official disapproval of particular works.

At the opposite end of the political spectrum lies the music of Nazi Germany and Austria in the 1930s and 40s. Here, in another kind of totalitarian society, other (and certainly no less ruthless) forms of censorship were applied. Music that challenged the existing order, like Kurt Weill's settings of texts by Bertolt Brecht, was not permitted, and here too experimentation of almost any kind was regarded as degenerate. Forward-looking composers (and not only Jewish ones like Schoenberg and Weill) fled the country; most of those who remained and were approved have faded into a proper obscurity, and with them their music.

The dust has now begun to settle on the first half of the twentieth century, and it is growing easier, in spite of the very great diversity of musical style and idiom, to see what lies in common between the various composers of the time. Doubtless it will be easier still a hundred years from now. But it is too soon for us to establish much of a perspective on music since 1950. Many composers pressed further the movements of the preceding years, like the "total serialists" and the Soviet bloc composers who developed a popular, patriotic vein that often drew on folksong. But after World War II, as after World War I, the younger generation strove to find fresh means of expressing in their music the ethos of their times, dominated by new and alarming technologies and the uncertainties to which they gave rise.

One technological development of the war years particularly important to musicians was, of course, tape recording: not only for performance but also for composition. A composer could now conceive and execute a piece without depending on performers to play and interpret it. In the early days, this was chiefly done (by a group based in Paris) with sounds from everyday life, like traffic noise or leaves rustling in the wind. With tape recording, the sounds could be manipulated –

Totalitarian regimes

Electronics

speeded up, slowed down, superimposed, played backwards, given an echo, and so on. The term *musique concrète* was used for "compositions" of this kind. Later, these techniques were applied to musical sounds, notably by Stockhausen in *Gesang der Jünglinge* ("Song of the youths" – it uses the biblical story of the three boys in the fiery furnace, and is entirely made up from a tape of one boy singing a hymn), and in America by composers at the influential Columbia-Princeton center. With the advent of the synthesizer a large range of sounds could be generated and processed electronically, giving the composer a new comprehensiveness of control over how his music would sound.

Not all composers, in fact, wanted that kind of control. Some preferred exactly the opposite. Even in the electronic world, a device called the ring modulator was sometimes used which would distort the sound in ways that could not always be calculated in advance. And some composers combined a pre-existing tape with live music-making, while others used electronic devices like amplifiers or throat microphones to introduce deliberately random elements into their music. In this area the most influential and revolutionary figure is probably the American composer John Cage. Cage has systematically questioned all the assumptions on which our musical culture is based: he has proposed the elevation of noise and silence to the level at which we hold music, has opposed the idea of the formal concert in favor of musical "happenings", and has used in his own compositions such elements as radio receivers randomly tuned to produce crackles and snatches of haphazard speech or music.

Many of Cage's suggestions have been followed up by younger men. In the turbulent late 1960s and early 70s, especially, audiences earnestly (though sometimes impatiently) listened to such events as a player on an amplified cello sounding one note continuously for two hours, perhaps with occasional accompaniment from others using instruments or noise-makers. In terms of traditional artistic values such events meant little; but certainly they served to sharpen one's awareness of the nature and the effects of sound.

Other composers of this period – not necessarily disciples of Cage – moved along similar lines. Some, recognizing and wishing to extend the role of the performer, abandoned traditional methods of notation in favor of symbolic graphic ones which the player could interpret exactly as he felt inclined; nothing is "wrong" and anything that reflects the player's feelings, on seeing the music, is "right". A piece of music might even be presented to the player as a piece of prose, to which he would react by playing something. Many other composers, however, were attracted to the idea of random elements in a much less extreme form – in a string quartet by Lutoslawski, for example, the players are asked to improvise on given phrases until the first violinist gives a signal to move on, and in a Stockhausen piano piece the player is required to make decisions, while he is performing, on which sections he will include and in what sequence.

There are limited analogies for ideas such as these in the other arts. Some modern poets have had their works printed in such a way as to leave the reader free to choose the sequence of sections. The graphic arts do not embody the time element that is vital to such procedures, but there are obvious parallels to be drawn between the art of Jackson Pollock (1912–56), who let paint fall at random on canvases lying on the floor, and the music of Cage.

There has, understandably, been a substantial reaction among composers against the experimentalist generation. Several, like David del Tredici in the United States

Random music

or Robin Holloway in England, have found what might be called a neo-Romantic idiom in which, without denying the more recent past, traditional values are affirmed. Other composers have looked, in these times of rapid world communications and ethnic mixing, to non-Western cultures for fresh inspiration – to the ragas of Indian music, for example, with their quality of timeless meditation, or to the strangely mystical clangor of gongs in the gamelan music of Indonesia. Still others have sought a coming-together with rock music, a notion that is particularly attractive because it implies an ending to the social and intellectual divisiveness hinted at by the existence of different music systems and the different publics that support them. Certainly it seems that music is at a crossroads; but then, looking back over the last four hundred or so pages of this book, it is hard to escape the conclusion that it nearly always has been.

The Second Viennese School

One area in which music has most conspicuously changed since 1900 is that of harmony. The change, once it came, came fast. In the nineteenth century composers had introduced an ever greater variety of chords and an ever faster rate of harmonic change. The major–minor system had been threatened in Wagner's *Tristan und Isolde* (see p. 353). In the music of composers otherwise as different as Richard Strauss and Debussy, Mahler and Scriabin, there began to be times when the pull of the tonic was so weak as hardly to be felt at all. To keep their music going, composers had to use ever larger orchestras and bigger forms, as in Mahler's symphonies; the alternative was the almost atonal miniature, as practiced by Scriabin. In 1908, the decisive break to atonality (see p. 423) was made by a slightly younger composer, who was thereby to establish himself as one of the dominant influences on the music of the twentieth century: Arnold Schoenberg (1874–1951).

Schoenberg

Schoenberg was a reluctant revolutionary. He was born in Vienna in 1874, at a time when Brahms was working there, and he always remained devoted to the Viennese tradition as expressed in the music of Haydn, Mozart, Beethoven, Schubert and Brahms. Indeed, he saw himself not as overturning that tradition but rather as perpetuating it, continuing a natural process of development. Just as Brahms's harmonies were more complex than Haydn's, Schoenberg's had to be more complex than Brahms's. But the aims stayed the same. Music must unfold with symphonic logic, stating its themes, developing them and then recalling them in an altered state. And the vehicle for the most profound musical thinking would have to be chamber music. A good half of Schoenberg's output falls into this category.

A further taste Schoenberg shared with his great Viennese predecessors was for playing chamber music as well as writing it. He started violin lessons when he was eight and was soon composing little duets and trios to play with friends. Because the family was not well off, however, there was no opportunity for him to study as a composer. Instead he had to leave school and work in a bank while he pursued his musical education through books and discussions with friends, among them the composer and conductor Alexander von Zemlinsky (1871–1942). So he developed the vigorous enthusiasm and the offbeat attitudes of one who has learned his art for himself: there would be no betrayal of the ideals of the great Viennese tradition, but

127 Arnold Schoenberg: self-portrait, 1910. Arnold Schoenberg Institute, Los Angeles.

Arnold Schoenberg	Life
1874	born in Vienna, 13 September
1890	began working in a bank; contact with musicians including Alexander von Zemlinsky who became a lifelong friend and musical influence
1899	*Verklärte Nacht*
1900	conducted choirs, orchestrated operettas; began work on *Gurrelieder*
1901	married Mathilde Zemlinsky; Berlin
1902	composition teacher at the Stern Conservatory, Berlin
1903	Vienna; began giving private composition lessons, Alban Berg and Anton Webern being among his pupils; met Mahler
1908	composed first atonal pieces: Piano Pieces op. 11. *The Book of the Hanging Garden*
1910	Second String Quartet greeted with incomprehension; mounted exhibition of his expressionist paintings
1911	Berlin; published harmony treatise
1912	*Pierrot lunaire*
1913	*Gurrelieder* first performed in Vienna
1915	Vienna; joined army as volunteer
1918	founded the Society for Private Musical Performances
1923	first serial works: Piano Pieces op. 23; his wife died
1924	married Gertrud Kolisch
1926	composition teacher at the Prussian Academy of Arts, Berlin; period of prolific composition
1933	left Germany because of Nazi anti-semitism; emigrated to the USA, to Boston
1934	moved to Hollywood because of health; took private pupils
1936	professor at the University of California at Los Angeles; Violin Concerto, Fourth String Quartet
1944	health began to deteriorate; left professorship
1951	died in Los Angeles, 13 July

nor would there be any compromising of the new musical ideas that came rushing into the young composer's mind.

Throughout the 1890s Schoenberg produced a stream of piano pieces, songs and chamber works, but only at the end of the decade did he start writing music he considered worthy. *Verklärte Nacht*, a symphonic poem for string sextet, was the first instrumental score he acknowledged. It was also the first of his works to create a scandal. In combining program music with orthodox form and medium, the sextet brought together the Wagner–Strauss tradition and that of Brahms. It brought *Tristan*-style harmonies into chamber music, and that for Schoenberg's contemporaries was unacceptable: the Composers' Union in Vienna declined to perform it.

For Schoenberg, however, *Verklärte Nacht* was a determinedly conventional piece. He saw the need to extend the boundaries of the central tradition, to make it possible for the language of Wagner to be spoken with the logic of Brahms. The fulfillment of this aim, in which he included elements from the languages of

---

Arnold Schoenberg   Works

Operas Erwartung (Expectation, 1909), Die glückliche Hand (The blessed hand, 1913), Von Heute auf Morgen (From one day to the next, 1930), Moses und Aron (1932, unfinished)

Choral music Gurrelieder (1911); A Survivor from Warsaw (1947); Die Jakobsleiter (1922, 1944, unfinished)

Orchestral music Verklärte Nacht (Transfigured night, 1917); Pelleas und Melisande (1903); 5 Pieces, op. 16 (1909); Variations (1928); Violin Concerto (1936); Piano Concerto (1942); 2 chamber symphonies

Chamber music 4 string quartets; string trio; wind quintet

Vocal music Das Buch der hängenden Gärten (15 songs, 1909); Pierrot lunaire (1912); cabaret songs; c75 others

Piano music 3 Pieces, op. 11 (1909); 6 Little Pieces, op. 19 (1911); 5 Pieces, op. 23 (1920, 1923); Suite (1923)

Unaccompanied choruses   *Canons*

Debussy and Stravinsky, as well as some of his own, was to be his effort for the rest of his life. *Verklärte Nacht* also set the pattern of his music in its heavy emotional load and its density of feelings in conflict, achieved through a web of polyphonic lines that strain out of the harmony.

By this time Schoenberg had left the bank and was earning his living by conducting choirs and orchestrating operettas. In October 1901 he married Zemlinsky's sister Mathilde, and the following December the couple moved to Berlin, where he had a job as musician at a rather literary cabaret. He took with him his most Wagnerian work, the *Gurrelieder*, a sort of concert opera of furious passion and tragic destiny which he had composed in 1900–1 but only partly scored.

Schoenberg returned to Vienna in 1903 and soon began giving composition lessons privately. Among his first pupils were Alban Berg (1885–1935) and Anton Webern (1883–1945), both of whom were to stay close to him, musically and personally, for the rest of their lives. The presence of such sympathetic colleagues might well have contributed to the speed with which Schoenberg's music now developed, though change had already been rapid after *Verklärte Nacht*. This work, in effect a one-movement symphony, was soon followed by a string quartet where the thematic development is intensively pursued through music embracing the conventional four movement-types, and where the absence of a justifying program helps make the expressive contortions still more intense. There is a note almost of hysteria as the music races away from disintegration, using its clearly chiseled themes and its bounding polyphony to sustain coherence and progression.

The same style is continued in the First Chamber Symphony (1906), which again plays continuously through sections that correspond to the normal symphonic movements: sonata allegro, scherzo, slow movement and finale. Again, too, the music is made tonal only with severe strain, and this contributes to the sense of hectic turmoil in so much of Schoenberg's music. For example, one of the main themes of the Chamber Symphony is a sequence of 4ths, which immediately strikes out from any given key: as first sounded by a horn it is D–G–C–F–B♭–E♭, pulling the music round from F major into the home key of E♭ major, but creating a dangerous precedent in hopping so freely among distant tonalities.

This work brings us the voice of Schoenberg as the unheeded prophet Cassandra, pointing out that the tonal system was about to collapse at the very moment when others were creating within it giant monuments (Mahler, for instance, was at work on his Eighth Symphony). Against that trend, Schoenberg's piece is scored for just 15 soloists, a crack team who can tackle the emphatic dynamism and the complex counterpoint of this music more effectively than could larger forces. It is significant, too, that Schoenberg wrote no "normal" symphonies but preferred to bring the genre within his favored sphere of chamber music.

His next chamber work, String Quartet no. 2, completes the move into atonality foreshadowed by the Chamber Symphony. After two tonal movements, the third has little feeling of key and the finale is wholly atonal until its drawn-out final settling into the work's home key of F♯: Schoenberg needs 40 slow bars to complete this. The revolution was indeed a momentous one, as momentous as that of Sigmund Freud (1856–1939) in psychology, and for similar reasons. Schoenberg and Freud both pull the carpet out from under our feet, show that accepted certainties (the major–minor system, moral categories) may be artificial. Freudian, too, is the analysis of extreme emotional states that Schoenberg accomplishes in his first fully atonal works. Among these are the short opera *Erwartung* (1909), a monologue for a woman seeking her lost lover in a wood, and *Pierrot lunaire* (1912).

The use of a key had always given music a feeling of progress. On the crudest level, the listener knew that a piece was aiming finally for its tonic (see p. 24). But if key and mode were to be relinquished, then progress would also be lost, or become less smooth as its end could no longer be foreseen. That made it hard to create satisfactory instrumental forms, since there was now no obvious goal: that is one reason why Schoenberg at this time preferred to use words to give him structural backbone. He even introduced song into the world of the string quartet, adding a soprano, singing settings of poems by Stefan George, in the last two movements – which are virtually atonal – of his path-breaking no. 2.

Schoenberg's high moral seriousness and his restless search for the indefinable are linked with religious searching in the work that should have crowned this period but was never completed, the oratorio *Die Jakobsleiter* ("Jacob's Ladder", 1917–22). Schoenberg had been brought up an orthodox Jew, but he was no longer practicing his religion (though he made a formal return in 1933, soon after he had been ejected from Berlin on Hitler's rise to power). Nevertheless, a Jewish sense of the divinity, urging mankind to a perpetual search after truth, underlies *Die Jakobsleiter*. The same feeling pervades the later opera *Moses und Aron* (1932), again written to the composer's own text, again concerned with the thorny road to God, and again significantly unfinished. For though *Die Jakobsleiter* was interrupted because of the war (Schoenberg had spent almost a year in the army), the real reason for its incompleteness is the impossibility of adequately describing the soul's eventual union with God.

Pierrot lunaire shows us instead the soul lost. The 21 brief poems speak in fractured terms of alienation, uncertainty, madness and disquiet. They draw from Schoenberg a particular musical world of shifting values: ambiguous sound – the soloist's *Sprechgesang* (a kind of delivery halfway between song and speech); ambiguous genre, suspended between cabaret and concert hall, opera and chamber music; ambiguous harmony, hovering around keys or other marks of stability. The cabaret element is important. Perhaps Schoenberg was remembering his experiences in Berlin a decade before (*Pierrot lunaire* was written during a second period of residence there from 1912 to 1915). After all, *Sprechgesang* of some sort is the stock-in-trade of the popular singer, and the accompaniment is for an agile band of flute, clarinet, two string instruments and piano. Cabaret, too, provides the background for what Schoenberg called the "light, ironic, satirical tone" of the work, for all its savagery, macabre humor, isolation and hopeless nostalgia. The whole thing presents itself as an image of nightmare fantasy, not the real thing that had seemed to be dredged up in the earlier atonal works (see Listening Note X.A). Those earlier works had enjoyed the freedom to abandon, with tonality, all other kinds of order and symmetry: the rhythm owes no allegiance to meter, instrumentation is rich and flexible, and repetition of any sort is avoided in forms that live by constant change. By contrast, in *Pierrot lunaire* a certain fixity begins to come back, in metrical regularity, in clear formal structure and in contrapuntal cunning. Already Schoenberg was looking for some way to build music logically without the help of major–minor tonality, for otherwise there could be no developed musical form.

Gradually, while working on *Die Jakobsleiter* and teaching in Vienna, he evolved the basic principles of 12-tone serialism, which was intended not so much as a system as an aid to extended composition without tonality. We have already seen (p. 62) something of how this system works and the variety of possibilities it offers. For Schoenberg, serialism made it possible once again to compose in the large instrumental forms, and so the appearance of the new method came with a certain neo-classicism that was a hallmark of music in the 1920s.

A notable early example is the Piano Suite (1923), Schoenberg's first wholly serial work, though here, typically, the reference back to Bach goes by way of Brahms. As he insisted, "one uses the series and then one composes as before" – before the intervention of atonality had overturned previous conventions. Within

128 The Kolisch Quartet rehearsing Berg's *Lyric Suite* in the presence of Schoenberg and the composer, before its first performance in Vienna, 8 January 1927: drawing by Benedict Dolbin. Meyer Collection, Paris.

Listening Note X.A

Schoenberg: *Pierrot lunaire* (1912), "Mondestrunken"
reciter, flute, violin, cello, piano

This is the first of 21 settings of poems from Albert Giraud's collection *Pierrot lunaire* in the German translations of Otto Erich Hartleben. The words are delivered in what Schoenberg's preface calls a *Sprechmelodie* ("speech-melody", also referred to as *Sprechgesang* or "speech-song"): the idea is that the notated pitches should be sung, but that the voice should immediately change to a speaking character.

Mondestrunken	Moondrunk
Den Wein, den man mit Augen trinkt, giesst nachts der Mond in Wogen nieder, und eine Springflut überschwemmt den stillen Horizont.	The wine one drinks through opened eyes pours down from the moon at night in waves, and a spring tide overflows the still horizon.
Gelüste, schauerlich und süss, durchschwimmen ohne Zahl die Fluten! Den Wein, den man mit Augen trinkt, giesst nachts der Mond in Wogen nieder.	Desires, terrible and sweet, arrive countless in those floods! The wine one drinks through opened eyes pours down from the moon at night in waves.
Der Dichter, den die Andacht treibt, berauscht sich an dem heilgen Tranke, gen Himmel wendet er verzückt das Haupt und taumelnd saugt und schlürft er den Wein, den man mit Augen trinkt.	The poet, lost in his devotions grows dizzy on the holy drink, and heavenwards turns in ecstasy and staggering sucks and sips the wine one drinks through opened eyes.

This, like every other poem set in the work, is a rondeau: i.e. the first two lines of the first stanza become the last two lines of the second, and the final line of all repeats the first. Usually Schoenberg draws on this to create a two-part musical form, the first part closed by the internal repetition at the end of the second stanza, and the second part, often more violent, closed by the further repetition at the very end of the poem.

mm.

1–14   The movement begins with a quiet ostinato in the piano (ex. i) and pizzicato violin, an image of the cascades flowing coldly from the moon. The voice enters, and then the flute with its own trickle. Under the second and third lines the ostinato is expanded, and a longer run from the flute joins these two lines. The word "stillen" brings a rare instance of pure sung tone, and the "still horizon" is pictured in a soft 3rd sustained by the flute and violin (harmonic) with chiming piano. At this point the flute takes up the ostinato, followed by the violin. The flute returns with a run up to the high G♯ with which the ostinato can start again.

15–28   The ostinato alternates between flute and piano while the violin plays a melody in the alto register. When the voice enters for the second stanza, the piano continues in trickles based on the ostinato while the violin melody comes to the forefront. The stanza ends with the flute and piano again sharing the ostinato music.

29–39   The final stanza opens with a sudden forte and a new sound: that of the cello, in an impassioned melody doubled and accompanied by the piano. This music, joined by the violin, reaches a climax at "Haupt", and then quickly dies away in preparation for the last line, where the ostinato in piano and flute is again restored.

ex. i   **Moderate**

the next few years came a Third String Quartet in the expected four movements and a set of Variations for Orchestra, which seem to have been designed in part to show how the serial method could produce results not far removed from the great tradition.

This was also a period of preparation for the opera *Moses und Aron*, with which various choral pieces of the 1920s are associated. Its biblical theme was close to the heart of Schoenberg as man and musician: it is the insoluble problem of communicating the most important truths. Moses' tragedy is to be a prophet who perceives divine truth but lacks the means to tell it; Aaron's curse is to be articulate but blind, so that he inevitably distorts and even destroys his brother's vision. The whole opera, nearly two hours of music, is based on a single series, used with the mastery of variety recently foreshadowed in the Variations for Orchestra. And in a sense serialism was the most appropriate technique for the work, since its possible forms are infinite, just as Jehovah is infinite: the voice in the burning bush, heard at the start of the work, is only one representation.

It is plain that Schoenberg felt himself to be much more a Moses (a prophet) than an Aaron (a communicator – though he was able to admire such Aarons of the musical world as George Gershwin). He had known ridicule since the rejection of *Verklärte Nacht*, and it had scarcely abated. An attempt to create a sympathetic, semi-private environment for the performance of new music in Vienna had had some success in 1919–21, but it foundered, and in Berlin, where Schoenberg moved in 1926 to take a master class in composition at the Prussian Academy of Arts, racial intolerance was mixed with musical. When he left in 1933 he went first to France and thence to the USA, with his second wife, Gertrud Kolisch (Mathilde had died in 1923).

In 1934 Schoenberg settled in California, his home for the rest of his life. This late period was one of continued teaching, both of private pupils (among them John Cage) and of students at the University of Southern California. These were the years too of Schoenberg's most complex and coherent serial works, including the Violin Concerto (1936), the Fourth String Quartet (1936), the Piano Concerto (1942), the String Trio (1946) and the Phantasy for violin and piano (1949). In all these he extends his serial practice to take command of large spans. In the last three he even feels confident enough to go back to his earlier technique of combining several movements into one: the standard four in the Piano Concerto, a more erratic grouping in the Trio and the Phantasy, which approach again the violent gestures of the period around 1910.

It may be significant that Schoenberg was able to recapture structural wholeness just when he found it possible to return to tonal composition, in works intended for student performers (a suite for string orchestra and a Theme and Variations for concert band). Both tonal and serial works certainly prove that Schoenberg was himself, whatever the style: intransigent, insistent, and always in search of a complex beauty and order.

The religious nature of his quest also became fully apparent during his American years. There was a liturgical piece, *Kol nidre*, for rabbi, chorus and orchestra (1938), and at the end a set of "modern psalms", setting his own words. But these too, like all his most profoundly spiritual works, were not to be finished: at his death in 1951 he had left the first of them in mid-air, on the words "and still I pray".

Berg

If testimony to Schoenberg's powers as a teacher were required, one only need look at the example of Alban Berg. Born in 1885 into a family wealthy enough to have a summer estate, Berg had dabbled in composition from his teenage years, but until he came to Schoenberg in 1904 he had written nothing but songs and had only the merest acquaintance with real compositional technique. Four years later, as an unofficial graduation exercise, he could write a single-movement Piano Sonata of Mahlerian dimensions. Within the next few years his development was astounding.

Equally astounding, though, was Berg's hankering after a past that he had only recently come to understand – unlike Schoenberg, who had been playing chamber music from his boyhood (Berg was no instrumentalist). His String Quartet (1910) is atonal in the manner of Schoenberg's contemporary scores, but the fulness of its two movements is partly due to a shaky grounding in tonality. The combination of novelty with nostalgia was to remain distinctively Berg's.

Berg dedicated his quartet to his wife Helene, whom he married in 1911. The next year he set some tiny, quizzical poems by his friend Peter Altenberg for soprano and orchestra. This must count as one of the most extraordinary first orchestral scores in musical history, filled with new, exactly imagined gestures within the context of five very short movements. The Three Pieces for orchestra of 1915 are different again: leaning more towards Mahler than Debussy, broad and developed whereas the songs are fleeting. The first is a musical palindrome – reading the same backwards as forwards – beginning and ending in the noise of untuned percussion; the second is a dance, both sensuous and cynical; and the massive finale is a funeral march, written on the very eve of World War I.

During the war Berg spent more than three years as a soldier, an experience that revived his earlier interest in making an opera out of Georg Büchner's play *Woyzeck*. Like everything he wrote, this first opera (called *Wozzeck*) is a work of direct emotional involvement and of conscious pattern-making, even on the largest scale: Act 1 scene 4 is a passacaglia, the whole second act a five-movement symphony. On another level, the musical materials are similarly diverse. A D minor Adagio, salvaged from an unfinished symphony, expresses feeling as in the old tonal tradition. There are also alarming parodies of café music in the manner of Mahler, stretches of *Sprechgesang* out of *Pierrot lunaire* (p. 429) and exercises in brutal constructivism. What makes it possible to use so wide a range of styles is the divergence at the heart of the opera. Some characters – notably Wozzeck's mistress Marie (soprano), but also the humble, surly, much abused Wozzeck himself (low baritone) – deeply engage the sympathies of the audience, while others, like the strutting Captain (comic tenor) and the manically obsessed Doctor (comic bass: the

---

Alban Berg   Works
born Vienna, 1885; *died* Vienna, 1935

Operas Wozzeck (1925), Lulu (1937)
Orchestral music Chamber Concerto (1925); Violin Concerto (1935)
Chamber music String Quartet (1910); Lyric Suite, for string quartet (1926, later orchestrated)
Songs 4 Songs, op. 2 (1910); Altenberg Songs, with orchestra (1912); c75 others
Piano music Sonata (1908)

passacaglia is his scene), are pure caricature. The world of *Wozzeck* is one in which human beings are at the mercy of inhuman forces, whether as victims or agents. It could have come only as it did, at a time when music and the world seemed to have run out of control. It was also much the biggest of the works created by Schoenberg and his pupils during the period of non-serial atonality (roughly 1908–22), and after its first performance, in Berlin in 1925, it began to be performed widely and so to guarantee its composer an income.

Berg's next work was the Chamber Concerto for piano, violin and 13 wind instruments (1925), a piece riddled with "three-ness" to honor the trio of Schoenberg, Berg and Webern. Its order and balance are carried in sweeping romantic gestures that weld the tonal and the atonal more firmly than had been the case in *Wozzeck*. This new style gained a certain clarification from Berg's adoption of serialism, which he used in parts of his Lyric Suite for string quartet (1926). The passionate intimacy of this music is sustained at a high pitch, high enough to invoke *Tristan* in the finale. Not until half a century later, after Helene Berg's death, did it become known that the work had a secret program alluding to Berg's emotional affair with another woman, Hanna Fuchs-Robettin.

Hanna's importance in his life affected everything Berg wrote in his last decade, not least his second opera *Lulu*, begun in 1929 and not quite finished when he died in 1935. Drawing on two plays by Frank Wedekind, pioneer of sexual candor in the theater, Berg fashioned his own libretto in three acts containing a characteristically symmetrical plot. In the first half of the opera Lulu is on the ascent, rising through several connections with men to become the wife of the wealthy Dr Schön. In the second half, after she has shot Schön, her fortunes fall, through prison, harlotry and cheap prostitution to death at the hands of Jack the Ripper (roles are neatly doubled, so that Jack is identified with Schön). But this is not a simple morality. Lulu, like Wozzeck, is more prey than predator. She is the spirit of natural woman, and her destruction is inevitable in a civilization that can exist only by the suppression and perversion of the urgings of raw sex.

By the time of *Lulu*, conditions were starting to deteriorate in Vienna, where Berg lived all his life. After 1933 *Wozzeck* was banned from German theaters; this placed him in financial difficulties. He also interrupted work on the opera to complete a concert aria on three Baudelaire poems and a Violin Concerto (1935). Both of these are marked by something of the musical and emotional atmosphere of *Lulu*, and both of them – like *Lulu*, like the Lyric Suite and the String Quartet, like the middle dance of the Three Pieces – look through the tawdry surface to what Berg perceived as the sensual essence of human existence.

Webern

Anton Webern's background was not so different from Berg's. He came from a middle-class family; he arrived in Schoenberg's classes with a clutch of juvenile compositions of no great merit; and he left as the composer of a big instrumental piece. This, his orchestral *Passacaglia* (1908), is already typical in its brevity, its thinness of texture, its close organization and its urgent climaxes. The difference was that Webern had enjoyed an education in musicology at the University of Vienna, his native city, and that he took from it a liking for strict canon and thorough motivic working along the lines of the Renaissance Netherlands school.

He was therefore naturally disposed towards serialism, which he brought to an extreme of concentration and calculation in such works as his Symphony (1928), Concerto for nine instruments (1934) and String Quartet (1938). The symphony is

Anton Webern   Works
born Vienna, 1883; *died* Mittersill, 1945

Orchestral music Passacaglia, op. 1 (1908); 6 Pieces, op. 6 (1909); 5 Pieces, op. 10
(1913); Symphony, op. 21 (1928); Variations, op. 30 (1940)

Choral music Das Augenlicht (Eyesight, 1935); 3 cantatas

Chamber music 5 Movements for string quartet (1909); 6 Bagatelles for string
quartet (1913); 3 string quartets (1905, 1929, 1938)

Vocal music George Songs, op. 3 (1909), op. 4 (1909); Rilke Songs, op. 8 (1910);
Jone Songs, op. 25 (1934)

Piano music Variations, op. 27 (1936)

129 Anton Webern: black
chalk drawing, 1918, by
Egon Schiele. Private
collection.

scored for a small orchestra, of clarinets, horns, harp and strings. There are only two movements, the first in sonata form but characteristically also a four-part canon, the second a set of variations that pivots at its halfway point, after which the music goes backwards and ends as it began.

Though palindromes of this kind also appealed to Berg (the middle movement of his Chamber Concerto turns on its tail in a similar manner), Webern's structures are much more obvious. His music is an architecture of polyphonic lines, playing constantly on the tiniest motifs (six notes in the case of the symphony) and closely organized in instrumentation, rhythm and dynamic level. At the start of the symphony, for example, instrumental coloring is used to divide separate parts in the same way, so drawing attention to units of two or four tones (in ex. X.1 the music is redrawn to show the double canon more clearly). But since Webern's expressiveness is retained even in the tiny gestures of his music, the impression is not so much one of engineering in sound as of created equivalents to the things he liked to bring home from his walks in the Austrian Alps: bright mountain flowers and mineral crystals.

It took Webern a while to achieve this purity. After leaving Schoenberg's class in 1908 he took a variety of short-lived and unsatisfactory conducting jobs, while

ex. X.1

Listening Note X.B

Webern: *Six Bagatelles* op. 9 (1913), no. 4
string quartet

mm.

1–3   The B♭ with which the movement opens, in extreme slowness and quietness, is the first note of a phrase played by the second violin (ex. i). Around this are placed even smaller and still very soft phrases in the other instruments: first the first violin oscillating through an octave and a half (E♭–A), then the viola stepping downwards (E–B–C), and then the cello (D–C♯–F♯–F). Thus each of the 12 notes is represented once, discounting the repetitions of the first violin ostinato. There is similarly a fine variegation of color. All the instruments play with mutes, but the first violin plays *sul ponticello* (towards the bridge), the viola *pizzicato* (plucking) and the cello towards the tail-piece.

3–5   Towards the end of the second violin phrase the first violin re-enters with another ostinato, still played *sul ponticello* but now consisting simply of a repeated E. On this is placed a wide-spaced chord, just for an instant, adding notes not tonally related (B♭, F, B).

5–8   Like the first part of the movement, this is a melody with accompaniments, but this time the accompaniments come first: a repeated harmonic F♯ in the cello, a repeated *pizzicato* G in the viola, and an oscillating minor 9th in the second violin *sul ponticello* (C♯–D). The melody, in harmonics on the first violin, covers six of the remaining notes, and the last two (B♭ and A) are supplied by second violin and viola twice over in plucked chords. For a second time the 12 notes have been completed, in a movement of sustained *pianissimo*.

All the other bagatelles are similarly composed of tiny phrases, ostinatos and single chords, and all are similarly compact in form (they each occupy a page of score). Together they make up a miniature string quartet, with an *A–B–A* first movement, two scherzos, two slow movements and a quick finale.

ex. i

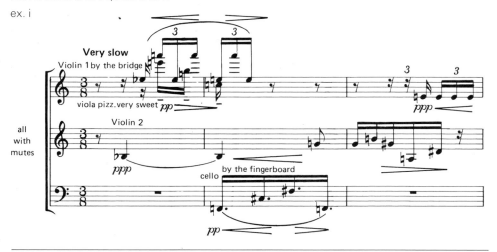

closely following his teacher's compositional development within his own briefer manner: this was the period of such miniatures as his Six Bagatelles for string quartet (1913), each occupying only a small page of score (see Listening Note X.B). Like Schoenberg, Webern found it easier to compose atonally when he was working with a text. For a decade after 1914 the only works he completed were songs, usually with the accompaniment of an ensemble that might range from a pair of clarinets in the severe Five Canons op. 16 (1924) to a brightly colored little orchestra in the Four Songs op. 13 (1916). Here the flow and delicacy contribute to the finely shaded expressiveness typical of Webern's songs.

In 1918 Webern settled near Schoenberg in Vienna, where he lived for the rest of his life. During the 1920s and early 1930s he held various conducting appointments, notably with the Workers' Symphony Concerts, but gradually he lost his posts as the Nazis gained control of Austria. Meanwhile he was writing his alpine serial compositions, including not only the instrumental pieces but also a series of settings of verses by Hildegard Jone; the nature symbolism and tremulous mysticism of her work obviously struck a chord in him. There were two sets of Jone songs and three little choral works, all responding to her imagery with eagerness disciplined by the mechanics of serialism. He was working on a further Jone cantata in 1945 when he was shot in error by an American soldier.

The radical alternative

Stravinsky

In terms of both creative accomplishment and influence, there can be no doubt that Igor Stravinsky (1882–1971) must stand with Schoenberg as one of the two dominant figures in twentieth-century music. His influence, indeed, has probably been the greater, for where Schoenberg's principal effort was towards continuing the Austro-German symphonic tradition, Stravinsky interested himself in radical alternatives to that tradition. Revolutionary change has been much more a feature of music in this century than has evolutionary growth.

The difference in musical temperament is partly to be explained by a difference of cultural background. Though Stravinsky spent much of his life in France, Switzerland and the USA, he was very much a Russian composer, with a Russian's hesitancy over western European values. His independence from the central tradition went far beyond that of Tchaikovsky and Mussorgsky, both potent influences on him. Another strong influence in his early years was Rimsky-Korsakov, with whom he had lessons between 1902 and Rimsky's death in 1908.

His work took off with two short orchestral pieces (*Scherzo fantastique* and *Fireworks*) performed in St Petersburg in 1908. They echo the French music that impressed Stravinsky at the time (that of Debussy and Dukas especially), but full too of a youthful brilliance in the handling of the orchestra. They certainly caught the attention of one member of the audience, Sergei Diaghilev, who at once commissioned Stravinsky to orchestrate some pieces by Grieg and Chopin for a ballet season he was mounting in Paris in 1909. This was the beginning of an association that bore immediate fruit. Three one-act ballet scores took Stravinsky out of Rimsky's kind of musical picture-making and into a quite new understanding of the art: *The Firebird* (1910), *Petrushka* (1911) and *The Rite of Spring* (1913).

If *The Firebird* still shows several directions Stravinsky was not to take (there is Scriabin in it as well as Rimsky), *Petrushka* is his first wholly individual creation. Interestingly, the central character is a Russian equivalent of the Western Pierrot, who was being addressed at the same time by Schoenberg (see p. 429). It might be supposed that both composers were looking for a puppet figure who could display human emotions more intensely than any real human being; Stravinsky found his in the tale of a doll brought to wretched life just as Schoenberg found his in poems for spoken song. But the comparison points up the differences between the

Igor Stravinsky	Life

1882	born in Oranienbaum (now Lomonosov) 17 June
1901	law student at St Petersburg University but chiefly interested in music
1902	met Rimsky-Korsakov, who became his mentor
1906	married Katerina Nossenko
1907	*Scherzo fantastique* and *Fireworks* acclaimed in St Petersburg and heard by Diaghilev, who commissioned music from Stravinsky, starting a long association with the Ballets Russes
1910	*The Firebird* (Paris) secured him an international reputation
1911	*Petrushka* (Paris)
1913	*The Rite of Spring* – riot in Paris theater
1914	settled in Switzerland
1917	Revolution made it impossible for him to return to Russia; *The Wedding* completed
1920	France; *Pulcinella*, the first of his "neo-classical" works, performed
1921	first European tour with Ballets Russes
1925	first American tour as conductor and pianist
1927	*Oedipus rex*
1935	second American tour
1936	*The Card Party* (New York) led to several American commissions, including the "Dumbarton Oaks" Concerto
1939	professor at Harvard University; his wife died
1940	married Vera de Bosset; settled in Hollywood
1945	naturalized American
1946	Symphony in Three Movements first performed in New York
1948	Robert Craft became Stravinsky's aide
1951	*The Rake's Progress* (Venice)
1957	*Agon* (New York)
1958	began international conducting tours
1962	well received in Russia
1966	*Requiem Canticles*
1971	died in New York, 6 April; buried in Venice

composers as well as the similarities. Stravinsky's orchestral score is flamboyant in gesture, brilliant in color and crisp in outline. It makes no pretence at Schoenberg's constant development. Instead, Stravinsky is happy to cut from one idea to another and back again, to give his music a kaleidoscopic quality. So, lacking long-term growth, the score can accommodate a great variety of materials. It includes both Russian peasant-style dances and more intimate mime sequences in which Petrushka's dual nature is expressed in the superimposition of opposed keys, or "bitonality".

The Rite of Spring takes all the novelties of *Petrushka* suddenly to a giant extreme. Scored for a very large orchestra, it is a dance-play of spring festivities in pagan Russia, ending with the sacrifice of a virgin in a tearingly self-destructive final dance. This also completes a musical revolution as profound as Schoenberg's at the same time. For just as Western music had hitherto been dependent on concepts of mode or key, so its rhythmic foundation had depended on meter, or an underlying stable pattern of beats. Stravinsky dispenses with that in the most overwhelming sections of *The Rite of Spring*, including the "Dance of the Earth" at the end of the first part and the "Sacrificial Dance" at the end of the second. Rhythm here is much more a matter of single impulses and short motifs built into irregular sequences, as in ex. X.2, from the "Sacrificial Dance". The emphasis on rhythm is enhanced by the unchanging harmony, instrumentation and dynamic level, and through their

130 Igor Stravinsky: drawing by Pablo Picasso, Paris, 31 December 1920. Private collection.

ex. X.2

restless alteration the rhythmic units give a powerful sense of pulse.

Of course, by no means the whole of *The Rite of Spring* is as "barbaric" as this. But such inventions as ex. 2 did provide Stravinsky with a rhythmic energy that he could use elsewhere in the score in more complex ways. Moreover, the heftily pulsating dances are set off by introductions to each part in which rhythmic detail is lost in seamless polyphonic flow. It is, even so, the new, violent rhythm of *The Rite of Spring* that was immediately admired or detested by Stravinsky's contemporaries: the first performance, in Paris on 29 May 1913, was the occasion of one of the greatest riots in the history of the theater, with audience reaction to match the noise coming from the pit.

The outbreak of World War I the next year severed Stravinsky from Russia. He set up home with his wife and children in Switzerland, and in exile his thoughts turned intensively towards Russian folk traditions. He had already decided that the subject of his next ballet for Diaghilev would be a Russian peasant marriage. Though the score of *Les Noces* ("The wedding") was complete in outline by 1917, it took another six years for Stravinsky to find the right orchestration. He then settled on a small percussion orchestra, led by four pianos, to join the chorus – an efficient, quick-moving, machine-like ensemble for music that jumps freely among different repeating patterns geared to an unchanging pulse. In this respect *The Wedding* is a prolonged development of one rhythmic principle from *The Rite*. It shares with its predecessor too its ritual solemnity, heightened at the end by a characteristic reference to the sound of bells.

Most of Stravinsky's other works from his time in Switzerland are satellites of *The Wedding*. The most important is a smaller-scale stage work which lies between categories. Just as *The Wedding* is both ballet and cantata, *The Soldier's Tale* is a short play with substantial musical interludes and dances. Breaking with the established genres was just one expression of Stravinsky's breaking with tradition.

He soon began, however, to find his own ways of re-using the past. Diaghilev's next project for him, once the war was over and the Ballets Russes could start up again, was an arrangement of pieces by Pergolesi, but what he provided in *Pulcinella* was not merely an orchestration. The music is newly imagined for a modern chamber orchestra, the harmony changed to add piquancy, the scoring thought out afresh to heighten contrast and character. The result is that the ballet sounds much more like real Stravinsky than an eighteenth-century retrieval: it was, as he said later, a confrontation with himself "in the mirror of the past", and it made possible numerous other reconsiderations of musical styles and forms. It opened the way, in other words, to neo-classicism.

There is a striking parallel with Picasso, who designed *Pulcinella* (it was Diaghilev's policy to use only the most gifted composers and artists). However, whereas Picasso's reinterpretations of the nineteenth-century Ingres or the seventeenth-century Velázquez occupy a relatively small part of his output, Stravinsky's neo-classicism was to last all his life. Indeed, there is hardly a major work of his after 1920 that does not refer clearly to the music of other composers. Only rarely is this a matter of direct quotation, for in his hands neo-classicism is not an appeal to timeless precepts of form, but rather a way of showing how much things have changed. For example, the ballet *Apollo* (1928) evokes the French Baroque in its stately rhythms and sonorous harmony, but it also expresses a gap between that world and its own. There is no question of imitation.

Among Stravinsky's early neo-classical works was his Octet for wind instruments, dedicated to Vera Sudeikina, with whom he spent a great deal of time from 1921 onwards and whom he married in 1940, a year after the death of his first wife. He had now settled in France, having left Switzerland in 1920. But his works were still intensely Russian: this was the period when he was giving *The Wedding* its final scoring and also writing *Mavra*, a short comic opera to a Russian libretto. One

131 Picasso's stage design for Stravinsky's *Pulcinella*, first staged at the Opéra, Paris, 15 May 1920: Musée Picasso, Paris.

striking tendency in these works is that the strings have very little importance. Stravinsky prefers the mechanical exactness of the piano and the harder outlines of wind instruments. The two are brought together in his Concerto for piano and wind (1924), where, as in the Octet, classical forms and Baroque counterpoint are the scaffolding for music of modern verve and aloofness.

The return to the full orchestra came in *Oedipus rex* (1927), the last of Stravinsky's works written for Diaghilev. This time it was not a ballet but an "opera-oratorio". Describing it thus, Stravinsky calls attention to the particular manner of staging he envisaged for the work. The principal characters stand like statues on plinths, and the musical-dramatic action is recounted by a narrator in modern evening dress, speaking in the language of the audience and so associating himself with them rather than with the myth itself, which is retold in Latin. Everything thus conspires to convert the play, by Jean Cocteau after Sophocles, into a monument, which the audience is invited to observe but not become involved in: the language is alien and ancient, the action deliberately artificial. So too is the music, where Stravinsky draws on the Handel of *Messiah* and the Verdi of *Aida*.

If the oratorio aspect of the work carries a hint of sacred music, it would not be unexpected, for in 1926 Stravinsky rejoined the Russian Orthodox Church, and that same year he wrote a setting for unaccompanied chorus of the Lord's Prayer in Church Slavonic. This was followed by the Symphony of Psalms for choir and orchestra (1930), in three movements each of which sets a Latin psalm. Solemn in tone, lacking violins lest they introduce too expressive an effect, the Symphony of Psalms is a sort of liturgy for the concert hall, a Vespers never intended for the church. It also marks a stage on Stravinsky's path back towards the Austro-German tradition, against which everything he had written in his maturity had been a decisive reaction.

A "real" symphony duly emerged a decade later in the Symphony in C (1940), where the presence of four movements serves only to exhibit, in typical neo-classical fashion, how very unconventional the music is. This is not a symphony in C like those of Haydn, Mozart, Beethoven and Schubert, or even Bizet. The piece goes through the proper motions: there is a first movement with sections corresponding to those of normal sonata form, followed by a slow movement, a scherzo and a finale with a slow introduction. However, this is only the skeleton outline, and its skeleton nature is made clear by the unsuitable nature of the material used to fill it.

Most important, Stravinsky does not develop his ideas but rather alters them: continuity is simply not an aim here in music that works by brisk shift. For example, the whole first movement, despite its outward show of sonata form, is a patterning of two tiny motifs that are forever being viewed afresh, the more important of them the unit B–C–G (or leading note–tonic–dominant). If this had been G–B–C it would be a trivial cadence: Stravinsky's characteristic fresh view of a cliché produces an arresting idea, but one that remains restless, accentuating the dominant as so much neo-classical music does. It thus lends itself admirably to Stravinsky's non-developing, constantly varying music. The oboe solo near the beginning of the movement (see Listening Note X.C, ex. ii) gives a sense of running on the spot. It keeps remembering its starting-point, and the accompaniment is harmonically static (it also, very typically, avoids the tonic, so that the music stays in the air).

One effect of the harmonic changelessness, as in the earlier example from *The Rite of Spring*, is to draw attention to the rhythm, and Stravinsky's neo-classical

Listening Note X.C

Stravinsky: *Symphony in C* (1940), first movement

piccolo, 2 flutes, 2 oboes, 2 clarinets, 2 bassoons
4 horns, 2 trumpets, 3 trombones, tuba; timpani
1st violins, 2nd violins, violas, cellos, double basses

The movement is based on orthodox sonata form.

Exposition (mm. 1–147)   The first four measures (ex. i) state the germinal material of the movement: the insistent repetition of a single pitch, the motif of leading tone–tonic–dominant, and its expanded, harmonized answer. After an introduction in which these ideas are briefly developed, the first subject in its full form is stated (ex. ii, m. 26) by a solo oboe; it is taken up by other instruments and groups. Later (m. 74) the strings take up a staccato of the repeated-tone figure while the winds develop a dotted-rhythm motif. This leads to a cadence (m. 94), soon followed by the second subject, in F, on the horns (ex. iii), which is developed with counterpoints based on the first subject; the horn theme is heard on violins, in a more orthodox G major.

Development (mm. 148–225)   A measure of silence introduces the development, which ranges widely in key and usually keeps some reference to exx. i and ii (oboe, m. 159, in G, and m. 173 in e♭, flutes at m. 181 in C and e, oboe at m. 192 and then violins, in G); later (m. 199) the music is locked in e♭, with gruff chords and a theme constricted to a narrow range (ex. iv). The section ends with a tutti.

Recapitulation (mm. 226–353)   The recapitulation is fairly exact, with the necessary changes for the key plan, and with the second-subject material being recapitulated before rather than after the repeated-tone material of m. 74ff.

Coda (mm. 354–78)   Ex. ii is heard from flute and clarinet, two octaves apart; the music quietens, then five measures of loud orchestral chords round out the movement.

2nd movement (Larghetto): Ternary form, F – leading to

3rd movement (Allegretto): Ternary form, G.

4th movement (Largo–Tempo giusto): partly a sonata-form basis, but also drawing on first movement material, C.

ex. i

ex. ii

ex. iii

ex. iv

music, reintroducing a background of stable meter, is full of such "motor rhythms" where the pulsation is divorced from any harmonic movement.

The rest of the symphony shows the same dislocations of rhythm, which gives it an oddly balletic flavor, and which has helped to make not only this work but others of Stravinsky's neo-classical scores highly suitable for dancing. Having reached

Igor Stravinsky	Works

Operas Oedipus rex (1927), The Rake's Progress (1951)

Ballets The Firebird (1910), Petrushka (1911), The Rite of Spring (1913), Pulcinella (1920), The Wedding (1923), Apollon musagète (1928), The Fairy's Kiss (1928), Jeu de cartes (The card party, 1937), Orpheus (1947), Agon (1957)

Music-theater The Soldier's Tale (1918)

Orchestral music Symphonies of Wind Instruments (1920); Concerto "Dumbarton Oaks" (1938); Symphony in C (1940); Symphony in Three Movements (1945); Violin Concerto (1931); Ebony Concerto for clarinet (1945); Concerto for strings (1946)

Choral music Symphony of Psalms (1930); Mass (1948); Cantata (1952); Threni (1958); A Sermon, a Narrative and a Prayer (1961); Requiem Canticles (1966)

Vocal music (with ensemble) Pribaoutki (1914); Abraham and Isaac (1963)

Chamber music Duo concertante for violin and piano

Piano music Sonata (1924); two pianos – Concerto (1935); Sonata (1944)

Songs

132 Stravinsky's *Apollon musagète*: scene from the first European production by the Ballets Russes (choreographed by George Balanchine; with Serge Lifar, Lubov Tchernicheva and Felia Doubrovska), Paris, 12 June 1928.

maturity as a ballet composer, he seems to have found strongly marked rhythm an indispensable part of his musical thinking. Here his music is a sprightly dance even when, in the slow movement, it is concerned also with florid, song-like lines for solo instruments, more in the manner of a concerto grosso than a symphony. This is followed by a scherzo and then a finale, whose opening duet for low bassoons is just one instance of the inventiveness of timbre that animates all Stravinsky's orchestral compositions. Nearly always he carefully chooses a different ensemble each time to give each work a particular color. In the case of the Symphony in C, though, he writes for a straightforward symphony orchestra, showing in this respect as in others his capacity to make the ordinary sound extraordinary.

During the decade between the Symphony of Psalms and the Symphony in C Stravinsky had become a French composer, having taken French citizenship in 1934. However, the outbreak of World War II caused him to move west again, to the USA, where the last two movements of the Symphony in C were composed.

He arrived in New York in September 1939 and settled the next year in Hollywood, finding, like Schoenberg, that the Californian climate suited him. The two composers were thus near neighbors for a dozen years, though it seems they set eyes on each other only on one occasion, at the funeral of the writer Franz Werfel.

Stravinsky was no stranger to America. Several of his works had been commissioned by American patrons, including *Apollo* and a concerto (*Dumbarton Oaks*) for chamber orchestra, a modern re-creation of the spirit and manner of Bach's Brandenburg Concertos (1938). Moreover, Stravinsky had used the specifically American genre of jazz in several of his works, beginning with the *Ragtime* (1918) and including *The Soldier's Tale*, with many further allusions helping to give an edge of streamlined modernity to his music.

Stravinsky was keenly aware of what he was worth, and not averse to taking on any compositional task if the money was right. He was involved with various film projects, though none materialized, and the music composed found its way into the few more weighty works of the period, including the Symphony in Three Movements (1945). After 1945, when he became an American citizen, Stravinsky also showed his financial canniness by making new versions of many of his works, thus re-establishing his claim to copyright in them. Involved thus in re-examining his own past, he created three major works to crown the three decades of neo-classicism: an austerely beautiful Roman Catholic Mass for chorus and wind instruments (1948), the ballet *Orpheus* (1947) and the opera *The Rake's Progress* (1951). For the opera he set a libretto on an eighteenth-century subject (Hogarth's famous engravings) by W. H. Auden and Chester Kallman, alluding unmistakably to the world of Mozart's comic operas, even to the extent of incorporating recitative with harpsichord accompaniment.

After this, his largest work, Stravinsky suddenly began to move in two new directions at the same time, even though he was nearly 70. He developed an interest in medieval and Renaissance music, already hinted at in the Mass but brought right to the surface of a new cantata on late-medieval English poems. Parallel with this, he began to investigate the possibilities of serialism, to which his own style, with its great dependence on tonality, had seemed utterly opposed. Possibly he felt freer to do this after Schoenberg's death, shortly before the première of *The Rake's Progress*. Certainly he had the opportunity to acquaint himself thoroughly with the music of Schoenberg, Berg and Webern through his friendship with the young American conductor Robert Craft from 1947 onwards: Craft soon became an indispensable part of the Stravinsky household, a musical assistant and tireless chronicler.

Stravinsky's gradual adoption of serialism is charted in his works of the 1950s, for example the *Canticum sacrum* written as a ceremonial honoring of St Mark in his own basilica in Venice; yet he remained very much himself despite the great change in manner. Within his interpretation of serialism it was still possible for small motifs or single pitches to be reiterated, rather as in the quotations above from *The Rite of Spring* and the Symphony in C (see ex. X.2 and Listening Note X. C, ii). Serialism also did nothing to curb his exact, always imaginative instrumentation or his rhythmic vitality. Indeed, since he was not above learning from composers two generations his junior – Pierre Boulez and Karlheinz Stockhausen – he found the stimulus for highly elaborate polyphonies of complex rhythms.

Most of Stravinsky's serial compositions are sacred or intended as funerary tributes. There was a last mixed-media dramatic piece, belatedly following in the wake of *The Soldier's Tale* and *The Wedding*: this was *The Flood*, a laconic telling for television of the Noah story in narration, song, dance and orchestral imagery. There was also a sequence of epitaphs for distinguished literary friends, including Dylan Thomas, T. S. Eliot and Aldous Huxley: Stravinsky had always maintained the Diaghilev habit of keeping the company of stars. His last memorial, however, was to himself, and it took the form of a typically compact and austere Mass for the Dead, the *Requiem Canticles* (1966). This was sung at his funeral, which he directed was to take place in Venice, scene of the first performances of *The Rake's Progress* as well as the *Canticum sacrum*, and last resting place too of Diaghilev.

The Central European crossroads

Schoenberg and Stravinsky, like Brahms and Wagner in an earlier age, seemed to offer clear alternatives to their contemporaries: either to ground their music in the past, or to make a clean break. In art, however, no either/or can ever be clear-cut, and it is notable that several of the greatest composers of the first half of the twentieth century found a way to steer some kind of middle course. The three composers next considered, a Hungarian and two Germans, belong to this group.

Bartók

Béla Bartók (1881–1945), Hungarian by birth, followed a career loosely matched by the history of his country. During his youth, Hungary was a part of the

Béla Bartók	Life
1881	born in Nagyszentmiklós, Hungary (now Sînnicolau Mare, Romania), 25 March
1899	Budapest Royal Academy of Music; began career as concert pianist and started composing
1902	influenced by hearing Richard Strauss's music; *Kossuth*
1905	met Zoltán Kodály, with whom he began collecting Hungarian folk music
1906	first folk-music collection published
1907	professor of the piano at the Budapest Royal Academy
1909	married Márta Ziegler
1917	*The Wooden Prince* produced in Budapest, the first of his works to be received favorably
1918	*Duke Bluebeard's Castle*; established as an international figure
1920	toured Europe as a pianist
1923	*Dance Suite* composed to mark the union of Buda and Pest; divorced; married Ditta Pásztory
1926	*The Miraculous Mandarin* causes stir; First Piano Concerto
1934	commissioned by the Hungarian Academy of Sciences to publish folksongs
1940	emigrated to the USA
1942	health deteriorated
1943	Concerto for Orchestra
1945	died in New York, 26 September

Plate 31 *Opposite Orphée* by Gustave Moreau (1826–98) (private collection): the Symbolist painter's version of the legend. It also appealed to Debussy (p. 411), who wrote sketches for a work on the subject.

Habsburg Empire, ruled from Vienna, and Bartók was much influenced as a young composer by the Austro-German tradition stretching from Haydn and Mozart to Reger and Strauss, with a nationalist dash of Liszt. However, in 1904 he discovered that the real peasant music of Hungary had little to do with the gipsy fiddle-playing that Brahms and Liszt would have heard in Hungarian restaurants and put into their "Hungarian" dances and rhapsodies. As one who had set himself the task of becoming a Hungarian composer – he had studied at the conservatory in Budapest rather than go to Vienna for his training, as was normal – Bartók set about using true folk music in his creative work. But since he had first to collect and study this music, he became at the same time one of the founders of modern ethnomusicology (the study of the music of different ethnic groups).

Folk music had for Bartók a purity and naturalness that gave it a special legitimacy, and he was careful to base his own music on it in almost every particular of melody, rhythm, ornamentation, variation technique and so on. However, he almost never quotes a folktune direct: the process had to be one of analysis followed by an independent drawing-together on the basis of what had been discovered. Bartók was ready to learn not only from his fellow Hungarians but also from Romanians, Slovaks, Turks and north African Arabs. All these, with their different modalities and rhythmic styles, contribute to the richness of material in such a work as String Quartet no. 2 (1917), one of the first in which almost everything seems to spring from a lesson in folksong. Clearly, though, Bartók had been learning too from his great contemporaries: from Debussy in his liking for ancient and newly invented modes, from Stravinsky in the rhythmic force and brilliance of the central scherzo and perhaps from Schoenberg in the wandering harmony of the first movement.

This work came in the middle of a cycle of theater pieces: an opera (*Bluebeard's Castle*), ballet (*The Wooden Prince*) and a mime drama (*The Miraculous Mandarin*), all of which show the same awareness of folk music and of current developments in Paris and Vienna. All are unusually self-revealing works for a composer who – whatever the explosive fury at times of his music – was of an unusually reserved personality. The opera, dedicated to his young wife, is almost too blatantly a warning: in it Bluebeard's young wife Judith demands to know all the secrets of his heart and thereby loses all chance of happiness with him, for what she discovers appals her. Bluebeard's mysterious concealments are neatly symbolized as a row of seven doors, and the music is in effect a sequence of vivid tone-poems depicting Bluebeard's bloodstained jewels or his procession of former wives or his other secrets, linked by dialogue which finds a Hungarian operatic style by way of folksong.

The Wooden Prince and *The Miraculous Mandarin* are also concerned with man–woman relationships, and both too expose the difference between natural sexual passion and civilized flirtation or perversion. In *The Miraculous Mandarin*, for example, the exotic and enigmatic Chinese is lured up to a garret in some big Western city by a girl compelled to play the whore. Just as the stage action is motivated by oppositions between what is naturally prompted and what is socially acceptable, so the music wields pentatonic and other modal ideas within a context of rich chromaticism and wild, exuberant color, influenced by *The Rite of Spring* and by the tone poems of Strauss, but thoroughly individual. This unusually flamboyant piece is filled with intuitive discoveries that the composer was to spend the rest of his working life sorting out.

Plate 32 *Left The Golden Cockerel* by Rimsky-Korsakov, title-page of the first edition of the vocal score (Moscow, 1908). See p. 378.

| **Béla Bartók** | **Works** |

Opera Duke Bluebeard's Castle (1918)

Ballets The Wooden Prince (1917), The Miraculous Mandarin (1926)

Orchestral music Kossuth (1903); Dance Suite (1923); Music for Strings, Percussion and Celesta (1936); Divertimento for strings (1939); Concerto for Orchestra (1943); piano concertos – no. 1 (1926), no. 2 (1931), no. 3 (1945); violin concertos – no. 1 (1908), no. 2 (1938); Viola Concerto (1945)

Chamber music string quartets – no. 1 (1908), no. 2 (1917), no. 3 (1927), no. 4 (1928), no. 5 (1934), no. 6 (1939); Contrasts for violin, clarinet and piano (1938); Sonata for solo violin (1944); rhapsodies for violin and piano; duos for two violins

Piano music 14 Bagatelles (1908); Allegro barbaro (1911); Suite (1916); Sonata (1926); Out of Doors (1926); Mikrokosmos vols. 1–6 (1926–39)

Choral music Cantata profana (1930)

Unaccompanied choruses   *Songs*

Folksong arrangements

For Bartók the years after World War I were generally years of stocktaking. His field trips to collect folksongs, which had brought him great happiness before the war, he now abandoned: he had enough material in his sketchbooks and on phonograph cylinders, besides which the peasants were no longer so unspoiled. He devoted himself to the task of organizing what he and other collectors had gathered. He also set himself to analyzing the various styles of folksong to be found within

133 Bartók transcribing folksongs from an Edison phonograph, *c*1910.

ex. X.3

any one culture, the influences between different cultures and the ways in which a tune would be varied as it passed from village to village. Through this work he gained a formidable understanding of the possibilities of musical variation, which had always been one of his favorite techniques. His music of the 1920s and 30s is ever more coherently based on the constant variation of one or more small motifs.

A case in point is Bartók's Music for Strings, Percussion and Celesta (1936), a four-movement piece laid out for two chamber orchestras of strings and percussion, one including piano and celesta, the other xylophone and harp. This grouping provides typically varied and precise sounds. Though his own instrument was the piano, Bartók was always a challenging but thoroughly knowledgeable writer for string instruments, introducing various new effects in his quartets and orchestral works; he also gave unusual attention to the percussion. Equally characteristic is the form of the Music for Strings and its dependence on variation. For instance, the principal idea of the canonic first movement reappears at the climax of the dance-like finale, taken from four solo violas to full, double strings and from unharmonized chromatic darkness into abundant diatonic light (ex. X.3). This same theme also turns up in disguise in the other two movements, an Allegro in sonata form and an Adagio, so that the whole work is bound by similarity of material into a tight slow–fast–slow–fast structure.

That kind of form, alternating slow music with quick rhythmic dancing, is to be found also in String Quartet no. 3. But still more typical of Bartók, as of Berg and Webern, are palindromic structures (see pp. 433, 436). String Quartet no. 4 (1928), for instance, has the pattern Allegro–scherzo–slow movement–scherzo–Allegro. The two outer movements share themes and the two scherzos are distinguished not only by character but also by their unusual sound – the first is muted, the second all plucked. Broadly similar arrangements of movements exist in several other works, where, in the quartet, the large-scale mirroring is reflected in the small-scale thematic detail, so that motifs seem naturally to call forth their inversions. Here one may discern the influence of neo-classicism, which left few composers untouched in the period between the wars. Certainly Bartók was a great admirer of J. S. Bach. However, his speculative approach to basic musical material must have been stimulated too by his work on folksong, by the intensive analysis that made possible the closely reasoned character of his mature compositions.

In addition to his studies as an ethnomusicologist, Bartók worked for much of his professional life as a piano teacher, first at the conservatory in Budapest where he himself had studied. This is one reason why he produced so much educational music, including most importantly the six volumes of *Mikrokosmos* (1926–39), which range from the most elementary exercises to big pieces suitable for concert performance by virtuosos. The latter are also well catered for by Bartók's other piano works, most of which were written for his own recitals and concerto appearances internationally during the 1920s and 30s. Along with Stravinsky – particularly in *The Wedding* – Bartók was one of the great pioneers of the percussive piano, his music suggesting hammered precision rather than a smooth, singing style: after all, the piano was numbered among the percussion in the Music for Strings. This concept of the piano was fully developed by the time of the stamping

---

Listening Note X.D

Bartók: *Concerto for Orchestra* (1943), first movement
3 flutes/piccolo, 3 oboes/english horn, 3 clarinets in B♭/bass clarinet, 3 bassoons
4 horns, 3 trumpets in C, 2 tenor trombones, bass trombone, tuba
timpani, cymbal, harp
1st violins, 2nd violins, violas, cellos, double basses

The movement is in sonata form with a slow introduction.
Introduction (mm. 1–75)   Cellos and double basses in octaves play a pentatonic arch whose intervals are all 4ths and major 2nds (ex. i). This is expanded, and expanded again, but still with the same restriction as to intervals. A solo flute then plays a brief melody before the pentatonic music is developed by the strings with soft trumpet commentary. The opening idea of both flute and trumpet music gives rise to a powerfully orchestrated theme, from beneath which an accompaniment figure in the low strings is gradually speeded up to create the launch for the first subject of the Allegro.
Exposition (mm. 76–230)   The first part of the Allegro introduces three themes, beginning with the one sparked off by the accelerated accompaniment figure: this is sounded by all the violins in unison, and starts out from a modal F minor (ex. ii). Typically, its second element is a varied inversion of its first. The second theme (m. 95) is in longer values, scored for full strings, and grounded in a modal C minor. Finally a trombone (m. 134) announces a theme in C♯ related to the first theme (ex. iii).
At a slower tempo (*Tranquillo*) a solo oboe plays what is effectively the second subject, in B (ex. iv, m. 154). The theme is taken up by other instrumental groups—clarinets, flutes, low strings.
Development (mm. 231–385)   Vigorous development of the first theme, particularly of the scale fragment with which it opens; at m. 272 there is a return to the tempo of the second subject (*Tranquillo*) but for a variant of the first theme as a clarinet melody, taken up by other woodwinds. At m. 313 there is a rushing re-entry of the first theme, but it is stopped by the third, again on solo trombone. This is then played in canon by trumpets and trombones, and after a further eruption of the first theme, the four horns play the third theme in inversion. Trumpets and trombones join in for a further discussion in canon, again brought to a halt by the . . .
Recapitulation (mm. 386–487)   The first theme is only briefly heard; soon (m. 401) we are on to the second subject, in A, at its original *Tranquillo* tempo but now played by solo clarinet. Again the theme is taken up by other woodwinds. Towards the end of the passage it is gradually invaded by the first theme, which brings about an acceleration to its own allegro tempo.
Coda (mm. 488–521)   The first theme (ex. ii) now reappears in a vigorous tutti, and the third is heard from all the brass, in F.

2nd movement (Allegretto scherzando): subtitled "Giuoco delle coppie" ("Game of the couples"), it presents the instruments in pairs.

3rd movement (Andante non troppo): an elegy, using material from the first movement; it is in three episodes, framed by a "misty texture of rudimentary motifs" (Bartok's words).

4th movement (Allegretto): an "interrupted intermezzo" in rondo form.

5th movement (Presto): based on sonata form.

Allegro barbaro (1911), and remains vital in all the later solo works and concertos, as well as in the electric tension of the Sonata for two pianos and percussion (1937).

It will be clear that much of Bartók's music is instrumental. Indeed, after *Bluebeard's Castle* he wrote only a handful of important vocal works, preferring to exercise his methodical technique in genres unencumbered by words. No doubt this was partly a matter of practicality. By the early 1920s, at least, Bartók was a composer of world renown whose works were performed throughout Europe and the USA. He must have been aware that his native language (which is extremely complex in structure) would be an obstacle to the wider appreciation of any vocal works. Nevertheless, his preference seems also to answer deeper needs in Bartók's personality: his secretiveness, his irony, his liking for strict creative rules and his wish to balance interior reflection with vigorous activity, whether in the alternating panels of the Music for Strings or the cycle of String Quartet no. 4. He also found instrumental forms better fitted to his structural thinking; and he preserved harmonic centers with only a hint of traditional tonality. There is a similarity here with the Stravinsky of the 1930s, also a composer mostly of instrumental music.

Like Stravinsky, and like Schoenberg, Bartók left Nazi Europe for the USA, though he waited until October 1940 before he went, with his second wife, Ditta Pásztory (he had divorced his first wife and married another young pupil in 1923). His American years were overshadowed by leukemia and serious financial hardship. The money problem was partly alleviated by a grant from Columbia University enabling him to make a study of a huge archive of Yugoslav folk music lodged there. Despite all the difficulties, though, his American works display a great deal of exuberance and a new simplicity of harmony and construction.

It would be possible to see Bartók's music very crudely as becoming steadily more inward-looking and chromatic, reaching an extreme around the time of String Quartets nos. 3 and 4. Thereafter there is a more diatonic feel and a more relaxed style, this change being marked already by the time of Piano Concerto no. 2. In America this process continued, with a further piano concerto and especially the boisterous Concerto for Orchestra (1943). This work, with its brilliant orchestral style, is another example of mirror symmetry grounded in a structure of five movements (see Listening Note X. D). Bartók died, in a New York hospital, in 1945.

Hindemith

Paul Hindemith, born in 1895, was another of those composers who, like Bartók, viewed Schoenberg's atonality (see p. 429) as a challenge to a new interpretation of tonality. But whereas Bartók found his guidelines in folk music, Hindemith as a German was closer to the central tradition, and tended to look first within that. No other composer of this period, for instance, was so classically neo-classical. After a phase of trying out various styles, including Schoenberg's, he began in 1924 to write music that featured Bach-type counterpoint, Baroque form and that mechanical even-value rhythm that turns up so often when the twentieth century imitates the eighteenth. This is the "motor rhythm", which propels the music along without any clear harmonic progress, and it is very much a feature of Hindemith's quick movements.

Hindemith was an exceedingly productive composer, and every phase of his development is represented by dozens of major works. However, his Bach–

Paul Hindemith   Works
born Hanau, near Frankfurt, 1895; *died* Frankfurt, 1963

Operas Cardillac (1926), Mathis der Maler (Matthias the painter, 1938), Die Harmonie der Welt (1957)

Ballets Hérodiade (1944), The Four Temperaments (1946)

Orchestral music Symphonic Metamorphosis on themes by Weber (1943); symphonies based on his operas; concertos for various instruments

Chamber music Kammermusik 1–7, concertos for different instruments (1922–7); 6 string quartets; sonatas for each orchestral instrument with piano (1936–55)

Piano music 3 sonatas (1936); Ludus tonalis (1942)

Organ music 3 sonatas (1937, 1940)

Vocal music (with instruments) Die junge Magd (The young servant, 1922); Das Marienleben (The life of Mary, 1959)

Choral music   *Songs*

Stravinsky style of neo-classicism is summed up in the series of seven works with the title *Kammermusik* ("chamber music"), most of them concertos for various instruments, and all of them written between 1922 and 1927. These have an unflagging contrapuntal energy and a sheer ebullience in the making of music that point to a connection with the Brandenburg Concertos. Like Bach, too, Hindemith has a feeling for dance rhythms, including the then new rhythms of American jazz. However, where Bach's orchestra was based on the strings, Hindemith follows the contemporary example of Stravinsky and shifts the emphasis to wind and percussion, giving his music a forceful, heavy-footed, modern profile.

Hindemith, who was a viola player of professional standing, was concerned that his music should be useful beyond international festivals or star performances. Ever since the last works of Beethoven there had been an evident gap between the interests of composers and the taste of the general musical public: one effect of Schoenberg's atonality was to bring the rift out into the open. Hindemith suggested that composers ought to write with the non-specialist and the amateur in mind, and he formulated a concept of *Gebrauchsmusik*, or "music for use", with a decisive function (film scores, radio music) or aimed at performance by children or amateurs. In the late 1920s and early 1930s, particularly, he wrote a lot of music of both kinds, but these activities were cut short by the arrival in power of the Nazis. In 1938 he left Berlin, where he was professor of composition at the conservatory, and from 1940 to 1953 he made his home in the USA as a professor at Yale.

The problems faced by a creative artist in an immoral, strife-ridden state are explored in Hindemith's most important work for the theater, his opera *Mathis der Maler* ("Mathias the painter", 1938). The central character is the sixteenth-century painter Mathias Grünewald, who decides that he must forsake his art to engage in political activity on behalf of the German peasants; but he discovers that his greatest need is the exercise of his creative talent, in which may also lie his greatest usefulness to society. The opera is evidently a personal document, and it marks too the start of a period of greater stability. Hindemith's harmony was becoming more smoothly tonal, less bitter and biting, and his ironic use of Baroque forms as framing devices was also giving way to a mellower kind of continuity.

Hindemith's emigration to the USA brought little change in this style, though he did adapt himself to his new environment in his choice of texts for setting. His most important American work was a *Requiem* for the dead of World War II, setting Walt Whitman's elegy on the death of President Lincoln, *When Lilacs Last in the Door-yard Bloom'd*. America also provided the opportunity for several large-scale orchestral works.

Other pieces have an educative, useful purpose. A flute sonata of 1936 eventually became the starting-point for a cycle of sonatas for all the normal orchestral instruments, not omitting such rarities as the english horn or the tuba. Meanwhile the *Ludus tonalis* ("Tonal play") for piano (1942) offered a set of "studies in counterpoint, tonal organization and piano playing", following Bach's *Goldberg Variations* and 48 Preludes and Fugues but exploring Hindemith's own expanded notion of tonality. Like Schoenberg, Hindemith believed that the time had come for all 12 tones of the chromatic scale to be kept in play, but he held to the idea, grounded in natural acoustical phenomena, that a hierarchy existed among the intervals, from the perfect 5th as the least dissonant to the tritone (or augmented 4th) as the most. An awareness of this hierarchy directed his compositional practice from the mid-1930s onwards.

Even though he had become an American citizen in 1946, Hindemith returned to Europe in 1953 and made his home in Switzerland; he died in Germany in 1963. The main work of his last years was a second opera concerned with a visionary from the Renaissance: *Die Harmonie der Welt* ("The harmony of the world", 1957), on the life and beliefs of Johannes Kepler. Here the "studies in tonal organization" have taken on a mystical fervor, and Hindemith seems to hope with his hero that an understanding of natural harmony will unlock the secrets of the universe.

Weill

Both Bartók and Hindemith were concerned with their music as the product of a society. In Bartók's case the concern took the form of a successful effort to create a national style; for Hindemith the need was to make music that would fit modern media or would give people something to play and respond to. For a more radical solution to the problem of artistic communication, however, we must turn to Kurt Weill (1900–50), whose musical background was somewhat similar to Hindemith's. Both men were attracted by the expressionism of Schoenberg's pre-serial atonal works and by corresponding trends in the German theater of the time. Both too were powerfully influenced by neo-classical ideals, Hindemith gaining his from Max Reger (1873–1916) and Stravinsky, Weill his from his teacher Ferruccio Busoni, with whom he studied in Berlin between 1920 and 1923.

The personal and musical connection between Hindemith and Weill was close enough for them to collaborate in 1929 on a setting of *Der Lindberghflug* ("The Lindbergh flight") by the German dramatist Bertolt Brecht (1898–1956). However, where Hindemith seems to have been happiest when engaged in pure music-making, Weill was very much a man of the theater, and he recognized in Brecht one who shared not only his political ideals but also his esthetic. In their joint opera *Rise and Fall of the City of Mahagonny* (1929), they show in exaggerated image the monstrous exploitation of money, power, rank and sex in the real world. Set in a mythical America, the work aspires in part to the style of the American popular song of the period. There is a delicate irony in the use of debased styles to criticize the society depicted. At the same time, Weill's tonal harmony, spiked with dissonances, is a pervading symbol of decadence and corruption.

This style reached its most acute form in the works Weill created with Brecht, but it had been more than foreshadowed in his earlier output and it spills over into compositions that have nothing to do with the dramatist, such as the Second Symphony. In any event, Weill's period of working with Brecht was quite brief. It

Kurt Weill   Works
born Dessau, 1900; *died* New York, 1950

Operas, musicals Mahagonny (1927), The Threepenny Opera (1928), Rise and Fall of the City of Mahagonny (1929), Happy End (1929), Knickerbocker Holiday (1938), Lady in the Dark (1941), Street Scene (1947)
Ballet Seven Deadly Sins (1933)
Orchestral music symphonies – no. 1 (1921), no. 2 (1933)
Choral music Der Lindberghflug (The Lindbergh flight, 1929); cantatas, choral songs
Chamber music String Quartet, op. 8 (1923)
Film and radio scores   *Songs*

began with *Mahagonny* and *The Threepenny Opera* (1928), whose great popular success enabled Weill to give up his occasional critical work and live off his earnings as a composer; it ended five years later with *Seven Deadly Sins*, a song cycle-cum-ballet that was staged for the first time in Paris in June 1933, three months after Weill had left Germany.

In September 1935 Weill moved on to the USA, and spent the rest of his life in New York as a composer for Broadway. On the face of it, this seems a curious fate for the composer of the insidiously ironic *Mahagonny*, but Weill merely shows in extreme form how the activity of an artist is conditioned by the society in which he lives. As a German Jew living under the crumbling Weimar Republic and under the constant threat of Nazism, Weill felt compelled to address himself to the strains in that society. As an American in a time of comparative prosperity and stability under Roosevelt's "New Deal", he was able to be more relaxed, even unashamedly entertaining. Moreover, America had nothing like the rich operatic life of the German cities. If Weill wanted to reach a large audience, as he did, it was the musical that offered him the best chance. Hence the succession of shows he wrote for Broadway, including *Knickerbocker Holiday*, *Lady in the Dark* and *One Touch of Venus*. The style he had once adopted, with a sort of love-hate relationship, as in "Mack the Knife" from *The Threepenny Opera*, now had to become the whole Weill, and the success of such a number as "September Song" is a mark not only of his musical skill but also of his artistic conscience.

Some contemporaries

Bartók, Hindemith and Weill were by no means alone in being influenced by Stravinsky. Indeed, few composers of the twentieth century have escaped being touched by the musician above all who has shown mastery of so many styles.

Orff

One very particular case is that of the German Carl Orff (1895–1981), who lived nearly all his life in Munich, working not only as a composer but also in music education: he pioneered the use of simple percussion instruments in schools to enable children to make music without having much theoretical or technical background. His compositions display a rude simplicity derived from the exultant choral chanting of Stravinsky's *The Wedding*. He took this style to one logical conclusion in the pounding, *ostinato*-based rhythms of his *Carmina burana* (1936), a dramatic cantata on low medieval verse.

Poulenc

Naturally Stravinsky was even more readily absorbed in Paris than in Munich. Among French contemporaries none followed him so completely or so profitably as Francis Poulenc (1899–1963). Poulenc's early works, such as his Sonata for two clarinets, are very Stravinskyan and the relationship is close even in such mature, large-scale pieces as *Dialogues des Carmelites* (1956), an opera which sympathetically treats the reactions to the persecution and impending death of the members of a Carmelite convent. However, Poulenc's is a softer, sweeter art than Stravinsky's. His harmony is more comfortably diatonic and the whole flow of his music is gentler.

Les Six, Satie

Poulenc and five of his contemporaries were known as Les Six: the others were Arthur Honegger (1892–1955), Darius Milhaud (1892–1974), Georges Auric (1899–1983), Germaine Tailleferre (1892–1983) and Louis Durey (1888–1979). Of these, Honegger was one of the outstanding symphonists of the interwar years while Milhaud became one of the most prolific composers of the century. Their model was in a sense the French composer Erik Satie (1866–1925), who wrote light-hearted, intentionally inconsequential music that possesses a certain charm.

Falla

The musical influence of Paris, dominated first by Debussy and then by Stravinsky, seems to have been almost inescapable for composers in the first four decades of the century. Certainly Paris enlarged the outlook of the century's leading Spanish composer, Manuel de Falla (1876–1946). Before he went to Paris, in 1907, he had achieved little: his hot-blooded, intensely Spanish opera *La vida breve* ("Life is short") had been composed but not performed. Paris came as a liberation, giving him the means and the encouragement for a small but steady output of works all markedly Spanish in subject and style. Like Bartók, Falla believed that his country needed a music based on its rich folk heritage, and, again like Bartók, he found the task of creating such a music facilitated by Debussy and Stravinsky.

Falla returned to Spain on the outbreak of World War I and composed a second opera, *El amor brujo* ("Love the Magician"), rooted in the primitive, highly charged music of southern Spain. Then came a ballet, *The Three-Cornered Hat*, which was another Diaghilev production and which made Falla's name. More than the operas, it conveys in its big dance numbers the excitement, vigor and brilliance associated with Spanish music. The influence of Debussy's orchestration is now strikingly joined by that of Stravinsky's. This was, however, more an end than a beginning. Settled in Granada, Falla began to dissociate himself from the public splendor of his earlier scores and to prefer much leaner forces, as well as a more severe harmonic style. Always a slow composer, he spent his last 20 years on a huge cantata, *Atlántida*, a mystical history of the Hispanic world. It remained unfinished when in 1946 he died, in Argentina, where he had taken refuge in 1939 at the end of the Spanish Civil War.

America: the "ultra-moderns"

A remarkable number of great composers from Europe were driven by Nazism and war to seek a better life in the Americas – Schoenberg, Stravinsky, Bartók, Hindemith, Weill and Falla among them. Their presence did much to stimulate the development of music in the New World: Schoenberg and Hindemith were both teachers, and apart from anything else, the presence of such names, like the earlier presence of Dvořák (see pp. 383–5), was a boost to the morale of American composers. However, American music was in fact quite strong enough to take care of itself: decades before it had produced its first genius in Charles Ives (1874–1954).

Ives

A close contemporary of Schoenberg in his musical character, Charles Ives also owed much to his upbringing. His father, George Ives, had been a young bandmaster in the Civil War. Living in the small Connecticut town of Danbury, he was a musician of extraordinary open-mindedness who encouraged his son to sing in a key different from that of the accompaniment, and in other ways to take nothing for granted. This urge to experiment was eagerly pursued by the young Ives in a group of psalm settings he composed around the age of 20, some of them in several keys at the same time or vaguely dissonant. However, Ives also had the benefit of a more normal musical education at Yale, where he was a pupil of

Charles Ives   Works
born Danbury, Connecticut, 1874; *died* New York, 1954

Orchestral music symphonies – no. 1 (1898), no. 2 (1902), no. 3 (1904), no. 4 (1916); First Orchestral Set (Three Places in New England) (1914); Second Orchestral Set (1915); The Unanswered Question (1906); Central Park in the Dark (1906); Emerson Overture (1907); Washington's Birthday (1909); Robert Browning Overture (1912); Decoration Day (1912); The Fourth of July (1913)

Choral music Psalm 67 (?1894); The Celestial Country (1899)

Chamber music From the Steeples and the Mountains (1902); string quartets – no. 1 (1896), no. 2 (1913); violin sonatas – no. 1 (1908), no. 2 (1910), no. 3 (1914), no. 4 (1916)

Piano music sonatas – no. 1 (1909), no. 2, "Concord" (1915); Studies (1908)

Organ music Variations on "America" (?1891)

Songs The Circus Band (?1894); General William Booth Enters into Heaven (1914); c180 others

Horatio Parker (1863–1919), one of a group of gifted but quite unadventurous composers in New England at the time. The result of this was a creative splitting. While at Yale, between 1894 and 1898, he continued his experiments, but he also composed works and studies of a more conventional kind, such as his First Symphony (1898). This was in no way unfortunate. Academic training gave Ives the technique to improve and enlarge his experiments, and the orthodox background – especially in the later symphonies, quartets and sonatas – provides a frame against which his departures can seem all the more extraordinary.

On leaving Yale, Ives went into the insurance business. Most American composers at this point would have gone to Europe for further training, but Ives felt no such need. Equally he would probably have found it too limiting to take up either of the two professional courses open to a composer: teaching or serving as a church musician. Insurance gave him the livelihood which made it possible for him to compose in his spare time, and he had also a firm belief in the moral virtue of insurance as the way for a man to safeguard his and his family's future. Certainly, together with his business partner Julian Myrick, he prospered, and his music silently prospered with him. Most of his output dates from the two decades up to 1918, when he suffered a heart attack, but almost nothing of it was known outside a small circle of musicians whom Ives invited occasionally to play pieces through.

Ives's achievements, though, were immense. At the center stands a body of around 150 songs, ranging from gentle hymn-like pieces (*At the River*) to robust philosophical meditations (*Paracelsus*), from student imitations of German *lieder* (*Feldeinsamkeit*) to exuberant pictures of an America that had disappeared with Ives's boyhood (*The Circus Band*). In responding to a text, he was able and willing to use any materials that seemed suitable, and his enthusiastic identification with such a great range of poems was responsible for the vast range of his musical technique. The more nostalgic pieces may be filled with quotations from hymns, parlor songs, marches and dances, whereas the more strenuous mental exertions tend naturally to go with dissonant chords and complex rhythms that are awkward and difficult to grasp. These sometimes suggest the atonal Schoenberg, though Ives worked in ignorance of what was happening in Europe during the years of his most hectic compositional activity.

Because he was not building up a professional body of work, he had the freedom to make different versions of the same piece, often for very different forces. This sprang in part from his conviction that what mattered in music was, to use his own terminology, the "substance" and not the "manner". He could even be impatient of the physical practicalities of music-making: "Why can't music go out in the same way it comes into a man", he wrote, "without having to crawl over a fence of sounds, thoraxes, catguts, wire, wood and brass? . . . Is it the composer's fault that man has only ten fingers?" For him, therefore, there was an ideal beyond the notation (again there is a connection with Schoenberg): hence his continued revision of his scores, and his readjustment of them from one medium to another.

A key work, typical in its marriage of personal vision and national destiny, is the set *Three Places in New England*. The first is a slow march, generously filled with quotations to capture the impressions made by a monument to a black regiment in the Civil War. Then comes "Putnam's Camp", a graphic musical scene that presents a boy hearing jolly, brassy marches on a Fourth of July outing, then going off by himself and having a vision of ghostly soldiers from the time of the Revolutionary War (see Listening Note X. E). The finale is a slow tone-poem in

---

Listening Note X.E

Ives: *Three Places in New England* (1914, rev. 1929), no. 2 "Putnam's Camp"
Flute/piccolo, oboe/english horn, clarinet, bassoon
2 or more horns, 2 or more trumpets, 2 trombones, tuba
piano, timpani, drums, cymbals
1st violins, 2nd violins, violas, cellos, double bass

The original scoring, reconstructed by James B. Sinclair in his edition of 1976, was for a rather larger orchestra.

mm.

1–63	Ives's own program note provides the information that the piece is an impression of a Fourth of July picnic at the place near Redding Center, Connecticut, where General Israel Putnam had his winter quarters in 1778–9. A full orchestral flourish in quick-step time prepares the way for a dance tune played by strings and horns (ex. i). Other tunes are superimposed on this, until there are as many as five metrically independent lines being played at once (m. 27). Gradually the complexity abates, and instrumental groups drop out until just the double bass is left on a low E: a boy has wandered away from the festivities.
64–88	He sees a tall woman who reminds him of the Goddess of Liberty (m. 64: sustained 9-note chord in strings and piano). She is pleading with some soldiers that they should not abandon their cause (ex. ii), but they start to march out of camp to a popular tune of the day, *The British Grenadiers* (ex. iii).
89–114	A stirring call on the brass (ex. iv) announces the arrival of Putnam, and the soldiers turn back: there is a vigorous collage of march tunes, including most notably *The British Grenadiers* again.
114–63	The boy suddenly wakes from his dream: the marches stop in the middle of a fully orchestrated fortissimo, and are replaced by one of the earlier dance tunes softly played by the strings. Again more tunes are superimposed, until by m. 126 the music has returned to a similar complexity to that of m. 27. But this time *The British Grenadiers* enters the mixture as well (m. 133). The confusion is broken briefly by an episode for brass and drums (mm. 141–3), but then continues as before. Finally, starting at m. 157, the rhythms are flattened to produce streams of dense chords going simultaneously in even 8ths, 16ths and dotted triplet 8ths. The movement ends with a loud 8-note chord spread across the orchestra.

Within the *Three Places* as a whole, "Putnam's Camp" is a scherzo between two slow movements. The first of these is "The 'St Gaudens' in Boston Common (Col. Shaw and his Colored Regiment)", which contemplates a memorial to heroes of the Revolution, and the finale is a more autobiographical piece, "The Housatonic at Stockbridge", in which Ives recalled a walk by the riverside with his wife.

which Ives remembers a walk he had with his wife along a river bank, the music rippling statically around a steadily moving melody in the middle of the texture.

Many of Ives's other orchestral works, especially those for small ensembles, are similarly memories of place and time: *Central Park in the Dark*, with the darkness presented in the atonal strings which circle unperturbed while the other instruments enter in mounting clamor, or *All the way around and back*, a musical skit on a baseball maneuver. However, there are also the symphonies, in which illustration plays only a secondary role. The first two, by Ives's standards, are mild and more than somewhat academic, but the third is more individual.

The fourth symphony is one of his greatest and most demanding works. It is also one of his most all-embracing. The third movement is a moderately well-behaved fugue that had been composed originally to open a string quartet and that functions here as a resting-place between much more ambitious movements. The second movement is the most complex of those jumbles of quotations that represent Ives in most vital spirits. "Putnam's Camp" from the *Three Places* and "The Fourth of July" from the *Holidays* symphony are other examples, though in the Fourth Symphony the raucous enjoyment of these pieces is rather modified by the density of marches, hymns and dances woven together. Instead of depicting a particular moment, as "Putnam's Camp" and "The Fourth of July" seem to, this second movement of the symphony is a vast panorama of mundane existence. If we accept Ives's own suggestion that the symphony is asking the reason for human existence, then its second movement might well give as its answer earthly pleasure, whereas the third, the academic fugue, responds only with formal correctness. The finale then returns to the slower, quieter, more distanced manner of the brief and preludial first movement. But where that opening had appeared to ask the questions, with its hymn fragments (the symphony requires a chorus as well as a huge orchestra), the finale is a departure into higher realms of transcendent vision, with muted percussion and far-off voices. A similar sort of music, though necessarily on a smaller scale, had ended Ives's String Quartet no. 2, and is present in other works where contemplation comes at the end of strenuous questioning or in answer to abundantly physical music with quotations strewn throughout.

Another, more condensed product of the philosophical Ives is the orchestral piece *The Unanswered Question*, where, as the title indicates, there is no meditative finale to complete the catechism. Instead, the "question" is posed several times by a solo trumpet, while offstage strings proceed through slow-motion diatonic chords, as if ignorant that any question is being asked (or perhaps not understanding that there is any need to answer), and a quartet of flutes rushes about in vain panic (ex. X. 4).

ex. X.4

Composed in 1906, this work antedates Schoenberg's first properly atonal compositions. It provides just one extraordinary instance of Ives's prefiguring of many of the techniques and interests that have guided the course of music in this century. For the trumpet solo is in pointed contradiction to the blissfully harmonized strings, not only in its atonality but also in its independence from the governing meter. The flute music too has nothing to do with any key, and though one may detect motivic links with the trumpet – compare the first flute chord with the last four notes of the "question" – the impression is that the woodwinds are avoiding the issues so austerely proposed by the trumpeter.

Ives's position as a precursor, as has already been suggested, is borne out by many other features. His use of recognizable scraps of musical quotations – to be found in most of his larger orchestral, chamber and piano pieces at some point – looks forward as far as Stockhausen and Berio (see pp. 491, 496) in the 1960s. He experimented too with tuning a piano in quarter-tones, with the close calculation of pitch, interval and rhythm structures (*Tone Roads* nos. 1 and 3, 1911 and 1915) and with many devices in his songs. He seems to have felt that his musical "substance" should not be compromised by convention or technique. If a piano sonata demanded impossible spreads and the introduction of subsidiary instruments (like a flute in the finale), then so it must be: hence the colossal breadth and difficulty of his Second Sonata, sub-titled "Concord" and picturing the personalities of four writers associated with that Massachusetts town. First comes Ralph Waldo Emerson, the far-seeing thinker, then Nathaniel Hawthorne, in a stream of activity taken up again in the third movement of the Fourth Symphony. The Alcotts provide a slow movement of domestic tranquillity, and finally there is Henry Thoreau, the plain man's seer.

The "Concord" Sonata had a prominent place in the belated discovery of Ives and his music. In 1920 Ives published it, privately, and in 1922 followed it with a volume of 114 songs: in both cases he sent his music off to anyone who might be interested, and asked for no financial recompense. It was only very gradually that performances began to take place, and not until the 1940s did Ives begin to be recognized as the first great American composer, the man who, in the great mix of styles and materials he cultivated, created musical images that could have come only from America. By then, though, he had long stopped composing: his poor health caused him to abandon composition in 1926 and insurance in 1930, even if he continued to dream of a *Universe Symphony* which would have been a still more comprehensive undertaking than any he achieved.

Cowell

Ives is the model of the truly American composer: unfettered by European norms, ready to go his own way, unashamed of the incongruous. The music of Henry Cowell (1897–1965) is, in these broad ways, similar. Like Ives, Cowell was an experimenter from his boyhood. A Californian, he gave his first piano recital just before his 14th birthday, by which time he had already worked with "clusters" of adjacent notes in the bass to be played with the flat of the hand or the whole forearm. Later he introduced the idea of playing directly on the strings of the piano, wrote much for percussion in unusual combinations with other instruments, and developed techniques for creating atonal melodies and then providing rhythmic structures on the same mathematical basis. All these methods, and others, were discussed in his influential book *New Musical Resources* (1930).

Henry Cowell   Works
born Menlo Park, California, 1897; *died* Shady, New York, 1965

Orchestral music 21 symphonies; Ensemble (1925); Synchrony (1930); Rhythmicana (1931); Schoonthree (1939); Hymn and Fuguing Tune (1943–63); Piano Concerto (1929); Percussion Concerto (1959)

Instrumental music string quartets – no. 1, "Pedantic" (1916), no. 2 (1934), no. 3, "Mosaic" (1935), no. 4 "United" (1936), no. 5 (1956); Ensemble for five strings (1924); Ostinato pianissimo for four percussionists (1934); Hymns and Fuguing Tunes; wind ensemble pieces

Piano music Aeolian Harp (1923); Amarind Suite (1939); educational pieces

Partsongs   *Songs*

Cowell's later work tended to be less adventurous, except in geographical terms. He wrote what is probably the first example of an "aleatory" composition – one with chance elements – in his *Mosaic Quartet* for strings (1935), to be played "alternating the movements at the desire of the performers, treating each movement as a unit to build the mosaic pattern of the form". More typical of his later concerns, however, is his next string quartet, the *United Quartet* (1936), in which he sought to bring about a junction of different musical cultures: the high European in the choice of genre, various kinds of folk music in the modalities and drones of the material. Near the end of his life he looked back on American traditions in his set of 18 works with the title *Hymn and Fuguing Tune*, conceived for a variety of instrumental groups.

Besides composing a great deal of music, Cowell was active as a teacher and promoter of other composers. In 1927 he launched the New Music Edition, publishing challenging new works on a subscription basis and bringing to public attention the music of Ives, Carl Ruggles (1876–1971) and Edgard Varèse among American contemporaries.

Varèse

Varèse (1883–1965) should be considered an American composer, because although he was born in Burgundy, France, and spent the first 32 years of his life in Europe, almost all his surviving music dates from after his emigration to New York in 1915. His earlier works, including an opera to a text by Strauss's librettist, Hugo von Hofmannsthal, and several big orchestral scores, were lost or destroyed, with the exception of a solitary song. Varèse was therefore born as a composer with his first American work, significantly entitled *Amériques* (1921), scored for an enormous orchestra and "symbolic of new discoveries – new worlds on earth, in the sky, or in the minds of men". The work is not without its memories of the old world: having spent some time in Berlin as well as Paris, Varèse was familiar with the atonal Schoenberg as much as with Debussy and Stravinsky. However, the importance of the percussion ensemble is something quite new, as is the rhythmic complexity of this many-stranded percussion music.

Amériques shows too Varèse's prodigious orchestral imagination. Ideas are not passed from one group of instruments to another: instead they are as if welded to a particular type of sound, and if there is a change in the sonority then there has to be a change of idea. Those changes come, too, with characteristic brusqueness and violence. Like Stravinsky in *The Rite of Spring*, Varèse aims towards a chopped form of distinct blocks in sequence; but where Stravinsky's blocks usually have pulse preserved from one to the next, Varèse's music very often gains power from the brutal interruption of one kind of music by another. In the most characteristic

---

Edgard Varèse   Works
born Paris, 1883; *died* New York, 1965

Orchestral music Amériques (1921); Hyperprism (1923); Octandre (1923); Intégrales (1925); Arcana (1927); Ionisation (1931); Déserts (1954)
Vocal music (with orchestra) Ecuatorial (1934); Nocturnal (1961)
Instrumental music Density 21.5 for flute (1936)
Electronic music Poème électronique (1958)

moments of *Amériques* this conveys the impression of the composer working directly with his raw material of sound, and it is not surprising that even at this early date Varèse was thinking of new instruments adequate to his new kind of music.

The most compact of Varèse's works from the 1920s is *Hyperprism* (1923), scored for flute, clarinet, seven brass and seven percussion players – all the percussionists using untuned instruments except for the indefinitely pitched siren. The avoidance of strings is typical: Varèse distrusted expressive nuances and liked the intensity that high woodwind and brass instruments could give him. They could also be used more effectively in simultaneous events that present themselves less as "chords" than as sounds in the raw. As for the percussion, they provide the framework of intricate rhythmic activity, with up to four independent parts, against which the wind sounds are heard (ex. X. 5). The searing high dissonance here is characteristic; so too is the conflict between this and the snarl in the bass trombone, and the complementing of static pitch with jostling rhythmic movement. Also to be noted is the progress achieved not by harmonic change but by the rude collision of sounds: the trombone's *fortissimo* seems to cause the disruption of the woodwind into shrill insistence.

134 Cartoon recording impressions of Varèse's *Hyperprism* after the first performance at the Klaw Theater, New York, on 4 March 1923.

ex. X.5

The fierce energy of *Hyperprism* went out of Varèse's music when he returned to Paris in 1928 and stayed there for five years. During this period his interest in percussion received maximum expression in *Ionisation* (1931), one of the first Western works for percussion orchestra. Typically the music is concerned above all with intricate rhythmic polyphony, pitched sounds entering only at the work's final plateau. In Paris, too, Varèse made the acquaintance of inventors who were developing electronic instruments, and he used two of these in his *Ecuatorial* (1934), setting a Maya incantation for bass voice or voices, brass, piano, organ, theremins (or ondes martenot) – these were newly invented electronic instruments – and percussion. However, the theremin and the ondes martenot were limited achievements by the standards of the technological breakthrough Varèse was looking for: they merely added new colors to the orchestra and extended the dependable reach into the high treble. In 1936 Varèse wrote a flute solo, *Density 21.5* (so called because it was written for a flute made of platinum, which has that density), but after that he composed almost nothing for more than a decade.

What reawakened Varèse's creativity was the arrival of the tape recorder. Earlier he had experimented with altering sounds recorded on disc by playing them backwards or at different speeds, but the tape recorder at once made such techniques simple, for tape could be cut up and edited into musical compositions. Using this procedure, he composed *Déserts* (1954), where three "windows" of electronic music are let into a score for wind, piano and percussion. Given his earlier optimism about electronic music, however, the expressive effect of the juxtaposition is curious. The title for him meant "not only physical deserts of sand, sea, mountains and snow, outer space, deserted city streets ... but also this distant inner space ... where man is alone in a world of mystery and essential solitude". Correspondingly, the outlook from the electronic windows is bleak, the orchestral music being much more subtle in form and sonority. Even so, Varèse did go on to create one of the few masterpieces of music on tape, his *Poème électronique* (1958), before finally returning to live media for various projects on the subject of night, none of them completed.

The American mainstream

Various as they may be, Ives, Cowell and Varèse all represent the strand of what was called "ultra-modern" music in the USA between the wars. But there was much else to be heard. This was, for instance, a golden age for popular song and musical comedy in New York: certainly to Weill, as we saw (p. 456), this seemed the most vital feature of the American musical scene. This repertory is discussed in a broader context in the next chapter – including the music of its greatest exponent, George Gershwin.

Copland

If the divide between popular and art music is not fully bridged in Gershwin's works, it is at least crossed in the music of Aaron Copland (b. 1900). Born, like Gershwin, in Brooklyn, Copland came from a more prosperous family and had the benefit of formal musical training from early boyhood. At the age of 20 he went to Paris, where he was a pupil of Nadia Boulanger for four years – one of the first disciples of a famous French teacher who was to instill her precepts of clarity and complete technical command into many more American composers, from Walter Piston to Philip Glass. In 1924 he returned to New York and formed the intention of becoming a specifically American composer. From jazz he borrowed syncopated rhythms and certain harmonic peculiarities in his Piano Concerto (1926), so approaching Gershwin's efforts of the same period from the opposite standpoint. He also set the words of various American poets in small choral pieces and songs.

At the same time, like Cowell and Varèse, Copland was active in support of his fellow composers, and joined with Roger Sessions in sponsoring a series of concerts of new music in New York between 1928 and 1931. He also took a serious interest

Aaron Copland   Works
born Brooklyn, 1900

Ballets Billy the Kid (1938); Rodeo (1942); Appalachian Spring (1944)

Operas The Tender Land (1955)

Orchestral music symphonies – no. 1 (1928), no. 2 (1933), no. 3 (1946); El salón México (1936); Lincoln Portrait (1942); Fanfare for the Common Man (1942); Orchestral Variations (1957); Music for a Great City (1964); Inscape (1967); 3 Latin American Sketches (1972); Piano Concerto (1926); Clarinet Concerto (1948)

Chamber music Vitebsk, Study on a Jewish Theme (1928); Violin Sonata (1943); Piano Quartet (1950); Nonet for strings (1960); Threnody I: Igor Stravinsky, in memoriam (1971)

Piano music Variations (1930); Sonata (1941); Fantasy (1957); Night Thoughts (1972)

Songs 12 Poems of Emily Dickinson (1950)

Choral music   *Film scores*

in the development of music within the southern neighbors of the USA, and it was a visit to a nightclub in Mexico City that gave him the stimulus for his first essay in light music, *El Salón México* (1936), catching the exuberance of the dance music he heard there.

The opportunity soon came for a similar hybrid of popular material and serious setting on an American theme in the ballet *Billy the Kid*. This was followed by another, rowdy cowboy ballet, *Rodeo*, and then by a treatment of the theme of

135 Aaron Copland (right) with Elliott Carter: photograph. Coll. G. D. Hackett, New York.

Stravinsky's *Wedding* in pioneer New England: *Appalachian Spring* (1944). In all these works the basic material is much as it is in Ives: folksong, traditional dance and hymn, joined by modern notions of rhythm, harmony and orchestration. The difference is that Copland, welding all these together, created a musical style in which he could move freely from quotation into original music and back again. This happens particularly in *Appalachian Spring*, where the Shaker hymn "The Gift to be Simple" provides the music with something like an underlying mode from which much of its substance derives. Indeed, *Appalachian Spring* is much the most sophisticated of the three ballets. Where *Billy the Kid* and *Rodeo* are both boldly scored for full orchestra and divided into separate episodes, *Appalachian Spring* is more continuous in its flow and unfolds as chamber music within a group of just 13 players, though its success led Copland to make it available for orchestral performance.

Its success also led him to contemplate more ambitious works in the same style, notably his Third Symphony (1946). No doubt this was encouraged too by the recent example of Stravinsky's Symphony in C, for the neo-classical Stravinsky had been a central influence on Copland since his time with Boulanger. Copland's rhythm is more deeply ingrained than Stravinsky's, not seeming to dance in sprightly fashion on the surface of his music. But his energy is similarly owed to interruptions and displacements of a marked meter: both composers, of course, had learned from jazz. In his orchestral sonorities, too, Copland is closer to Stravinsky than to any other contemporary. Simple chords – most effectively in *Appalachian Spring* – can be completely refashioned by unusual wide spacing and luminous orchestration, so that even a major triad becomes something new, belonging only to the sound-world of this work.

One aspect in which Copland went beyond Stravinsky was in the range of levels at which he composed, especially in the late 1930s and 1940s, immediately after the release of *El Salón México*. The *Lincoln Portrait* for speaker and orchestra and the *Fanfare for the Common Man* (both 1942) represent the public composer, addressing the nation at a time of crisis and using a language that presents no difficulties, even though it is definitely his own. At the other extreme are the more searching and rarefied chamber and instrumental pieces. Right at the end of this period came two sets of utterly simple arrangements of Old American Songs (1952) and the exploratory Piano Quartet (1950) in which Copland, like Stravinsky at this time, began to test the waters of serialism. This was not an entirely unexpected departure, for as far back as 1930 Copland had used a seven-tone motif in quasi-serial manner. With the greater importance of serialism in his music came a decline in his use of the popular style of the ballets and film scores. Copland also became much less prolific and after *Inscape* for orchestra (1967) he composed little. Like Stravinsky, he used serialism not as a leveling-out but rather as a technique for deriving clear-cut ideas and patterns that can move, change and reassemble as purposefully as before.

Carter

The outstanding characteristic of American music is, as we have seen, its diversity. But there are rare composers who draw from that diversity to build up their own style, and one such, the most notable, is Elliott Carter (b. 1908). Like Ives, with whom he was in contact from his schooldays onwards, he developed a firm independence and a willingness to use highly complex ideas. Like Copland, he was greatly impressed by the neo-classical Stravinsky. Like Copland too, he was greatly concerned in his youth with creating a specifically American music. As it happened,

Elliott Carter   Works
born New York, 1908

Ballets Pocahontas (1939); The Minotaur (1947)

Orchestral music Symphony no. 1 (1942); Holiday Overture (1944); Variations (1955); Concerto for Orchestra (1969); A Symphony of Three Orchestras (1977); Double Concerto for harpsichord and piano (1961); Piano Concerto (1965)

Chamber music string quartets – no. 1 (1951), no. 2 (1959), no. 3 (1971); Elegy for viola or cello and piano (1943, later orchestrated); Wind Quintet (1948); Brass Quintet (1974); Cello Sonata (1948)

Piano music Sonata (1946)

Vocal music (with ensemble) A Mirror on which to Dwell (1975); Syringa (1978)

Songs   *Choral music*

Copland-like folklorism was to be replaced in Carter's music by a much more individual style, though one no less American in its essential difference from the European tradition: its openness, its freedom from preconceptions.

Carter studied at Harvard and then followed the trail blazed by Copland to Paris and Nadia Boulanger, whose pupil he was from 1932 to 1935. He returned to the USA as musical director for a dance company. In 1950 he set off for Arizona to compose in relative isolation, determined to strike his own path and not be troubled by the needs and tastes of potential audiences. The result was a 40-minute string quartet (1951) whose powerful newness is only partly indicated in the Piano Sonata and Cello Sonata that had previously been Carter's most strenuous works. However, in satisfying himself, he turned out to be creating music that also spoke broadly, if in a difficult style, and the quartet was soon recognized as a major achievement.

It is a work with bigness written into it. During its course it seems to run through every possibility of textural arrangement provided by the four instruments: it begins with an unaccompanied cello solo that is completed only at the very end by the first violin alone, and includes in between everything from unadorned 5ths to the extreme separation (in the slow movement) of high, becalmed, muted violins from the effortful recitative of the lower instruments (ex. X. 6).

The vertical complexity seen here has its natural horizontal expression in fluidity of rhythm and form. Carter had introduced in his Piano Sonata the technique of "metrical modulation", by which meter is changed while the pulse remains the same, and in the quartet this becomes an almost constant feature, so that the time-signature never stays unchanged for more than a few measures. On the level of form, Carter makes an elementary but subtle and far-reaching discovery in realizing that a "movement" need not be the same thing as a chunk of music separated in time. His First Quartet is divided by double bars into three sections – I Fantasia, II (untitled) and III Variations – but the division into movements is different. The Fantasia consists of the cadenza introduction, a combative Allegro and the beginnings of the scherzo. This is then continued in the second marked section, which also includes a slow movement and the start of the final Variations – these creating change in so fantastic a way that they have begun before their nominal beginning.

Carter pursued this quicksilver variation technique in his next major work, the

ex. X.6

Variations for orchestra; indeed, much in his subsequent music has its roots in the First Quartet. The idea of bringing together different movement types is carried much further in, for instance, the Symphony of Three Orchestras (1977), where the separate ensembles converge and diverge in a kaleidoscope of 12 movements arranged within a single span. The rhythmic and textural intricacies – also the variety of the ideas and their sheer energy – are present in all Carter's later works. Not for nothing did Stravinsky single out his Double Concerto for harpsichord and piano, each with its own group of instruments (1961), as perhaps the finest musical achievement to date by any American.

Bernstein

If Carter belongs to the intellectual wing of American composition, one who embraces a multiplicity of traditions is Leonard Bernstein (b. 1918). His music looks to the twentieth-century symphonic tradition of Mahler and Shostakovich, to American jazz, to Jewish sacred music, to the rhythmic verve and clear scoring of Copland and Stravinsky, to the snappy melody of the Broadway musical. Usually these various strands are moderated according to the nature of the work, and Bernstein has shown an unusual ability to compose in quite different genres almost at the same time. Moreover, he has combined his career as a composer with that of one of the outstanding conductors of his generation, though most of his works date from before or after the period of his musical directorship of the New York Philharmonic (1958–68), and he has also been uniquely distinguished as a popularizer of music through his brilliant television programs.

The earlier group includes two symphonies, sub-titled *Jeremiah* (1943) and *The Age of Anxiety* (1949). The latter has a solo piano and a program derived from Auden's long poem: it was the first evidence of Bernstein's willingness, like Copland, to address the great issues of the day, in this case the conflicts and tensions of the cold war (also reflected, incidentally, in Menotti's *The Consul*). Both these symphonies are in the Mahler–Berg–Shostakovich line of Bernstein's music; his Broadway style is more in evidence in the ballet *Fancy Free*, in the musical *On the Town*, and most successfully of all in the musical *West Side Story* (1957), an updating of the story of Romeo and Juliet where the warring families become rival gangs in

Leonard Bernstein   Works
born Lawrence, Massachusetts, 1918

Stage music On the Town (1944), Candide (1956), West Side Story (1957), Mass (1971)

Ballet Fancy Free (1944)

Orchestral music The Age of Anxiety [Symphony no. 2] (1949); On the Waterfront (1955)

Choral music Jeremiah Symphony [no. 1] (1943); Symphony no. 3, "Kaddish" (1963); Chichester Psalms (1965)

Piano music Seven Anniversaries (1943); Four Anniversaries (1948)

Chamber music Clarinet Sonata (1942)

Songs

New York. With its strong plot, its hit tunes and its big dance numbers, *West Side Story* has all the ingredients needed for the genre. It has taken its place among the classics of the American musical, while the brilliant overture to another stage work of this period, the operetta *Candide*, immediately gained a place in the repertory.

Bernstein's more serious works of the 1950s and 60s are broadly of two kinds, reflective and declamatory. The *Chichester Psalms* are melodious settings in Hebrew for choir and orchestra. Another Hebrew work, the *Kaddish* Symphony, his third (1963), belongs however stylistically and expressively with its two predecessors, though benefiting from the heightened grasp of different idioms that Bernstein had now achieved.

His *Mass* (1971) is a much more startling mix of styles. Using the words of the Roman Catholic Mass and enacting the ritual on stage, Bernstein attempts to explore the meaning of the ceremony for a contemporary audience: this brings the world of the *Chichester Psalms* into contact with that of *West Side Story*. In later works, however, Bernstein has been more selective in his style and has chosen to compose only to mark special occasions: his *Songfest*, for example, is an anthology of American poetry set to celebrate the Bicentennial.

Menotti

Perhaps the most successful opera composer working in America is Gian Carlo Menotti (b. 1911), an Italian who arrived in the country as a teenager and found his new environment a source of color and spice to reinvigorate the tradition of Puccini. His most successful works date from the immediate postwar years and

Gian Carlo Menotti   Works
born Cadegliano, 1911

Operas Amelia goes to the Ball (1937), The Medium (1946), The Telephone (1947), The Consul (1950), Amahl and the Night Visitors (1951), The Saint of Bleecker Street (1954), Maria Golovin (1958), Help, Help, the Globolinks! (1968), The Most Important Man (1971)

Choral music The Death of the Bishop of Brindisi (1963); cantatas

Orchestral music concertos

Songs   *Chamber music*

include *The Consul* (1950) and the children's opera *Amahl and the Night Visitors* (1951); the former is representative of his bold melodrama, the latter of his tunefulness. Menotti has also been active as a festival administrator (Festival of Two Worlds at Spoleto, Italy, and Spoleto, Charleston, South Carolina), opera producer and librettist for other composers: he wrote *Vanessa* (1957–8) for Samuel Barber (1910–81), a fellow conservative. Barber's roots are in the late Romantic symphonism of Strauss, Mahler and Elgar rather than the *verismo* of Puccini; correspondingly, his finest works are not his operas but his orchestral works and songs, and his best-known piece is his *Adagio* for strings.

Latin America

The fact that Copland should have found his way in Latin America, with *El Salón México*, is not insignificant, for just as the USA was experiencing a musical rebirth in the years between the wars, so too were its neighbors. One of the first Latin American composers to make a mark was the Brazilian Heitor Villa-Lobos (1887–1959), who seems to have had little formal education but produced a huge quantity of music: over 3000 works, it is said. He is best known for his *Bachianas brasileiras* (1944), a series of nine pieces for various combinations, all of them dreaming of Bach from within an easy-going style rooted in Brazilian folk music.

Villa-Lobos

Ginastera

The Argentinian Alberto Ginastera (1916–84) has been a powerful musical force in the area, through his own works and his teaching in his native Buenos Aires. In his earlier years he emulated Bartók and tried in the same way to build a complete, versatile musical language out of folk music. He reached, however, beyond local dance styles to a fervent expressiveness that is the most deeply Latin characteristic of his music. In the 1950s he began to apply serial methods and the new orchestral usages appearing in the works of younger men. The resulting operas (notably *Bomarzo*, 1967) have an abundance of extreme sexual passion, depicted vigorously in a style that uses modern techniques within a dramatic background inherited from Verdi.

Britain and the Soviet Union

If America's position to the far west of the European musical centers has tended to make her composers more adventurous, then Britain and Russia, on the fringes of Europe, have traditionally been musically rather conservative and mistrustful of home-grown originality. Hence, to some degree, the continuation in those countries of genres widely considered obsolete around the middle of the twentieth century: opera (Britten, Tippett, Prokofiev) and symphony (Shostakovich, Prokofiev, Tippett).

Vaughan Williams

The rebirth of English music at the very end of the nineteenth century provided encouragement for such young composers as Ralph Vaughan Williams (1872–1958), Gustav Holst (1874–1934) and Frederick Delius (1862–1934), who together dominated English music between the wars and, in Vaughan Williams's case, long after. Vaughan Williams's influence was also the deeper because he put forward a general approach, whereas Holst and Delius were musical loners. That approach was the absorption of English folksong, which he began to collect at the

Ralph Vaughan Williams

born Down Ampney, Gloucestershire, 1872; *died* London, 1958

Works

Operas Hugh the Drover (1924), Sir John in Love (1929), The Pilgrim's Progress (1951)

Ballets Job (1931)

Orchestral music 9 symphonies – A London Symphony (1913), Pastoral Symphony (1921), no. 4 (1934), no. 5 (1943), no. 6 (1947), Sinfonia antartica (1952); Fantasia on a Theme by Tallis (1910); The Lark Ascending (1914); Flos campi (Flower of the field, 1925); Fantasia on Greensleeves (1934)

Choral music A Sea Symphony [no.1] (1909); Serenade to Music (1938); cantatas

Incidental music The Wasps (1909)

Vocal music (with ensemble) On Wenlock Edge (c1923)

Chamber music 2 string quartets; Violin Sonata (1954)

Hymn-tunes   *Unaccompanied choral music*

Piano music   *Songs*   *Film scores*

very beginning of the century and which had given his music a distinctive melodic and harmonic flavor by the time of such early works as the song cycle *On Wenlock Edge*, to words by A. E. Housman, for tenor and piano quintet.

Vaughan Williams wrote that work while a mature student of Ravel in Paris, more than a decade after his formal training under Hubert Parry and Charles Stanford in England. But Vaughan Williams's roots were all English: like Falla, he looked not only to folksong but also to the art music of his country's Renaissance, and in particular to the sacred music of Byrd and Tallis. A notable example is the Fantasia on a Theme by Thomas Tallis for string orchestra (1910). This work utilizes the most harmonious chords in a quite original way, motivated by the modal relationships its composer discovered as much in English folksong as in Tallis. Bartók at the same time was also struck by the potential usefulness of folk-music modality: the difference between the two composers is essentially the difference between their two musical cultures, the Hungarian colored with abrupt 4ths and emphatic dance rhythms, the English preferring soft 3rds and even flow.

A further aspect of Vaughan Williams's Englishness is the feeling for landscape his music sometimes conveys, particularly the feeling for the flat, still vistas of eastern England, which proved a rich collecting ground for folksong. *The Lark Ascending* (1914) is a work of this kind, and one of Vaughan Williams's most perfect, with its solo violin etching the bird's flight against the warm, immobile orchestral accompaniment. There was also a cycle of nine symphonies and the opera *The Pilgrim's Progress*. Vaughan Williams worked for much of his creative life on this; it displays over the longest span his identification with the simple, visionary nonconformist religion of the seventeenth-century writer John Bunyan. His similar regard for William Blake found expression in the ballet *Job* (1931), which, in its combination of modal blessedness and chromatic Satanic fury, is one of his strongest works.

Holst, Delius

English folksong was an influence on several other composers, of whom the most important are Holst and Delius. Holst is best known, however, for his "astrological suite" *The Planets* (1916), which consists of a series of colorful movements depicting, in the fashion of a tone poem, the characteristics associated with each planet – Mars, for example, is treated as the bringer of war, Uranus as the magician. He uses a large orchestra, as in *The Rite of Spring*, and with something of the same rhythmic forcefulness. Delius, on the other hand, was a master of dappled orchestral effects, like Debussy, and wrote dreamy, rhapsodic music with chromatic melodies wandering through the rich textures. His nature poem *On Hearing the First Cuckoo in Spring* (1912) is typical of his work.

Prokofiev

Whereas the nationalism of Vaughan Williams, Holst and Delius is largely a rural matter – a matter of folksong and landscape – for Russian composers the assumption of a national identity has been politically essential. The career of Sergei Prokofiev (1891–1953) shows this clearly. His early music, often wild and uncontrolled, reflects vividly the condition of Russia on the threshold of the 1917 Revolutions. In 1918 he left the new Soviet Union, but unlike Stravinsky he did not sever his links for ever. Starting in 1927, he made return visits, confirming an enthusiasm for the Soviet state that had already been expressed in some of his works, for example a ballet incorporating exultant machine music. Then in 1936 he returned definitively, and had to contend with the increasingly tight cultural policy of Stalin's Russia: the condemnation of anything that did not speak optimistically to the masses.

Prokofiev was inevitably affected by these various changes in his life, but at an early stage he had established a musical personality that could flourish whatever the surrounding circumstances. By the time he completed his studies at the St Petersburg Conservatory, in 1914, he had several published works to his credit, including his headily romantic First Piano Concerto. He had also established a reputation as a flouter of convention, with a vein of bitter irony. Naturally enough, he attracted the attention of Diaghilev, but he enjoyed a much less fruitful relationship with the great impresario than did Stravinsky. A project composed for the Ballets Russes in 1915 was *Chout*, in a favorite Prokofiev mode of fantastic

---

Sergey Prokofiev   Works
born Sontsovka, Ukraine, 1891; *died* Moscow, 1953

Operas The Love for Three Oranges (1921), The Fiery Angel (1928), The Gambler (1929), War and Peace (1944)

Ballets The Prodigal Son (1929), Romeo and Juliet (1938), Cinderella (1945)

Orchestral music symphonies – no. 1, "Classical", D (1917), no. 2, d (1925), no. 3, c (1928), no. 4, C (1940), no. 5, B♭ (1944), no. 6, E♭ (1947), no. 7, c♯ (1952); Peter and the Wolf (1936); piano concertos – no. 1, D♭ (1912), no. 2, g (1913), no. 3, C (1921), no. 4, B♭ (1931), no. 5, G (1932); violin concertos – no. 1, D (1917), no. 2, g (1935); Cello Concerto, e (1938)

Choral music Alexander Nevsky (1939)

Chamber music string quartets – no. 1, b (1930), no. 2, F (1941); Flute Sonata (1943); Violin Sonata (1946); Cello Sonata (1949)

Piano music sonatas – no. 1, f (1909), no. 2, d (1912), no. 3, a (1917), no. 4, c (1917), no. 5, C (1923), no. 6, A (1940), no. 7, B♭ (1942), no. 8, B♭ (1944), no. 9, C (1947)

Songs   *Incidental music*   *Film scores*

136 Prokofiev's *The Love for Three Oranges*: scene from the Glyndebourne production, designed by Maurice Sendak, 1983.

comedy and keen satire, but war held up its production until 1921.

Political developments also upset Prokofiev's operatic plans. His first full-length opera, *The Gambler*, was being rehearsed in St Petersburg (now Leningrad) when the February 1917 Revolution broke out, and so this rich adaptation of Dostoyevsky's novel, erupting into violent caricature, was not staged until 1929 (in Brussels). But Prokofiev was composing a great deal else. In a style quite different from the powerful and noisy *Gambler* was a piece in which he opened a door into the world of Haydn: his First Symphony, the *Classical* (1917). Antedating Stravinsky's first neo-classical works, this symphony is in four short movements emulating eighteenth-century form, gracefulness of pattern and lightness of orchestration. It did not, however, lead Prokofiev into a neo-classical period. His ideas were too diverse for that, his creative temper too quick.

Instead his next major work was another opera, *The Love for Three Oranges* (1921), composed after Prokofiev had left Russia and settled briefly in the USA: it had its first performance in Chicago. The plot of the opera is exceedingly complicated and almost entirely nonsensical. It served merely to stimulate Prokofiev to create a variety of musical and musical-dramatic situations suited to his sharp mockery and brilliant technique. Conventional operatic emotions of longing and love are exaggerated to a point of absurdity, and the orchestra takes on a toy-like quality of crisp definition and color. But then, changeable as ever, Prokofiev launched himself immediately into an opera of a very different kind, *The Fiery Angel* (1923), a tale of high passion and religious hysteria. It was not heard complete until after his death, but some of its music went into his Third Symphony.

During the composition of *The Fiery Angel*, Prokofiev had returned from

America to Europe, and after his marriage to a Spanish singer in 1923 he settled in Paris. His Second Symphony (1925) and a ballet follow the fashion for heavy-engineering music, with massive sonorities and chugging motor rhythms – something quite different, except in rhythmic manner, from the delicate brittleness of the First Symphony. Once he had taken up residence again in the Soviet Union, he gained a new stylistic balance, even if he continued to compose as prolifically as ever. Partly, of course, this can be put down to the natural development of an artist in his mid-40s: one might say that Prokofiev had merely enjoyed a prolonged period of adolescent instability. Partly, though, the smoother, more fulsomely Romantic style of his works from the mid-1930s onwards was a necessity in Russia.

The turning-point was marked by the four-act ballet *Romeo and Juliet* (1938), written for the Bolshoy Theater in Moscow. At first rejected, it won eventual popularity for the vitality and variety of its dancing rhythms, its skillfully etched orchestral sounds and its glamorous love music, launched on the kind of streamlined melody that had been a feature of Prokofiev's style since *The Gambler*. Other major works of Prokofiev's early Soviet years include a dramatic score for Eisenstein's film *Alexander Nevsky* and one of the very few masterpieces of music for children, *Peter and the Wolf* (1936), where the gifts for musical illustration exhibited in the ballet and the film score are applied to a simple story.

With the outbreak of war most Soviet artists were evacuated to the provinces, where in 1941 Prokofiev began an operatic setting of scenes from Tolstoy's epic novel *War and Peace*. Official encouragement spurred him to make it into a patriotic panorama. This in no way detracts from the value of the opera, which occupied Prokofiev off and on for the rest of his life. His patriotism was genuine, and it is expressed with genuine forcefulness in the choral scenes, while the "peace" scenes, focusing on the loves of the heroine Natasha, provide opportunities for the lyrical impulse that was also part of his creative personality.

Another wartime work, the Fifth Symphony, was effectively a return to the abstract design of the First Symphony, though with the grander, more Romantic gestures of Prokofiev's Soviet style, and with the triumphantly affirmative conclusion that would suit a time of new hope. But the contrary feeling of grim challenge comes over powerfully in some of his piano sonatas of the time. There was also a second full-length ballet, *Cinderella* (1945), which does not pretend to the fierce musical excitement of *Romeo and Juliet*. Generally, the works of Prokofiev's last decade are milder repetitions of things he had done before. A second score for Eisenstein, *Ivan the Terrible* (1945), is less pointed than *Alexander Nevsky*, and the last two symphonies are relaxed in terms of invention.

Again it may be supposed that political conditions played some part. The war inevitably heightened the demand from government quarters for music to be cheerful, inspiriting and direct. After the war came the darkest hour of suppression when Andrey Zhdanov, speaking for the Central Committee of the Communist Party, in 1948 condemned Prokofiev and most of his outstanding colleagues for their pursuit of "formalism" – a term applied to anything the government disliked, but particularly to tendencies associated with the newest music of the West. Feeling himself ever more narrowly cornered by official policy, Prokofiev was driven to works of bland character, like his opera about the heroism of a World War II pilot. Even this, however, was not acceptable, and after a private preview the opera was withdrawn until after Stalin's death in 1953. Prokofiev, ironically, died on the same day.

Shostakovich

The effect of Russian cultural dictates was even stronger in the case of Dmitry Shostakovich (1906–75) than in that of Prokofiev. Unlike Prokofiev, who returned to the Soviet Union in the 1930s with his reputation well made, Shostakovich lived all his life in Russia, and musically he grew up with the Soviet state: his op. 1, an orchestral Scherzo, was written in 1919. Moreover, he lived not only under Stalin's dictatorship but also under Khrushchev's and Brezhnev's, and so had to deal with subtler forms of intervention than the blanket censorship of the 1930s and 40s. There is, however, little point in trying to imagine what Shostakovich's music might have been like had he not been subject to so much state supervision. The constraints became an indissoluble part of his musical personality, as did the irony and cynicism with which he extricated himself from them.

The irony, as with Prokofiev, is there from his earliest works. No official persecution was needed to bring it out: irony had been a quality of Russian music at least since Mussorgsky. The other characteristic of Shostakovich's art that emerged early was his prolific inventiveness, in which he again paralleled Prokofiev. Indeed, after Prokofiev's departure in 1918 Shostakovich soon took over as the bold young innovator of Russian music. By the time he finished at the Leningrad Conservatory, in 1925, still only 18, he had composed a variety of instrumental works, including his First Symphony (1925). This at once brought him international renown, but it is a curious début, and a curious start for a symphonic cycle that was over the next half-century to unfold as the most important since Mahler's. The First Symphony begins with a tune of ambling casualness and then picks up the clear-cut outlines of Prokofiev's *Classical Symphony*. It has none of the grand over-reach one might expect of a teenage composer's first symphony; it is, rather, disarmingly curt and comic. But it established at once the central vein of self-mockery in Shostakovich's music, a trait still more openly revealed in his First Piano Concerto (1933), where the official soloist is cheekily rivaled by a trumpet against an accompaniment for string orchestra.

Meanwhile, in other works, Shostakovich had associated himself with the movement in Russia that saw artistic revolution as the necessary companion of political revolution. Its followers took a keen interest in what was being done by Stravinsky, Schoenberg, Hindemith, Bartók and other leaders of Western musical

---

Dmitry Shostakovich   Works
born St Petersburg, 1906; *died* Moscow, 1975

Orchestral music symphonies – no. 1, f (1925), no. 2, "To October", B (1927), no. 3, "The first of May", E♭ (1929), no. 4, c (1936), no. 5, d (1937), no. 6, b (1939), no. 7, "Leningrad", C (1941), no. 8, c (1943), no. 9, E♭ (1945), no. 10, e (1953), no. 11, "The year 1905", g (1957), no. 12, "The year 1917", d (1961), no. 13, "Babi-Yar", b♭ (1962), no. 14 (1969), no. 15, A (1971); October (1967); piano concertos – no. 1, c (1933), no. 2, F (1957); violin concertos – no. 1, a (1948), no. 2, c♯ (1967); cello concertos – no. 1, E♭ (1959), no. 2 (1966)

Operas The Nose (1930), Katerina Izmaylova (1963) [revision of Lady Macbeth of the Mtsensk, 1932]

Chamber music 15 string quartets; Piano Quintet (1940); 2 piano trios

Piano music sonatas – no. 1 (1926), no. 2 (1942); 24 Preludes (1933); 24 Preludes and Fugues (1951)

Songs   Choral music   Incidental music   Film scores

advance. It was, however, a movement that was to be briskly quenched once the Stalinism of the arts got underway in the mid-1930s. Shostakovich's connection with it is strongest in such works as his Second and Third Symphonies and his opera *The Nose*. The symphonies are both colossal and noisy, emulating the machine music of Prokofiev and many other Russian composers of the period who were impressed by the rapid industrialization of the young Soviet state. Both symphonies, too, have massive choral finales in praise of the revolution, the Second having the title "To October" and the Third "The First of May". Written between them, *The Nose* is no less adventurous: there is, for instance, an *ostinato* interlude for percussion instruments alone. Its overriding character, however, is that of grotesque parody: the libretto is based on a fantastic story by Gogol in which a man's nose takes on an independent existence. The story line is certainly clearer than in Prokofiev's *The Love for Three Oranges*, but the score is similarly a patchwork of brightly fashioned musical objects that satirize operatic convention or are just simply wilful and perverse.

Shostakovich's second opera, *Lady Macbeth of the Mtsensk* (1932), also contains a well-aimed dose of satire, but now within the context of a realistic tragedy, not an absurd carnival. It is the bourgeois world within which the "Lady Macbeth" finds herself that is mocked, while she herself is a strong, urgent character, driven to desperate acts by her stifling situation. After its first production, at Leningrad in 1934, the opera was loudly praised as a major achievement in Soviet art, and it was quick to travel outside Russia, confirming the international reputation Shostakovich already enjoyed with his First Symphony and First Piano Concerto. However, in 1936 *Lady Macbeth* was suddenly subjected to violent castigation in the official party newspaper, *Pravda*, and hurriedly taken from the stage. It was not seen again in Russia until it was revived in 1963, under the different title of *Katerina Izmaylova*.

The enforcement of the policy of "socialist realism" affected Shostakovich's other works too. He withdrew his Fourth Symphony, a vast work mingling the heavy orchestration of the previous two with the intense intimacy of Mahler: it was not heard until 1961. He then offered his Fifth Symphony (1937) as "a Soviet artist's practical creative reply to just criticism", where the "finale resolves the tragically tense impulses of the earlier movements into optimism and joy of living". On the face of it, this was a bow to state demands, but one can also detect Shostakovich's irony infiltrating the underlying structure even of his splendid, optimistic last movement. The "joy of living" seems pressured and hysterical, and the symphony ends by being an empty victory for Stalinist compulsion. The style is indeed more diatonic than in any of Shostakovich's previous works, but the substance is uncompromising beneath its veneer of good behavior.

Shostakovich found another way of declaring the overriding importance of the self in his Sixth Symphony, where a long lament is succeeded by two short and rather flippant quick movements: optimism fails now by being insufficient. After this, Shostakovich decided to cultivate chamber music as a less public, less exposed platform. In 1940 came his first weighty chamber piece, the Piano Quintet, followed in 1944 by the start of a succession of string quartets: one appeared every two or three years until by the end of his life there were 15, equal in number to the symphonies. However, the quartet–symphony distinction does not exactly reflect a split between private and public works. In Stalin's Russia all music was public and subject to scrutiny. Moreover, though the spirit of Shostakovich's quartets may often be personal, the style is one of public address. On the other hand, the

137 Shostakovich at work on his Symphony no. 7 in 1941.

symphonies include works that are just as private, along with others conceived as national monuments.

Among the latter are two program symphonies concerned with critical events in the birth of the Russian Revolution: the Eleventh, "The Year 1905" (1957) and the Twelfth, "The Year 1917" (1961). Similarly expansive is the "Leningrad" Symphony, no. 7 (1941), which interprets current events in order to edify and encourage its audience. Its subject is the German invasion, depicted in immense, obsessive repetition and overcome in a grand finale that truly conveys the optimism undercut in the Fifth Symphony. Shostakovich's Eighth Symphony (1943) is the private counterpart to this public affirmation, interpreted widely as speaking of appalled horror and gruff determination in the face of the war; it trails off into hopeless, resigned detachment. While the Seventh Symphony was positively welcomed by the authorities – and promoted abroad quickly enough for it to be bitingly parodied in Bartók's Concerto for Orchestra (1943) – the Eighth was denounced and not played again until the 1950s. The Ninth Symphony (1945), too, disappointed the Kremlin, since it was not the hoped-for celebration of victory but instead a brittle, gay, brief work close to the tradition of Prokofiev's *Classical Symphony* once more.

After this Shostakovich wrote no more symphonies for eight years – the longest hiatus in his symphonic output – until in 1953, after Stalin's death, he composed his Tenth. In this he returned to the powerful forces and large forms of the Fourth from nearly 20 years before: the earlier one was a black entry into the years of Stalinist oppression, the later a strenuous, not very hopeful emergence. The Tenth Symphony is also signed all through with a motif that Shostakovich derived from his initials spelt in German as D–S–C–H (i.e. D–Eb–C–B). This musical monogram also occurs in several string quartets, especially the autobiographical no. 8 which is interspersed with quotations from other works going right back to the First

Symphony. To some extent quartets filled the gap between the Ninth and Tenth Symphonies, but during this period, the period of Zhdanov's pronouncement, Shostakovich was obliged also to offer blatant praise to the state in banal and inferior works.

On Stalin's death Shostakovich might have been expected to take advantage of the looser controls, but he had been too much bullied to come out into the open in any way but cautiously. He did bring forward his powerful First Violin Concerto (1948), held in reserve since its completion, but otherwise his works of the next few years avoided political dangerousness. So the Thirteenth Symphony (1962) came as all the more of a bombshell. In it Shostakovich set poems by Evgeny Yevtushenko, outspokenly critical of the government. The first movement is an Adagio lament for bass and chorus bitterly sorrowful at Russian complicity in the massacre of the Jews at Babi-Yar, the second a scherzo satire on the hypocrisy of rulers, the third an identification with Russian women bearing the burden of deprivation, the fourth a rebuke to those who fear the truth, and the last a cheer for those who speak it. Here at last was powerful optimism, but not of a kind to commend itself to the authorities. The symphony was withdrawn and Yevtushenko was forced to change some of the text, but Shostakovich was now sufficiently respected abroad for his music to be untouchable.

He did not take political advantage of his immunity. Instead his creative thoughts were turning towards death, the goal of most of the music of his last decade. His Fourteenth Symphony (1969) is a cycle of songs on the subject, his Fifteenth (1971) a purely orchestral work with enigmatic quotations from Rossini, Wagner and others. The mood of this late period, however, was one that favored chamber music, and the years 1968–74 saw the composition of his last four quartets, works with many original features of form and an increasingly elegiac tone.

Britten

Shostakovich dedicated the most explicit of his late meditations on death, his Fourteenth Symphony, to Benjamin Britten (1913–76), who had inscribed to him his "church parable" *The Prodigal Son* (1968). Their respect was not only mutual but deep, for both had persevered in finding continued usefulness within tonality, even in the 1950s and 60s when tonality was widely regarded as played out. Shostakovich, of course, had little option. Full atonality could never have been countenanced in Russia, least of all from the leading light of Soviet music, and right to the end all his works find their homes in some key or other even if there may be long stretches where no key definitely prevails. For Britten, too, tonality was not simply an esthetic choice. For example, the plain, luminous key of C major is associated in each of his three string quartets (1941, 1945, 1975) with an ideal world, one that is glimpsed but lost in the First and Third Quartets, and attained in the Second only at the end of a huge chaconne – by using that antiquated form he identifies himself with the English predecessor he most admired, Purcell.

Britten had studied under Frank Bridge (1879–1941), an English composer of the Vaughan Williams generation, who was open-minded enough to learn from Berg and Bartók. The young Britten was impressed by those composers, and by Stravinsky. From them he drew a style of vital rhythm, formal elegance, brilliant technique and, at times, satirical wit – all exemplified in his *Variations on a Theme of Frank Bridge* for string orchestra (1937), which move through the shadows of the Rossini aria, the Strauss waltz and the Mahler funeral march. Also from this period is the song cycle *Les illuminations*, to words by the French symbolist poet Arthur Rimbaud, for high voice and string orchestra (1939). Here Britten sets the original French, as later he was to set Michelangelo in Italian, Hölderlin in German and Pushkin in Russian.

The approach of war in 1939, and the example of Auden, led Britten to emigrate to the USA. However, he became homesick, and the feeling was sharpened by his discovery of the subject for a more ambitious work: he read an article on George Crabbe, like himself from the county of Suffolk, and author of the verse tale *Peter Grimes*. He returned to England in 1942 and in 1944 began the composition of his

138 Benjamin Britten and a Squirrel during a rehearsal for *Noyes Fludde*. Aldeburgh, 1958.

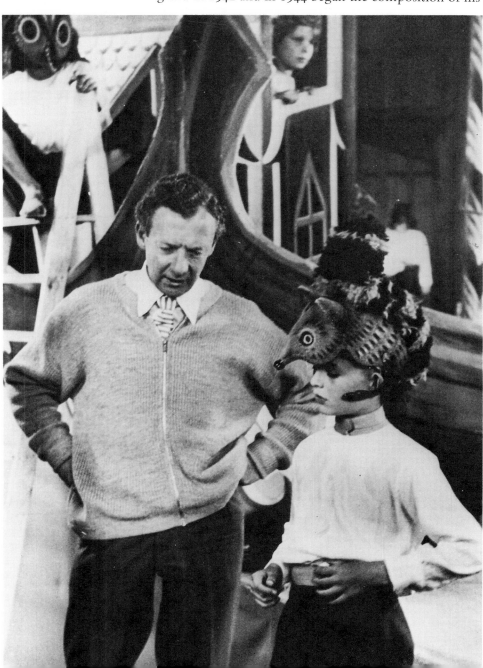

Benjamin Britten   Works
born Lowestoft, 1913; *died* Aldeburgh, 1976

Operas Peter Grimes (1945), The Rape of Lucretia (1946), Billy Budd (1951), Gloriana (1953), The Turn of the Screw (1954), A Midsummer Night's Dream (1960), Death in Venice (1973)

Church parables Curlew River (1964), The Burning Fiery Furnace (1966), The Prodigal Son (1968)

Orchestral music Variations on a Theme of Frank Bridge (1937); Sinfonia da Requiem (1940); Four Sea Interludes and Passacaglia from "Peter Grimes" (1945); The Young Person's Guide to the Orchestra (1946); Cello Symphony (1963); Piano Concerto (1938)

Choral music A Boy was Born (1933); Hymn to St Cecilia (1942); A Ceremony of Carols (1942); Spring Symphony (1949); Cantata academica (1959); War Requiem (1961)

Vocal music (with orchestra) Our Hunting Fathers (1936); Les illuminations (1939); Serenade (1943); Nocturne (1958)

Song cycles Seven Sonnets of Michelangelo; The Holy Sonnets of John Donne (1940); Canticles I–V (1947–74); Winter Words (1953); Songs and Proverbs of William Blake (1965); The Poet's Echo (1965)

Chamber music string quartets – no. 1 (1941), no. 2 (1945), no. 3 (1975); Six Metamorphoses after Ovid for oboe (1951); Cello Sonata (1961); 3 cello suites

Piano music   *Folksong arrangements*   *Incidental music*

opera on the same subject. *Peter Grimes* is the story of a man hounded by small-town society because he cannot contain his violence, and because he is an "outsider": it can readily be understood as a metaphor for Britten's own feeling of being an outcast because of his homosexuality. However that may be, its first performance in London, soon after the victory in Europe in 1945, continued the history of English opera after an interruption of two and a half centuries since the death of Purcell. Britten himself acknowledged a debt to Purcell's extravagant vocal style, and the opera contains some evidence of his admiration for Berg's *Wozzeck* in the presentation of two suffering central characters in a world where "ordinary people" are seen as grotesques. But these elements, together with Britten's continuing orchestral brilliance, are fused into a quite new style that belongs only to *Peter Grimes* and the operas that followed it.

At the same time, the role of Peter Grimes was the first of many that Britten wrote for his lifelong companion Peter Pears, for whom he had already composed his settings of Michelangelo and his *Serenade*, an anthology of English verse for tenor, horn and strings. Pears's distinctive voice – a razor-sharp lyric tenor of unusual expressive potential – colors almost the whole of Britten's output from this point onwards. Another musical effect related to Britten's homosexuality is seen in his versatile use of boys' voices, whether in chorus (for example in *A Ceremony of Carols*), or as soloists in several of his operas.

The *Serenade* (1943) shows the depth of Britten's feeling for English verse – its sounds, its rhythms, above all its meaning, expressed in the rich imagery of the tenor line, fluid and wilful, and the colorful, pointed, poetic writing for the solo horn and the string orchestra. The poems range from a fifteenth-century dirge (where the voice sings the same words in each verse while the accompaniment grows increasingly menacing) to Tennyson's Romantic vision in "The splendour falls on castle walls", with its mysterious echoing fanfares on the horn. Others of the songs treat the subject of evening and darkness and their images more lightly, except for the setting of Blake's Elegy, a haunting and masterly miniature about the worm at the heart of the rose, the rottenness that is buried within beauty and can eat it away and destroy it (see Listening Note X. F).

Listening Note X.F

Britten: *Serenade* op. 31 (1943), "Elegy"
solo tenor, solo horn
1st violins, 2nd violins, violas, cellos, double basses

This is the third movement of a song cycle setting English poems of the fifteenth to nineteenth centuries. Here the poem is by William Blake.

> O Rose, thou art sick;
> The invisible worm
> That flies in the night,
> In the howling storm,
> Has found out thy bed
> Of crimson joy;
> And his dark, secret love
> Does thy life destroy.

mm.

1–6	The first section of the orchestral introduction states and develops the basic musical idea: a downward chromatic slip that causes a significant harmonic change. At the start, for instance, the strings play the 5th E–B with octave doublings, in a low register and a slow march rhythm. The horn enters with the major 3rd (G♯), but then falls to the minor (G♮), suggesting already the insidiously destructive worm at the center of the rosebud.
7–11	The introduction continues with a repetition of mm. 2ff down a major 3rd, but there is then a sudden octave rise.
12–17	The last part of the introduction lingers over another harmonic slippage already explored: the strings are in B♭ major, and the horn turns down from the 5th (F) to the tritone (E).
18–25	The tenor takes over the horn's role in rotting the string harmony. At the opening of the poem there is a repetition of the E major–minor change from the opening of the introduction; later, at the words "Has found out", one hears again the C major–minor of mm. 7ff. Altogether the sung part of the movement is a condensed repetition of the introduction: the "dark, secret love" recalls the important B♭ episode. Finally the chromatic slip is upwards, from G to G♯, changing E minor back to E major.
25–40	The horn re-enters for a repeat of mm. 2–17, so completing a tripartite form.
41–2	The coda has the horn twice falling again to convert E major into E minor, but then it slides back, as the tenor had at the end of his contribution, to end in E major.

The success of *Peter Grimes*, and the realization that he could write operas, caused Britten to turn away from instrumental genres. The only important orchestral score of the next 30 years was his Cello Symphony (1963), written for Mstislav Rostropovich, who was the dedicatee also of a sonata and three suites for cello. Other instrumental works were occasional or else written, like the Rostropovich pieces, for friends. Songs, too, Britten composed with particular performers in mind: chiefly Pears, with whom he regularly gave recitals including his own cycles, the songs of his beloved Schubert and arrangements that he made of English folksongs and works by Purcell. Pears was also one of the intended soloists for his biggest choral work, the *War Requiem* (1961), written for performance in the rebuilt Coventry Cathedral in memory of the dead of World War II, and adding a personal melancholy to the obsequies by the insertion of war poems, often ironic in tone, by Wilfred Owen amid the traditional, impersonal ritual of the Latin Mass for the dead.

Otherwise the major works were all operatic. For the Royal Opera House in London's Covent Garden Britten wrote *Billy Budd* (1951) on Herman Melville's story of an innocent seaman, the victim of envy and injustice. This is his starkest and most symphonic large-scale operatic score, and since the entire action unfolds on an eighteenth-century man-o'-war, the cast is all male. Large projects, however, were becoming less to Britten's taste. He preferred working with a small troupe of a few singers and a dozen instrumentalists, eventually established as the English Opera Group, for whom he wrote a series of chamber operas, culminating in *The Turn of the Screw* (1954). This last, based on a story by Henry James, is a chilling study of childish fantasy and one of Britten's most theatrically effective works. The tight pressure of its musical form – the literal 'turn of the screw' – is achieved by its construction as a passacaglia on a 12-tone theme, though one that (like some of Shostakovich's) serves to accentuate rather than dissipate tonal tensions, for the struggle among the main characters is conducted in a struggle among rival key centers. It is a struggle, moreover, that reflects Britten's own troubled search, in so many of his works, for readmission to the blissful innocence of childhood. The power of the opera resides too in its recognition that the innocence is only superficial, that children have the potential for alarming evil.

Britten's work with the English Opera Group, and with other chosen performers, became centered on the festival which he and several friends established in 1948 in the Suffolk coastal town of Aldeburgh, where he and Pears had recently settled. Aldeburgh gave him the isolation and privacy he craved, and its festival gave him the opportunity to introduce his works on his own terms. Many had their first performances there, including his adaptation of *A Midsummer Night's Dream* (1960), his set of three "church parables", slung in somewhat Stravinskyan fashion between the world of opera and that of Japanese *nō* drama (1968), and his last opera, *Death in Venice* (1973). This provided Pears with one last star part as the German writer Thomas Mann's character, Aschenbach, infatuated with a boy who in this version is a dancer and hence outside the constrained, sweetly decaying realm of the opera: instead he gambols to lithe and brilliant music for tuned percussion instruments.

Tippett

In some ways Michael Tippett (b. 1905) represents Britten's opposite. Where Britten had written several fully individual works by the time he was 20, Tippett composed nothing that satisfied him until he was in his mid-30s, and his output has remained modest in relation to Britten's fecundity. There is also a clear difference of tone. Britten's characteristic expression is intimate and personal: hence his particular success in song, chamber music and chamber opera. Tippett, on the other hand, would see himself very much as a public artist, dealing with issues of public concern, and correspondingly the weight of his output falls on his large-scale operas, symphonies and oratorio-like works.

It was the first of these oratorios, *A Child of our Time* (1941), that effectively started his career. Written in response to a case of Nazi vindictiveness, it is not a

139 Scene from Tippett's opera *The Knot Garden*, first performed at Covent Garden, 2 December 1970.

simple condemnation of evil but an attempt to comprehend: "I must know my shadow and my light". Tippett's aim is to involve his audience, and he chooses his materials accordingly. Spirituals interrupt and round out the narrative, rather in the ways that chorales do in a Bach Passion.

Most of Tippett's larger works are philosophically related to *A Child of our Time* in that they put forward self-understanding and empathy as a cure for aggressiveness. *The Midsummer Marriage* (1952), the first of his operas, is a symbolic drama of enlightenment catching up a young couple on the eve of their wedding. Filled with imagery ranging from Blake to the psychologist Jung, the work is similarly rich in its musical textures. It opened a short period of opulence marked also by the rippling woodwind and leaping violins of the Piano Concerto and Second Symphony. *King Priam* (1962) fixed these colorful ideas into tight blocks of sound, matching recent developments in the music of Stravinsky and Messiaen, and again there was a sequence of instrumental works belonging to the same world. Since the early 1970s, however, Tippett has been working to reconcile his various inventions within larger spans again, expressing a need for reconciliation – political, cultural, national, racial – that is the subject of his opera *The Ice Break* (1976). Here again, as in his Third Symphony, it is from black American music, specifically the blues, that healing comes.

Since 1945

Though the careers of many composers extend across the end of World War II – Stravinsky, Shostakovich, Carter, Copland, Britten and Tippett are among those already mentioned – 1945 is still a useful boundary. Bartók and Webern died in that year, Schoenberg soon afterwards, and the next few years saw the first acknowledged works of the Frenchman Pierre Boulez, the German Karlheinz Stockhausen and many others who were to play leading roles in the development of music. Even composers active before the war – including the six mentioned above – went through periods of stylistic change in the postwar years, when serialism, hitherto a specialty of the Schoenberg circle, began to gain the enthusiastic attention of all.

Messiaen

In Europe the center for the most radical musical ideas of the late 1940s and early 1950s was the class taught at the Paris Conservatoire by Olivier Messiaen (b. 1908). At that time he was an organist-composer whose works suggested a fixation on the mysteries of the Catholic faith and the marvels of modality rather than on new-fangled techniques. However, Messiaen's subsequent career has proved his readiness to bring into his music the fruits of his constant inquisitiveness. From stable foundations in the "church modes" or invented scales, as in his music of the early 1930s, he has gone on to incorporate serialism, rhythms calculated according to the patterns of ancient Indian music or Greek verse, dense harmonies chosen with his eye for the "color" of sounds, birdsongs collected in the field and transcribed, even sacred messages coded in musical notation. All these elements are applied, ultimately, to the celebration of the mysteries of the Roman Catholic Church, the central force behind Messiaen's music. They come into play in his hugely extended, hugely virtuoso meditation on the Christ child, *Vingt regards sur l'Enfant-Jésus* ("Twenty glimpses of the infant Jesus", 1944) (see Listening Note X. G).

Such a wealth of materials could not be accommodated in smooth, continuous

Olivier Messiaen	Works
born Avignon, 1908	

Orchestral music L'ascension (1933); Turangalîla-symphonie (1948); Oiseaux exotiques (Exotic birds, 1956); Chronochromie (1960); Couleurs de la cité céleste (1963); Et exspecto resurrectionem mortuorum (1965); Des canyons aux étoiles (1974)

Choral music Trois petites liturgies de la Présence Divine (1944); La Transfiguration de Notre Seigneur Jésus-Christ (1969)

Vocal music Poèmes pour Mi (1936, later orchestrated); Harawi, chant d'amour et de mort (1945)

Piano music Vingt regards sur l'enfant Jésus (1944); Catalogue d'oiseaux (1958); two pianos – Visions de l'amen (1943)

Organ music Le banquet céleste (1928); L'ascension (1934, version of orch. work); Le nativité du Seigneur (1935); Le corps glorieux (1939); Livre d'orgue (1951); Méditations sur le mystère de la Sainte Trinité (1969)

Instrumental music Quatuor pour le fin du temps (Quartet for the end of time, 1940)

Opera St François d'Assise (1983)

Listening Note X. G

Messiaen: *Vingt regards sur l'Enfant-Jésus* (1944), no. 18 "Regard de l'onction terrible"
piano solo

The "Regard de l'onction terrible" ("Glimpse of the dreadful anointment") is one of 20 pieces that make up a two-hour cycle of meditations on the Child Jesus.

mm.	
1–22	The right hand climbs down a chromatic scale in chords of a tritone plus a 4th, and, after a first rush of 16ths, in progressively longer values: 8th, dotted 8th, quarter, and so on. At the same time, the left hand reverses this process: the climb is upwards, and, beginning with a whole note, the values become progressively shorter. After this introductory section, an upward glissando and a downward chain of arpeggiated chords prepare the main body of the movement.
23–37	The main subject is a chorale (ex. i) harmonized in organum style, i.e. with 5ths and octaves only. Its constituent elements are separated by flamboyant bursts of decoration, overflowing the severe pitch limitations of the chorale itself, which uses the notes of one of Messiaen's symmetrical modes (ex. ii: the numbers indicate the widths of the intervals in semitones).
38–52	Repeat of the preceding section, but with the chorale in a different mode.
53–67	Variations of the *a* and *b* fragments of the chorale, with a new decorative element.
68–82	Further repeat of mm. 23–37, transposed up a major 3rd.
83–97	Variations of the *c* fragment of the chorale, with a new decorative element.
98–112	Repeat once more of mm. 23–37, transposed up a minor 6th.
113–27	Repeat of mm. 53–67, up a minor 6th.
128–42	Repeat yet again of mm. 23–37, transposed up by an octave.
143–57	Varied repeat of the preceding section.
158–77	Varied repeat of mm. 83–97, ending in loud affirmation of C♯.
178–98	Reversal of the introductory section: the left hand now falls and decelerates while the right hand rises and quickens.

The entire form can be represented as: *X–A–A–B–A–C–A–B–A–A–C–X.*

forms. Messiaen's structures typically are made up of distinct blocks, often in alternation or other symmetrical arrangements. For the same reason his textures tend to be heterophonic rather than homophonic or contrapuntal. In ex. X. 7, from his *Turangalîla-symphonie* (1948), for example, there are three separate levels: a melodic line carried by bassoons, trombones and double basses, an *ostinato* toccata for an ensemble of tuned percussion sounding something like an Indonesian gamelan, and a zig-zag of glissandos crossing between the cellos and the electronic ondes martenot. Also to be noted here is a characteristic instance of rhythmic calculation, where the durations of the first melodic motif (*x*: eighth-note –

ex. X.7

quarter–note) are multiplied by one and half for the second (*y*: dotted eighth –
dotted quarter).

This is in keeping with the meaning of the title, made up of two Sanskrit words
connoting "rhythm" and "play" (or "love"). However, the sort of abstract
speculation represented by ex. 7, from the movement "Turangalîla I", is only one
face of this ten-movement work. Messiaen has described it also as a *Tristan*
symphony, and in certain of the movements, notably the sixth, "Jardin du sommeil
d'amour" ("Garden of the sleep of love"), he is not afraid to wallow in lush string
music bedded in the sensuous key of F♯ major. Indeed, the co-existence of the
mathematical and the erotic is frequent in Messiaen, as it must be if he is to praise
God both as architect of the universe and as creator of the human body as his
choicest work.

The *Turangalîla-symphonie* summarizes Messiaen's early manner, which had been
revealed for the most part in similar cyclical works for piano, two pianos or organ.
But the symphony also, not least in its "Turangalîla" movements, looks forward to
the serial constructions in which Messiaen was to interest himself for the next two or
three years, following up the interest of Boulez and others among his pupils.
Beginning here, he applies serialism to rhythm by making successions of durations
chosen from an arithmetical series (e.g. from one to 12 thirty-second notes), and
then performing serial operations of reversing and so on. The furthest he went in
this direction was in his *Mode de valeurs et d'intensités* ("Mode of durations and
volume") for piano, a crystalline mixture of three lines passing through series of
pitches, rhythmic values and dynamic levels.

This highly structured but formally elusive music had an enormous influence on
Boulez and Stockhausen. For Messiaen himself it was an isolated event and has
remained his least characteristic work. His next move was to withdraw to his
personal world of the organ, and to bring together the old modality and the new
constructivism, in his *Livre d'orgue* ("Organ book", 1951). After this he turned for a
while to birdsong for his material, used almost exclusively in the *Catalogue d'oiseaux*
(1956–8), a collection of impressions of different birds in their habitats around

140 Olivier Messiaen
collecting birdsong, 1961.

France, worked into substantial pieces each of which represents 24 hours of activity.

Most of Messiaen's later works have absorbed interests from his output of the 1930s, 40s and 50s, and in most of them a religious intention is clear. Messiaen is resistant, however, to description of himself as a mystic, preferring to appear as a musician-theologian who expounds the truths already revealed to the church. In his immense *La Transfiguration* (1969), for example, each of the 14 movements is an illustration of a text from the New Testament or St Thomas Aquinas. Though the range of reference is intensely personal – including birdsong along with the complex rhythmic apparatus, percussion ensemble, color chords, evocations of nature and modality – the usual building-block forms convey a sense of inevitability and objectivity.

Boulez

It is a measure of Messiaen's qualities as a teacher, as it is of Schoenberg's, that his pupils have not been imitators except where imitation has proved most useful to them. Thus Pierre Boulez (b. 1925) has been able to learn much from Messiaen's calculated approach to rhythm, from his vibrant piano writing and from his scoring for pitched percussion, but in terms of harmony and form his style is wholly

Pierre Boulez   Works
born Montbrison, Loire, 1925

Orchestral music Doubles (1958); Pli selon pli (Layer upon layer, 1962); Eclat/
Multiples (1970); Livre pour cordes (1968–); explosante-fixe . . . (1972–4);
Mémoriales (1975); Répons (1981)

Vocal music (with instruments) Le marteau sans maître (The hammer without
master, 1955); Improvisations sur Mallarmé I–III (1957–9); e.e. cummings ist der
Dichter (1970–)

Instrumental music Livre pour quatuor (1949); Eclat (1965); Domaines (1968)

Piano music sonatas – no. 1 (1946), no. 2 (1948), no. 3 (1957); two pianos –
Structures I–II (1952–61)

Electronic music Etudes (1952); Symphonie mécanique (1955)

different. At an early stage Boulez became a serialist, while drawing on a
Schoenbergian passion and turbulence; he soon moved on to "total serialism",
applying rules, analogous to those that Schoenberg's 12-tone system applies to
pitch, to other elements, like rhythm, loudness and color, notably in his *Structures*
for two pianos (1952). But then he moved towards a different kind of elaboration,
in which typical features of flexibility in time, ornamentation and sudden violence
return. The climax of this development came in *Le marteau sans maître* ("The
hammer without master", 1955), a setting of three short, surrealist poems by René
Char, consisting of nine movements (the songs are interleaved with instrumental
commentaries), for contralto voice, alto flute, viola, guitar, vibraphone, xylorimba
(large xylophone) and unpitched percussion. The tone colors recall Debussy and
Schoenberg, but also the worlds of Asian and African music: yet the style is Boulez's
own, with fast tempos, clear and brittle sounds, highly intricate structures (too fast-
moving for the ear to grasp) and an expressive manner in which extreme
excitement is conveyed with complete coldness. There is, too, a collision between a
Western notion of time and progress and an oriental feeling of stillness – most
striking where a rhythmic movement is started only to be suddenly stilled in a
pause, when Boulez can indulge his liking for resonating sounds (ex. X.8).

This taste is evident on a larger scale in his next completed major work, *Pli selon
pli* ("Layer upon layer", 1962), devised as a portrait of Mallarmé, the symbolist
poet, for soprano and an ensemble strong in pitched percussion. The gestures are
larger and the nervous energy is reduced; but it is replaced by a flexibility deriving
from Boulez's introduction of choice for his performers (for example in options
over the order of sections): all stimulated by Mallarmé's thinking on chance as well
as a new awareness of the experiments of the American composer John Cage. He
did not go far in that direction, however, and indeed has completed few
compositions since *Pli selon pli*, though many have been begun: Boulez has said that
music consists of the proliferation of simple basic ideas in a variety of directions, so
he must see it as a process easier to begin than to finish. But in the 1960s and 70s he
devoted much of his time to conducting (he was chief conductor of both the New
York Philharmonic and the BBC Symphony orchestras), and in the 1980s he has
chiefly been occupied in running an advanced computer-music studio in Paris. His
first work from there, *Répons*, suggests a reawakening of creative vitality and a
feeling – inherited from Varèse – that only the advent of sophisticated electronic
equipment could allow music to move forwards.

ex. X.8

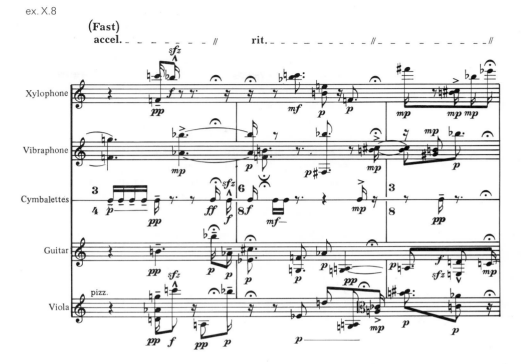

Stockhausen

The involvement of Karlheinz Stockhausen (b. 1928) with electronic music has been more continuous than Boulez's, though for both of them the starting-point was the same: the studio run in Paris by Pierre Schaeffer (b. 1910). Schaeffer was the first to create effective examples of electronic music from disc recordings in 1948, and the studio he operated for French radio became a center of *musique concrète*, music made out of recorded natural sounds (see p. 425). Boulez worked there briefly in 1951, and Stockhausen in 1952, during his year in Paris studying with Messiaen. But both found the techniques of *musique concrète* too primitive: Boulez was writing his first book of *Structures* at the time, and Stockhausen's response to Messiaen's *Mode de valeurs* was the equally difficult *Kreuzspiel* ("Crossplay") for piano, percussion and two woodwinds.

Stockhausen found a more congenial studio in his native Cologne, and there in

Karlheinz Stockhausen   Works
born Burg Mödrath, near Cologne, 1928

Orchestral music Spiel (1952); Punkte (1952); Gruppen (1957); Mixtur (1964)

Instrumental music Kontra-Punkte (1953); Zeitmasze (1956); Zyklus (1959); Aus den sieben Tagen (From the seven days, 1968); Alphabet für Liège (1972); Inori (1974)

Vocal music Carré (1960); Momente (1964); Stimmung (1968)

Electronic music Electronic Studies (1953): Gesang der Jünglinge (Song of the youths, 1956); Kontakte (1960); Telemusik (1966); Hymnen (1967)

Piano music Klavierstücke I–XI (1953–6); Mantra for two pianos and electronics (1970)

1953–4 he composed two studies which are among the first pieces of music realized entirely by electronic means: that is, the sounds are electronically synthesized, not recorded from nature. No less significant, though, was the instrumental work Stockhausen completed in Cologne, his *Kontra-Punkte* for ten players (1953). In it he reached beyond the single events of the earlier works to take charge again of note groupings, and he established a flexible style of writing for mixed instrumental ensemble that influenced all his European contemporaries. His pre-eminence was then secured by three works produced almost simultaneously in the mid-1950s: *Gesang der Jünglinge* ("Song of the Youths", p. 425), a brilliant tape piece merging a treble soloist into textures of synthetic sound (see Listening Note X. H); *Gruppen* ("Groups"), which divides an orchestra into three ensembles situated around the audience, their streams of music sometimes separate, sometimes joined; and *Piano*

Listening Note X.H

Stockhausen: *Gesang der Jünglinge* (1956), opening sequence

This is a piece of electronic music, composed on tape in the studios of West German Radio. There is no published score, but the source materials are usually clearly identifiable as a boy's voice and electronically generated sounds. The boy sings words from the canticle *Benedicite, omnia opera*, in German translation.

Preiset (*or* Jübelt) den (*or* dem) Herrn, ihr Werke alle des Herrn:	O all ye works of the Lord, bless ye the Lord:
lobt ihn und über alles erhebt ihn in Ewigkeit.	praise him and magnify him for ever.
Preiset den Herrn, ihr Engel des Herrn:	O ye angels of the Lord, bless ye the Lord:
preiset den Herrn ihr Himmel droben.	O ye heavens, bless ye the Lord.
Preiset den Herrn, ihr Wasser alle die über den Himmeln sind:	O ye waters that be above the firmament, bless ye the Lord:
preiset den Herrn, ihr Scharen des Herrn.	O all ye powers of the Lord, bless ye the Lord.
Preiset den Herrn, Sonne und Mond:	O ye sun and moon, bless ye the Lord:
preiset den Herrn, des Himmels Sterne.	O ye stars of heaven, bless ye the Lord.
Preiset den Herrn, aller Regen und Tau:	O ye showers, and dew, bless ye the Lord:
preiset den Herrn, alle Winde.	O ye winds of God, bless ye the Lord.

time	
0' 00''	The piece opens with a characteristic flourish of purely electronic sounds.
0' 11''	The boy's voice is heard in the distance, singing what can just be recognized as the word "jübelt". Stockhausen makes great play throughout the piece with ways in which verbal comprehension can be hampered: by placing the voice in the distance, as here, by breaking up the text or by combining the singing voice with other vocal or electronic sounds.
0' 29''	The boy is heard as a soloist at the left, followed by an artificial "chorus" of boys at the right. A sustained *n* sound is heard chorally.
1' 01''	A new chorus enters at the right, followed by the soloist on the words "Preiset den Herrn".
1' 30''	There is again a choral entry at the right, followed by a pair of soloists, also at the right, singing around the words "ihr Scharen des Herrn".
1' 45''	Choruses are heard across the sound picture.
1' 57''	A soloist in the middle sings "Preiset den Herrn", as before. After this comes a short "development section" which recalls some of the events already heard: the opening "jübelt", the "Scharen" duet and the soloist's "Preiset den Herrn".
2' 45''	Out of this emerges a solo *n*, which recedes into the background as electronic flourishes enter.
3' 02''	The *n* returns in electronic facsimile, and the music becomes both slower and less richly textured. Solo voices contribute words from the last two verses printed above.
4' 19''	The extract ends: this is approximately a third of the whole composition.

ex. X.9

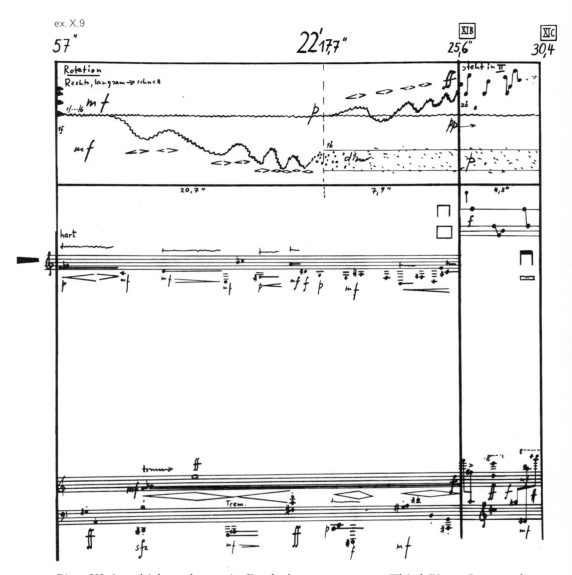

Piece XI, in which, rather as in Boulez's contemporary Third Piano Sonata, the soloist has to decide the order of the provided fragments.

The culmination to this period of parallel electronic and instrumental exploration came in *Kontakte* ("Contacts") for piano, percussion and tape (1960), where, as Stockhausen has said: "The known sounds ... function as traffic signs in the unbounded space of the newly discovered electronic sound-world". A printed quotation can convey only the vaguest idea of this, since Stockhausen's score gives no more than an impression of the electronic part, and since the work depends not only on sound but on space: on various levels of events seeming to take place behind the loudspeakers, on the rotation of electronic sounds around the audience, and on the contrast between the actual placing of the piano-percussion sounds and the merely imaginary location of the electronic components. However, ex. X. 9 may give some indication of the processes involved. Here two constituents split off from

141 Karlheinz
Stockhausen at his
electronic control panel.

a steady electronic sound, one wavering downwards, one later taking an upward course. The path of the first is charted by piano and marimba; the fate of the second, cut off into blobs of sound, is shared by noise percussion and high piano.

Kontakte is characteristic of Stockhausen's work in its emphasis on the collaboration of live and electronic components (most of his works need electronic equipment, though none, after the early studies, is purely electronic). Equally characteristic is the way the music achieves a form from a process, in this case one of sound transformation. Stockhausen's distrust of prescribed, outer form led him soon after *Kontakte* to develop the notion of "moment form", in which "moments" were to succeed each other without anyone worrying about their succession. But in fact his awareness of process has always led him to modify this ideal, even in the work entitled *Momente*, so that the moments are arranged according to some pattern of resemblance and change.

During the later 1960s Stockhausen's methods became increasingly free, particularly in the works he was writing for his own performing ensemble of players on conventional instruments and electronic appliances. This process culminated in *Aus den sieben Tagen* ("From the Seven Days"), in which the players are provided only with short texts as guides to their musical intuition. The only conceivable next step could have been silence, but in fact Stockhausen drew back and suddenly wrote an hour-long, fully notated score for two pianos and electronics: *Mantra*.

This was the first of his works created around a melodic theme or formula. The technique is somewhat akin to that of serialism, but with the crucial difference that a Stockhausen formula has a definite profile and is presented as a melody: the similarity lies in the way the whole composition is built out of this material by means of transposition, inversion and other transformations. A typical example is *Inori* for orchestra (1974), where the formula is gradually built up and then used in various richly harmonized combinations, the whole process being seemingly governed by two dancers who go through ritual gestures of prayer on platforms above the players.

Most of Stockhausen's later works offer the same mix of music and drama, ritualized and selfconsciously portentous. *Licht* ("Light"), the large-scale project on which Stockhausen expects to be working until the end of the century, is a cycle of seven stage works devised to be presented on consecutive evenings. It is concerned with a personal mythology centered on the figures of the Archangel Michael, Eve and Lucifer.

Henze

By contrast, Hans Werner Henze (b. 1926) is principally a composer of operas. For him too the Italian vocal tradition has been a major influence, ever since he moved from Germany to Italy in 1953, spurred by lack of understanding and by the rise of the Boulez–Stockhausen group to dominate the German festivals of new music. Henze was briefly attracted by their brand of serialism, as he had earlier been by Schoenberg's, but compositional practice mattered for him less than the demands of the theater, and he has been happy to cultivate a wide-ranging style with roots also in Stravinsky, Italian music, Debussy (for sensuous orchestration), jazz and Caribbean folk music.

Immediately after completing his studies Henze began working in the theater. He scored an early success with his opera *Boulevard Solitude* (1951), a retelling of the Manon Lescaut story in which the patchwork musical style, merging Berg and Stravinsky, allows classical arias and jazz dances to emerge within a 12-tone serial framework. When Henze moved to Italy two years later, pulled by the northerner's dream vision of the hot, serene, classical south, he began to compose over broader spans, with a much richer harmonic and instrumental range. The first major fruit was the opera *König Hirsch* ("King Stag", 1955, later revised in Italian), a fantasy exploring labyrinths of magical happening and orchestral fulness.

The early 1960s saw Henze's assimilation of all these influences into a smooth, luxuriant style, capable of taut, earnest expression in such works as his Fifth Symphony (1962). But he used it more characteristically to develop moods of nostalgia, romantic love and aloneness. To a libretto written by W. H. Auden and Chester Kallman he then produced *The Bassarids* (1966), a version of an ancient Greek play (Euripides' *Bacchae*) treating the conflict between cool restraint and manic self-indulgence. Henze composed the opera in the form of an unbroken four-movement symphony. It embraces the decadence of his Mediterranean style as well as the rude vigor of the Bacchic dances, the charade of a mock eighteenth-century pastoral interlude, and quotations from Bach which suggest a link between the destruction of the puritanical Pentheus and the crucifixion of Christ.

After *The Bassarids*, Henze felt a sense of loss and self-doubt, as his aims in traditional opera seemed to be completed. The outcome was a realization of the need for political activity, a need sharply focused when, in 1968, opposition to the Vietnam War fueled a wave of protest movements across Europe and America. Henze vehemently aligned himself with this trend in his dramatic oratorio *Das Floss der "Medusa"* ("The Raft of the Medusa", 1968), characteristically confronting its audience with a noble working-class hero pitted against a bourgeoisie of grotesquely caricatured effeteness and greed. His next opera was *We Come to the River* (1976), created with the English playwright Edward Bond as a violent attack on capitalist militarism and praising the good sense and peacefulness of the working class. This, however, brought to an end Henze's period of extreme political expression. He turned next to chamber music, and in subsequent orchestral works he has returned to his ripe style of the earlier 1960s, though with sharper elements.

Berio

The Italian composer Luciano Berio (b. 1925) joined the Boulez–Stockhausen circle towards the end of the 1950s. Typically Italian, his music generally shuns angularities in favor of static or smooth and malleable musical forms, usually led by voices or instrumental soloists. Berio has been concerned with connections between vocal and non-vocal sounds, as Stockhausen was in *Gesang der Jünglinge*. One of his finest pieces is *Circles* for soprano, harpist and two percussion players (1960), in which the sound and sense of poems by e. e. cummings circle out of the voice and into the instruments (ex. X. 10). An important feature of *Circles* is its dramatization of the concert platform, for the soprano is required to move nearer the ensemble as the two come more nearly to occupy the same musical landscape.

ex. X.10

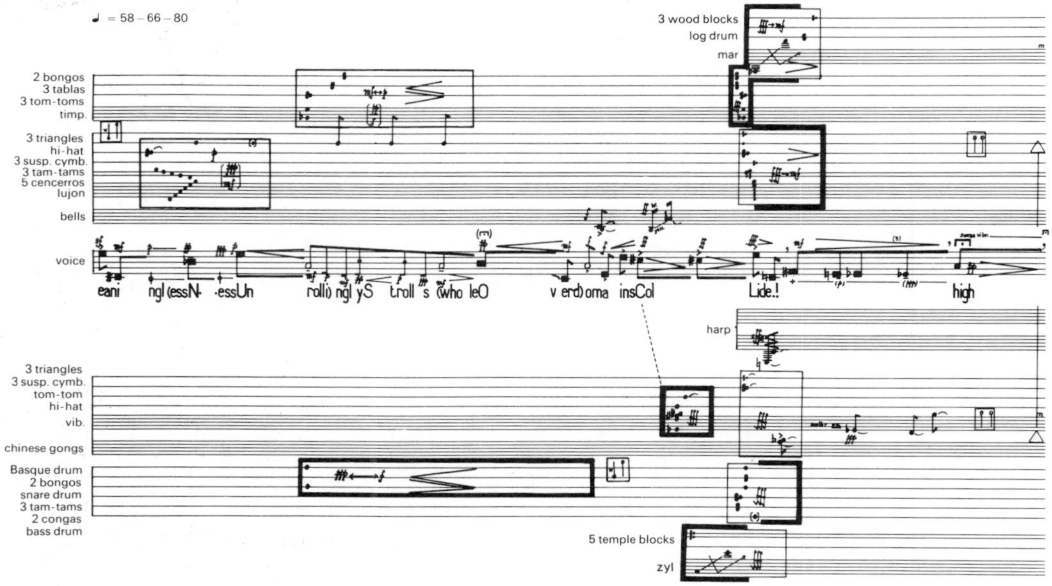

Even without such imposed activity, Berio's work shows a response to the physical business of making music. His *Sequenza* ("Sequence") series for soloists are not merely essays in virtuosity but dramatic scenes deploying a soloist, whether the ambience be comic as in *Sequenza V* for trombone, frantic as in *Sequenza VII* for oboe, or hopelessly trapped as in *Sequenza IX* for clarinet. Indeed, Berio's dramatic sense has been more often exercised in concert works than in music for the stage, though his output does include theater works.

Cage

Although there was little personal contact at the time, the aims of Boulez and Stockhausen in applying serialism to other elements than pitch in the late 1940s and early 50s were matched in America by Milton Babbitt (b. 1916). Sometimes regarded as Babbitt's precise opposite, John Cage (b. 1912) has spent most of his life trying to free music from mental control, not endeavoring to make it serve the mind ever more faithfully and completely. However, besides studying with Cowell (see p. 463), Cage had lessons from Schoenberg in 1934 and wrote some serial compositions in his youth. Serialism even contributed, along with his awareness of Balinese and other exotic musical traditions, to the repetitious (or *ostinato*) style he

John Cage
born Los Angeles, 1912

Works

Piano music Metamorphosis (1938); Sonatas and Interludes (1948); Music of Changes (1951); Music for Piano (1952); Seven Haiku (1952); Water Music (1952); Cheap Imitation (1969, later orchestrated)

Percussion music First Construction (in Metal) (1939); Second Construction (1940); Third Construction (1941); Imaginary Landscape nos. 1–5 (1939–52)

Electronic music Fontana Mix (1958); Cartridge Music (1960); Rozart Mix (1965); Bird Cage (1972)

Other music 4'33" (1952); Variations I–VI (1958–66); Music for Carillon nos. 1–5 (1952–67); Musicircus (1967); Atlas eclipticalis (1961); HPSCHD (1969); Quartets I–VIII (1976); Score (40 Drawings by Thoreau) and 23 Parts (1974)

developed in works for percussion ensemble such as his *First Construction (in Metal)* of 1939. Around the same time, he discovered the possibilities of the piano as a one-man percussion ensemble, if miscellaneous objects are placed between the strings: the result he described as the "prepared piano", and used most ambitiously in various works of the 1940s.

By that time Cage had settled in New York (earlier he had lived on the West Coast), where he was active as a teacher, ballet musician (beginning a long association with the choreographer Merce Cunningham) and composer. Partly through his association with other New York composers, partly through his contacts with the painters working there, and partly through his studies of Eastern

142 Cage's prepared piano.

thought, he came to see a need to remove from music every trace of personal intention. This led him into a laborious process of coin-tossing to decide the nature and layout of events in his *Music of Changes* for piano (1951). In *Imaginary Landscape no. 4* (also 1951) he made the musical outcome still more arbitrary by scoring the work for 12 radio sets. Then, in *4' 33"* (1952), he realized a long-cherished ideal in creating a piece that has no sounds at all: the performer sits or stands as if to play, but nothing is heard, except the environmental sounds and any audience reaction. These, in Cage's view, have quite as much value as anything he might propose in their place: the function of the artist becomes that of pointing people towards the potential art surrounding them in life.

Logically Cage might have ended his career with *4' 33"*, but he proved too fertile with new ideas, particularly concerning the involvement of electronics in music-making. In this field he was a pioneer. As an offshoot of his work with percussion ensembles, he produced the first example of live electronic music in his *Imaginary Landscape no. 1* (1939) for variable-speed phonograph turntables, muted piano and cymbal. This was followed during the next few years by other works using simple electronic devices. These had their mature successor in *Cartridge Music* (1960), for several performers amplifying the "small sounds" they can make with objects to hand, using phonograph cartridges to pick them up. Later works of the 1970s continue this trend, using seashells and plant materials.

Meanwhile another main thrust of Cage's activity has been in the direction of freeing music from the concert. This was a special concern of his in the 1960s, when he was responsible for stimulating jamborees bringing together various musical performers, video and light shows, and so on. These extended Ives's all-inclusiveness to a larger scale, and celebrated rather than condemned the electronic age of short attention-span and "omni-attentiveness". The main "work" remaining from this period is *HPSCHD* for harpsichords and tapes (1969), to which other phenomena may be added at will.

Although Cage produced very few works in the later 1950s and 60s, in the 1970s he became prolific again, partly in response to a reactivated conscience about the orchestra. As a body of highly trained professionals, the orchestra might seem an unsympathetic environment for Cage's music of non-intention and freedom: indeed, a performance by the New York Philharmonic of his *Atlas eclipticalis* (1961), where the parts consist of star maps (from which the musicians play as the spirit moves them), had proved disastrous (ex. X. 11). In *Cheap Imitation* (1972),

ex. X.11

therefore, Cage tried to provide a model of what an orchestra might be in the new age of musical democracy: not ruled by the composer (the material is a "cheap imitation" of another man's work, Satie's *Parade*), not swayed by the conductor, but working together harmoniously at a common task. This phase in Cage's work was however brief, and in later works for orchestra he has returned to looser forms of notation, as in the self-explanatory *Score (40 Drawings by Thoreau) and 23 Parts.*

Though their intellectual and musical concerns have been so divergent, Cage and Babbitt have both had a great influence on other composers, primarily in America but also more widely. As a teacher at Princeton University since 1948, Babbitt has had a hand in the training of many young colleagues, whereas Cage's message has been carried by his music and by writings enjoying the same happy disorder.

Texture music

The boom in serialism in the early 1950s was a west European and American phenomenon: there was no comparable movement in eastern Europe because of official policy (already observed in its effects on Shostakovich and Prokofiev). However, in the later 1950s artistic constraints began to be loosened, and in Poland, in particular, the result was a sudden flowering of avant-garde activity, marked by boldly new textures. Witold Lutoslawski (b. 1913), as the most distinguished of Polish composers, played a leading part in this movement; Krzysztof Penderecki (b. 1933) produced some of the most striking effects in music of raw sound.

Lutoslawski, Penderecki

The effect of the change can be judged by referring to two Lutoslawski scores indebted to Bartók: his Concerto for Orchestra (1954) and his *Funeral Music* for string orchestra (1958), a homage to the Hungarian master. For where the concerto is bright, agile and cheerful, influenced not only by Bartók's similar work but by the Stravinsky of such pieces as the Octet, the *Funeral Music* is a severe canonic treatment of a chromatic seed. Neither work, though, is quite typical of Lutoslawski, for his mature style became defined a little later in *Venetian Games* for small orchestra (1961). This was the first work in which he used "aleatory counterpoint", asking instrumentalists to repeat phrases out of synchronization to generate textures in which details reappear in an atmosphere of constant, teeming change. Almost all Lutoslawski's later works have combined sections in "aleatory counterpoint" with fully composed sections, using the latter to steer among the necessarily stationary harmonies of the fluid, dappled passages. Most of these later works have been orchestral, sometimes with solo voice, but there is also a String Quartet (1964) and some small instrumental pieces.

Penderecki's output is much broader, and differs from Lutoslawski's too in doing without the expressive refinement that is the older composer's most profoundly French trait. Moreover, whereas Lutoslawski has generally worked with new textures contrived from traditional instrumental usages, Penderecki has been interested in quite new color effects, particularly in his writing for strings. A notable early example is his *Threnody for the Victims of Hiroshima* for string orchestra (1960), with its alarming massed glissandos, pizzicatos, back-of-the-bow effects and so on. In his *St Luke Passion* (1966) he found a focus for such violent expressive gestures to operate over a wider span, illustrating in graphic terms the trial and crucifixion of Christ. The same style also served to make a melodramatic opera of religious hysteria in *The Devils of Loudun* (1969). But shortly afterwards Penderecki began to feel the force of thematic working and tonal harmony, which lend his works of the late 1970s and early 1980s a flavor of Bruckner oddly remote from the furious imagery of his earlier style.

Penderecki's change of direction was not an isolated eccentricity. One of the most conspicuous features of music in the 1970s was a seeking after simplicity and uniformity: it may be discerned too in Davies's move from expressionist theater to symphony, or in the greater thematic content of Berio's later music. It may be found as well in the music of the Greek composer Iannis Xenakis (b. 1922), previously associated with the kind of texture music composed by Lutoslawski and Penderecki. Indeed, he may be deemed the originator of the style, for his orchestral *Metastaseis* (1954) was the first work to treat each string player as a soloist in complex waves of glissandos. This sort of mass effect is Xenakis's abiding concern, and it remains so in his later works, though now with the addition of modal melodies and driving regular rhythms.

Xenakis

Ligeti

A similar if more refined development can be detected in the music of György Ligeti (b. 1923). Born a Hungarian, Ligeti was subject to the same limitations as Lutoslawski and Shostakovich in the late 1940s and early 1950s, but he left Budapest after the Russian invasion of November 1956 and nearly all his published music dates from after this event. Coming upon the new serial music of Boulez and Stockhausen, he was struck by the leveling-out that takes place when the elements of music are all in processes of rapid change: the brilliant detail merges into a gray generality. He determined, therefore, to give his attention to the generalities. In his orchestral piece *Atmosphères* (1961), he thus removed all trace of harmony, melodic profile or rhythm: the work is compounded entirely of orchestral cluster-chords, constantly shifting in weight and color. Its awesome effect created a sensation when the work was new, and served well in Stanley Kubrick's film *2001* a few years later. But Ligeti was also working in quite another direction in his *Aventures* and *Nouvelles aventures* (1962–5), a pair of crazy theater pieces for three soloists, singing nonsense syllables, and seven instrumentalists.

A combination of the two styles was not possible until it could be managed on the large scale of an opera in *Le grand macabre* (1976). Meanwhile Ligeti's "serious" works began to be undercut with the irony and humor of his skits, just as they began to readmit the basic materials of music. A second orchestral study, *Lontano* (1967), worked now with definite harmonic colors, and in *Melodien* for small orchestra (1971) there came the return of melody in tangles of leaping lines. Last to come back was functional harmony, of which there are hints in the concluding passacaglia of the opera, based on the ground bass from the finale of Beethoven's *Eroica* Symphony – but though the chords are tonal, they are arranged so as to defy any stable sense of key.

**The
Minimalists**

However, the clearest indications of the new simplicity are to be found in the music of certain American composers sometimes classified as "minimalists": they include LaMonte Young (b. 1935), Terry Riley (b. 1935), Philip Glass (b. 1937) and Steve Reich (b. 1936). In Reich's music of the late 1960s, for example, the aim is the projection of a simple process of change involving repeating patterns in pure tonal harmony. Ex. X. 12, from *Violin Phase* for four violins (1967), indicates one stage on one such process. Here the first three violins are all playing the same idea, but spaced out at time intervals of a half-note, the process being one of "phasing", or gradually separating parts from an opening rhythmic unison. The fourth violin is to pick out the patterns that result at each particular stage of the phasing process (only one such pattern is shown in the example).

There are evident signs, however, that for Reich and his colleagues such

ex. X.12

simplicity is only a stepping-stone to complexity of another sort, for in later works, such as *Drumming* (1971), Reich has created much more ambitious and complicated processes while retaining the mesmeric intensity of his repetitive rhythm and glowing harmony. It is characteristic of our enigmatic times that this is one of the directions that music is now taking.

Chapter XI

The Traditions of Popular Music

Popular music, or "pop music", means "music of the populace". The term embraces all kinds of "folk" music which, originally made by illiterate people, were not written down. In most societies throughout European history different types of folk music have co-existed, usually in a rural environment, with "art" music, usually centered on courts, aristocratic houses or towns. For many centuries there was give and take between folk and art music, just as there was between a peasant society and an urban one.

The creation of a popular music that aims simply at entertaining large numbers of people is a product of industrialization, in which music may become a commodity to be bought and sold. It is in the rapidly industrialized nations, notably Britain and the USA, that we first encounter composers who have devoted themselves to fulfilling a demand for popular, entertainment music.

A transition from the old world to the new is represented by the Vauxhall Gardens in London, for which such eighteenth-century composers as Handel and J. C. Bach supplied music for people seeking relaxation from toil. Although the music was not radically different from that which they composed for more august occasions, it was on the way to what we now call "easy listening". Early in the nineteenth century, in Britain and still more in America, some composers became professionally occupied with the production of popular pieces which may be defined according to their social purpose: music for the chapel, the pub, bar and eating-house, the pleasure-garden and music hall, the parlor. We may further define them in terms of the needs they serve; they encourage various forms of hedonism (physical delight in the present moment) and of nostalgia (sentimental regret for what is past). These areas of experience, which continue to feature in popular music, are not necessarily discreditable. Human beings need forms of escape. And even in an industrial community the borderline between "art" and "entertainment" is hazy.

That is particularly true of what might be described as religious music. A Mass by Byrd, in Shakespeare's England, or a cantata by Bach in Lutheran Germany, is an act of worship that embraces man's deepest needs and highest aspirations. One cannot say the same of most of the evangelical hymns of the Victorian age, the purpose of which is to comfort us with a repetitive, predictable tune and to lull us with cozy harmonies, marshaled by a four-square, metrical beat. Such music reminded laboring people of their humble place while referring to their rewards in

Heaven. Yet the music is not insincere, and it may be moving. The musically strong envangelical hymn-tunes pack more punch than the trite ones, but emotional impact is usually disproportionate to musical merit. This is still more true of the "escapist" music of the Victorian parlor, which by the later nineteenth century was dedicated to sentimental, often foolish ballads, or to superficial, brilliant piano pieces of no real technical difficulty or musical substance.

In America, where the production of parlor pianos increased prodigiously during the nineteenth century, the manufacture of music to match the instruments became an industry in itself. Charles Grobe, who emigrated from Weimar in 1839, has been described as "the most productive piano-piece factory that ever existed"; he turned out operatic transcriptions and pot pourris, piano arrangements of missionary hymns and military marches, along with dubiously original compositions that extend to opus 1995. Instantly dispensable, his music is an early example of planned obsolescence: it was designed to become out of date.

Of the numerous composers of nineteenth-century popular music, three figures stand out for their modest genius. All are "escapist": Stephen Foster by way of nostalgia, John Philip Sousa by hedonism, and Louis Moreau Gottschalk by a mixture of the two.

Foster

Stephen Foster was born in 1826, near the steel-producing town of Pittsburgh. It was an urban industrial community, "full of dirt and smoke", on the edge of the wilderness; the Indians had left but their memory lingered. Foster worked as a journalist, composing songs in the spare time from his office and printing press. He had little formal training in music. His aim was to amuse the middle-class public; since this society wanted no more from art than a respite from work, those conventions that were handiest, and most familiar through use, seemed the best. The well-worn clichés were derived from British composers of the early nineteenth century, from evangelical hymns and military marches, from Italian Romantic opera, and from salon music for piano which was a reworking of European classical conventions. Foster's public was a mixture: English, Irish, German, Italian by ancestry, with a heavy leaning towards Puritan heritage.

Yet although Foster had no ambition other than to give the public what it wanted, he understood those wants better than did the people themselves. This discovery he made in his "Ethiopian" songs, based not on real black spirituals but on the songs of the Christy minstrel shows. These were an exploitation of the black man by white men with blackened faces, in an idiom closer to English ballad, march and hymn than to black music. The conventional form of the Christy show, with its comic presenter and two stooges armed with tambourine and bones, crystalized the white myth of the wide-grinning, dazzling-toothed, red-lipped black man, lazy and good for nothing, yet happy in his innocence. Foster's genius lay in his revealing the other side of this myth: the black man, although happy, was also homeless, and therefore sad. The minstrel show took the savagery out of his merriment, making him a harmless figure of fun. At the same time, Foster's songs tell us that the black man's homesickness is related to the frustration and nostalgia in everyone, of whatever color, especially in a raw industrial city with an uncertain future. All Foster's songs yearn for the "good old days". But their yearning is not innocent, as real folk music is, since they express modern man's consciousness of loss. That is why, in no discreditable sense, they are sentimental and why their technique is at once simple and artificial. The ballad is an artistic contrivance

143 Title-page of Stephen Foster's song *Willie we have missed you* (1854).

combining elements from English music hall, French waltz and light Italian opera. In Foster's finest songs, however, heartfelt simplicity transforms artifice into something like folk art; that is why some of them have achieved enduring, worldwide fame.

The most celebrated of Foster's "Ethiopian" songs, *Old folks at home* (1851), presents the theme of lost innocence in basic terms. The tune is restricted to five tones and the harmony does not depart from the rudimentary tonic, dominant and subdominant of evangelical hymn-books. Yet this song, epitomizing the instinct to return to one's roots, is known all over the world. It owes its obsessive quality to its very simplicity: the phrases are repeated four times, making their effect because they are worth repeating, for the leaping octave followed by a declining minor 3rd contains an age-old yearning, while the closing phrase brings us safely to the security of home. The other internationally celebrated "Ethiopian" song, *My old Kentucky home* (1853), is no less elementary structurally, and melodically uses only six tones. It has nothing to do with genuine black music, not even in the Westernized form of the plantation song. The words are not literally true, but the singer's longing for release from weariness has preserved the song's potency.

Foster's music is a quintessence of the common man's yearning for Eden. In spite of the fabulous appeal of his music, his life was a failure both materially and spiritually. He was unable to establish relationships, especially with women; after the failure of his marriage he relapsed into alcoholic despair, and died in New York in 1864. The most deeply touching of his songs, *Jeanie with the light brown hair* (1854), is a dream-image of his lost wife. It is perhaps the only one of his songs in which the gracefully undulating melody has the haunting simplicity of a real Scots or Irish folktune, imbued with tender regret in the little cadenza that takes us back to the repeat of the first section, to end with the fleeting sigh of a closing chord of the 13th. The simplicity of the art matches the fragility of the dream. The song may still bring tears even to sophisticated eyes.

Sousa

Stephen Foster is the poet of American nostalgia. At the opposite, "hedonistic" pole stands John Philip Sousa, who was born in Washington, DC, in 1854. He was the son of a Spanish trombonist in the US Marines band; he refuted the legend that his father's name was originally Antonio So, the "USA" being appended as a tribute to his adopted country, but it should be true, because Sousa had no doubt that although he was a professional composer with experience in operetta and symphonic music, his durable works were his marches for his military band. Inaugurated in 1892, this band soon became internationally famous; it did so because it epitomized the youthful optimism of America, making the maximum appeal to body and nerves, the minimum to head and heart. Sousa said that his marches were "music for the feet instead of the head. . . . A march should make a man with a wooden leg step out"; a march must be as "free from padding as a marble statue. . . . There is no form of composition wherein the harmonic structure must be more clear-cut. . . . There must be a melody which appeals to musical and unmusical alike". Sousa died in Reading, Pennsylvania, in 1932.

Sousa's marches (except for some of the late ones) generally follow the same pattern. After four or sometimes eight measures of introduction, the "verse" section of the march falls into two groups of 16 measures. The first, like a classical sonata, modulates perkily to the dominant. After the double bar the second 16 rarely depart from the tonic and are usually broader and more song-like, with richer harmony and a few chromatic passing notes. The "trio" section, derived from the classical minuet, is usually in the more "passive" subdominant and is melodically more lyrical and quieter in rhythm. After its own brief middle section, often rhythmically and harmonically more strenuous, the chorus trio is restated, still in the subdominant but very loud. The most famous of Sousa's marches, *The Stars and Stripes Forever* (1896), represents this type. The four-measure introduction, with its aggressive unison and cocky syncopation, makes us take notice; the verse section proceeds in a jerky triple meter over a swinging bass. When, in the second 16, the bass becomes the top line, transformed into a wide-intervaled tune, the effect is like chest expansion. The bass has become the top, and this gives a sense of physical and moral well-being. The trio begins in a narrower melodic range. In its final statement, however, animated by a prancing bass and by fierce descending chromatics, its majesty ("molto grandioso") carries all before it. The mixture of sentiment such a piece evokes – private and public, personal and communal, domestic and national – is finely judged, and brought to a unity by the overall design.

Gottschalk

Nostalgia and hedonism, the poles represented by Stephen Foster and John Philip Sousa, meet in the career of Louis Moreau Gottschalk, who of the three has the closest ties with Europe and its art music. Born in 1829 in New Orleans, of German-Jewish-French-Creole descent, Gottschalk was a child prodigy who was sent to study the piano and composition in Paris, where he was admired by Chopin, Berlioz and Liszt. Back in his native land, this technically proficient musician became a figure rather like an American Liszt, traveling the length and breadth of the continent publicizing himself, his music and the rapidly expanding American piano industry. He spent his last years in South America, dying there in 1869.

In spite of Gottschalk's affluent background and European experience, in industrialized America he was a man of commerce as much as of art. Drawing on his cosmopolitan origins he incorporated into his music elements from black rag, French waltz and quadrille and Spanish habanera; often he used authentic Creole or black melodies for his elegantly pianistic pieces. Even his contributions to the sentimental parlor genre have substance to support their delicate filigree. His greatest hit, *The Last Hope* (1854), treats a Presbyterian hymn-tune with seductive yet disciplined luxuriance. Interestingly, Gottschalk wrote it as a parody of the popular *The Maiden's Prayer*, but he played it, eyes closed, with total dedication. It sold 35,000 copies in a few years and is still in print: it pleases the player in being rewardingly pianistic but not as difficult as it sounds; it pleases the listeners in entertaining them while also making them feel good morally.

All Gottschalk's pieces fulfill the prescription for entertainment music since they delight by their skill, enliven by their wit, and charm with their pathos, while never radically disturbing emotional equilibrium. They often disturb physical equilibrium, especially in barnstorming pieces like *Union, paraphrase de concert* (1862), in which a solo virtuoso hilariously becomes several Sousa bands in vainglorious blaze. Though Gottschalk means us to take his thundering octaves half-seriously, a sense of the ludicrous breaks in. Cliché and invention weigh even.

In *Souvenir de Porto Rico* (1857) he hit the balance exactly. It is a set of variations in the popular convention of the arriving and departing procession. As the band approaches, the "chromatic grapeshot and deadly octaves", with which Gottschalk attracts our attention, fill us with the childish wonder of watching fireworks. But they are for fun, not a real conflagration. As the procession departs into the distance, we know our lives will go on when the rockets are spent.

That Gottschalk came from the Southern, European-affiliated city of New Orleans is significant; so too is the fact that his music incorporated elements from that of the city's black population. For its provides a transition to jazz: the origins of what was to become the popular music of "global" industrial society were also rooted in the music of another race.

144 US Marine Band,
*c*1880, with J. P. Sousa
(*front right*).

Blues and ragtime

Though jazz is a twentieth-century phenomenon, mainly associated with cities, its origins were in Africa, in societies quite different from those of the West. Stravinsky's *Rite of Spring*, Bartók's *Cantata profana*, Orff's *Carmina Burana* and many elements in the visual art of such men as Pablo Picasso and Amedeo Modigliani might suggest that there had been a move away from the ego-conscious values of Western civilization from the beginning of the twentieth century. Yet that would not explain why the music of black Africans became a mouthpiece for white men too, throughout the Westernized world. Perhaps we are all, in some ways, if not black and enslaved, at least alienated and dispossessed. The black man's music, transmuted into the white man's world, asserted the violence of dispossession, that very violence which was exploding in the monstrously mechanized wars; at the same time it reaffirmed man's roots in the earth and in Nature. That is why the techniques of "primitive" music could be transplanted to a strange land.

We have seen in earlier chapters how tonal progression has been used in Western music. The techniques of African music have evolved rather differently. Forms tend to be circular rather than linear, repetitive rather than progressive. Melody is usually basically pentatonic, restricted to the five pitches (paralleled by the black notes on a piano; see p. 12) which for acoustical reasons are the most natural to sing. Almost always, African music avoids leading tones, so the harmonic finality of dominant–tonic cadences is impossible. Textures are not so much polyphonic as heterophonic – several different versions of the same melody are stated simultaneously. The resulting harmony therefore happens by chance and is non-developmental. African music expresses a communal way of life. People dance together. Unlike Western music, when solo voices sing or play they are seeking to lose, rather than to assert, personal identity. The singer is a mouthpiece for his

145 Caricature of one of Gottschalk's "monster" concerts, performed by 56 pianists and two orchestras at the Teatro Lyrico Fluminense, Rio de Janeiro, 1869.

people's culture and history. If he sings of himself or of topical and local events it is to affirm his oneness with the group to which he belongs, or to assuage his distress at having left it.

In his new, white American world the black man, enslaved, inevitably used the musical techniques he had been reared on. He danced to express solidarity with his fellows; alone, he hollered to the empty fields. His wailing cries, on the cotton plantations, in labor camps or in prisons, were virtually unchanged from those he had uttered in his homeland, but his oppressed state lent a sharper edge to the distortions of pitch and flexibilities of rhythm typical of folk music conceived as a single line. As an outcast, he no longer sings a tribal song but, seeing himself as belonging to the suffering tribe of mankind, calls on ancient vocal formulas of the pentatonic roulade and a tumbling descent from a high note, and on traditional techniques of vocal production – modified because he sings in the American, rather than in an African, language.

But in the white world the black man's African heritage was to suffer a change more radical than one of language. Inevitably it came into contact, and then conflict, with the musical manifestations of the New World, especially the march and hymn. The hymn, as we saw when discussing Foster's music, followed a pattern of tonic, dominant and subdominant harmony, while the march, as we saw with reference to Sousa, also provided a four-square beat. When the American black, responding to these types of music, took over the white man's guitar, the blues was born, and with it the heart of jazz.

Blues

There was no decisive break between the folk holler and the blues. Pete Williams, for instance, a black man in a Southern prison, uses the guitar to accompany himself in what he calls "Prisoner's talkin' blues" and "Levee camp blues", but these are still hollers in which speech in heightened, with the guitar providing a repeated figure. "Levee camp blues", a labor song (that is, intended to be sung during hard, strenuous work), is metrically more regular and melodically more defined, but the guitar still plays mainly a tonic chord, with only fleeting touches of subdominant and dominant. The poetic theme is the familiar one of the faithless woman. The words of vocal blues often concern the agony of desertion, betrayal and unrequited love and sexual references are frequent. Blind Willie Johnson sings the hymn *Mother's child* in a deeply guttural growl, reducing the tune to brief pentatonic moans; another hymn, *Dark was the night*, he croaks with the intensity of a voodoo shaman. Here again there is no more than a touch of white harmony on the guitar to balance the plangent black vocal line. Although he is not here singing blues, he uses his voice in dialogue with his guitar; the instrument can sing-speak with the intimacy of a human voice and can strum the fundamental chords of European, and especially white American, hymnody. Blues "form", as it evolved, tends to fall into a pattern, as shown:

```
           a                a'               b'
Bars    1   2   3   4    5   6   7   8    9   10   11   12
Chords  I————————         IV—  I—         V—   I————
```

But the form is not static. It provided a harmonic framework against which the black singer could interpret his words or the instrumentalist could improvise. Thus black melody and white harmony interact.

This interaction may be heard in Robert Johnson's blues *At the crossroads* (1936). Johnson was a neurotic black, addicted to wine and women no less than to song, who was murdered in 1937 at the age of 21. Both the rasping timbre of his voice and the contours of the improvised melody are profoundly African. Launching the phrase on a high, pinched note, he "tumbles" wildly from it, while his chittering guitar brokenly attempts to affirm a march-like beat and to establish the tonic, dominant and subdominant fundamentals of white tonality. Unlike the examples cited above, this is a real 12-bar blues, effecting a compromise between black melody and rhythm and white harmony and meter. But the compromise is agonizing; vocal and instrumental elements cannot fit – not surprisingly, since Johnson yells "ain't nobody seem to know me, everybody pass me by". Yet the desperate repetitions are still therapeutic. Strength springs from contradiction, in clashes of minor and major 3rd. These clashes happen by chance because black pentatonic and modal melody favors the vocally "natural" flat 7th while white guitar harmony prefers the sharpened leading tones appropriate to the closing cadences of the march and hymn. These "false relations" (see p. 16) became an important feature of jazz idioms, where they are known as "blue notes".

Ragtime

The basic form of the country blues came from the Mississippi Delta. The pieces we have discussed come into the category of folk rather than popular music; but as black men moved into cities, the white elements of harmony and meter grew more obtrusive and barriers between folk and pop were scarcely discernible. This is evident if we compare a classic bluesman like Blind Lemon Jefferson with a Memphis singer like Furry Lewis, whose source materials include minstrel-show music and white ballads as well as blues. We have seen in discussing Foster that minstrel shows included black-faced songs and dances which blacks themselves emulated in the convention of piano rag. It is not surprising that American blacks, holding on for grim life, should in the early years of the century have evolved their own version of the white march. Ragtime, basically piano music though often played by bands, was the black's attempt to make a "civilized", notated music that could compete with that of his white masters. Significantly, the most celebrated rag

Scott Joplin

composer, Scott Joplin (1868–1917), known as the "King of Ragtime", moved from the South to the urban North. He took his musical convention from the white military two-step, more or less identical with Sousa's march form. But Joplin's music, both in the *Maple Leaf Rag* (1899) that made him famous and in more harmonically sophisticated pieces like *Euphonic Sounds* (1909), has an improvised feel mostly because the rhythms are "ragged" in being syncopated. The manner is dandified. In the music of the notable rag composers, for example James Scott (1886–1938) and Eubie Blake (1883–1984) as well as Joplin, a wistful vulnerability hides beneath the mirth. The music has pathos but not sentimentality.

Piano jazz

Blues and rag meet in the evolution of piano jazz. When blacks came across broken-down pianos in shanty-town bars they treated them as mechanized guitars, sometimes using them mainly as drone-like backgrounds to song or speech. "Barrelhouse" pianists came to make basic, usually very fast use of the harmonies of the 12-bar blues and to seek pianistic substitutes for the guitar's expressiveness by way of "crunched" tones, slides and displaced accents. The pianist exploited the power of a percussive keyboard, creating momentum with a pounding left hand, usually in patterns of repeated tones or unequal rhythms that came to be known as boogie basses. Gradually, the piano's capacity for polyphony, harmony and rhythm encouraged barrelhouse pianists to explore complexities of texture as well as to exploit rhythmic force.

Physical exuberance could hardly be carried further than in Mead Lux Lewis's famous *Honky tonk train blues*. No more sexy music could be conceived than this rip-roaring boogie blues. Though Jimmy Yancey, a less virtuoso but more expressive Chicago pianist, also played frenetic train pieces, he was one of the few barrelhouse men to specialize in slow blues, achieving music of tough sinew yet of airy grace. His *At the window*, with its fragmented texture and electrically hesitant rhythm, is marvelously moving. Leroy Carr, as singer and pianist, shows how white art may lend elegance to black passion, as the rumbustiousness of the barrrelhouse piano comes to terms with the artfulness of rag. Most early bluesmen were not professional musicians but itinerants who made their music at street corners or in bars and brothels, but Carr became a professional, working in nightclubs and speakeasies. The same is true of James P. Johnson, trained in both barrelhouse and ragtime traditions and distinguished for his command of an irresistibly "striding" bass and for the delicate precision of his right-hand figurations. With equal facility he played ragtime and minstrel-show numbers and, significantly, he moved to New York to work in white cabaret, even trying his hand at composing symphonies and musicals.

Blues singing

The fusion of blues and rag exemplified in Johnson's playing is crucial to the evolution of jazz, especially during the 1920s. The blues were now centered on traveling shows, and the most revered singers were women. A matriarchial image is fundamental to black American music, since African matriarchy (society ruled by women) offered an alternative to the white patriarchy on which Western culture had been founded. The earliest of the great women blues singers, Gertrude Rainey, received her nickname "Ma" at the age of 18, and she soon began to fulfill a role as Earth Mother and Priestess. Her searing vocal timbre often has a liturgical flavor; despite her secular material, in the early 1920s she worked with guitarists or pianists with church affiliations. Performing the traditional *Boeval blues* or *See, see rider*, she found no barriers between country blues, gospel and minstrel-show music.

Bessie Smith

Bessie Smith (1894–1937), the most famous blues singer of the 1920s, was known as the "Empress of the Blues". A neurotic type with a gargantuan appetite for sex and alcohol, she demonstrated what happened to the blues when it entered the city. Though her musical roots are black, she was a sophisticated performer within her convention and became a committed urban American. Like all the finest jazz, her music sprang from tension: between country and town, black and white, art and entertainment. That tension is both creative and self-destructive, and in this too Smith is representative.

Like other women blues singers, Smith usually performed not only with a piano and perhaps drums but also in dialogue with a melody instrument which both intensified and depersonalized the vocal line. She gave superb versions of folk blues like *Careless love* and *Reckless love* with Louis Armstrong playing a cornet obbligato, and of her own *Young woman blues* and *Poor man blues* with the cornet of Joe Smith, her favorite collaborator. In later years she sometimes used minstrel-show numbers, imbuing their white formality with black and blue potency, most movingly in her quasi-autobiographical version of *Nobody knows you when you're down and out* (which she was herself after squandering a fortune).

Jazz

New Orleans

Since women blues singers worked with jazz players and used conventions from both jazz and minstrel show, their work had many features in common with the music of the early jazz band. This began in New Orleans where, as we have seen, a lively black population mingled with a cosmopolitan society of white Americans, Frenchmen, Spaniards, Italians and Germans. Blacks played waltzes, quadrilles, polkas and "mazookas" at white junketings, and also played in parade bands. From these cross-fertilizations the New Orleans (or Dixieland) jazz band became established, with instruments from the white military band. Typically, it was a group of five to eight players. The cornet (later trumpet), clarinet and trombone were the main melody instruments. A tuba (later string bass) provided the bottom line, reinforced by drums and other percussion instruments. The banjo substituted for the guitar as harmonic fill-in, perhaps because it was easier to play, jauntier and less "expressive", for jollity rather than pathos was the aim. Later, when bands no longer marched, the piano became the main harmony instrument, combined with the plucked strings.

The music of the New Orleans band compromises between the 12-bar blues and a 32-bar form. Sometimes the band played traditional material with folk origins, at others it started from composed numbers, re-creating them in folk style. The musical substance lies in the tension between the thumping military beat and the symmetries of white harmony on one hand, and on the other the black solo lines which, with their African flexibility of pitch and rhythm, try to override the basic form. Each tune is repeated several times, the cornet, clarinet and trombone usually improvising a solo in turn and combining in noisy abandon for the last statement.

The supreme New Orleans soloists – Louis Armstrong (cornet and trumpet), Johnny Dodds (clarinet) and Sidney Bechet (soprano saxophone) – attain a levitating ecstasy with their soaring improvised melodies. They also affirm their humanity in imbuing their instruments with the expressivity of the voice. This **Louis Armstrong** becomes obvious if we compare Armstrong's trumpeting with his gravelly singing, or recall how he played dialogue on equal terms with the women blues singers. The voice and instrument speak, the body moves: so the heart of the music is in the spoken and unspoken word and in physical movement.

What is remarkable about New Orleans jazz, especially after the players migrated, under economic pressure, north to grimmer cities like Chicago, is that this word–body relationship flourished within the context of Westernized commercial music. We can hear this in the supreme achievements of band jazz, the recordings made by Louis Armstrong with his Hot Five and Hot Seven in 1926–8. *Tight like this*, for instance, exhilaratingly demonstrates how a black man hits back through a military two-step tingling in sonority, nervous in syncopated rhythmic agility, hilarious in the skill with which it teeters on a tightrope. This is high comedy on the brink of tragedy. And tragedy is overt in Armstrong's famous unaccompanied solo opening to *West End blues*. A military fanfare is transformed into a lament, the false-related arpeggios being poignant in intensity, heroic in span and sonority.

That the consummation of New Orleans–Chicago jazz involves a marriage between black folk melody and the harmony of white art music is revealed in Armstrong's recording of "King" Oliver's *Weather bird*, which he presents simply

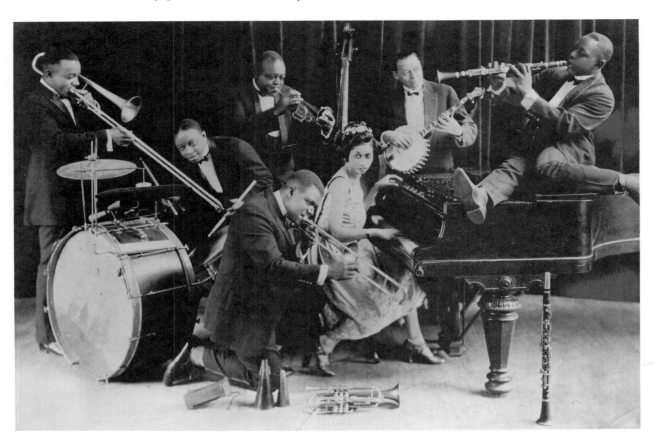

146 King Oliver's Creole Jazz Band, early 1920s; Oliver plays the cornet, Louis Armstrong the trombone (*center*), Lil Hardin the piano, Johnny Dodds the clarinet, and "Baby" Dodds the drums.

as a duet with Earl Hines, the most eminent jazz pianist of the time. We might expect, from only two players, rhapsodic improvisation, but we get a sequence of choruses artfully planned to lead to a climax of disrupted repeated notes. The piano part is sometimes melodic and agile, sometimes merely a background to, and inspiration for, the wildly spurting trumpet. The stuttering repeated tones and the rising scale of the coda fuse exaltation and frustration, at once comic and tragic. Since the music has this effect it must, in spite of its basis in undeveloping variation, have some sense of beginning, middle and end. Armstrong and Hines have proceeded from the folk heterophony of early jazz to a true improvised polyphony, which creates tension between melodic direction and harmonic progression.

These tracks were recorded in 1928, just before Armstrong left Chicago for New York, later to embark on a career as a show-business entertainer as well as a jazzman. Such rapprochement was inevitable and has been essential to jazz's development. That becomes clear if we consider those men who, working within black folk traditions while being influenced by white entertainment music, appropriated white elements to their own ends, composing numbers that could serve as bases for jazz improvisation. Jelly Roll Morton, a light-skinned New Orleans black, produced, between 1926 and 1930, a series of recordings with his Red Hot Peppers. He composed most of the numbers in the convention of the Sousa march and trio and even wrote down 12-bar blues with precise indications of harmony and figuration, if he wanted to modify established patterns. Starting from skillfully devised and notated arrangements, the music involved jazz improvisation, though Morton, as pianist-director of his still basically New Orleans ensemble, controlled the performance. Whether in a militarily derived piece like *King Porter Stomp*, in a real, acerbic blues like *Smokehouse Blues*, or in a cross between the two like *The Chant*, they generate passion while managing to sound blithely carefree. Their improvised composition, as distinct from Louis Armstrong's composed improvisation, is an irresistible affirmation of the human spirit.

Duke Ellington

A further refinement of Morton's approach occurs in the music of Duke Ellington who, born in Washington, DC, of a modestly genteel if not affluent black family, worked mostly in New York nightclubs, for a predominantly white audience. If Morton was the first, Ellington was the second composer in jazz history; he remains the finest. Playing in a politer environment than that of the Chicago bars in which Armstrong and Morton performed, he scored for a bigger band, using a choir of saxophones blending, or playing in contrast, with brass and reeds, supported by string bass and percussion; Ellington directed from or beside the keyboard.

Ellington composed almost all the band's material, using a 32-bar format rather more than the 12-bar blues, and creating enlivening permutations between them. The more artful quality of Ellington's music, compared with Morton's, lies first in the tunes, which are memorable and recognizably his. *Black Beauty* (1928), for instance, has a most touching melody that attains, through an unobtrusive irregularity, a delicate balance between innocence and sophistication. Similarly Ellington's nocturnal tunes, like *Solitude* and *Mood Indigo* (1930), have prototypes in Tin Pan Alley's "lonesome" numbers, yet acquire a distinctive flavor since melody is inseparable from harmony and scoring. For although Ellington starts from the clichés of white march and hymn, he adds chromatic richness that can plumb our emotions. In spite of the art of its composition, the music remains folk improvisation, in tune with the spirit of the blues and at heart profoundly African.

147 Duke Ellington at the Royal Albert Hall, London, 1967.

Although the sequence of musical events is written down, each event is conceived in terms of a particular member of Ellington's ensemble, singing or speaking in his own voice and making a spontaneous utterance.

In a piece like *The Mooche* (1928), the moochers are simultaneously sleazy loafers in New York bars and fierce felines in a jungle. Ellington's ripply piano prelude sets us comfortably in the city cocktail lounge. Yet when the tune emerges it is very blue in feeling, and its passionate descending chromatics are reinforced by the mutes and "plungers" through which the trumpeter and trombonist gibber and growl. In Ellington's band (as in commercial dance-band music of the period), the oily saxophones begin to rival the sharper clarinets, enhancing the sensuous colors that smoothe over the hard reality of the blues. The orchestral colors are dreamily romantic, yet the piece remains sinister because of the padding cat beat and the cross-rhythms of the guitar. The wordless singing sounds merry but also dangerous. The symmetry of form, with a clear recapitulation, disciplines such elements in the music.

One of the finest examples of this ambiguity is the *Black and Tan Fantasy* (1927), a piece Ellington recorded several times. Here the dream is contained in the atmospheric background of liquid "creole" clarinet, saxophone and muted brass, through which the trumpet's 12-bar blues tune, a transformation of the popular anthem *The Holy City*, speaks painfully of the heart's truth. The piece is an elegy of the lost world the black man allegedly cannot inherit, which is why the quotation of Chopin's well-known funeral march in the coda seems appropriate. In the original version of the piece this coda is played in a manner simultaneously comic and pathetic, like so much authentic New Orleans funeral music. In a later (1938) version the coda becomes loud and wild. Ellington fuses the spirit of New Orleans jazz with the precise realization of art. Compromise between black jazz and white art entails the acceptance of white show business which, in an industrial society, is art's popular manifestation. There are two complementary strands in this process. One develops black jazz into a mechanized powerhouse; the other combines popular conventions with the escape art of musical comedy. The two streams converge, as did blues, minstrel show and rag in the earlier generation.

American musical

The jazz musicans we have discussed have all been black, indirectly of African descent. The musicians who worked in music theater on Broadway during the same decades were all white, mostly of Jewish European ancestry. Musical comedy had its roots in European operetta, Viennese, French and English. One of the earliest and most talented of Broadway composers, Jerome Kern, though born in New York in 1885, studied in Europe, intending to become a classical composer. When he returned to the USA and to Tin Pan Alley, he did not forget his musical education. He produced his first show in 1912 and during the next 30 years composed such musicals as *Sunny* (1925), *Showboat* (1927) and *The Cat and the Fiddle* (1931), which gave "classic" formulation to musical comedy conventions. Even the format of musical comedy steers it towards escapism, since a spoken play with musical interludes has two separate elements: the play, which is naturalistic, and the song-and-dance, which may be thought of as dream. In this, Broadway musical comedy emulates the operettas of such composers as the Strausses, Lehár, Offenbach and Sullivan, transplanting both themes and forms into an American environment. Like those of minstrel show and vaudeville, the themes are again either hedonistic or nostalgic. The forms follow a predictable pattern, the tunes constructed within rigidly diatonic, symmetrical eight-plus-eight-measure periods, though the harmony and modulations, especially in the middle eight, may be more adventurous than those of the old minstrel music. Verse and refrain have a relationship similar to that of the main section and the contrasting one in a Sousa march. A faintly jazzy element now comes from the syncopated pianism of the black rag. The escapism of musical comedy is not necessarily negative. Men of talent, like Kern and Irving Berlin, may demonstrate, as had Foster, how dreams may represent our real feelings. We shall understand this better if we consider two composers who represent opposite but complementary poles.

Irving Berlin

Irving Berlin, born in Russia as Israel Baline in 1888, was taken to New York as a baby and grew up the hard way in the Bowery and lower East Side. He had no musical training except what he picked up as a singing waiter in Bowery saloons; when he discovered that he had a gift for writing words and tunes he was content to pick out the melody with one finger on the piano, leaving harmonization and notation to a professional.

As we would expect, Berlin's songs have only two basic themes: an adolescent pleasure in the present moment and an equally adolescent nostalgia, sometimes tinged with self-pity. In songs like *Top Hat* and *Cheek to Cheek* (from the Ginger Rogers and Fred Astaire musical *Top Hat* of 1935), we can recognize or remember the experience. The tunes, with their narrow range and stepwise movement, more or less sing themselves. Yet this cannot be all there is to them or they could not have retained their appeal over half a century. However empirical his early efforts, Berlin acquired some expertise as a composer. He was able to achieve such subtleties as the gradual extension of the repeated phrase in *Cheek to Cheek* until it reaches its highest point on the words "hardly speak". Such songs do not deny that love may hurt; they seek pleasure from the hurt itself and create an illusion that we can live on the surface of our emotions.

Cole Porter

The world of musical comedy seldom gets beyond, or wants to get beyond, this illusion, which is why it is most convincing when making an ironic point of its illusory nature. Cole Porter (1891–1964), unlike Berlin, the poor boy who made good, was a rich boy who, in becoming a theatrical playboy, made bad but richer. The cynical title of Porter's musical *Anything Goes* (1934) is typical; so too is the fact that it conveys the mood of the 1930s with carefree irresponsibility, with no trace of the bitterness of the social-political art of the time. The story, improbably based on a novel by the English comic writer P. G. Wodehouse, satirizes the Establishment, the English lord and all representatives of authority. Its hero is an American outcast, a gangster of whom the heroine, a slightly blowsy English rose, expresses moral disapproval; but the gangster turns out to be an inefficient public enemy, a figure of fun, shorn of the savagery he really represents. There is no positive element except the rudimentary boy–girl relationship, as expressed in the song "All through the night". Its tune is merely a descending chromatic scale that, prompting dreamy modulations, induces trance, making the love seem almost too innocent to be true. Porter's chromatics cast an ironic reflection on the diatonic love-songs of Berlin.

The satirical elements in Porter's songs are not sharp; they tend to defuse passion and violence, and become part of the American dream. Yet his irony sometimes carries an uneasy honesty that we do not find in later musicals such as Richard Rodgers's *Oklahoma* (1943), though that ostensibly deals with ordinary folk in a commonplace world, or in Rodgers and Hammerstein's *South Pacific* which, affected by World War II, attempts to embrace serious themes. Occasionally, for instance in "Night and Day", Porter allowed wit to be disturbed not only by passion but also by something not far from fright. Over a tom-tom beat, which is also the ticking of a clock, the tune's repeated tones might sound comic but for the restless modulations. As the repeated tones grow into the refrain, we realize that the point is in fact a yearning actually to be free of repetition. The Latin-American rhythm drives the music to a sensuality rare in this type of music, though the return to the tonic for the cadence phrase is unconvincing. If the song does not finally have the courage of Porter's passion, at least it shows that he knew passion exists.

George Gershwin

Only one composer of Broadway and Tin Pan Alley overrode the illusory nature of the conventions to produce works of genius: George Gershwin (see p. 466). Many songs he contributed to ephemeral musicals have survived in their own right, for example "The man I love", one of many numbers written with his brother Ira as lyricist; it is a song of remarkable melodic, harmonic and tonal subtlety which treats the stock theme of the adolescent dream with irony and compassion, though making no overt departures from Tin Pan Alley. Evidence of Gershwin's percipience lies in his discovery of his essential theme in a novel by Dubose Heywood dealing with life among the blacks in New Orleans. From it was made a libretto for *Porgy and Bess* which, starting out as an ambitious musical, ended up as a full-fledged opera exploiting an interplay of speech, recitative, arioso and pop "aria" and exhibiting a musical-theatrical craft to rival Puccini, if not Verdi. Within the sophisticated harmonic and orchestral textures Gershwin finds scope for the tunes, which serve their dramatic function while having separate identity as numbers performable in dance-hall or cabaret. Art and entertainment are one, in a tale about corruption, oppression, alienation and the inviolability of a radical innocence of spirit. Gershwin himself was not, like his hero Porgy, a physical cripple; but he was a poor boy who (neurotically) made good, a Jew who knew about spiritual isolation and had opportunity to learn about corruption. Perhaps he wrote such fresh music because even in the face of temptation he preserved, like Porgy, a modicum of innocence. This is manifest in the radiant lullaby, "Summertime", that opens the opera; and it is still present when, at the end, Porgy sings his heart-rending lament "Bess, O where's my Bess", before he pathetically trundles off in his go-cart, seeking his eternal beloved. She has been lost to the neatly named Sportin' Life and his Happy Dust; he and his dope may be equated with the lure of commerce and the deceit of the American dream.

Swing era

That Gershwin's understanding of the black blues, though intuitive, was profound is indicated by the fact that his tunes have always been favored material for jazz improvisation. *Porgy and Bess* itself has been given superb jazz treatments by such distinguished musicians as Louis Armstrong and Ella Fitzgerald, Miles Davis and Gil Evans, Ray Charles and Cleo Laine. This provides a link to the evolution of jazz, now both black and white, in the 1930s and 40s: the era of swing, during which the relationship of band to soloists changed. Even Ellington's band, though treated in

148 Scene from the first performance of Gershwin's *Porgy and Bess*, Colonial Theater, Boston, 10 October 1935. Coll. G. D. Hackett, New York.

chamber-music style, grew to considerable dimensions and has affiliations with the big white bands that were more a part of show business than of jazz. The earliest was the concert band of Paul Whiteman, for which Gershwin composed *Rhapsody in Blue*, and to which some of the most talented of white jazz wind players contributed; notable among them was Bix Beiderbecke, who produced a sound on his cornet that was characteristically "white" in being pure, clean and vulnerable. Dominating the era of World War II was the big band of Glenn Miller. More interesting both musically and sociologically is Benny Goodman, a white clarinetist who directed big and small bands and who looked, from the world of commerce, towards both jazz and art. In his small groups he played with many talented black jazzmen. He also flirted with serious music, as a concerto soloist and as commissioner of jazz works from "straight" composers. It is significant that Goodman, himself a fine musician, was the first white impresario to promote black jazzmen on equal terms.

Count Basie

However, the supreme achievements of jazz during the swing era remain black, notably the Kansas City bands of Count Basie. The Basie band is an authentic successor to the barrelhouse music of the shanty-town piano thumpers; the obliviousness of the city takes over from the deprivation of earlier days. The machine-made energy of the massed brass is now set against the wiry agility of Basie's piano playing, as tenuous in texture as the brass is massively remorseless. Basie's line and rhythm, though nervously fragmented, are strong as steel. Thus, in *Tickle toe* (1940), his thin, sinewy, boogie-rhythmed piano solo, sharp as glinting glass, is shattered by the explosive shouts of brass chords; or Lester Young's tenor saxophone, expressive but pallidly "lost", tries to hold its own against the streamlined precision of the lashing brass interjections. In the Chicago music of Armstrong and Bechet the soloists' ecstasy flowered over the ensembles and tension led to the recognition that the individual ought to triumph. In Basie's music, which is more blues-influenced than Ellington's, the outcome is more dubious. Rhythmic momentum liberates the soloist but at the same time threatens his individuality. Basie is not only a superb soloist himself; he also allows scope for tenor saxophone or trumpet solos of a kind that speak the more intimately the more the brass batters, and the most vibrant rhythm section in jazz history carries all before it.

Cabaret singers

It is no accident that the big band era was also the age of the great jazz cabaret singers. Basie worked with male blues "shouters" such as the great Jimmy Rushing, creating a fiercely urban complement to the primitive country blues. He also worked with Billie Holiday, the finest female jazz singer since Bessie Smith, who, restricting herself mostly to pop standards, nonetheless revealed, especially in dialogue with Lester Young, emotional depths beneath the corniest material. In *If dreams come true* (1938), her simple enunciation of the words suggests that she wants to believe, but the lingering phrasing shows that she cannot. Her continually shifting verbal stresses are echoed by Young's saxophone, and she in turn answers his echoes almost instrumentally. Holiday died young, of heroin, but other great cabaret singers of the 1940s and 50s, notably Ella Fitzgerald, Sarah Vaughan and Betty Carter, have carried on performing into the 1980s. The individual voice and the spoken or sung word may still triumph. In the 1970s Basie himself made some magnificent traditional blues recordings with trio or quartet.

Instrumen-talists

149 Billie Holiday, one of the last photographs. Coll. G. D. Hackett, New York.

We have seen that the story of jazz has veered between the private and the public life. The big band seemed to sell out to a commercially manipulated world, yet sometimes discovered in it new identities for the individual. During the 1950s and 60s what came to be called Modern Jazz reverted to private values. A pianist-composer like Thelonious Monk had some of the attributes of a high priest, literally turning his back on his audience as he created a nervously tight, harmonically and tonally contorted revamping of old barrelhouse styles, whether in dialogue with a few brilliantly driving wind and percussion players, or as soloist, in the fragmented austerity of a blues with the pertinent title of *Functional* (1957). Miles Davis, in his "cool" jazz of the 1950s, tempered jazz heat with the muted sonority of his trumpet and with the grave modality of his melodic lines, akin to Spanish flamenco dance. Often he was abetted by the swinging lilt, the lucid chromaticism and the controlled filigree of Bill Evans's piano-playing. Evans was a white man. So is the composer-arranger Gil Evans, with whom Davis collaborated in some of the most beautiful jazz "tone poems" since Ellington, notably the suite derived from *Porgy and Bess* (1958).

Among the saxophonists of modern jazz Charlie Parker stands supreme, the most inventive and influential jazz soloist since Armstrong. Although he used blues and pop conventions, his rapid chord changes and flexible meter steered jazz improvisation once more towards a linear approach. This is evident too in the playing of Stan Getz, a white man who experiments in Latin-American as well as Afro-American idioms; and in that of John Coltrane and Ornette Coleman, who revealed relationships between country blues and the melodic arabesques of Indian and other Asiatic music. Nor did players of the percussive and harmonic piano avoid Parker's influence, as we can hear in the jittery linearity of the playing of Bud Powell who, like Parker, was a drug-infected vicitim of jazz neurosis. More positively, McCoy Tyner, starting in the 1960s in duo with Coltrane as a brilliant exponent of blues and standard forms, became, as soloist or with his own groups, pervasively African in his drone-dominated techniques.

White country music

Black jazz began as the music of an alien people in a vast industrial land. Originally a minority activity, in its true forms it has remained one, though it has also been absorbed into the white entertainment business. In the eighteenth and nineteenth centuries the original white settlers on the American continent brought their folk music with them, and they too have been transformed into an industry: the pop music known as country and western. The music originated, however, in the Eastern states, where emigrants from Britain had sung their old songs, rendered scrawnier and more rasping by the tough conditions of pioneer life. Even in the mid-twentieth century this is still evident in the singing of men and women living in remote areas of the Carolinas, Kentucky and Virginia. Aunt Molly Jackson, Sarah Ogan Gunning or Nimrod Workman, all from the Virginian and Kentuckian mining fields, sang a "monody of deprivation" which remains folk, not pop, music. The instrumentalists, however, who made music not so much to alleviate loneliness as to stimulate communal activity, transformed their old-world models more radically. Georgian, Arkansas and Virginian fiddlers such as Fiddlin' John Carson played the old Scots and Irish reels with wild abandon, making a music of almost manic cheerfulness. To keep their spirits up, the old music had to be defused of pain and passion – and therefore, to a degree, of truth.

This provided a recipe for pop or entertainment, as distinct from folk, music. Whereas the singing of Jackson or Workman pares the old world's experience to its barest bone, the fiddling of the string bands of the 1920s abandons everything to hedonism. This euphoria is no less evident in the banjo and guitar pickers who often support the fiddlers or themselves play European-based dance music, or accompaniments to songs, some derived from British sources, others newly invented. Both fiddle music and plucked string music tends to be fast, regular in meter and diatonic. The modal inflections of old folk music are banished, though they occasionally creep back through the influence of the singing and playing of itinerant blacks. The musical interest of this functional music, existing to stimulate dancing, increases with such influence. We can hear this, for example, if we compare Uncle Dave Macon, a traveling singer, banjoist and story-teller who belonged to minstrel-show traditions, with blind Doc Watson, a guitarist of high virtuosity who discovers danger within his pyrotechnics. Whereas the typical white country banjoist or guitarist, such as Doc Boggs, adopts an impassive stance, Watson's music tells us that jollity, like life, must be precarious. This becomes more poignantly evident in the "high lonesome sound" of the great mountain singer and player, Roscoe Holcomb.

Bluegrass

Some fiddlers and string players formed string bands such as the Skillet Lickers, the Gully Jumpers or the North Carolina Ramblers. The music they made in the 1920s

150 The Gully Jumpers (Burt Hutcherson, Roy Hardison, Charley Arrington, Paul Womack), c1938.

and 30s was still a medley of old British songs and dances drained of hurtful elements and seasoned with bits of American hymnody, march and ballad, with exotic intrusions from new and old Mexico and from French Louisiana. At first this concerted music was still folk music in that, played by amateurs, it served the needs of the community. During the 1940s it became more streamlined, exploitable on radio and recording. It was named "bluegrass" in homage to its Eastern mountain origins. Bluegrass music was performed by a lead singer who also played the guitar, banjo or mandolin, vigorously supported by other players of guitar, banjo and harp, with an interlacing of fiddles. Tunes were fast and plainly diatonic; in the work of the Monroe Brothers, and still more the legendary Flatts and Scruggs, breathtaking virtuosity may again bring a whiff of danger, and therefore of nervous reality, to the cozy themes of hearth and home, mother, love and duty. There may be a hint of desperation in the way in which the most melancholy local events – railway accidents, hangings etc – are recounted with headily impervious glee. One finds something similar in the more jazz-influenced string bands that, in the 1940s, came to be known as "western swing".

Bob Willis, an academically trained fiddler who used his technique to enhance his music's folky abandon, and the Monroe Brothers were not merely intinerant entertainers but stars on the radio networks. So were the Carter Family, a Virginian mountain family centered on A. P. Carter, who collected and arranged old-time hymns and ballads and sang quavery bass in the vocal trio. This was led by the low, rasping voice of his wife Sarah; Maybelle, musically the most gifted of the family, played banjo, fiddle, lute, autoharp and guitar. All the Carters' songs, whatever their origin or theme, come out at moderate-to-fast tempo, regular in meter and in unsullied diatonicism. Enunciation is flat, tone pinched, whether the numbers are

Carter Family

based on British ballads, gospel hymns or parlor songs in barbershop harmony. The Carters' importance is attributable not to exceptional talents but to their incorruptible integrity. Though popularized, even commercialized, they were little changed between the 1920s and the 1950s.

With the Carters and the frail, clown-like figure of Jimmie Rodgers the Lonesome Cowboy, country music became an industry in which those opposite poles of pop music, hedonism and nostalgia, were identified. Country singers like Dolly Parton and Lacy J. Dalton, mountain girls who began by singing music imbibed at their mother's knee, have entered big business in becoming pop stars, without destroying the folklike creativity they started from.

Rock

The rock explosion that occurred in the wake of World War II and came to fruition in the 1960s was an attempt to re-create music as orgiastic magic. White country music, having become an industry, tried to absorb the life-giving primitivism of black jazz. Black–white integration worked both ways. If white culture engulfed black, black culture was now eager to take advantage of white technology to boost its growing self-confidence. From this process emerged what came, appropriately, to be called soul music: the traditional passion and pain of black gospel music and of the blues are given greater punch by electric rather than acoustic guitars and keyboards, in powerful amplification. The most distinguished male and female soul singers – Otis Redding and James Brown, Nina Simone and Aretha Franklin – maintain contact with black folk traditions both in their vocal production and jazz-oriented rhythm and phrasing, and also in their use of gospel-style antiphony between lead voice and backing group. Also, in the 1960s blacks established their own record-producing industry, based in Detroit, manufacturing their own black style, called Motown. This fast, regular-metered, cheerily diatonic music, reflecting the black's self-assurance, is best represented by Diana Ross and her Supremes. It is a mechanized version of the appeal typical, half a century earlier, of ragtime, a black music that had sprung from competition with whites. The sound of Motown has been widely imitated by pop groups on both sides of the Atlantic from the late 1970s.

But the emergence of rock and roll in the mid-twentieth century was a white phenomenon, in that young whites listened to black rhythm and blues out of frustration with their own society. It is possible to see Elvis Presley as a successor to the country singer Hank Williams. Both were Southern white boys with an

Hank Williams

evangelical background; both were or became nervously distraught. Williams composed most of his own material in an idiom related to that of the Carter Family, though with a touch of the black blues that gave a darker shade to the hymn-like and ballad style. He found a pleasurable zest in the sincerity of his corniness, reflected in his transitions between country waltz and blues, folk fiddle and electric guitar. His songs of disappointed love spring from the same emotion that informs his devotional songs, as we can hear in comparing *Last night I dreamed of you* (1951) with *Long gone lonesome blues* (1953). In each he comes through by walking a tightrope between an obvious sincerity and irony.

Elvis Presley

Occasionally the black elements in Williams's songs, reinforced by the electric beat, guide him towards early Presley-style rock and roll, as in *Move it on over*. Born a decade later than Williams, Elvis Presley responded to a non-conformist small-town background far more rebelliously. Whereas Williams created his own songs, mostly about broken loves, frustrated attempts to deal with them and appeals for God's succor when all else fails, Elvis, a pampered mother's boy, at first used other people's modes and manners to evoke an image of narcissistic self-esteem. Dressed extravagantly, he brought it off because he had abilities to bolster his charisma.

Presley's confidence in his voice projected his image, making it possible for him at once to conform and to rebel. *Heartbreak Hotel*, the number that brought him instant fame in 1956, was in origin a Southern country song. He sings it lyrically, with a ripe romanticism almost comparable with that of a concert artist; he thus invites us to take the love experience straight. At the same time he rebelliously undermines it by rhythmic displacements derived from the triple drag-style of piano boogie and by conscious pitch distortions suggested by gospel singing. Presley uses both black barrelhouse and white Pentecostal styles as part of his performing expertise. Straight romantic lyricism is held in tension. The performance stimulates because it is precarious.

This also applies when Presley starts from black material, as in his version of *Hound Dog*, originally associated with Big Mama Thorton. He was always a performer, never a composer. The gyrations of the body followed the voice and the face, for his ecstasy became sexual rather than godly. The two poles of his nature – white dream-maker and black rebel – were both attempted escapes from routine. Slowly he succumbed to drink, drugs and near-infantilism.

151 Elvis Presley in the film *Jailhouse Rock*, 1957.

Rolling Stones

Presley was a solo performer; he could brook no competition. But as rock music developed it increasingly took over from gospel music the concept of the group. Interestingly, the rock group reached its climax not in the USA but in traditionally conservative Britain. The Rolling Stones, whose heyday was in the 1960s, still represent the closest approach pop has made to an orgiastic music comparable with that created in tribal societies. This is seen in the group's singer Mick Jagger's Africanized yelling and bodily gyrations, as well as in the fact that he adapted much of his material from black bluesmen like Muddy Waters (who enjoyed a revival during these years because they offered something that young whites desperately needed). The Rolling Stones' instrumental resources also have rudimentary origins, electric guitars and keyboards being vastly amplified versions of blues guitar, country harmonica, bagpipes and autoharp. Amplification intensifies primitivism, since electronics may create a nightmarish inflation of the pitch distortions typical of folk music. Just as the black voice, emulated by the white Jagger, substitutes aggression for passion, so instrumental forces follow suit. Percussion is more violent than real tribal drumming, both because it is metrically cruder and because, in amplification, it is so loud, passing the threshold of tolerance, to render one deaf as well as stunned. Breaking the sound barrier may become not a permissive euphoria but a destructive force relatable to voodoo. In 1970 Jagger's rendering of *Under my thumb* triggered a Hell's Angels ritual murder at the site of the performance. Not surprisingly, primitive pentatonic melody here relies mainly on the driving beat for its momentum; harmony, as in real tribal music, is minimal or non-existent, reduced to one or two reiterated chords. This is powerfully evident in the Stones' albums *Let it bleed* or *Their Satanic Majesties request* (1968); it may be observed too in "hard" American rock groups such as the Doors, the Grateful Dead and the drug-oriented Velvet Underground. Although language plays a part in the activities of these groups it is for the most part inaudible or, if audible, negative and deflatory.

As with genuine tribes, submission to the devil may lead to driving him out. This may be why the Stones' music has retained its virility over 20 years. The celebrants at a concert by the black Jimi Hendrix, who identified his musical with his sexual instrument, regarded his violent magnificence as prelude to an affirmative act. The same might be said of the music of The Who, even as they concluded their performance by burning their instruments. This instance of conspicuous waste and planned obsolescence contained latent ironies; the instruments were destroyed as a protest against the obsolescence encouraged by a civilization based on industrial commodities, yet the waste could be afforded only because the performers were promoted by that society. Later more unorthodox groups like the Mothers of Invention offered a purgative experience in which song, dance, acrobatics, mime and clowning combine with narcotics and with what is usually called obscenity. A parallel with the Ancient Greek satirist Aristophanes, as well as with some Red Indian cults, is clear, though the satire is more derisive. But Frank Zappa, the super-mother consciously cultivating a white matriarchy to balance the unconscious black version in the city blues, has said that what is being promoted is independent of the words. He has given support to this in the impressively jazz-like qualities of his music from *Hot Rats* (1969) onwards.

Sometimes attitudes are more benign. Groups such as the Incredible String Band, Moody Blues, the Pentangle and Steeleye Span were triggered off not so much by black blues and voodoo violence as by European folk-cults and the traditional comic play of the Italian *commedia dell'arte*. Medieval and Renaissance techniques meet those inherited from folk styles – European, American, African, Middle and Far Eastern. From such fusions of techniques, both straight and electronic, springs a world of fairy-tale. The gentle modal tunes and sonorities are not escape into daydream, as is the nostalgia of Irving Berlin, but they do imply a return to the child within us all. Militantly hard rock and dreamily soft folk both opt out of a society considered hostile because materialistic. Yet both depend on that society.

Music-theater, rock musicals

Just as the energy of the Rolling Stones seem to have weathered the years, so something survives from the happier and hippier cults of the 1960s. There is a direct return, if in simple form, to the Greek concept of music-theater ritual. This is also demonstrated in the "tribal musicals" of which Galt McDermott's *Hair* (1969) was the first to achieve artistic as well as material success. *Hair* has much the same form as a Dionysiac initiation ceremony, consisting of a *pompē* (novice's departure), an *agon* (contest, death, rebirth) and a *komos* (return of the initiate). It offered a hippy's purification from the enemies, war and society, by way of freedom, sex and drugs. (The pop hero of the 1960s bore a resemblance to the Greek god Dionysos, who was often depicted as "a youth of effeminate appearance, with luxuriant hair".) The same theme and structure appear in The Who's *Tommy* and in Andrew Lloyd Webber's *Jesus Christ Superstar*, which boldly transmutes Christianity's patriarchal Son and Father into emissaries of the new matriarchy. More conventionally rooted musicals of the 1970s, notably Sondheim's brilliant *Sweeney Todd* (1979), veer towards the "tribal" concept, turning a Victorian melodrama into a late twentieth-century myth of ritual murder. The use of multiple media – word, sound, movement, lighting – and of improvisation and audience participation means involvement rather than passive reception.

Most pop concerts have become theater ritual in this sense. Audiences will no longer tolerate a pop concert without visual as well as audible appeal. The Yes's performance of their *Tales from Topographic Oceans* (1973) has something in common with the later music rituals of Stockhausen, in intention as well as in technique and technology. Two movements are called "The Revealing Science of God" and "The Ancient Giants under the Sun"; the point is the remoteness of such cosmic-astrological concerns from Western consciousness. The young echo the prophets and seers who have maintained that man, to survive, must rediscover ancient truths. The music is ethnically African and Middle Eastern as well as American-British.

There is a difference between a ritual that supports inherited beliefs and one that seeks to destroy or attains fulfillment only in dream or regression. Pop is ritual in an emergent stage, and its ambiguity may be a strength. The long-playing record, tape and audio-visual are more radical innovations than we once realized. They transplant ritual from temple or theater to any place. Individuals may create one, as do The Who in *Quadraphenia* (1965) or Pink Floyd in *Atom Heart Mother* (1968) and *The Wall* (1979). Intellect and technology are combined with feeling and instinct.

The Beatles

The most successful group in pop history, the Beatles, was the best. Their quality depended on the fact that, although they were four young men who represented their culture, they made songs of pronounced individuality. The return to origins in the basic beat, the often modal tunes, the side-stepping harmonies, were given a location and a name. American blues and country music interlaced with British hymn and music hall in the memorable melodies. The innocence of the early, wide-eyed *I saw her standing there* (1963), the unsentimental nostalgia of *Yesterday* (1965),

152 The Beatles recording
Day Tripper, 1965.

Bob Dylan

the witty pathos of *Eleanor Rigby* (1966), the magical mystery of *Strawberry Fields Forever* (1967), the regenerative lyricism of *Because* (1969) are all beyond the range of time and tarnish. With *Sergeant Pepper's Lonely Hearts Club Band* (1967) the Beatles made history with the first self-contained cycle prompted by the long-playing disc; they explored with instinctive verbal articulateness and in fresh, original music the perennial problems of adolescence: loneliness, fear, friendship, sex, the generation gap, alienation, nightmare. They could do this because, although a group, they were also four individuals, two of whom, John Lennon and Paul McCartney, had immense creative gifts. The cycle is about "A Day in the Life" of any young person in a divided and distracted world; and the contrast between the tender pentatonic tune with which the song opens and the inhumane hubbub that simulates the atomic bomb remains as potent and as poignant as ever.

Alongside tribal pop has flourished the music of solo performers, who affirm the validity of the individual spirit. With the Beatles, Bob Dylan is probably the most remarkable pop musician. He has consistently written his own words and music. Opting out from college and the Establishment, he became a spokesman for American youth, starting from the minimal conventions of white country music and black blues. He at first castigated a sick society in "protest" songs in part

153 Bob Dylan at Slane, July 1984.

inspired by those of his master, Woody Guthrie. Variations of pitch and inflection were part of the composition. The narrative *Ballad of Hollis Brown* (1964) told a true story of deprivation and alienation through means identical with those of a real folk ballad, except for the amplification necessary for communicating with a mass audience.

The social validity of Dylan's songs is deepened, not denied, when he moves from protest against the world outside to self-confrontation. This is initiated in *Mr Tambourine Man* (1965) which, related to white hillbilly music rather than to blues, looks like an escape from life to dream, and in a sense it is so, in that a tambourine man is a dope pedlar. His Pied Piper myth encourages us to follow the unconscious, as is movingly suggested by the wavery refrain and the irregularity of the verbal and musical clauses. In the next phase of Dylan's work, notably the double album *Blonde on blonde* (1966), the tambourine man leads him into dream and nightmare, in rich poetry that prompts comparably rich permutations of country music and blues, calling on electric technology in the process. In *John Wesley Harding* (1968) Dylan abandons this gadgetry, returning to his country roots and acoustic guitar; but dream and nightmare are not expunged, for the verses now have a fundamentalist Christian background. The political protest, having passed through the fire of the inner life, merges in religious consciousness and conscience. This is not the same as faith, of which there is little evidence on this powerful record, even in the magnificent, doom-laden *All along the watchtower*. But the love songs that follow – on *Planet waves* (1974), *Blood on the tracks* (1974) and *Desire* (1975), in which Dylan makes haunting use of the mythology of the movie Western – are "songs of redemption".

Not only *Nashville Skyline* (1970), a deliberate compromise between the folk and the commercialized country world, but also *John Wesley Harding* and the later Wild West songs were "produced" in Nashville, factory of the pop music industry. The ethnic qualities of Dylan's songs become more, not less, marked after his flirting with commerce. The gospel songs of his "born again" phase contain some of his blackest music, close to pentatonic yell and tumbling strain, abrasive in vocal production. The black elements in *Slow train coming* (1979) reveal affinities with the age-old, pinched-toned cantillation of his Jewish ancestry, linked in turn with the Moorish-Spanish incantation of the Arizonan and New Mexican desert songs.

Joni Mitchell

It is not surprising that some of the finest singing poet-composers should be women. Joni Mitchell matriarchally complements Dylan's white-Jewish-black patriarchy, creating verses dedicated to woman as lonely seagull, seeking flight from conformity. The pathos of her verses in early songs like *To a seagull* and *Margie* (1968) flows into modal tunes and empirical, guitar-derived harmonies that sound at once hopeful and vulnerable. In feminine passivity, she does not "grow", as Dylan does, and in her middle phase, especially in *Hejira* (1976), she was prone to self-pity. Yet that was a response to a deep-felt frustration which could not destroy her poetic gift, and from which she emerged with the help of black jazz rather than rock. The process begins with her disc *Mingus* (1979), named after the neurotically brilliant composer-performer Charles Mingus who made the record with her; the fusion of her white lyricism with black jazz's physical and nervous vivacity brings rich dividends. In recent songs Mitchell's ethnic qualities are as varied as Dylan's, embracing white folk, black jazz and South American music along with a ghost of the aboriginal Amerindians. Dylan and Mitchell are not alone in these travelings through space and time. Among their colleagues and successors are the white black-comedian, Randy Newman, whose musical spontaneity complements the rigor of his verbal wit; Tom Waits, the gravel-voiced bard of late-night New York bars; Bruce Springsteen, rockstar of "the darkness at the edge of town"; and the West Indian Bob Marley, who gave international status to his people's pop music, reggae (a Caribbean derivative of soul and Motown), and so became a national political hero. Among the women we must note another West Indian, the British Joan Armatrading, whose creative intensity is in part attributable to her ethnically varied roots; and Tania Maria, another hybrid, dazzling alike as jazz pianist and as a singing composer in an idiom somewhere between a New York jazz club and the Rio bars she came from.

For the first time in history, pop offers an art that is the prerogative of youth. That is not because of the young's financial independence but because pop youthfully demonstrates how man's life is. In the 1980s, "groups" are appearing who, like the Beatles, speak on behalf of the individual as well as the tribe. Notwithstanding their ironic name, the Police are verse-makers, composers and performing musicians of subtlety and high intelligence who, especially on their record *Synchronicity* (1983), deal with "serious" themes in a witty and poetic idiom. *Tea in the Sahara* is as mysteriously evocative as the writings of Paul Bowles, by which it was inspired. Synthesizers are used with such imagination that the music "sounds" in total lucidity, in spite of the rapid, nervous tempos; and that is still more true of the Eurhythmics, whose ethnic connotations – British, American, North African, Polynesian, West Indian, Balinese – combine to make a music of rejuvenating grace. It says much for today's young that groups like the Police and the Eurhythmics should have achieved popular success.

Further Listening

The Listening Notes throughout the book (listed in the contents pages) treat in detail certain representative works or movements which should be listened to above all. The first priority for further listening should be the remaining movements of works of which only one or two are discussed in the Listening Notes. The lists below, which correspond with the arrangement of the historical chapters in the book, offer suggestions of works that may appropriately be used for following up. Most of them are mentioned, and some are discussed, in the text; all are relevant to points made in the text, nearly all are readily available in good recordings. And all should give pleasure to the listener.

Chapter IV
Any examples of plainsong
VITRY *Impudenter/Virtutibus* (motet)
MACHAUT *Douce dame jolie* (virelai)
DUNSTABLE *Veni sancte Spiritus* (motet)

Chapter V
DUFAY *Ave regina coelorum* (motet); Mass *Se la face ay pale*
BINCHOIS *Filles à marier* (chanson)
OCKEGHEM *Ma bouche rit* (chanson)
JOSQUIN *Ave Maria . . . virgo serena* (motet); *Mille regrets* (chanson)
JANEQUIN *Le chant des oiseaux* (chanson)
LASSUS *Salve regina, mater misericordiae* (motet); Lamentations
PALESTRINA *Tu es Petrus* (motet); *Missa Papae Marcelli*
VICTORIA Mass *Laetatus sum*
GIOVANNI GABRIELI *In ecclesiis* (motet)
GESUALDO Responsories; *Deh, coprite il bel seno* (madrigal)
BYRD Mass in Four Voices; *Sing joyfully* (anthem); *This sweet and merry month of May* (madrigal); *The Carman's Whistle* for virginals
MORLEY *Now is the month of maying* (madrigal)
WILBYE *Draw on, sweet night* (madrigal)
GIBBONS *O clap your hands* (anthem); *The silver swan* (madrigal)
DOWLAND *Lachrimae* (fantasia for strings)

Chapter VI
MONTEVERDI Vespers (1610); *Lamento d'Arianna*; *Chiome d'oro* and *Zefiro torna* (madrigals)
CARISSIMI *Jephte* (oratorio) (*excerpts*)
SCHÜTZ *Veni, sancte Spiritus* (motet); *St Matthew Passion*
PURCELL *Come, ye sons of art* (ode); *My heart is inditing* (anthem)
LULLY *Te Deum*; *Armide* (*excerpts*)
COUPERIN Harpsichord music, e.g. *Les barricades misterieuses, Soeur Monique*
CORELLI Concerto grosso in g op. 6 no. 8, "Christmas"
VIVALDI *Gloria* in D; Violin Concertos, *The Four Seasons*, op. 8 nos. 1–4
DOMENICO SCARLATTI Harpsichord sonatas
TELEMANN *Musique de table* (*excerpts*)
BACH Toccata and Fugue in d for organ; Brandenburg Concerto no. 5 in D; Partita no. 1 in B♭; Cantata no. 80, *Ein feste Burg*; *St Matthew Passion* (*excerpts*)
HANDEL *Water Music*; Organ Concerto (e.g. op. 4 no. 4 in F); *Giulio Cesare* ("Julius Caesar") (*excerpts*); *Jephtha* (*excerpts*)

Chapter VII
GLUCK *Orfeo ed Euridice* (*excerpts*)
HAYDN String Quartet in f op. 20 no. 5; Symphony no. 44 in e; *The Creation* (*excerpts*)
MOZART String Quartet in G K387; String Quintet in C K515; Symphony no. 40 in g K550; *Die Zauberflöte* ("The Magic Flute") (*excerpts*)

BEETHOVEN Piano Sonata in c op. 13, "Pathétique", String Quartet in F op. 59 no. 1; Symphony no. 5 in c; Symphony no. 9 in d, "Choral" (finale); String Quartet in a op. 132; *Fidelio* (*excerpts*)

Chapter VIII

SCHUBERT Songs, e.g. *An die Musik* ("To Music"), *Der Erlkönig* ("The Erlking"), *Die Forelle* ("The Trout"), *Heidenröslein* ("The Little Rose in the Heather"), *Tod und das Mädchen* ("Death and the Maiden"); *Wanderer* Fantasia for piano; Symphony no. 9 in C, "Great C major"

MENDELSSOHN Overture *A Midsummer Night's Dream*; Symphony no. 4 in A, "Italian"

SCHUMANN Piano Concerto in a; *Carnaval* for piano

CHOPIN Nocturne in E♭ op. 9 no. 2; Ballade no. 1 in g op. 23; Waltz in D♭ op. 64 no. 1

LISZT Piano Sonata in b

BERLIOZ *Fantastic Symphony*

ROSSINI *Il barbiere di Siviglia* ("The Barber of Seville") (*excerpts*)

VERDI *Rigoletto* and *La traviata* (*excerpts*)

WAGNER *Die Meistersinger* ("The Mastersingers") (*excerpts*)

BRAHMS Violin Concerto; Clarinet Quintet

Chapter IX

TCHAIKOVSKY *Romeo and Juliet* (overture)

MUSSORGSKY *St John's Night on the Bare Mountain*

RIMSKY-KORSAKOV *Sheherazade*

RACHMANINOV Piano Concerto no. 2 in c

SMETANA *Vltava*

DVOŘÁK Symphony no. 9 in e, "From the New World"; String Quartet in F op. 96, "American"

JANÁČEK *Katya Kabanova* (*excerpts*)

BRUCKNER Symphony no. 7 in E

MAHLER Symphony no. 4 in G

STRAUSS *Der Rosenkavalier* (*excerpts*)

SIBELIUS Symphony no. 5 in E♭

ELGAR Variations on an Original Theme "Enigma"

FAURÉ *Requiem*

DEBUSSY *La cathédrale engloutie* (Préludes, i)

RAVEL *La valse*

PUCCINI *Tosca* (*excerpts*)

Chapter X

SCHOENBERG *Verklärte Nacht* ("Transfigured Night")

BERG Violin Concerto

WEBERN Symphony op. 21

STRAVINSKY *The Rite of Spring*

BARTÓK Music for Strings, Percussion and Celesta; String Quartet no. 4

HINDEMITH *Mathis der Maler (suite)*

WEILL *The Threepenny Opera* (*excerpts*)

IVES *The Unanswered Question*

COWELL String Quartet no. 4, "United"

VARÈSE *Hyperprism*

COPLAND *Appalachian Spring*

CARTER String Quartet no. 1

VAUGHAN WILLIAMS Fantasia on a Theme by Thomas Tallis

PROKOFIEV *Romeo and Juliet*

SHOSTAKOVICH Symphony no. 5

BRITTEN *Peter Grimes* (*excerpts*)

MESSIAEN *Turangalîla-symphonie*

STOCKHAUSEN *Kontakte*

CAGE *4′ 33″*

BERNSTEIN *West Side Story* (*excerpts*)

LUTOSLAWSKI *Venetian Games*

Further Reading

Below is listed a selection of books which should help the reader who wants to look more deeply into any particular topic. The reference books contain fuller bibliographies which may usefully be followed up. Publication dates are normally those of the most recent edition.

There exist numerous biographies and other studies of individual composers. Here we confine ourselves mainly to the rather factual biographies in the *New Grove* series (largely reprinted from *The New Grove Dictionary*), which have comprehensive lists of works and full bibliographies. Other composer studies are cited only when they have something rather different to offer on a major figure; similarly, a number of non-biographical books (including the subject's own writings) are listed where they afford particular insights.

In the "Composers" section below, studies treating groups of composers are listed first, then books on individual composers in chronological order by composer.

Reference

The New Grove Dictionary of Music and Musicians, ed. Stanley Sadie (Washington, DC: Grove's Dictionaries; London: Macmillan, 1980)
Harvard Dictionary of Music, ed. Willi Apel (Cambridge, Mass. and London: Harvard UP, 1973)
Baker's Biographical Dictionary of Musicians, ed. Nicolas Slonimsky (New York: Schirmer; Oxford: Oxford UP, 1985)
The New Oxford Companion to Music, ed. Denis Arnold (New York and London: Oxford UP, 1983)

Special topics

INSTRUMENTS
Anthony Baines, ed.: *Musical Instruments through the Ages* (Baltimore and Harmondsworth: Penguin, 1966)
Robert Donington: *Music and its Instruments* (New York and London: Methuen, 1982)
Sybil Marcuse: *A Survey of Musical Instruments* (New York: Harper & Row; Newton Abbot: David & Charles, 1975)
Mary Remnant: *Musical Instruments of the West* (New York: St Martin's; London: Batsford, 1978)

ELEMENTS, FORM
See individual subject articles in *The New Grove Dictionary of Music and Musicians* and the *Harvard Dictionary of Music* (cited above)

AMERICAN MUSIC
Charles Hamm: *Music in the New World* (New York and London: Norton, 1983)
H. Wiley Hitchcock: *Music in the United States: a Historical Introduction* (Englewood Cliffs, NJ, and London: Prentice-Hall, 1974)

JAZZ
James Lincoln Collier: *The Making of Jazz* (New York: Houghton, Mifflin; London: Granada, 1978)
Donald D. Megill and Richard S. Demory: *Introduction to Jazz History* (Englewood Cliffs, NJ, and London: Prentice-Hall, 1984)
Paul Oliver, Max Harrison and William D. Bolcom: *Ragtime, Blues and Jazz* [The New Grove] (New York: Norton; London: Macmillan, 1986)

OPERA
Donald Jay Grout: *A Short History of Opera* (New York: Columbia UP, 1965)
Earl of Harewood, ed.: *Kobbé's Complete Opera Book* (New York and London: Putnam, 1972)
Joseph Kerman: *Opera as Drama* (New York: Vintage, 1956)
Stanley Sadie, ed.: *Opera* [The New Grove] (New York: Norton; London, Macmillan, 1986)

NON-WESTERN MUSIC
William P, Malm: *Music Cultures of the Pacific, the Near East, and Asia* (Englewood Cliffs, NJ, and London: Prentice-Hall, 1977)
Bruno Nettl: *Folk and Traditional Music of the Western Continents* (Englewood Cliffs, NJ, and London: Prentice-Hall, 1973)
Elizabeth May, ed.: *Music of Many Cultures: an Introduction* (Berkeley, Los Angeles and London: U. of California Press, 1980)

History

GENERAL
Gerald Abraham: *The Concise Oxford History of Music* (New York and London: Oxford UP, 1980)
Edith Borroff: *Music in Europe and the United States: a History* (Englewood Cliffs, NJ, and London: Prentice-Hall, 1971)
Donald Jay Grout: *A History of Western Music* (New York: Norton; London: Dent, 1974)
Paul Henry Lang: *Music in Western Civilization* (New York: Norton; London: Dent, 1941)

PERIODS
Richard H. Hoppin: *Medieval Music* (New York and London: Norton, 1978)
Howard Mayer Brown: *Music in the Renaissance* (Englewood Cliffs, NJ, and London: Prentice-Hall, 1976)
Claude V. Palisca: *Baroque Music* (Englewood Cliffs, NJ, and London: Prentice-Hall, 1981)
Charles Rosen: *The Classical Style: Haydn, Mozart, Beethoven* (New York: Norton; London: Faber, 1972)
Leon Plantinga: *Romantic Music* (New York and London: Norton, 1985)
Gerald Abraham: *A Hundred Years of Music* (Chicago: Aldine; London: Duckworth, 1974)
William W. Austin: *Music in the Twentieth Century* (New York: Norton; London: Dent, 1966)
Nicolas Slonimsky: *Music since 1900* (New York: Scribner, 1971)
Eric Salzman: *Twentieth-Century Music: an Introduction* (Englewood Cliffs, NJ, and London: Prentice-Hall, 1974)
Paul Griffiths: *A Concise History of Modern Music from Debussy to Boulez* (New York and London: Thames & Hudson, 1978)
Paul Griffiths: *A Guide to Electronic Music* (New York and London: Thames & Hudson, 1979)
John Vinton, ed.: *Dictionary of Contemporary Music* (New York: Dutton; London: Thames & Hudson, 1974)

Composers

MIDDLE AGES, RENAISSANCE, BAROQUE
David Fallows: *Dufay* [Master Musicians] (London: Dent, 1983)
Joseph Kerman and others: *High Renaissance Masters* [Byrd, Josquin, Lassus, Palestrina, Victoria; The New Grove] (New York: Norton; London, Macmillan, 1984)
Denis Arnold and others: *Italian Baroque Masters* [Monteverdi, Cavalli, Frescobaldi, A. and D. Scarlatti, Corelli, Vivaldi; The New Grove] (New York: Norton; London: Macmillan, 1984)
Joshua Rifkin and others: *North European Baroque Masters* [Schütz, Froberger, Buxtehude, Purcell, Telemann; The New Grove] (New York: Norton; London: Macmillan, 1985)
Malcolm Boyd: *Bach* [Master Musicians] (London: Dent, 1984)
Christoph Wolff and others: *The Bach Family* [The New Grove] (New York: Norton; London: Macmillan, 1983)
Winton Dean: *Handel* [The New Grove] (New York: Norton; London: Macmillan, 1982)

CLASSICAL
Jens Peter Larsen: *Haydn* [The New Grove] (New York: Norton; London: Macmillan, 1982)
Wolfgang Hildesheimer: *Mozart* (New York: Farrar, Straus & Giroux, 1982; London: Dent, 1983)
Stanley Sadie: *Mozart* [The New Grove] (New York: Norton; London: Macmillan, 1982)
Emily Anderson, ed.: *The Letters of Mozart and his Family*, 3rd edn. (New York: Norton; London: Macmillan, 1985)

Maynard Solomon: *Beethoven* (New York: Schirmer; London: Cassell, 1977)

Alan Tyson and Joseph Kerman: *Beethoven* [The New Grove] (New York: Norton; London: Macmillan, 1983)

Joseph Kerman: *The Beethoven Quartets* (New York: Knopf; London: Oxford UP, 1967)

ROMANTIC

Nicholas Temperley and others: *Early Romantic Masters I* [Chopin, Schumann, Liszt; The New Grove] (New York: Norton; London: Macmillan, 1985)

John Warrack and others: *Early Romantic Masters II* [Weber, Berlioz, Mendelssohn; The New Grove] (New York: Norton; London: Macmillan, 1985)

Philip Gossett, Andrew Porter and others: *Masters of Italian Opera* [Rossini, Bellini, Donizetti, Verdi, Puccini; The New Grove] (New York: Norton; London: Macmillan, 1983)

Deryck Cooke and others: *Late Romantic Masters* [Bruckner, Brahms, Wolf, Dvořák; The New Grove] (New York: Norton; London: Macmillan, 1985)

Michael Kennedy and others: *Turn of the Century Masters* [Strauss, Sibelius, Mahler, Janáček; The New Grove] (New York: Norton; London: Macmillan, 1984)

Maurice J. E. Brown: *Schubert* [The New Grove] (New York: Norton; London: Macmillan, 1982)

Hector Berlioz: *Memoirs*, ed. David Cairns (New York: Knopf; London: Gollancz, 1969)

Leon Plantinga: *Schumann as Critic* (New York: Da Capo, 1976)

John Deathridge and Carl Dahlhaus: *Wagner* [The New Grove] (New York: Norton; London: Macmillan, 1983)

Barry Millington: *Wagner* [Master Musicians] (London: Dent, 1984)

Julian Budden: *Verdi* [Master Musicians] (London: Dent, 1985)

John Warrack: *Tchaikovsky* (New York: Scribner; London, Hamish Hamilton, 1973)

TWENTIETH CENTURY

Oliver Neighbour and others: *Second Viennese School* [Schoenberg, Berg, Webern; The New Grove] (New York: Norton; London: Macmillan, 1983)

László Somfai and others: *Modern Masters* [Bartók, Stravinsky, Hindemith; The New Grove] (New York: Norton; London: Macmillan, 1984)

Edward Lockspeiser: *Debussy: his Life and Mind* (London: Cassell, 1962)

Charles Rosen: *Arnold Schoenberg* (New York: Viking; London: Boyars, 1975)

Arnold Schoenberg: *Style and Idea*, ed. Leonard Stein (New York: St Martin's; London: Faber, 1984)

John Kirkpatrick, ed.: *Charles E. Ives Memos* (New York: Norton; London: Calder & Boyars, 1972)

Robert Craft: *Stravinsky: Chronicle of a Friendship* (New York: Vintage; London: Gollancz, 1972)

John Cage: *Silence: Lectures and Writings* (Middletown, CT: Wesleyan UP; London: Calder & Boyars, 1961)

Glossary of Musical Terms

Words given in capitals refer to other glossary entries. Page references are given for terms discussed more fully in the main text of the book.

absolute music Music with no extra-musical association or PROGRAM.

a cappella A Latin term, applied to choral music without accompaniment.

accent The emphasizing of a note in performance.

acciaccatura A "crushed" note, sounded just before the main one, used as a musical ornament.

accidental A sharp, flat or natural sign occurring during a piece, temporarily altering the pitch of a note.

adagio Slow; a slow movement.

aerophone A generic term for a wind instrument.

air A simple tune for voice or instrument; also AYRE.

aleatory music Music in which chance or randomness is an element (pp. 425, 499).

allegretto Less quick than allegro; a movement in moderately quick tempo.

allegro Quick; a movement in lively tempo.

allemande A moderately slow Baroque dance in quadruple meter, often the opening movement of a SUITE; also *almain*, *almand* etc.

alto 1 A female voice with a range lower than a soprano, or a high male voice (p. 33). **2** A term used for an instrument whose range is analogous to the alto voice, e.g. alto saxophone; hence *alto clef*, used by the viola.

andante At a moderately slow pace; a movement in moderately slow tempo.

andantino A little faster than andante.

answer A musical phrase that responds to one previously heard, particularly in a fugue (p. 68).

anthem A choral work in English for performance in church services; a *national anthem* is a patriotic hymn.

antiphony Music in which two or more groups of performers are separated to create special effects of echo, contrast etc; hence *antiphonal*.

appoggiatura A "leaning" note, usually a step above (or below) the main note, creating a DISSONANCE with the harmony, used as a musical ornament.

arco A direction to bow rather than pluck the strings of a string instrument.

aria An air or song for solo voice with orchestra, usually part of an opera, cantata or oratorio (p. 80).

arioso A style of singing between RECITATIVE and ARIA.

arpeggio The notes of a chord sounded in succession rather than simultaneously.

Ars Nova A Latin term, meaning "new art", used for the new style of fourteenth-century French and Italian music (p. 96).

art song A composed, written-down song (as opposed to a folksong).

atonality Without TONALITY, not in any KEY; hence *atonal*.

augmentation The lengthening of time values of the notes of a melody (usually by doubling them), particularly of a medieval *cantus firmus* or a fugue subject.

augmented interval An interval that has been increased by a semitone (p. 16).

avant-garde A French term used to describe composers (also artists and writers) whose work is radical and advanced.

ayre An English song (or air) for solo voice with lute or viols (p. 80).

bagatelle A short, light piece, usually for piano.

ballad A traditional song, often with a narrative; hence *ballad opera*, which has spoken dialogue and uses popular tunes.

ballade 1 An instrumental piece in narrative style, usually for piano. **2** A medieval polyphonic song form.

ballata A late thirteenth- and fourteenth-century Italian poetic and musical form.

ballett A Renaissance part song with a dance-like rhythm and a "fa-la" refrain; also *balletto*.

bar MEASURE.

baritone A male voice with a range between a tenor and a bass (p. 33).

barline The vertical line marking off one MEASURE from the next.

bass 1 A male voice with the lowest range (p. 33). **2** An instrument of bass range, or the lowest of a group of instruments, e.g. bass clarinet; hence *bass clef*, used by bass instruments and a pianist's left hand. **3** The lowest-pitched part in a piece of music, the basis of the harmony.

basse danse A medieval and Renaissance court dance, usually in slow triple meter.

basso continuo The term for which the more commonly used CONTINUO is an abbreviation.

beat The basic pulse underlying most music (p. 18).

bel canto A style of singing, particularly in Italian opera, that allows the voice to display its agile and sensuous qualities; hence *bel canto opera*.

binary form The form of a piece of music with two sections, *AB* (p. 63).

blues A type of black American folk or popular music (p. 509).

bourrée A fast Baroque dance in duple meter with a quarter-note upbeat.

break In jazz, a short solo passage (usually an IMPROVISATION) between passages for ensemble.

bridge 1 A linking passage in a piece of music. **2** The part of a string instrument over which the strings pass.

cadence A progression of notes or chords that gives the effect of closing a passage of music (p. 24).

cadenza A virtuoso passage (sometimes an IMPROVISATION) towards the end of a concerto movement or aria.

canon A type of polyphony in which a melody is repeated by each voice or part as it enters (p. 30).

cantata A work for one or more voices with instrumental accompaniment (p. 82); hence *church cantata*, with a sacred text (p. 77).

cantus firmus A Latin term, meaning "fixed song", used for a borrowed melody on which composers from the late Middle Ages onwards based polyphonic compositions (p. 61).

canzona A short sixteenth- and seventeenth-century instrumental piece.

capriccio A short instrumental piece; also *caprice*.

chaconne A moderate or slow dance in triple meter, usually with a GROUND BASS.

chamber music Music for a chamber (or small room) rather than a hall; hence music played by small groups – duos, trios, quartets etc (p. 71).

chance music ALEATORY MUSIC.

chanson The French word for "song", used specifically for French medieval and Renaissance polyphonic songs (p. 80).

chant PLAINSONG.

characteristic piece A short piece, usually for piano, representing a mood or other extra-musical idea; also *character piece*.

chorale A traditional German (Lutheran) hymn-tune.

chorale prelude An organ piece based on a chorale.

chord The simultaneous sounding of two or more tones (p. 27).

chordophone A generic term for a string instrument.

chorus 1 A choir. **2** The music a choir sings. **3** The REFRAIN of a song.

chromatic Based on an octave of 12 semitones rather than a DIATONIC scale; hence *chromaticism, chromatic scale, chromatic progression* (p. 16).

clef The sign at the beginning of the staff that indicates the pitch of one of its lines and therefore determines all of them; hence *treble clef, alto clef, tenor clef, bass clef* (p. 15).

coda An Italian term, meaning "tail", used for a movement's closing section added as a rounding-off rather than an integral part of the form.

coloratura A rapid, decorated style of singing, often high-pitched.

common time 4/4 time, i.e. four quarter-notes in a measure (p. 20).

compound meter A meter in which the main beats are grouped in threes (e.g. 6/8), unlike SIMPLE METER (p. 20).

con brio With spirit.

concertino 1 The small group of soloists in a CONCERTO GROSSO. **2** A small-scale concerto.

concerto Originally, a work (vocal or instrumental) with effects of contrast, but now a work in which a solo instrument is contrasted with a large ensemble or orchestra; hence *solo concerto* (p. 70).

concert overture An overture written as a self-contained concert piece, not as the opening of a larger work.

consonance An interval or chord that sounds smooth and harmonious, as opposed to a dissonance; also *concord* (p. 28).

continuo 1 A term (abbreviated from *basso continuo*) for a type of accompaniment played, usually on a keyboard or a plucked instrument with or without a sustaining instrument, from a notated bass line to which figures may have been added to indicate the required harmony. **2** The group of instrumentalists playing a continuo part.

contralto A female voice with a range lower than a soprano (p. 33).

counterpoint The simultaneous combination of two or more melodies, or POLYPHONY; hence *contrapuntal* (p. 29).

countersubject A subsidiary theme played simultaneous with the subject of a fugue (p. 193).

countertenor A male voice with the highest range, similar to that of an alto (p. 34).

courante A moderately fast Baroque dance in triple meter, often the second movement of a SUITE; also *corrente*.

crescendo Getting louder.

cyclic form A form in which themes recur in more than one movement of the same work.

da capo An Italian term, meaning "from the head", placed at the end of a piece as an instruction to the performer to repeat the first part of the music up to a given point; hence *da capo aria* (p. 80).

development The process of developing (expanding, modifying, transforming etc) themes and motifs; the section of a movement in which development takes place (p. 65).

diatonic Based on a major or minor scale rather than a CHROMATIC one; hence *diatonic scale* (p. 16).

diminished interval An interval that has been reduced by a semitone (p. 16).

diminuendo Getting quieter.

diminution The shortening of time values of the notes of a melody (usually by halving them).

dissonance An interval or chord that sounds rough, not harmonious like a consonance; also *discord* (p. 28).

dominant The fifth step or degree of the scale (p. 24).

dotted note In notation, a note after which a dot has been placed to increase its time value by half (p. 20).

double 1 Lower in pitch by an octave; hence *double bass*. **2** A VARIATION.

double bar A pair of vertical lines to mark the end of a piece or a substantial section of it.

downbeat The accented beat at the beginning of a measure, indicated by a downward stroke of a conductor's stick, and sometimes anticipated by an UPBEAT.

duo A work for two performers (or a group who play such a work); also *duet*.

duple meter A meter in which there are two beats in each measure (p. 19).

duplet A pair of notes occupying the time normally taken by three of the same note value.

dynamics The gradations of loudness in music (p. 31).

electronic music Music in which electronic equipment plays a part.

electrophone A generic term for instruments that produce their sound by electric or electronic means.

ensemble 1 A small group of performers. **2** A number in an opera or large choral work for two or more solo singers (p. 81). **3** The quality of coordination in a performance by a group.

episode An intermediate passage, e.g. a section of a fugue or a rondo between entries of the subject.

étude The French term for a STUDY.

exposition The first section of a work, particularly of a movement in sonata form, in which the main themes are stated (p. 64).

expressionism A term borrowed from painting and literature for music designed to express a state of mind.

fanfare A ceremonial flourish for trumpets or other brass instruments.

fantasia In the Renaissance, a contrapuntal instrumental piece; later, a piece in free, improvisatory style; also *fantasy, phantasia, fancy*.

fermata The sign (⌒) indicating that a note or rest should be prolonged; also *pause*.

figured bass A system of notating the harmonies in a CONTINUO part.

finale The last movement of a work or the closing ensemble of an act of an opera.

flat In notation, the sign (♭) indicating that the pitch of a note should be lowered by a semitone; also *double flat (♭♭)* (p. 16).

florid A term used to describe a melody that is highly ornamented; also *fioritura*.

form The organization or structure of a piece of music (p. 59).

forte, fortissimo (f, ff) Loud, very loud.

French overture A piece in two sections (a pompous, jerky introduction followed by a fugue) that originated in the late seventeenth century as an introduction to an opera or ballet (p. 70).

fugato   A passage in fugal style.

fugue   A type of composition (or a technique) in which imitative polyphony is used systematically (p. 67).

galant   A term for light, elegant, tuneful eighteenth-century music of no great emotional weight (p. 220).

galliard   A lively sixteenth- and early seventeenth-century court dance in triple meter, often paired with a PAVAN.

gavotte   A fast Baroque dance in quadruple meter, beginning on the third beat of the measure, often a movement of a SUITE.

Gebrauchsmusik   A German term, meaning "functional music", used in the 1920s for music with a social or educational purpose.

Gesamtkunstwerk   A German term, meaning "total art work", which Wagner used for his later music-dramas in which music, poetry, drama and the visual arts were unified in his concept.

gigue   A fast Baroque dance usually in compound meter, often the last movement of a SUITE; also *jig*.

glissando   A rapid instrumental slide up or down the scale.

Gregorian chant   A repertory of PLAINSONG associated with Pope Gregory I, during whose reign chants were categorized for use in the Roman Catholic church (pp. 61, 89).

ground bass   A bass melody repeated several times while upper parts have varying music (p. 66).

group   A group of themes in a sonata form exposition; hence *first group*, *second group* (p. 64).

harmony   The combination of tones to produce chords, and the relationship of successive chords; hence *harmonic, harmonize* (p. 26).

harmonics   The sounds heard together when a tone is produced by a vibrating string or air column, through its vibration in parts (two halves, then thirds etc); hence *harmonic series*.

heterophony   A texture in which several different versions of the same melody are stated simultaneously; hence *heterophonic*.

hocket   A medieval technique of staggering rests and short phrases between two or more voices to give a "hiccup" effect.

homophony   A texture in which the parts generally move together, a melody with accompanying chords; hence *homophonic* (p. 29).

hymn   A song of praise, usually in several stanzas, sung congregationally.

idée fixe   A term used by Berlioz for a recurring theme in his symphonic works (p. 326).

idiophone   A generic term for instruments that, when they are struck, produce the sound themselves.

imitation   A polyphonic technique in which the melodic shape of one voice is repeated by another, usually at a different pitch; hence *imitative counterpoint* (p. 30).

impressionism   A term borrowed from painting to describe music that is intended to convey an impression (often of natural phenomena) rather than a dramatic or narrative idea.

impromptu   A short piece, usually for piano, that suggests improvisation.

improvisation   Spontaneous performance without notated music, but often with reference to a tune or chord progression.

incidental music   Music composed as a background to, or interlude in, a stage production (p. 85).

indeterminacy   The compositional principle of leaving elements to chance (ALEATORY MUSIC) or at the discretion of the performer.

interval   The distance between two notes (p. 16).

inversion 1   The rearrangement of the notes of a chord so that the lowest note is no longer the fundamental one.   **2**   The performance of a melody "upside-down", with the intervals from the starting note applied in the opposite direction.

isorhythm   A fourteenth-century technique whereby a scheme of time-values is repeated, usually to a plainsong melody; hence *isorhythmic motet* (pp. 61, 96).

Italian overture   A piece in three sections (fast – slow – fast/dance) that originated in the early eighteenth century as an introduction to an opera or other vocal work (p. 70).

jig   GIGUE.

Kapellmeister   The German term for the musical director of a prince's private chapel or other musical establishment.

key 1   The TONALITY and major or minor scale of a passage of music according to the note to which it is gravitating; hence *key note* (pp. 24, 60).   **2**   The lever depressed by the player on a keyboard instrument.

key signature   The group of sharp or flat signs at the beginning of each staff indicating the KEY (p. 25).

largo, larghetto   Slow and grandly, slightly less slow; a slow movement.

lai   A medieval song form.

leading tone   The seventh degree of the scale, a semitone below the tonic, to which it therefore gives a feeling of leading.

legato   Smoothly, not STACCATO, indicated by a SLUR.

leger lines   Small extra lines above or below the staff for notes too high or low to be accommodated on the staff itself; also *ledger line* (p. 15).

leitmotif   A German term, meaning "leading motif", used (chiefly by Wagner) for a recognizable theme or musical idea that symbolizes a person or a concept in a dramatic work (p. 351).

lento   Very slow.

libretto   The text of an opera (or oratorio), or the book in which the text is printed.

lied   The German word for "song", used specifically for nineteenth-century German songs for voice and piano; plural *lieder* (pp. 82, 285).

madrigal   A Renaissance secular contrapuntal work for several voices that originated in Italy and later also flourished in England (p. 80).

maestro di cappella   The Italian term for the musical director of a prince's private chapel or other musical establishment.

Magnificat   The hymn to the Virgin Mary, often set to music for liturgical use.

major   The name given to a SCALE in which the distance from the first note to the third is four semitones, applied to keys, chords, intervals (pp. 16, 25).

manual   A keyboard played with the hands, as opposed to a pedalboard, chiefly used with reference to the organ and harpsichord.

Mass   The main service of the Roman Catholic church, frequently set to music for liturgical use (pp. 77, 89).

mazurka   A Polish dance in triple meter.

measure   A metrical division of music marked off by vertical lines (barlines); also *bar* (p. 20).

Meistersinger   A member of a guild of German merchant musicians which flourished from the fourteenth century to the seventeenth.

melisma   A group of notes sung to the same syllable; hence *melismatic*.

mélodie   A French word for "song", used specifically for nineteenth- and twentieth-century French songs for voice and piano.

melody   A succession of notes of varying pitch with a recognizable shape or tune; hence *melodic* (p. 21).

membranophone   A generic term for instruments that produce their sound from stretched skins or membranes.

meter   The grouping of beats into a regular pulse; hence *metrical* (p. 18).

metronome A device (mechanical or electrical) that sounds an adjustable number of beats per minute; hence *metronome mark*.

mezzo- Half, medium; hence *mezzo-forte* (*mf*), *mezzo-piano* (*mp*).

mezzo-soprano A female voice with a range halfway between a soprano and a contralto or alto (p. 33).

Minnesinger The German equivalent of a TROUBADOUR.

minor The name given to a SCALE in which the distance from the first to the third notes is three semitones, applied to keys, chords, intervals (pp. 16, 25).

minuet A moderate dance in triple meter, often a movement of a Baroque SUITE and later the third (occasionally second) movement of Classical forms like the symphony, string quartet and sonata.

mode A term used to describe the pattern of tones and semitones within an octave, applied particularly to the eight church modes used in the Middle Ages; hence *modal, modality* (p. 26).

moderato At a moderate pace.

modulation The process of changing from one KEY to another in the course of a piece (p. 26).

monody A term for music consisting of a single line, applied to the type of accompanied song that flourished in Italy around 1600 (p. 141).

monophony A single line of melody without accompaniment, as opposed to polyphony; hence *monophonic* (pp. 29, 93).

motet A polyphonic choral work, usually with a Latin text, for use in the Roman Catholic church, that was one of the most important forms from the thirteenth century to the eighteenth (pp. 77, 95).

motif A short, recognizable musical idea; also *motive*.

motto A brief motif or phrase that recurs during a work.

movement A self-contained section of a larger composition.

music-drama Wagner's term for his later type of opera.

musique concrète Music in which real (or "concrete") sounds are electronically recorded.

mute A device used on instruments to muffle the tone (Italian *sordino*).

natural In notation, the sign (♮) indicating that a note is not to be sharp or flat (p. 16).

neo-classical A term describing the music of some twentieth-century composers whose techniques draw on those of the Baroque and Classical periods (p. 423).

neume A sign used in medieval notation showing the groups of notes to which a syllable should be sung (pp. 14, 90).

nocturne A piece that evokes night, usually a short, lyrical piano piece (pp. 76, 318).

nonet A work for nine performers.

note The written symbol for a tone of definite pitch; also the tone itself.

obbligato A term for an instrumental part that is essential to a composition, second in importance only to the principal melody.

octave The interval between two notes of the same name, 12 semitones (an octave) apart (p. 15).

octet A work for eight performers.

ode In ancient Greece a sung celebratory poem; in the seventeenth and eighteenth centuries, a cantata-like work celebrating events, birthdays etc.

Office The eight daily services (apart from Mass) of the Roman Catholic church.

opera A drama set to music (p. 82).

opera buffa Italian eighteenth-century comic opera.

opéra comique French opera, normally with spoken dialogue (not just "comic opera" and not necessarily comic at all).

opera seria Italian eighteenth-century opera on a heroic or tragic subject.

operetta Light opera with spoken dialogue, songs and dances.

opus The Latin word for "work", used with a number to identify a work in a composer's output.

oratorio An extended setting of a text on a religious topic for soloists, chorus and orchestra (p. 79).

orchestration The art and technique of writing effectively for an orchestra or large group of instruments.

Ordinary The parts of the Mass with fixed texts that remain the same each day, as opposed to the Proper (table, p. 89).

organum A type of medieval polyphony in which one voice or more is added to a plainsong (p. 93).

ornament One or more notes used to embellish a melody.

ostinato A musical figure that is persistently repeated while the other elements are changing; hence *basso ostinato*, a GROUND BASS.

overture A piece of orchestral music introducing a larger work; also CONCERT OVERTURE, FRENCH OVERTURE, ITALIAN OVERTURE.

part 1 The written music for a performer or performing section in an ensemble, e.g. the violin part. **2** In polyphonic music a "strand", line or voice, e.g. two-part harmony, four-part counterpoint; hence *part-writing, partsong*, a song for several parts.

passacaglia A GROUND BASS movement, in slow or moderate triple meter, in the Baroque period.

passing tone A tone, foreign to the harmony with which it sounds, linking by step two tones that are (normally) part of the harmony.

Passion An extended oratorio-like setting of the story of the crucifixion (p. 79).

pavan A slow, stately sixteenth- and early seventeenth-century court dance in duple meter, often paired with a GALLIARD; also *pavane*.

pedalboard A keyboard (e.g. on an organ) played by the feet.

pedal point A sustained tone, usually in the bass, round or above which the other parts proceed.

pentatonic A term used for a mode or scale consisting of only five tones (p. 17).

phrase A group of tones, often a unit of a melody, longer than a motif.

piano, pianissimo (p, pp) Quiet, very quiet.

pitch The highness or lowness of a sound (p. 14).

pitch class A term for all notes of the same name, such as C or A♭.

pizzicato A direction to pluck rather than bow the strings of a string instrument.

plainsong Liturgical chant to Latin texts used since the Middle Ages, also known as GREGORIAN CHANT.

polonaise A stately Polish dance in triple meter.

polyphony A texture in which two or more independent melodic lines are combined, as opposed to heterophony, homophony, monophony; hence *polyphonic* (pp. 29, 93).

prelude A short instrumental work originally intended to precede another, but from the nineteenth century a short, self-contained piece usually for piano.

presto, prestissimo Very fast, very fast indeed.

program music Instrumental music that is narrative or descriptive of some non-musical idea, often literary or pictorial (p. 284).

progression A musically logical succession of chords; hence *harmonic progression, chord progression*.

Proper The parts of the Mass text that vary from day to day according to the church calendar, as opposed to the Ordinary (table, p. 89).

quadruple meter A meter in which there are four beats in each measure (p. 20).

quarter-tone An interval half the size of a semitone.

quartet A work for four performers (or a group that plays such a work).

quintet A work for five performers.

ragtime A type of early twentieth-century American popular music characterized by syncopated melody, usually for piano (p. 510).

rallentando Slowing down.

recapitulation The third main section in a movement in sonata form in which the thematic material stated in the exposition is repeated in the home key (p. 65).

recitative A type of writing for the voice with the rhythm and inflections of speech, used in opera, oratorio and cantatas by the soloists (p. 82).

refrain A verse of a song or vocal work that recurs after each new verse or stanza.

Requiem The Roman Catholic Mass for the dead, frequently set to music (p. 77).

resolution The progression from dissonant, unstable harmony to consonant harmony.

rest In notation, one of several symbols corresponding to a given number of beats or bars, indicating a period of silence (p. 20).

rhythm The distribution of sounds into groups with a perceptible meter or pulse (p. 17).

rhythm and blues A type of black American pop music of the 1950s.

ricercare A Renaissance instrumental work that usually displays skillful application of counterpoint; also *ricercar*.

ripieno The large group of instrumentalists in a CONCERTO GROSSO.

ritardando Becoming slower.

ritenuto Held back.

ritornello A passage that recurs, particularly the instrumental section of an aria or a passage for orchestra in a Baroque or Classical concerto; hence *ritornello form* (p. 65).

Rococo A term borrowed from art history to describe the decorative, elegant style of music between the Baroque and Classical periods (p. 220).

rondeau 1 A medieval polyphonic song form. 2 A seventeenth-century instrumental form, forerunner of the RONDO.

rondo A form in which a main section recurs between subsidiary sections (p. 64).

round A sung CANON in which the voices all sing the same melody at the same pitch.

row SERIES.

rubato The Italian word for "robbed", used as an indication that the meter may be treated with some freedom by a performer for expressive effect.

sarabande A slow Baroque dance in triple meter often with a stress on the second beat of the measure, normally a movement of a SUITE.

scale A sequence of notes going upwards or downwards by step; hence *major scale, minor scale, chromatic scale* (p. 16).

scherzo 1 A lively movement in triple meter that came to replace the minuet as a symphony movement. 2 In the nineteenth century, a self-contained instrumental piece, usually for piano.

score The music-copy of a piece for several performers; hence *full score*, containing complete details of every participating voice and instrument, *short score*, a compressed version of a full score; *conducting score, miniature score, piano score, pocket score, vocal score*.

semitone Half a tone, the smallest interval commonly used in Western music.

septet A work for seven performers.

sequence 1 The repetition of a phrase at a higher or lower pitch than the original. 2 A medieval and Renaissance polyphonic setting of a religious text.

serialism A method of composing using a series of tones (usually all 12 of the chromatic scale), or other musical elements, which are heard only in a particular order; hence *serial* (pp. 62, 430).

series A fixed set of tones used as the basis of a serial composition (p. 62).

sextet A work for six performers.

sforzato, sforzando (sf, sfz) Strongly accented.

sharp In notation, the sign (♯) indicating that the pitch of a note should be raised by a semitone; also *double sharp*, x (p. 16).

simple meter A meter in which the main beats are grouped in twos (e.g. 2/4), unlike COMPOUND METER (p. 20).

sinfonia The Italian word for "symphony", used to designate a wide range of instrumental pieces; hence *sinfonia concertante*, a sinfonia with a concerto element; *sinfonietta*.

Singspiel A German eighteenth-century opera with spoken dialogue.

slur In notation, a curved line over a group of notes indicating that they should be smoothly joined in performance.

sonata A piece in several movements for small ensemble, soloist with accompaniment or solo keyboard; hence *sonata da camera* ("chamber sonata") and *sonata da chiesa* ("church sonata"), seventeenth- and eighteenth-century instrumental works in three or four movements; *sonatina* (pp. 71–2, 75).

sonata form A form used from the Classical period onwards, chiefly for the first movements of large instrumental works (e.g. symphonies, string quartets, sonatas) (p. 64).

sonata–rondo form A form that combines elements of sonata form and rondo (p. 65).

song cycle A group of songs unified by their texts, a general idea, a narrative or musical features.

soprano 1 The highest female voice (p. 33). 2 A term used for an instrument of high range, e.g. soprano saxophone.

Sprechgesang A German term used to describe a vocal style between speech and song, used extensively by Schoenberg (p. 429); also *Sprechstimme*.

staccato Detached, not legato, indicated by a dot or a dash over a note.

staff The set of lines on and between which music is written; also *stave* (p. 14).

stretto 1 The overlapping of entries in the subject of a fugue. 2 A direction to the performer to increase the tempo, or a passage containing such an increase; also *stretta*.

strophic A term applied to songs in which each stanza (verse) of the text is sung to the same music.

study A piece, usually for solo instrument, intended to demonstrate or improve an aspect of performing technique; also *étude*.

Sturm und Drang A German expression, meaning "storm and stress", used for an eighteenth-century literary and artistic movement the ideals of which were to convey emotion and urgency (p. 234).

subdominant The fourth step or degree of the scale.

subject A theme or a group of themes on which a work is based; hence *subject group*.

suite An instrumental work in several movements, usually a set of dances, which in the seventeenth and eighteenth centuries often took the form ALLEMANDE–COURANTE–SARABANDE–optional dance movements–GIGUE (p. 75).

suspension A harmonic device whereby a tone or tones of one chord are held while the next, with which the prolonged tones are dissonant, is sounded; there is a RESOLUTION when the suspended tones fall to those of the new chord.

symphonic poem An orchestral piece based on a non-musical (literary, narrative etc) idea, or program (p. 70).

symphony An extended orchestral work usually in several (most often three or four) movements (p. 69).

syncopation The stressing of beats of a meter that are normally unstressed.

synthesizer A machine that produces and alters sounds electronically.

tablature A system of notation by symbols that represent the position of a performer's fingers (e.g. on a guitar) rather than the tone to be played (p. 14).

tempo The speed of a piece of music (p. 18).

tenor 1 The highest normal male voice (p. 33). **2** A term used for an instrument whose range is analogous to the tenor voice, e.g. tenor saxophone; hence *tenor clef*, used by the cello.

tenuto A term telling the performer to hold a tone to its full length.

ternary form A form with three sections, the third a repetition of the first, *ABA* (p. 63).

texture The way in which the individual strands of a work are blended.

thematic transformation A nineteenth-century process whereby themes are modified during a movement (p. 323).

theme A musical idea on which a work is based, usually with a recognizable melody; hence *thematic, theme and variations* (p. 59).

thoroughbass CONTINUO.

through-composed A term applied to songs in which each stanza (or verse) is set to different music, as opposed to STROPHIC songs.

tie In notation, a curved line linking two notes of the same pitch, indicating that they should be one continuous sound.

timbre TONE-COLOR.

time signature The figures on the staff at the beginning of a piece indicating the meter and unit (p. 20).

toccata An instrumental piece in free form, usually for keyboard, intended to display the performer's technique.

tonality The feeling of gravitational pull towards a particular tone, determined by the KEY of the music.

tone 1 A sound of definite pitch and duration. **2** The interval equal to two semitones. **3** The timbre or quality of a musical sound.

tone-color The quality of the sound of a particular instrument or voice, or a combination of them.

tone-poem SYMPHONIC POEM.

tonic The main note of a major or minor key (p. 24).

transition A subsidiary passage that leads from one more important section to another, e.g. a BRIDGE passage in sonata form.

transpose To write down or play music at a pitch other than the original one; hence *transposing instrument*, which plays a tone at a fixed interval from the written one, e.g. a clarinet in B♭ (p. 24).

treble 1 A high voice, usually a child's (p. 33). **2** A term used for an instrument of range similar to the treble voice, e.g. treble recorder; hence *treble clef*, used by high instruments and a pianist's right hand.

tremolo A rapid reiteration usually of a single tone, e.g. by the trembling action of a bow of a string instrument; also *tremolando*.

triad A three-note "common" chord consisting of a fundamental tone with tones at the intervals of a 3rd and 5th above (p. 27).

trill The rapid alternation of two adjacent tones, used as a musical ornament; also *shake*.

trio 1 A work for three performers, or a group that plays such a work. **2** The middle section of a minuet, scherzo, march etc.

trio sonata A Baroque sonata for two melody instruments and continuo (p. 72).

triple meter A meter in which there are three beats in each measure (p. 20).

triplet A group of three notes occupying the time normally taken by two of the same note value.

tritone The interval of three whole tones.

trope A passage, with or without a text, introducing or inserted into Gregorian chant.

troubadours, trouvères French poet-musicians who performed songs of courtly love at the feudal courts of Europe during the Middle Ages (pp. 90–92).

tune A simple, singable melody.

tutti An Italian term, meaning "all the performers", used (e.g. in a concerto) to designate a passage for orchestra rather than the soloist.

twelve-tone A term used to describe a technique of composition (SERIALISM) in which all 12 notes of the chromatic scale are treated equally (pp. 62, 430).

unison A united sounding of the same tone or melody; hence *unison singing*.

upbeat A weak or unaccented beat preceding the main beat (the DOWNBEAT), particularly the beat before a barline, indicated by an upward stroke of a conductor's stick.

variation A varied (elaborated, embellished etc) version of a given theme or tune; hence *theme and variations* (p. 66).

verismo An Italian term, meaning "realism", applied to some late nineteenth-century operas that feature violent emotions, local color etc (p. 368).

verse 1 A stanza of a song. **2** In Anglican church music, a term used for the passages for solo voice rather than choir; hence *verse anthem*.

vibrato A rapid fluctuation in pitch and/or volume, used for expressiveness and richness of sound, e.g. the "wobble" of a string player's left hand on the strings.

virelai A medieval polyphonic song form.

vivace Vivacious.

vocalise A wordless solo vocal piece.

voice-leading The rules governing the progression of the voices in contrapuntal music; also *part-writing*.

waltz A nineteenth-century dance in triple meter.

whole tone The interval of two semitones; hence *whole-tone scale*, a scale progressing in six equal tones (p. 414).

word-painting The musical illustration of the meaning of a word, or its connotation, in a vocal work.

Acknowledgements

John Calmann & King Ltd wish to thank the institutions and individuals who have kindly provided photographic material for use in this book. Museums, galleries and some libraries are given in the captions; other sources are listed below.

Alinari, Florence: 21; 51
Artothek, Munich: pl. 23; pl. 27
Clive Barda, London: 32
Imogen Barford, London: 8
Bartók Archive, Budapest: 133
BBC Hulton Picture Library, London: 111
Biblioteca Nacional, Rio de Janeiro: 145
Bibliothèque Nationale, Paris: 61; 71; 87; 106; 107; 109; 121
Bridgeman Art Library, London: pl. 7
Trustees of the British Library, London: pl. 1; pl. 5; pl. 32; 5; 15; 33; 38; 39; 45; 46; 47; 56; 59; 62; 63; 67; 73; 82; 85; 95
Bulloz, Paris: pl. 31; 66
Bureau Soviétique d'Information, Paris: 114
Giancarlo Costa, Milan: pl. 30; 126
Brian Dear, Lavenham: 6; 7; 24 (Oxford University Press); 28; 29 (Macmillan Publishers Ltd, London)
Department of the Environment, London: pl. 15 (reproduced by gracious permission of Her Majesty The Queen)
Dover Publications Inc., New York: 97
Edison Institute, Henry Ford Museum and Greenfield Village, Dearborn (Mich.): 143
Editions Alphonse Leduc, Paris: 140
EMI Ltd, London: 124
Fotomas, London: 90
Freie und Hansestadt Hamburg: 69
Fürstlich Oettingen-Wallerstein'sche Bibliothek und Kunstsammlung, Schloss Harburg: 35
Mrs Aivi Gallen-Kallela, Helsinki/Akseli Gallen-Kallelan Museosäätiö, Espoo: 123
Gemeentemuseum, The Hague: 22
Giacomelli, Venice: pl. 19
Giraudon, Paris: pl. 9; 72; 104
Glyndebourne Festival Opera/Guy Gravett: 136
G. D. Hackett, New York: 133; 148; 149
Hansmann, Munich: pl. 17
Heritage of Music: pl. 2; pl. 5; pl. 20; pl. 25; pl. 29; 64; 101; 106; 107; 117; 142
Hungarian Academy of Sciences, Budapest: 105
Peter Hutten, Wollongong/Kurt Hutton: 138
Master and Fellows of St John's College, Cambridge: 42
Kerkelijk Bureau de Hervormde Gemeente, Haarlem: 26
Collection H. C. Robbins Landon, Cardiff: pl. 18; 101
Les Leverett, Goodlettsville (Tenn.): 150
Mander and Mitchenson, London: 81
Bildarchiv Foto Marburg: 48
Federico Arborio Mella, Milan: 75
Museen der Stadt Wien: pl. 20; 83; 89; 100
Museo Teatrale alla Scala, Milan: 108
Godfrey MacDomnic, London: 3
Ampliaciones y Reproducciones MAS, Barcelona: 64
National Library of Ireland, Dublin: 116
New York Public Library, Lincoln Center: 142
Novosti, London: 137
Öffentliche Kunstsammlung, Basel/SPADEM: 130
Österreichische Nationalbibliothek Bildarchiv, Vienna: 96; 118
Photo Service, Albuquerque: 27
The Photo Source, London: 152; 153 (Seán Hennessy)
Reiss Museum, Mannheim: 86
Réunion des Musées Nationaux, Paris: pl. 16; 17; 131 (SPADEM)
Roger-Viollet, Paris: 125; 132

Harold Rosenthal/Opera Magazine: 115
Royal Collection (reproduced by gracious permission of Her Majesty The Queen): 88
Royal Opera House Covent Garden/Stuart Robinson: 139
Scala, Florence: pl. 10; pl. 11; pl. 13; pl. 14; pl. 26; pl. 28; 53
Robert-Schumann-Haus, Zwickau: 103
Sotheby's, London: 11; 40
Staatliche Museen Preussischer Kulturbesitz, Berlin: 4
Staatliches Kunstsammlungen, Weimar: 109
Denis Stevens, Berkeley (Cal.): 76
Mrs Sivvy Streli, Innsbruck: 129
Stuart-Liff Collection, Isle of Man: 113
Universitäts- und Landesbibliothek Sachsen-Anhalt, Halle: 78
University of Texas at Austin (Theater Arts Library, Harry Ransom Humanities Research Center): 144; 151 (from the MGM release Jailhouse Rock © 1957, Loew's Incorporated and Avon Productions Inc.)
Mrs Louise Varèse/W. W. Norton & Co., New York (from L. Varèse, Varèse: a Looking-glass Diary, 1972): 134
VEB Deutsche Verlag für Musik, Leipzig: 31
Courtesy of the Board of Trustees of the Victoria and Albert Museum, London: pl. 21; 41; 80
Richard-Wagner-Museum, Bayreuth: 112
Allan Dean Walker, Santa Monica (Cal.): 127
© Galerie Welz, Salzburg: 119
Val Wilmer, London: 147
Joseph P. Ziolo, Paris: 128

Examples of copyright music in Chapters IX and X are reproduced by kind permission of the copyright-owners, as follows:

Bartók, Concerto for Orchestra (p. 453): copyright © 1946 by Hawkes & Son (London) Ltd. Extract reprinted by permission of Boosey & Hawkes Music Publishers Ltd. Specifically excluded from any blanket photocopying arrangements.
Bartók, Music for Strings, Percussion and Celesta (p. 451): © Universal Edition, by permission of Boosey & Hawkes Inc, assignee of copyright and renewal in USA.
Berio, Circles (p. 496): Universal Edition AG Vienna (Afred A. Kalmus Ltd).
Boulez, Marteau sans Maître (p. 491): Universal Edition (London) Ltd.
Cage, Atlas Eclipticalis (p. 498): © 1962 by Henmar Press Inc, 373 Park Avenue South, New York, USA. Reproduced by kind permission of Peters Edition Ltd, London.
Carter, String Quartet no. 1 (p. 470); by arrangement with Associated Music Publishers Inc, New York.
Ives, Three Places in New England (p. 461); The Unanswered Question (p. 462): Theodore Presser Company (Alfred A. Kalmus Ltd).
Messiaen, Vingt regards sur l'Enfant-Jésus (p. 487); Turangalîla-symphonie (p. 488): reproduced by permission of Durand SA/United Music Publishers Ltd.
Puccini, Tosca (p. 421): reproduced with permission of Ricordi.
Reich, Violin Phase (p. 501): Universal Edition (London) Ltd.
Schoenberg, Pierrot lunaire (p. 431): Universal Edition AG Vienna (Alfred A. Kalmus Ltd).
Sibelius, Symphony no. 4 (p. 407): Breitkopf & Hartel Ltd.
Stockhausen, Kontakte (p. 493): Universal Edition (London) Ltd.
Strauss, Till Eulenspiegel (p. 401): © 1932 by C. F. Peters, reproduced by kind permission of Peters Edition Ltd, London.
Stravinsky, Symphony in C (p. 444): © 1948 B. Schotts Söhne, Mainz, and Schott & Co. Ltd, London.
Varèse, Hyperprism (p. 465): © Colfranc Music Publishing Corporation, New York, Agent E. C. Kerby Ltd, Toronto; Ricordi, London: reproduced by arrangement.
Webern, Symphony op. 21 (p. 436); Six Bagatelles op. 9, no. 4 (p. 437): Universal Edition AG Vienna (Alfred A. Kalmus Ltd).

Index

Page numbers in *italic* indicate main
references; those with an asterisk ★
refer to Listening Notes

Abel, C. F., 229
Adam de la Halle, 91
Agoult, Countess Marie d', 322
Albéniz, 367
Albert, Prince Consort, 307
Albrecht V, Duke of Bavaria, 118
Albrechtsberger, J. G., 262
Aldeburgh, 484
Altenberg, Peter, 433
Amati family, 34
Amsterdam, 179, 242
Angiolini, 223
Ansfelden, 388
anthems, 77–8
Aquinas, St Thomas, 489
arias, 80–2
Arcadelt, Jacques, 118, 125
Armatrading, Joan, 528
Armstrong, Louis, 51, 511, *512–14*,
    517, 519
Arnstadt, 185
Ars Nova, 96–9
Astaire, Fred, 516
atonality, 423
Auden, W. H., 447, 481, 495
Auric, Georges, 457
Ávila, 128
ayres, 80

Babbitt, Milton, 496, 499
Bach, Anna Magdalena, 187–8
Bach, Carl Philipp Emanuel, 76, 186,
    202, 226, *227–8*, 230, 231
Bach, Johann Christian, 76, 188, 226,
    228–30, 242, 254, 502
Bach, Johann Christoph Friedrich,
    188, 226
Bach, Johann Ludwig, 196
Bach, Johann Sebastian, 28, 31, 43, 63,
    66, 67, 68, 70, 75, 79, 105, 144, 154,
    181, *184–204*, 190–1★, *192–3*★, 214,
    220, 247, 305, 359, 423, 451, *454–5*
Bach, Maria Barbara, 185, 186, 187
Bach, Veit, 184
Bach, Wilhelm Friedemann, 186, 226
Balakirev, Mily, 369–71, 374, *375*, 376,
    379
Baldwin, John, 132
ballet, 85–6
Balzac, Honoré de, 316, 368
bands, 56–7
Barber, Samuel, 472
Barezzi, Margherita, 337
Baroque era, 140–221
Bartók, Béla, 71, 73, 74, 77, 422, 423,
    448–54, *452–3*★, 456, 473, 477, 479,
    480, 486, 499, 507
Basie, Count, *518–19*
bassoons, 44–5
Baudelaire, Charles, 434
Bayreuth, 349–50, 411
BBC Symphony Orchestra, 490
Beatles, *525–6*
Beaumarchais, 257, 335
Bechet, Sidney, 512, 519
Beethoven, Carl Caspar van, 265, 276
Beethoven, Johann van, 265, 280
Beethoven, Karl van, 276, 280
Beethoven, Ludwig van, 40, 60, 64,

65, 67, 69, 72, 73, 76, 77, 82, 219,
    261–80, 268–9★, 283, 284, 285, 286,
    296, 323, 326, 335, 358, 360–1, 389
Beiderbecke, Bix, 518
Bellini, Vincenzo, 316, 336
Berg, Alban, 85, 422, 423, 428, *433–4*,
    436, 480, 482, 495
Berg, Helene, 433, 434
Bergamo, 336, 337
Berio, Luciano, 62, *496*
Berlin, 202, 221, 222, 227, 228, 263,
    300, 302, 306, 315, 406, 432, 455,
    456
Berlin, Irving, *516*
Berlioz, Hector, 69, 70, 77, 84, 284,
    310, 316, 320, 323, *325–33*, 328–9★,
    347, 350, 366, 369, 372
Bernstein, Leonard, *470–1*
Beverly Hills, 380
binary form, 63
Binchois (Gilles de Bins), *113*, 114
Birmingham, 307, 409
Bizet, Georges, 33, 84, 334, 367, 368
Blake, Eubie, 510
Blake, William, 473, 483, 485
Blow, John, 162
blues, 507–11
Boccherini, Luigi, 74, *260–1*
Boehm, Theobald, 43, 45
Boggs, Doc, 520
Böhm, George, 184
Boito, Arrigo, 344–5
Bologna, 334, 336
Bond, Edward, 495
Bonn, 261–2, 356
Bononcini, Giovanni, 209
Bordoni, Faustina, 213
Borodin, Alexander, 369, 375, 377, *378*
Bouilly, J. N., 274
Boulanger, Nadia, 466, 469
Boulez, Pierre, 21, 77, 423, 447, 486,
    488, 489–90, 491, 496, 500
Bowles, Paul, 528
Brahms, Johannes, 65, 67, 69, 70, 72,
    74, 76, 77, 309, 314, *356–65*, 361–3★,
    367, 383–4, 389, 392
Brandenburg, Margrave of, 189
brass instruments, 49–52
Brecht, Bertolt, 424, 456
Brentano, Antoine, 275
Breslau, 300
Brezhnev, Leonid, 477
Bridge, Frank, 480
Britten, Benjamin, 56–7, 67, 77, 85,
    480–4, 483★
Brno, 388
Brown, James, 522
Bruckner, Anton, 69–70, 356, 368–9,
    388–91, 398, 406
Brunsvik, Josephine von, 275
Büchner, Georg, 433
Budapest, 392, 449, 452, 500
Bull, John, 137–8, 138★
Bülow, Hans von, 324, 349, 361
Bunyan, John, 473
Burgundian school, 109
Burlington, Lord, 207
Burney, Charles, 154
Busnois, Antoine, 114
Busseto, 337, 341
Busoni, Ferruccio, 423, 456
Buxtehude, Dietrich, 67, *160–1*, 185,
    206

Byrd, William, 66, 77, 78, 80, *129–33*,
    132–3★, 136, 137, 473, 502
Byron, Lord, 323, 328, 371, 374

cabaret singers, 519
Caccini, Giulio, 141–2, 145, 166, 175
cadence, 24, 61
Cage, John, 17, 86, 425, 432, 490,
    496–9
Cairo, 344
Calvin, Jean, 107
Calzabigi, Raniero de, 223, 225
cantatas, 77–8, 82
cantus firmus, 61
Cara, Marchetto, 118
Carissimi, Giacomo, 79, 155, 175, 217
Carl Theodore, Elector Palatine, 225
Carr, Leroy, 511
Carson, Fiddlin' John, 520
Carter, A. P., 521
Carter, Betty, 519
Carter, Elliott, *468–70*
Carter family, 521–2
castrati, 34
Catherine the Great, 260
Cavalieri, Emilio de', 155
Cavalli, Francesco, 83, *154–5*
Cavour, Camillo Benso di, 342
cellos, 35
Cesti, Antonio, 154
Chabrier, Emmanuel, 416
chamber ensembles, 58
chamber music, 71–4
Chandos, Duke of, 208
chanson, 80
Char, René, 490
Charles, Ray, 517
Charles I, Duke of Bourbon, 113
Charles VII, King of France, 113
Charles VIII, King of France, 113
Charles the Bold, Duke of Burgundy,
    109
Charlotte, Queen, 229
Charpentier, Gustave, 79, 155
Charpentier, Marc-Antoine, 168,
    368
Chausson, Ernest, 411
Cherubini, Luigi, 303
Chicago, 475, 512–13, 519
Chopin, Frédéric, 40, 76, 261, 284,
    309, *315–20*, 318★, 366, 379, 381,
    416, 438
chorales, 61–2
chords, 27
Christina, Queen of Sweden, 175
Ciconia, Johannes, *100*
Cimarosa, Domenico, 259
clarinets, 46–8
classical era, 218–80
classicism, 218–20
Clementi, Ignace, *261*
Cocteau, Jean, 443
Colbran, Isabella, 335, 336
Coleman, Ornette, 519
Colette, 418
Colloredo, Count Hieronymus, 245
Cologne, 314, 491–2
color, 31
Coltrane, John, 519, 520
concertos, 70–1
consonance, 28
continuo, 142
Copland, Aaron, 67, 424, *466–8*

Corelli, Arcangelo, 72, 144, 169, 175,
    177, 207
cornetts, 50
Cöthen, 186–94
Counter-Reformation, 107–8
counterpoint, 29–31
country music, 520–2
Couperin, François, 64, 75, *168–70*
Couperin, Louis, 168
Coventry, 484
Cowell, Henry, *463–4*
Crabbe, George, 481
Craft, Robert, 447
Cremona, 149
Cristofori, Bartolomeo, 39
Cui, César, 369, 375, 376, 377, 378
Cunningham, Merce, 497
Cuzzoni, Francesca, 209
Czerny, Karl, 320

Dalton, Lacy J., 522
dance, 85–6
D'Annunzio, Gabriele, 416
Dargomïzhsky, Alexander
    Sergeievitch, 376, 377
Darmstadt, 300
Davies, Peter Maxwell, 500
Davis, Miles, 517, 519
Debussy, Claude, 17, 72, 73, 77, 85,
    356, 367, *411–17*, *412–13*★, 418, 426,
    449, 458
del Tredici, David, 425
Delibes, Léo, 374
Delius, Frederick, 472, *473–4*
Detmold, 357
Diabelli, Anton, 276
Diaghilev, Sergei, 85, 416, 418, 438,
    441–3, 448, 458, 474
Dibdin, Charles, 259
dissonance, 28
Dittersdorf, Carl Ditters von, 259
Dodds, Johnny, 512
dominant, 24
Donizetti, Gaetano, *336–7*
Doors, 524
Dostoyevsky, Fyodor, 375, 475
double bass, 35
Dowland, John, 80, *138–9*, 139★
Dresden, 156, 179, 202, 203, 222, 263,
    300, 311, 313, 347–8, 379
drums, 54
Dublin, 214
Dufay, Guillaume de, 77, 80, *109–13*,
    111★, 114
Dukas, Paul, 411
Duncan, Isadora, 86
Dunstable, John, *101–3*, 102★, 104
Duparc, Henri, 411
Dürbach, Fanny, 369
Durey, Louis, 457
Düsseldorf, 305, 313–14, 315, 356
Dvořák, Antonín, 69, 365, 381, *383–6*,
    388, 405, 409
Dylan, Bob, *526–7*
dynamics, 31

Eisenach, 182, 184
Eisenstein, Sergei, 476
Eleanor of Aquitaine, 87
electronic instruments, 55
electronic music, 424–5, 491–5
Elgar, Edward, 67, 80, *408–10*
Eliot, T. S., 448

Elizabeth I, Queen of England, 106,
    129–30, 131
Ellington, Duke, 514–15, 518
Emerson, Ralph Waldo, 463
Enlightenment, 221–2
Ercole I, Duke of Ferrara, 114
Erkel, Ferenc, 381
escapism, 283–5
Este, Isabella d', 118
Esterházy, Count Johann, 288
Esterházy, Prince Nikolaus, 232, 235
Esterházy family, 230, 232–4, 238–9,
    295, 320
Euripides, 495
Evans, Bill, 519
Evans, Gil, 517, 519
exoticism, 367

Falla, Manuel de, 458
Fauré, Gabriel, 72, 411
Field, John, 261, 318–19
Fingal's Cave, 305
Fitzgerald, Ella, 517, 519
Flatts, 521
Flaubert, Gustave, 376
Florence, 117, 142, 153, 206, 207
flutes, 43–4
Foster, Stephen, 503–5
Francis I, King of France, 106
Franck, César, 333, 411
Franco of Cologne, 20
Frankfurt, 182
Franklin, Aretha, 522
Frederick the Great, King of Prussia,
    202, 227
Freiberg, 300
Frescobaldi, Girolamo, 67, 153–4, 160
Freud, Sigmund, 368, 388, 429
Fricken, Ernestine von, 309
Friedrich Wilhelm II, King of Prussia,
    260
Froberger, Johann Jacob, 67, 160
Fuchs-Robettin, Hanna, 434
fugue, 67–8

Gabrieli, Andrea, 78, 80, 108, 125–6,
    136
Gabrieli, Giovanni, 78, 79, 108, 125–6,
    126*, 136, 141, 155–6
galant, 220–1
Galuppi, Baldassare, 260
Garrick, David, 223
genres, 69–86
George, Stefan, 429
George I, King of England, 207–8
George II, King of England, 213
Gershwin, George, 424, 466, 517, 518
Gesualdo, Carlo, 80, 127–8, 146
Getz, Stan, 519
Geyer, Ludwig, 345
Giardini, Felice de, 260
Gibbons, Orlando, 78, 136
Gilbert, W. S., 334
Ginastera, Alberto, 472
Giraud, Anna, 179
Glass, Philip, 466, 500
Glinka, Mikhail, 369
Gluck, Christoph Willibald, 34, 84,
    85, 174, 223–5, 230, 326, 333
Goethe, Johann Wolfgang von, 282,
    286–8, 300, 303, 306, 315, 323, 331,
    333, 345, 369, 388, 398, 411
Gogol, Nikolai Vasilievich, 478
Goldoni, Carlo, 232, 260
Golenishchev-Kutuzov, Count
    Arseny, 377
Golitsin, Prince, 279
Gonzaga family, 144, 149

Goodman, Benny, 48, 518
Gottschalk, Louis Moreau, 367, 503,
    506
Gounod, Charles, 84, 333
Granados, Enrique, 367
Grateful Dead, 524
Graupner, J. C., 189
Gregory I, Pope, 89
Grétry, A. E. M., 259
Grieg, Edvard, 367, 405, 438
Grillparzer, Franz, 289, 299
Grobe, Charles, 503
ground bass, 66–7
Guicciardi, Countess Giulietta, 275
Guiot de Dijon, 92, 92*
guitars, 36
Gully Jumpers, 520
Gunning, Sarah Ogan, 520
Guthrie, Woody, 527

Halle, 205, 226
Hamburg, 83, 145, 182–3, 184, 188,
    206, 221, 227–8, 356, 357, 365, 392
Hamburg Philharmonic, 358
Hämeenlinna, 406
Hammerstein, Oscar, 517
Handel, George Frideric, 28, 34, 43,
    68, 70, 79–80, 82, 84, 144, 155, 183,
    196, 204–17, 209*, 216*, 223, 247,
    305, 306, 358, 359, 502
Hanover, 207
harmony, 26–9, 61
harps, 37–8
harpsichords, 39–41
Hartmann, Victor, 378
Harvard, 469
Hasse, Johann Adolf, 204, 223
Hawthorne, Nathaniel, 463
Haydn, Franz Joseph, 64, 65, 69, 72–3,
    76, 77, 80, 219, 230–42, 237–8*, 240,
    247, 259, 260, 261, 262, 270, 284,
    285
Haydn, Michael, 300
Heidelberg, 300, 309
Heiligenstadt, 265
Heine, Heinrich, 312, 316, 320
Helsinki, 406–8
Hendrix, Jimi, 524
Henze, Hans Werner, 495
Henry VIII, King of England, 106, 107
Heywood, Dubose, 517
Hiller, Johann Adam, 259
Hindemith, Paul, 72, 74, 423, 454–6,
    458, 477
Hines, Earl, 513
Hoffmann, E. T. A., 311
Hofmannsthal, Hugo von, 400–3, 464
Holiday, Billie, 519
Holloway, Robin, 426
Holst, Gustav, 472, 473–4
Honneger, Arthur, 457
horns, 50–1
Housman, A. E., 473
Hugo, Victor, 320, 340, 342
Hukvaldy, 386
Hummel, Johan Nepomuka, 300, 315
Humperdinck, Engelbert, 356
Hüttenbrenner, Anselm, 290
Huxley, Aldous, 448

Ibsen, Henrik, 405
Iglau, 392
imitation, 30
Imperial Russian Music Society, 369
Impressionism, 367–8
incidental music, 85
Innsbruck, 117

instruments, 32–58
intervals, 16–17
Isaac, Heinrich, 117–18
Ives, Charles, 423, 458–63, 460–1*
Ives, George, 458

Jackson, Aunt Molly, 520
Jagger, Mick, 524
James, Henry, 484
Janáček, Leoš, 85, 368, 383, 386–8
Janequin, Clément, 118
jazz, 512–15
Jefferson, Blind Lemon, 510
Jenkins, John, 162
Jennens, Charles, 215
Joachim, Eduard, 356, 359, 365
Johann Georg, Elector of Hanover, 156
Johnson, Blind Willie, 509
Johnson, James P., 511
Johnson, Robert, 510
Jommelli, Nicolò, 223, 225
Jone, Hildegard, 438
Joplin, Scott, 510
Josquin Desprez, 30, 77, 80, 106,
    114–16, 116*, 117
Julius III, Pope, 120
Jung, Carl, 485

Kalischt, 392
Kallman, Chester, 447, 495
Kansas City, 518
Karevo, 376
Kassel, 156, 276
Keiser, Reinhard, 217
Kern, Jerome, 515–16
key, 24–6, 60
keyboard instruments, 39–41
keyboard music, 74–6
Khrushchev, Nikita, 477
Klopstock, Friedrich Gottlieb, 394
Kolisch, Gertrud, 432
Konstanz, 118
Kotek, Josif, 374
Kubrick, Stanley, 500

Laine, Cleo, 517
Lalande, Michel Richard de, 168
Landi, Stefano, 155
Landini, Francesco, 80, 99*, 100, 104
Lassus, Orlande de, 77, 80, 118–20,
    120*, 125
Le Sueur, Jean-François, 326
Leipzig, 144, 182, 183, 188, 194–202,
    227, 307, 309, 345, 346, 392
Leipzig Gewandhaus Orchestra, 306,
    307
Leningrad, 477, 478
    see also St Petersburg
Lennon, John, 526
Leoncavallo, Ruggiero, 368
Léonin, 93–4
Leopold, Prince of Cöthen, 186, 188
Lewis, Furry, 510
Lewis, Mead Lux, 511
Lichnowsky, Prince, 263
lieder, 82
Ligeti, György, 500
Linz, 293, 388
Lisbon, 181
Liszt, Franz, 67, 70, 76, 284, 285, 315,
    316, 319, 320–5, 332, 348, 350, 356,
    368, 381, 405, 417
Litomyšl, 381
Lloyd Webber, Andrew, 525
Locke, Matthew, 162
London, 83, 84, 144, 207–17, 222, 223,
    229, 235–8, 242, 305, 320, 332–3,
    338, 349, 384

Louis XI, King of France, 113
Louis XIII, King of France, 55
Louis XIV, King of France, 83, 166
Louÿs, Pierre, 412
Loyola, Ignatius, 128
Lübeck, 160, 185, 206
Lucca, 260
Ludwig II, King of Bavaria, 349
Luis, Don, prince of Spain, 260
Lully, Jean-Baptiste, 79, 83, 85, 166–8,
    169
Lüneburg, 184, 185
lutes, 36–7, 138
Luther, Martin, 106–7
Lutoslawski, Witold, 425, 499, 500
Lyadov, Anatoly, 379
Lyapunov, Sergey, 379
Lyons, 325

McCartney, Paul, 526
McDermott, Galt, 525
MacDowell, Edward, 367
Machaut, Guillaume de, 80, 97–8, 98*
Macon, Uncle Dave, 520
Madrid, 181, 260
madrigals, 80
Maeterlinck, Maurice, 414
Magdeburg, 346
Mahler, Gustav, 69–70, 368–9, 375,
    389, 391–9, 396–7*, 420
Mahler, Alma, 394
major keys, 25–6
Malatesta, Carlo, 112
Mallarmé, Stéphane, 367, 411, 412–13,
    418, 490
Manchester, 320
Mann, Thomas, 484
Mannheim, 225–6, 246
Mantua, 118, 144, 145–9
Manzoni, Alessandro, 344
Marcabru, 91
Marenzio, Luca, 80, 126–7, 128*, 146
Maria, Tania, 528
Marley, Bob, 528
Marxsen, Eduard, 356
Mascagni, Pietro, 368, 420
Mass, 77, 89
Massenet, Jules, 84, 356, 368, 411, 420
Mattheson, Johann, 206
Maximilian I, Emperor, 117
Mayr, J. S., 336
Mayrhofer, Johann, 289
Meck, Nadezhda von, 372, 374
Medici, Lorenzo de', 117
Medici family, 206
Meiningen, 361–5, 399
melody, 21–4
Melville, Herman, 484
Mendelssohn, Felix, 70, 72, 74, 76, 80,
    85, 284, 295, 302–7, 312
Mendelssohn, Moses, 302
Menotti, Gian Carlo, 470, 471–2
Messiaen, Olivier, 71, 486–9, 487*, 491
Metastasio, Pietro, 223
meter, 18–20
Meyerbeer, Giacomo, 315, 316, 347,
    348
Michelangelo, 323, 481, 482
Mickiewicz, 318
Middle Ages, 87–104
Milan, 114, 229, 242, 334, 337–8, 344,
    345, 419–20
Milhaud, Darius, 457–8
Miller, Glen, 518
Milyukova, Antonina, 372
Mingus, Charles, 527
minimalism, 500–1
minor keys, 25–6

Mitchell, Joni, *527–8*
modes, 26
modulation, 26
Moke, Camille, 326, 328
Molière, 402
Moniuszko, Stanislaw, 381
Monk, Thelonius, 519
Monroe Brothers, 521
Mons, 118
Monteverdi, Claudio, 78, 80, 81, 144, *145–53*, 147–9★, 154, 155, 156
Moody Blues, 524
Moravská Ostrava, 388
Mörike, 388
Moritz, Landgrave of Hesse-Kassel, 155, 156
Morley, Thomas, 80, 131, 133–4
Morton, Jelly Roll, 513–14
Morzin, Count, 231–2
Moscow, 369, 374, 376, 379, 476
motets, 77–8, 95–6
motif, 59–60
Motown, 522
Moulins, 113
Mozart, Constanze, 247
Mozart, Leopold, 242, 245–6, 255
Mozart, Wolfgang Amadeus, 61, 64, 65, 67, 69, 71, 72, 73, 74, 76, 77, 82, 84, 219, 230, *242–59*, 249–51★, 252–3★, 261, 270, 284, 285, 300, 350
Muffat, 217
Mühlfeld, Richard, 365
Mühlhausen, 185, 186
Munich, 118, 222, 242, 246, 257, 300, 315, 349, 399
musicals, 515–17
Musset, Alfred de, 316, 420
Mussorgsky, Modest, 70, 84, 369, 375, *376–8*, 380, 418, 438
Myrick, Julian, 459

Naples, 83, 145, 175–7, 181, 222, 259, 305, 306, 335, 336–7, 342
Napoleon I, Emperor, 242, 266–7
Nardini, Pietro, 260
Nashville, 527
nationalism, 366–7
nature, 283–5
Neefe, C. G., 261
Nelahozeves, 383
neo-classicism, 423–4
New Orleans, 506, 512, 515
New York, 384–5, 392, 395, 421, 447, 454, 457, 464, 466, 497, 511, 513, 514–15, 516
New York Philharmonic, 395, 490, 498
Newman, Cardinal, 409
Newman, Randy, 528
Nielsen, Carl, 405, 408
Nietzsche, Friedrich Wilhelm, 394
Nijinsky, Vaslav, 416
North Carolina Ramblers, 520
notation, 14–17
Nuremberg, 355

oboes, 44–5
Obrecht, Jacob, 114
Ockeghem, Johannes, 80, 113–14, 115, 116
octaves, 15
Offenbach, Jacques, 85, 334
Ohrdruf, 184
Oliver, King, 512
opera, 82–5, 144–53, 208–13, 222–3, 256–60, 273–6, 332–56
oratorios, 79–80, 213
orchestral music, 69–71

orchestras, 55–6
Orff, Carl, 457, 507
organs, 52–3
Ossian, 287
Ottoboni family, 177
overtures, 70
Owen, Wilfred, 484
Oxford, 213

Pachelbel, Johann, 160
Paganini, Nicolò, 67, 285, 315, 320, 328
Paisiello, Giovanni, 260, 335
Palestrina, Giovanni Pierluigi da, 30, 67, 77, 78, 80, 108, *120–5*, 122–3★
Palma, 319
Pamphili family, 177
Paris, 93, 145, 154, 170–1, 222, 225, 226, 235, 242, 246, 302, 315–20, 326–33, 336–7, 340, 342, 346–7, 348–9, 411–19, 424, 457–8, 465, 469, 486, 490, 491, 506
Parker, Charlie, 519, 520
Parker, Horatio, 459
Parry, Hubert, 473
Parton, Dolly, 522
passions, 79
Pásztory, Ditta, 454
patronage, 144
Paul, Jean, 309, 310
Pears, Peter, 482, 483–4
Pélissier, Olympe, 336
Penderecki, Krzysztof, *499–500*
Pentangle, 524
percussion, 53–5
Pergolesi, Giovanni Battista, 183, 204, 223, 441
Peri, Jacopo, 145
Pérotin, *94*, 95★
Pesaro, 334
Petrarch, 80
Petrucci, Ottaviano, 109
Philadelphia Orchestra, 380
Philharmonic Society of London, 277, 280, 384
Philidor, F. A. D., 259
Philip the Good, Duke of Burgundy, 109, 113
phrase, 59–60
piano sonatas, 75–6
pianos, 39–41
Picasso, Pablo, 442
Piccinni, Niccolò, 260
Pink Floyd, 525
Piston, Walter, 466
pitch, 14–15
plainsong, 61, 89–90
Planer, Minna, 346
Pleydel, Ignace, 261
Ployer, Barbara, 254
Poe, Edgar Allan, 380
polyphony, 29–31, 93–5
Ponte, Lorenzo da, 257, 258
popular music, 502–29
Porpora, Nicola, 231
Porter, Cole, *516–17*
Potocka, Countess Delfina, 316
Poulenc, Francis, 457
Prague, 179, 223, 255, 256, 258, 263, 300, 346, 381, 383, 386, 392
Presley, Elvis, 522, *523–4*
Princeton, 499
printing, 108–9
Prokofiev, Sergei, 85, 379, 423, 424, *474–6*, 477, 478
Promnitz, Count of, 182
Puccini, Giacomo, 84–5, 368, *419–21*

Purcell, Henry, 66, 78, *162–6*, 165★, 215, 482
Pushkin, Aleksander Sergeievitch, 377
Pythagoras, 15

Quantz, J. J., 227

Rachmaninov, Sergey, 67, *379–80*
ragtime, 507–10
Rainey, Gertrude "Ma", 511
Rameau, Jean-Philippe, 84, 85, *170–4*, 172–3★
random music, 425
Ravel, Maurice, 77, 367, 378, *417–19*, 424, 473
Razumovsky, Count, 271
realism, 368–9
recitative, 82
recorders, 42–3
Recio, Marie, 331, 333
Redding, Otis, 522
Reformation, 106–7
Reger, Max, 456
Reich, Steve, 500
Reicken, J. A., 184, 188
Reményi, Eduard, 356
Renaissance, 104–39
requiems, 77
rhythm, 17–18
Richter, J. P. F., 309
Ricordi, Giulio, 338, 344, 420
Riga, 346
Riley, Terry, 500
Rimbaud, Arthur, 481
Rimsky-Korsakov, Nikolay, 367, 369, 375, 377, *378–9*, 438
Riquier, Guiraut, 91
ritornello, 65–6
rock music, 522–8
Rococo, 220–1
Rodgers, Jimmy, 522
Rodgers, Richard, 517
Rogers, Ginger, 516
Rohrau, 231
Roller, Alfred, 394
Rolling Stones, *524–5*
Romantic era, 281–365
Rome, 118, 120, 125, 126, 143, 144, 145, 153, 155, 175, 177, 179, 206–7, 259, 305, 324, 328
rondo, 64
Rore, Cipriano de, 125
Ross, Diana, 522
Rossetti, Dante-Gabriel, 411
Rossini, Gioacchino, 84, 260, 289, *334–6*, 337, 344
Rostropovich, Mstislav, 483
Rubinstein, Anton, 369
Rückert, Friedrich, 293, 394
Rudolph, Archduke, 277, 279
Ruggles, Carl, 464
Rushing, Jimmy, 519
Russolo, Luigi, 423

Sachs, Hans, 355
sacred music, 77–80
St Germain-en-Laye, 411
St Petersburg, 222, 260, 279, 342, 369, 376, 378, 379, 438, 474, 475; see also Leningrad
St Pölten, 289
Salieri, Antonio, 286, 320
Salomon, J. P., 235, 238
Salzburg, 143, 242, 245–6, 252, 300
Sand, George, 319–20
Satie, Erik, 458, 499
saxophones, 48–9
Sayn-Wittgenstein, Princess Carolyne, 323, 324

scales, 16
Scarlatti, Alessandro, 82, 83, 144, *175–7*, 181, 207, 223
Scarlatti, Domenico, 60, 63, 75, 175, *181–2*, 207
Schaeffer, Pierre, 491
Scheidt, Samuel, 156
Schein, J. H., 156
Schikaneder, Emanuel, 259, 273
Schiller, Friedrich von, 277–9, 287, 323, 336, 342
Schindler, Anton, 279
Schober, Franz von, 288, 289, 293
Schoenberg, Arnold, 62, 67, 74, 77, 85, 365, 400, 402, 418, 422, 423, *426–32*, 431★, 433, 434, 438, 447, 454, 455, 458, 477, 486, *489–90*, 495, 496
Schoenberg, Mathilde, 428, 432
Schubert, Ferdinand, 295
Schubert, Franz, 23, 65, 69, 72, 74, 76, 82, 284, *285–99*, 297–8★, 306, 312, 324, 389
Schumann, Clara, 309, *311–14*, 356, 359
Schumann, Robert, 69, 72, 284, 295, 306, *307–14*, 312–13★, 314, 324, 356, 366
Schuppanzigh, Ignaz, 279
Schütz, Heinrich, 79, *155–60*
Schwind, Moritz von, 289, 295
Scott, James, 510
Scott, Sir Walter, 282
Scriabin, Alexander, 76, 379, 381, 426, 438
Scribe, Eugène, 342
Scruggs, 527
Sechter, Simon, 388, 389
Semyonovo, 379
serialism, 62, *430–8*, 488, 490, 499
Sermisy, Claudin de, 118
Sessions, Roger, 466
Sforza family, 114
Shakespeare, William, 70, 85, 304, 323, 326, 330, 331, 333, 340, 344, 345, 346, 408, 410
Shaw, Artie, 48
Shield, William, 259
Shostakovich, Dmitry, 70, 424, *477–80*
Sibelius, Jean, 70, 405, *406–8*
Simone, Nina, 522
Skillet Lickers, 520
Smetana, Bedřich, *381–3*, 384, 405
Smith, Bessie, *511*, 519
Smith, J. J., 23
Smith, Joe, 511
Smithson, Harriet, 326, 328, 330, 331, 333
sonata form, 64–5
Sondheim, Stephen, 525
Sonnleithner, Joseph von, 273–4
Sorau, 182
Sousa, John Philip, 503, *505–6*
Spaun, Josef von, 287–8
Spohr, Louis, 300
Spontini, Gaspare, 315
Springsteen, Bruce, 528
Stalin, Josef, 476, 477, 478, 479
Stamitz, Johann, *225*, 226
Stanford, Charles, 473
Stasov, Vladimir, 375
Steeleye Span, 524
Stenhammar, William 405
Steyr, 289, 293
Stirling, Jane, 320
Stockhausen, Karlheinz, 77, 425, 447, 462, 486, 488, *491–5*, 492★, 496, 500
Stockholm, 222

storm and stress, 234–5
Stösslová, Kamila, 386, 388
Stradivari family, 34
Strauss, Johann, 85
Strauss, Johann jnr, 334
Strauss, Richard, 70, 84, 85, 356,
    368–9, 392, 398, 399–405, 400–1*,
    409, 426
Stravinsky, Igor, 21, 28, 70, 77, 85, 86,
    379, 386, 416, 417, 418, 419, 422,
    423, 424, 438–48, 444–5*, 449, 452,
    455, 457, 458, 468, 477, 480, 495,
    499, 507
Strepponi, Giuseppina, 340–2, 345
String Band, 524
string instruments, 34–9
string quartets, 72–3, 233–4
Stuttgart, 222, 300
Sudeikina, Vera, 442
Sullivan, Sir Arthur, 85, 334
Sweelinck, Jan Pieterszoon, 160
Swieten, Baron Van, 247
swing era, 517–19
Symbolism, 367–8
symphonic poems, 70
symphonies, 69–70
Szymanowski, Karol, 381

Tailleferre, Germaine, 457
Tallis, Thomas, 129, 130, 473
Taneyev, Sergey, 379
Taverner, John, 130
Tchaikovsky, Modest, 372
Tchaikovsky, Pyotr Ilyich, 65, 69, 70,
    84, 85, 369–75, 372–3*, 379, 380,
    406, 438
Telemann, Georg Philipp, 79, 182–3,
    186, 189, 204, 217, 227
tempo, 18
ternary form, 63
texture music, 499
theme, 59–60

Thibault IV, King of Navarre, 91–2
Thomas, Dylan, 448
Thoreau, Henry, 463
Thornton, Big Mama, 523
Thurber, Jeannette, 384
Tippett, Sir Michael, 484–5
Tolstoy, Leo, 388, 476
tonic, 24
totalitarianism, 424
Traetta, Tommaso, 223, 225
Tregian, Francis, 132
triads, 27–8
Tribschen, 349
trio sonatas, 72
Tromb’cino, Bartolomeo, 118
trombones, 52
troubadours, 91–2
trouvères, 91–2
trumpets, 51
tubas, 52
Turina, 367
twelve-tone music, 62, 430–8, 488,
    490, 499
Tyner, McCoy, 520

Varèse, Edgard, 423, 464–6, 490
variations, 66–7
Vaughan, Sarah, 519
Vaughan Williams, Ralph, 423, 472–3
Velvet Underground, 524
Venice, 125–6, 145, 149–50, 154–5,
    156, 157, 175, 179–80, 222, 259, 305,
    334, 342, 350, 447, 448
Ventadorn, Bernart de, 91
Verdi, Giuseppe, 77, 84, 335, 337–45,
    367, 368
Verga, Giovanni, 368
Verlaine, Paul, 411
Versailles, 168
Victoria, Queen of England, 307, 325
Victoria, Tomás Luis de, 128–9
Vienna, 117, 145, 179, 222, 223, 231,

238, 242, 243, 245, 246–57, 258–9,
    261, 262, 273–6, 286–99, 301, 311,
    315, 320, 337, 349, 358, 368,
    388–405, 406, 426–38
Vienna Philharmonic Orchestra, 361
Vienna Philharmonic Society, 295,
    296, 359
Villa-Lobos, Heitor, 472
violas, 35
violence, 422–3
violin sonatas, 72
violins, 34–5
viols, 36
Virgil, 333
Vitry, Philippe de, 96, 97
Vivaldi, Antonio, 66, 70, 175, 177–81,
    180*, 189, 196, 204
vocal music, 33–4, 77–85
Vogl, J. M., 288, 289
voice, 33–4

Wackenroder, W. H., 283
Wagner, Cosima, 324, 349
Wagner, Friedrich, 345
Wagner, Minna, 346, 349
Wagner, Richard, 17, 28, 33, 84, 284,
    302, 323, 324–5, 330, 332, 337, 344,
    345–56, 354–5*, 366, 367, 383, 388,
    389, 399, 411, 426
Waits, Tom, 528
Walsh, John, 214
Warsaw, 222, 315
Washington, 505, 514
Waters, Muddy, 524
Watson, Doc, 520
Weber, Carl Maria von, 84, 282,
    300–2, 306, 347
Webern, Anton, 67, 74, 422, 423, 428,
    434–8, 437*, 486
Wedekind, Frank, 434
Weelkes, Thomas, 80, 133–5, 135*
Wegelius, Martin, 406

Weill, Kurt, 424, 456–7
Weimar, 185, 186, 285, 300, 323–4,
    332, 348, 356, 503
Wert, Giaches de, 145
Wesendonck, Mathilde, 348
Wessenfels, 205
Whistler, James MacNeill, 414
Whiteman, Paul, 518
Whitman, Walt, 455
Who, The, 525
Wieck, Friedrich, 309, 310
Wilbye, John, 135
Wilde, Oscar, 368, 400
Wilhelm Ernst, Duke, 186
Willaert, Adrian, 118, 125
Williams, Hank, 522, 523
Williams, Pete, 509
Willis, Bob, 521
Winckelmann, J. J., 218
wind instruments, 41–53
Wodehouse, P. G., 516
Wolf, Hugo, 356, 388
woodwind instruments, 42–9
Worcester, 408, 409
Workman, Nimrod, 520

Xenakis, Iannis, 500

Yale, 455, 458–9
Yancey, Jimmy, 511
Yevtushenko, Evgeny, 480
Young, LaMont, 500
Young, Lester, 518, 519

Zachow, 206
Zappa, Frank, 524
Zelter, Carl Friedrich, 305
Zemlinsky, Alexander von, 426
Zhdanov, Andrey, 476, 480
zithers, 38–9
Zola, Emile, 368
Zürich, 348
Zwickau, 309

1750–1875 Music		Art and literature	History and philosophy

1750–1875   Music

C. P. E. Bach: *Essay on the True Art of Playing Keyboard Instruments*

D. Scarlatti dies (71); J. Stamitz dies (39)
Handel dies (74)

Gluck: *Orfeo*; J. C. Bach moves Milan–London

Haydn becomes *Kapellmeister* to Esterházys

Boccherini settles as chamber composer in Madrid

Mozart visit to Mannheim and on to Paris

Haydn: String quartets op. 33; Mozart settles in Vienna

Mozart begins great series of piano concertos
Mozart: *Marriage of Figaro*
Mozart: last three symphonies

Haydn's first London visit; Mozart: *The Magic Flute*, dies (35)

Haydn returns from second London visit (Symphonies 99–104); rejoins
   Esterházys (late Masses, 1796–1802)
Paris Conservatory founded
Haydn: *The Creation*

Beethoven: Symphony no. 3
Beethoven: *Fidelio*

Beethoven: Symphony no. 5
Haydn dies (77)

Vienna Philharmonic Society founded
(Royal) Philharmonic Society, London, founded
Schubert: *Erlking* (and about 150 other songs)
Rossini: *The Barber of Seville*

Weber: *Der Freischütz*
Beethoven: Choral Symphony
Schubert: Great C major Symphony
Beethoven: late string quartets; Weber dies (39); Mendelssohn: Overture
   Midsummer Night's Dream
Beethoven dies (56)
Schubert: String Quintet in C, *Winterreise*, dies (31)
Berlioz: *Fantastic Symphony*; Bellini: *Norma*
Chopin: Nocturne in E♭
Mendelssohn: *Italian Symphony*
Schumann: *Carnaval*; Donizetti: *Lucia di Lammermoor*; Bellini dies (34)

Schumann: *Dichterliebe*
New York Philharmonic Symphony Society founded
Leipzig Conservatory founded

Berlioz: *The Damnation of Faust*
Mendelssohn dies (38)
Chopin dies (39)

Verdi: *La traviata*; Liszt: Piano Sonata in b

Schumann dies (46)
Liszt: *Faust Symphony*
Offenbach: *Orpheus in the Underworld*
Wagner: *Tristan und Isolde*; Gounod: *Faust*
Brahms: Piano Concerto no. 1

Smetana: *The Bartered Bride*

Brahms: *German Requiem*; Grieg: Piano Concerto; Wagner: *Mastersingers*

Mussorgsky: *Boris Godunov*; Smetana: *Vltava*; J. Strauss: *Fledermaus*; Verdi: *Requiem*
Bizet: *Carmen*, dies (36); Tchaikovsky: Piano Concerto no. 1

Art and literature

(1750)

Voltaire: *Candide*

Fragonard: *The Swing*

(1775)

Beaumarchais: *Le mariage de Figaro*

Reynolds: *Master Hare*
Blake: *Songs of Innocence*

(1800)

Schiller: *William Tell*

Goethe: *Faust*, part 1; Friedrich: *Winter*

Byron: *Childe Harold*
Austen: *Pride and Prejudice*
Goya: *The Third of May 1808*

Constable: *The Haywain*

(1825)

Delacroix: *Liberty leading the people*
Pushkin: *Eugene Onegin*

(1850)

Dickens: *David Copperfield*
Beecher: *Uncle Tom's Cabin*
Thoreau: *Walden*
Whitman: *Leaves of Grass*
Baudelaire: *Fleurs du mal*; Flaubert, *Madame Bovary*

Hugo: *Les misérables*

Moreau: *Revelation*
Dostoevsky: *Crime and Punishment*
Ibsen: *Peer Gynt*; Zola: *Thérèse Raquin*
Tolstoy: *War and Peace*

Degas: *Ballet Rehearsal*
Twain: *Tom Sawyer*

(1875)

History and philosophy

Diderot and others begin the *Encyclopédie*

Rousseau: *Discourse on Inequality*
Johnson: *Dictionary*

America becomes independent

Kant: *The Critique of Pure Reason*

French Revolution

Louisiana Purchase

Napoleon invades Russia

Battle of Waterloo; Congress of Vienna

Schopenhauer: *The World as Will and Idea*

Hegel: *The Philosophy of Right*

Bolivar liberates South America

Faraday discovers electrical induction

Marx: *The Communist Manifesto*; Revolutions
   sweep Europe; California Gold Rush

Darwin: *Origin of Species*
American Civil War begins; Unification of Italy
Emancipation of slaves in USA

Marx: *Das Kapital*

Franco-Prussian War
Unification of Germany